Date Due

Feb 16			
Oc. 3 '7			
	PRINTED IN U. S. A.		

THE AMERICAN BOOK OF DAYS

The
AMERICAN BOOK OF DAYS

A COMPENDIUM OF INFORMATION ABOUT
HOLIDAYS, FESTIVALS, NOTABLE ANNIVER-
SARIES AND CHRISTIAN AND JEWISH HOLY
DAYS WITH NOTES ON OTHER AMERICAN
ANNIVERSARIES WORTHY OF REMEMBRANCE

By

GEORGE WILLIAM DOUGLAS, A.M., Litt.D.
MEMBER OF THE HISTORICAL SOCIETY OF PENNSYLVANIA

Revised by

HELEN DOUGLAS COMPTON

*As it is the commendation of a good huntsman to find
game in a wild wood, so it is no imputation if
he hath not caught all.*—Plato

THE H. W. WILSON COMPANY
NEW YORK - - - NINETEEN HUNDRED FORTY - EIGHT

Copyright 1937
By George William Douglas
Copyright 1948
By Helen Douglas Compton

Published 1937
Second Printing 1938
Third Printing 1940
Fourth Printing 1943

Revised Edition 1948
Second Printing 1952
Third Printing 1957

Printed in the United States of America

Library of Congress Catalog Card No. 48-28210

DEDICATED

To all those interested in the history of their
country and in the customs of
its citizens

PREFACE

It occurred to me about thirty years ago that a book of this kind should be written. I then began assembling the necessary data and have continued at the task until the last word was put down on paper. I hope that the story of the anniversaries observed in the various states will assist the reader in forming a properly balanced view of the history of his country. Some of the most important have little more than a local fame. For example, Halifax Resolution Day in North Carolina is observed in celebration of the adoption of the first declaration by any colony of a belief in independence. The resolutions were adopted a few weeks after the battle of Moore's Creek Bridge, which, in its way, was as important as the Battle of Concord and Lexington. It was a pitched battle and not a mere skirmish of farmers behind fences and stone walls with British troops. And Georgia Day, celebrating the landing of General Oglethorpe, marks the beginning of a colonization by free men to whom freedom of speech and worship was guaranteed, which rivals the colonization of Pennsylvania by William Penn.

I have included among the anniversaries the dates of the births of the Presidents and Chief Justices of the United States, although public notice is taken of only a few. I have thought that a record of the men holding these high offices should not be omitted from a book of this kind. As the date of the birth of Chief Justice John Rutledge is not known I have written of him on the date of his death. President Washington evidently regarded him as the most distinguished lawyer in the country next to John Jay for when he appointed Jay as the first Chief Justice he named Rutledge as the first Associate Justice and when Jay retired from the court he named Rutledge in his place. I have included other anniversaries worthy of remembrance although there may be no formal note taken of them.

Furthermore, I have taken note of the feast days of the holy men and women of the Church usually called saints. They belong to the history of the progress of Christianity, and although they lived in other parts of the world they are venerated by millions of Americans. I have told also of other holy men and women the anniversary of whose birth or death is celebrated but who have not yet been formally classed among the saints in the calendar of any church. It is desirable that everyone, whatever be the nature of his religious belief, should be reminded that the lives of these consecrated individuals illustrate the possibilities of devotion and

vii

PREFACE

sacrifice which are inherent in human nature when striving for high ideals.

There are many movable religious festivals falling on different days in different years. And there are several other celebrations falling on a fixed Sunday or other day in the month. As the date of these changes from year to year I have, for the sake of convenience, told about them on the date on which they were observed in 1934. [In the revised edition the year 1945 is used, for the most part, instead of 1934.] Their story can be found by consulting the table of contents.

It may seem to some that I have given too much space to the New Orleans Mardi Gras observance. As this is the most elaborate and picturesque celebration in the country I have thought it worth while to record in detail what was done in a typical year when neither war nor economic depression forced a curtailment of the program. While its origins are European, in crossing the ocean it has suffered a sea change into something rich and strange which the fertile imagination of those in charge has been able to interpret to the wonder and delight of tens of thousands who visit the city in the carnival season.

While I was engaged in the work I had many delightful experiences in serendipity. This word was invented by Horace Walpole to describe the practices of the heroes of the fairy story, "The Three Princes of Serendip," who "were always making discoveries, by accident or sagacity, of things they were not in quest of." On one occasion after reading a review of a life of Montaigne made up from the autobiographical parts of his letters and essays I turned to my copy of Montaigne and read at random in the Third Book. There I found his remarks on the change in the calendar made by Pope Gregory which I have included as an interesting contemporary comment. Again, while looking for some information about fast days I ran across the fact that Frederick County, Maryland, the courts of which repudiated the Stamp Act when it was passed, continues to this day to celebrate the anniversary of the repudiation, the story of which I have told in the proper place.

If the readers get as much pleasure from this book as I have derived from writing it I shall be more than delighted. They will learn why a set piece of fireworks is called a Catherine wheel, why the Escorial in Spain was built on the general plan of a gridiron, and that one of the Popes, when including a traditional hero among the saints, said with engaging frankness that the saint was among those who should be venerated by men, but that his "actions were known only to God."

I have consulted all available sources of information—books, newspaper files and individuals. If I should give a list of the individuals to whom I am indebted for assistance, including Gover-

PREFACE

nors, United States Senators, Cabinet officers, Generals in the Army, and private citizens, it would take too much space, and if I should give a list of the books I have consulted it would savor too much of pedantry. I must be content, therefore with expressing my thanks to all who have helped me during the long years in which I have been engaged on this work.

G. W. Douglas

May 1, 1937

PREFACE TO THE SECOND EDITION

A long time ago, when I was a little girl, my father told me about this book, saying wistfully that he was afraid someone else might think of writing it before he had the time. No one else did, although he was an elderly man when he finally commanded the leisure for the task. As a newspaper editor, consulting books of fact and reference almost daily, he had been surprised to find no complete compilation of American holidays and festivals, and thus conceived the American Book of Days. That the book supplied a felt need was immediately evident upon publication, and my father was pleased and gratified by the consistent annual sales proving the worth of his patiently cherished idea.

It was his intention to bring out a new edition, including the holidays that had been inaugurated since publication of the original text, and many more of the picturesque festivals and local celebrations which reflect the American scene. However, World War II intervened and, before it was over, his death at the ripe age of eighty-two put an end to his labors. It therefore devolved upon me to complete them, rounding out his theme of American history and folklore with the great dates, and biographical sketches of the great leaders, of the last war. This edition brings the book up to date, amplifying it with copious fresh material which I hope, out of sentiment for my father's sentiment, will make The Book of Days even more useful and interesting.

Helen Douglas Compton
Coral Gables, Florida

July 27, 1948

CONTENTS

	PAGE
PREFACE	vii
PREFACE TO SECOND EDITION	ix

JANUARY

Origin of the Name... 1

JAN.
1. New Year's Day; Philadelphia Mummers' Parade; Pasadena Tournament of Roses; Pasadena Rose Bowl Football Game; Emancipation Proclamation; New Year ·in Mobile; Feast of the Circumcision 2
2. The First Flag of Washington's Army 13
3. Battle of Princeton................................. 14
4. Feast of St. Titus.................................. 14
5. Epiphany Eve...................................... 15
6. Feast of Epiphany; Twelfth Night Revels; Blessing of the Sponge Divers at Tarpon Springs, Florida; The Four Freedoms 15
7. Millard Fillmore's Birthday; The Panama Canal........ 22
8. Jackson Day 24
9. The First Balloon Ascension........................ 26
10. League of Nations Day............................. 27
11. Birthday of Alexander Hamilton.................... 28
12. La Salle's Last Journey............................ 30
13. Birthday of Salmon P. Chase; Festival of St. Veronica... 30
14. Feast of the Holy Name........................... 33
15. Vermont's Declaration of Independence............. 34
16. France Recognizes the United States; Prohibition and Repeal 35
17. Franklin's Birthday; Feast of St. Anthony the Great.... 36
18. Birthday of Daniel Webster........................ 42
19. Birthday of Robert E. Lee; Birthday of Edgar Allan Poe; The Greek Church of Epiphany 43
20. Eve of St. Agnes; Inauguration Day................ 48
21. Birthday of "Stonewall" Jackson; Feast of St. Agnes.... 50
22. Ohio's First Legislature; Birthday of Frederick Moore Vinson 51
23. Feast of St. Ildefonsus............................ 54
24. Feast of St. Timothy 54

CONTENTS

                                                                  PAGE
25. Birthday of Robert Burns; Feast of the Conversion of
    St. Paul 55
26. Michigan Day; Birthday of Douglas MacArthur 57
27. Feast of St. Chrysostom............................. 60
28. The United States Withdraws from Cuba............. 61
29. Kansas Day; Carnation Day, Birthday of William Mc-
    Kinley; Emanuel Swedenborg's Birthday; Thomas Paine
    Day 62
30. A Royalist Fast Day in Virginia; Birthday of Franklin D.
    Roosevelt 69
31. Birthday of James G. Blaine........................ 73

FEBRUARY

          Origin of the Name............................. 75
FEB.   1. Festival of St. Bridget........................... 76
       2. Candlemas; Ground Hog Day...................... 77
       3. Creation of the Territory of Illinois............... 79
       4. Birthday of Mark Hopkins...................... 79
       5. Arrival of Roger Williams in America.............. 80
       6. Birthday of Aaron Burr; Twentieth Amendment....... 81
       7. Birthday of Charles Dickens..................... 82
       8. Boy Scout Day................................. 86
       9. Birthday of William Henry Harrison.............. 87
      10. The Spanish Peace Treaty; The Gasparilla Carnival..... 88
      11. Birthday of Melville W. Fuller; Birthday of Thomas Alva
          Edison 90
      12. Lincoln's Birthday; Georgia Day; Charro Fiesta in
          Brownsville, Texas; Chinese New Year............ 92
      13. Shrove Tuesday or Mardi Gras..................... 104
      14. Ash Wednesday; St. Valentine's Day; Arizona Admission
          Day 119
      15. Temple University Founder's Day; Destruction of the
          "Maine" 123
      16. Birthday of Cushing Eells; Republic of Lithuania Day... 130
      17. Frances E. Willard Day........................... 133
      18. Inauguration of Jefferson Davis................... 135
      19. Decision on Validity of the Initiative and Referendum;
          Ohio Admitted to Union 135
      20. Birthday of Joseph Jefferson...................... 136
      21. Dedication of the Washington Monument............ 136
      22. Washington's Birthday; Lowell's Birthday............ 137
      23. Birthday of Emma Willard; Battle of Buena Vista...... 142
      24. Feast of St. Matthias; Birthday of Chester William Nimitz 143
      25. The National Bank Act; The Sixteenth Amendment.... 146

CONTENTS

PAGE

26. Birthday of William F. Cody...................... 147
27. Longfellow's Birthday 147
28. Explosion of the "Peacemaker"...................... 149
29. Birthday of Ann Lee; Leap Year.................... 150

MARCH

Origin of the Name............................... 152

MAR. 1. St. David's Day; Nebraska State Day................. 153
2. Texas Independence Day; Festival of St. John Maro.... 156
3. Birthday of Alexander Graham Bell; Hundredth Night at West Point... 157
4. Birthday of Pulaski; Vermont Day 159
5. The Boston Massacre............................. 160
6. Alamo Day....................................... 161
7. Luther Burbank's Birthday......................... 161
8. Birthday of Oliver Wendell Holmes; Birthday of Simon Cameron 162
9. Edwin Forrest's Birthday; Fast of Esther............. 163
10. Albany Becomes the Capital of New York; Feast of Purim 164
11. The Blizzard of 1888.............................. 166
12. Girl Scout Day................................... 167
13. Birthday of Joseph Priestly........................ 168
14. Eli Whitney Patents the Cotton Gin................. 169
15. Maine Admitted to the Union; Birthday of Andrew Jackson 169
16. Birthday of James Madison; Founding of the United States Military Academy 170
17. St. Patrick's Day; Birthday of Roger B. Taney; Evacuation Day... 173
18. Birthday of Grover Cleveland; DeMolay Day.......... 178
19. Birthday of William Jennings Bryan................. 181
20. Birthday of Neal Dow............................. 182
21. The First Indian Treaty........................... 183
22. Signing of the Stamp Act.......................... 184
23. Patrick Henry's Speech for the Revolution............. 184
24. Birthday of Fanny Crosby......................... 184
25. Maryland Day; Palm Sunday; Lady Day or The Feast of the Annunciation................................. 185
26. Birthday of Count Rumford........................ 188
27. Rebuilding the Navy.............................. 189
28. President Jackson Censured; Daffodil Festival in Washington 189

CONTENTS

PAGE

29. Birthday of John Tyler.............................. 191
30. Good Friday; Seward Day in Alaska................. 192
31. Widows of the Presidents Pensioned; Transfer of Virgin
   Islands 196

APRIL

   Origin of the Name............................... 198
APR. 1. All Fool's Day; Easter............................. 199
   2. Pasch Monday; Establishment of the Mint; Mule Day in
      Columbia, Tennessee............................ 202
   3. Birthday of Washington Irving...................... 206
   4. Adoption of the Present Flag....................... 207
   5. Birthday of Elihu Yale; Founder's Day at Tuskegee Insti-
      tute 207
   6. Army Day; Founding of the Mormon Church; Greek In-
      dependence Day 208
   7. The Alabama Claims.............................. 212
   8. Ponce de Leon Seeks the Fountain of Youth.......... 212
   9. Appomattóx Day 213
   10. Salvation Army Founder's Day..................... 214
   11. Birthday of Charles Evans Hughes.................. 215
   12. Halifax Resolutions Day 217
   13. Jefferson's Birthday; Huguenot Day; Bird Day........ 218
   14. Pan American Day................................ 222
   15. Expatriation Treaty with Great Britain.............. 223
   16. Endowment of College Teachers Pension Fund........ 224
   17. Chartering of the American Academy of Arts and Letters 225
   18. The San Francisco Fire; Pasch or The Feast of the Passover 225
   19. Patriot's Day.................................... 227
   20. Gift of The Hague Peace Palace.................... 229
   21. San Jacinto Day 229
   22. Arbor Day; The Opening of Oklahoma Territory...... 232
   23. Birthday of James Buchanan; Shakespeare's Birthday;
      St. George's Day.............................. 235
   24. The British Burn Washington...................... 239
   25. St. Mark's Day.................................. 240
   26. Confederate Memorial Day; Fast Day in New Hampshire;
      Birthday of John James Audubon; Cape Henry Day... 240
   27. Grant's Birthday................................. 245
   28. Birthday of James Monroe......................... 246
   29. Birthday of Oliver Ellsworth...................... 248
   30. Feast of St. Catherine of Siena.................... 249

xiv

CONTENTS

MAY

PAGE

Origin of the Name............................... 250

MAY 1. May Day; Dewey Day; Child Health Day; Feasts of
St. James the Less and St. Philip; Americanism Day
in Pennsylvania 251

2. First Paid Fire Department in New York; Rural Life
Sunday 258

3. First Medical School in America; Shenandoah Valley
Apple Blossom Festival......................... 259

4. Rhode Island Declaration of Independence; McDonogh
Day in New Orleans; Wenatchee Apple Blossom Festival 261

5. Derby Day; Cinco de Mayo...................... 263

6. Birthday of Robert E. Perry; Feast of St. John before the
Latin Gate 267

7. Sinking of the Lusitania........................ 268

8. Feast of the Apparition of St. Michael; V-E Day; Birthday of Harry S. Truman........................ 268

9. Birthday of John Brown......................... 271

10. The First Transcontinental Railroad; Ascension Day;
Philadelphia Centennial Exposition............... 272

11. The Connecticut Charter........................ 275

12. Hospital Day; American Indian Day.............. 276

13. Mother's Day; First Permanent English Settlement...... 279

14. Rockefeller Foundation Chartered.................. 282

15. Festival of St. Peter and His Companions........... 282

16. The Memphis Cotton Festival.................... 282

17. Norwegian Independence Day.................... 284

18. Feast of Pentecost.............................. 286

19. I Am an American Day; First American Confederation 286

20. Mecklenburg Declaration of Independence; Dolly Madison
Day; Founder's Day at Girard College; Whitsunday 287

21. Lindbergh Lands at Paris........................ 294

22. National Maritime Day.......................... 295

23. The Hanging of Captain Kidd................... 298

24. British Empire Day............................. 299

25. Emerson's Birthday............................. 301

26. Feast of St. Augustine of Canterbury.............. 302

27. Fiesta de la Senora Conquistadora; St. Bede's Day 303

28. Birthday of Louis Agassiz....................... 305

29. Birthday of Charles II.......................... 306

30. Memorial Day; Festival of St. Joan of Arc........... 308

31. Walt Whitman's Birthday; The Seventeenth Amendment 314

CONTENTS

JUNE

PAGE

Origin of the Name............................. 317
JUNE 1. Statehood Day in Kentucky; Statehood Day in Tennessee;
Pere Marquette Day 318
2. Birthday of John Randolph of Roanoke............... 322
3. Birthday of Jefferson Davis..................... 323
4. Jacksonville, Texas, Tomato Festival; Jack Jouett Day... 325
5. Repeal of the Gold Clause...................... 326
6. D-Day 327
7. Boone Day; Royal Poinciana Festival in Miami........ 328
8. The Yoakum, Texas, Tomato Tom-Tom.............. 332
9. Feast of St. Columba; Petersburg Memorial Day; Birthday of Jennie Casseday.......................... 332
10. Children's Day; Rose Day at Manheim, Pennsylvania.... 335
11. Kamehameha Day in Hawaii; Feast of St. Barnabas.... 336
12. The Portland Rose Festival...................... 338
13. Feast of St. Anthony of Padua................... 340
14. Flag Day................................... 341
15. Asheville Rhododendron Festival; Idaho Pioneer Day;
Magna Charta Day 343
16. Father's Day; Organization of the World Court........ 347
17. Bunker Hill Day; Blessing the Berries............... 349
18. Susan B. Anthony Fined for Voting................. 351
19. New Church Day.............................. 351
20. West Virginia Day............................. 352
21. The Constitution Ratified; Riot of Unpaid Revolutionary
Soldiers; Birthday of Daniel Carter Beard.......... 353
22. The Beginning of Osteopathy..................... 355
23. The Penn Treaty with the Indians................. 355
24. St. John's Day; Swedish Midsummer Festival.......... 356
25. The Custer Massacre 358
26. American Troops Land in France.................. 359
27. Birthday of Helen Keller....................... 359
28. World War I 360
29. St. Peter's Day 361
30. St. Paul's Day............................... 362

JULY

Origin of the Name............................. 364
JULY 1. Battle of Gettysburg........................... 365
2. First Exhibition of Hussey's Reaper................ 366
3. Birthday of John Singleton Copley; Idaho Admitted to
Union 367

CONTENTS

PAGE

4. Independence Day; Philippine Independence; Birthday of Calvin Coolidge.. 367
5. Birthday of Admiral Farragut.................................. 380
6. The Founding of the Republican Party........................ 380
7. The Opening of Columbia University; Annexation of Hawaii 382
8. Birthday of John D. Rockefeller............................. 383
9. Braddock's Defeat 384
10. The Whistler Centenary; American Troops Land in Sicily; Wyoming Admitted to Union 384
11. Birthday of John Quincy Adams.............................. 387
12. Orange Day.. 389
13. Birthday of Nathan B. Forrest.............................. 389
14. Bastille Day 390
15. St. Swithin's Day 392
16. Birthday of Mary Baker Eddy; Feast of Our Lady of Mt. Carmel 394
17. Florida Ceded to the United States; Birthday of John Jacob Astor 397
18. Birthday of John Paul Jones................................ 398
19. The National Cherry Festival; First Woman's Rights Convention; Feast of St. Vincent de Paul................... 400
20. Italians Lynched in Louisiana.............................. 403
21. The Destruction of Jerusalem; Loyal Temperance Union Day 404
22. Feast of St. Mary Magdalen................................. 406
23. Death of John Rutledge..................................... 407
24. Pioneer Day in Utah; Mormon Pioneer Day in Idaho.... 408
25. Frontier Day in Cheyenne; Feast of St. James the Greater; Feast of St. Christopher; Pony Penning on Chincoteague Island 411
26. Festival of St. Anne.. 415
27. First Successful Atlantic Cable............................. 416
28. The Fourteenth Amendment; Founder's Day of the Volunteers of America 416
29. Feast of St. Martha; Days of Ezra Meeker................. 417
30. Crater Day 419
31. Feast of St. Ignatius de Loyola; Bretton Woods Agreements 420

AUGUST

Origin of the Name.. 423
AUG. 1. Colorado Day; Swiss Independence Day.................. 424
2. First Street Letter Boxes................................... 425
3. Columbus Sails... 426

xvii

CONTENTS

PAGE

4. Feast of St. Dominic; Acquittal of John Peter Zenger... 426
5. Birthday of John Eliot; First Use of the Atomic Bomb... 428
6. Feast of the Transfiguration........................... 430
7. Creation of the War Department; Chautauqua Day..... 431
8. Birthday of Charles A. Dana....................... 432
9. Birthday of Izaak Walton........................... 432
10. Birthday of Herbert Clark Hoover; Feast of St. Lawrence 433
11. Fulton's Steamboat Sails; John Alden Day............. 435
12. Feast of St. Clare................................. 437
13. Feast of St. Hippolytus............................ 437
14. V-J Day; The Atlantic Charter...................... 438
15. Feast of the Assumption of the Virgin............... 440
16. Battle of Bennington; Festival of St. Roch........... 441
17. Birthday of David Crockett; Jousting Tournament in Virginia 443
18. The First Government Exploring Expedition Sails....... 445
19. National Aviation Day; The "Constitution's" Great Victory 445
20. Birthday of Benjamin Harrison..................... 447
21. Feast of St. Jane Frances de Chantal................ 448
22. The "America" Wins the Cup...................... 449
23. Birthday of Oliver Hazard Perry................... 449
24. Festival of St. Bartholomew....................... 450
25. Feast of St. Louis................................ 451
26. Soldiers' Hospital Day; The Nineteenth Amendment.... 451
27. Petroleum Day 453
28. Festival of St. Augustine.......................... 454
29. Birthday of Oliver Wendell Holmes; Decollation of St. John the Baptist............................. 455
30. Inter-Tribal Indian Ceremonial; Banishment of Anne Hutchinson; Birthday of Huey P. Long............... 456
31. The Charleston Earthquake 460

SEPTEMBER

Origin of the Name................................ 461
SEPT. 1. The Santa Fe Fiesta................................ 462
2. Birthday of Eugene Field; Labor Sunday............. 464
3. Labor Day 465
4. Los Angeles Birthday Celebration................... 466
5. First Continental Congress......................... 467
6. Lafayette's Birthday 468
7. Birthday of James Fenimore Cooper................. 471
8. The Galveston Tornado; Feast of the Nativity of the Virgin Mary 472

CONTENTS

PAGE

9. Admission Day in California...................... 472
10. John Smith Elected President of the Council; Jewish New
    Year 474
11. Battle of Brandywine............................ 475
12. Maryland Defenders' Day; Francis E. Clark Recognition
    Day 476
13. Anniversary of the Death of Commodore John Barry; The
    Pendleton Round-up 478
14. Feast of the Exaltation of the Cross................. 481
15. Birthday of William Howard Taft................... 481
16. Cherokee Strip Day in Oklahoma................... 483
17. Constitution Day; Birthday of Baron von Steuben...... 484
18. Laying the Cornerstone of the Capitol............... 489
19. Feast of St. Januarius; Day of Atonement............ 490
20. Panic of 1873.................................. 492
21. Feast of St. Matthew............................ 493
22. Hanging of Nathan Hale.......................... 494
23. Birthday of William H. McGuffey.................. 494
24. John Marshall's Birthday; Schwenkfelder Thanksgiving
    Day; Feast of the Tabernacles.................... 495
25. Discovery of Pacific by Balboa..................... 498
26. Feast of St. Isaac Jogues......................... 498
27. Women in National Politics....................... 499
28. Frances E. Willard's Birthday; Cabrillo Day in California 499
29. Michaelmas Day or The Feast of St. Michael and All
    Angels 501
30. Feast of St. Jerome.............................. 502

OCTOBER

Origin of the Name 504
OCT. 1. Missouri Day; Mountain State Forest Festival.......... 505
2. The Veiled Prophet Festival at St. Louis.............. 506
3. Founder's Day at Lehigh University; Ending of the Siege
   of Leyden..................................... 508
4. Birthday of Rutherford B. Hayes; Feast of St. Francis of
   Assisi 510
5. Birthday of Chester A. Arthur; Birthday of Edward L.
   Trudeau 514
6. German Day................................... 517
7. Birthday of James Whitcomb Riley; Founder's Day at the
   Berry Schools................................. 519
8. Birthday of John Clarke 521

xix

CONTENTS

PAGE

9. Chicago Fire Day; Fraternal Day in Alabama; Leif Erikson Day 522
10. Oklahoma Historical Day 525
11. Pulaski Day; Y.M.C.A. Founder's Day; Birthday of Harlan Fiske Stone 525
12. Columbus Day; University of North Carolina Day; Farmers' Day 529
13. Laying the Cornerstone of the White House 534
14. Birthday of Dwight David Eisenhower 534
15. Feast of St. Theresa; Ether Day 537
16. Apple Tuesday 538
17. Opening of the Delaware and Chesapeake Canal 539
18. Carnegie Institute Founder's Day; Alaska Day; Feast of St. Luke 540
19. Birthday of John Adams; Yorktown Day; Peggy Stewart Day 543
20. Birthday of Daniel E. Sickles 548
21. Will Carleton Day; The English Thanksgiving Day 549
22. Revocation of the Edict of Nantes; Anniversary of the Death of Jean Grolier 551
23. Birthday of Francis Hopkinson Smith 551
24. Pennsylvania Day; The United Nations Charter; Thursday of Fair Week in South Carolina; Panic of 1929 552
25. Feast of St. Crispin 557
26. Laying the Cornerstone of Dartmouth Hall 558
27. Navy Day; Birthday of Theodore Roosevelt 558
28. Feast of St. Simon; Republic of Czechoslovakia Day; Dedication of the Statue of Liberty 562
29. A Historic Election 563
30. John Mitchell Day 564
31. Hallowe'en; Protestant Reformation Day; Admission Day in Nevada 565

NOVEMBER

Origin of the Name 575
NOV.   1. Feast of All Saints 576
2. Birthday of James K. Polk; Birthday of Warren G. Harding; All Souls' Day 576
3. Birthday of Edward Douglas White 580
4. Feast of St. Charles Borromeo; Will Rogers Day in Oklahoma 581
5. Guy Fawkes Day 583
6. Election Day; Appointment of the First Catholic Bishop .. 584

CONTENTS

PAGE

7. American Troops Land in Africa.................... 585
8. Mount Holyoke College Founder's Day.............. 586
9. Sadie Hawkins Day................................ 588
10. United States Marine Corps Day................... 588
11. Armistice Day; Martinmas; Washington Admission Day 590
12. Birthday of Joseph Hopkinson...................... 594
13. Edwin Booth's Birthday............................ 595
14. A Protestant Episcopal Anniversary; Birthday of Jacob
    Abbott 596
15. The First Constitution............................ 597
16. Feast of St. Edmund.............................. 598
17. Congress Finds a Permanent Home................. 598
18. Birthday of Asa Gray............................. 599
19. Birthday of James A. Garfield; Dedication of the National
    Cemetery at Gettysberg.......................... 599
20. First National G.A.R. Encampment................. 603
21. Invention of the Phonograph...................... 603
22. Feast of St. Cecelia.............................. 604
23. Birthday of Franklin Pierce; Repudiation of the Stamp
    Act; Feast of St. Clement........................ 604
24. Birthday of Zachary Taylor........................ 608
25. Feast of St. Catherine; Evacuation Day in New York.... 619
26. John Harvard Day................................ 612
27. Thanksgiving Day 613
28. Feast of St. Stephen the Younger.................. 618
29. Birthday of Morrison R. Waite; Death of Marcus Whitman 619
30. Birthday of Mark Twain; Feast of St. Andrew.......... 622

DECEMBER

Origin of the Name.............................. 626
DEC. 1. Mother Seton Day................................ 627
2. Beginning of Advent; Promulgation of the Monroe Doctrine 628
3. Birthday of Gilbert Stuart......................... 629
4. Washington Takes Leave of His Officers............. 629
5. Birthday of Martin Van Buren..................... 630
6. Feast of St. Nicholas............................. 631
7. Pearl Harbor; Delaware Day; Library Day in West Virginia 633
8. Feast of the Immaculate Conception................ 635
9. Birthday of Joel Chandler Harris.................. 636
10. Birthday of Thomas H. Gallaudet; Wyoming Day...... 637
11. Indiana Day; Hanukkah or the Festival of Lights...... 639

CONTENTS

PAGE

12. Birthday of John Jay; Feast of the Virgin of Guadalupe.. 640
13. Feast of Santa Lucia................................. 643
14. Death of Washington............................... 643
15. Adoption of the Bill of Rights...................... 644
16. The Boston Tea Party.............................. 644
17. Aviation Day; Whittier's Birthday.................. 645
18. Birthday of Lyman Abbott......................... 648
19. Washington Encamps at Valley Forge............... 648
20. Louisiana Purchase................................. 650
21. Feast of St. Thomas................................ 650
22. Forefathers' Day; St. Frances Xavier's Day........... 651
23. Birthday of Joseph Smith, Jr....................... 655
24. Christmas Eve...................................... 657
25. Christmas or the Feast of the Nativity............... 657
26. Battle of Trenton; Feast of St. Stephen.............. 666
27. Feast of St. John the Evangelist..................... 668
28. Birthday of Woodrow Wilson; Childermas........... 669
29. Birthday of Andrew Johnson........................ 673
30. Gadsden Purchase.................................. 674
31. New Year's Eve; Feast of St. Sylvester............... 675

APPENDICES
    Calendar 679
    Days of the Week.................................. 681
    Rhymes of the Days and Seasons.................... 683
    Signs of the Zodiac................................ 685
    Holidays in the United States....................... 686

INDEX 689

Battle of New Orleans

JANUARY

There is snow on the windowpane
Framing my room,
And the trees are heavy
With frosty bloom.

—ANNE MARY LAWLER

January is the first month in the modern calendar. The name—in Latin it is Januarius—is derived from the two-faced Roman god Janus. The Anglo-Saxons called January Wulf-monath in allusion to the hunger of the wolves which made them bold enough to leave the forests and enter the villages in search of food. Janus is one of the principal deities in Roman mythology. The name is often explained as the masculine form of Diana. Janus was originally the god of light and day, but he gradually became the god of the beginning of things. There are many other theories about him. It was once believed that the worship of him, which existed as a local cult before the foundation of Rome, was introduced by Romulus and that Numa dedicated a temple to him. This temple, however, was only an arch or gate which stood at the northeast end of the Forum. It was kept open during war and closed in time of peace. The Romans were so often at war that it is said that the archway was closed only four times before the Christian era. The beginning of the year was sacred to Janus and a festival in his honor called Agonia, was celebrated on January 9. His aid was invoked at the beginning of any important undertaking. All gateways, doors and other entrances were under his protection. He was worshipped as the guardian of trade and shipping and he was the inventor of agriculture. His head and the prow of a ship adorned Roman coins. He is usually represented with two faces, one looking to the past and the other to the future, but was sometimes represented with three and even four faces.

JANUARY FIRST

NEW YEAR'S DAY

January 1 was fixed as the beginning of the year without relation to the position of the sun. The ancient Egyptians, however, began their year on September 21, the date of the autumn equinox, and the ancient Greeks began their year on June 21, the date of the summer solstice. For a short time December 25 was the date of the beginning of the year in New England.

That the year might have an auspicious beginning the Romans offered sacrifices to Janus and exchanged friendly greetings with their kinsfolk and acquaintances. They also made presents to one another called "strenae" from Strenia, the goddess of strength. This custom, according to tradition, originated in 747 B.C., when the Romans presented to Tatius, king of the Sabines, branches from the trees consecrated to Strenia as tokens of good omen. Later branches of bay and palm were gathered on the first of the year, and in the course of time gifts of a more elaborate character took their places. Those who sought favor with the emperor gave him presents of great value. Under the Caesars these gifts became a source of personal profit to the emperor. Claudius, aware of the burden which these gifts laid upon the people—the giving of them began as a voluntary tribute, but came to be regarded as a duty—issued a decree limiting the amount which might be given. The Christian emperors kept up the custom of observing the new year, but the people continued so many idolatrous rites that the church soon prohibited Christians from participating in the social customs of the day. Finally, after December 25 had been fixed as the day of the nativity, the church made January 1 a religious festival in commemoration of the circumcision of Jesus. The Feast of the Circumcision has been observed in the Roman church since 487 and in the Anglican church since 1549.

The Druids distributed branches of the sacred mistletoe, cut with peculiar ceremonies, as new year's gifts to the people and the Saxons observed the day with gifts and festivals. The Roman custom of making gifts to the emperor was introduced into England as early as the time of Henry III and Queen Elizabeth is supposed to have supplied herself with her jewels and wardrobe almost entirely from these gifts. As late as 1692 the English nobility were accustomed every new year to send to the King a purse with gold in it. Under the Tudors and the Stuarts it was the habit of all classes to give presents to friends with the wish that the new year might be happy. Ladies received presents of gloves or pins which were then expensive. Sometimes the gift was compounded in money and from this practice we have the terms "pin money" and "glove money."

On New Year's Day in Scotland it was an ancient custom for the boys to go from house to house asking for money or something to eat and singing this ditty:

> I wish you a Merry Christmas
> And a Happy New Year,
> A pocketful of money
> And a cellar full of beer,
> And a good fat pig
> To serve you all the year.
> Ladies and gentlemen
> Sitting by the fire,
> Pity us poor boys
> Out in the mire.

This ditty was brought to the United States and the first four lines at least were used by boys in rural New York and elsewhere as a sort of jocular holiday greeting.

It has been the custom from the beginning for the President of the United States to welcome the new year by holding a reception open to the general public. On the first New Year's Day after his inauguration President Washington opened his house to receive the people. Throughout the seven years during which Washington lived in Philadelphia as the capital of the nation he continued this custom. One of the Senators from Pennsylvania wrote the following in his diary on January 1, 1791:

> Made the President the compliments of the season; had a hearty shake of the hand. I was asked to partake of the punch and cakes, but declined. I sat down and we had some chat. But the diplomatic gentry and foreigners coming in, I embraced the first vacancy to make my bow and wish him a good morning.

Thomas Jefferson, the first Democratic President, followed Washington's example, as the following newspaper report of his reception in 1804 indicates:

> About 12 o'clock the President was waited upon by the heads of departments and other officers, civil and military, foreign diplomatic characters, strangers of distinction, the Cherokee chiefs at present on a mission to the seat of government, and most of the respectable citizens of Washington and Georgetown. Some time after the company had assembled, Colonel Burrows, at the head of the Marine Corps, saluted the President while the band of music played the President's march, went through the usual evolutions in a masterly manner, fired sixteen rounds in platoons and concluded with a general *feu-de-joie*. The band at intervals during the morning played martial and military airs. After partaking of the abundant refreshments that were distributed, and enjoying pleasure which may be truly said to have been without alloy, the company separated about 2 o'clock, and betook themselves to the various places of entertainment provided for the celebration of the day.

In contrast with this brief report the account of President Taft's first New Year's reception in 1910 filled more than eight columns of the Washington *Star*. According to its account the President and Mrs. Taft led the receiving party from the upper part of the White House to the blue room at a few minutes past 11 o'clock. They were preceded by the military attachés, walking in couples. A bugle call announced their descent, according to the old custom, and "The Star Spangled Banner" was played by the Marine Band, which functioned then as it had in the days of President Jefferson. In the receiving line, in addition to the President and Mrs. Taft, were Vice President and Mrs. Sherman, the members of the Cabinet who were in Washington, with their wives, and Miss Helen Taft, the daughter of the President. The New Year's reception at the White House, however, is no longer a fixture in Washington social life. The custom was suspended by President Franklin D. Roosevelt on January 1, 1934, as his lameness made it difficult for him to stand in the receiving line for any length of time.

Following the reception at the White House the wife of the Vice President and the wives of several members of the Cabinet were in the habit of holding receptions for their friends at their own homes, thus continuing in a limited way the very old New Year's custom of paying New Year's calls. This custom was introduced into New York by the Dutch who settled first in that city, and it spread to other parts of the country. The people kept open house on that day, and their friends called to give them the compliments of the season. Refreshments were provided which usually consisted of punch made in accordance with the favorite recipe of the host and served from a large bowl. When the city was small the hospitality of those who opened their houses was not abused. After a time it became the custom of those who intended to receive their friends and acquaintances to send their names to the newspapers with the hours when they would be "at home" so that the intending callers might know in advance what houses would welcome them. In the latter part of the nineteenth century these lists of houses filled many columns, and contained the names of persons of fashion as well as of those who made no pretense of moving in fashionable society. It frequently happened that young men, after having made six or eight calls and stopping at six or eight punch bowls, became intoxicated, causing distress in the houses which they next visited. Even when the young men did not get intoxicated they showed slight courtesy to their hostesses. A group of them would hire a carriage and ride from house to house wherever one of them knew the people, rush in, with a brief greeting, exclaim "This is our forty-seventh call," rush out again and urge the driver to hasten to another house for their forty-eighth. And bibulous young men, attracted by the prospect of free punch, would force their way into houses where they were not known, linger for a time over the punch and depart. Because of these abuses the custom was finally abandoned; so that New Year's calls are exchanged now only by intimates without any public announcement of an intention to receive. In Philadelphia, according to a man of fashion, New Year's calls were virtually compulsory in the seventies for those who wished to keep their place in

4

the society of the city. "A grand custom and good liquor, too," he remarked in a reminiscent mood, "and at sundown this fine old town was in a mellow mood." The custom was abandoned, however, in Philadelphia as well as in New York.

Long after the custom was abandoned by private citizens James Cardinal Gibbons of Baltimore, Md., continued it. It was his habit for years to receive the public on New Year's Day at his residence in Charles Street. He said mass in the cathedral in the morning and in the afternoon welcomed many thousands of citizens who called to pay their respects, both Protestants and Catholics. He was always friendly with the newsboys and scores of them called to pay their respects to him, along with the others, and were welcomed graciously as the most distinguished citizens.

The first of January is a legal holiday in all the states and the District of Columbia. It was not until after 1918, however, that the day was made a legal holiday in Massachusetts. It is also a holiday in the army and navy. The navy regulations read:

> The first of January, the twenty-second of February, the thirtieth of May, the fourth of July, the first Monday in September, the twenty-fifth of December and such other days as may be designated by the President, including the day of National Thanksgiving, shall be designated as holidays on board ships of the Navy and at all naval stations.

Americans abroad celebrate the day in accordance with the customs of the country in which they are living or which they may be visiting. The report of the celebration in Berlin in 1910 contained an account of a call made by David Jayne Hill, the American Ambassador, on the Kaiser and the return of the call by the Kaiser and the Crown Prince. Ambassador Hill received American citizens at the embassy in the afternoon. The day and the evening before were celebrated by the Germans in their usual boisterous manner on what is known as Sylvester Abend. Ladies who ventured into the street were likely to be kissed by strangers, and silk hats worn by men were smashed. The police were in the habit of shutting their eyes to much that went on and arrested only those who were so drunk and disorderly that they could not be ignored.

THE PHILADELPHIA MUMMERS' PARADE

The mummers' parade in Philadelphia on New Year's Day had its origins, according to Dr. Francis Burke Brandt, who has written its history, in the old Swedish custom of welcoming the New Year and in the old English mummers' play of the holiday season. The celebration of Christmas by the Swedes, who were among the earliest settlers on the Delaware River, was continued until the New Year. Roaming bands of masqueraders and merrymakers marched about the country making sport for everyone. The English families brought with them the traditions of

5

JANUARY 1

the mummers' play with St. George killing the dragon. In Philadelphia, after the Revolution, Washington was substituted for St. George and along with him, in the company of players, was a character known as Cooney Cracker. Few details of this mummery have been preserved, but it is known that the first two lines of Washington's speech were:

> Here am I, great Washington!
> On my shoulders I carry a gun.

As soon as the character representing Washington had said this, Cooney Cracker interrupted with:

> Here comes I, old Cooney Cracker!
> I swear to God my wife chews terbacker!
> A pipe is good; cigars are better;
> When I get married, I'll send you a letter.

And there was a character representing the devil who cut various antics. In the records of an old Quaker family appears this account of the way the mummers were treated:

> It was considered the proper custom in those days to give the leading mummers a few pence as a dole, which, in the language of the present time, they would pool and buy cakes and beer. It was also regarded as the right thing to do to invite them into the house and regale them with mulled cider or small beer and homemade cakes. It was considered a great breech of decorum or of etiquette to address or otherwise recognize the mummer by any other name than the name of the character he was assuming. I remember a little girl who, with all the curiosity of her sex, had discovered a neighbor's boy in the party; and with childish impetuosity she broke out with, "Oh, I know thee, Isaac Simmons! Thee is not George Washington!" This departure from the proprieties of the occasion was made the subject of comment on many returning holidays.

These bands of mummers were not organized and consisted of small groups of masqueraders parading within the neighborhood of their homes. In the southern part of the city the new year was welcomed by roving bands of men who went about shooting off firearms and making all the din possible. Later they donned fancy costumes and were called Shooters, a name which survived for years as the proper one for the great parade which gradually developed. The beginning of the parade in its present form was on January 1, 1876, the centennial year. The Silver Crown New Year's Association had been organized a short time before and was the first of the large societies which now participate in the demonstration. The report of the parade appeared in the *Public Ledger*, among other paragraphs, under the heading "Local Affairs." Here it is:

> On New Year's Day the weather was as uncomfortable as usual lately, but it seemed to have little or no effect on the spirits of our citizens who crowded the streets and made the city very lively during the entire day and evening. The Fantasticals or "Shooters" were out in force during the whole day and caused much boisterous amusement. Indians and squaws, princes and princesses, clowns, columbines and harlequins. Negroes of the minstrel hall type, Chinese and burlesque Dutchmen, bears, apes and other animals promenaded the streets to the

6

music of the calethumpian cowbell or the more dignified brass bands, and kept up the racket until late at night. Independence Hall was the grand objective for them all, and the old building received many a cheer and serenade, both burlesque and serious. In the middle of the day several of these parties united in one grand parade and made quite a striking display.

But the parade was not yet organized, as is evident from a description of the mummers in an article in *Scribner's Magazine* for July 1881 by Maurice F. Egan, a Philadelphian, later United States Minister to Denmark, who wrote:

On New Year's Eve crowds of men and boys dress themselves in fantastic costumes and roam through the Neck (a name given to a district in the southern part of the city) and lower parts of the city all night. This custom, doubtless a remnant of the old English Christmas "mumming," grows year by year in Philadelphia, and the mummers, becoming bolder, penetrate as far north as Chestnut Street.

The mummers were not formally recognized by the city government until the parade of 1901. They then received permits for their parade and forty-two clubs, multiplied to that number since the formation of the Silver Crown twenty-five years earlier, combined their forces and paraded together on Broad Street. The newspapers, however, did not regard the parade of enough importance to describe it on the front pages. Here is the report of it that appeared on the inside pages of one of them:

For two hours yesterday, almost to a minute, the official section of Philadelphia, represented by the public buildings, was given over to mummery so fantastic that the shades of the staid Quakers, who gave it its sobriquet, must have cloaked themselves in their winding sheets and stalked to bournes more sedate. Beneath the eyes of William Penn, at the very knees of Stephen Girard, about the Reynolds statue, three thousand men and boys in outlandish garb frolicked, cavorted, grimaced and whooped, while the Mayor and members of Councils, Judges and other officials, State and municipal, looked on, laughed and applauded. How many thousands of ordinary citizens did the same no one can compute. The grand plaza about the City Hall and the streets converging were choked with people—a healthy, clean and orderly congregation. The city had put its official seal upon mummery, the lawmakers were there as sponsors and directors and from the windows of the courts of justice wives and daughters of the Judges viewed and enjoyed the scene.

Money prizes were given by the city for the best costumes, comic and otherwise and for the best bands and most amusing antics. It was said of the paraders that the city had known them a century earlier when they were ragamuffins and that half of them looked like ragamuffins still. But it was agreed that "Philadelphia saw on the first day of the twentieth century a procession that Momus himself could not have devised." The parade was led by the Silver Crown New Year's Association. Its members were dressed in elaborate costumes, and in this division were also the George A. Furnival Association, the Elkton Association and the John F. Slater Association. In the comic division led by the Dark Lanterns were other associations known as the Hardly Ables, the Early Risers, the Mixed

7

Pickles, the White Turnips, the Katzenjammer Band, the White Caps, the Energetic Hoboes, the Red Onions, the Ivy Leaf, the Corinthians, the Half and Half and the Cucumbers. By 1930 the parade had become an elaborate affair. There were twelve thousand marchers in line and a crowd estimated at more than three hundred thousand watched them from the sidewalks of Broad Street and from the windows of the abutting buildings. Prizes amounting to $30,000 were awarded. The costumes worn by the presidents of the clubs in the fancy dress division are most curious affairs. The president wears what is called a cape, which consists of great sections of embroidered silk extending twenty or thirty feet before and behind the wearer and supported by scores of pages who hold it parallel with the surface of the street. He wears an elaborate head dress of feathers and plumes. In the comic division, current events and men and women in the public eye at the time are burlesqued. The parade attracts visitors from all the neighboring states. It is one of the most notable demonstrations in honor of the advent of the new year. And the newspapers print many columns of description of the affair with pictures.

THE PASADENA TOURNAMENT OF ROSES

The first Tournament of Roses in Pasadena, Calif., was held on January 1, 1886, by the Valley Hunt Club, founded by the late Charles Frederick Holder. Mr. Holder was a naturalist and author of many books on natural history. He was born in Lynn, Mass., in 1851. He served for five years as associate curator of zoology in the American Museum of Natural History in New York and in 1885 went to Pasadena to become a teacher of zoology. He suggested to the members of the Valley Hunt Club that on January 1 they decorate their carriages with natural flowers and drive them over a prearranged route and that after this parade athletic sports be engaged in. In a letter explaining his connection with the tournament Mr. Holder wrote:

The first parade was in 1886 and consisted of a long line of carriages beautifully decorated with natural flowers, and which, I am told, was the finest thing of the kind ever seen either in this country or in Europe. The following year we not only had private carriages decorated with flowers, but floats of various kinds.

The Valley Hunt Club had charge of the tournament for several years and bore the cost of it. When it became so elaborate that the cost was burdensome to the members, the city of Pasadena assumed responsibility for it. Finally a Tournament of Roses Association was formed to take charge of the celebration. Mr. Holder's original intention was to arrange what he called "an artistic celebration of the ripening of the oranges in California," which occurs at about the beginning of the year. New Year's Day was chosen as the date as that day is a holiday when people are free to celebrate.

The tournament has passed through several stages in the course of its development. At first it was merely a parade of decorated private carriages followed by athletic sports. Then floral floats were entered for a parade in the morning, with a chariot race or football in the afternoon and a ball in the evening. Prizes were awarded for the floats and for the winners in the chariot races. The prizes were presented at the ball over which a Queen of the Tournament presided. In 1902 the afternoon entertainment had been provided by a football game between the University of Michigan and Stanford University.

The following year the first chariot races were run with amateur drivers and a prize for the winner of $750 and smaller prizes for the next three. After four or five years, professional drivers were employed and the prizes were made larger. There were burlesque races between burros to give a comic element to the spectacle. But as the celebration was intended to be an amateur affair, interest in the professional chariot races gradually died out and they were abandoned. In 1916 the afternoon football game permanently took the place of the races. It was played in that year between Washington State College and Brown University. (See Pasadena Rose Bowl Football Game below.)

With the increase in population of the city the annual parade grew larger from year to year. In 1920 it was two and a half miles long and it was estimated that more than a million five hundred thousand separate blossoms were used to decorate the floats. On January 1, 1935, the floats stretched over more than four miles of streets and no one tried to estimate the number of millions of blossoms used, but the float of the Tournament of Roses Association on which Miss Muriel Gowan, the Queen of the Tournament, rode, was said to contain two hundred and fifty thousand blossoms. It was called the Russian Firebird. The bird was fashioned from thousands of yellow chrysanthemums and lavendar sweet peas. Behind this bird were three Russian churches made of pink, white and lavender stocks and sweet peas. The domes were made of yellow pompons. This float led the procession, the grand marshal of which was Harold Lloyd, the popular moving picture actor. It was followed by flower-bedecked automobiles containing the city officials of Pasadena, Los Angeles, Long Beach, and Glendale. A float representing the Bird of Paradise, entered by Los Angeles, led the second division. On it sat Miss Helen Waters as the Queen, between two birds of paradise made of blossoms representing their natural colors, and before her were three white floral cranes stretching their long necks aloft, standing among talisman roses and maidenhair ferns. Portland, Oregon, was represented by a float showing Miss Barbara Williams as Cinderella on a coach made of heather, sweet peas and white carnations surrounded by pink roses. A scene from the opera "Martha" was the subject of the float entered by Los Angeles County. Glendale had a float representing the mythical roc, with wings spreading twenty-five feet, made of blue delphiniums. Its beak was yellow pompons and its crest poinsettias. San Diego, which was planning an international exposition for 1935, entered a floral representation of the tower of the California building at its fair. And the Metropolitan Water Commission, with a float called the River of Destiny, showed the Boulder Dam and the Colorado river in blue delphiniums surrounded by mountains of heather and colored pompons. Notable floats in the other divisions represented the legend of King Arthur, with Kenneth Boettcher as the King, drawing a huge floral broadsword from an anvil of blue delphiniums; a scene from "Midsummer Night's Dream," with Miss Ailene Lytle as Titania standing in the heart of a huge blossom, and Jackie Harris, as Puck, astride a floral butterfly; the Hawaiian legend of the sacrifice to Pele, with Miss Farla Nell Clayton, as the goddess standing beside Kilauea which was belching forth flames, made from poinsettia blossoms; the Court of the Lions in the Alhambra with floral lions and fountain; a floral sea serpent sixty feet long composed chiefly of poinsettia blossoms; and a pelican twenty-five feet long and fifteen feet tall composed of white chrysanthemums and yellow pompons. The first prize was won by the Santa Barbara float called the Peacock. It represented a section of a formal garden approached by a flight of floral steps on each side of the landing of which were floral urns. At the end of a path and standing in front of a floral temple there was a floral peacock with its tail fully spread. The tail was made of blossoms which suggested the natural colors of the bird. In the center of the path was a fountain. There were sixty-four floats in all, representing various cities as well as business corporations, hotels and schools. It was characterized as one of the most beautiful demonstrations in the whole history of the annual tournament and attracted hundreds of thousands of visitors from all parts of the country.

PASADENA ROSE BOWL FOOTBALL GAME

One of the most interesting collegiate sporting events of the year is the football game arranged as an attraction to visitors to supplement the Tournament of Roses, and played in the Rose Bowl at Pasadena on January 1. The first game was played in 1902, when the University of Michigan football team was on a barnstorming tour in the West. They were invited to play with Stanford University and accepted. The score was 49 to 0 in favor of the University of Michigan. This score was tied in 1948 when Michigan beat Southern California 49 to 0, the largest score which had ever been made in the Rose Bowl. A chariot race was substituted for the football game the next year, and continued as the afternoon attraction until January 1, 1916, when the games became an annual event. They were played at Tournament Park until 1923, when the Rose Bowl, a great stadium seating eighty-five thousand persons, was dedicated at the game between Southern California and Pennsylvania State College. The profits of the game are divided, one third to each football team and one third to the Tournament of Roses Association, to be devoted to the cost of the tournament and toward liquidating the debt on the stadium. The championship team of the Pacific Coast Intercollegiate Conference is selected as the western contender in the game and it invites the Eastern contender from among the teams which have made the best records in the autumn playing.

Following are the scores of the games from 1916 when the regular annual series began:

1916—Washington State 14, Brown 0
1917—Oregon 14, Pennsylvania 0
1918—Mare Island Marines 19, Camp Lewis 7
1919—Great Lakes Naval Training Station 17, Mare Island Marines 0
1920—Harvard 7, Oregon 6
1921—California 28, Ohio State 0
1922—Washington and Jefferson 0, California 0
1923—Southern California 14, Pennsylvania State 3
1924—Washington 14, Navy 14
1925—Notre Dame 27, Stanford 10
1926—Alabama 20, Washington 19
1927—Alabama 7, Stanford 7
1928—Stanford 7, Pittsburgh 6
1929—Georgia Tech 8, California 7
1930—Southern California 47, Pittsburgh 14
1931—Alabama 24, Washington State 0
1932—Southern California 21, Tulane 12
1933—Southern California 35, Pittsburgh 0
1934—Columbia 7, Stanford 0
1935—Alabama 29, Stanford 13
1936—Stanford 7, Southern Methodist 0
1937—Pittsburgh 21, Washington 0
1938—California 13, Alabama 0
1939—Southern California 7, Duke 3
1940—Southern California 14, Tennessee 0
1941—Leland Stanford 21, Nebraska 13
1942—Oregon State 20, Duke 16 (Played in Durham, N.C., because of the war)
1943—Georgia 9, U.C.L.A. 0
1944—Southern California 29, Washington 0
1945—Southern California 25, Tennessee 0
1946—Alabama 34, Southern California 14
1947—Illinois 45, U.C.L.A. 14
1948—Michigan 49, Southern California 0

The Rose Bowl was the first of many football "bowls" which include the Orange Bowl, the Sugar Bowl, and numerous others.

THE EMANCIPATION PROCLAMATION

On January 1, 1863, President Lincoln issued a proclamation freeing the slaves in those states and parts of states which were in rebellion on that date. The President had announced by proclamation, dated September 22, 1862, that he would pronounce the slaves free in such parts of the nation as were not represented in Congress by members chosen at elections wherein "a majority of the qualified voters" had participated.

11

JANUARY 1

January 1 is the date generally observed by Negroes as Emancipation Day, although September 22 is sometimes celebrated. In various parts of the country other days are observed as Emancipation Day. The Negroes of Texas celebrate June 19, the date in 1865 when General Robert S. Granger, in command of the military district of Texas, issued a proclamation notifying the Negroes that they were free. Emancipation Day is celebrated in some states on the anniversary of the adoption of the Thirteenth Amendment to the Constitution by those states. Slavery was abolished in Illinois on August 2, 1824. This anniversary is celebrated in that state and in some adjoining states. Emancipation Day has been celebrated in accordance with the differing dates of emancipation or ratification of the Thirteenth Amendment on May 22, May 29, May 30, June 19, August 4, August 8, September 12, September 22 and October 15, as well as on January 1.

The proclamation of January 1, 1863, omitting the preliminary whereases, follows:

Now, therefore, I, Abraham Lincoln, President of the United States, by virtue of the power in me vested as Commander-in-Chief of the Army and Navy of the United States in time of actual rebellion against the authority and government of the United States, and as a fit and necessary war measure for suppressing said rebellion, do, on this first day of January, in the year of our Lord one thousand eight hundred and sixty-three, and in accordance with my purpose so to do, publicly proclaimed for the full period of one hundred days from the date first above mentioned, order and designate as the States and parts of States wherein the people thereof respectively this day are in rebellion against the United States, the following, to wit:

Arkansas, Texas, Louisiana (except the parishes of St. Bernard, Plaquemines, Jefferson, St. John, St. Charles, St. James, Ascension, Assumption, Terre Bonne, Lafourche, St. Marie, St. Martin and Orleans, including the City of New Orleans), Mississippi, Alabama, Florida, Georgia, South Carolina, North Carolina and Virginia (except the forty-eight counties designated as West Virginia and also the counties of Berkeley, Accomac, North Hampton, Elizabeth City, York, Princess Anne and Norfolk, including the cities of Norfolk and Portsmouth), and which excepted parts are, for the present, left precisely as if this proclamation were not issued.

And by virtue of the power, and for the purpose aforesaid, I do order and declare that all persons held as slaves within said designated States and parts of States are, and henceforward shall be, free; and that the Executive Government of the United States, including the military and naval authorities thereof, will recognize and maintain the freedom of said persons.

And I hereby enjoin upon the people so declared to be free, to abstain from all violence, unless in necessary self-defense; and I recommend to them that, in all cases when allowed, they labor faithfully for reasonable wages.

And I further declare and make known that such persons, of suitable condition, will be received into the armed service of the United States, to garrison forts, positions, stations, and other places, and to man vessels of all sorts in said service.

And upon this act, sincerely believed to be an act of justice, warranted by the Constitution upon military necessity, I invoke the considerate judgement of mankind and the gracious favor of Almighty God.

In testimony whereof I have hereunto set my name and caused the seal of the United States to be affixed.

12

THE NEW YEAR IN MOBILE

There was a spontaneous and impromptu celebration of the new year in Mobile, Ala., in 1831, out of which developed many of the carnival customs in that and other Southern cities. On New Year's eve Michael Kraft and a few other merry citizens of Mobile dined at a famous Creole restaurant where the wine flowed freely. On their way home in the early morning of New Year's Day they passed a hardware store belonging to one of the number. Rakes, scythes, gongs and cow bells were hanging outside to indicate what was for sale within. These were seized and the merrymakers visited the houses of numerous sleeping citizens where they made all the racket possible with the gongs and rakes and other implements. As the man of the house appeared to beseech them to stop the din he was forcibly impressed into the ranks of the serenaders and compelled to assist in the noisy sport. The last house to be visited was that of the Mayor. He recognized the men and invited them in for breakfast. The next year a large group of jolly fellows dined at the same Creole restaurant and again in the early morning they serenaded the town with every kind of device which could be used for making a noise. The third year the celebration was organized in advance and those taking part were masked. Then a burlesque society called the Cowbellian de Rakian was formed and the celebrations became more elaborate. Out of this grew the Mobile carnival. In 1881 the society observed the fiftieth anniversary of the celebration.

FEAST OF THE CIRCUMCISION

According to the Jewish custom Jesus was circumcised. The account in the Gospel of St. Luke says: "And when eight days were accomplished for the circumcising of the child, his name was called Jesus, which was so named of the angel before he was conceived." The rite was given to Abraham as a sign of the covenant which Jehovah had made with him. It was after the date of Christmas had been fixed for December 25 that the Christian church began to observe January 1 the anniversary, as a feast day. It was first observed by the Roman church in 487 but was not introduced into England until 1549 after the Anglican church broke with Rome.

JANUARY SECOND

THE FIRST FLAG OF WASHINGTON'S ARMY

George Washington, who was chosen commander in chief of the Continental Army by Congress on June 15, 1775, on the nomination of Thomas Johnson of Maryland, left Philadelphia on June 21, arrived at Cambridge, Mass., on July 3, and took command of the sixteen thousand men assembled there. He devoted himself to organizing them for service and to obtaining uniforms and other equipment. He decided that they should have a flag and on January 2, 1776, one of his choosing was run up for the first time on the flag staff before his headquarters. It had thirteen stripes of red and white representing the thirteen colonies with the British Union Jack of the Crosses of St. George and St. Andrew in the corner now occupied by forty-eight stars.

JANUARY THIRD

BATTLE OF PRINCETON

After the defeat of the British at Trenton on December 26, 1776, Washington learned that Cornwallis with an army of eight thousand had arrived near that city. Washington had a much smaller force, and the ice in the Delaware river prevented his retreat although he had been able to cross the river before the Battle of Trenton. He therefore decided to attack the British forces at Princeton and New Brunswick instead of waiting for Cornwallis to attack him at Trenton. He left his camp fires burning on the night of January 2, 1777, and marched, in the darkness, around the British left. He reached the Stony Brook bridge at about sunrise on January 3 and sent General Mercer with about four hundred men to destroy the bridge. Mercer met the British force from Princeton at the bridge on its way to join Cornwallis at Trenton. The Americans opened fire and the British replied with a bayonet charge. General Mercer was fatally wounded and his men retreated, pursued by the British. A force of regulars and militia under Washington met the British and dispersed them, some fleeing by a roundabout way to Trenton and others to New Brunswick. Washington then entered Princeton and seized the military stores. When Cornwallis advanced, Washington retreated and took up a strong position at Morristown. The battle is regarded as of strategic importance as it forced Cornwallis to return to New York and left New Jersey in the possession of the Americans. The anniversary of the battle is observed periodically in Princeton.

JANUARY FOURTH

FEAST OF ST. TITUS

In the calendar of the Roman Catholic Church, January 4, the Octave of the Holy Innocents, is set down as the birthday of St. Titus. Titus shared with Timothy the confidence and affection of St. Paul. There is little biographical detail in the New Testament. It is known, however, that he was a Gentile and converted to Christianity through Paul and that he went with Paul and Barnabas on the mission from the church at Antioch to the council of the Apostles in Jerusalem. Paul sent him from Ephesus on two if not three missions to the church at Corinth. He went with Paul to Crete to strengthen the churches on that island. According to tradition he was bishop of Crete and died there at the age of ninty-three years. The church there is now under the control of the Greek bishops.

JANUARY FIFTH

EPIPHANY EVE

One of the most interesting Christian legends is connected with the eve of Epiphany. It is related that when the Three Wise Men from the East were on their way to Bethlehem from Jerusalem they passed an old woman cleaning her house. She asked them where they were going and when they told her, she asked them to wait until she had finished her work and she would go with them. They replied that they could not wait and advised her to follow them. When she had finished her work, she started, but they were out of sight, and ever since that day she has been wandering about the world seeking the child Jesus. According to the folklore of Russia and Italy she goes down the chimneys of houses leaving gifts for the children in imitation of the gifts of the Wise Men, in the hope that at last she may find the Child whom she is seeking. In Italy she is known as Befana, a corruption of the word Epiphany. Citizens of Italian descent have brought this legend to America with them and their children have faith in Befana as other children believe in Santa Claus. Epiphany Eve is a rustic festival in England, observed in order to obtain a blessing on the crops of the coming year.

This day is also the feast of St. Simeon Stylites, the founder of a small order of monks known as pillar-saints. Simeon lived for thirty years on a pillar about sixty feet high and three feet in diameter at the top, surrounded by a railing to prevent him from falling. People assembled twice a day to watch him at his devotions. When he died in the middle of the fifth century his body was taken to Antioch where it was buried.

JANUARY SIXTH

FEAST OF THE EPIPHANY

The feast of the Epiphany, falling on the twelfth day after Christmas, is observed by all branches of the Christian church. The word "epiphany" comes from the Greek and means a manifestation. It is applied to the manifestation of Jesus as the Christ. This occurred at three different times. The first was when the Three Wise Men from the East came to worship Him in the cradle at Bethlehem; the second, when at His baptism in the Jordan by John the Baptist the Holy Spirit descended upon Him in the form of a dove, and a voice proclaimed Him the Son of God; and the third was when He began His miracles by changing water into wine at the wedding feast at Cana. All three manifestations are supposed to have occurred on the same day of the year.

In the Greek Church the day is called the Theophany, or the Appearance of God. This church also calls it the Feast of the Jordan as well as the Feast of the Lights, referring to the tradition that lights appeared on the river at the time of the baptism of Jesus. In Germany it is known as the Festival of the Three Holy Kings.

The feast of the Epiphany is first mentioned by Clement of Alexandria late in the second century when he wrote that the Basilidians, an Alexandrine sect of Gnostics, followers of Basilides, had a feast on the day of the baptism of Jesus, preceding it with scripture readings. The day they observed was either January 6 or January 10. Professor Conybeare is of the opinion that Basilides selected the date because it corresponded with the date of the blessing of the Nile in Egypt and the heathen festival could therefore easily be transformed into a Christian observance. This theory is supported by the belief of St. Chrysostom that the water drawn from the rivers on Epiphany was holy and could be preserved much longer than water drawn on other days, a literal acceptance of the Egyptian belief about the waters of the Nile. St. Chrysostom's belief about the sacredness of the waters on Epiphany survives to this day in the Greek Church. Before the Tsar was dethroned in Russia the ceremony of blessing the Neva, in commemoration of the blessing of the Jordan by the baptism of Christ, was observed with great pomp in St. Petersburg. A pavilion was built on the frozen river opposite the Winter Palace and the Tsar and his court went there. A hole was chopped in the ice large enough to admit a cross, and the Metropolitan and his clergy blessed the waters with prayers that they might fertilize the earth and benefit mankind during the ensuing year. At one time the devout peasants would also break holes in the ice and throw themselves into the water in the belief that they would be cured of their diseases and remain immune to illness for the next year. Not only was the Neva blessed but the local clergy blessed the Don, the Volga and other rivers, and the people, following the example of those in St. Petersburg, bathed in the streams, regardless of the temperature.

January 6 was kept as the anniversary of the physical birth of Jesus as early as the fourth century and the Christians in Palestine observed both the birth and the baptism on that date. There is extant a copy of a letter from the Bishop of Jerusalem to the Bishop of Rome saying that the faithful met in Bethlehem before dawn on that date to celebrate the birth and then hurried off to the Jordan, thirteen miles east of Jerusalem, to celebrate the baptism. The Bishop asked his brother in Rome to look in the archives of the Jews, taken there after the destruction of Jerusalem, and find out if possible the real date of the birth of Jesus. The Bishop of Rome made the necessary investigation and replied that December 25 was the date of the birth.

It is uncertain whether the feast of the Epiphany was first celebrated by the Basilidians or by the Christians in Palestine. It is possible that the Palestinians instituted it first for there is a tradition that it was observed by the disciples of John the Baptist who were present at the baptism. The Gnostic theory of a spiritual birth at baptism may have been responsible for the celebration of the anniversary of the physical birth on the same day as the celebration of the baptism.

The visit of the Magi has received chief attention in the observance of the day in the Western Church since the fourth century, as the event has come to be regarded as the manifestation of the divine purpose to extend the benefits of the gospel to the Gentile world as well as to the Jews. There grew up a body of legends concerning these Three Wise Men, each version adding a little to the last till the men became the Three Kings, sometimes called the Three Kings of Cologne. Names were given to them and one was called Caspar or Jaspar, King of Tarsus, the land of myrrh; another was called Melchior, King of Arabia, rich in gold; and the third was known as Balthasar, King of Saba, or Sheba, where frankincense flowed from the trees. When they beheld the wondrous star, said by some astronomers to have been what is now known as Halley's comet which made its most recent appearance in the solar system in 1910, they mounted their dromedaries and set out on their journey. They followed the star till it took them to Jerusalem and there it disappeared. Herod learned that the Three Kings were asking about a child whom they called the King of the Jews. He sent for the learned men among the Jews and asked them where their Messiah was to be born. They told him that it was in Bethlehem. Thereupon he sent for the Three Kings and told them to go to Bethlehem and if they found the new king to return and report to him. They departed and as they were leaving the city of Jerusalem, according to one form of the tradition, they were accosted by an old woman engaged in cleaning her house. She wanted to know where they were going and when she was told she besought them to wait till she had finished her work so that she might go with them. But they refused to wait, telling her that she might follow them at her leisure. So when her work was finished she started after them but could not find them. It is said in the legend that she has been wandering about the earth ever since seeking the child Jesus. (See Epiphany Eve, January 5.)

The star reappeared to guide the Three Kings to Bethlehem as soon as they were outside the walls of Jerusalem. When Mary heard the tramping feet of the dromedaries she took Jesus in her arms lest he should be taken from her and it was in this attitude that the seekers found the mother and child. They knelt and adored Jesus as God and the Savior of the world. Caspar gave gold to Him to indicate that he regarded the child as King. Melchior gave frankincense to show that he looked upon the child as God, and Balthasar presented myrrh, prophetic of the time when He should lie in the tomb. Jesus in return for the gold bestowed the gift of charity and spiritual riches; for the frankincense he bestowed faith and for the myrrh he gave the gift of truth and meekness. The Three Kings, warned in a dream, returned to their homes without going back to Herod.

According to one tradition, when they reached their own countries they resigned their high offices, distributed their goods to the poor and went about preaching the gospel of the Prince of Peace. St. Thomas, when traveling in India forty years later, is said to have found the Three Wise Men and baptized them and ordained them as priests. They suffered martyrdom for their faith and were buried together. Empress Helena found what she was convinced were their bones and carried them to Constantinople and put them in the church of St. Sophia. At the time of the First Crusade the bones were rescued and taken to Milan, and Barbarossa, when he captured Milan, took possession of them and laid them in the cathedral at Cologne. When the old cathedral was burned the relics were saved and were deposited in the new one. They now rest there in a golden shrine decorated with precious gems.

TWELFTH NIGHT REVELS

Epiphany marks the close of the Advent season (see Advent, December 2) during which strict observance of their religious duties is enjoined on the faithful. It also once marked the beginning of the carnival season which continued until Shrove Tuesday (see Shrove Tuesday, February 13) the day before Ash Wednesday (see Ash Wednesday, February 14). In recent years the carnival season in Europe has been confined to the three days before Lent, a custom which has been followed in the arrangements for the New Orleans carnival. It has been the custom in the United States for many secular organizations to have a Twelfth Day frolic. A celebration arranged by the Lotus Club of New York is typical of them all. On this occasion a company of trumpeters marched through the corridors and rooms of the club house sounding the call to the dinner in the banquet room. When the guests gathered the lights were turned down and a spot light was played on the boy choristers from Christ Church who sang "While by my sheep I watch at night," and "Lo, how a rose ere blooming" and "The First Noel." When the lights were turned on the president of the club was seen sitting on a throne beneath a Christmas canopy. He raised the wassail cup and commanded every one to forget his cares, and rejoice. During the first course of the dinner four waits standing under a street lamp which had been set up in the room sang of the sorrows of Solomon over his many wives and other merry songs. The room was darkened again and chimes from the galley played Tom Moore's ballad, "Believe me if all those endearing young charms." After a time the musicians clad in Elizabethan costume were seen to make their way to the kitchen. In a few moments they returned blowing their oboes and French horns at the head of a procession led by the chef. This functionary wore a sprig of holly in his cap and a cleaver and carver hung from a belt about his waist. Behind him came two under cooks bearing on their shoulders a litter decorated with greens and holly berries and containing great barons of beef. A third cook marched behind these two holding high over his head a trencher containing a boar's head. The scullions followed carrying ladles and gravy boats. The procession marched about the room and through the aisles between the tables and then returned to the kitchen where the beef was carved. While the waiters were bringing in the beef the diners sang "The Roast Beef of Old England," keeping time by pounding the table with their knives. When the beef was served four cellarmen brought in a great brass bowl filled with flaming Jack Ketch punch. The bowl was put in its place, the lights were lowered again, and the orchestra played the fire music from "Die Walkure." Then the lights were turned on and the choir boys sang more carols. Nat Wills, a well known comedian of the time, acting as the king's jester, told some merry stories, and there were more songs and more music from the orchestra. The feast ended with plum pudding, and was followed by the singing of songs by Reinald Werrenrath and Signor Ferrara.

In New Orleans Twelfth Night is observed as the beginning of the carnival season, preliminary to the fasting of Lent. The word carnival comes from the Latin *carnem levare*, meaning to put away flesh although other derivations have been suggested. It is applied to the season of feasting and revelry preceding the abstinence of Lent. The Twelfth Night Revelers, headed by the Lord of Misrule, have been accustomed to give an annual ball in the French Opera House in New Orleans. At a typical celebration the ball was preceded by a series of stage pictures of "The Garden of the Gods." The first scene showed a corner of the garden on the shores of a lake. Swans swam on the water but suddenly something startled them and they swiftly swam away while from the other side of the lake several of the gods appeared rowing. As they floated idly about, the scene changed to another part of the garden. Flower-bordered walks were shown with the gods strolling along them. As the gods approached the plants the buds opened and soon the garden was a riotous mass of bloom. The third scene showed what was described as the holy of holies of the garden. High on his golden throne sat the Lord of Misrule. On each side of the throne a fountain poured forth a crystal stream which changed its colors as it fell into the basin below. Eight golden lions with flashing eyes, spitting fire from their open jaws, stood on high pedestals. Statuary and vases with flowers adorned a terrace and the garden seemed to stretch into infinite space. Here on this terrace were assembled all the carnival gods: Venus, the goddess of love; Old Sol and his retinue; Selene, the moon, and Aurora, the dawn; Vulcan, the god of fire; Neptune, god of the sea; Momus, the god of laughter; Comus, the leader of the revelry and all the others.

The queen of the previous year's ball was escorted to the throne beside the Lord of Misrule along with her maids of honor. Then the gods formed into platoons and executed an intricate march about the stage. At the end of the march each took a dancing partner and they all assembled at the front of the stage. Thereupon the cook brought in the king's cake after the fashion of the old custom in England and France. In those countries a large cake, in which a bean was put, was baked for Twelfth Day. When the cake was cut and divided among the guests the person who received the piece containing the bean was the king for the celebration. Sometimes a small doll was used instead of a bean. The New Orleans cake was an imitation affair filled with small boxes, one containing a golden bean and other silver beans. The ladies drew the boxes from the cake. The one drawing the golden bean became the queen and she was escorted to the throne, took her seat beside the king, and was crowned by the queen of the previous year. Those who drew the silver beans became the queen's maids. After these ceremonies were concluded the ball began.

BLESSING OF THE SPONGE DIVERS AT TARPON SPRINGS, FLORIDA

One of the most beautiful and interesting observances of the Epiphany ceremony, long celebrated by the Greek Orthodox church, occurs each year on January 6 at Tarpon Springs, Florida. It is known locally as the Blessing of the Sponge Divers and the ceremonies are unique in the United States; are, in fact, observed nowhere else in the same manner except in Greece. After masses have been said at the Church of St. Nicholas, a procession of ecclesiastical dignitaries in magnificent robes, led by the parade marshall, proceeds to the bayou on the Gulf of Mexico. The gospel is read, first in Greek by the archbishop and then in English by an interpreter. Next a white dove is released over the waters, signifying the Holy Spirit, and at the same time the archbishop casts the cross into the bayou in symbolism of the baptism of Christ. The sponge divers plunge after the crucifix and the one to retrieve it is blessed by the archbishop. Thousands of visitors come to Tarpon Springs annually to witness the ceremonies, which invariably take place at noon on the sixth of January in a natural amphitheatre on the banks of the bayou, against a backdrop of palms and tropical sky.

In 1945, the forty-second observance at Tarpon Springs, Bishop Gerasimos, head of the Greek Orthodox diocese of Chicago, officiated, admonishing the sponge-fishing captains to pray for peace and for the return of the five hundred servicemen of the community. The Greek prelate was an impressive figure of patriarchal dignity in the jeweled miter of the Eastern church, his long, white beard flowing over brocaded, hand-embroidered vestments. He carried a silver staff surmounted by entwined serpents, symbolic of the serpent Moses lifted from the wilderness. His prayer asked a blessing upon the five thousand present, upon the sponge fleet, and upon the mothers who had sent sons overseas in World War II. A fifteen-year-old Greek high school boy of Tarpon Springs, the youngest ever achieving the honor, retrieved the golden cross, emerging from the bayou in youthful triumph to pose for newspaper cameramen assembled from all over the United States. The procession from the church to the bayou, which preceded the ceremony, was headed by the marshall in the costume of a native Evzone warrior; pleated, starched, white skirt, black velvet bodice, and red-tasseled slippers. Following him were the church dignitaries, the acolytes, the black-robed, chanting choir, flag bearers, Boy Scouts, Legionaires, representatives of the Allied nations in the persons of young Greek women of the community wearing the native costumes of each country, and many other colorfully garbed participants. After the ceremony, the young diver who retrieved the cross spent the afternoon visiting houses throughout the city so that the faithful might kiss the golden symbol and place flowers upon it.

The origin of the sponge divers at Tarpon Springs goes back to 1905 when they were imported directly from Greece and the Greek islands at the instigation of John Corcoris, the first Greek diver to join the growing industry. Prior to this, sponges had been found at Key West as early as 1849, but sponge-fishing on a commercial basis was not started in the Gulf waters until 1890 when John K. Cheynes, one of the early settlers, sent out the first "hooker" boat and later established the first packing house. During the Spanish-American war the Key West sponge fleet, fearing Spanish warships, disposed of their cargo at Tarpon Springs. From these small beginnings there developed the Tarpon Springs Sponge Exchange, said to be the largest sponge market in the world. The sponge fleet comprises about one hundred and seventy-five boats and some six hundred men who make trips, often of several months duration and sometimes from fifty to eighty miles from land, in craft only twenty-five to forty-five feet in length.

THE FOUR FREEDOMS

On January 6, 1941 President Franklin D. Roosevelt made an address to Congress which was widely quoted and discussed, his phrase, the four freedoms, subsequently being used to epitomize the ideology of the democracies as opposed to Nazism. The President said:

In the future days, which we seek to make secure, we look forward to a world founded upon four essential human freedoms.

The first is freedom of speech and expression—everywhere in the world.

The second is freedom of every person to worship God in his own way—everywhere in the world.

The third is freedom from want—which, translated into world terms, means economic understandings which will secure to every nation peaceful life for its inhabitants—everywhere in the world.

The fourth is freedom from fear—which, translated into world terms, means a worldwide reduction of armaments to such a point and in such a thorough fashion that no nation will be in a position to commit any act of aggression against any neighbor—anywhere in the world.

JANUARY SEVENTH

MILLARD FILLMORE'S BIRTHDAY

Millard Fillmore, the thirteenth President of the United States, was born at Locke, Cayuga County, N.Y., on January 7, 1800. He was the oldest son and second child of Nathaniel Fillmore who had moved to Locke from Bennington, Vt., in 1798. He was named for his mother, Phoebe Millard. The family name was originally spelled Phillmore when its first known American member bought an estate at Beverly, Mass., in 1704. Millard worked on his father's farm and as an apprentice to a clothier with short periods spent in school. When he was eighteen he began to study law in the office of a Cayuga County judge. The family moved to East Aurora and the youth continued the study of the law there, teaching school at the same time. He was admitted to the bar of Erie County in 1823, and opened an office in East Aurora. He practiced his profession there until 1830 when he moved to Buffalo where he made his home for the rest of his life. He had interested himself in politics and in 1828, through the influence of Thurlow Weed, he was elected to the State Legislature on the Anti-Masonic ticket. He served three terms in the Legislature and in 1832 was elected to the national House of Representatives. He declined reelection, but in 1836 he was again sent to Congress from his district and was twice reelected. He was a follower of Henry Clay in Congress, but refused to go along with his leader in his fight for the reestablishment of the United States Bank. When the Whigs obtained a majority in the House in the election of 1840 Fillmore was made chairman of the Ways and Means Committee and took an active part in framing the protective tariff law of 1842. An attempt was made to nominate him for Vice

President in 1844, but it failed and he was nominated for governor of New York against Silas Wright, the Democratic candidate, but was defeated. In 1847 he was elected Comptroller of New York; and in 1848 he was nominated for Vice President on the ticket with Zachary Taylor and elected. He resigned his state office on February 20, 1849, to take up his duties in Washington. He succeeded to the presidency on July 9, 1849, on the death of President Taylor. He had believed that the election of 1848 had put an end to all ideas of disunion as it raised up "a national party, occupying middle ground, and leaves the fanatics and disunionists, North and South, without the hope of destroying the fair fabric of our Constitution." As President he sought to occupy a middle ground and favored the compromise measures, including the Fugitive Slave Law. The extreme anti-slavery advocates in the North denounced him bitterly, but it is now admitted that he strove with all the power at his command to avert the conflict which began ten years later. His supporters, chiefly the Southern Whigs, sought to bring about his renomination in 1852, but failed. He was nominated, however, by the Whigs in 1856, the last presidential candidate of the party, while the new Republican party nominated John C. Fremont. He received 874,534 votes, Fremont received 1,341,264, and Buchanan, the Democratic candidate, received 1,838,169, or about 375,000 votes less than were polled by the combined opposition. He opposed Lincoln's conduct of the war and supported General McClellan for President in the campaign of 1864, and during the reconstruction period he was in sympathy with the policies of President Johnson. He was the first Chancellor of the University of Buffalo, one of the founders of the Buffalo Historical Society and of the Buffalo General Hospital. Oxford University offered the degree of Doctor of Civil Laws to him in 1855, but he declined it on the ground that he had no literary or scientific attainments which would justify accepting it. He died on March 8, 1874.

THE PANAMA CANAL

On January 7, 1914, the self-propelled crane boat, Alex La Valley, made the first passage through the Panama Canal. The first ocean steamer passed through on August 3, and the canal was officially opened August 15, 1914. This opening solved a problem of international commerce which originally presented itself to the Western World in 1453 when Constantinople fell to the Turks and the great land routes to India and the Orient were closed to Christian Europe. Within half a century Columbus set forth in search of a route to the East, and later Balboa explored the Isthmus of Panama for a legendary strait. But to Hernando Cortez, conqueror of Mexico, belongs the honor of first proposing the

23

construction of a water route between the Gulf of Mexico and the Pacific. The subsequent founding and rapid growth of the United States emphasized the need of such a waterway and several times during the nineteenth century a canal under American control seemed assured, but political difficulties invariably arose to prevent it. While this country was still struggling to recover from the Civil War the French undertook to engineer and finance the project. In 1879 a French company was organized with Count Ferdinand de Lesseps as its president. The plan was for a sea-level canal and excavations were actually started; however, it proved impractical from an engineering standpoint and the French company, in financial difficulties, became corrupt and was finally declared bankrupt. A new company was eventually formed, and in June 1902 the Spooner Bill was passed in Congress authorizing President Theodore Roosevelt to acquire the rights and property of the New Panama Canal Company from the French. On May 4, 1904, the United States took formal possession of the site and property, and in 1906 work was started on a canal with high-level locks which was successfully completed in 1914.

JANUARY EIGHTH

JACKSON DAY

The anniversary of the Battle of New Orleans is a legal holiday in Louisiana. It is known as Jackson Day, or Old Hickory's Day, in honor of Andrew Jackson who commanded the victorious American forces in the battle.

This was the last battle in the War of 1812, and was fought after the treaty of peace had been signed. American representatives, including John Quincy Adams, James A. Bayard, and Henry Clay, had been sent to Europe to negotiate a peace. They met the British representatives at Ghent and after long negotiations signed a treaty on December 24, 1814, ending the war. Methods of communication, however, were so slow that news of the signing of the treaty did not reach this country for several weeks.

The New Orleans adventure had been undertaken by the British against the advice of the Duke of Wellington. Nevertheless, his brother-in-law, Major General Packenham, was put in command of the expedition. He arrived off the coast of Louisiana with a fleet of fifty ships and seven thousand soldiers on December 10. On December 23 he reached a point eight miles from New Orleans with a detachment of troops. He was attacked by General Jackson but successfully resisted the assault. The next morning General Jackson fell back behind a disused millrace at Chalmette, near New Orleans, and ordered his troops to fortify themselves by throwing up earthworks. Cotton bales were used in the embrasures of some of the batteries and around the magazines. On January 1 the British tried to break the American lines by cannonading them, but were unsuccessful. On January 8 they attempted to take the American position by assault, but were met by such vigorous resistance that within half an hour they lost two thousand men, and General Packenham himself was killed along with two other generals. Ten days later the British retreated to their ships.

The victory made General Jackson a national hero and laid the foundation for the political strength which later made him President. Jackson was born on the border line between North and South Carolina on March 15, 1767, of Scotch-Irish parentage. His birthday is observed as a legal holiday in Tennessee. His father, a farm laborer, died a few days before Andrew's birth. His mother died while he was small and his two brothers were killed in the Revolutionary War, so that in his early youth he was left alone in the world. In 1784, at the age of seventeen, he began to study law in Salisbury, S.C., and was admitted to the bar when he was less than twenty years old. At the age of twenty-one he was appointed public prosecutor in the region now forming the State of Tennessee. At the age of twenty-nine he was a member of the convention which framed a constitution for Tennessee and in the same year he was elected to the national House of Representatives. He was a Jeffersonian and was one of the twelve members of the House who opposed the adoption of an address to Washington at the close of his administration. He was elected to the United States Senate in 1797, but resigned after serving about a year. He held various offices in Tennessee and engaged in private business until the declaration of war against Great Britain in 1812. He then offered his services and the services of the militia which he commanded. They were accepted with the result that he was the victor in the Battle of New Orleans which is regarded in Europe as the most famous battle in the war. His military career continued for five or six years.

He reentered political life by reelection to the Senate in 1823. In 1824 he was a candidate for the presidency, but as there were three other candidates and none received a majority of the electoral votes the choice was thrown into the House of Representatives in accordance with the Constitution. Each state had one vote which was cast in accordance with the will of the majority of the Representatives from that state. Jackson was defeated by the vote of Stephen VanRensselaer of New York. He had agreed to vote for Jackson, but as he was a rich man the supporters of John Quincy Adams told him that all property would be in danger if Jackson were elected. VanRensselaer, as Martin VanBuren tells the story in his autobiography, did not know what to do. But he was a pious man and when he took his seat in the House on the day when the vote was to be taken, he bowed his head in prayer and asked for divine guidance. When he opened his eyes he saw on the floor in front of him a ballot with the name of Adams on it. He took this for an answer to his prayer and his vote for Adams gave the vote of New York against Jackson. Jackson, however, was elected by a majority of the electors in 1828 and again in 1834. He was the first President to be chosen from what was then regarded as the West and the first representative of what the politicians call "the plain people" to sit in the White House. His administration was notable for his assault upon the United States Bank and his opposition to a central banking system. He aroused so much hostility to such an arrangement that it persisted until the administration of another Democratic President, Woodrow Wilson, under whom the Federal Reserve Banking System was organized.

In Louisiana, Jackson Day is observed by special exercises in the public schools in celebration of the victory at the Battle of New Orleans. In other parts of the country the day has come to be an occasion for Democratic jubilation. In the principal cities the Democrats arrange dinners at which party orators declaim party doctrines. The Democratic National Committee usually arranges a dinner in Washington on the anniversary, and in the year of a presidential campaign the aspirants for the party nomination to the presidency are invited to be present to set forth their views. One of the most notable Jackson Day dinners held outside of Washington in the present century was that in Baltimore in 1911, after the Democratic victory at the congressional elections in the preceding November. Distinguished party leaders were present and outlined what they regarded as the proper policy for the party. There were a thousand guests present, and the people of the city were so deeply interested in the amount of food needed to feed them that the Baltimore newspapers reported that seven thousand oysters, seventy-five gallons of terrapin, fifteen hundred pounds of capon, five hundred canvasback ducks, forty-five Smithfield hams, three thousand cigars and five hundred bottles of champagne were provided.

One of the most notable early celebrations of the anniversary occurred in New Orleans on January 8, 1828, during Jackson's campaign for the presidency. Jackson had gone to that city in the course of his campaign, taking with him James A. Hamilton, as the representative of the Tammany Society of New York. The general was naturally the guest of honor and since it was a political gathering then, as the celebration has been in subsequent years, he was praised highly by his party associates.

JANUARY NINTH

THE FIRST BALLOON ASCENSION

The problem of flight was solved in America by the Wright brothers, but the first successful balloon ascension in this country was made by a Frenchman, François Blanchard, in Philadelphia on January 9, 1793. There had been a previous attempt made by a man named Carnes from Baltimore at a Fourth of July celebration in Philadelphia in 1784, but it failed and Carnes narrowly escaped with his life. Blanchard had tried in 1784 to build a balloon with wings or sails and a rudder. In 1785 he crossed the English channel in a balloon, and in the same year he used a parachute in descending from the air. He came to America in 1792 where his fame had preceded him, and arranged to make an ascent. The yard of the old Walnut Street Prison in Philadelphia was put at his disposal. Tickets of admission were offered at $5, but not many were sold at that figure and the price was reduced to $2. About two hundred spectators assembled within the yard and a large crowd gathered outside to see the balloon rise into the air. A company of artillery was stationed in the yard, and when President Washington arrived at nine o'clock a salute of fifteen guns was fired in his honor. Two guns were fired every fifteen minutes until the time of the ascension. At five minutes after ten o'clock President Washington gave Blanchard a written message to take up with him. Blanchard then entered the car, threw out some ballast and when the balloon began to rise, cannon were fired and the band played a lively air. The balloonist landed at Cooper's Ferry, N. J., forty-five minutes later. He returned to Philadelphia in the evening and presented his respects to the President. The enterprise was financially unsuccessful for it cost Blanchard about $2000 more than he received. An effort to reimburse him for his loss by popular subscription failed, and he made two or three more ascents in an endeavor to recover what he had lost.

The one hundred and forty-fourth anniversary of Blanchard's ascent was celebrated in Philadelphia on January 9, 1937, by the release of a balloon from Independence Square opposite the site of the jail from the yard of which the original ascent was made. The balloon, filled with hydrogen gas, was in charge of four policemen dressed in eighteenth century costumes. In the basket was a doll in colonial dress made to represent Blanchard. After the balloon was released and had floated in the direction in which the first balloon had been carried by the wind one hundred and forty-four small balloons, one for each year, were released from the top of the Penn Mutual Insurance Company building, which stands where the jail once stood. A navy blimp from Lakehurst and a squadron of airplanes from the Philadelphia Navy Yard flew above the square while the ceremonies were in progress. The celebration was arranged to mark the opening of an airplane exhibition in the city to show the progress in aviation since Blanchard made his flight.

JANUARY TENTH

LEAGUE OF NATIONS DAY

The League of Nations for the establishment of which the Treaty of Versailles provided, came into existence on January 10, 1920, the date of the deposit of the ratification of the treaty by Germany. The insertion of provisions for such an organization in the treaty between the Allies and Germany was proposed by President Wilson. He took a draft of a covenant to Paris with him when he went there to attend the Peace Conference. It was at first welcomed coldly, but the President insisted that it be included. Finally a commission was appointed composed of two delegates each from the United States, France, Great Britain, Italy and Japan with representatives of five smaller powers subsequently added, to study the different forms of covenant which had been submitted. After several sittings a final draft was agreed upon and inserted in the treaty. The primary purpose of the Covenant was to bring about a reduction of armaments in the interest of peace with penalties for any power which began a war. The treaty with the Covenant was ratified by the European powers involved. President Wilson sought to induce the United States Senate to ratify it but failed. Many reservations were proposed in the Senate. The advocates of international cooperation in the interest of peace urged ratification. Indeed, a plan for a league had originated in the United States long before World War I and had the support of many influential leaders in public and private life. President Wilson objected to the reservations proposed in the Senate and when the question of ratification with the reservations came to a vote the supporters of the President in the Senate voted in the negative and the treaty was rejected. The issue of joining the League entered the presidential campaign of 1920, with the Democratic candidate favoring it and the Republican candidate taking an equivocal position. The Republicans won by a large majority, and the United States never joined the League.

On April 18, 1946, the League was officially disbanded, having been eighteenth amendment, went into effect on December 5, 1933, after being following World War II.

JANUARY ELEVENTH

BIRTHDAY OF ALEXANDER HAMILTON

Alexander Hamilton, one of the most brilliant figures of the Revolutionary era, was born at Charles Town, on the island of Nevis in the West Indies on January 11, 1757, the son of a Scotch father and a French Huguenot mother. When he was twelve years old—a year after the death of his mother—he was put in a counting room at Christiansted, on the island of St. Croix. Sometime later he wrote a description of a West Indian hurricane in such a brilliant manner that he was sent to America to be educated. He arrived at Boston, in October 1772, when he was in his sixteenth year and from there went to a grammar school at Elizabethtown, N. J. He spent a year at Elizabethtown and then entered

King's College, now Columbia University. On July 6, 1774, when he was only seventeen years old, he attended a meeting in the City Hall Park at New York, called to consider a congress of the colonies, and made an extemporaneous speech favoring it that was so well reasoned as to attract general attention. Soon afterward he published anonymously two pamphlets defending the action of the colonies. These were at first attributed to Jay and Livingston and when it was known that young Hamilton had written them the reputation won by his speech was increased. He enlisted in a company of volunteers and was soon put in command of an artillery company. He was present at the battles of Long Island, Trenton and Princeton and on March 1, 1777, he was made an aide on the staff of General Washington with the rank of lieutenant colonel, and acted as confidential secretary. He was a member of the Continental Congress in 1782 and 1783. Before entering the Congress he had been admitted to the bar and had begun to practice in New York. He was a delegate to the Annapolis Convention in 1786 and wrote the report which led to the assembling of the convention in Philadelphia to draft a constitution for the new government. He was a delegate to that convention and it was his influence that brought about the ratification of the Constitution by New York. When Congress created the Treasury Department President Washington appointed him as the first Secretary of the Treasury where he made a brilliant reputation. He resigned from the Cabinet on January 31, 1795, and resumed the practice of law in New York. When danger of war with France arose he was appointed, in 1798, as the virtual head of the army with the rank of major general and the duties of inspector general, a position which he held until June 1800, perfecting plans for the defense of the country. In the presidential election of 1800 he favored John Adams against Aaron Burr and when it appeared that the two men had received an equal number of electoral votes he threw his influence in favor of the choice of Adams by the House of Representatives. In 1804, Burr, who insisted that he had been insulted, challenged Hamilton to a duel. Although he was opposed to dueling, Hamilton accepted the challenge lest he should get a reputation for cowardice. The two met at Weehawken, N. J., on July 11. Hamilton fired into the air, but Burr aimed directly at his opponent and wounded him so seriously that he died on the next day. There are many biographies of him, and his complete works have been published. Social and political clubs have been named for him and his "Report on Manufactures," made while Secretary of the Treasury, is generally regarded as a justification for the protective tariff policy of the United States. He argued for the establishment of factories so that a market might be found among the industrial workers for the product of the farms, of which there would be a large surplus unless they could be sold to residents in the towns engaged in a different occupation. It is customary for the Secretary of the Treasury to place a wreath at the base of Hamilton's statue in Washington on the anniversary of his birth.

JANUARY TWELFTH

LA SALLE'S LAST JOURNEY

René Robert Cavelier, Sieur de La Salle, distinguished French explorer, began his last heroic journey from Matagorda Bay on the coast of what is now Texas, on January 12, 1687. He had been abandoned by part of his companions and set out with his brother, two nephews and thirteen others, to walk back to Canada where he had possessions. His followers mutinied when he had advanced as far as Trinity River in Texas, and killed one of his nephews in an ambush. When LaSalle turned back to look for him he was shot and killed on March 19, 1687.

La Salle was born in 1643, the son of a wealthy merchant family of Rouen, but lost his right to inherit when he became a novice in a monastery. He migrated to Canada at the age of twenty-four where he received the grant of a large tract of land at Lachine on the St. Lawrence River from the superior of the Seminary of St. Sulpice. He heard stories from the Indians about a large river which they called the Ohio and he conceived the idea of exploring it in the belief that it might provide a water route to China. He is credited with discovering the river and with being the first explorer of the greater part of the Mississippi. He did much exploration in the West and through the Mississippi Valley. In April 1682, he took possession of the valley in the name of France, planted fleur de lys at the mouth and erected a cross. Some months later he returned to France with a plan for colonizing the new territory. His plans were received with favor, and four vessels with four hundred men were put at his disposal and he was authorized to govern the country from the mouth of the Mississippi to Lake Michigan. The fleet sailed from La Rochelle on July 24, 1684, but there was soon a disagreement between LaSalle and the naval officer of the fleet. When they arrived in the Gulf of Mexico they were unable to find the mouth of the Mississippi and LaSalle became convinced that the naval officer was trying to thwart his plans. He had his men landed at Matagorda Bay, mistaking it for the entrance to the great river. He soon realized his mistake and he began a fruitless search for the Mississippi. In April 1686, he started for Canada but was compelled to turn back and it was on January 12, 1687, that he made his final effort, resulting, as already indicated, in his death at the hands of the men with him.

JANUARY THIRTEENTH

BIRTHDAY OF SALMON P. CHASE

Salmon Portland Chase, sixth Chief Justice of the United States, was born at Cornish, N. H., on January 13, 1808, the son of Ithamar

Chase, a farmer, who held various state and local offices. He was the eighth of eleven children. While he was still a child the family moved to Keene, N. H., where his father became a tavern keeper. When the boy was nine years old his father died, and he was soon sent to live with his uncle, Philander Chase, Protestant Episcopal bishop of Ohio and the founder of Kenyon College. He studied in the church school which his uncle conducted at Worthington, near Cincinnati. When his uncle became president of Cincinnati College in 1821 he entered the college. In 1824 he entered the junior class of Dartmouth College and was graduated in 1826, at the age of eighteen. He unsuccessfully besought Dudley Chase, an uncle and United States Senator from Vermont, for appointment to a governmental clerkship in Washington. He then opened a school for boys in the national capital and at one time had the sons of all but one of the members of the Cabinet of John Quincy Adams as his pupils. He decided to be a lawyer and studied under the direction of William Wirt. He was admitted to the bar in 1829, and in 1830 opened an office in Cincinnati. He organized the Cincinnati Lyceum which conducted a course of lectures, some of which he delivered. He tried to establish a literary magazine for the West, but failed in this attempt. Then he compiled the Statutes of Ohio in three volumes. As a lawyer he defended slaves who had escaped into Ohio and carried the case of one of them to the United States Supreme Court, joining with William H. Seward in arguing that a Negro who had escaped into or been taken into a free state thereupon became free. He was active in the Free Soil movement and drafted that part of the platform of the Buffalo convention of 1848 which declared for "no more slave states and no more slave territory."

He was elected to the United States Senate in 1849, by the votes of the Democratic and Free Soil members of the Ohio Legislature. In the Senate he opposed the compromise measure of 1850 and denounced Senator Douglas's Nebraska Bill as "a criminal betrayal of precious rights." He had been a Whig but when the Republican party was formed he associated himself with that. He was nominated for governor of Ohio in 1855 and although opposed by the old school Whigs and the Democrats he was elected, and was reelected as a Republican in 1857. He had sought the Republican nomination for President in 1856, but did not have the undivided support of the Ohio delegation, and again in 1860, with the Ohio delegation split, he received only forty-nine votes on the first roll call in the Chicago convention which nominated Lincoln. When the nomination of Lincoln seemed impending he threw his strength to the Illinois candidate. The Ohio Legislature again elected him to the Senate in 1860, but he resigned to accept appointment as Secretary of the Treasury in the Cabinet of Lincoln, in which position he served until July 1864. With the cooperation of Jay Cooke, a Philadelphia

31

banker, he succeeded in financing the Civil War. He was responsible for the creation of national banks with power to issue currency supported by government bonds, a plan which facilitated the floating of governmental loans, and incidentally suppressed the issue of currency by the state banks.

There was hostility between Chase and William H. Seward, Secretary of State. At a caucus of Republican Senators certain supporters of Chase expressed lack of confidence in the President and demanded a reconstruction of the Cabinet. The President summoned the discontented Senators to a Cabinet meeting and gave them an opportunity to state their grievances. Chase, although he had been complaining of lack of harmony, felt impelled to deny the existence of discord. As a result of this incident both Chase and Seward resigned, but the President refused to accept their resignations. In 1864 a movement was started to bring about the nomination of Chase for President by men who believed that Lincoln's administration had failed. Chase wrote to Lincoln that his attitude toward the movement was passive and expressed both respect and affection for him. After the renomination of Lincoln a disagreement arose between him and Chase over the appointment of a subordinate in the Treasury Department and Chase offered his resignation, which was accepted. Influential Republican leaders, convinced that Lincoln could not be reelected, sought to bring about his withdrawal in favor of Chase, but it came to nothing. When Chief Justice Taney died, on October 12, 1864, Lincoln appointed Chase to succeed him. The political gossips said that Lincoln had put Chase in the Supreme Court to take him out of the political arena, but Chase's friends in succeeding years were still active in their efforts to obtain a presidential nomination for him. He presided with impartiality over the impeachment trial of President Johnson and in 1870 he wrote the opinion of the Court declaring unconstitutional the Legal Tender Act of 1862 under which the greenbacks had been issued. As Secretary of the Treasury he had reluctantly consented to the issue of them. The court in 1871, differently constituted, reversed this decision and Chief Justice Chase filed a dissenting opinion. He voted for Horace Greeley, the Liberal Republican candidate for President, in 1872, in opposition to General Grant. While visiting New York he died of a paralytic stroke on May 7, 1873.

FESTIVAL OF ST. VERONICA

St. Veronica de Binasco of Milan is honored on January 13. She was a member of the Order of St. Augustine. As a girl she worked in the fields about the city during the day and at night received religious instruction from her pious parents. She decided to devote herself to a religious life and was admitted to the nunnery of St. Martha and in the course of time became the head of it. She is said to have wept continually for her sins until her eyes became fountains of tears.

Her name has been connected with the interesting legend of the woman who wiped the face of Jesus with a towel at the time of the crucifixion. The towel is said to have received the imprint of his features so that it contained the vera iconica, or the true image. Tradition says that she took the towel to Rome with her where it was long exposed to public veneration. The Italian version of the tradition is that she went to Rome at the summons of the Emperor Tiberius who was ill and that he was cured by the touch of the sacred portrait. She remained in Rome with Peter and Paul and when she died she bequeathed the portrait to Pope Clement. A French version is that she married Zacheus and accompanied him to Rome and then to Quiercy where Zacheus became a hermit. There is still a towel or handkerchief at Rome containing a portrait of Jesus. It is admittedly of ancient origin but there is no agreement among antiquarians about its age.

JANUARY FOURTEENTH

FEAST OF THE HOLY NAME

The Feast of the Holy Name is celebrated by the Roman Catholics on the second Sunday after Epiphany, which fell on January 14, in 1934 and in 1945. It originated toward the end of the fifteenth century when it was instituted by the private authority of some bishops in Germany, Spain, Belgium, Scotland and England. The feast was officially granted to the Franciscans on February 25, 1530, and spread over a great part of the church. It was kept by the Franciscans, Carmelites and Augustinians on January 14 and by the Dominicans on January 15, At Salisbury, York and Durham in England and at Aberdeen in Scotland it was celebrated on August 7 and at Liege on January 31. In the middle of the seventeenth century it was fixed for the Carthusians for the second Sunday after Epiphany. Its observance on that date was extended to the whole church in the first quarter of the eighteenth century. It is one of the feast days the observance of which is particularly enjoined upon the members of the Confraternity of the Most Holy Name of God and Jesus, commonly called the Holy Name Society. These members usually hold a parade on the day and attend mass in a body.

The feast had its origin in the Council of Lyons in 1274. This council prescribed a special devotion to the Holy Name of Jesus "that reparation might be made for the insults offered by the Albigenses." The primary object is to beget love and reverence for the Holy Name and its secondary object is to suppress blasphemy, perjury and all improper language and to prevent these vices in others. Gregory X selected the Dominicans to preach the devotion; and John of Vercelli, master general of the order, immediately after receiving the commission in September

33

1274, wrote to all the provincials impressing upon them the duty of carrying out the wishes of the Pope. It was ordained that an altar to the Holy Name should be erected in every Dominican church and that societies with the title of the Holy Name of Jesus should be organized. Andrea Diaz, a retired Dominican bishop, preached devotion to the Holy Name in Lisbon during a plague in 1432. The ravages of the plague were stopped and the people of the city, in gratitude for their deliverance, paraded through the streets. This is said to be the first public procession in honor of the Holy Name, and set the example for the annual parades in this and other countries. At about this time a Spanish Dominican, Didacus of Victoria, founded a society known as the Holy Name of God the purpose of which was to suppress blasphemy. It was approved by the Pope and was later incorporated into the older society to which its name was added.

The society has always had the favor of the Bishop of Rome. Pope Leo XIII, by a decree of May 20, 1896, greatly strengthened it by permitting the organization of more than one confraternity in a city. There are more than 500,000 members of the society in the United States. The symbol for the Holy Name has passed through a curious transformation. The word Jesus was originally written in abbreviated form in Greek, with the first three letters, "iota, eta and sigma." As the capital form of the Greek "eta" is like the letter "H" it was ignorantly assumed by those unfamiliar with Greek that it was an "H" and they read IHS as an abbreviation of "Jesus Hominum Salvator." The Jesuits formed a cross through the middle letter and made the abbreviation the symbol of their society. Another interpretation of the letters is that they stand for "In Hoc Signo," the words which Constantine is said to have seen in the heavens under a cross on the eve of the Battle of Milvian Bridge in 312.

JANUARY FIFTEENTH

VERMONT'S DECLARATION OF INDEPENDENCE

Sovereignty over the territory that is now Vermont was in dispute for many years. But on January 15, 1777, a convention of the settlers declared it an independent state under the name of New Connecticut which was changed to Vermont by a convention meeting in the following June. The dispute over control of the territory grew out of the conflicting terms of the grants made by the King. The Massachusetts and Connecticut charters placed their western boundaries at the Pacific Ocean. The grant of Charles II to the Duke of York placed the eastern boundary of New York at the Connecticut River. After a great deal of controversy the boundary between New York and Massachusetts and Connecticut was fixed at a line twenty miles east of the Hudson River. New

York, however, still claimed the territory as far east as the Connecticut River, north of Massachusetts. New Hampshire disputed this claim and Governor Benning Wentworth in 1749 gave a patent to settlers to land in what is now the town of Bennington and issued other patents to land known in history as the New Hampshire Grants. The Governor and Council of New York protested against the extension of the authority of New Hampshire, but Governor Wentworth ignored the protest and claimed all the region as far west as the extended boundary of Massachusetts and Connecticut. The dispute was referred to the King in 1764 who decided in favor of New York. Thereupon New York declared the New Hampshire grants void and issued orders for the sale of the farms of the settlers. Ethan Allen organized a force known as the Green Mountain Boys to resist the eviction of the settlers and to oust the New Yorkers who had tried to take possession of their lands. This was in 1771. The Vermonters, as already indicated, called a convention to assert their independence and did so in 1777, applying for admission to the confederation of states fighting Great Britain. A constitution was drafted and approved. Admission to the confederation was opposed by New York and by the Southern states which objected to another Northern state. In 1780 Vermont again appealed to the Continental Congress for admission with the announcement that if it were denied the Vermonters would propose to the other New England states and New York an alliance for mutual defense independent of Congress and the other states, and that if their wishes were not respected they would be at liberty to propose a cessation of hostilities with Great Britain. The British learned of this and communicated with Ethan Allen in an effort to get his support for their plan to make Vermont a British province. Allen made no reply to the communication, and in 1781 informed Congress of the efforts of the British. He insisted on his loyalty to his country but declared "Vermont has an indubitable right to agree on terms of a cessation of hostilities with Great Britain, provided the United States persist in rejecting her application for an union with them." But it was not until February 18, 1791, that Congress voted to admit Vermont. New York had in the meantime withdrawn opposition and Vermont had appropriated $30,000 to indemnify the New York settlers who had been ousted.

JANUARY SIXTEENTH

FRANCE RECOGNIZES THE UNITED STATES

Vergennes, French Minister of Foreign Affairs, sent Conrad A. Gerard to Benjamin Franklin and Silas Dean, the American agents in Paris, on January 16, 1778, with the draft of a treaty recognizing the independence of the United States. Some changes were made in it and it was finally signed on February 6. Gerard was sent to America as the first French minister. The American agents had been seeking recognition for a long time. The news of the surrender of Burgoyne at the Battle of Saratoga was taken to France by a fast ship and the French received it with enthusiasm. On December 12, 1777, Franklin and Dean had an interview with Vergennes who praised Washington's strategy highly and promised to make a treaty with the United States. He had been using Franklin's landlord as a spy, and had learned that negotiations with England to end the war were in progress and decided to hasten his own agreements with this country in order to prevent an immediate peace which would relieve Great Britain. It was then that he had the treaty drafted and submitted to Franklin and Dean, ending all uncertainty about the recognition of the independence of the new nation.

PROHIBITION AND REPEAL

The eighteenth amendment to the Constitution was proposed to the state legislatures by the 65th Congress in 1917, and on January 29, 1919, the Secretary of State proclaimed its adoption by thirty-six states and declared it in effect January 16, 1920. It prohibited the manufacture, sale, or transportation of intoxicating liquors within the United States and all territories subject to its jurisdiction, and also forbade their importation and exportation. The amendment was ultimately adopted by all the states except Connecticut and Rhode Island, but unfortunately it proved to have more or less the opposite effect to that designed by its sponsors. The years following witnessed an almost universal flouting of the law; "speakeasies" flourished and "rumrunning" became a remunerative racket inciting violence in the underworld between mobs of gangsters importing and transporting liquor, and hijackers who attempted to "muscle in" on the monopolies of rival gangs. Eventually it became apparent to even the most ardent temperance advocates that the eighteenth amendment had failed to accomplish its purpose and the pressure of public opinion gradually brought the issue to the point of legislation for repeal. The twenty-first amendment, embodied in a joint resolution of the 72nd Congress in February 1933, was transmitted to the Secretary of State who at once sent copies to the governors of the states. This amendment, repealing the eighteenth amendment, went into effect on December 5, 1933, after being adopted by thirty-six states.

JANUARY SEVENTEENTH

FRANKLIN'S BIRTHDAY

One of the earliest celebrations of the anniversary of the birth of Benjamin Franklin, on January 17, 1706, occurred in Boston, his birthplace, in 1826. It was arranged by the Franklin Typographical Society, an organization formed for the relief of needy printers. The celebration began with a meeting in Concert Hall, Boston, at which an address in honor of Franklin was made by Jefferson Clark, a printer. He did not attempt to deliver a eulogy of Franklin as he professed his lack of the proper qualifications for such an effort. He talked about printers and printing. The report of the celebration, which was printed in a pamphlet for circulation among the members of the society, states that a supper was served after the address. Twenty-nine toasts were proposed at the supper, the first being in honor of Franklin. While the supper was in progress a song, written by Thomas G. Fessenden, was sung by Mr. Williams. It is printed in full in the report. Following is the first stanza with the chorus:

> While the Press is the theme of our festal lay
> We should be sublime and should be sonorous—
> To the top of our voices we'll quaver away,
> And hope this assemblage will shout in the chorus.
>
> Chorus:
> That art 'tis confessed
> Is the brightest and best
> Which preserves and proclaims and transmits all the rest.
> Unblest with the rays
> Which flow from its blaze
> The Sun of the Mind would set in the West.

The Franklin Typographical Society has continued to observe the anniversary every year. The Old Time Printers Association of Chicago began to celebrate the day in 1885, and printers in other cities hold periodic if not yearly celebrations in honor of the man whom they regard almost as their patron saint. The International Benjamin Franklin Society with headquarters in New York honors him every year for his manifold achievements.

The most notable celebration of the anniversary is naturally in Philadelphia where Franklin went when he ran away from Boston after having a quarrel with his brother, and where he became, in the course of time, the city's most distinguished citizen. The Poor Richard Club, named for the almanac which Franklin published, observes the day with memorial services in Christ Church, with the decoration of his grave in the church burying ground, and a dinner in the evening. The President of the United States usually sends a wreath to be placed on the grave. The services in the church are always attended by representatives of the institutions in the city which Franklin was influential in founding, including the American Philosophical Society, the Library Company of Philadelphia, the *Saturday Evening Post*, the University of Pennsylvania and the Philadelphia Contributionship for Insuring Houses from Loss by Fire. A memorial address is delivered by a representative citizen. On one occasion the orator was Russell Duane, a great-great-great grandson of Franklin. The exercises are always attended by as many of Franklin's descendants as can conveniently reach the city on the date of the anniversary. They usually occupy the pew in the church in which their distinguished ancestor sat when he attended the services, a pew not far from that occupied by General Washington while he lived in Philadelphia.

The University of Pennsylvania, which owes its origin to suggestions made by Franklin for the education of youth, also celebrates the anniversary. There is a society in the university named for Franklin, and a Kite and Key Society, named in honor of Franklin's experiments in the relation between lightning and electricity. His memory is still further kept green by a statue on the campus, representing him as a boy with a staff and a bundle as he appeared when he first entered the city in 1723 at the age of seventeen. Soon after it was erected, the Sophomores introduced the custom of compelling every Freshman to kiss the toe of the statue.

In 1921 the New York City Thrift Week Committee adopted a resolution that "the citizens of the United States should plan annually to celebrate Dr. Franklin's birthday, January 17, which always begins National Thrift Week." The committee drafted a memorial listing the many organizations and institutions which it believed should cooperate in the movement, and commended it to them by name. It reads in part:

To Congress is recommended the holding of appropriate annual Franklin birthday exercises, also the consideration of a suitable Franklin memorial to be built in Washington.

To the State Department, because Franklin in France and England was America's greatest diplomat in history, is urged acknowledgment of Dr. Franklin's accomplishments in statesmanship.

To the Treasury Department, Franklin's claims for suitable recognition are here pointed out. Franklin raised America's first real "Liberty Loans."

To the Post Office Department, attention is called to Franklin's record as Postmaster General.

To the Navy Department is referred the consideration of a plan also to honor Franklin by naming a modern battleship Bon Homme Richard, thus reviving 'Poor Richard's" nom de plume of immortal renown.

To France, our sister Republic, and to the city of Paris which has a large statue of Benjamin Franklin, is suggested appropriate mention of the man who so well loved their country and was so highly regarded personally in return.

To Great Britain, because Franklin's father was born in Ecton, England, and because of Franklin's earnest efforts before the Revolutionary War to preserve peace between the Mother country and the Colonies.

The memorial also suggested the observance of the day:

To his successors in the newspaper and magazine field; to the modern advertising profession he so much helped to found; to the printers of whom Franklin was proudest to call himself one; to the colleges of the world as Franklin was the founder of one and the recipient of five honorary degrees from five others, both here and abroad; to the organizations of scientists for Franklin's many investigations and also for his launching the American Philosophical Society; to the electrical societies because Dr. Franklin "snatched the lightning from the skies" as well as "the sceptre from tyrants"; to the libraries of the United States since Franklin started the first public library in America; to the firemen because Franklin established a fire company and later an insurance company in Philadelphia; to the policemen, as Franklin organized a police department, also a State militia of which he was colonel; to the postmen, as Franklin was once Postmaster General; to the colored citizens of the United States, as although he owned and sold slaves, he was the leading abolitionist of his time; to the labor organizations, because Franklin began his life as a candlemaker and later said "he that hath a trade hath an estate"; to Boston and Massachusetts, whose son Franklin was; to the churches as Franklin wrote this creed: "I believe in one God the Creator of the Universe, that He governs by his Providence; that He ought to be worshipped; that the most acceptable service we render to Him is doing good to His other children; that the soul of man is immortal and will be treated with justice in another life respecting its conduct in this."

The connection between Franklin and thrift is obvious because of the many maxims inculcating thrift which appeared in *Poor Richard's Almanac*. The people in many cities were called upon by their mayors to observe the week for their own good as well as in honor of Franklin.

There are statues of Franklin in many American cities but the most notable physical memorial in his honor is the building of the Franklin Institute in Philadelphia. It was erected to house the Franklin Institute, founded in 1824, and also to house a mechanical museum and a planetarium. It is a large structure in the classic style erected at a cost of about $3,000,000 and completed in 1934.

The two hundredth anniversary of Franklin's birth was celebrated by the American Philosophical Society in April 1906, by a series of meetings extending over four days. Plans for it were begun in 1903 by the appointment of a committee of which George F. Edmunds was chairman. Among his committee men were Alexander Graham Bell, Andrew Carnegie, Grover Cleveland, Charles William Eliot, Arthur T. Hadley, John Hay, Captain A. T. Mahan, Simeon Newcomb, Andrew D. White and Woodrow Wilson. The State of Pennsylvania appropriated $20,000 toward the expenses of the celebration and Congress appointed a committee of six Senators and ten Representatives to attend. Henry Cabot Lodge was chairman of the Senate committee and M. E. Olmstead was the head of the committee of the House. The celebration, which was included in the proceedings of the regular spring meeting of the society, began with a reception to delegates from the great scientific societies of this country and Europe who had come to the United States to honor the memory of Franklin. At one of the sessions Andrew Carnegie, Lord Rector of the University of St. Andrews, conferred the honorary degree of Doctor of Laws upon Agnes Irwin, dean of Radcliffe College. There was a military parade through the streets of the city to Franklin's grave on which wreaths were placed by official representatives of the organizations and institutions which he had started. This was followed by a national salute fired by the guns of the battleship "Pennsylvania," anchored in the Delaware river. The ceremonies ended with memorial addresses in the Academy of Music by H. H. Furness, Charles William Eliot and Joseph Hodges Choate, and the presentation to France of a medal voted by Congress. The presentation was made by Elihu Root.

Secretary of State, and Jules J. Jusserand, the French Ambassador, accepted it in behalf of his country.

Franklin comes as near to being a universal genius as any man this country has produced. The list of his activities contained in the memorial of the Thrift Week Society indicates the variety of his interests. His unusual intellectual qualities began to manifest themselves early in life. At the age of fifteen he was writing satirical articles for his brother's newspaper in Boston. At the age of seventeen, while on his flight from Boston to Philadelphia, he reflected that he was glad that man was a reasoning creature, as "he could find a reason for anything he wanted to do." He reached this conclusion when he abandoned his vegetarian practices and ate of the fish which the cook on the boat on which he was sailing had caught and fried. He had seen the cook clean the fish and find a smaller fish inside it. He then reflected that if it was right for the big fish, acting according to natural instinct, to eat the little one it could not be wrong for him to eat the big one. It was his habit to the end of his days to put into effect the result of his observations and to reach his conclusions in his own way regardless of what other men thought. He was the first American to win an international reputation and he won this because of his scientific investigations.

Franklin was the fifteenth of the seventeen children of his father, Josiah Franklin, and the tenth son. His father wanted him to become a clergyman, but the boy had no taste for the profession. After working for a year in his father's tallow chandler's shop he was apprenticed at the age of twelve to his brother James, a printer and the founder of the New England *Courant*, one of the earliest American newspapers. The terms of the apprenticeship required him to serve until he was twenty years old, but he quarreled with his brother when he was seventeen and ran away to New York. Although he had learned his trade thoroughly he was unable to find work in New York and continued his flight till he reached Philadelphia. He was almost penniless, but he soon found friends and employment. In 1725, when he was nineteen, Governor Keith of the colony, told him that if he would go to London money would be provided for him to buy the equipment for a printing office to be brought back to Philadelphia, but Governor Keith did not keep his promise and Franklin had to find work for himself. He remained in London, working at his trade for a year and a half, when he returned to Philadelphia and soon had a printing establishment of his own, and in 1729 he got control of the *Pennsylvania Gazette* which he edited with distinction. This was really the beginning of his career, the details of which are known to most school children.

FEAST OF ST. ANTHONY THE GREAT

St. Anthony the Great, one of the most widely known saints of the Roman church, whose feast is celebrated on January 17, was born in

Koma, Upper Egypt, in about the year 251. The exact date is unknown. His parents were wealthy Christians and gave him a religious education. They died when he was twenty years old, leaving their property to him. He was religiously inclined and one day when he heard the Gospel read in church containing the words, "If thou wilt be perfect, go and sell all thou hast" he took the injunction to himself and sold his property and distributed the proceeds to the needy. He had a sister whom he sent to a religious house, after providing for her with part of his estate. This is said to be the first setting apart of a nun to the Christian life.

Anthony then withdrew from the world and adopted various ascetic practices in his native town. Then he began to live in one of the tombs near the village, where he was subjected to various temptations. The story of them is told by Athanasius in his life of the saint. According to this account the devil by confusing his thoughts strove to force him to reconsider his determination to become a monk. But this failed. Then he appeared in the form of a handsome woman who sought to beguile him into violating his vow of chastity. And this failed. Then Satan, accompanied by a number of attendant fiends, attacked him during the night, and he was found almost dead in his cell in the morning. Later the fiends transformed themselves into the shape of wild beasts which roared furiously at him and mangled his body, but he taunted them until the roof of his cell opened and a ray of light shot through, silencing the beasts. Anthony's wounds were healed and the roof closed again. He lived in this cell for about fifteen years when he decided to retire entirely from human society. He took up his abode in an old fort at Pispir on the east bank of the Nile where he lived twenty years without looking on the face of man. Food was thrown to him over the walls of the fort. Pilgrims visited the place and those who would be his disciples lived in caves and huts in the neighborhood. They begged him to come forth and be their leader. He at length yielded to their importunities and for five or six years devoted himself to the instruction of the great body of monks which had gathered about his retreat. Then he withdrew to the desert between the Nile and the Red Sea where he spent the last forty-five years of his life. Here he received those who went to visit him and made occasional trips to the scene of his early retirement at Pispir. He is said to have visited Alexandria twice, once to encourage the Christian martyrs in 311 and again in 350 to combat heretical preaching. He died in 356, venerated by the Christian church.

He is regarded as the founder of monasticism and he is also recognized as the patron saint of animals. It is the custom in many European, Mexican and South American cities for the priests to bless the animals owned by the faithful on the anniversary of his feast. In the year 1089 a plague of erysipelas swept over France and, according to tradition, those who visited the church of LaMotte St. Didier, near Vienne, Dauphine, where St. Anthony's relics were said to be preserved, were cured of the disease. And the afflicted throughout France prayed to the saint for relief.

Because of this the disease came to be known as St. Anthony's fire. The next year the Order of the Canons Regular of St. Anthony, which survived in France until 1790, was founded for the relief of those suffering from the ailment.

JANUARY EIGHTEENTH

BIRTHDAY OF DANIEL WEBSTER

Daniel Webster, who won fame as an orator, statesman and constitutional lawyer, was born in Salisbury (now Franklin), N.H., on January 18, 1782, of a father who had been a soldier in the Revolutionary army. He received a preliminary education in the schools of his neighborhood and was graduated from Dartmouth College in 1801 at the age of nineteen. He studied law and was admitted to the bar in 1805, and in 1807 he began to practice at Portsmouth. He was elected to Congress from the Portsmouth district in 1812 by the party opposed to the war with England, and reelected in 1814. He moved to Boston in 1816 where he devoted himself to his profession for about seven years. In 1822 he was elected to Congress from a Boston district and twice reelected by an almost unanimous vote. In 1827 he was elected to the United States Senate from Massachusetts, where he denounced the theory of nullification. He opposed Jackson's bank policy and enunciated the principles of sound banking legislation some of which have been embodied in the laws.

He received the electoral vote of Massachusetts for President as the candidate of the Whigs in 1836 and in 1840 the nomination for Vice President was offered to him, but he declined it. President Harrison made him Secretary of State in his Cabinet, a post which he retained under President Tyler after the death of Harrison. But when President Tyler broke with the Whigs, Webster resigned and resumed the practice of law in Boston. He entered the Senate a second time in 1845 as the successor of Rufus Choate where he opposed the war with Mexico and the annexation of Texas. He aspired to the nomination for President in 1848 and denounced the selection of Zachary Taylor as "not fit to be made," but he supported Taylor in the campaign. His last notable speech in the Senate was made in March 1850, known in history as the "Seventh of March Speech," in which he advocated compromise on the issue of the extension of slavery. He was roundly denounced for it in the North, and Whittier, an ardent abolitionist, wrote a bitter poem which he named "Ichabod," a Hebrew name meaning "the glory has departed." It began:

> So fallen! so lost! the light withdrawn
>   Which once he wore!
> The glory from his gray hairs gone
>   Forevermore!

42

The poem continued in this vein for eight more stanzas and ended with:

> Then pay the reverence of old days
> To his dead fame;
> Walk backward, with averted gaze,
> And hide the shame!

When he died, broken in health at his home at Marshfield, Mass., on October 24, 1852, there was widespread mourning at the passing of one of the most brilliant men which America had produced.

JANUARY NINETEENTH

BIRTHDAY OF ROBERT E. LEE

The anniversary of the birth of Robert E. Lee was made a holiday by the State of Georgia in 1889. Virginia followed her example in 1890. The anniversary is now a holiday in Alabama, Arkansas, Florida, Georgia, Kentucky, Louisiana, Mississippi, North Carolina, South Carolina, Tennessee, Texas, and Virginia.

Lee, who is regarded by many military authorities as the ablest strategist developed during the Civil War, was born at Stratford, the family estate in Westmoreland County, Va., on January 19, 1807. He was the son of Henry Lee, known as "Light-Horse Harry," one of the distinguished soldiers of the Revolution. His mother, his father's second wife, was Anne Hill Carter, a daughter of Charles Carter, belonging to a Virginia family as famous as the Lees. His father, because of unfortunate investments, was forced to leave Stratford in 1811, when the boy was four years old. He moved to Alexandria, where the boy went to school. The father died in 1818 and as Robert grew up he had to look after his invalid mother. Inspired by his father's military career he sought admission to the Military Academy at West Point, which he entered in 1825, and was graduated next to the head of his class in 1829. He entered the army as a brevet second lieutenant of engineers. He was assistant engineer at Fort Monroe, Va., from May 1831, to November 1834. While there he married, on June 30, 1831, Mary Ann Randolph Custis, the only daughter of George Washington Parke Custis, grandson of Martha Washington, who lived on the estate known as Arlington, across the Potomac from Washington. He was assigned to various engineering duties until 1846 when he was ordered to San Antonio, Tex., as assistant engineer under General John E. Wool, Commander of the army which was engaged in the Mexican War. When he was attached to the Vera Cruz expedition he won the esteem and admiration of General Winfield Scott, its commander, and he performed valuable service in planning for the capture of Mexico City. He had already

43

risen to the rank of captain and on his return to the United States he was promoted for gallantry to the rank of brevet colonel, and was put in charge of the construction of Fort Carroll, in Baltimore Harbor.

After he had served there for not quite four years the post of superintendent of the Military Academy at West Point became vacant and he was appointed to fill it, much against his wishes. He remained there for three years, when at his solicitation, Jefferson Davis, Secretary of War, obtained his transfer to the line and his assignment as lieutenant colonel of the Second Cavalry Regiment in March 1855. He was in Washington at the time of the John Brown raid on Harpers Ferry in 1859 and was sent there to put down the uprising. He was a Whig, loyal to the Union, and when the secession movement began to take form he hoped that the issue might be settled amicably. He, however, believed that his first duty was to his state and if Virginia seceded he would go with it as a matter of course. General Scott put him on waiting orders in Washington in February 1861, with the intention of promoting him at once if there should be war. On March 16 he was made colonel of the First Cavalry Regiment, a commission which he gladly accepted. On April 18 Francis P. Blair told him that he was authorized to offer him the field command of the United States Army. He declined the offer and discussed the situation with General Scott. The general told him that he should either resign from the army or accept whatever duty was assigned to him.

In the meantime a Virginia convention had voted in favor of secession and to submit the issue to the people for ratification. Lee, persuaded that secession would not wait for the referendum, resigned from the army on April 20. Three days later Virginia made him commander of her forces. At that time he had never commanded more troops in the field than four squadrons of cavalry, and that for only a short scouting expedition in Texas. He was soon made military adviser to Jefferson Davis, the President of the Confederacy, with the rank of general. It was not long before he was in command of the Confederate armies. A history of his conduct of the war does not belong here. It is enough to say that after the first reverses he won the confidence of the South and in spite of lack of men and supplies conducted the war with great brilliancy. His biographers, however, say that his great weakness was his habit of surrendering his views to the views of those who disagreed with him in planning a battle or a campaign. They lay his defeat at Gettysburg to the reorganizing of the command of his army with inexperienced men forced upon him by the death of General "Stonewall" Jackson, his ablest supporter. His surrender to General Grant at Appomattox Court House on April 9, 1865, virtually brought the war to an end. He returned to Richmond as a paroled prisoner of war. He could not return to Arlington as that place had been sold for non-payment of taxes in 1863. In September he accepted the presidency of Washington College at Lexington, Va., and devoted the remaining years of his life to lifting its standards of scholarship and increasing the number of its students. He died on October 12, 1870, at Lexington where he is buried. After his death the trustees of Washington College changed its name to Washington and Lee. Virginia has placed a statue of him in Statuary Hall in the National Capitol and another statue adorns the rotunda of the State House in Richmond. He did his duty as he saw it and consequently, in the North as well as in the South, he is regarded as one of the great Americans of his generation.

The celebration of the anniversary of the birth of General Lee is more elaborate in Virginia, his native state, than in any of the other eleven states which observe the day. Services are usually held at Stratford Hall, his birthplace, to purchase which as a memorial the school children have contributed funds. Washington and Lee University, of which he was President, does not let the day pass without appropriate ceremonies and eulogistic addresses. And in Richmond, organizations of Confederate veterans and sons and daughters of veterans gather in the Hall of Delegates in the State Capitol to honor his memory. The Virginia Historical Society, which occupies the house in Richmond in which General Lee lived with his family, pays annual tribute to him, and the Confederate Museum, in the house occupied by Jefferson Davis as President of the Confederacy, is opened to the public without admission fee on the anniversary and is visited by thousands who inspect the Lee relics there. And there is usually a memorial service in St. Paul's Episcopal Church in Richmond, which Lee attended during his residence in the city. A stained glass window in his honor has been placed in the church.

BIRTHDAY OF EDGAR ALLAN POE

The honors paid to the memory of Edgar Allan Poe multiply with the passing years. When he died in Baltimore on October 7, 1849, he was buried in an unmarked grave in the cemetery attached to a Protestant Episcopal church in that city. The grave was not marked until 1875 when the Baltimore school teachers erected a modest headstone over it with an appropriate inscription. Spasmodic attempts to celebrate the anniversary of his birth followed this action of the school teachers, but it was not until the first quarter of the twentieth century that the observance of the anniversary became somewhat regular. There are Poe societies in New York, Philadelphia, Boston and other cities which observe the anniversary either unitedly or separately. There is an International Poe Society and a French society of Les Amis d'Edgar Poe. The Poe Society of Philadelphia, founded by Richard Gimbel, who bought and preserved the Poe house in that city, celebrated the one hundred and twenty-fifth anniversary of the birth of Poe with a dinner in 1934 at which representatives of the Poe societies of New York, Boston and Chicago were present. Addresses were made by distinguished men and women of letters and by collectors of Poe manuscripts and first editions. A dealer had on exhibition at the dinner a collection of first editions valued at half a million dollars, including a copy of *Tamerlane*, Poe's first book, which is worth a small fortune.

Poe was born in Boston, on January 19, 1809, the same year in which Abraham Lincoln was born. His father was David Poe, the son of a Revolutionary patriot. Both his father and mother were strolling actors and he was carried about the country with them in his infancy. While he was still a small boy his mother died and he was adopted by Mrs. John Allan, the wife of a business man of Richmond, Va., He was taken to England in 1815, when he was six years old and entered in the Manor House School near London. Five years later the Allans returned to Richmond and the boy received instruction from private tutors. In 1826 he entered the new University of Virginia established by Thomas Jefferson at Charlottesville, where he showed great proficiency in the study of Latin, Greek, French, Spanish and Italian. The students were accustomed to drink heavily and to gamble for large sums and he joined them in these dissipations. He accumulated a gambling debt of $2500 which Mr. Allan refused to pay and he was taken out of college and put to work in his adoptive father's counting room. He did not stay there long but ran away to Boston where in 1827 *Tamerlane* was published in paper covers. In the same year he enlisted in the United States army as a private, served for two years and was honorably discharged. He returned to Richmond and was reconciled with Mr. Allan, and in 1829 published in Baltimore *Al Aaraaf*. Mrs. Allan had died in the meantime and Mr. Allan had married a second wife. In an effort to provide permanently for the youth, Mr. Allan obtained an appointment for him to the United States Military Academy at West Point in 1830. Poe neglected his military duties, was frequently under arrest and at the end of six months was dismissed. He then began his attempt to support himself by his pen. He lived with Mrs. Clemm, the widowed sister of his father, whose daughter, Virginia, he married when she was only thirteen years old. In 1833 he won a prize of $100 offered by the *Saturday Visitor*, a monthly literary journal. He soon returned to Richmond, which he always regarded as his home, and was for a time editor of the *Southern Literary Messenger*. He tried his fortune unsuccessfully in New York in 1837 and in 1838 he went to Philadelphia where he was employed as editor of *Graham's Magazine*. During his editorship its circulation increased from 5,000 to 50,000 and it became the leading literary magazine in the United States. About this time he won a second prize of $100 for a story, "The Gold Bug," which was printed in the *Dollar Newspaper*; it was so popular that the publisher had to print more than 300,000 copies to meet the demand. When he retired from the editorship of *Graham's Magazine* he had no resources and was often in dire need for the necessities of life. In 1844 he went to New York and rented a small cottage at Fordham. His wife died there in January 1847, leaving him overcome with grief. In June 1849, he

46

went to Richmond where he was received with kindness and recovered his spirits. In late September he started for New York, but on October 3 he was found in a desperate condition in a Baltimore saloon and taken to a hospital where he died four days later.

His tales and poems were acclaimed in Europe as the finest of the kind which America had produced and his peculiar genius was recognized there before it was generally admitted in this country. The Baltimore school teachers probably began the popular tributes to Poe when they marked his grave in 1875. Ten years later an actors' memorial to Poe was erected in New York as a recognition of the association of his parents with the American theater. In 1891 a bust of Poe was unveiled at the University of Virginia from which Mr. Allen had withdrawn him, and a tablet set up in the room which he had occupied. In 1902, as the centennial anniversary of his birth approached, interest in him and in his career became acute and in 1909, the centennial year, his bust was set up in the Hall of Fame of New York University. His cottage in Fordham was restored and moved to a small park at about this time. And a Poe Memorial Door was set in the library of the Military Academy at West Point from which he had been expelled. In Baltimore a tablet was placed in the room in the hospital in which he died. Richmond, his childhood home, dedicated an Enchanted Garden and Poe Shrine in 1921, and on January 19, 1924, the Authors' Club of Boston erected a tablet announcing that Poe was born in that city. In 1933 Richard Gimbel, a collector of Poe manuscripts and first editions, and founder of the Poe Society of Philadelphia, bought the Poe cottage in Philadelphia, restored it to its original condition and opened it to the public as a museum. The house has a telephone which is listed in the directory as "Edgar Allan Poe, residence, 530 North Seventh Street," with the name of the exchange and the number of the telephone.

THE GREEK CHURCH EPIPHANY

Those branches of the Greek church which have not adopted the Gregorian calender for their festivals observe Epiphany on January 19, with many of the ancient ceremonies. It is the custom on this day to bless the waters in the vicinity of the church by dipping into them a crucifix. It was once believed that the waters so blessed would cure many diseases. This rite is said to be symbolic of the baptism of Jesus in the Jordan. It is celebrated by the Greek churches in the United States. For example, on the Sunday nearest Epiphany in 1935 Bishop Arsenius headed a procession which marched from the Greek Orthodox Church of St. Nicholas in New York City to the Battery. He was accompanied by Archbishop Francis of the Old Catholic Church, and a company of priests, deacons and archdeacons and white robed acolytes chanting hymns. Bishop Arsenius boarded a raft moored near shore and threw a crucifix into the water, and released two white doves. Two men previously selected for the duty dived into the water to rescue the crucifix and struggled for its possession. The man who rescued it had the honor of carrying it back to the church.

JANUARY TWENTIETH

EVE OF ST. AGNES

The eve of the feast of St. Agnes is one of those occasions when charms and incantations are supposed to have peculiar virtues. The feast is observed on January 21. It was long regarded as an auspicious time for the employment of those charms which are potent in revealing to young women the names and faces of their future husbands. Many such charms are described in the old books. One custom which was supposed to be certain to produce the desired result was for the maid to take a row of pins and pull them out one by one and stick them in her sleeve, singing a pater noster. Another custom, adopted by such as were able, was for the maid to go into a different district from that in which she lived and spend the night. Before going to bed she took her stocking from her right leg and knitted it to the garter from the stocking on her left leg, singing as she did so:

> I knit this knot, this knot I knit
> To know the thing I know not yet,
> That I may see
> The man that shall my husband be,
> Not in his best or worst array,
> But what he weareth every day;
> That I to-morrow may him ken
> From among all other men.

Then she was to lie on her back in bed with her hands under her head. If she had observed the formalities with precision she was assured that her future husband would appear to her in a dream and press a warm kiss upon her lips. If the maid went supperless to bed the charm was supposed to work with greater certainty. Keats founded his romantic poem, "The Eve of St. Agnes" upon these superstitions. Those maids who could not get away from home for the night would take a sprig of rosemary and a sprig of thyme, sprinkle each thrice with water and put one in each shoe. Then a shoe with its sprig was put on each side of the bed, while the maid repeated:

> St. Agnes, that's to lovers kind,
> Come, ease the trouble of my mind.

Then she was certain to dream of her husband, seeing his face clearly so as to be able to identify him without difficulty.

INAUGURATION DAY

The term of the President of the United States started on March 4 until the adoption of the Twentieth Amendment to the Constitution in 1933. Presidents elected since that date take office on January 20. Washington, the first President, was not inaugurated until April 30, 1789. He took the oath of office on the steps of the old City Hall, at the corner of Wall and Nassau Streets in New York City which was then the national capital. At the beginning of his second term he took the oath in front of Independence Hall in Philadelphia, then serving as the capital. John Adams was also inaugurated in Philadelphia, but by the time Thomas Jefferson was elected the seat of government had been removed to Washington. Jefferson was escorted to the Capitol by a body of militia and a procession of citizens and took the oath of office in the Senate Chamber. James Madison was the first President to take the oath in the hall of the House of Representatives and it was in his honor that the first inaugural ball was held. This ball became in the course of time one of the established features of Inauguration Day, or of the preceding evening. And in the course of time also March 4 was made a quadrennial holiday in the District of Columbia by Act of Congress. The holiday was automatically changed to January 20, when inauguration day was changed.

President Monroe was the first to deliver his inaugural address and take the oath on the eastern portico of the Capitol. Since his time it has been customary for the inaugural address to be delivered from this place in the presence of a large crowd assembled on the plaza. The inauguration of Andrew Jackson drew to Washington thousands of his admirers from the West and the South. They crowded the White House at the reception following the inaugural address.

The development of the inaugural day parade was slow. The new President was at first escorted to the Capitol. Later, because of the many organizations which wished to march, the parade followed the inauguration and was reviewed by the President from a stand erected in front of the White House. Probably the most imposing parade up to that time was on the occasion of the inauguration of General Grant in 1869. Large bodies of soldiers and members of political organizations from various parts of the country were in the line. When a Republican President succeeds a Democrat or a Democratic President succeeds a Republican his partisans flock to Washington for the inauguration with organizations marching and waving banners, rejoicing, as the cynical put it, at the opportunity once more to share in the distribution of offices.

The ceremonies at the induction into office of the President of the United States do not resemble those attending the coronation of a hereditary monarch, but they are more elaborate than those at the entrance into office of the elected head of any other country.

49

JANUARY TWENTY-FIRST

BIRTHDAY OF "STONEWALL" JACKSON

Although Thomas Jonathan Jackson, better known as "Stonewall," was born in Clarksburg in what is now West Virginia, the State of Virginia regards him as one of its heroes and observes the anniversary of his birth in conjunction with the anniversary of the birth of Robert E. Lee, who was born two days earlier. (See Birthday of Robert E. Lee, January 19.) When Sunday intervenes the celebration usually lasts three days with secular exercises on Saturday and Monday and religious services on Sunday.

Jackson was born on January 21, 1824, the son of Jonathan Jackson, a lawyer. He was named Thomas and when he was in his teens he added Jonathan in memory of his father. Both his father and mother died while he was a small boy and he was reared by an uncle. In 1842 he entered the United States Military Academy at West Point handicapped by inadequate preparation, but he worked hard and was graduated in the upper third of his class. He was sent almost immediately to Mexico and distinguished himself at Vera Cruz, Cerro Gordo and Chapultepec and was brevetted a major within eighteenth months of his graduation. He was stationed at Fort Columbus and Fort Hamilton in New York harbor from 1848 until 1851. When he was ordered to Florida in the latter year he accepted appointment as professor of military tactics at the Virginia Military Institute at Lexington and resigned from the army. It is said that he was not successful as a teacher, but that as he was deeply religious his influence over the students was good. He commanded the cadet corps at the hanging of John Brown on December 2, 1859. At the outbreak of the Civil War he was ordered by the Confederate commander to Richmond with part of the cadet corps and was sent to Harpers Ferry as a colonel of infantry. On June 17, 1861, he was promoted to the rank of brigadier general, and took part in the first battle of Bull Run. He successfully resisted the assault of the Federal troops and conducted himself so gallantly that General Barnard E. Bee cried out as his own troops retreated, "There is Jackson standing like a stone wall." Thereafter he was known as "Stonewall Jackson. His subsequent career as a soldier was brilliant. He cooperated with General Lee who depended on him to carry out many of his plans. While he was reconnoitering in front of his lines on the evening of May 2, 1863, his own men mistook the party for Federal officers and fired on it wounding Jackson in the left arm and right hand. His left arm was amputated and he seemed in a fair way to recovery when pneumonia set in and he died at Guinea Station on May 10. In his military maneuvers he was courageous to the point of rashness. He is regarded as one of the most brilliant military geniuses produced by the Civil War.

FEAST OF ST. AGNES

There are many conflicting stories of the life and martyrdom of St. Agnes of Rome, one of the four great virgin martyrs of the Christian church. They all agree, however, on her extreme youth. It is not known definitely whether she met her martyrdom in the third century or early in the fourth century. The many legends concerning her all say that she was the daughter of a rich Roman. She became a Christian and when the son of a prefect fell in love with her she refused to marry him as she was the "bride of Christ." The young man fell sick and his father tried all sorts of persuasion to induce the young girl to change her mind, even threatening her with death. She remained true to her vow and in a final attempt to overcome her resistance the young man's father is said to have taken her to a place of infamy to subject her to the outrages of its frequenters. According to the tradition the soldiers who dragged her to the place stripped her of her garments. When she saw herself thus exposed she bent her head in prayer and immediately her hair spread itself about her covering her body like a garment. Those who looked on were seized with awe and cast their eyes on the ground. She was then locked in a chamber and an angel appeared to her with a white robe which she put on. It was finally ordered that she be burned and when she was put on the pyre and the fire lighted the flames did not touch her, but the two soldiers who guarded her were burned to death. She was finally slain by the sword. A church named for her was erected over her tomb in Rome.

She has been included in the list of Christian martyrs since 354. Since the Middle Ages she has been represented in Christian art with a lamb at her feet, suggesting either her name or her innocent purity. Her feast day is observed by the Latin church and there is a procession in her honor in Rome every year. On this day two lambs are solemnly blessed and from their wool the palliums sent by the Pope to the archbishops are woven.

JANUARY TWENTY-SECOND

OHIO'S FIRST LEGISLATURE

The Ordinance of 1787, setting up a government in the Northwest Territory, provided that not less than three and not more than five states might be formed from the territory, and fixed the boundaries of the proposed states. The Ordinance also provided that when in any of the districts thus outlined there should be five thousand free male inhabitants they might "elect representatives from their counties or townships to represent them in the general assembly," and that this general assembly might elect a delegate to Congress who should have the right to debate but not to vote. In 1798 there were the requisite number of free male inhabitants in Ohio and a general assembly was elected. It met for the first time at Cincinnati on January 22, 1799. After organizing, it chose William Henry Harrison, afterward President of the United States, as its first delegate to Congress.

The Ordinance of 1787 further provided that whenever any of the territories formed out of the Northwest Territory should have sixty thousand free inhabitants "it should be admitted, by its delegates, into the Congress of the United States, on an equal footing with the original states, in all respects whatever." Congress in 1802 passed an act to enable the people of Ohio to form a state government. Such a government was formed and by an act approved on February 19, 1803, Ohio was admitted to the Union as a state. Its first capital was Chillicothe. In 1810 the capital was removed to Zanesville but within a few years Columbus was made the capital. The legislature met there for the first time in 1816.

BIRTHDAY OF FREDERICK MOORE VINSON

Frederick Moore Vinson, the thirteenth Chief Justice of the United States, was the fifth Kentuckian to sit on the bench of the Supreme Court and the only one to become Chief Justice. He was born January 22, 1890, at Louisa, Ky., a little hill town on the edge of the Big Sandy River, son of James and Virginia Ferguson Vinson. His father was the town jailer and Mr. Vinson first saw the light of day in the front part of the jail building where his parents made their home. James Vinson died when his son was very young, but Mrs. Vinson, by taking in boarders, made enough money to send Fred to college with the help of his own earnings. In 1908 he was graduated from the Kentucky Normal School. However, he changed his mind about becoming a teacher and took his B.A. from Centre College, being graduated first in the class of 1909 and carrying off the Ormond Beatty alumni prize. He went on to acquire his LL.B. degree at Centre, in 1911, together with the Jacobs Junior Law Prize and the Senior Law Prize and, in that same year, hung out his shingle at Louisa, Ky. By 1913 he was city attorney of Louisa; in 1921 he became commonwealth attorney for the 32nd Judicial District of Kentucky, an office he held three years. In November 1922 he was elected to Congress from the old 9th Kentucky District. The Hoover landslide of 1928 swept him out of the House, but two years later he was elected for the second time from the old 9th Kentucky District and was returned to Washington as Representative from this District at every succeeding election until his resignation from Congress in 1938. He was appointed to the District of Columbia Court of Appeals and in March 1942 became chief justice of the three-member Emergency Court of Appeals which was to handle cases arising under the Emergency Price-Control Act. In May 1943 he resigned from the Court of Appeals to become Director of the Office of Economic Stabilization. His appointment was regarded favorably by all factions since his activities in Congress had given him the necessary training and experience for this responsible position. A current periodical commented:

> With his knowledge of the coal industry, his legal slant on the issues involved in price control, and more importantly, his training for a dominant role in taxation, Vinson may well be able to carry on where Byrnes left off.

However, his determined efforts to hold the line against a threatened inflationary spiral soon aroused opposition from labor and management alike; he invariably persisted in whatever he deemed the most advantageous decision for the country as a whole, whether it was a question of wages or prices and regardless of whose toes he stepped on. In the ensuing three years Mr. Vinson was appointed to several important posts in rapid succession. He became Federal Loan Administrator and, a few days after Mr. Truman took the presidential oath upon the death of Franklin D. Roosevelt, he was chosen as War Mobilization Chief. In July 1945 President Truman nominated him as Secretary of the Treasury upon the retirement of Henry Morgenthau. Early in 1946 he became United States governor of both the International Monetary Fund and the International Bank for Reconstruction and Development provided in the Bretton Woods agreement. This put Mr. Vinson in the top policy-making job to guide the country's international financial agreements. Essentially the Fund was to be operated as a pool of world currencies and gold from which member countries may draw when temporarily short of another member's currency. It was designed to tide members over short-term trade difficulties when otherwise they might have to curtail imports, to subsidize exports, impose exchange controls or take other restrictive action. Mr. Vinson was also chairman of the National Advisory Council created in 1945 to coordinate public financial policy, foreign and domestic.

In June 1946 President Truman chose him as Chief Justice of the Supreme Court of the United States to fill the vacancy made by the death of Chief Justice Harlan Fiske Stone. The Justices of the Supreme Court at that time were divided into so-called "liberal" and "conservative" blocs and there was considerable dissension among them. Mr. Vinson's middle of the road tendency, and his personal tact and diplomacy, were generally considered as suited to resolving these difficulties.

JANUARY TWENTY-THIRD

FEAST OF ST. ILDEFONSUS

The Spanish missionaries converted many Indians in the Southwest to Christianity, and in New Mexico one of the pueblos was named San Ildefonso for the Spanish saint, Ildefonsus. He died on January 23, 667, and his feast is celebrated on that day by a ceremonial dance by the Indians of the pueblo, in which pagan rites are combined with Christian ceremonies.

St. Ildefonsus, or as the Spanish have it, San Ildefonso, was born of a distinguished Spanish family. In spite of the opposition of his family he embraced the monastic life in the monastery of Agli, near Toledo. He endowed a monastery of nuns while still a monk. He was ordained a deacon about 630 and thereafter became abbot of Agli. He was made archbishop of Toledo in 657 and when he died about nine years later he was buried in the basilica of St. Leocadia. This is about all the authentic information concerning him which is known. His successor as archbishop of Toledo, however, toward the end of the eighth century, wrote some legends about him. One is that when he was praying before the relics of St. Leocadia the saint rose from her tomb and thanked him for his devotion to the Virgin Mary. Another is that the Virgin appeared to him in person and presented to him a priestly vestment to reward him for his zeal in honoring her. These legends, particularly the latter, have been favorite subjects with poets and painters. Philip V of Spain built a palace about thirty-four miles northwest of Madrid and a village grew up about it which was named San Ildefonso in honor of the saint.

JANUARY TWENTY-FOURTH

FEAST OF ST. TIMOTHY

Timothy was one of the most trusted assistants of Paul, who is said to have made him bishop of Ephesus in charge of the churches in Asia. His feast day is observed on January 24. He was a native of Lystra in Lycaonia, the son of a Gentile father and a Jewish mother. Nothing is known of his conversion to Christianity. On Paul's second visit to Lystra, Timothy was favorably known among the Christians and Paul persuaded him to go with him as an assistant. He was intrusted with important missions to the churches at Berea, Athens, Thessalonica, Corinth and Ephesus. He went with Paul to Jerusalem and visited him in Rome. Two lives of him were written. According to one of them St. John went to Ephesus during the persecutions by Nero and lived with Timothy until he was exiled to Patmos by Domitian. Timothy was unmarried and lived until he was eighty years old. The story of his death is told in this way by Polycrates, bishop of Ephesus in the second century: "Under the Emperor Nerva, in the year 97 . . . Timothy was slain with stones and clubs by two heathen while he was endeavoring to oppose their idolatrous ceremonies on one of their festivals called Catagogia, kept on January 22, when the idolators called in troops carrying in one hand an idol and the other a club." There is a tradition that his bones were removed from Ephesus to Constantinople in 356.

JANUARY TWENTY-FIFTH

BIRTHDAY OF ROBERT BURNS

Scotchmen the world over, the United States included, gather on January 25, the anniversary of the birth of Robert Burns, to glorify the poet and the country which produced him. The celebration in the United States usually takes the form of a dinner during which Scottish songs are sung and after which speeches are made by distinguished men of Scotch ancestry.

Burns was born in 1759 in a cottage about two miles from Ayr, the eldest son of William Burns, a man of fine integrity who was oppressed by poverty. Robert worked on his farm as a plow boy till he was fifteen. The family moved from one farm to another. The boy was eager to learn and he read the *Spectator*, Locke's *Essays* and Pope's translation of the *Iliad*. He went to school for a time and learned a little Latin and French. In 1781 he was apprentice to a flax dresser, but before he began to work the shop burned and he was left without work or money. In his twenty-fifth year his father died and he wrote for him an epitaph the last line of which declared that "even his failings leaned to virtue's side."

He took a farm at Mossgiel with his brother and toiled there for four years earning a bare living. In 1786, discouraged by his lot, he decided to emigrate and accepted a place as bookkeeper on an estate in Jamaica and bought his ticket for the West Indies. But at about that time his first small volume of poems was published. It received so hearty a welcome that he abandoned his intention to leave Scotland. The financial return from the book was only £20, but the social returns were much greater. Because of it he was invited to Edinburgh and welcomed by the literary society of the city. Sir Walter Scott, then a boy of fifteen, saw him and has described him in this way: "His countenance was more massive than it looks in any of his portraits. There was a strong expression of shrewdness in his lineaments; the eye indicated the poetic character and temperament. It was large and of a dark cast, and literally glowed when he spoke with feeling or interest. I never saw such another eye in a human head."

The second edition of the volume of poems, which appeared in 1787, yielded him £400 and with the proceeds he took a walking tour throughout the border towns of England and the eastern Highlands of Scotland and returned to Ayrshire. Here he took a farm and in 1788 formally married Jean Armour with whom he had had an affair a few years earlier. The next year he received appointment as excise officer of the district at £50 a year and two years later he was promoted to a similar post at Dumfries at a salary of £70. At about this time he was asked to write words for Scotch airs collected by George Thompson. He wrote about a hundred songs for which he received a shawl for his wife, a painting and £5 in money. He had been in the habit of drinking to excess for years and he now began to indulge in extreme dissipation. His strength failed, and he died on July 21, 1796, an old and worn out man at the age of thirty-seven. His fame has grown with the years and he is regarded as one of the great lyric poets of his race.

FEAST OF THE CONVERSION OF ST. PAUL

It is not known just when the church began to observe the anniversary of the conversion of Paul. The festival is mentioned in the calendar and missals of the eighth and ninth centuries and Pope Innocent III (1198-1216) urged that it be celebrated with great solemnity. It is mentioned as a solemn festival in the records of the Council of Oxford in 1222, held during the reign of Henry III, and it continued to be observed by the Anglican church after its separation from Rome. Yet curiously enough it had no official recognition from the English church until the Diocesian Synod at Exeter in 1827, when its observance with that of other feasts was formally ordered.

The account of the conversion of Paul appears in the Acts of the Apostles. He was a member of the tribe of Benjamin and he was named Saul for the first King of the Jews. This is the Hebrew form of his name. The Latin form, Paul, is that by which he is now known, a form which it is supposed that he adopted when he began to preach to the Gentiles. Following is the story of the event which is celebrated on this day:

And Saul, yet breathing out threatenings and slaughter against the disciples of the Lord, went unto the high priest and desired of him letters to Damascus to the synagogues, that if he found any of this way, whether they were men or women, he might bring them bound to Jerusalem. And as he journeyed, he came near Damascus; and suddenly there shined about him a light from heaven: and he fell to the earth, and heard a voice saying unto him, "Saul, Saul, why persecutest thou me?" And he said, "Who art thou, Lord?" And the Lord said, "I am Jesus whom thou persecutest; it is hard for thee to kick against the pricks." And he trembling and astonished said, "Lord, what wilt thou have me to do?" And the Lord said unto him, "Arise and go into the city, and it shall be told thee what thou must do." And the men which journeyed with him stood speechless, hearing no voice and seeing no man. And Saul arose from the earth; and when his eyes were opened, he saw no man; but they led him by the hand and brought him into Damascus. And he was there three days without sight, and neither did he eat or drink.

An interesting ceremony is performed at St. Paul's Chapel, at Broadway and Fulton Street, New York, every year on the eve of the festival of the conversion of St. Paul. There is a large burying ground around the chapel, enclosed by an iron fence with gates. The public passes through the burying ground along the paths, using it as a thoroughfare. When there is uninterrupted use of such a right of way for a term of years the owner of the property loses control over it. Therefore, the gates of the church yard are closed for forty-eight hours every year, ending with the eve of the festival. Then the rector of the chapel, in full vestments, takes his stand at the gates, reads four verses from the sixty-eighth Psalm and the whole of the ninety-first Psalm, and then says, "Open the gates that the people may enter." The gates are opened and there is a service in the chapel appropriate to the day, preceding the special service on the day of the festival.

JANUARY TWENTY-SIXTH

MICHIGAN DAY

Michigan was organized as a territory in 1805 and admitted to the Union as a state on January 26, 1837. The Michigan country was probably first visited by white men when the Frenchman Jean Nicolet reached Sault de Ste. Marie in 1634. Here the first permanent white settlement was made by Father Marquette in 1668 for a Jesuit mission. Detroit was founded in 1701 by a French colony under Cadillac. The lands now within the boundaries of the State of Michigan passed to the English in 1760, and to the United States in 1796; it was again occupied by Great Britain in 1812, but was recovered by the Americans the next year, becoming a permanent part of the United States.

With a coast line on four of the Great Lakes, and encircling Lake Michigan except for the part of the western shore bordered by Wisconsin, transportation facilities are excellent and have promoted and fostered industrial development. The leading industry is the manufacture of the automobile, centered chiefly in Detroit. In 1925, of the nearly five million cars representing the world output, Michigan accounted for over three million, and has continued to lead the industry up to the present time. In the mining of ore the state is second only to Minnesota, producing pig iron and copper in important quantities, and is the foremost state in the salt industry.

57

BIRTHDAY OF DOUGLAS MACARTHUR

In Arkansas January 26 has been designated General Douglas Mac-Arthur Day and is proclaimed annually by the governor. Douglas Mac-Arthur, commanding general of the United States Armed Forces in the Far East during World War II, comes of a celebrated army family. Born in Little Rock, Ark., on January 26, 1880, he is the son of Mary P. Hardy and Lieutenant General Arthur MacArthur. His father helped to drive the Spaniards out of the Philippine Islands and served there as Governor General for two years. Thus, it was natural that young Mac-Arthur should attend West Point. He was graduated in 1903, the number.one honor man of his class, commissioned a second lieutenant and sent to the Philippines. The following year he was promoted to the rank of first lieutenant, returning to the United States in October to spend several months with the California Debris Commission, and also serving as chief engineering officer of the Pacific Division. Then came a year in Japan as aide to his father, another year as Theodore Roosevelt's aide in Washington, and in 1908, after being graduated from the Engineering School of Application, he joined Company K, 3rd Battalion of Engineers, at Fort Leavenworth, Kan. He served at that station, at San Antonio, Tex., and on detached service in the Canal Zone until August 1912, and until November 1912 was an instructor of engineering at Army Service Schools, Fort Leavenworth. Meanwhile, in February 1911, he had acquired the rank of captain. From Fort Leavenworth he was ordered to Washington where he was appointed to the General Staff Corps and, from April to September 1914, served with the Engineering Corps in the Vera Cruz Expedition. In December 1915 he was raised to the rank of major and in September 1917, after the United States entered the first World War, was appointed chief of staff of the 42nd (Rainbow) Division with the rank of colonel of infantry.

During the war the thirty-seven-year-old colonel participated in the Champagne-Marne and Aisne-Marne defensives. He was given the temporary rank of brigadier general in June 1918 and placed in command of the 84th Infantry Brigade, leading it in the St. Mihiel, Essey, Pannes, Meuse-Argonne and Sedan offensives. He was twice wounded in action and created a sensation by insisting on going into battle with his men. The citation for "extraordinary heroism against an armed enemy" accompanying his Distinguished Service Cross reads: "When Company D, 168th Infantry, was under severe attack in the salient du Fays, France, he voluntarily joined it upon finding that he could do so without interfering with his normal duties, and by his coolness and conspicuous courage aided materially in its success." The Armistice of 1918 found General Mac-Arthur temporarily commanding the 42nd Division once more before being put in command of the 84th Infantry Brigade and stationed with the Army of Occupation in Germany until April of the following year.

Returning to the United States Military Academy, he immediately began to work toward the mechanization of the "horse and saber department." Then, in January 1920, he was made a brigadier general in the regular army, and in 1922 he left for the Philippines again to serve for three years as commander of the District of Manila, the 23rd Infantry Brigade and Philippine Division. Promoted to the rank of major general in January 1925, he spent the next five years commanding the Fourth Corps Area in Atlanta, the Third Corps Area in Baltimore and, from 1928 to 1930, the Philippine Department. Finally, in November 1930, President Hoover made him Chief of Staff of the United States Army— the only chief of staff in United States history whose father had held the same post, and the youngest man to hold it since World War I. At the same time the four-star insignia of a general was bestowed upon him, making him the youngest general since Grant.

In 1935 General MacArthur, due to retire as Chief of Staff of the United States Army, became director of the organization of national defense of the Philippine Commonwealth. The next year a bill made him military adviser to the Commonwealth, and in August of that same year President Quezon commissioned him field marshall of the Philippine Army. The General was not only confident that the defense of the islands could, in a few years, be built up so effectively that conquest would cost an invader some half million men and ten billion dollars, but also that Japanese militarism would be a very real threat in the near future, and he continued energetically with his program. On December 31, 1937, he retired from the army at his own request, but remained with the Philippine Army as field marshall, undiscouraged by hints in 1940 from Commissioner Francis B. Sayer, and even from President Quezon, that the islands were practically indefensible. However, by 1941 relations between the United States and Japan were growing so strained that even former critics expressed little but gratitude when, in July, President Roosevelt placed the land and sea forces of the Philippine Commonwealth under United States military and naval command for the duration of the emergency and appointed General MacArthur commander of the United States Army in the Far East. Thereafter frequent conferences took place with President Quezon over the incorporation of the Philippine Army reservists into the United States Army, and with Sir Robert Brooke-Popham over Anglo-United States military plans. When the Japanese attack occurred in 1941, commentators praised the work the General had done in the Philippines over a number of years and the quality of resistance met by the enemy; and on December 19, 1942, he became a full general in the Army of the United States for the second time.

Shortly before the fall of Bataan and Corregidor he was ordered out for the defense of Australia and left on a PT boat, making the declaration which subsequently became famous: "I came through and I will return." On September 25, 1942, he launched a counter attack on New Guinea, driving the invaders back, and six weeks later airborne Americans descended into the swamps of New Guinea. The Japanese were killed one by one in no-quarter fighting and General MacArthur announced his victory January 23, 1943. His offensive then went into full swing and the year 1943 with its leap-frog operations opened the way to the Philippines and the Marianas, the front door to Japan. True to his promise, he returned to the Philippines, wading ashore on the east coast of Leyte on October 20, 1944, and calling on the Filipinos to "rise and strike." The Second Battle of the Philippines, the greatest naval battle of the war and also the greatest in American naval history, dissipated the naval threat to the Americans and the MacArthur forces continued their advances. The decisive blow came on Christmas Day and the General announced that the Japanese army had suffered its most severe defeat with 125,000 killed. Eventually, after bitter fighting and heavy casualties, the Philippines were cleared of the enemy July 5, 1945. By the middle of August Japan surrendered, defeated on land and sea, and General MacArthur, acting for the Allies as Supreme Commander in the Far East, signed the formal articles aboard the battleship Missouri in Tokyo Bay. On September 7, American troops entered Tokyo and the Stars and Stripes were raised over the General's headquarters. He immediately announced that he was taking over the entire Japanese government, including the Emperor, in accordance with the terms of surrender.

JANUARY TWENTY-SEVENTH

FEAST OF ST. CHRYSOSTOM

St. John of Constantinople, or St. Chrysostom, as he is better known, was one of the learned men of the early Christian church and is frequently compared with St. Jerome. He was born at Antioch in about 345, the son of the commander of the imperial army in Syria, and died in 407. His feast is celebrated by the Roman church on January 27 and by the Greek church on November 13. The Protestant Episcopal church honors him by including one of his prayers in its order of service. He was not called Chrysostom, the golden mouthed, until about 680. His reputation as one of the most brilliant orators of his time had survived till then and a church council decided to honor him by adding "chrysostom" to his name.

When he was a baby his father died and he was reared by his mother. When he was old enough he studied oratory under a Roman rhetorician as he intended to become a lawyer, and soon excelled his teacher. But he felt called to the religious life and began to devote himself to the study of the Bible. On his mother's death about 375, he retired to the desert around Antioch and lived in the simplest possible manner. The rigors of his asceticism brought on an illness and he returned to Antioch in 381 where he was ordained as a deacon. His preaching attracted wide attention and in 398 he was made bishop of Constantinople. He used the greater part of the revenues of his office in charity and came to be known as John the Almoner. He also sought to bring about reforms in the life of the clergy and of the people, and because of this he aroused the enmity of his political and ecclesiastical superiors and was banished from Constantinople to a little town in the Armenian highlands. He was received kindly by the resident bishop and continued his Christian work among the people. His banishment was resented by the faithful Christians and this resentment enraged the emperor who ordered that he be sent to a town on the northeast coast of the Black Sea, at the very edge of the Roman Empire. He set out on foot to make the journey of hundreds of miles, but after traveling for three months he could go no farther and died at the chapel of Basiliscus, six miles from Comana, in Pontus, on September 14, 407. He left a large number of written works, including homilies, commentaries, treatises and liturgies.

JANUARY TWENTY-EIGHTH

THE UNITED STATES WITHDRAWS FROM CUBA

Following the war with Spain in 1898 the United States took temporary possession of Cuba. For the next three years the affairs of the island were administered by the War Department through General Leonard Wood as Governor General. The people of the island adopted a constitution in 1901 and elected Estrada Palma as president in 1902. On May 20 of that year the United States formally withdrew from the island. But political troubles arose and grew more acute from year to year until in August 1906, there was a violent outbreak. In September President Palma appealed to the United States for intervention, professing to be unable to suppress the insurrection, and on September 12 the United States cruiser "Des Moines" was sent to Havana. President Theodore Roosevelt sent Secretary of War Taft to the island to act as a mediator and he landed at Havana on September 19. Secretary Taft decided that the election of 1905 was void with the exception of the election of a President. President Palma thereupon resigned and Mr. Taft assumed the office of provisional governor. United States troops were sent to the island and the belligerents were disarmed. The troops remained in control until January 28, 1909, when order had been restored and a new government set up. Then the United States withdrew from the island for the second time.

JANUARY TWENTY-NINTH

KANSAS DAY

Kansas was organized as a territory by an Act of Congress approved on May 30, 1854, and it was admitted to the Union as a state by an act approved on January 29, 1861. The anniversary of statehood has been celebrated by the Republicans since 1892. Their clubs meet in Topeka, the capital, elect officers in the afternoon, and listen to partisan speeches at a dinner in the evening. There is a Men's Kansas Day Club and a Women's Kansas Day Club, and there are other Republican clubs of men and women, all of which take part in the annual celebration. In 1935 the Women's Kansas Day Club, after electing its officers, presented two pageants. The first was called "Today's Harvest from Pioneer Soil." The scenes represented were: "Seed Sowing—justice, freedom, law; Growing Grain—organized strength, individual progress. Blossom Beauty—the fine arts; Harvest Riches—spiritual strength; Garnered Grain—social grace and culture; A Tableau—seed for tomorrow's harvest." The second was "A Dream of Fair Women." The Kansas Women's Republican Club celebrated the anniversary by holding its annual meeting and giving a reception in the executive mansion. The women were welcomed to the state capitol by Governor Landon and by John Hamilton, the Republican National Committeeman for Kansas.

The Kansas Republican Service Men's League also held its annual meeting on the anniversary and, in addition to transacting routine business, it gave a luncheon attended by prominent leaders of the party in and out of the state, including Patrick J. Hurley of Oklahoma, Secretary of War in the Hoover Administration; Hanford MacNider of Iowa, past national commander of the American Legion, and Colonel Frank Knox of Chicago. The Men's Kansas Day Club at its business meeting received pledges of partisan support from the Young Republican Club of the state and messages of congratulation from distinguished Kansans who were unable to be present. The principal speaker at the dinner in the evening was Colonel Frank Knox who made a Republican address, condemning the policies of the Democratic national administration.

The greater part of the present area of Kansas came into the possession of the United States by the Louisiana Purchase in 1803. The southwestern part of the state was ceded to the Federal Government by Texas in 1850. Lewis and Clark passed through the region in 1804. Fort Leavenworth was erected in 1827 and in 1831 the Baptists founded a mission among the Shawnee Indians. Emigrant trains on the way to California crossed the region in 1844. The population was estimated .at seven hundred in 1854. What is now Kansas was part of Missouri until 1821. It remained without organized government until it became a territory in May 1854. While the territorial bill was pending in Congress a large number of immigrants from Missouri and Arkansas and from the Northern states entered Kansas and the struggle between them over whether the territory was to permit slavery began. Anti-slavery men had settled in Lawrence, Topeka and Ossawatomie, and advocates of slavery founded Leavenworth and Atchison. On March 30, 1855, an election of a territorial legislature was held and 5427 pro-slavery votes were cast out of a total of 6218, although there were only 3000 legal voters in the territory. Governor A. H. Reeder set aside the election in six of the districts and ordered a new election which resulted in the victory of the anti-slavery candidates. When the first territorial legislature met at Pawnee on July 2, 1855, it was controlled by a pro-slavery majority. This majority expelled the members chosen at the second election ordered by the governor. It passed acts making it a capital offense to assist slaves in escaping either to or from the territory and a felony to circulate anti-slavery publications or to deny the right to hold slaves, and requiring all voters to swear to support the Fugitive Slave Law. The anti-slavery men refused to recognize the legality of the Territorial government and in a convention at Topeka on October 23, 1855, they adopted a constitution prohibiting slavery after July 4, 1857, and excluding Negroes from the state, although Congress had not yet granted statehood. The constitution was adopted at an election in December in which the pro-slavery men took no part. A Governor and a Legislature were chosen at an election in January 1856. The supporters of this government wished to avoid armed conflict, but when a sheriff under the Territorial government was shot at Lawrence while trying to seize a prisoner, the anti-slavery leaders were indicted for treason and imprisoned; and on May 21 a mob of pro-slavery men sacked Lawrence.

Two days later John Brown and his sons killed five men on Pottawatomie creek and civil war between the two factions began and continued throughout the month of June when United States troops intervened and restored order. The Free State Legislature met at Topeka on July 4, 1856, but was dispersed by Federal troops. This legislature made another attempt to meet on January 6, 1857, but its members were arrested. Robert J. Walker, the fourth Governor of the Territory since 1854, succeeded in arranging a compromise with the men who had adopted a constitution for a state government, and they agreed to take part in an election for a territorial legislature in October, 1857. The anti-slavery party won the election. The pro-slavery party, however, had called a convention to meet in Lecompton and this convention adopted a constitution on November 7 declaring that the right of slaveholders in Kansas to their slaves was inviolable and prohibiting the Legislature from passing any act of emancipation. The document was not submitted to the people for their approval, but on December 21 the question of whether they would have a constitution with slavery or a constitution without slavery was submitted. The vote for a constitution with slavery was 6226, more than one-half of which was polled along the Missouri border where there were not more than 1000 qualified voters. The great body of anti-slavery advocates refrained from voting as they regarded the election as farcical so that the opposition vote was only 569. The Lecompton constitution was submitted to the voters by the Territorial Legislature on January 4, 1858, when 10,226 votes were cast against it to less than two hundred for it. The issue was taken to Congress where the Senate voted to admit Kansas as a satte with the Lecompton constitution. The House of Representatives rejected the bill and a compromise measure was passed. The disputed constitution was again submitted to the voters and again rejected by a majority of more than 10,000. This ended the struggle for the establishment of slavery in Kansas. An anti-slavery constitution was adopted on October 4, 1859. On January 29, 1861, Kansas was admitted to the Union as a free state.

CARNATION DAY, BIRTHDAY OF WILLIAM McKINLEY

This is the anniversary of the birth of William McKinley, twenty-fifth President of the United States. He was born at Niles, Ohio, January 25, 1843, of Scotch-Irish ancestry, the seventh of nine children. His great-grandfather, David McKinley, was a soldier in the Revolution. His father and grandfather were engaged in the iron industry, and he worked with his father when a boy. He prepared for college at Poland Academy and entered Allegheny College at Meadville, Pa., but was unable to complete his course for lack of money and obtained employment as a teacher. He was teaching when the Civil War broke out. On June 11, 1861, he enlisted in the Twenty-third Ohio Volunteer Regiment of which William S. Rosecrans was colonel. Rutherford B. Hayes, who was to become President, succeeded Colonel Rosecrans as commander. The regiment saw service and on September 23, 1862, McKinley was commissioned second lieutenant by Colonel Hayes, for gallantry on the field. He continued with the regiment throughout the war, reaching the rank of captain. On March 13, 1865, he was brevetted major, a title by which he was known in after life.

When he was mustered out he began the study of law in the office of Judge Glidden and completed his preparation in the Albany Law School. He was admitted to the bar in 1867 and opened an office in Canton, Ohio. In 1869 he was elected prosecuting attorney for Stark County as a Republican, although the county was normally Democratic. He supported the candidacy of Hayes for governor in 1875 and his speeches in favor of the resumption of specie payments attracted national attention. He was elected to the national House of Representatives in 1876 and served seven successive terms. He rose to the chairmanship of the Ways and Means Committee and a tariff act drawn by that committee is known by his name. In a reapportionment of the Congressional districts in the state the Democrats in control of the Legislature gerry-mandered his district in such a way as to give their party a majority and he was defeated in the election in 1890. The Republicans nominated him for governor in 1891 and he was elected, and re-elected in 1893. He was nominated for the presidency by the Republicans in 1896 and elected over William Jennings Bryan by an electoral vote of 271 to 176. Conditions in Cuba precipitated a war with Spain in 1898, which he car-ried to a successful end. The treaty of peace provided for the withdrawal of Spain from Cuba and ceded Porto Rico, the Philippine Islands and the island of Guam to the United States upon the payment of an indemnity of $20,000,000 to Spain. He was reelected in 1900 with Bryan as the Democratic candidate. He was fatally shot while holding a public re-ception at the Pan American Exposition in Buffalo, N.Y., on September 6, 1901, and died on September 14.

The anniversary of his birth has been observed as Carnation Day since 1903. The celebration was proposed by Lewis G. Reynolds of Dayton, Ohio. In a letter to the editor of the New York *Tribune*, pub-lished on January 22, 1903, he said:

It is proper that some annual observance be held in memory of William McKinley. The same loyal impulse that prompted the stoppage of almost all the wheels of industry for those few moments on the day of his burial may find annual expression in this tribute suggested by the Carnation League. The plan of the movement is a simple, inexpensive and attractive one and can be taken part in by the old and the young of either sex. A beautiful, fragrant flower worn in the lapel of the coat or at the throat or in the hair in silent memory of a public servant whose life was forfeited because he was our servant is what is contemplated. The fact that the carnation was President McKinley's favorite flower and was always found in his buttonhole is the reason for its choice as a league symbol. On all other days of the year it will be what it is today—the common people's flower—but on September 14 (it was first proposed to observe the day of McKinley's death)—it becomes especially the President's flower and will be worn in silent tribute to his memory. . . . If the Carnation League of America serves the purpose of a perennial memorial to a faithful public servant and at the same time fosters a national brotherhood of patriotism it will be worthy of our people. It will do all that and it will accomplish its purpose silently with almost unconscious effort.

The Carnation League was formally organized on January 29, 1903, with the President of the United States, the Governor of Ohio and the Ohio Senators as honorary trustees and with the following as active trustees: Marcus A. Hanna of Ohio, Henry C. Payne of Wisconsin, Dr. William R. Harper of Illinois, George B. Cortelyou of New York, William R. Day of Ohio, Charles W. Fairbanks of Indiana, David R. Francis of Missouri, Myron T. Herrick of Ohio, H. H. Kohlsaat and Alexander H. Revell of Illinois, and S. S. Rankin and Lewis G. Reynolds of Ohio.

While the anniversary in 1903 was known as Carnation Day, there had been an observance of the anniversary of McKinley's birth in the previous year. A memorial association had been organized to raise money for erecting a monument to his memory. The association persuaded the governors of many states to issue proclamations calling upon the people to gather in some public place in their respective communities to do honor to the memory of the dead President, and suggesting that special services be held in the schools. Such public meetings and memorial services were widely held. Many who attended them wore a carnation in the buttonholes of their coats. The carnation was McKinley's favorite flower. During his presidency he had several fresh blossoms sent to him every day from the White House conservatories. Callers would frequently ask him for the flower which he was wearing as a souvenir of their visit. With his usual graciousness he granted their request. Many of these blossoms were preserved by their recipients.

The observance of the anniversary grew in importance from year to year while the contemporaries of McKinley were still alive. Special attention is still paid to it in Ohio. One of the most notable celebrations was that of the Tippecanoe Club of Cleveland in 1908, a club which continues to observe the anniversary. William Howard Taft, then Secretary of War, was the principal speaker. He said in part:

I shall endeavor to speak to you tonight on that which I think will be ever remembered as the great and distinguishing characteristics of McKinley's administration—the expansion of the United States into a world power. Those who look at McKinley's administration find it difficult to separate from his administration the great battle for honest money and for the integrity of the nation's plighted faith with which his administration was ushered in. While this was a most important point in the history of the country, it was rather an electoral victory than one of the administration of McKinley. That which really distinguishes the administration of McKinley is the war with Spain and the expansion which followed it. . . . Our action in assuming our part of the responsibility of the world powers for the development of the world has added to our influence the world round and has made our voice influential in all international councils. So great has been this growth that the immediate successor of William McKinley, Theodore Roosevelt, has been able to accomplish more in the preservation of the peace of the world than any president that ever administered or any monarch that ever reigned. The influence that we are exerting in South America, in Central America, in Europe and in China, is, much of it, the result of the policy of expansion adopted under William McKinley. It is said that this policy has entailed upon us the enormous burden of a navy. I believe that it has increased the necessity for a great navy. I believe that a navy is the greatest insurer of peace that we could possibly have—a navy commensurate with our resources and commensurate with the number of dependencies we have and commensurate with our population and commensurate with our influence as a world power. The expression "World Power" has been made an occasion for ridicule and sneers, but it has a real meaning and a real significance. It means an influence throughout the world, and so long as that influence is wielded for the betterment of mankind, for the uplifting of our unfortunate fellow creatures, for the maintenance of peace, for the promotion of morality and civilization, we may be proud to have taken any part in the change of our national policy which made us a world power. The highest claim of William McKinley for the gratitude of his countrymen is that in spite of the abuse and contumely that was heaped upon his head for this policy he placed our country in the forefront of nations as a civilizer and uplifter of unfortunate peoples.

The city of Niles, his birthplace, dedicated a memorial building in his honor on October 5, 1917.

EMANUEL SWEDENBORG'S BIRTHDAY

The Church of the New Jerusalem, or the New Church, as it is usually called by its members, celebrates the anniversary of the birth of Emanuel Swedenborg, one of the greatest mystics of historic time. The exercises consist of an address on some phase of his religious views. Reference is frequently made to Carlyle's *Heroes and Hero Worship*, in which there is an enthusiastic appraisal of this remarkable man.

Swedenborg was born in Stockholm on January 29, 1688. His father the Reverend Jesper Swedenborg, was a regimental chaplain and court preacher. In 1696 his father was appointed Chancellor of the University of Upsala and bishop over the Swedish churches in London, Pennsylvania, Delaware and New Jersey. The boy was interested in religious matters and he once wrote that from his sixth to his twelfth year he used to delight in talking with clergymen about faith, saying that the life of faith is love, and that the love which imparts life is love to the neighbor. There is a tradition that while he was a child, angels, invisible to others, appeared to him and played with him in his father's garden. He was educated at Upsala and on his graduation traveled four years in England, Holland, France and Germany. When he returned to Sweden, Charles XIII appointed him as an assessor of mines. He held the office for eleven years writing much on mineralogy, mathematics, astronomy, physics and chemistry, as well as upon anatomy and physiology. In 1745 he professed to have had his spiritual senses opened and claimed to be consciously an inhabitant of the spiritual world, and in 1759 he published the *Arcana Coelesta* which is an exposition of the internal or spiritual significance of Genesis and Exodus. He insisted that there is a spiritual sense in the greater part of the Bible, that the Jewish dispensation ended with the appearance of Jesus and that the church which Jesus established came to an end in 1757 when a new dispensation began with a new church identified with the New Jerusalem described in the Revelation of St. John the Divine. His later writings set forth and expound the doctrines of the New Church. One of those doctrines is that hell is not merely a place of punishment for the sins done in the body but is a provision of divine love, and the only place where the unregenerated natural man would feel comfortable. This view is similar to that expressed by Mark Hopkins, the famous president of Williams College. When a student asked him who would go to heaven Dr. Hopkins replied that he did not know but he was sure that only those would go who would feel at home there.

Swedenborg did not found a church, but those who read his writings came together and organized themselves into religious societies. The first church in America was organized in Baltimore on April 1, 1792, when the Reverend James Wilmer, an Episcopalian clergyman, preached the first New Church sermon on this continent. There are two branches of the church, one organized on the Episcopalian basis with a bishop and the other using the Congregational form of government.

Swedenborg was stricken with paralysis in London in December 1771, and died there on March 29, 1772. He was buried in the vault of the Swedish church. Many years later the government of Sweden sent a warship to England to take the body to Sweden where it was buried with honors at the University of Upsala (see New Church Day, June 19).

THOMAS PAINE DAY

Thomas Paine was born of Quaker parents at Thetford, Norfolk, England, on January 29, 1737. He left school at the age of thirteen and joined his father at the trade of stay making for ships. He followed this trade for some time. He was successively an exciseman, a tobacconist and a grocer. In October 1774, he emigrated to America with a letter from Benjamin Franklin to Richard Bache of Philadelphia. Bache introduced him to Robert Aitkin who made him editor of the *Pennsylvania Magazine or American Monthly Museum*. He attached himself to the Patriot party and on January 6, 1776, he published his pamphlet *Common Sense* in which he argued that the American colonies owed no allegiance to the British crown and "should forthwith be independent." He had a brief military experience and held some subordinate political offices and wrote much in defense of the cause of the colonies. In 1781 he went to France as secretary of a commission seeking financial aid, which was obtained. At the suggestion of Washington, Congress voted $800 to him on condition that he should write in defense of the country. Two years later the State of New York presented to him a farm of 277 acres at New Rochelle, and Pennsylvania gave him £500 and in 1785 Congress voted to him $3000. In 1787 he went to France again, this time to enlist the interest of the French in an iron bridge of his invention. He became involved in revolutionary politics and was elected to the convention which discussed the deposition of the king. When the party with which he was acting fell from power he was arrested and imprisoned on December 28, 1793, and narrowly escaped the guillotine. He had finished the first part of *The Age of Reason*, his exposition of deism, just before his arrest.

He returned to America in 1802 and landed at Baltimore on October 30. He discovered that although his services to the cause of freedom had not been wholly forgotten his attacks upon the accepted religious views of the people had made him extremely unpopular. He died in New York on June 8, 1909, and was buried in New Rochelle, N. Y., where a monument was erected to him in 1839. His body, however, had been removed to England in 1819 at the direction of William Cobbett.

It was not long after his death that religious radicals began to observe the anniversary of his birth. In Boston it was the custom of such to decorate their houses and their places of business with flags on that date. At a dinner in New York on the anniversary in 1910 there was prominently displayed a fragment of his brain with this inscription:

> Tuesday, January 7, 1833, I went to 11 Bott-Court, Fleet Street, and there I saw the remains of Mr. Thomas Paine——and from his skull I took a portion of his brain—which was almost black. A. Tilley.

A wax statue of Paine was unveiled on this occasion. It was later set up in the Paine National Museum at New Rochelle where many relics are assembled. This museum is in the house on the farm which the state presented to him. The Boston *Index* raised a fund to pay for a marble bust of Paine to be presented to Independence Hall in Philadelphia in 1876, the centennial year. It commissioned Sydney H. Morse to make the bust. Among the contributors to the fund were the Unitarian clergymen, Edward Everett Hale, O. B. Frothingham and Robert Collyer. The authorities in charge of Independence Hall declined to accept the bust, and it remained in the possession of Mrs. Carrie Kilgore of Philadelphia after unsuccessful attempts had been made to place it in the galleries of the Pennsylvania Academy of the Fine Arts and Memorial Hall, the museum built for the centennial celebration. In 1905, however, Mrs. Kilgore once more offered the bust to Independence Hall and it was accepted, but not before the inscription on its base had been changed. It had originally read:

THOMAS PAINE

Presented to the City of Philadelphia, October 13, 1876
by the Liberals of America

After it was rejected a line was added, "But rejected by the Select Council." This line was removed from the inscription and the presentation was changed from "By the Liberals of America" to "By the Patriots of America."

The bust remained in the Supreme Court Chamber of Independence Hall for several years, but it was removed along with a number of other busts and in 1934 was in a storage warehouse.

JANUARY THIRTIETH

A ROYALIST FAST DAY IN VIRGINIA

The Virginia General Assembly, in 1662, passed an act making January 30, the anniversary of the beheading of Charles I, a fast day to be observed every year. It thus followed the lead of Charles II who, on his restoration in 1660, issued an edict that January 30 should receive

69

special observance in the Anglican Church as "the day of the martyrdom of the Blessed King Charles I." This day was observed in England until the edict was repealed by Parliament in 1859. Its observance in Virginia, which was a royal colony when the act was passed, was an act of loyalty to the monarchy in the mother country. Virginia had received its charter from James I, the father of Charles, the martyr, and the interval of the Cromwellian Commonwealth apparently did not weaken its loyalty to the House of Stuart.

Charles was born at Dumferline, Scotland, on November 19, 1600. As a child he was tongue-tied and weak, but he outgrew his physical defects. The only evidence of his original defect of speech which remained was a slight stutter. He developed artistic and musical tastes and when he reached the age of twenty-two years he was noted for his modesty and morality. His father died on March 27, 1625, and he succeeded to the throne. On May 1 he married by proxy, Princess Henriette Marie of France, who took with her to England a Catholic retinue of four hundred and fifty persons. This offended the people and within a year Charles sent the retinue back to France. He was a firm believer in the divine right of kings and was supported in that view by Buckingham, his prime minister. He dissolved three parliaments within four years because they would not agree to his demands on them. After the assassination of Buckingham he governed without a parliament for eleven years. He sought by force to impose the episcopacy upon the Scotch Presbyterians who resisted. The Scotch defeated his army at Newburn-upon-Tyne and occupied Durham and Newcastle. He summoned the Long Parliament, which met on November 3, 1640, took measures to redress many popular grievances, and compelled the King to approve a bill which provided that parliament was not to be dissolved without its consent. There were threats to impeach the Queen who had appealed to Rome for help and the King entered the House of Commons with an armed force and demanded the surrender of Pym, Hampden and others whom he accused of treason. The accused men had taken refuge in a place of safety and the King had to retire. The nation prepared to defend itself against the royal tyranny and Charles was compelled to flee for safety to Hampton Court. Civil war followed with the royal forces victorious at first but they were completely overcome at Naseby on June 14, 1645. A little less than a year later he surrendered himself to a Scottish army and was delivered up to the English Parliament. He escaped to the Isle of Wight where he was imprisoned. Cromwell and his supporters compelled Parliament to charge the King with treason. He was taken to Westminster Hall on January 20, 1649, to be tried. He refused to plead to the indictment on the ground that the court was illegally constituted, but on January 27, he was found guilty and sentenced to death. Protests were at once made by Scotland, France and the Netherlands, but in vain. He was beheaded at Whitehall on January 30, 1649. His last words were a reiteration of his views on the right of kings. He said:

"I must tell you that liberty and freedom consist in having of government those laws by which the lives and goods of the people may be their own. It is not in having share in the government; that is nothing pertaining to them."

The General Assembly, when the news of the beheading of the King reached Virginia denounced "the treasonable principles and practices" of the party in England responsible for what it characterized as a crime. The General Assembly also proclaimed that anyone in Virginia heard defending the "murder" of the monarch should be taken as an accessory after the fact and that anyone who should cast any reflections upon the conduct of Charles during his life should be subject to such penalties as the Governor and Council should think proper. Everyone known to have questioned the right of Charles II to succeed his father was arrested and punished for high treason. The people of Virginia believed that Charles had been fighting for the preservation of his inherited rights against a multitude of rebels. Sir William Berkeley, who had been governor of the colony since 1641, exerted himself to the utmost to strengthen this belief. As Virginia had refused to recognize the authority of Cromwell, Captain Dennis was ordered to sail from the Barbadoes with a squadron of war ships to force recognition. Sir William resisted, but the Council finally agreed to the captain's demands after he had let two of its members know that he had valuable goods of theirs in his possession, the delivery of which depended on their favorable action. A new governor was appointed and Sir William lived in retirement until March 21, 1660, when he was elected as governor by the General Assembly. He accepted on the promise of the members to venture their lives and property in defence of the King, and Sir William immediately proclaimed Charles II King of England, Scotland, France, Ireland and Virginia. This was two months before the restoration in England. It was two years later that the General Assembly made the anniversary of the beheading of Charles I a fast day.

The annual services in the Anglican church on the anniversary of the death of Charles kept alive the consciousness of his martyrdom. And although these services have been abandoned there are still Stuart loyalists who keep the day in some form, not only in England but in the United States.

BIRTHDAY OF FRANKLIN D. ROOSEVELT

Franklin D. Roosevelt, thirty-second President of the United States, was born at Hyde Park on the Hudson, New York, on January 30, 1882. The anniversary of his birth is a legal holiday in Kentucky. He was stricken with infantile paralysis in August 1921, while at his summer home on Campobello Island, New Brunswick, and for a time his life was despaired of. He survived, however, but with both legs paralyzed. In the course of years he reduced the paralysis so that he could walk with crutches and then with a cane while his legs were supported by iron braces. He found help in the baths at Warm Springs, Ga., and established a foundation there for the benefit of similar sufferers without money. During the first year of his presidency arrangements were made to give balls on his birthday in various cities, the proceeds of which were to be devoted to the maintenance of the Warm Springs Hospital. So on January 30, 1934, there were more than five thousand balls which raised about $1,000,000. The Legislature of South Carolina made the day a holiday for that year. The balls were given in succeeding years during his presidency, with satisfactory financial results.

Mr. Roosevelt was a descendant of Claes Martenszan van Rosenvelt, who arrived in New Amsterdam in about 1649 from the Netherlands. Theodore Roosevelt, the twenty-sixth President, was descended from the same ancestor. Franklin Roosevelt was graduated from Harvard University in 1904 and from Columbia Law School in 1907. He was the Democratic candidate for the Senate of New York from the Dutchess County district in 1910 and was elected and served two terms from a district which was usually Republican. He was a delegate to the Democratic National Convention which nominated Woodrow Wilson for President in 1912, and voted for Wilson, who made him Assistant Secretary of the Navy in 1913. The Democratic National Convention, which nominated James W. Cox of Ohio for President in 1920, nominated Roosevelt for Vice President. At the Democratic Convention in 1924 he made the speech putting Alfred E. Smith in nomination, calling him "the happy warrior." But Smith did not receive the nomination. In 1928, however, Roosevelt again made the nominating speech for Smith at the Democratic Convention and Smith was nominated. At the solicitation of Smith, Roosevelt consented to become the Democratic candidate for Governor of New York in that year and was elected although Smith lost the state. He was reelected in 1930, and in 1932 he was nominated for President and elected by an overwhelming majority over Herbert Hoover, the incumbent.

Mr. Roosevelt was renominated by acclamation in the Democratic National Convention held in Philadelphia in June 1936, and was reelected in November by a majority of 10,000,000 in the popular vote and with all but eight of the electoral votes, carrying every state except Maine and Vermont. Again in 1940 he was renominated, although he had sent a message to the delegates at the convention in Chicago saying that he had no desire for a third term and they were free to vote for any candidate. His nomination was unanimous on the first ballot. His Republican opponent, Wendell L. Willkie, carried only ten states in the November election and Mr. Roosevelt became the first Chief Executive chosen for more than two terms. The fourth term nomination was made at the Chicago convention in 1944 with Harry S. Truman as a running mate. Once more the President was reelected, this time against the Republican nominee, Thomas E. Dewey. When Mr. Roosevelt died on April 12, 1945, at Warm Springs, Ga., he had been in office more than four years longer than any other President of the United States.

His body was taken to Washington and remained briefly in a flag-draped coffin in the East Room of the White House, while on the Capitol the flag flew at half-staff for the seventh President to die in office. Later the body was taken to Hyde Park, N.Y., the family estate, and buried in a quarter-acre rose garden, the grave marked by a plain white marble tombstone bearing his name and the dates of his birth and death and, below this, the name and date of birth of his wife, Anna Eleanor Roosevelt.

Mr. Roosevelt took office as President during the depression of the thirties when banks were closed in thirty-eight states and some twelve million persons were without employment. He established numerous government agencies to put men into jobs, to insure better farm income, and to protect home owners and investors. In this term the United States went off the gold standard and diplomatic recognition was extended to Soviet Russia. In his second term World War II was drawing near and the President abandoned the theory of American isolationism. He began to rearm the country and called for heavy Navy expansion and a new Atlantic fleet. He promoted revision of the Neutrality Act so that Great Britain and France could buy arms and ammunition on a cash-and-carry basis. Military conscription was inaugurated in 1940. His third term was marked by the Pearl Harbor disaster and the declaration of war against the Axis. President Roosevelt obtained passage of the Lend-Lease Act and promulgated the Atlantic Charter with Prime Minister Churchill of Great Britain in August 1941. A few days after his fourth term inauguration the President left for Yalta in the Crimea where he met Prime Minister Churchill and Premier Stalin of Russia, and the future course of the war was charted. He did not live to see the successful conclusion of the war, but at the time of his death the Allies were pushing forward on all fronts and victory was in sight.

JANUARY THIRTY-FIRST

BIRTHDAY OF JAMES G. BLAINE

James G. Blaine, who at the height of his career was the most popular political leader in the country, was born at Brownsville, Pa., on January 31, 1830. He was graduated from Washington College at Washington, Pa., at the age of seventeen. He spent the next seven years as a teacher in Kentucky and Pennsylvania, and in 1854 he moved to Augusta, Me., and became part owner of the Kenebeck *Journal* which he edited for three years. In 1857 he became editor of the *Advertiser* in Portland.

Me., a position which he held for three years. He was elected to the larger house of the State Legislature in 1858, rising to the post of Speaker. In the meantime he had been made chairman of the Republican State Committee. He was elected to the national House of Representatives in 1862 and served there until 1877 and was its Speaker from 1869 to 1875. He was an aspirant for the Republican presidential nomination in 1876 but the publication of what are known as the "Mulligan letters," indicating that he had used his political influence for his personal profit, weakened his support and he lost the nomination, but the Legislature of Maine elected him to the United States Senate. He was again a candidate for the presidential nomination in 1880, but failed a second time to receive it. He won the nomination, however, in 1884 and ran against Grover Cleveland, whom the Democrats had named. The independent Republicans opposed his election, and Cleveland was successful. President Garfield, elected in 1880, made him Secretary of State but after the assassination of Garfield he resigned. He became Secretary of State a second time under President Benjamin Harrison. While holding this office he presided over the first Pan American Conference and successfully defended the rights of American citizens in foreign countries. He wrote *Twenty Years of Congress*, an autobiographical work, and published a volume of political addresses. He died in Augusta, Me., on January 27, 1893.

Lincoln

FEBRUARY

The trees stand wistful in the square,
Wearing a half-expectant air;
The sky is a slender silver bell
That waits to sound the knell
Of Winter.

—ANNE MARY LAWLER

This month derives its name from the Latin verb, februare, meaning to purify. On the fifteenth day the Romans held a festival at which a goat was sacrificed. After the sacrifice the priests went around the Palatine striking the women on the hands with a strip of the skin of the goat, a proceeding which was believed to insure fertility and a safe delivery. Candlemas Day, occuring on February 2, is the Christian Feast of the Purification of the Virgin Mary. The Saxons called the month Sprote-kale from the fact that kale sprouted at that season. They later changed the name to Sol-monath, in recognition of the returning sun. The month, which has twenty-eight days except in leap years when it has twenty-nine, was not in the early Roman calendar. It was added to the end of the year, by Numa, following December. Numa also made another new month, January, which he placed at the beginning of the year before March. The order of these two months was changed in 453. According to the ancient British weather lore, the weather on the twelfth, thirteenth and fourteenth days of the month indicated the weather for the year. If the days were fair it would be a stormy year and if the days were stormy the weather would be fair.

The month is notable in American history, for in it occur the anniversaries of the birth of Abraham Lincoln and George Washington, whose fame is worldwide because of their connection with human freedom and political liberty. Portraits of them are frequently found in the homes of people in China and Russia.

FEBRUARY FIRST

FESTIVAL OF ST. BRIDGET

The scholars of the church insist that the proper spelling of the name of this Irish saint, whose festival is observed on February 1, is Brigid. The name is also spelled Bride. She is reverenced in Scotland, England, and the United States, but especially in Ireland where she shares honors with St. Patrick with whom she was associated in religious work. There is an ancient well adjoining St. Bride's Church in Fleet Street, London, known as Bride's well. A palace, erected near it, was known as Bridewell. The palace was given to the city by Edward VI as a workhouse for the poor and as a house of correction. Nowadays "bridewell" is a common name for a jail, and thus the name of the holy Irish woman is associated with a place of confinement for unholy persons.

Saint Bridget or Brigid was born of princely ancestors near Dundalk, County Louth, Ireland, in 451 or 452. When she was of marriageable age she received many offers, but decided to become a nun and took the veil from St. Macaille. With seven other virgins she lived for a time at the foot of Croghan Hill, but later removed to Druin Criadh, in the plains of Magh Life where under an oak she erected what subsequently became the famous convent of Cill-Dara, or "the church of the oak." The city of Kildare was built there and a cathedral erected in it. St. Bridget founded two monastic institutions, one for men and another for women. St. Conleth, bishop of Kildare, shared jurisdiction over them with her and for centuries there were abbot-bishops and abbesses jointly ruling in Kildare. St. Bridget also founded a school of art including metal work and illumination. There is a tradition that the Book of the Gospels illuminated in her scriptorium was one of the most beautiful ever made. A Welsh ecclesiastic who saw it in the twelfth century said that it left the impression on him that "all this is the work of angelic and not human skill." It disappeared after the Reformation. She died on February 1, 525, and was buried at the right of the high altar in Kildare cathedral. Because of the Scandinavian raids in the late ninth century her remains were taken to Downpatrick and buried with those of St. Patrick and St. Columba. About three hundred years later they were transferred to Downpatrick cathedral in the presence of a cardinal, fifteen bishops and numerous other ecclesiastics. Many places in Ireland are named for her and many Catholic churches in this country are called in her honor, and more Irish girls are known by her name than by any other, unless it be Mary.

FEBRUARY SECOND

CANDLEMAS

Candlemas, or the Feast of the Purification of the Blessed Virgin, is observed on February 2 by the Roman, the Greek, and the Anglican churches. It is in celebration of the visit of Mary to the Temple in Jerusalem for purification which, according to the Jewish ritual, took place forty days after the birth of Jesus and which is described in the second chapter of Luke. Simeon, a holy man living in Jerusalem, had been longing for the appearance of the Messiah and as the record says, "It was revealed unto him by the Holy Ghost that he should not see death before he had seen the Lord's Christ. And he came by the spirit into the temple; and when the parents brought in the child Jesus, to do for him after the custom of the law, then took he him up in his arms and blessed God and said, 'Lord, now lettest thou thy servant depart in peace, for mine eyes have seen thy salvation which thou hast prepared before the face of all the people; a light to lighten the Gentiles, and the glory of thy people Israel.' " Simeon blessed the child and his parents. And Anna, a prophetess living in the Temple, also blessed them and gave thanks for the birth of the child.

The church historians are of the opinion that the day was celebrated from very early times by the Christians in Jerusalem. For many years the celebration was on February 14 for Jesus was supposed to have been born on the day of the Epiphany. But when it was decided that Christmas fell on December 25, the Feast of the Purification was celebrated on February 2. It is called Candlemas as candles are blessed in the churches on that day, symbolical of Simeon's reference to the "light to lighten the Gentiles." There have been many changes in the ritual observed on the day, and various views have been held about the candles that are blessed. One is that if they are preserved in the homes of the people they will ward off evil. This view prevailed in Europe and it has been brought to America. Not many years ago a maid asked her mistress on an evening when a thunder storm was brewing if she might light a candle in the night. The maid explained that the candle had been blessed on Candlemas and that if she lighted it she would suffer no harm from the storm.

There is a theory that the feast is a Christianized form of the Roman Lupercalia which was celebrated in February. The *Catholic Encyclopedia* says that "The feast was certainly not introduced by Pope Gelasius to suppress the excesses of the Lupercalia." Pope Gelasius occupied the chair from 492 to 496. There is extant, however, what purports to be a sermon by Pope Innocent XII (1691-1700) in which he says: "Why do we in this feast carry candles? Because the Gentiles dedicated the month of February to the infernal gods, and as at the beginning of it Pluto

77

stole Proserpine, and her mother Ceres sought her in the night with lighted candles, so they, at the beginning of the month, walked about the city with lighted candles. Because the holy fathers could not extirpate the custom, they ordained that Christians should carry about candles in honor of the Blessed Virgin; and thus what was done before in the honor of Ceres is now done in honor of the Blessed Virgin."

GROUND HOG DAY

In the United States Candlemas is also known as Ground Hog Day, a time for forecasting the weather for the next six weeks. The custom of observing the weather on this day to discover what the future weather would be was brought to America by immigrants from Great Britain and Germany. The theory is that if the ground hog, or woodchuck, comes out of his winter quarters on this day and sees his shadow there will be six more weeks of winter, but that if the day is cloudy he will not return to his winter quarters for a long sleep as the winter weather will soon give way to balmy spring. In Germany it was the badger which broke its hibernation to observe the skies; in the United States the belief was transferred to the woodchuck. The English and the Scotch have many rhymes in which the belief is embodied. Here are some of them:

If Candlemas Day be dry and fair,
The half o' winter's to come and mair;
If Candlemas Day be wet and foul,
The half o' winter's gone at Yule.

If Candlemas Day be fair and bright,
Winter will have another flight;
But if it be dark with clouds and rain,
Winter is gone, and will not come again.

The hind had as lief see
His wife on the bier
As that Candlemas Day
Should be pleasant and clear.

The last rhyme is the English variation of a German saying that "The shepherd would rather see the wolf enter his stable on Candlemas Day than the sun." The belief that the weather on February 2 foreshadows by contraries the weather of the succeeding weeks has no connection with any religious festival or saint. In this respect it differs from the belief in the relation between the weather on St. Swithin's day and that to follow (See St. Swithin's Day, July 15).

In the early part of the present century a group of merry wags living in and around Quarryville, Lancaster County, Pa., organized the Slumbering Groundhog Lodge. On the morning of February 2 its members don silk hats and carry canes and go into the fields seeking the burrow of a woodchuck. When one finds a burrow he calls to the others and they all assemble to await the awakening of the animal from his hibernation and his emergence into the outer air. They watch his behavior and then return to the village where they interpret his actions and report them to the public. According to the records of the lodge the woodchuck's prognostications have been verified by the weather eight times, have been indefinite five times and have been wrong seven times since the observations began.

FEBRUARY THIRD

CREATION OF THE TERRITORY OF ILLINOIS

What is now the State of Illinois was included in the Northwest Territory by the Ordinance of 1787 which provided that not less than three nor more than five states might be organized out of that territory and that a territorial government might be set up when the region within the boundaries for the states fixed by the Ordinance contained five thousand free males. Ohio, Indiana and Michigan had been organized prior to 1809, leaving Illinois to await the action of Congress. On February 3, 1809, an act setting up the Territory of Illinois was approved by the President and Ninian Edwards became its first governor, with Kaskaskia on the Mississippi as the first capital. An Act of Congress of April 18, 1818, authorized the people of the territory to form a constitution preliminary to admission to the Union as a state. The constitution was framed and Illinois became a state on December 3, 1818.

FEBRUARY FOURTH

BIRTHDAY OF MARK HOPKINS

Mark Hopkins, one of the most distinguished educators of his generation and president of Williams College from 1836 to 1872, was born at Stockbridge, Mass., on February 4, 1802, the son of a farmer. He entered Williams College as a sophomore and was graduated in 1824 and began the study of medicine, but was recalled to Williams as a tutor in 1825, and taught for two years. He then entered the Berkshire Medical College at Pittsfield, Mass., from which he was graduated in 1829. He opened an office in New York City and soon moved to Binghamton, N.Y., but Williams College needed him and he was called there in 1830 as professor of moral philosophy and rhetoric. He was licensed as a Congregational minister in 1833 and ordained in 1836. When he resigned as president of the college in 1872 he retained the professorship of moral philosophy and continued as pastor of the college church. He died on June 17, 1887. He was not a profound scholar but as a teacher he was able to arouse the interest and enthusiasm of the students. Gar-

79

field, a graduate of this college, is credited with saying at a dinner of the alumni of Williams in New York that a log in the woods with Mark Hopkins on one end and a student on the other would be a university. What Garfield did say in discussing the physical equipment of colleges was that a log cabin with such a teacher as Mark Hopkins would be a university. It is said of Hopkins that when a student in his moral philosophy class asked him who would go to heaven he replied that he did not know but that he was sure that no one would go there who would not feel at home.

FEBRUARY FIFTH

ARRIVAL OF ROGER WILLIAMS IN AMERICA

Roger Williams, one of the most famous defenders of religious liberty in America, was born in England, probably in London, in 1604 or 1605. The exact year and day are not known. As a youth he attracted the attention of Sir Edward Coke by his shorthand notes of sermons and speeches and Sir Edward sent him to Sutton's Hospital, now the Charterhouse School, in 1621. He entered Pembroke College four years later and won the degree of bachelor of arts in 1627. It is supposed that he took orders in the Church of England, but it is known that he became a Puritan and decided to leave England. He arrived at Boston on February 5, 1631, at the age of about twenty-six. As the members of the congregation at Boston with which he associated himself refused to express their repentance for having once been in communion with the Church of England he went to Salem as an assistant preacher, but he got in trouble there for denying the right of magistrates to punish persons for religious offenses. As the Massachusetts Bay government insisted on this right he went to Plymouth where he assisted the minister. In 1633 he returned to Salem as pastor of the church where he argued that the power of the civil magistrate extends only to the bodies and goods of men and not to their consciences. He was, therefore, banished from the Massachusetts Bay Colony in 1635 and plans were made to send him back to England, but he fled south to the shores of Narragansett Bay accompanied by a few followers, bought land from the Indians, founded the city of Providence in 1636 and established a government founded on complete religious toleration. He came to believe in the baptism of believers by immersion and was baptized by a layman whom he then baptized along with ten others and in 1639 founded in Providence the first Baptist church in America. He later withdrew from the church because he doubted the validity of his own baptism. He went to England in 1643 and again in 1651 in the interest of the colony which he had founded. In 1654 he was elected as its president, holding the office for three years. He wrote much on religion and on the languages of the

Indians, and died in 1683. Roger Williams Day was observed by the Baptists in 1919 when plans were announced for raising a fund to build a Roger Williams Memorial Church in Washington. The money was raised and the church has been built.

FEBRUARY SIXTH

BIRTHDAY OF AARON BURR

Aaron Burr, whose popularity and political skill almost made him President of the United States and who died friendless and alone at the age of eighty years, was born at Newark, N.J., on February 6, 1756. His father was the Reverend Aaron Burr, the second president of Princeton College, and his maternal grandfather was Jonathan Edwards, the distinguished New England clergyman. He prepared for college and entered the sophomore class at Princeton when he was thirteen and was graduated when he was sixteen. He studied theology for a while and toyed with the idea of following his father's profession, but in 1774 he began the study of law. When the Revolutionary War began he enlisted in the army. Two years later he was on the staff of Benedict Arnold with the rank of captain. Then he was on General Washington's staff for a few weeks. He remained in the army until March 1779, when he resigned because of ill health. The next year he resumed the study of law, was admitted to the bar in 1782, and opened an office in Albany. In the autumn of 1783 he moved to New York where he devoted himself to his profession for six years.

Governor Clinton made him Attorney General of the State of New York, in 1789, and he was United States Senator from 1791 to 1797. In the presidential election of 1792 he received one electoral vote and in the election of 1796 he received thirty. He was an active candidate in 1800, running with Thomas Jefferson against John Adams and two other Federalist candidates. When the vote was counted it was found that Jefferson and Burr, the two Republican candidates, had received seventy-three votes each. The electors at that time voted for two candidates, the one receiving the highest number of votes to be President and the one receiving the next highest to be Vice President, with the House of Representatives deciding when there was a tie. The election of a President thus went to the House which was controlled by the Federalists. For a time they thought of throwing their support to Burr but after balloting for six days they consented to the election of Jefferson and Burr automatically became Vice President. In this capacity he presided over the impeachment trial of Justice Samuel Chase of the Supreme Court. Jefferson wanted Justice Chase removed and the friends of the administration sought to influence Burr by obtaining appointments to office for members

81

of his family.   Burr, however, presided "with the dignity and impartiality of an angel and with the rigor of a devil" and the Justice was acquitted.

Burr had dreams of various kinds about the West and about Mexico. He made plans to carry them out which resulted in his arrest and trial on the charge of treason.   When the treason charge failed he was charged with misdemeanor.   He was acquitted, but was held for trial in Ohio. He kept out of the state and the charges were not pressed.   He went to England in 1808 and sought help in his plans to drive the Spanish from Mexico, and when he failed to get it he took his plans to France but was equally unsuccessful there.   He returned to the United States in 1812 and resumed the practice of law in New York.   While he was still Vice President he killed Alexander Hamilton in a duel, an act which destroyed much of his popularity.   In July 1833, he married the widow of Stephen Jumel of New York, a woman twenty years younger than he, but after four months they separated as Burr was threatening to squander her fortune.   She brought suit for divorce and the decree was issued on the day of his death which occurred in a hotel on Staten Island on September 14, 1836.

THE TWENTIETH AMENDMENT

The twentieth amendment to the Constitution of the United States, known as the "lame duck" amendment, provides that the terms of the President and Vice President shall begin on January 20, and those of senators and representatives on January 3 instead of on March 4; and that Congress shall convene on January 3 of each year instead of the first Monday in December.   The amendment was proposed by the 72nd Congress in March 1932 and was proclaimed in effect on February 6, 1933, thirty-six of the forty-eight states having ratified it.   By October 15, 1933, it had been ratified by all the states.

When the Constitution was adopted the date of March 4 for the inauguration had been selected in order to provide time for election returns to be assembled and for newly elected candidates to reach the Capital.   Due to improved methods of transportation and communication this long delay was no longer necessary and the short session of Congress beginning in December and attended by members who had been defeated in the November elections, popularly called "lame ducks," had been outdated.

FEBRUARY SEVENTH

BIRTHDAY OF CHARLES DICKENS

The anniversary of the birth of Charles Dickens is observed on February 7 by the branches of the Dickens Fellowship throughout the world. He was born on that day in 1812. The Fellowship was organized in London in October 1902, by descendants of the novelist. Its membership later included admirers of the man and his work. Its original purpose was to promote the reforms in which he had been interested. There are seventeen branches of the Fellowship in continental United States and one in the Hawaiian islands. They are in Bethlehem, Chester, Nazareth, Philadelphia, and Pittsburgh, Pa.; Boston and Worcester, Mass.; Chicago, Ill.; East Bay, Berkeley, Los Angeles, Pasadena, and Sierra Madre, Calif.; Madison and Marinette, Wis.; New York City; and Orono, Me. The purpose of them all is similar to that of the Philadelphia Fellowship which is "to knit in a common bond of friendship lovers of that great master of humor and pathos, Charles Dickens; to spread the love of humanity which is the keynote of all his work; to take such measures as may be expedient to remedy or ameliorate those existing social evils which would have appealed so strongly to the heart of Charles Dickens, and to help in every possible direction the cause of the poor and the oppressed."

The nature of the celebration of the anniversary varies from year to year. Sometimes a public dinner is given at which addresses are made by admirers of Dickens. At other times the members of the various branches of the Fellowship assemble privately to do honor to him. A committee of the Philadelphia branch makes a pilgrimage every year to the Dickens statue in Clark Park, at the corner of Forty-eighth Street and Chester Avenue, and places a wreath at its base. This statue, erected by the Fairmount Park Art Association, was the first to be set up in honor of Dickens in any part of the world. It represents the novelist seated in an arm chair with Little Nell leaning on his knees. Not only was the first statue of Dickens erected in Philadelphia, but it was in that city that the second story which he wrote was first published in America, and it was also there that the *Pickwick Papers* were first published in this country. The story, "Mrs. Joseph Porter, 'Over the Way,'" appeared in Waldie's *Select Circulating Library* for August 26, 1834, and Carey, Lea & Blanchard began publishing *Pickwick Papers* in 1836, when their London agent sent to them some of the first monthly parts. The complete book was printed in three volumes, bound in boards, four parts in each volume. It sold so well that the publishers wrote to Dickens in London telling him to draw on them for £25, "not as compensation but as a memento of the fact that unsolicited a bookseller has sent an author, if not money, at least a fair representative of it." Dickens wrote in reply: "I should not feel, under the circumstances, quite at ease in drawing upon you for the amount you so liberally request me to consider you my debtors in, but I shall have very great pleasure in receiving from you an American copy of the work, which, coupled with your very handsome letter, I shall consider a sufficient acknowledgment of the American sale." The first portrait of Dickens to appear in America was also printed in Philadelphia in the *Gentleman's Magazine* in August 1837. Its title is "Boz," and it represents a smooth-faced man seated at a table with his right arm over the back of his chair. Although it is a lithograph assigned to "Phiz," it is regarded as an imaginary portrait, not drawn from life.

The career of Dickens is one of the most remarkable in the history of literature. He was born on February 7, 1812, at Landport, England, in a house which on July 22, 1904, was opened as a Dickens museum. His father, who is described as Wilkins Micawber in *David Copperfield*, was a clerk in the navy pay-office at a salary of £80 a year. Charles was the second of eight children. The family moved in 1814 to London and four years later was established near the dockyards at Chatham where it remained until 1821. During this time the father received £250 a year. Charles' mother taught him to read and he found among his father's books, *Roderick Random, Peregrine Pickle, Tom Jones, The Vicar of Wakefield, Don Quixote,* and *Robinson Crusoe.* He read these and played at being the characters in them, sometimes pretending to be the same character for a month at a time. The family fell on evil times, with the father in prison for debt and with Mrs. Dickens trying to run a school. Charles had to go to work in a blacking house, labeling pots of blacking for six shillings a week. From 1824 to 1826 he was able to attend an academy and in May 1827, when he was fifteen years old, he entered a solicitor's office at thirteen shillings and sixpence a week. He spent his spare time mastering stenography and reading in the British Museum. After eighteen months in the solicitor's office he became a reporter covering the police courts for a newspaper and in 1831, when he was nineteen, he was employed by the *True Sun* as its parliamentary reporter. He was then the most rapid and accurate stenographer in London. He ended his newspaper career as a reporter for the *Morning Chronicle.* At about this time he began to write a series of sketches of London life which were later published in book form with the signature "Boz." In 1836 he began the publication of *The Posthumous Papers of the Pickwick Club*, in monthly parts. When Sam Weller was introduced in the fifth part they became immensely popular. When the book was completed publishers on the continent immediately brought out French and German translations of it, and, as already noted, its publication was begun in America soon after the first parts had appeared in London. "Pickwick" was soon followed by *Oliver Twist, Barnaby Rudge,* and *Nicholas Nickleby,* and as the years succeeded each other the books which made him the most popular novelist of his generation were produced one after another. He visited the United States in 1842 on a lecture tour, and again in 1867, when he read from his novels. He was an amateur actor and it is said that he read most dramatically, moving his audiences alternately to laughter and to tears. He was also in demand in England as a reader and he kept his engagements in the last year of his life in spite of physical weakness. His last reading was in St. James Hall, London, on March 15, 1870. Soon after this appearance he was received in private audience by Queen Victoria who presented to him her *Leaves from a Journal of Our Life in the Highlands* with the inscription, "From one of the humblest of authors to one of the greatest." She had tried to persuade him to accept a title, but when he refused she begged him to accept appointment as a privy councillor. He died at Gads Hill on June 9, 1870, and was privately buried in Westminster Abbey on June 14. In his will he asked that no monument be erected to him, a request that was honored until the monument was set up in Philadelphia. He said he wanted only his name and his dates on his tomb. "I rest my claim to the remembrance of my countrymen on my published works." His novels have been sold by the millions and are still selling. He created more characters which live in the consciousness of the people than any other English writer with the possible exception of Shakespeare.

One of the most interesting Dickens relics in America is the marble tombstone which the novelist placed over the grave of his daughter's pet bird at Gad's Hill. It contains the following inscription:

"This is the Grave of Dick, the Best of Birds. Born at Broadstairs, Mid's, 1851. Died at Gad's Hill Place 14th Oct'r, 1866."

The stone is in the possession of the estate of Charles Sessler of Philadelphia, one of the founders of the Philadelphia branch of the Dickens Fellowship. It was given to him in 1913 by Mrs. Kate Perugini, a daughter of Dickens who was one of Mr. Sessler's friends. She wrote him a letter telling its history, as follows:

July 22, 1913.
32 Victoria Road,
Kensington, West.

Dear Mr. Sessler:—

In accordance with the promise I made, I write to tell you the history of the little tombstone I gave you, which has on it an inscription composed by my father, and which was placed by him over the grave of my sister's little bird Dick in the garden at Gad's Hill Place. When we left Gad's Hill after my father's death my sister (Mamie) brought away with her the little tombstone, and after her death it came into my possession.

Meanwhile, my oldest brother, Charles, had gone to live at Gad's Hill with his family. Wishing that everything there should be as it was in his father's lifetime he had a copy made of the tombstone and placed it where the original, now in your possession, once stood.

Hoping that you will find satisfaction in this true and particular account, and with the very best regards to Mrs. Sessler and your son, I beg to remain,

Very sincerely yours,
KATE PERUGINI,
Nee Katie Dickens, daughter of Charles Dickens.

F. Hopkinson Smith visited Gad's Hill during one of his visits to England and in his book, *In Dickens's London,* he says that one of the men on the grounds at Gad's Hill showed him the grave in which the bird had been buried. He continues: "There is now a wooden tombstone over it about as large as a shingle—it might have been made of one—and a bed of pansies lend their fragrance."

FEBRUARY EIGHTH

BOY SCOUT DAY

The anniversary of the chartering of the Boy Scouts of America, February 8, 1910, is observed every year by the members of the organization. In 1935, the twenty-fifth anniversary was observed with special ceremonies including an address over the radio by President Franklin D. Roosevelt, praising the Scouts and the work which they have done. The organization of boys into the society of scouts is due to Sir Robert S. S. Baden-Powell, an English army officer. While serving in South Africa he wrote a book called *Aids to Scouting*. When he returned to England he learned that the book was being used in schools for boys to help in character training. It occurred to him that boys might be organized into scout troops to keep them out of mischief and to train them in habits of industry, courtesy and general helpfulness. He thereupon formed a company of seven or eight boys and called them Boy Scouts. This was in 1908. Out of this grew the scout movement which spread rapidly throughout England.

William D. Boyce, a Chicago publisher, was in London on a foggy day in 1908, standing uncertainly on the sidewalk, when a boy accosted him and offered to show him his way. Mr. Boyce gave the boy the address he was seeking and was guided to it. He then offered the boy a shilling.

"Oh, no, sir," the lad replied, saluting. "A Scout never takes money for courtesies."

Asked to explain what he meant, he told of the British Boy Scout Association and offered to take Mr. Boyce to its headquarters. At the Scout Office Mr. Boyce met Sir Robert Baden-Powell and learned about the organization. He returned to America and early in 1909 started the organization of the Boy Scouts of America. A permanent organization was perfected and chartered under the laws of the District of Columbia on February 8, 1910, as already indicated. There stands in Gilwell Park in England a bronze statue of a buffalo, the gift of the Boy Scouts of America, and on its base is the inscription: "To the Unknown Scout whose faithful performance of the 'Daily Good Turn' brought the Scout Movement to America."

Since 1910 more than five million boys have received the Scout training and in 1934 about a million boys were active members of the Scout troops. Before 1910 there were two organizations intended to interest boys in wholesome things. One was Ernest Thompson Seton's "Woodcraft Indians" and the other was Dan C. Beard's "Sons of Daniel Boone." These were incorporated into the Boy Scouts of America when it was chartered, as the Boy Scout movement was based on a broader foundation.

Boys from twelve to eighteen years of age are eligible for membership. On admission they take the Scout Oath: "On my honor I will do my best to do my duty to God and my country; and to obey the scout law; to help other people at all times; to keep myself physically strong, mentally awake and morally straight." There are three, or possibly four classes of scouts—tenderfoot, second class and first class. The possible fourth class comprises the Eagle Scouts who are those who have won twenty-one merit badges. The Scout Law requires a boy to be trustworthy, loyal, helpful, friendly, courteous, kind, obedient, cheerful, thrifty, brave, clean and reverent. In order to pass from one class to another a boy must submit to certain tests. For example, to become a first class scout a boy must have a small sum of money in a savings bank, must understand various kinds of first aid to the injured, must be able to cook various kinds of food, must be able to read a map correctly and to draw a rough sketch map and must know how to fell a small tree and be familiar with other kinds of woodcraft. The Scouts wear a prescribed uniform when on scouting duty. They also wear a badge which resembles the fleur-de-lys of France, although it is really the sign of the North which appears on the mariner's compass and is intended to represent steadfastness of purpose. The Scout salute is made with three fingers brought smartly to the brim of the hat and pointing upward. It symbolizes the three parts of the Scout oath and the aspiration of the Scout for higher things.

The Boy Scouts of America are directed by a National Council with headquarters in New York. The country is divided into twelve districts each with a District Council. The President of the United States, beginning with President Taft, has been the honorary head of the Scouts since the start in 1910.

FEBRUARY NINTH

BIRTHDAY OF WILLIAM HENRY HARRISON

William Henry Harrison, ninth President of the United States, was born at the plantation of Berkeley in Charles County, Va., on February 9, 1773. He was the third son of Benjamin Harrison, the fifth of the name in the direct line of descent, whose ancestors came to America from England in 1633. Benjamin was Governor of Virginia and one of the signers of the Declaration of Independence. His son William Henry entered Hampden-Sidney College in 1787. In 1790 he went to Richmond to study medicine and a few months later went to Philadelphia where he studied under Dr. Benjamin Rush. After his father's death in 1791 he decided to enter the army and was commissioned as an ensign in the first United States infantry regiment. He served in the Northwest Territory, rose to the rank of lieutenant, and was acting aide-de-camp to

Anthony Wayne. He resigned from the army in 1798 and was appointed secretary of the Northwest Territory. The next year he was elected as its first delegate to Congress. He was influential in obtaining the passage of the act setting up the territories of Ohio and Indiana and in 1800 was appointed Governor of the Territory of Indiana. As Governor he succeeded in obtaining from the Indians grants of millions of acres of land in Indiana and Illinois. The Indians, however, resented the influx of white settlers and Tecumseh, a Shawnee chief, formed a confederation of Indian tribes to prevent the occupation of their lands. In October 1811, Harrison led a force of about a thousand men against the Indians gathered at Tippecanoe, defeated them, and took possession of the settlement. When the war with Great Britain began he saw active service in the battles with the British forces and their Indian allies. His victory at the battle on the Thames river in 1813 virtually ended the British activities in the Northwest and was followed by the pacification of most of the Indians of the region. He was succeeded as Governor of Indiana in March 1813, by Thomas Posey, and was raised to the rank of major general. In May of the next year he resigned from the army for the second time and took up his residence on his farm at North Bend, Ohio, near Cincinnati. He was elected to the national House of Representatives in 1816, and in 1825 he was elected to the United States Senate. He remained in the Senate for three years and in 1828, through the influence of Henry Clay, he was appointed United States Minister to Colombia. He arrived in Bogota when the enemies of Bolivar were actively revolting against him. He was charged with sympathizing with the revolutionists and was recalled after about a year. In 1836 he was nominated for President by the anti-Van Buren forces and received seventy-three electoral votes to one hundred and seventy for Van Buren, although his popular vote was large. His supporters immediately began to organize a movement to bring about his nomination in 1840. The three leading Whig candidates were Harrison, Daniel Webster and Henry Clay. Webster withdrew in December 1839, and his influence, along with that of Thurlow Weed of New York, was strong enough to win the nomination for Harrison. John Tyler was nominated for Vice President. Harrison was elected with two hundred and thirty-four electoral votes to sixty for Van Buren, the Democratic nominee. He was inaugurated on March 4, 1841, and died from pneumonia a month later.

FEBRUARY TENTH

THE SPANISH PEACE TREATY

At the conclusion of the war with Spain in 1898 a commission was appointed to negotiate a treaty of peace. It met the Spanish commissioners in Paris and a treaty was written under which Spain ceded to the United States the Philippine Islands and the island of Guam in the Pacific Ocean and the island of Porto Rico in the Atlantic in consideration of payment of $20,000,000. Spain also agreed to withdraw from Cuba and leave the settlement of the affairs in that island to the United States. The treaty was submitted to the Senate by President McKinley on January 4, 1899, for ratification. Debate on it was conducted in open session. Senator Hoar of Massachusetts opposed ratification on the ground that the United States had no constitutional power to hold the Philippine Islands. Senate Spooner of Wisconsin said that the islands constituted the bitter fruits of the war." He insisted that the United States had the right to acquire territory, but he did not think it expedient for the country to hold "permanent dominion over far distant lands and people." While the debate was in progress William Jennings Bryan, who had been the Democratic candidate for President in 1896, went to Washington and advised the Democratic Senators to vote for ratification of the treaty. As the Republicans did not have two-thirds majority Democratic votes were necessary. The debate continued for several weeks and on February 6 the vote was taken. It showed fifty-seven for the treaty and twenty-seven against it. Of those voting for it ten were Democrats. Three Republicans voted against ratification. The treaty was returned to the President and on February 10, 1899, he signed it thus completing the act of ratification and ending the war.

THE GASPARILLA CARNIVAL

Tampa, Fla., began in 1904 to hold a Gasparilla Carnival celebrating the exploits of José Gasparilla, a Spanish pirate of the early eighteenth century. In that year a company of sixty young business men organized a club which they called Ye Mystic Krewe of Gasparilla and on a day during the State Fair in February they entered the harbor of the city in a "pirate" ship, took possession of it and held high revels, including a ball over which the mock Gasparilla presided with a queen selected from the young women of the city. Since then the Mystic Krewe has been increased to one hundred and sixty with a consequent increase in the elaborateness of the carnival. The festivities in 1936, which began on February 10, lasted for three days. The pirate crew landed and took over the city amid storms of confetti. The Mayor gave the keys of the city to Gasparilla. There was a parade through the streets with the members of the Mystic Krewe followed by fantastic floats with other floats entered by business houses, civic organizations and neighboring cities. At the ball the Gasparilla for the preceding year is dethroned and hanged in effigy, and the new Gasparilla is crowned along with his queen.

Gasparilla was born in Ponferrada, a province of Leon, in the early part of the eighteenth century of what are described as poor but honest parents. While he was still in his teens, he and a group of neighboring youths ran away from their native village after getting into trouble with the officers of the law. According to tradition the youths went to sea in a merchant ship, incited the sailors to mutiny and murder the captain. Gasparilla then took command and began to prey on shipping as a pirate. He crossed the ocean and sailed into the Gulf of Mexico where he found an island a hundred miles south of Tampa which he made his headquarters. The island was later named for him and is known as Gasparilla to this day. Among the legends about him is one that he maintained a harem on the island and that when he tired of its inmates he sailed for Tampa, then a small settlement, and seized a young woman and carried her away with him. On one such occasion he carried off a popular young woman bethrothed to a young Spaniard. The indignant lover fitted out a ship and took with him the other men whose daughters or sweethearts had been carried away. They sailed for the island, entered its harbor at night, captured Gasparilla and killed or captured his entire band which had been surprised at a drunken feast. The young woman was rescued and carried back to Tampa unharmed. And the pirate and those of his band who had not been killed were hanged at what is now the foot of Lafayette street. Then a great celebration was held at which the people rejoiced over the removal of the danger which had threatened them and from which they had suffered for a long time.

The Gasparilla Carnival attracts to Tampa visitors from all parts of the South every year.

FEBRUARY ELEVENTH

BIRTHDAY OF MELVILLE W. FULLER

Melville Weston Fuller, eighth Chief Justice of the United States, was born in Augusta, Me., on February 11, 1833. His father, grandfather and great-grandfather had been leading citizens of the state. His grandfather sat on the Supreme Court bench of Maine from 1820 to 1841 and for the last seven years was Chief Justice. He was educated at Bowdoin College graduating in the class of 1853. He began the study of law in the office of his uncle, George Melville Weston, in Bangor, and then took a course of lectures in the Harvard Law School. On his admission to the bar in 1855 he began the practice of law in the office of another uncle, Benjamin G. Fuller, in Augusta. He was president of the Common Council of the city in 1856 and served as City Solicitor. Late in the same year he moved to Chicago and opened an office in that young city. His practice and his reputation grew with the growth of the city. The extent of his practice is indicated by the presence in more than one hundred volumes of the state law reports of cases in which he had appeared. He was a member of the convention of 1862 called to revise the Constitution of the State, and a member of the larger house of the State Legislature in 1863. He was a delegate from Illinois to the Democratic National Conventions of 1864, 1872, 1876 and 1880. In 1876 he made the speech proposing the nomination of Thomas A. Hendricks for President. He took no active part in politics after the convention of 1880. When the office of Chief Justice became vacant by the death of Morrison R. Waite on March 23, 1888, there were political complications in Illinois which could be resolved only by the appointment of a citizen of that state to a high office. The Illinois politicians stated the case to President Cleveland and they stated it so convincingly that the President, who had decided to appoint George Gray of Delaware to the chief justiceship and was about ready to send Judge Gray's name to the Senate, yielded and named Mr. Fuller on April 30, 1888. The appointment was confirmed and the commission issued to him on July 20. A little more than a year after taking his seat on the bench he was selected to deliver the address in commemoration of the one hundredth anniversary of the inauguration of Washington before both houses of Congress. In 1899 he was a member of the Arbitration Commission which sat in Paris to settle the Anglo-Venezuelan boundary dispute, and in 1904 he was chosen by Great Britain as arbitrator at The Hague in the dispute with the French over the jurisdiction at Muscat. He served with distinction in all his functions until his death in 1910.

BIRTHDAY OF THOMAS ALVA EDISON

Edison Day is observed annually on February 11 in many schools throughout the United States, in accordance with a resolution passed by Congress which also ordered that flags be flown from Government buildings in honor of the birthday of the great American inventor. Thomas Alva Edison was born at Milan, Ohio, on February 11, 1847, of Dutch ancestry on his father's side and Scottish on his mother's. His education was limited to three months in the Port Huron, Mich., public school and at the age of twelve he became a railroad newsboy. At fifteen he began to earn his living as a telegraph operator, but during his spare time he constantly studied and experimented. His first patent was for an electrical vote recorder, in 1868. During the next few years he devised stock tickers, duplex, quadruplex, and automatic telegraph systems, and the electric pen which developed into the mimeograph for the multiplication of typewriting. In 1877 and 1878 his invention of the carbon transmitter, in which compressed lamp-black buttons were used to obtain the necessary variable resistance in the circuit, marked an important advance in the development of the telephone, aiding materially in bringing the Bell telephone into practical use.

Most modern inventions result from contributions by many persons and it is often difficult for the courts to determine priority, but when Mr. Edison made application in 1877 for a "phonograph or speaking machine" the United States Patent Office could discover no previous record of this sort. The original model, which cost $18, was a primitive affair consisting of a cylinder covered with tinfoil and turned with a hand crank. Ten years later he perfected a motor-driven machine with cylindrical wax records and this rapidly came into popular use. Subsequently he invented a disk form reproducing with a diamond point for music, and the "Ediphone" for office dictation.

On October 21, 1879, after expending more than $40,000 in fruitless experiments, he succeeded in making an incandescent lamp in which a loop of carbonized cotton thread glowed in a vacuum for over forty hours. The following decade was devoted almost entirely to the invention and exploitation of methods for the generation and distribution of electric light, heat and power, including the three-wire system, underground mains, improved dynamos and motors, and an electric railway. From 1891 to 1900 this persistent and tireless genius was chiefly engaged on a magnetic method of concentrating iron ores, and from 1900 to 1910 in the development of a new kind of storage battery using an alkaline solution with nickel hydrate as the positive and iron oxide as the negative material. Meanwhile, in 1891, he had applied for a patent on a "kinetescopic camera" for taking motion pictures on a band of film to be viewed by peeping into a box, and later for projecting them on a screen. Thus a great industry, the modern moving pictures, got its start. Even earlier, in 1883, he had patented what became known as "the Edison effect," the passage of electricity from a filament to a plate of metal inside an incandescent lamp globe which was a forerunner of the radio tube.

In 1927, Mr. Edison was admitted to the National Academy of Sciences. By April 1928 he had taken out over one thousand patents. He died on October 18, 1931, having spent the greater part of his eighty-four years on scientific experiments which materially altered and improved the daily life, not only of Americans, but of people everywhere.

FEBRUARY TWELFTH

LINCOLN'S BIRTHDAY

The first formal celebration of Lincoln's birth after the original one in Hardin County, Kentucky, on February 12, 1809, when Nancy Hanks Lincoln gave thanks that a man child was born, was held in the Capitol of the United States in Washington in 1866. There were present at this celebration President Johnson, members of his Cabinet (with the exception of the Secretary of State who was too ill to leave his house), the Justices of the Supreme Court, the Diplomatic Corps, the members of the United States Senate and the House of Representatives, the Governors of the States, and the military and naval officers who had been mentioned by name in resolutions of thanks by Congress, besides a large number of citizens crowding the galleries. The occasion was the gathering of both Houses of Congress to listen to a memorial address in honor of the dead President. The anniversary of his birth had been selected as the most appropriate date for the tribute. The flags on all the public buildings were displayed at half mast and the whole city of Washington was pervaded by a funeral atmosphere. The officers of the government and the invited guests gathered in the hall of the House of Representatives silently and reverently and waited for the proceedings to begin as though they were at a religious service in a church.

The exercises began at noon with the playing of a selection from "Il Trovatore" by the Marine Band. Then the Reverend Charles E. Boynton, chaplain of the House of Representatives, offered a prayer, after which Lafayette S. Foster, president pro tempore of the Senate, who presided, made a brief speech, referring to the assassination of Lincoln and to its effect upon the country, concluding as follows:

The Senate and House of Representatives thought proper to commemorate this tragic event by appropriate exercises. This day, the birthday of him we mourn, has properly been selected. An eminent citizen, distinguished by his labors and services in high and responsible positions at home and abroad, whose pen has instructed the present age in the history of his country and done much to transmit the fame and renown of that country to future ages, the Honorable George Bancroft, will now deliver a discourse.

Mr. Bancroft, who had been selected on brief notice after Edwin M. Stanton, Lincoln's Secretary of War, had declined to serve, delivered his famous review of the career of the Great Emancipator. The New York *Tribune* of the next day, February 13, 1866, in commenting on the exercises, said of Mr. Bancroft's address that:

It deals with him (Lincoln) as one who was molded by events and acted as their agent rather than as one whose force of character made the times take shape in accordance with his will. It is well known that Mr. Lincoln had the same view of his own relation to affairs. He thought himself put at the head of the Republic in order to execute the will of the people as from time to time indicated—not to take the lead in public business, not to announce a policy, not in a single instance to transcend popular expectation, not to show himself guided and uplifted by prophetic inspiration.

These memorial exercises in Washington constituted the official celebration of the anniversary of Lincoln's birth as well as the official tribute to him on his passing. On the same day in Jersey City, N.J., the Lincoln Association, composed of private citizens, was holding the first of many such celebrations to be held there and in other parts of the country. This association was formed in the autumn of 1865 by several residents of the old Third Ward of the city who had been in the habit of meeting periodically in a small club room. Among them were William B. Dunning, Samuel Stilsing, Henry Lee, David Peloubet, Dr. Lane, Joseph Acton, Daniel Shea and Clay Tilden. They decided that something should be

93

done in memory of the dead President and agreed to change the name of their club to the Lincoln Association and to observe the anniversary of Lincoln's birth with a dinner every year. The first president of the reorganized club was William B. Dunning and the first dinner was held on February 12, 1866, as already indicated. At this dinner James Gopsill was elected president and under his leadership the club grew until its Lincoln dinners were attended by three hundred or more. They were held at Taylor's Hotel until that building was torn down. Then they were transferred to the Jersey City Club. Some of the most noted men of the country addressed the association at its annual dinner. William Walter Phelps said, in the course of an address at the Association's twenty-third annual dinner, that it was "the one association in this broad land that has never failed to celebrate his birthday since his death."

The name of Lincoln has been one to conjure with. It was used by the newly organized Republican Club of New York City in 1887 to attract attention to itself when it announced that its first dinner was to be in celebration of Lincoln's birthday. This dinner was described by the press as "the most notable celebration of the day ever held in the city." "With such a start" said the *Tribune*, "it seems most likely that the celebration may become an established custom," a prophecy which has been fulfilled.

At this first dinner, held at Delmonico's Restaurant, two hundred and eighty persons were present including many of the most prominent Republicans of the country. Addresses were made by Senator Hawley of Connecticut, Senator-elect Frank Hiscock of New York, Governor Foraker of Ohio, Senator Benjamin Harrison of Indiana, destined to become President of the United States in a short time; Chauncey M. Depew, later a Senator from New York; Governor Oglesby of Illinois, and Henry Cabot Lodge of Massachusetts, then serving his first term in the House of Representatives. James G. Blaine of Maine, who had been the Republican candidate for the presidency in 1884, and was one of the most popular leaders of his party, wrote a letter of regret in the course of which he referred to the widening interest in the career of Lincoln and to the tendency of men of all parties to honor him. Among other things he wrote:

> The Republican party makes no attempt to narrow the possession of a fame that is recognized on all continents, that will last through the centuries, that belongs to humanity. But the political organization which supported Mr. Lincoln has the right to claim the prestige of his name as it continues to labor in the great field where he wrought until all the harvests of his plantings are gathered and garnered.

By the time the hundredth anniversary of his birth arrived in 1909 the memory of Lincoln had become a precious heritage to the people of the whole nation, regardless of geographical section or political belief. The private and unofficial celebration of the day had become general before this date. At the dinner of the Lincoln Club of New York in 1891 Hannibal Hamlin of Maine, who was Vice President during Lincoln's first term as President, made the journey to New York, undeterred by his great age—he was eighty-one—for the purpose of making an address. In the course of it he urged that the anniversary be made a national holiday, a suggestion which was greeted with enthusiastic applause. The next year, 1892, the legislature of Illinois, the state in which Lincoln spent his mature years and in which he is buried, made the anniversary a legal holiday. Four years later the legislatures of New Jersey, New York, Minnesota and Washington followed the example set by Illinois and many others have since then taken formal recognition of the propriety of observing the anniversary by making it a legal holiday. Massachusetts, however, instead of making it a legal holiday authorized the governor, by law in 1905, to call upon the people by proclamation to observe the day with appropriate exercises. One of the early proclamations issued under this authority bore the signature of Curtis Guild, Jr., and appeared on February 1, 1908. It contained a long eulogy of Lincoln and ended in this way:

> Let cannon and bell at high noon call the people from sport or study or toil, to reflection on that great life so nobly lived. Let the universal display from tenement to State House of the flag of the United States of America remind the people that our country is the United States because of Abraham Lincoln.

Elaborate preparations were made for observing the hundredth anniversary. A Memorial Association had been organized to buy the Lincoln farm in Hodgenville, Ky., containing the log cabin in which he had lived. Congress on February 11 made the day a national holiday in the District of Columbia and the territories, and the Post Office Department issued a memorial two-cent postage stamp.

Theodore Roosevelt, then President of the United States, went to Hodgenville, as the guest of the Memorial Association to lay the cornerstone of a marble structure to inclose the famous log cabin and to deliver an eloquent tribute to Lincoln. In introducing President Roosevelt, Joseph Folk, former Governor of Missouri, president of the Association, explained that it was the intention to preserve the cabin as Mt. Vernon is preserved in memory of Washington, as the Hermitage is kept in the state in which Jackson left it, and as Monticello is the Mecca of the followers of Jefferson.

While the exercises were in progress at the place of Lincoln's birth they were also going on at Springfield, Ill. Memorial tablets were placed on the building in which Lincoln had his law office and on the Presbyterian church which he attended, and an elm was planted in his honor on the grounds of the Court House in which he tried his cases. A mass meeting in the afternoon was addressed by Jules Jusserand, the French Ambassador, James Bryce, British Ambassador, and William Jennings Bryan, three times the candidate of the Democratic Party for the presidency. And the Springfield Chapter of the Daughters of the American Revolution held a reception in Lincoln's old home.

It was estimated that a million persons took part in the various exercises of the day in New York. The official celebration of the city was held in Cooper Union where Lincoln made the famous speech in 1860 which displayed his breadth of vision and marked him for the presidency. Mayor George B. McClellan, son of one of the generals prominent in the Civil War who was the Democratic candidate against Lincoln for the presidency in 1864, presided. Addresses were made by Joseph H. Choate, the leader of the New York bar, and by the Reverend Lyman Abbott, who succeeded Henry Ward Beecher, one of Lincoln's most efficient supporters, as pastor of Plymouth Church in Brooklyn. A memorial tablet was placed on the center column at the back of the stage reciting the fact of the historic appearance of Lincoln in the hall. With peculiar appropriateness the celebration in the Republican Club in the city was addressed by Booker Washington, president of Tuskeegee Institute, a Negro who was born a slave and freed by the Emancipation Proclamation.

In Chicago fifty public meetings were held by as many different organizations. The city was "fairly buried beneath flags," according to the newspaper accounts. The show windows of the stores were filled with Civil War relics and portraits of Lincoln, and the streets were crowded with marching paraders. The principal exercises were held in the auditorium, with Woodrow Wilson, a Democrat and president of Princeton University, making the chief address. Mr. Wilson in 1912 was elected to the presidency as a successor of Lincoln, and he won over two opposition candidates as Lincoln had won the first time over three.

In Boston the official celebrations included a meeting under the auspices of the city addressed by John D. Long, a former governor, at which Julia Ward Howe, author of "The Battle Hymn of the Republic," read a poem, and a meeting of the Government of the Commonwealth in the State House addressed by United States Senator Henry Cabot Lodge. At one o'clock a company of cornetists mounted the belfry of the Park Street Congregational Church and played "The Battle Hymn of the Republic" and "America" while a crowd that filled the streets and the corner of the Common near the church stood with uncovered heads.

The anniversary was observed on the battlefield at Gettysburg with exercises held on Seminary Ridge where some of the fiercest fighting occurred. The famous address made by Lincoln on November 19, 1863, on the occasion of the dedication of the National Cemetery there was read.

Vice President Fairbanks spoke at a celebration in Pittsburgh and Vice President-elect Sherman was the chief speaker at the exercises in Harrisburg, the Pennsylvania capital. President-elect Taft was the guest of honor at a dinner in New Orleans, a city which had not yet begun to celebrate Lincoln day, but Mr. Taft made appropriate reference to the

anniversary. In other Southern cities, however, the day was observed.
In Birmingham, Ala., Lincoln exercises were held in the public schools
for the first time and, in Texas, for the first time in the history of the
state, many cities celebrated the day. In Arkansas it was observed as a
semi-holiday and a dinner was given in Little Rock at which prominent
Confederate soldiers responded to Lincoln toasts.

Considerable notice of the anniversary was taken abroad. The Mayor
of Lincoln, England, cabled greetings to President Roosevelt: "The Lincoln City flag waves over the Guild Hall to-day in sympathetic commemoration of the event." An address on Lincoln was delivered at the
University of Berlin by Professor Felix Adler of New York, and he
unveiled a bust of Lincoln by Volks which had been presented to the
University. In Paris the Americans held a celebration with an address
by Professor Henry Van Dyke of Princeton University and it was similarly celebrated in Rome with Lloyd Griscom, the American Ambassador,
as the speaker. And the Brazilian Government paid a tribute to Lincoln
by displaying the national flag on all the public buildings in Rio de
Janeiro and by firing a salute of twenty-one guns from the warships in
the harbor.

The great Doric structure in Potomac Park in Washington, enshrin-
ing a heroic statue of Lincoln, grew out of the interest aroused by the
celebration of the hundredth anniversary of his birth. Senator Shelby M.
Cullom of Illinois introduced in Congress in 1910 a bill providing for
the erection of a memorial in the National Capitol. It was passed in
1911, creating a commission, with William H. Taft as its chairman, to
have charge of the work. This commission approved a design for the
building by Henry Bacon, an architect of New York, and employed
Daniel Chester French, one of the most noted American sculptors, to
make the statue. The cornerstone was laid on February 12, 1915, without ceremonies. Among the articles placed within the stone was a sketch
of the life of his father by Robert Todd Lincoln. In the completed
structure the Gettysburg Address and the Second Inaugural are engraved
on the walls of the chamber containing the statue. There are in the
building also mural decorations by Jules Gurin showing in allegory the
principal events in Lincoln's life.

The building was dedicated on May 30, 1922, at exercises over
which Mr. Taft, the chairman of the Memorial Commission, presided.
Dr. Robert R. Moton, successor to Booker Washington as the head of
Tuskeegee Institute, was the first speaker. He paid a tribute to Lincoln
as the emancipator of his race. Edwin Markham read a poem, and Mr.
Taft presented the memorial to President Harding who received it as the
representative of the nation.

The anniversary of Lincoln's birth has come to be widely observed
by special exercises in the schools. A typical program, arranged for the
schools in West Virginia, begins with the singing of "The Battle Hymn
of the Republic." This is followed by the recitation of William Knox's

97

poem, "Oh, why should the spirit of mortal be proud," which was one of Lincoln's favorites, followed by the recitation of Walt Whitman's poem on the death of Lincoln, "O Captain! my Captain!" Then "The Star Spangled Banner" is sung, followed by the recitation of the Gettysburg Address. The exercises close with a brief address by the principal of the school, or by some visitor, on the lessons to be drawn from the public and private life of Lincoln.

Abraham Lincoln was born in a log cabin in Hardin County, Kentucky, the son of Thomas Lincoln and Nancy Hanks. Samuel Lincoln, his first American ancestor, came from Norwich, England, and settled in Hingham, Mass., in 1638. Descendants of Samuel, with the pioneering spirit of their progenitor, migrated westward and southward. Some settled in Berks County, Pa. Others moved on to Rockingham County, Va., and the President's grandfather went to Jefferson County, Ky. His father lived in various places in Kentucky and in 1816 moved to Spencer County, Ind. Fourteen years later, when Abraham was twenty-one, he moved to Illinois. The son worked as a farm laborer, but he must have impressed his neighbors with his ability for in 1832 he was chosen captain of a company of volunteers for service in the Black Hawk Indian war. When he returned from the campaign he settled in New Salem and became a partner in a general store in the village. He was also postmaster and a deputy surveyor. When he was twenty-five he was elected to the State Legislature. When the capital of the state was moved to Springfield in 1839, he settled there and opened a law office. He had been licensed to practice two years before. He was elected a Representative to Congress in 1846, when Stephen A. Douglas, later to become his rival, was in the Senate. When the issue of the extension of slavery into free territory arose he opposed such extension. At the State Convention in Bloomington, when the Republican party in Illinois was formed in 1856, he made a strong anti-slavery speech. He supported John C. Fremont for President and was one of the presidential electors in the state. He had previously been an elector for Harrison in 1840 and for Clay in 1844, indicating that while he was still a young man he had become one of the leading citizens of the state. In 1858 he was nominated for the United States Senate by the Republicans to run against Stephen A. Douglas, the Democratic candidate. During the campaign he and Douglas debated the issues with each other in a series of speeches which lifted Lincoln into the national consciousness. The next year his friends began to talk of him for the presidency. On February 27, 1860, he made an address in Cooper Union, New York, which was a statesmanlike discussion of the problems before the country and was highly praised in the East. He was nominated for the presidency at the convention in Chicago in May 1860, and was elected over two Democratic candidates and one

Union party candidate. He took office on March 4, 1861, and the Civil War broke out in a little more than a month. It was fought and won under his direction. In September 1863, he issued a proclamation declaring his intention of freeing all the slaves in the rebellious states on January 1, 1864. He was reelected to the presidency in November 1864, and on April 14, 1865, he was shot in Ford's Theatre in Washington by John Wilkes Booth, an actor, and died on the following morning. Edwin M. Stanton, his Secretary of War, said as he looked on the lifeless face: "He now belongs to the ages," a verdict which has been accepted by the world for he is now regarded as the great modern apostle of liberty and his name is venerated in the remotest parts of the earth.

The anniversary of his birth is observed as a legal holiday in thirty states, and in two others the people are called upon annually to celebrate it, by proclamation of the governor.

GEORGIA DAY

The anniversary of the landing of James Edward Oglethorpe at Savannah on February 12, 1733, is observed as Georgia Day by the state which he founded. It is a legal holiday observed by the public schools and the various patriotic societies. Oglethorpe, the son of Sir Theophilus Oglethorpe, a stanch Jacobite, was born in London on June 22, 1696. He was educated at Eton and at Corpus Christi College, Oxford. On graduation he was commissioned in the army in which he served until 1715. The efforts of the supporters of the son of James II to place him on the throne in that year failed and Oglethorpe crossed the channel to France. Two years later he enlisted under Prince Eugene of Savoy in a campaign against the Turks where he won distinction. At the close of the campaign he attached himself to the court of the Pretender in France and Italy and busied himself with an attempt to advance the fortunes of the Stuarts. In 1719, apparently deciding that he was engaged in supporting a losing cause, he returned to England and settled on the family estate of Westbrook in Godalming, Surrey. He was elected to Parliament in 1722 as a Tory and represented his district continuously for thirty-two years. He became interested in the fate of debtors and wrote a pamphlet exposing the evils of imprisonment for debt. He conceived the plan of sending to America as colonists the debtors discharged from prison, not only to give them a new start in life, but also to relieve unemployment at home. In June 1732, he and sixteen associates obtained a charter as trustees "for establishing the colony of Georgia in America." The Colony was named for King George II. While the motive of Oglethorpe was philanthropic the motive of the government was political. The Spaniards in Florida were making raids on Carolina and it was planned to create a new colony between Carolina and Florida to act as a buffer. Oglethorpe landed at Charleston with a company of settlers on January 13, 1733, and began negotiations with the Indians for a tract of land at the mouth of the Savannah river, the present site of the city of Savannah. He arrived there on either February 12 or 13, 1733, and began the settlement of the new colony with Englishmen. In that year a company of fifty Jewish colonists arrived, followed the next year by a company of Lutheran refugees from Salzburg, Germany. A company of Moravians also came, but after remaining in Georgia for a time most of them moved north into Pennsylvania. In 1736, John and Charles Wesley, along with a body of Scotch Presbyterians, joined the colony, but remained only a short time. George Whitefield, an English evangelist, visited the colony and founded the Bethesda Orphanage near Savannah. In spite of many difficulties the enterprise prospered and Oglethorpe returned to England for the last time in 1743. He was courtmartialed in 1745 for unsuccessful leadership in a campaign against the Young Pretender, but was acquitted. He was made a lieutenant general in 1746 and a general in 1765. He lived to the age of eighty-nine, dying on June 30, 1785. In his later years he was the friend of Samuel Johnson, Boswell, Goldsmith, Horace Walpole, Edmund Burke, and a large company of other distinguished persons. Boswell, in his life of Johnson, reports a conversation on the subject of dueling among the guests at dinner at General Oglethorpe's house in London in 1772. The general said, "Undoubtedly a man has a right to defend his honor." After the discussion had continued some time, writes Boswell:

> The general told us that when he was a very young man, I think only fifteen, serving under Prince Eugene of Savoy, he was sitting in a company at a table with a Prince of Wirtemberg. The Prince took up a glass of wine and, by a fillip, made some of it fly in Oglethorpe's face. Here was a nice dilemma. To have challenged him instantly might have fixed a quarrelsome character upon the young soldier; to have taken no notice of it, might have been considered as cowardice. Oglethorpe, therefore, keeping his eye upon the Prince, and smiling all the time, as if he took what his Highness had done in jest, said "Mon Prince—" (I forget the French words he used, the purport, however, was) "That's a good joke, but we do it better in England"; and threw a whole glass of wine in the Prince's face. An old general who sat by, said, "Il a bien fait, mon Prince, vous l'avez commencé"; and thus all ended in good humor.

There is a tradition that when the American colonies rebelled, General Oglethorpe was asked to command an expedition to suppress the rebellion, but declined to fight his "fellow countrymen."

In 1835 a university named for him was founded in Milledgeville, then the capital of Georgia. During the Civil War all the students enlisted in the Confederate army and the funds of the university were invested in Confederate bonds. The buildings were used for barracks and later were burned. An attempt was made to revive the university after the war but it was finally abandoned in 1872. In 1913, however, a new Oglethorpe University was founded at Atlanta by men who believed that the name of the great patron of the state should be thus honored. General Oglethorpe was a graduate of Corpus Christi College, Oxford. One of the buildings of the new university is a reproduction of the building of that college, even to the coat of arms over the main entrance. Dr. Thornwell Jacobs, the president of the university, after learning that there was no monument to Oglethorpe in England and that there was no definite information concerning the place where he was buried set about discovering the place of burial. All that was known was that Oglethorpe had been buried in the chancel of Cranham Church, Essex. That church had been burned and a new one built in its place. Dr. Jacobs satisfied himself and the church authorities that the new building had been erected on the foundations of the old and obtained permission to make an opening in the floor of the chancel to find the body of the general. The opening was made and on October 10, 1923, Dr. Jacobs descended into the vault and found two coffins, one containing the body of the general and the other the body of his wife, as indicated by the plates upon them. He planned to bring the body of the general to America, bury it on the campus of Oglethorpe University and erect a memorial tower over the grave, but the plan fell through, largely because the people of Savannah, the city founded by Oglethorpe, insisted that if the body were brought to America it should rest in Savannah. The university, however, has obtained the only known portrait of the general painted in his maturity, and copies, if not the originals, of all other known portraits, and has hung them in Lupton Hall, one of its chief buildings.

The two hundredth anniversary of the founding of the state of Georgia was celebrated in 1933. The celebration began in Savannah on February 12, which fell on Sunday. The Young People's Service League of the two Protestant Episcopal dioceses of the state attended a communion service at Christ Church in the morning, and the Right Reverend Henry J. Kirkell, Bishop of Atlanta, delivered a patriotic address. There were appropriate services in the other Protestant churches in the city, including Trinity Methodist Church, the successor of the church which John Wesley founded there. The senior bishop of the Southern Methodist church, the Reverend Warren A. Candler, delivered a memorial address at this service. The celebration, begun in Savannah, was continued in other parts of the state and the Federal Government issued a memorial postage stamp showing a portrait of General Oglethorpe.

CHARRO FIESTA IN BROWNSVILLE, TEXAS

A Texas-Mexican border fiesta, known as Charro Days, is held each year in Brownsville, Tex., during the weekend before Lent. In 1942 the

101

dates were February 12th through the 15th. The celebration is elaborate and picturesque, and attracts thousands of visitors annually. Brownsville is situated on the Rio Grande opposite Matamoros on the Mexican side of the river, and the proximity of the two cities suggested the idea of a fiesta recreating the color and romance of the old border where Latin-American and Anglo-American met. In the beginning it was purely local, but its fame spread until it soon drew tourists from all over the United States in much the same manner as the Mardi Gras in New Orleans. As with the latter celebration, visitors to Brownsville during the Charro fiesta frequently don costumes and participate in the festivities instead of remaining mere spectators.

Charro was originally the name of a costume worn by the Spanish dons, consisting of tight-fitting breeches, a brightly colored shirt, a serape, and a huge sombrero, but the term was later extended by popular usage to include the Mexican cowboy outfit, due to its similarity. The male residents of Brownsville wear variations of the Charro and grow beards for the fiesta. The China Poblana is the most popular costume for the women and its origin is even more colorful. According to legend, it was designed by a little Chinese girl who was befriended by the Mexican people and who became a sort of fairy princess to them. The most striking characteristic of the China Poblana is a full skirt, brilliantly colored and richly embroidered in glittering sequins. A blouse or bolero, or whatever the wearer fancies, vies with the skirt in vivid shades and gorgeous embroidery. Other striking costumes are those native to states in the southern part of Mexico, such as the Tejuana which is even gayer than the China Poblana. The youngsters also take part in the fiesta, wearing small replicas of their elders' costumes for the children's parade, a regular feature of the program with as many as six thousand children participating.

The program in 1942 was typical of the observance. At eight o clock on the evening of February 12 a Grand Charro Days Parade set forth along Elizabeth Street, lit by thousands of flares to enhance the extraordinary brilliance of the Charro, China Poblana, and other costumes. After the parade there was a costume street dance, and a Grand Fiesta Ball at the El Jardin Hotel. On the afternoon of the 13th the children marched in their parade, which was followed by a band concert, and, in the evening, the China Ball. The program for the 14th included the Grand Fiesta Parade in the morning, another band concert in the afternoon, and an inter-American ball in the evening. On February 15, the final day, there was a bull fight across the river at Matamoros, and the evening festivities were centered in the Plaza of the Mexican city. This part of the celebration is known as Noche Mexicana (Mexican Night) and features Mexican dancing and music. An international rodeo, street vaudeville acts, and strolling Mexican troubadours contributed action and glamor to the spectacular gaiety of the fiesta whose apt slogan is "A Charro Never Sleeps."

CHINESE NEW YEAR

Although the republican government in China officially adopted the Gregorian calendar the Chinese people at home and abroad continue to observe the beginning of the new year on the date fixed by the old Chinese calendar. The year, according to that calendar, has three hundred and fifty-four days and twelve lunar months, about one half of them with thirty days and the other half with twenty-nine. In order to make the months correspond with the movements of the planets a thirteenth month is inserted every two or three years and two months are added every five years. The new year begins on the twentieth day of the first moon and it may fall anywhere from January 21 to February 19, inclusive. The advent of the new year is celebrated by festivities continuing from one week to a month.

The Chinese New Year's Day in 1945 fell on February 12. It was celebrated by the Chinese in the United States with many of the old ceremonies. The use of fireworks, common in China, has been forbidden in American cities for several years but the rule is sometimes suspended for the festival. In some cities there was the parade of the dragon throughout the Chinese quarter. The dragon is a gruesome beast in which are concealed several men who make it move. The spectators drop money into its mouth to be sent to China for the relief of the needy. There is much feasting during the holiday season. Early in January 1934, a ship from China arrived in the harbor of New York with a cargo of food and drink valued at $1,000,000 to be consumed by the Chinese in different parts of the country during the celebrations of that year.

The New Year customs in Shanghai, as described by a traveler, are similar to those observed by the Chinese in this country. He says:

I was the guest of a Chinese family during the New Year ceremonies. I reached the compound just as the final house cleaning was in progress. This spasm of neatness was to impress the Kitchen God, who, later in the evening, was to be released from his duty over the household and sent back to heaven to report. He was represented by a lithograph. His features were done in the classic style, with long ear lobes that denote knowledge, the almond eyes and bushy whiskers. The lithograph hung over the great clay oven upon which were simmering many strangely shaped pots for the banquet to come. Red candles and incense were burned before him. The entire family, from the grandfather to a fat baby all of two years old, bowed gravely before him. I bowed also. Rumor has it that occasionally the Kitchen God was base enough to make unpleasant reports on high about the household during the previous year. That risk must be nullified. The Tai-tai, the old grandmother, wabbled up to him on

103

her tiny, bound feet, and, producing a small pot of honey, sealed his lips by smearing them with the viscid fruit of the bee. Now, if he were able to speak at all, it would be only sweet words. Next, the portrait was removed from the wall. A candle was touched to the paper. The Kitchen God blazed for a brilliant moment, then became a sheet of gray-brown ash, while a thin spiral of ascending blue smoke attested the flight of his soul heavenward. . . . Great horn lanterns with the shou character for longevity painted in splashy red ideographs were hung in the halls and corridors. Across the door vermilion strips with ideographs brushed in gold leaf were pasted. The legend read: "Life and Death, Adversity and Happiness, All Are Decided by Heaven." As the sun dropped into a clear, frosty western horizon, a sharp clatter arose at the outer gates. Congregated in the lane outside were a dozen men. All carried long, lighted tapers which they carefully shielded from the wind. One by one they approached my host and held out slips of flimsy paper on which had been brushed spidery ideographs. He examined these gravely. Then, extracting a fat, clinking purse from a girdle about his waist, he began to pay over various sums of money.

"Those were tradesmen," he told me. "They collect their debts at this time. As long as their candles remain alight they can continue to make their collections."

"What if the wind blows out the candle?" I asked.

He smiled. "Actually, if money is still due them they sneak down a side alley and light up again."

"But what happens if they reach the house of a bankrupt, some one with no money to pay them at this season?"

"That's bad," he said seriously. "If the debt is very large the creditor will make a loud outcry and attract the neighbors and the passersby in the lane. He will tell the throng that his debtor has just refused to pay. Thus he makes the person owing him lose face—such great face that the poor debtor dares not show himself during the next year. I know of several cases where debtors, to rehabilitate their repute, have committed suicide. By doing that they gain back their neighbors' esteem."

"You mean their spirits gain it," I said.

"Isn't that the same thing?" my host asked in some surprise. "Are not the spirits of our ancestors always around us?"

At the banquet hall the feast was ready. . . . Rice wine spouted hot and pungent from the narrow stems of chased pewter flagons. Lichens from the far south of China were eaten. Sharks' fins and Javanese bird-nest soup made their inevitable appearance. Twenty different varieties of sea food were interspersed with as many variations of duck, pheasant and bamboo partridges.

After the feast the members of the family paid their respects to its head, the grandfather. Then there was a puppet show followed by the antics of a small boy dressed as a tiger, and other divertissements.

These customs, originating no one knows how many thousand years ago, cannot be abolished instantly by a decree of the government. The observance of them by the Chinese in the United States serves to keep alive the memory of their native land.

FEBRUARY THIRTEENTH

SHROVE TUESDAY OR MARDI GRAS

This is a movable celebration, its date depending on the date of Easter (See Easter, April 1). It fell on February 13 in 1945. It is a legal holiday in Alabama and Florida and in the parishes of Orleans, St. Bernard, Jefferson, St. Charles and St. John the Baptist in Louisiana. It is the Tuesday immediately preceding the beginning of Lent on Ash Wednesday and it was and still is in some parts of the world the concluding day of the carnival festivities which preceded the Lenten season of fasting. The name Shrove Tuesday or Shrovetide is English and is derived from "shrive." In the Anglo-Saxon *Ecclesiastical Institutes* appears the following passage referring to it: "In the week immediately before Lent everyone shall go to his confessor and confess his deeds and the confessor shrive him." The French call the day Mardi Gras, or Fat Tuesday, and it is Fastnacht to the Germans. It is sometimes called Doughnut Tuesday and Pancake Tuesday. The name Pancake Tuesday is an allusion to the custom of making pancakes on the day. As no meat was to be eaten in Lent all the fats in the house were used in making pancakes. An account of this custom is contained in a seventeenth century English book protesting against the excesses practiced on the day. It reads:

> There is a thing called wheaten flower, which the sulphury necromantic cooks do mingle with water, eggs, spice and other tragical, magical enchantments, and then they put it little by little into a frying pan of boiling suet, where it makes a confused dismal hissing—like the Lernean snakes in the reeds of Acheron, Styx or Phlegeton—until at last by the skill of the cook it is transformed into the form of a flap-jack, which in our translation is called a pancake, which ominous incantation the ignorant people do devour very greedily—having for the most part well dined before—but they have no sooner swallowed that sweet, candied bait, but straight their wits forsake them and they run stark mad, assembling in routs and throngs of ungovernable numbers, with uncivil civil commotions.

It was the custom to insist that the wife or mother of the family should fry the cakes for her own household, and that when one side of the cake was cooked it should be tossed into the air in such a way as to turn it over and make it fall back into the frying pan with the uncooked side down. The name flap-jacks survives to this day in the United States where the cakes are made of buckwheat flour, cornmeal or rice as well as of wheat flour.

In England and Scotland it was customary to play a boisterous game of football in the streets of the towns on Shrove Tuesday, accompanied by much horseplay. There was a custom, too, of beating the cocks, when fighting cocks were taken to an agreed place where the spectators beat them to death. One theory is that this practice originated in a desire to punish the cocks vicariously for the cock which crowed and recalled to Peter that he had denied his Lord. Another theory is that it originated at the time of the victory of Henry V over the French, as the cock was the French symbol. Still a third theory is that the cocks were punished because in the days of the Danish domination in England the people planned to massacre their oppressors in the early morning of Shrove Tuesday while they were still asleep. But the Danes were awakened by the crowing of the cocks and the plan failed.

Mardi Gras, the end of the carnival season, is celebrated in New Orleans and Shreveport, La., Pensacola, Fla., Mobile, Ala., and Galveston, Tex., with regularity and in other cities occasionally. The New Orleans celebration is the most elaborate and the best known. It was introduced by a company of young men of French descent who had been sent to Paris to be educated. They had enjoyed the Mardi Gras festivities in that city and when they returned home in 1827 they organized a procession of street maskers which marched about the city on the day before Ash Wednesday. In the course of time this developed into a parade of boys armed with bags of flour and cudgels who marched about the streets indulging in horse play with other marchers. The wearing of masks dates back to the Roman Lupercallian feast and survived in the Mardi Gras festivities in France and Italy.

The custom of celebrating the day in America with a parade of floats carrying symbolical figures originated in Mobile. The plan was adopted in New Orleans and the first pageant of decorated floats was given in 1857 by the Mystic Krewe of Comus, a secret organization formed in that year. The subject illustrated in the pageant was Milton's "Paradise Lost." After the parade the members of the organization went to the old Gaiety Theatre and there presented a series of tableaux. It gave an annual parade until 1861, when the celebration was interrupted by the Civil War. It was resumed in 1866 and continued without interruption till 1884 when it was suspended until 1910 and again resumed. In 1870 another society, the Twelfth Night Revellers, was organized to celebrate the beginning of the carnival season (See Feast of the Epiphany, January 6). It gave a street parade for a while, preceding a ball in the French Opera House, but the parade has been abandoned. An organization known as Rex was formed during the visit of the Russian Grand Duke Alexis to New Orleans in 1872. For his entertainment it was proposed that the different bodies of maskers should be consolidated into a single group and arrange a parade in honor of the city's distinguished guest. This organization became permanent and its King was recognized as the King of the Carnival, the Sovereign Lord of Misrule. He usually arrives in the city on the day before Mardi Gras and is welcomed with elaborate ceremonies. There is a procession in his honor and on the next day a ball at the City Hall. At one time he was preceded in his march into the city by a float containing a fat ox with several butchers in white aprons gathered about him, in imitation of the European custom of parading an ox and then slaughtering it and roasting it for a feast for the revellers. The New Orleans ox was not slain, and the custom of having it in the parade has been abandoned. The Krewe of Proteus was organized in 1882 and gives an annual pageant followed by elaborate tableaux and a ball at the French Opera House on Monday night. The Knights of Momus give a ball on the Thursday of the preceding week, and other carnival societies, including the Krewe of Nereus, the Knights of Mithras, the Amphyctions, the Falstaffians, and the Atlanteans celebrate with balls. The Rex organization pretends that the King of the Carnival lives on Mount Olympus in Greece and that he visits New Orleans once a year in the carnival season.

There is no better way of indicating the elaborateness of the ceremonies than by describing the celebration in 1910, one of the most extensive, as reported in the New Orleans newspapers of the time. Rex "arrived" on the Mississippi River, opposite New Orleans, early on Monday morning in his "royal yacht." The "Isla de Luzon," the Louisiana Naval Brigade gunboat, borrowed for the occasion, went out into the stream to meet him. He was transferred to the gunboat without accident and his "loyal subjects" were presented to him. He welcomed them graciously, and they admired his gorgeous white silken costume, his golden scepter and sword. His escort was dressed in appropriate court costume. It included the Lord High Chamberlain, the Earl Marshall, the Duke of Maine, the Duke of Dunn, the Duke of Education, the Royal Jester, the Chancellor of the Exchequer and many others. The King's health was drunk in champagne and many toasts were proposed. Salutes were fired as the gunboat, serving as the royal flagship, started up the river at noon, and landed at Canal Street. Preceded by the royal band led by Ali Ben Dammit, the King, accompanied by his retinue, landed while the guns of the United States warship "Paducah" fired a welcoming salute. The King mounted his royal car on which was the throne of state, the members of his retinue mounted horses, the guests sat in carriages, and, escorted by a military parade, they entered the city. A detachment of the Ninety-first Coast Artillery was the first military organization in line. Sailors from the "Paducah" and detachments of the state militia followed. The procession marched through the streets to the City Hall where it arrived with Rex at three o'clock. Rex was received by Mayor Behrman who welcomed him in an address which described the improvements made in the city during the year and referred to the arrangements for entertaining the "royal" visitor in a suitable manner. At the conclusion of the address Miss Camille O'Connor presented the key of the city to Rex, and Rex gave to her a gold locket and a bouquet of flowers. Then the Duke of Education, on behalf of Rex, thanked the Mayor for the welcome and explained that the King had traveled over the greater part of the world since his last visit and was delighted to note what had been done in his loyal city during his absence, and hoped that there would be nothing but feast and gaiety during his presence among his subjects. In the evening the Krewe of Proteus, described as a cousin of Rex, held a spectacular parade in the streets, followed by a ball in the French Opera House. The City Hall was brilliantly illuminated and the Mayor reviewed the parade from a grand stand erected before it. All the balconies on the houses along the line of march were crowded with spectators and the streets were lined with people. As the parade moved through the crowds, according to the contemporary accounts, "abundant largess in the shape of necklaces, pins, bracelets, and other mementoes of Proteus's appearance were showered upon the women and girls along the route by the dukes and nobles of the train." The floats in the parade represented the various heavenly bodies. They were described in the explanatory program as follows:

Proteus. Emerging from a huge lotus, which is gracefully poised upon the marble steps of his palace near the island of Pharos, which, according to Homer, is a day's sail from the mouth of the Nile, Proteus greeted his subjects with a youthful and smiling face. Great streams of water flowed from fountains on each side of him and lotus flowers and lotus buds with their broad leaves were tastefully grouped about him. Three mighty dolphins, with flaming eyes and scales of emerald were before him, ready to carry him over the ocean waves. He seemed to be the personification of grace and beauty.

Title Car. Father Time, with folded wings and armed with his scythe, was watching an enormous globe upon which were seen all the stars and constellations of the universe. Like an ancient astrologer he appeared to be reading the fate of men, of nations and of worlds.

Hesperus, The Evening Star. Proteus transported his subjects first to the evening star, where perpetual twilight reigns and the landscape is forever tinted with the purple rays of the setting sun. It is the home of dreamers and of musicians. Hesperus is sitting upon a hill, surrounded by fair women and romantic youths, who are filling the air with sweet strains of music, making a beautiful picture.

Luna. This is the orb of reverie and of mystery, the torch destined to light the word "astrology." Reigning over the empire of silence and of peace it appeared more mysterious and solitary than any other. The queen of divinities, crowned with a silver crescent, was standing above the clouds. A long and glistening serpent was coiled beneath her feet, and pale blue flames were flashing forth from massive braziers. Winged maidens were floating about her doing homage to the queen of the night.

Polaris, The North Star. In a palace of eternal ice and snow, the spirit that governs this star was standing, scepter in hand, keeping guard over the firmament, for the Pole Star is the hold for the center of the immense whirlpool of stars that revolve around it every twenty-four hours. It is the celestial axis around which the firmament is forever turning.

Aries, The Ram. The ram is the first sign of the Zodiac, because at the time when this principal part of the celestial world was established the sun entered this sign at the Spring equinox. It is the ram with the golden fleece of the Argonaut expedition, the symbol of Spring and the opening of the year.

Standing upon a tall pedestal the ram was seen surrounded by trees covered with delicate leaves. Beautiful girls were disporting themselves near him, rejoicing in the return of Spring.

Taurus, The Bull. This is the animal which bore Europa over the seas to that country which derived from her its name. The fair daughter of Agenor, of whom Jupiter became enamored, was sitting upon his back adorned with garlands of flowers.

Gemini, The Twins. The twins, Castor and Pollux, sons of Jupiter, celebrated for their indissoluble friendship, for which they were rewarded with immortality. They were shown standing upon a bank of clouds and, to commemorate their participation with Jason in the celebrated contest for the golden fleece, the ship Argo was dancing beneath them upon the surface of the foaming sea.

Cancer, The Crab. The prevailing opinion is that while Hercules was engaged in his famous combat with the Lernaean monster, Juno, envious of the fame of his achievements, sent a sea crab to bite him and annoy the hero's feet, but the crab being soon despatched, the goddess to reward its services, placed it among the constellations. Juno was seen standing upon the back of the huge crustacean gazing scornfully upon Hercules who stood unmoved upon the hydra-headed monster he had just slain.

Leo, The Lion. The sun enters the Lion at the Summer solstice and causes it to disappear by covering it with his fires. This signifies the victory of Hercules over the lion of Nemea. Being the house of the sun during the month of July, it is the sign of burning heat, the symbol of strength and power. A golden lion was shown rampant, dancing upon a pillar of flame, while pretty women, gathered under a blossom-covered tree, fanned themselves and admired the glorious summer flowers gathered around them.

Virgo, The Virgin. According to the ancient poets, this constellation represents Astraea, the daughter of Jupiter and Themis, the goddess of Justice who lived upon the earth during the golden age. Offended at the wickedness and impiety of mankind during the bronze and iron ages of the world, she returned to heaven and was given a place in the starry zone through which the sun passes during the course of the year. She was represented with wings, holding in one hand a pair of scales and a sword in the other.

Libra, The Balance. It is generally supposed that the figure of the Balance has been used by all nations to denote the equality of the days and nights at the period of the sun's arriving at this sign of the Zodiac. The ancient husbandmen, according to Vergil, were wont to regard this sign as indicating the proper time for sowing the winter grain. Day was typified by huntsmen pursing wild gazelles over the hills, and Night was symbolized by revelers who, in a satin-curtained pavillion, were drinking and carousing.

Scorpio, The Scorpion. This sign was anciently represented by various symbols, sometimes by a snake, and sometimes by a crocodile, but most commonly by a scorpion. It was considered by the astrologers as a very evil sign. According to Ovid this is the famous scorpion which sprang out of the earth at the command of Juno and stung Orion.

Sagittarius, The Archer. This is the centaur, Chiron, the tutor of Achilles, Jason and Esculapius, and the inventor of the art of riding. This was the last lord of the ancient race. Doubtless the vicinity of the Scorpion influenced the opinion of those who studied the heavens with regard to this sign, for it is not represented under very favorable colors. Chiron was renowned for his knowledge of music, medicine and shooting, and was skilled in the knowledge of plants and medicinal herbs. Proteus here represented him in a beautiful forest, surrounded by fair-haired adolescents to whom he was teaching the science of archery.

Capricornus, The Goat. Capricornus is said to be Pan, who was feasting with some other deities near the banks of the Nile, when, suddenly, the giant Typhon came upon them and compelled them to assume a different shape in order to escape his fury. Pan led the way and plunged into the Nile and that part of his body which was under the water assumed the form of a fish and the other part that of a goat. To preserve the memory of this frolic Jupiter made him a constellation in his metamorphosed shape. He appeared seated in a grove with bunches of purple grapes suspended from twining vines around him, and the shepherds and shepherdesses who gathered near him were delighted with the tuneful airs which he played on his pipes.

Aquarius, The Waterbearer. This part of the eternal circle was represented by the figure of a man pouring out water from an urn. Aquarius is symbolic of the handsome Ganymede, who was raised by Jupiter's eagle to serve as cup-bearer to the gods after the fall of Hebe. Between two marble columns the master of Olympus was seated upon his throne. Near him were the divinities that help him govern the universe. They were quenching their thirst from the limpid stream which flowed from the golden vessel of the Waterbearer.

Pisces, The Fishes. This is the twelfth House of the Sun, before the renewing of the year. This was the time of the inundation of Egypt and that of fishing. It closes the circle of zodiacal constellations. Venus and her son Cupid were one day on the banks of the Euphrates when they were greatly alarmed at the appearance of the giant Typhon. Throwing themselves into the river they were changed into fishes and by this means escaped danger. To commemorate this event Minerva placed two fishes among the stars. Proteus depicted the fishes with scales of rubies and of sapphires, swimming gracefully over the heads of sprightly Undines who are watching their undulations.

The Wandering Comets. Proteus offered his subjects a sight of the vaga-bond comets. They are wild youths mounted upon steeds of blue and yellow and red and green, galloping madly across the sky and leaving behind them a trail of light. These mysterious apparitions which suddenly come to light up the firma-ment were long regarded with terror by the astrologers.

Lucifer, The Morning Star. This is the abode of perpetual Spring, where flowers never cease to bloom and where the leaves of trees and vines are always green. The rosy-fingered Dawn and her maids are awakening the world with the strains of music from their golden harps and announcing to the universe that a new day has been born to gladden the hearts of gods and men.

The Sun. In a chariot of pure gold, ornamented with precious stones, the Sun stands ready to start upon his course through the firmament. His steeds are prancing and are anxious to start on their journey. The deities who preside over the planets of astrological lore are grouped around him, making obeisance to their lord and master. Beams of light are flashing here and there and are casting an illumination over the entire scene.

This procession escorted Proteus to the French Opera House where he was to receive his Queen and open the ball. The Opera House was filled with invited guests and when the curtain rose on a darkened stage Jupiter and the other gods were there assembled in a woodland scene. There was a storm effect with floating clouds and flashes of lightning. When the clouds parted the throne room was disclosed in a blaze of light. The throne, which was a shell ornamented by iridescent gems, rested on branches of coral at the base of which were cornucopias.

Proteus wore a crown of palm branches and held his scepter in his hand as he awaited his Queen. She was escorted from a proscenium box by one of the courtiers and presented to Proteus along with her maids of honor. When this ceremony was concluded the dancing began.

The next day, Mardi Gras itself, there were two street pageants, one in the afternoon presided over by Rex, and the other in the evening, arranged by the Mystick Krewe of Comus, and there were two balls in the evening, one in the Athenaeum and the other in the French Opera House. The Rex pageant, presented on twenty floats, represented the freaks of fable. The ladies of the court of Rex were gathered on the balcony of the Boston Club and as the parade reached that point it halted while Rex paid his respects to his Queen. It then continued over the prearranged route. Following is a contemporary description of the floats:

Rex. Here upon a dazzling throne which occupied the highest position in the very center of the tableau, sat His Carnival Majesty himself, clad in robes of surpassing richness and wearing the scintillating jewels which the court artificers of New Orleans prepared expressly for the royal use. Sparkling draperies swept from the base of the throne caught in exquisite folds at each corner of the car where clusters of flowers and heraldic devices were affixed. A vast butterfly waved his Tyrian wings above the royal head.

The Title Car. Immediately after the royal car followed one of scarcely inferior interest, the one which revealed the theme, "The Freaks of Fable" which his Majesty deigned to illustrate. A mass of autumnal foliage, heaped together upon the car, assumed the form of a fantastic creature, half rustic, half animal, wholly extravagant, and upon its enormous wings the title of the pageant was illuminated in glowing letters.

The Griffin. In the works of the old poets and romantic writers, whether of the classic age or of medieval times, or of the renaissance, will be found descriptions of strange creatures, sometimes animals, sometimes birds, sometimes startling combinations of both, or even of beast and bird and human being. These chimeras are the freaks of fable which Rex illustrated. The first to be presented was the Griffin. The Griffin is mentioned in works written five hundred years before Christ, but the middle ages believed it to be the guardian of the buried treasure of Bactria. To it were attributed the body and hind quarters of the lion, and the head and neck of the eagle. Rex showed this grisly creature flying through the air and bearing on its back an armed man. It was about to attack the Moslem knights who had come to its lair in search of the treasures heaped in the rear of the car. Around the glittering heaps stood groups of winsome maidens.

Scylla and Charybdis. In the Straits of Messina, not far from the stricken city of that name, there were in the time of Homer—or so the poets would have us believe—on one side a terrible animal dwelling in a whirlpool and on the other a many-armed monster whose home was a rock and a cave. Every vessel passing between them—and all that entered the strait must pass between—paid its toll of sailors, those who did not fall victims to Scylla being snatched from the deck by Charybdis. Rex showed how those fabled animals wrought their will upon the mariners of antiquity. Scylla lifted her dreadful hands and threatened the occupants of a little vessel who vainly turned in the opposite direction only to confront Charybdis in a similarly menacing attitude. Sea monsters writhed their slimy but glittering lengths amidst the waves on every side.

The Hydra. In the marshes along the sea coast of Greece in ancient times there was supposed to exist a terrible creature, the offspring of Echidna and Typhon, having a hundred heads and spouting from its many mouths a subtle

111

and deadly venom. The destruction of this frightful beast was one of the labors accomplished by Hercules. In the exquisite tableau shown by Rex, Hercules, club in hand, was depicted as he advanced to the contest. Hydra sprawled in front of him; behind him a Grecian King and his attendants looked on in fascinated terror, while overhead curled the fronds of some singular form of Greek vegetation.

Pegasus and Chimera. A helmeted warrior riding upon a winged horse advanced valiantly to do battle with a horrible thing, which with its triple head of lion, goat and serpent, crouched dismally at the van of the car. It was the Chimera, mother of the Sphinx, who after ravaging the fertile fields of Lycia, was about to meet her deserved fate at the hands of Bellerephon. The hero having tamed the fleet Pegasus, with the help of Minerva, succeeded in overcoming his adversary; after which Pegasus ascended to heaven and became the bearer of the thunderbolts of Jove. In modern literature Pegasus is described as the horse of the Muses, but this is erroneous, and Rex was quite right in showing him as one of the participants in the great struggle with the Chimera.

The Phoenix. The Phoenix was contributed to the galaxy of fabulous freaks by Egypt, when a shrine dedicated to it existed at Heliopolis. Once in every five centuries the wondrous bird visited the spot and then withdrew to immolate itself upon the pyre which it had erected for that purpose. From the flames a new and youthful Phoenix arose, to live through the long years, revisit the shrine beside the Nile and eventually cremate itself and repeat the marvelous cycle of its existence. Rays of intolerable light rose from every corner of the car converging to the point where the flames burst around the nesting Phoenix. In front an Egyptian priest performed the ceremonies observed whenever the sacred bird was supposed to be undergoing fiery regeneration.

The Dolphins. Bacchus, or, as the Greeks called him, Dionysius, was the god of wine. Once, when asleep on the seashore, he was captured by pirates, who hurried him on board ship and sailed away, intending to sell their victim for a slave. After various experiences, the upshot of which was extremely uncomfortable for the kidnappers, as may be imagined, the captive god liberated himself and found refuge in the sea where shoals of dolphins had assembled around the vessel. They now received the god to bear him on their broad backs safe to land. This is the moment Rex has represented in this beautiful car. High rolled the azure billows and upon them frolicked not merely the dolphins, but lissome figures of mermaidens, while Bacchus himself, harp in hand, rode triumphant upon the mightiest dolphin of all.

Briareus. Thousands of years before the dawn of history, when from Olympus the gods ruled over the world, there was a rebellion against them, and at the head of the insurgents were the huge but courageous Titans. In their peril the gods enlisted Briareus, the son of Uranus and Gaea, who with his brothers routed the giants and saved the authority of Jupiter from the peril that had threatened it. Briareus possessed a hundred arms and fifty heads, and so was able to contend equally even against the huge Titans. Rex showed him at the supreme moment of his career, when with every hand grasping a separate spear he overrode his unwieldy foes, thrusting them down into the sulphurous smoke of Tartarus, while in the background the Olympians, surrounded by clouds, stars and rainbows, looked on in awe and wonder at the tremendous struggle.

The Minotaur. Warriors in splendid dress guarded the approaches to an ancient world. In the foreground smoked the altars dedicated to a blood-thirsty deity. Just beyond the sacred threshold a group of fear-smitten maidens found themselves face to face with a huge and terrifying figure, half man, half ox. Thus Rex represented the old myth of the Minotaur, that grisly beast, penned up in a labyrinth in Crete by the vindictive King Minos. To avenge wrongs done his son, Minos made war upon Athens and compelled the Athenians to send every year a tribute of young men and girls to be devoured by the Minotaur.

At length Theseus, indignant at the danger to which his friends were exposed, went to Crete and slew the Minotaur.

The Sphinx. The Sphinx gets its name from the Greek word meaning the "throttler." It was a figment of Egyptian imagination invested with the body of a winged lion, and the head and breast of a woman. Hera, angry at the crimes of Laius, sent the Sphinx from Ethiopia to Thebes, and there, making her home upon a rock, she intercepted the citizens of the town or any passing traveler, propounded a riddle to them, and when they failed to answer it aright flung them headlong to death on the plain below. But eventually Oedipus, the Greek hero, fell into her clutches and when he gave the right answer to her question the grisly beast in fury hurled herself from the rock and perished miserably. Rex showed the Sphinx as an Egyptian religious emblem, a serene figure carved in marble, guarded by Egyptian priests and surrounded by the flowers that grow beside the banks of the Nile.

The Midgard Serpent. When Thor went to the home of Asa and there in a contest of skill and strength lifted a huge old cat almost entirely from the floor, his giant hosts grew pale and trembled, for in the form of that cat the hero was contending with the Midgard serpent who holds the world in its folds. If Thor had lifted the cat clear of the pavement the grasp of the serpent upon the globe would have been loosened and chaos would have come. In the beautiful car which bore the name of this fantastic snake were seen princes and warriors and all the pomp of the world splendid in the sunshine, but far below, in the depths of the earth, the Midgard serpent held the world in its coils.

The Sea Horses. Neptune, god of the sea, scorns to use an automobile when he goes forth. He has instead a conch shell for a chariot and a school of sea horses to draw it. Hippocampus, as these fairy animals were called of old, has the body of a fish but the head and forelegs of a horse. We may well believe that when the monarch of the ocean had some important business to attend to, he was escorted by half a dozen or more attendants exquisitely dressed, executing fairy music upon wreathed horns, or riding as couriers upon the flourishing sea horses in the divinity's train, just as we beheld them in this superb car.

The Ogre. From the mythology of the middle ages we get the grim figure of the Ogre, a man of giant stature and brutish instincts, usually with a consuming appetite for human flesh. According to Rex the Ogre makes his home in forests. Sometimes, as on this charming car, in a bit of woodland lovely in its bright colors, vines and flowers. From amidst the beautiful and delicate vegetation appeared the huge head and gaping mouth of the monster and his great claw-like hands reaching hungrily towards the youths and maidens who, unconscious of nearing danger, frolicked in the shade of the blossom-covered thicket.

The Sea Serpent. The iridescent car to which Rex gave the name of the Sea Serpent told its own story. From the dark blue waves shot with silver and crested with foam issued the complex folds of an enormous serpent covered with scales that flashed in the sunshine, its back adorned with fins and singular, hair-like tentacles. In its forearms it carried its young. Masses of seaweed invested it in a sort of drapery, while spirits of the deep, some seemingly part human and part fish, and others with all the outward aspect of men and women, disported themselves upon the water, or rode joyously upon the back of the serpent itself. Cautious science hesitates to deny the existence of the sea serpent in view of the well-authenticated reports of seaman who have seen it; and so, perhaps, we ought not to include this particular freak among those of fable. Nevertheless some of the legends which are associated with it warrant doing so.

The Centaurs. The haunt of the Centaurs was Thessaly. They are described by the poet Pindar as animals with the head and trunks of men, but the body and legs of horses. They were a rude and bestial race, anyway. When Pirithous was wedded to Hippodamia, daughter of the King of Argos, he made a feast in his house to which he invited his neighbors, including the Centaurs of Pelion. But one of the latter, Eurytion, became intoxicated on the good wine copiously supplied the guests, and behaved so ill that a dreadful conflict arose in which many of the Centaurs were slain and the rest driven from Pelion and compelled to retire to other regions. In this car was represented the wedding feast of Pirithous, who like his semiferine guests is decked with garlands of grapes and crowned with chaplets of grape leaves. The car itself was a vast mass of grapes and grapeleaves emblematic of the rich liquor which wrought such confusion in the veins of Eurytion.

The Dragon. Here again Rex gave a splendid picture, the meaning of which called for no interpretation. The dragon appears in the mythology of almost every people, nearly always as the embodiment of the evil passions that work in the heart of man to his undoing. The serpent represents the smooth, deceptive evil that subtly undermines the good, but the dragon is the furious passion which rushes headlong and openly upon its prey. Here Rex portrayed this great worm, as the ancient Saxons termed him, with his fearful neck, flaming mouth and sinuous tail. He rode upon clouds and flames and with him were imps and other creatures of evil, bearing torches, spears and similar implements of destruction.

The Roc. Rex found the theme of this grandiose car in the Arabian Nights where, in the story of Sinbad the Sailor, the tale is told of a huge egg and the mighty bird that laid it, the latter so great that Sinbad might fasten himself to its leg and be carried far through the air, without the host being aware of the passenger. So immense a bird might of course become a menace to tiny things like man and so in this tableaux the carnival artist showed a group of armed men advancing to attack the Roc which awaited their onset in the midst of a thicket of spikey cactus. The idea of the Roc seems to have been developed in Arabia by untruthful travelers who brought home the leaves of certain varieties of palm found in other remoter parts of the East, which they passed off as feathers of the enormous bird.

Cerberus. Dark and strange, there rose above this car the roof of Hades, supported in the front by columns wreathed with serpents, and in the rear by mighty masses of fire and smoke. Here and there amid the fumes of burning sulphur and the jagged tongues of flame were the forms of priests, guards and imprisoned spirits, richly clad, indeed, but all kept in close confinement by the ghastly dog, Cerberus, Pluto's trusted lieutenant, who glared with all his three heads at his hapless prisoners. Cerberus was the offspring of Echidna and Typhon, and hence a brother of Hydra. He it was whom Orpheus lulled to sleep with the music of his lyre, and also that Hercules, in accomplishing the twelfth and last of his labors, dragged from his post.

The Unicorn. And now came the last, but not the least splendid of the long and sumptuous series of superb cars with which Rex presented his ideas of the "Freaks of Fable." Students tell that the Greeks got their idea of the fleet-footed horse with the long, twisted horn in the forehead from much distorted descriptions of the rhinoceros. They had never seen the rhinoceros and in striving to represent him hit upon the fantastic figure of the unicorn. However, be that as it may, Rex showed the unicorn as a marine animal, frolicking gaily in the waves, while groups of voyagers, half-armed and richly dressed made their way over the high-swelling waves in little boats of unique design. The waves glittered with silver and purple, their tips crested with snowy foam. Over the sleek bodies of the unicorns the sun cast tremulous lights, turning their colors to hues of celestial beauty. The joyous figures in the tiny ships danced happily, their burnished cuirasses and flowing robes revealing fresh glories with every hilarious movement.

As was customary the carnival pageants ended with the parade of the Mystick Krewe of Comus on Tuesday evening. This parade was followed by a formal reception to Rex in the Athenaeum and by the

Comus ball in the French Opera House, attended by Rex at the close of his reception. The floats in the pageant—there were twenty of them—dealt with the story of Mahomet. Comus himself led the procession. The subject of the various floats was described in the following manner:

Comus. As if speeding across the flat Arabian sands, the merry god came, seated in a sort of chariot harnassed to the floating pinions of those mighty birds of the desert, the ostriches. Unique in conception and design, the float was a marvel of beauty. Waving golden banana leaves gave atmosphere to the scene and seemed to waft one to Araby the blest.

The Title—Mahomet. The sword is Mahomet's emblem of faith and only recently was brought to mind in Constantinople how important in the crowning of Mahomet's representative is the ceremony of the girding on of the sword. The prophet's sword ended in a trail of fire, and at the time of his birth celestial lights illumined the heavens as far as the confines of Persia and many other signs portended the coming of a great man. The color of his mantle was green and to this day his descendants use that color as the sign of nobility and rank. Mahomet wore a turban, for he said turbans were worn by the angels. Whether believed to be a divine apostle, an unprincipled imposter, or simply a religious fanatic, he was a most remarkable man, changing the history of the world, and his influence extends over millions of people even unto today.

The Koran. The Koran is the Mohometan bible. It is the only miracle that Mahomet claimed, and is supposed to be a divine revelation. Much of it can be traced to the Bible, the Mishnu and the Talmud of the Jews. Mahomet claimed to be nothing more than an apostle, but Moslem writers assert otherwise and describe how he took from the horns of a bull a scroll containing one of the chapters of the Koran, and at another time a white dove whispered in his ear a message from the deity. By readers of the original, the Koran is said to be a piece of literature of incomparable merit, though as it exists to-day it has undergone many corruptions and interpolations.

The Mystic Shrine. When Adam and Eve were driven from Paradise, according to the Arabian traditions, they fell in different parts of the earth. They were finally permitted to meet each other again near the present city of Mecca. Here Adam implored the Almighty that a shrine be given him similar to the one at which he worshipped in Paradise. This was granted, the shrine being formed of radiant clouds and ever after Adam turned towards it when in prayer. The site of this heaven-descended tabernacle is that of the Caaba in Mecca to-day, a place of holiness even before the time of Mahomet.

Legend of Eyla. A tradition which made a powerful impression on the mind of Mahomet, when quite a lad, was that of the city of Eyla, situated near the Red Sea. This place had been inhabited by a tribe of Jews who lapsed into idolatry and profaned the Sabbath by fishing on that sacred day. For this they were turned into swine and monkeys. This divine judgment made the prophet very strict regarding idolatry and keeping the holy days.

Habib The Wise. Habib was a very rich and learned prince who in turn had been Jew, Christian and one of the Magi, and who lived to be over a hundred and forty years old. His daughter, Satiha, to whom he was devoted was very ill and hearing of the wonderful prophet he sent for him and as proof of his holiness demanded that he cure his daughter. This Mahomet did immediately, so claim the Moslem writers, and made of Habib not only a convert but a rich and powerful ally.

Cadijah. When about twenty-five years of age Mahomet was married to a very wealthy widow named Cadijah. She was many years his senior, but of very superior qualifications and aided him most effectually in every way in his career. Without her he would hardly have been what he was and doubtless he realized that. He was devoted and true to her to the last, only availing himself of the Arabian law regarding plurality of wives after her death. A silver palace was allotted to Cadijah in Paradise as a reward for her great faith and early service to the cause of Mahometanism.

The Genii. The vast solitudes of the desert are peopled with good and evil genii who are spiritual beings and liable like man to future rewards and punishments. They are created from fire and smoke. To keep them from prying into heaven, flames and darts are placed around the celestial confines. In the valley of Naklab a passing company of genii overheard Mahomet reading the Koran and became converted to his faith.

Al Borak. Texts in the Koran seem corroborative of the famous journey of the prophet to Jerusalem and thence to the seventh heaven. Tradition has it that he was awakened by the angel Gabriel who stood before him with radiant wings and dazzling garments. To Mahomet he had brought Al Borak, a steed of wonderful form and qualities and unlike any other known animal, with a human face, cheeks of a horse, and eyes as radiant as stars. From its splendor and incredible speed it was called Al Borak, or Lightning. Mounting this marvelous creature Mahomet makes the heavenly journey from the earth to the empyrean.

The Garden. For the true believer who has expiated all his sins is this paradise. The soil is of the finest, producing most beautiful flowers of exquisite colors and fragrant with perfumes. The air resounds with the voice of Israfel and the songs of his daughters. Here one can eat without satiety and drink without inebriation.

The Cock. In the first heaven were animals of all kinds. Among these was a cock of dazzling whiteness and of such marvelous height that his crest touched the second heaven. The bird salutes the ear of Allah each morning with his melodious chant. All creatures on earth, save man, are awakened by his voice and all the fowls of his kind chant hallelujahs in emulations of his note. When the last day is near this bird will close his wings and chant no more.

The Tree of Heaven. This is the wonderful tree of life, its boughs laden with delicious fruit, bending to the hands of those who seek to gather. Its branches extend wider than the distance between the sun and the earth, and its leaves of gold somewhat resemble in shape the ears of the elephant. Birds sport in its shade repeating the divine verses of the Koran. Its fruits are milder than milk and sweeter than honey. From this tree issue four rivers, two flowing into Paradise, the other two being the Nile and the Euphrates.

The Place of Adoration. This is called Al Mamour, and is flaming with red jacinths or rubies, and surrounded by innumerable lamps perpetually burning. As Mahomet entered here three vases were offered to him, one containing wine, another milk and the third honey. He took and drank of the vase containing milk and was commended therefor by the Angel Gabriel.

Solomon's Messenger. According to the Koran, Solomon, who understood the speech of birds, reprimanded the hoopoe, or lapwing, for not coming when he was called. The bird in explanation said that he was in the far away country of the Queen of Sheba. To prove whether this was the truth Solomon sent the bird with a message to the magnificent Balkis and received an answer which convinced him that there was such a person.

The Hegira. This, meaning the flight of the prophet, is the date from which time is calculated by the Moslems, corresponding to the year 622 of the Christian era. It was a time of trial to the prophet as he had to flee from his enemies and take refuge in Medina. The miracle of the acacia tree where pigeons had their nests and over which spiders wove their webs, protecting the prophet and saving him from his pursuers who sought to kill him, is of the whole hegira the story which is dearest to the minds of all true believers.

116

Ayesha. After the death of his first wife Mahomet became much interested in the beautiful child of his faithful adherent Aba Beher. After a betrothal of two years in which time Ayesha was instructed in the accomplishments of an Arabian maiden of distinguished rank, they were married. She is often spoken of as the favorite wife of the prophet and he doted upon her most intensely. She was young and very beautiful and it was she who soothed his last moments. The henna flower of Arabia seems most typical of Ayesha as Mahomet calls it the most perfect blossom of heaven and earth. And when one glances at shining minarets pointing silently and gleamingly upward one is reminded of the dual graces and virtues of the flower of the desert.

King of Abyssinia. Many of the relatives and friends of Mahomet took refuge from persecutions of opposing tribes of the country in Abyssinia. The King of this country—from whom Menelik of to-day claims descent—was a powerful potentate well able to take care of himself and any who came to him for protection. He was a Nestorian Christian and found Mahomet's precepts much like those of his own religion, so he took pleasure in confounding the prophet's detractors, dismissing them from his court, which was one of great magnificence.

The Sorcerer. At one time Mahomet had a long, languishing illness which is attributed by Moslem writers to the spells of a Jewish sorcerer. This necromancer, aided by his daughter, was exceedingly skilled in diabolical art. Under the influence of their spells Mahomet wasted to a shadow. By divine revelation he was able to free himself and eleven verses of the Koran deal directly with the subject, the last of which reads, praying to be delivered, "and from the evil Genii and men who deal in magic."

Contest of the Poets. The prophet was very susceptible to the charms of poetry. On one occasion a rebellious tribe dared the Moslems to a poetical contest. This took place in the presence of Mahomet and so pleased was he with the result that he forgave his opponents, releasing those he held as prisoners and dismissing them with presents. He was equally susceptible to the fragrance of flowers. One authority quotes him as saying in the Koran that if one possessed three pennies, one should give one to the poor, keep one for one's self and with the other buy narcissus blossoms because of their perfume.

Reward of the Faithful. Though strange to our way of thinking, the height of bliss was supposed to be what was given to true believers as reward for their faithful following of religion, according to Mahomet. After having tasted of the waters of life, the truly pious are admitted to Paradise by the angel Rushvan, and they are borne aloft on winged camels, white as milk, with saddles of pure gold. Their raiment is sparkling with jewels, and their crowns are of precious metals and gems.

The Carnival season which comes to a brilliant close on Monday and Tuesday before Ash Wednesday, begins on Twelfth Night in January when the Twelfth Night Revellers give a ball. This is followed during January by balls given by the Krewe of Nereus, the Knights of Mithras, and the Elves of Oberon, followed by a ball by the Atlanteans, and on the Thursday before Ash Wednesday by a ball and parade by the Knights of Momus. This parade really marks the beginning of the outdoor celebrations of the carnival season. The subject of the Momus pageant in 1910 was "The Winged World." The parade was led by Momus himself in a triumphal car. Each car was drawn by four mules caparisoned in flaming red and accompanied by a retinue of flambeaux bearers. Following is the official description of the car of Momus:

117

Momus. Momus was seated on a wonderful creature of magnificent proportions. Half dragon, half sea animal, it seemed to rise from the waves as graceful in movement as the sinuous waters themselves. Seated on its curving back, Momus waved aloft a glittering scepter. Grouped around him, surrounded by dashing spray, were odd appearing attendants, sparkling and dripping with the wave wash; queer looking individuals brought from the other world, they seemed ready to fly, swim or do aught else commanded by their ruler.

His car was followed by cars containing representations of wasps, butterflies, humming birds, dragon flies, night moths, mosquitoes, bumble bees, will o' the wisps, the winged nautilus, the pterodactyl, katydids, bats, devil horses, doves and hobgoblins.

These elaborate pageants are not the only features of the carnival season culminating on Mardi Gras. There are almost numberless carnival clubs which parade the streets in costume, and men, women, and children don masks and fancy dress and wander about the town making sport for themselves and others. Young men dress as women and young women dress as men, and prizes are offered for the best costume. It once happened that a young man disguised himself so successfully that he received the prize for the most tasteful costume worn by a lady. Persons prominent in the news of the time are impersonated and sometimes burlesqued to the delight of the crowds looking on.

The King of the Carnival in New Orleans is known as Rex. In Mobile he is called Felix and arrives at the city on his "royal yacht" after the manner of Rex in New Orleans. He is accompanied by a retinue of courtiers and is formally welcomed by his subjects. He selects his queen who is crowned and an organization known as the Infant Mystics arranges a pageant with numerous floats representing fantastic subjects. The King of the Carnival in Pensacola, who is called Pricus, arrives by water and enters the city escorted by troops and is formally welcomed by the Mayor. This is followed by a pageant of floats drawn through the streets, representing various phases of the subject chosen for exhibition. Memphis also celebrates Mardi Gras with parades and masked balls.

Invitations to the balls given by the clubs in New Orleans which arrange the pageants are highly prized. The tickets are not transferable and if it is known that anyone has given his ticket to another the guilty person never receives another ticket. It happened in 1866 that a man anxious to attend one of the select balls put an advertisement in one of the New Orleans newspapers offering a large price for a ticket, but was unable to get one. The railroad companies run excursion trains to New Orleans during the carnival to accommodate the tens of thousands of visitors attracted by the spectacle.

Memphis, Tenn., revived its Mardi Gras Carnival in 1872 after a lapse of several years. A committee had been sent to New Orleans in 1871 to inspect the carnival there and returned with an enthusiastic report, and the Memphis *Appeal* published a series of articles setting forth the benefit which would accrue to the city by such a celebration.

But the plan was slow in winning popular support. In January 1872, however, the business men had agreed to cooperate by paying for the floats to be used in the parade. Shrove Tuesday fell on February 13 and on the eve of that day all the hotels were filled with visitors. The city at that time had a population of forty thousand which was increased by twenty thousand during the carnival. The parade was held in the evening and it passed through streets crowded with cheering spectators. Many characters of fiction and history appeared on the floats, including Rip Van Winkle, the Sultan of Turkey, the Prince of Bagdad and scores of others. Prince Carnival sat in a huge wine glass on his float and threw balloons and whistles to the children. There were dances in many public halls and a masked ball was given to invited guests at the New Memphis Theatre. At the close of the ball it was announced by Prince Carnival that a secret society to be called the Memphi, after an Egyptian religious cult, had been organized to arrange for the carnival the next year. It managed the festival until 1881, and included in its membership virtually all the influential men in the city, the Farnsworths, the Hills, the Robertsons, and the Semmeses. Their identity was not known, however, for a long time. A different theme for the carnival was selected by the Memphi each year. One pageant illustrated the legendary history of Greece and another the discovery of the Mississippi by DeSoto. And the Memphi gave a masked ball every year, the invitations to which were sent out in the name of the organization. A Queen of the Ball was always chosen. The last elaborate celebration of Mardi Gras in Memphis was in 1881, but the day was observed fitfully until 1892, when the celebration was finally abandoned, to be revived in a different manner in 1931 as a Cotton Carnival (See Memphis Cotton Carnival, May 16).

FEBRUARY FOURTEENTH

ASH WEDNESDAY

Ash Wednesday is the first day of Lent. Its date depends upon the date of Easter (See Easter, April 1). In 1945 it fell upon February 14. The name, Dies Cinerum in Latin, dates from at least the eighth century. On the day all faithful Roman Catholics are exhorted to approach the altar before the beginning of Mass. The priest dips his thumb in ashes previously blessed, and marks the sign of the cross on the forehead and repeats in Latin, "Remember man that thou art dust and unto dust thou shalt return." The ashes used are made by burning the remains of the palms blessed on the Palm Sunday of the previous year. The day is not observed by the Protestant Church of Germany, but the Church of England and the Protestant Episcopal Church in America observe it, but without the use of ashes. That ashes were used in the ceremonies on

119

the day as early as the tenth century is evident from the record made by
an Anglo-Saxon writer of that period who wrote: "We read in the
books both in the Old Law and the New that the men who repented
of their sins bestrewed themselves with ashes and clothed their bodies
with sack cloth. Now let us do this little at the beginning of our Lent
that we strew ashes upon our heads to signify that we ought to repent
of our sins during the Lenten fast."

ST. VALENTINE'S DAY

The early martyrologies mention three Saint Valentines each associated with February 14. One of them is described as a priest of Rome
and another as Bishop of Interamna, now Terni. They suffered martyrdom in the second half of the third century and were buried in the
Flaminian Way. What was known to the ancient Romans as the Flaminian Gate was later called the Gate of St. Valentine from a church in the
immediate neighborhood dedicated to the saint. It is now known as the
Porta del Popolo, or the Gate of the People. Little is known of any
of these saints, and less is known of the third of the name who suffered
martyrdom with a number of companions.

There are various theories about how the name of Valentine came
to be connected with the day on which lovers send tokens to one another.
One is based on the belief throughout Europe during the Middle Ages
that the birds began to mate on February 14. Chaucer in his "Parliament
of Foules" refers to it in this way:

For this was Seynt Valentyne's day.
When every foul cometh ther to choose his mate.

English literature, following Chaucer, contains frequent references
to the day as sacred to lovers. In the Paston Letters, covering the period
from 1422 to 1509, appears a letter by Dame Elizabeth Brews to John
Paston with whom she hoped to arrange a match for her daughter which
runs in this way:

And cousin mine, upon Monday is St. Valentine's day and every bird
chooseth himself a mate, and if it like you to come on Thursday night and make
provision that you may abide till then, I trust God that ye shall speak to my
husband and I shall pray that we may bring the matter to a conclusion.

The affair must have been managed to her satisfaction for among
the letters is one addressed by the young woman herself "Unto my right-
well beloved Valentine, John Paston, Esquire."

Those who do not think that the old opinion about the mating of
the birds on February 14 is sufficient to explain the connection between
St. Valentine and the lovers suggest that the association grew out of the
similarity between the Norman word "galantin," meaning a lover of
women, and the name of the saint. They think that Galantin's Day with

the initial "g," frequently pronounced as "v," led to confusion in the popular mind.

Another theory is that the lover's custom is a survival and a Christianized form of a practice in the Roman feast of the Lupercalia occurring in February. The names of young men and women were put in a box from which they were drawn by chance, an arrangement under which a young man became the gallant of a young woman for the next year. It is said that the Christian clergy objected to this custom and substituted the names of saints for the names of the young people; each young person was to try to emulate the saint drawn for him or her during the next twelve months. As this drawing occurred on February 14, the day of the saint, the association with Valentine was established. But this does not explain the association with lovers. The theory connecting the day with the mating season of the birds seems the most plausible to a modern mind. The drawing of the names of young men and young women from a box on the day continued for many years after the custom of Christianizing pagan usages had been abandoned.

The youth and the lass who were paired by this method were once in the habit of giving presents to each other. Later the youth only gave a gift to the lass. Then the custom of sending valentines to the favorite grew up. These were originally simple. When the post offices were established and postal rates were reduced the mail was crowded with the sweet messages every year. The stores offered them in various designs and at various prices. Comic valentines, some of which were coarse and vulgar, could be purchased for a cent. In the early part of the present century the Chicago post office rejected 25,000 such on the ground that they were not fit to be carried through the mail, but it did accept 1,250,000 valentines that year and 750,000 were handled by the Philadelphia post office. By the first third of the twentieth century the custom of sending valentines was observed chiefly by children and for children. Their parents sent little love messages to them and they sent them to their playmates and to their parents. And the stores kept in stock gilt cupids and red hearts and colored papers which the children bought to make their own valentines. The children in the kindergartens were taught how to make them.

It frequently happens that costume balls are arranged for St. Valentine's evening. One such held by the Boston Conservatory of Music in Symphony Hall was attended by more than nineteen hundred dancers. The costumes were of various periods, from those worn by knights and gallants of the Middle Ages to those associated with the pirates of the Spanish Main, including fairies, butterflies, gypsies, characters from the operas and from the plays of Shakespeare. Prizes were awarded for the most beautiful costumes. A contemporary account of the grand march says

As they passed slowly, eight abreast, down the sides and across the center of the floor they appeared to be some ancient manuscript, wonderfully illuminated, come to life. Juliet smiled up at Weary Willie; a white robed nun of the fourteenth century paced demurely at the side of Charles II; Faust bent over the hand of a cowgirl; Hamlet joked with Carmen; the Arabian princess drew aside her veil to dimple at a plaided Scotchman.

ARIZONA ADMISSION DAY

In Arizona February 14 is a legal holiday, known as Admission Day, and commemorates the date on which President William H. Taft signed the proclamation admitting Arizona as a state. By an historical coincidence, the date of admission in 1912 was the fiftieth anniversary of the signing of a document by Jefferson Davis, declaring Arizona a Territory of the Confederate States. It lacked but ten days of being the forty-ninth anniversary of the approval of an Act of the Congress of the United States creating the Territory of Arizona. Aside from the usual observances of a legal holiday there are no established ceremonies on this date, but it is frequently celebrated in various ways by the schools and by patriotic groups.

The first white man to visit the region within the present boundaries of the State of Arizona was probably Fray Marcos de Niza, in 1539. He returned to Mexico with tall tales of the "seven cities of Cibola" where "gold and silver were the only metals" and in common use by the natives. It is historical fact that Coronado's Spanish army crossed Arizona in 1540 on an expedition organized in Mexico to seek the gold of Cibola. No gold was found, but detachments from his army reached the mouth of the Colorado and discovered the Hopi Indian towns and the Grand Canyon. Later, during the seventeenth century, Franciscan missionaries sought to convert the Hopis, and they were followed by the Jesuits. During the Mexican rule, from 1821 to 1856, the only important white settlements in Arizona were at Tubac and Tuscon, nearly all others having been abandoned because of Apache raids; but as early as 1826 Anglo-American fur trappers began coming in by way of the Gila valley. The region north of the Gila was ceded to the United States by Mexico in 1848 and became part of New Mexico Territory. Explorations for a proposed Pacific Coast railway indicated the acquisition of the south Gila valley, and accordingly the Gadsden Purchase was negotiated with Mexico in 1853, that part of Arizona between the Gila and the present Mexican boundary being added to New Mexico. In 1856 a convention at Tuscon petitioned Congress to grant separate territorial rights to Arizona, but without success. Thereafter, Texan Confederate troops occupied southern Arizona for a short time during the Civil War and finally, following their expulsion, Congress established the Territory of Arizona. In 1891 a movement for statehood began to take shape with the framing of a constitution by the legislature at Phoenix, the new territorial capital. However, it was nearly twenty years later that President Taft gave his approval to a new state constitution on the condition that a clause providing for the recall of judges be eliminated. The condition was accepted and Arizona formally admitted as the forty-eighth state on St. Valentine's Day, 1912, although within a short time the controversial provision was restored to the state's constitution.

FEBRUARY FIFTEENTH

TEMPLE UNIVERSITY FOUNDER'S DAY

After the death in 1925 of Dr. Russell H. Conwell, its founder, Temple University in Philadelphia began to celebrate February 15, the anniversary of his birth, as Founder's Day. In 1934, when the university was fifty years old, the exercises extended over a whole week and were attended by distinguished educators from all parts of the country. The orator of the occasion was Dr. Glenn Frank, then president of the University of Wisconsin. Temple University at that time had about twelve thousand students in its various schools. They include a college of liberal arts and sciences, a teachers college, schools of commerce, theology, law, medicine, dentistry, pharmacy, chiropody, and music, as well as a high school.

The university began with the visit of a working man to Dr. Conwell, pastor of Grace Baptist Church in Philadelphia. The man wanted to study to prepare himself for the Christian ministry but had no money and was compelled to work to support himself. After some discussion Dr. Conwell said to him "Come to me one evening a week and I will begin teaching you myself and at least you will in that way make a beginning." And he named the evening. The man thereupon asked if he might bring a friend with him and he was told to bring as many as he wished. On the appointed evening the man came with six friends and Dr. Conwell began to teach them the rudiments of Latin. By the third evening there were forty young men in the class and a room was hired in which to teach them. Within two years there were so many students that it became necessary to hire a separate building. In 1888 when the school obtained a college charter it had five hundred and ninety students. The right to grant degrees was obtained in 1891 and instruction which had been given at night began to be offered during the day. The physical plant has grown from a single building to a splendid group of modern structures in the heart of the city with a large stadium for athletic contests in the suburbs. Its expenses in its early days were paid almost entirely by Dr. Conwell from the proceeds of his lectures.

Dr. Conwell was one of the most remarkable men of his generation. He was born in 1843 in a two-room house on a farm in the Berkshire Hills at South Worthington, Mass. He attended the district school four miles away. When he learned to read he read the Bible and *Paradise Lost* and before he was ten years old had committed to memory the first

123

three books of Milton's great poem. When he was old enough he was sent to Wilbraham Academy where he was made drill master of the military corps and captain of the debating team. In his second year he was appointed to teach reading and elocution. While carrying on his studies he was teaching a district school, but was able to keep up with his work and was graduated in 1859 at the age of sixteen. He then entered Yale college where he had learned that a student could work his way. When President Lincoln issued his call for one hundred thousand men in 1862 Conwell decided that it was time for him to enlist and he left college and raised a company among the men in his home county. He was unanimously elected captain and Governor Andrew gave him his commission although he was only nineteen years old. Among the boys in the town was John Ring who was too small to be admitted to the company, but he was so anxious to go with the soldiers that Conwell took him along as his servant. He had an elegant sword which had been presented to him but which was too fine for use in the service and he kept it hanging on one of the poles of his tent. John kept it bright. One day, as Conwell related the incident, the Confederates attacked their camp near New Berne and they fled across the river burning the bridge behind them. Suddenly John was seen rushing back over the burning structure to Captain Conwell's tent to rescue the sword and then trying to make his way over the bridge again through the flames. When he was half way over the Confederate officer saw him and impressed by his heroic attempt ordered his men to cease firing. The Union and Confederate men then watched in silence while John struggled on. He reached the other side with the sword but was so badly burned that he died within a day or two. Dr. Conwell thereafter kept the sword hanging at the head of his bed to remind him of the unselfish heroism of the boy. He once said:

> When I stood beside the body of John Ring and realized that he had died for love of me, I made a vow that has formed my life. I vowed that from that moment I would live not only my own life, but that I would also live the life of John Ring. And from that moment I have worked sixteen hours every day— eight for John Ring's work and eight hours for my own. Every morning when I rise I look at the sword, or if I am away from home, I think of the sword, and vow anew that another day shall see sixteen hours of work from me. It was through John Ring that I became a Christian. This did not come about immediately, but it came before the war was over.

He was made a colonel and was seriously wounded in the battle of Kenesaw Mountain and had to go home. At the close of the war he entered the Albany Law School and on graduation was admitted to the bar. He went West and opened a law office in Minneapolis and to add to his income he became the Minneapolis correspondent of the St. Paul *Press.* With the aid of some business men he soon founded the Minneapolis *Daily Chronicle.* But he continued to attend to his growing law practice and to teach music and give lessons in elocution in his spare time. His health began to fail and he abandoned Minneapolis and spent a year in Europe but got no better. Finally a surgeon extracted a bullet from one of his lungs which had lodged there when he was wounded at Kenesaw Mountain. He recovered his health almost immediately and opened two law offices in Boston. He kept one of them open at night to give free legal advice to the poor who could not see him during the day. At times he would be visited by fifty or more in a single evening. In addition to his law practice he wrote for the Boston *Traveler* and the New York *Tribune.* During these years he learned six languages while traveling between his home and his office by train. In 1874 he took up his residence in Newton Center, a Boston suburb and the seat of the Baptist Newton Theological Seminary. It was there that he decided to become a minister. He closed his law office in 1878 and offered his services to a struggling Baptist church in Lexington where he was or- dained. There were eighteen persons in his first congregation. The next Sunday the church was crowded with people thronging the sidewalk in an effort to get in. On the third Sunday the services were held in the Town Hall and continued to be held there until a new and larger church was built. He remained in Lexington for eighteen months when he was called to become pastor of Grace Baptist Church in Philadelphia, formed by members of the Tenth Baptist Church. He entered on his work in Philadelphia on Thanksgiving Day, 1882. The congregations grew in size and crowded the building used as a church. And so many children flocked to the Sunday school that it was not easy to find room for them. One Sunday afternoon a little girl six years old was found by Dr. Conwell unable to get in the building. He took her on his shoulder and carried her inside and found a place for her. She had heard her parents talk about the need of a new church and she began to save her pennies to help pay for it. She died within a few months and her mother opened her little bank and found fifty-seven cents which the child had saved. She took the pennies to Dr. Conwell and told him about them. He told the story to friends of the church and it inspired them to buy the lot on which later was built Grace Temple, one of the largest Protestant church buildings in the country with a seating capacity of three thousand.

Edward Bok, for many years editor of the *Ladies' Home Journal,* established a trust fund, the proceeds of which are used every year to bestow on a citizen of Philadelphia a cash prize of $10,000 and a gold medal in recognition of what that citizen has done. It is known as the Philadelphia Award. The committee in charge selected Dr. Conwell as the worthy recipient of the distinction in 1923, with the hearty approval of the general public. Dr. Conwell used the money for philanthropic purposes as he had used all other money that came into his possession. He was a lecturer in frequent demand. It is estimated that he earned more than $10,000,000 on the lecture platform all of which save the money needed to pay his traveling expenses he gave away. His most famous lecture was "Acres of Diamonds" which he delivered more than six thousand times for which it is said he received more than $4,000,000.

This lecture was never twice the same, but it always began with a tale told to him by an Arab guide he had hired in Bagdad while traveling down the Euphrates river. This guide said that there once lived not far from the Indus river a Persian named Ali Hafed who owned a large farm and orchards, lent money at interest, and was happy and contented. One day a Buddhist priest visited Ali Hafed and told him how the world was made. It started with a bank of fog and then became a ball of fire and then rain fell on it and cooled the outer surface turning it to a solid shell, while the interior remained molten. If the molten mass burst through and cooled quickly it became granite, if less quickly it became copper and then silver and then gold and finally diamonds. The old priest said that a diamond was a congealed drop of sunlight and told Ali Hafed that if he had a mine of diamonds he could place his children on thrones because of his great wealth. He at once became discontented and asked the priest where he could find a mine of diamonds. The priest told him there were always diamonds in a river running over white sands between high mountains and Ali Hafed sold his farm and set out on his hunt for diamonds. He traveled all over the world, spent all his money and died in poverty. The man who bought his farm took his camel to drink in the brook in the garden and saw a flash of light from the white sands and picked up a stone with a bright spot in it reflecting all the colors of the rainbow. He took it in the house not knowing what it was, but the priest who had told Ali Hafed about diamonds happened to visit him and told him that it was a diamond. They rushed to the little stream and found other diamonds and out of this mine came the Kohinoor and Orloff diamonds and the crown jewels of England. And as Dr. Conwell concluded the tale he always said that his Arab guide explained to him that if Ali Hafed had remained at home and dug in his own garden, instead of wretchedness and starvation he would have had acres of diamonds. And the lecture was an elaboration of this moral with modern instances.

Dr. Conwell died on December 6, 1925. In February of that year Dr. William M. Lewis, president of George Washington University of Washington, D. C., included Dr. Conwell in a list of the ten Americans who would be regarded by future historians as "truly great." Among the ten were also Charles W. Eliot, Elihu Root and Oliver Wendell Holmes.

DESTRUCTION OF THE "MAINE

The American battleship "Maine," under command of Captain Charles G. Sigsbee, was sent to Cuba in January 1898, as a gesture of friendliness to Spain, as well as to be ready to rescue any Americans whose safety might be imperilled by the troubles on the island. It was anchored in the harbor of Havana. On February 15 the Spanish warship, "Alfonso XII," and the Ward line ship, "City of Washington," were anchored not far from it. The Cubans were in revolt against Spanish rule and the Spanish Governor was charged with intolerable cruelties. The people of the United States were in sympathy with the Cubans. Expeditions for their relief were frequently organized in the United States and the Government exerted itself to prevent their departure but it was not always successful. The Government in Washington, interested in the peace of the island, was in correspondence with the Government in Madrid in an attempt to find a way by which the Cuban troubles could be settled to the satisfaction of all‘ concerned. There was resentment in certain Spanish circles in Havana, however, over the presence of the "Maine" in the harbor.

February 15 had been unusually warm for the season. The evening was cloudy with neither moon nor stars visible and the heat was so oppressive that the officers and men on the two battleships and the passengers on the merchant ship were relaxing trying to keep cool. At nine o'clock Captain Sigsbee had just finished writing a report to Theodore Roosevelt, Assistant Secretary of the Navy, on the advisability of continuing the practice of placing torpedo tubes on cruisers and battleships and he was about to begin a letter to his wife. At ten minutes after nine the bugler began to blow taps. In describing the incident later the Captain wrote:

I had just laid down my pen to listen to the notes of the bugle which were singularly beautiful in the oppressive stillness of the night. The marine bugler, Newton, who was rather given to fanciful effects, was evidently doing his best. During the pauses the echoes floated back to the ship with singular distinctness, repeating the strains of the bugle fully and exactly.

As the hands of the clock indicated that it was forty minutes after nine everything was quiet on the ship and the Captain was folding the letter which he had written to his wife. In an instant, as the Captain explained afterward, "there came a bursting, rending and crashing sound or roar of immense volume, followed by a succession of heavy, ominous metallic sounds and reverberations." The explosion had occurred under the sleeping quarters of the crew and had wrecked the vessel so completely that it sank within a very short time. It had a complement of 26 officers and 328 men. Two of the officers and 250 of the men were killed outright and eight died later in a hospital. Captain Sigsbee was the last man to leave the ship. He took refuge on the "City of Washington" and sent the following despatch to the Navy Department:

Maine blown up in Havana harbor tonight and destroyed. Wounded and others on board Spanish man-of-war and Ward line steamer. Send lighthouse tenders from Key West for crew and few pieces of equipment above water. No one has clothing other than that upon him. Public opinion should be suspended until further report. All officers believed to be saved. Jenkins and Merritt not yet accounted for. Many Spanish officers, including General Blanco, now with me to express sympathy.

Charles W. Newton, a captain in the National Guard, was in Havana at the time of the explosion. He had gone there with General Arthur

L. Goodrich, the owner of the Hartford (Conn.) *Courant*, to see if conditions were as bad as reported. He and General Goodrich were seated in a park overlooking the harbor when the explosion occurred. His description of what he found and what he saw indicates the critical nature of the situation. He said:

> Thousands of natives, driven into the city by the Spaniards, were starving. Every morning the authorities would line up men suspected of inciting to revolt and shoot them down. There were street riots all the time. Nevertheless the Spanish officers had a gay time and there were bull fights all the time. That night (February 15) we left the Hotel Inglaterra and went to sit in the park. There was plenty of high feeling and we thought maybe the hotel would be blown up. However, nothing serious had happened and I said to Arthur: "We'll be leaving for home tomorrow and nothing much has happened. I wouldn't mind seeing some excitement, even if we had to swim out to the 'Maine' for protection." Just as I said these words there was a great flash out on the water and a few seconds later a big boom. We could barely see the "Maine" in the darkness. It began sinking slowly by the stern. Its powder magazines let go, just like a fireworks blast. It was awful. The ship continued to burn for hours, just that portion that remained out of water. Goodrich and I were afraid that would be a signal for a general fight, so we ran to a warehouse and took shelter until three o'clock in the morning. Then we got aboard the "City of Washington" to which Admiral Sigsbee was taken after every living man had been removed from the "Maine." Two days later we returned to the states.

The immediate impression in the United States was that the Spanish authorities were responsible for the destruction of the ship. This feeling together with the indignation at the Spanish cruelties led finally to the declaration of war, the expulsion of Spain from the island and to Cuban independence. A naval court of inquiry, however, which sat in the case, found that the explosion had been caused by a submarine mine but that it was impossible to fix the responsibility. The report of a Spanish investigation, made independently, was that the "Maine" had been wrecked by an interior explosion.

The anniversary has been observed regularly by the Navy and by the Spanish War Veterans Associations in Havana and in the United States. The wreck was allowed to remain in Havana harbor for fourteen years. On February 15, 1909, the Havana Camp of the Spanish War Veterans was organized and its first act was to adopt a resolution calling on Congress to lift the wreck, recover the bodies of the dead which were still in it, and tow the ruined hull out to sea and sink it. Similar resolutions were adopted by the Spanish War Veterans and by other bodies in the United States and on May 9, 1910, Congress authorized the work to be done. It was completed on March 16, 1912. On February 15 of that year memorial services were held in Havana over the bodies of sixty sailors taken from the wreck and temporarily resting in a casemate in Cabana fortress. And on the same day the corner stone of a monument to the "Maine" dead was laid at the Columbus Circle entrance to Central Park in New York.

The Government of Cuba erected a monument to the "Maine" in Havana which was dedicated on February 15, 1926. Memorial exercises are held at its base every year in recognition of the part taken by the United States in freeing the island from Spanish rule. During the Pan American Conference in Havana in the winter of 1928 the delegates from the Latin-American countries present participated in the celebration. In the United States the speakers at the anniversary celebrations have frequently urged the importance of the development of the American navy until it is equal to all possible demands that may be made upon it.

In support of the theory of the Naval Court of Inquiry that the "Maine" was wrecked by the explosion of a submarine bomb, the New York *Sun* on March 24, 1912, after the ship had been raised, the bodies recovered and the hull towed out to sea and sunk, printed what purported to be a detailed account of the placing of the bomb and explanation of its explosion. It was told by an unnamed naval officer who held high rank after the war and who, the *Sun* explained, was well known to its editors. He said he had obtained the account from a Spaniard who professed to have been a confidential messenger for Governor-General Blanco in Cuba, a position which he occupied because he and Blanco had been born in the same district in Spain.

According to this account, when Governor-General Blanco heard that the "Maine" had been ordered to Havana he called his staff together and told them that the Americans must be treated with courtesy for if there were any overt act the "Maine" might bombard the city. He said, however, that Captain Sigsbee might demand the release of a man or that they should refrain from executing a man because he was an American citizen, and threaten to fire on the city unless the demand were granted, in which case there would be serious trouble. To meet such a demand he proposed that a bomb be prepared and sunk near the place at which the "Maine" was to be moored. Then if the demand were made the bomb could be exploded before the captain had time to fire. The forts could not fire on the "Maine" as the shots would enter the city. So, according to this account a bomb was made from a disused boiler. The wires were run from it to a private house so that if they were found before anything happened the government could disclaim any responsibility. The rebels learned of this and they planned to use the bomb for their own purposes. Because of the currents in the harbor the "Maine" would swing about its anchorage. The plan of the rebels was to explode the bomb when the ship was far enough away from it to escape serious injury. The explosion would be regarded by the Americans as an attempt to blow up the ship and they would intervene on the side of those who were fighting Spanish rule. But the location of the bomb was miscalculated and when it was exploded it wrecked the ship.

The Boston *Herald* on March 25, 1912, printed a despatch from its Washington correspondent containing interviews with naval officers expressing the opinion that the account in the New York *Sun* was substantially accurate. An unnamed rear admiral was represented as saying "I have heard in whispers from persons who assured me that they had learned to their own satisfaction that the mine was manufactured and placed near the 'Maine' by the officers of the government in control then in Havana." Another officer told the story that he had from an officer who had been on duty in Havana for some time after the explosion. According to this officer the bomb was made from an old buoy or boiler and connected with the shore by an electric cable. It was made by the Havana authorities who planned to blow up the "Maine" if war were declared. It was carried to a spot near the "Maine" on a lighter, the lighter which, according to Captain Sigsbee before the Naval Court, had come near fouling the "Maine." It was running without lights contrary to harbor regulations. The lighter, however, had already placed the mine between two buoys marking the channel which the captain would have to take in leaving the harbor. According to this account the mine was placed on the night of February 14. The rebels learned of it the next day and they planned to explode the mine without hurting the ship.

These accounts, whether authentic or not, belong in any history of the event.

FEBRUARY SIXTEENTH

BIRTHDAY OF CUSHING EELLS

Cushing Eells, a missionary to the Indians in the Northwest and founder of Whitman College at Walla Walla, Wash., was once characterized by Dr. Theodore T. Munger, a distinguished Congregationalist clergyman, as "the greatest saint of modern times." He was born in Massachusetts on February 16, 1810. On the centennial anniversary of his birth there was a celebration in his honor at Whitman College. The anniversary has been observed every year since then at the college and by its graduates and by admirers of Dr. Eells throughout the United States. There were celebrations of the anniversary in 1935 in Europe, Asia and Africa as well as in this country.

Dr. Eells, familiarly known during the later years of his life as Father Eells, died in 1893 at the age of eighty-three years. At the time Dr. Stephen B. L. Penrose, who was president of Whitman College from 1894 until 1934, wrote a memorial pamphlet which he called *Father Eells*. On the title page are these lines from a well known hymn:

> Brothers, we are standing
> Where the saints have trod.

Dr. Penrose wrote that young Eells became a Christian when he was fifteen years old and decided to become a missionary. He graduated from

130

Williams College in 1834, and from Hartford Theological Seminary, at
the time the East Windsor Theological Institute, in 1837. He chose
South Africa as his field of work, and was commissioned as a missionary
to the Zulus, by the American Board of Commissioners of Foreign Missions. A war among the Zulus, however, prevented him from going to
Africa.

The churches in the East had become interested in the Indians
through the visit of some chiefs to St. Louis who sought information
about the white man's God. The Reverend Jason Lee started for Oregon
in 1834 to take the white man's Book to the Indians and in the same year
Dr. Samuel Parker was commissioned by the American Board to explore
the region and make a report. Two years later Dr. Marcus Whitman and
his wife organized a party of missionaries and crossed the continent in a
wagon and began their work among the Indians. In 1838 Cushing Eells
and his bride were sent to Oregon. It took them a year to reach what is
now Eastern Washington. They began their work among the Spokane
Indians in the spring of 1839. He built a log cabin with pine boughs for
a roof and a table of three boards on stakes. He lived there for nine
years, preaching to the Indians and teaching them. On November 29,
1847, Dr. Whitman, his wife and twelve others were killed in an Indian
uprising, and Eells and his family had to flee for their lives, and took
refuge in the Willamette Valley. As soon as the Indian wars were over
he returned to the Whitman mission. When he stood over the grave of
his friend he had a vision of a school for the Christian education of the
young people of the region, which became a reality in Whitman College
at Walla Walla, now an institution with about five hundred students and
an adequate faculty.

Eells had begun as a foreign missionary among the Spokane Indians.
He now became a home missionary without salary and devoted himself
to the white settlers who were moving into the Walla Walla valley. He
earned his living by farming on the old mission claim so that he might
preach on Sunday. Late in 1859 he obtained from the territorial legislature of Washington a charter for Whitman Seminary. It had been
intended to establish the school at the Whitman mission at Wailatpu,
but as Walla Walla was growing rapidly it was established there. The
first building was dedicated in October 1866, and Mr. Eells assumed
charge of the school soon after it was opened. He had been elected
school superintendent of the county, but he devoted five days of the week
to teaching and attended to his official duties on the sixth. He continued
his preaching and traveled about Washington founding churches. It is
said that every Congregational church in the state east of the Cascade
Mountains was either organized by him or helped by gifts from him.
It is estimated that out of his meager earnings he gave $12,000 to these
churches and when he died in 1893 he left $5000, about all that he

possessed, to Whitman College. He helped organize the churches at The Dalles, Walla Walla, Skokomish, Colfax, Chewelah, Cheney, Medical Lake, Spokane and Sprague and served as pastor of six of them. He gave bells to nine churches. When he died Lyman Abbott said of him: "A man of quiet and beautiful character, of unsurpassed consecration, and one to whom the republic of the United States owes a far greater debt than to many who have occupied a more conspicuous place in its history." If he had lived in the tenth century his name would have appeared in the calendar of saints of the church with a day set apart to be observed as his festival. His day is celebrated, however, by the inheritors of the beneficence of his life.

REPUBLIC OF LITHUANIA DAY

In 1935 a joint resolution of the General Assembly of Maryland directed that the governor should proclaim February 16 of each year for the observance and commemoration of the founding of the Republic of Lithuania. During the First World War Russian control of Lithuania was displaced by German, and on February 16, 1918, the Lithuanians declared themselves independent, the United States recognizing the government of the Republic of Lithuania *de jure* on June 28, 1922. The Honorable Antanas Smetona was elected the first president on April 6, 1919, and, except for a period of a few months in 1926, continued as president for upward of two decades.

This resolution of the Maryland Assembly followed the same form as that which directed observance of Republic of Czechoslovakia Day on October 28, a similar commemorative holiday also created in 1935. The resolution declared it fitting that the recurring anniversary of "this great sister Republic in Europe" should be commemorated with "suitable patriotic and public exercises." It further directed that the governor should call upon the state officials to display the flag of the United States on all government buildings on February 16, and that he should invite the citizens to observe the day in schools and churches with appropriate ceremonies.

Accordingly, in various communities in Maryland where persons of Lithuanian descent have settled, the anniversary is celebrated by banquets, special religious services, and patriotic speeches. In Baltimore a banquet is usually held at Lithuanian Hall, 851 Hollins Street, and there are special commemorative services at St. Alphonsus, the Lithuanian Roman Catholic Church. The Governor of Maryland, ex-governors, judges, the consul general of Lithuania, and other distinguished persons, are guests and speakers at the banquet, which is accompanied by a musical program with a well known orchestra and soloists who render songs suitable to the occasion.

FEBRUARY SEVENTEENTH

FRANCES E. WILLARD DAY

Miss Frances E. Willard, noted for her success in promoting the work of the Woman's Christian Temperance Union and in organizing the World Woman's Christian Temperance Union, died on February 17, 1898. At the national convention of the Union in St. Paul, Minn., in that year it was voted to observe annually the date of her death and to establish in her honor a memorial fund to be used in organizing new branches and strengthening weak ones and promoting the work in other ways. The money was to be raised by asking each local union in the United States to hold a public meeting on February 17 in commemoration of the life and work of Miss Willard, and to take up a collection from which $2 should be sent to the national treasury of the union. The suggestion was adopted and the memorial meeting has been held ever since. The fund thus raised is administered by the national corresponding secretary with offices in Evanston, Ill. It has been used to support the work of twenty-four state organizations and to promote it in three of the territorial dependencies of the United States.

The *Union Signal*, the official organ of the Woman's Christian Temperance Union, offered in its January number a program for the celebration in 1934. It began with the song, "O, Master, let me walk with Thee." This was followed by what was described as a Scripture Mosaic made up of passages from the Bible which Miss Willard had marked during her life. Then there was a brief talk on the outstanding memorial to Miss Willard in the state in which the meetings were held. Preceding an address on the secret of the influence of Miss Willard, the following poem by Ray Nance Smethers was read:

> Frances Willard—brave and fearless,
> Frances Willard, regal, peerless.
> Ever thy name shall honored be,
> Ever our love shall follow thee.
>
> Never soul more noble, royal;
> Never heart more true, loyal;
> Never one with courage stronger,
> Never Patience striving longer.
>
> None with vision more sublime,
> None such seer in her time,
> None more dauntless to inspire,
> None more quick to raise men higher.
>
> How we need thy faith, thy power,
> In the problems of this hour!
> How we crave thy radiant hope
> As in darkness now we grope!

133

Why should we not dangers dare
Since thy deeds beyond compare?
Why should we give up the battle?
We are men—not "driven cattle."

What's the secret of thy life?
"Trust in God nor shun the strife.
In His strength be not afraid;
Right will win; be not dismayed."

Give thy wisdom, leader peerless!
Give thy courage, leader fearless!
Eager, brave to do our part,
Let us ne'er be faint of heart.

We admire thine every trait;
Thy example we emulate;
Never will we quit the fight
Till He conquers with His might!

After the address a quartette sang "We are coming, dear leader," and there was a final address followed by the collection for the memorial fund.

Miss Willard was born in 1839 at Churchville, N.Y. She was graduated from the Northwestern Female College at Evanston, Ill., in 1859, and was principal of the Genesee Wesleyan Seminary at Lima, N.Y., in 1866 and 1867. She then traveled two years in Europe and on her return to this country became professor of esthetics at Northwestern University and dean of the Woman's College. In 1874 she was elected corresponding secretary of the Woman's Christian Temperance Union which had been organized that year at a meeting in Cleveland, Ohio, assembled in response to a call issued from Chautauqua, N.Y., signed by Mrs. Mattie McClellan Brown, Mrs. Jennie Fowler Willing and others. It was attended by women from sixteen states and was the first of a series of annual conventions which has continued to the present. Mrs. Annie Wittenmeyer was the first president. She was succeeded in 1879 by Miss Willard who held the office until her death. The declaration of principles of the organization, adopted when it was founded in 1874, was written by Miss Willard. Besides containing a pledge of total abstinence from all intoxicants the declaration stated that:

We believe in the golden rule and that each man's habits of life should be an example safe and beneficent for every other man to follow; we believe that God created man and woman in His own image, and therefore we believe in one standard of purity for both men and women, and in the equal right of all to hold opinions and to express the same with equal freedom; we believe in a living wage; in an eight hour day, in courts of conciliation and arbitration, in justice as opposed to greed of gain, and in "Peace on earth and good will to men."

Miss Willard became one of the most famous women of her time and when the State of Illinois decided to honor two of its citizens in

Statuary Hall in the National Capitol at Washington it selected her as one of them. And there she stands, a full length figure of white marble, the only woman thus honored. Katherine Lent Stevenson, after looking upon the statue, wrote:

> Stand, radiant soul!
> Here in the center of our Nation's heart,
> Forever of its best life thou'rt a part;
> Here shalt thou draw thy land to what thou art,
> Stand, radiant soul.

FEBRUARY EIGHTEENTH

INAUGURATION OF JEFFERSON DAVIS

Jefferson Davis, who was elected United States Senator from Mississippi in 1847, had become the acknowledged leader of the Southerners by 1857. In a speech in the Senate on January 10, 1861, he maintained that the states had the constitutional right to secede from the Union and that Congress had no right to interfere with the domestic institutions of any state. When Mississippi adopted its resolution of secession he left the Senate and cast his fortunes in with his state. On February 9, 1861, he was elected President of the provisional government of the Confederacy, formed at Montgomery, Ala. He was formally inaugurated on February 18, 1861, and began to organize the new government. He was recognized as the leader of the state's rights cause and the choice of him as the head of the Confederacy was generally approved throughout the South (see Jefferson Davis' Birthday, June 3).

FEBRUARY NINETEENTH

DECISION ON VALIDITY OF THE INITIATIVE AND REFERENDUM

A legislative device under which the citizens are allowed to propose laws and to pass them by popular vote, originating in Switzerland, was first adopted in the United States by Oregon in 1902. About a score of other states followed the example of Oregon. The validity of this method of legislation was disputed and a test case was taken to the Supreme Court of the United States for final decision. That court decided on February 19, 1912, that the initiative and referendum were political devices the adoption of which lay within the discretion of the people of the states and that when adopted the courts must accept them. When Ohio attempted to submit the question of the ratification of an amend-

135

ment to the Federal Constitution to the voters the validity of such ratification was disputed and this case was taken to the Supreme Court which
decided that a state had no power to change the method of amending
the Constitution laid down in that document which provides that amendments shall be submitted to the legislatures of the states or to conventions
in the states called for the purpose of considering them.

OHIO ADMITTED TO UNION

See January 22, Ohio's First Legislature

FEBRUARY TWENTIETH

BIRTHDAY OF JOSEPH JEFFERSON

Joseph Jefferson, one of the most distinguished actors of his generation, was born in Philadelphia, Pa., on February 20, 1829. His birthplace, at the corner of Sixth and Spruce Streets in that city, is marked by
a bronze tablet. His father, grandfather and great grandfather had been
actors before him. His career on the stage began at the age of three
when he played the child in "Pizarro." In 1838 his father began playing
in Western and Southern cities and died of yellow fever in Mobile, Ala.,
in 1842. The son spent the next few years as a strolling actor with
various companies. He became a member of Laura Keene's company in
New York in 1857 and played Dr. Pangloss in "The Heir-at-Law." The
next year he played with E. A. Sothern in "Our American Cousin," and
then began a search for a character both humorous and pathetic around
which a play could be written. He finally settled on Washington Irving's
Rip Van Winkle and wrote a short play about him, but as it was unsatisfactory he had Dion Boucicault amplify and rewrite it. The resulting play was acted by him throughout the United States for many years,
winning for him both fame and fortune. He owned a large plantation
in Louisiana and when not acting spent the winters there. He also owned
a summer place on Buzzard's Bay, Mass., adjoining that occupied by
President Cleveland and the two frequently went fishing together. He
wrote an autobiography. He was a member of the American Academy
of Arts and Letters. He died in 1905.

FEBRUARY TWENTY-FIRST

DEDICATION OF THE WASHINGTON MONUMENT

The project for a monument in the national capital in honor of the
first President originated early in the nineteenth century with the Wash-

ington National Monument Association. Robert Mills, who had supervised the construction of the post office, the patent office and treasury buildings, was chosen as the architect. He planned a granite shaft faced with white marble, six hundred feet high, fifty-five feet square at the base and thirty feet square at the top. The monument association asked for contributions of money to build the structure. After fifteen years it had obtained $87,000. A site was then selected—the site which Washington himself had chosen for a memorial to the American Revolution—and work was begun. The cornerstone was laid on July 4, 1848, and Robert C. Winthrop, Speaker of the House of Representatives, delivered an appropriate oration. Work was abandoned in 1856 as the funds of the association had been exhausted and an appeal for more had met with no response. The monument had risen to one hundred and fifty feet of the proposed height. Completion of the structure was authorized by Congress in 1877, and it was finished on December 6, 1884, when the capstone weighing thirty-three hundred pounds was put in place. Arrangements were made by Congress for its dedication and on Saturday, February 21, 1885, ceremonies were held at the base of the monument and in the House of Representatives. The orator of the occasion was Robert C. Winthrop who had spoken at the laying of the cornerstone thirty-seven years earlier. The monument is five hundred and fifty-five feet, five and one-eighth inches in height, and cost $1,300,000. The top is reached by a flight of eight hundred and ninety-eight steps and also by an elevator. Its white marble exterior, stained by the weather, was cleaned in 1934.

The first public monument to Washington was erected in Baltimore. The cornerstone was laid on July 4, 1815, but it was several years before it was completed. It gave to Baltimore the title of Monument City. But before the Baltimore monument was dedicated the people of Boonsboro, Md., erected a cairn of stones fifty-four feet in circumference and fifteen feet high on July 4, 1827, in honor of the father of his country. It was in North Carolina in 1775 that the first town was named for Washington when the Forks of Tar River voted to take the new name.

FEBRUARY TWENTY-SECOND

WASHINGTON'S BIRTHDAY

The custom of celebrating the anniversary of the birth of George Washington, now general throughout the United States, was of slow growth. The first observance of the day outside of Washington's immediate family of which any record has been found occurred at Valley Forge in the winter of 1778 when the band of the Fourth Continental Artillery marched to headquarters there and serenaded the commander. In 1781, Comte de Rochambeau, commander of the French forces aiding the revo-

137

lutionists, declared a holiday for his troops in honor of the anniversary, and the French and American officers celebrated at a dinner. This was on February 12, as February 11, the anniversary old style, occurred on Sunday. It was many years before the new calendar came into general use with the adoption of February 22 as the date of the anniversary. New York claims the honor of being the first to hold a celebration, as on the evening of February 22, 1783, a company of gentlemen met at a hotel for dinner, and made speeches in praise of Washington. They decided to meet annually thereafter for that purpose. But the claim of New York is disputed by Richmond, Va., where the anniversary was celebrated on February 11, 1782. There was a celebration in that year also at Talbot Court House, Md., and a celebration in Cambridge, Mass., in 1783, the year of the New York dinner. In 1790, during Washington's first year in the presidency, Congress adjourned in honor of the anniversary and extended its congratulations to him. The Tammany Society of New York celebrated the day in the same year. The day was observed in Philadelphia, then the national capital, in 1791 with a parade of militia. The *Gazette* in its report of the event said:

Yesterday being the anniversary of the birthday of the President of the United States, when he attained the fifty-ninth year of his age, the same was celebrated here with every demonstration of public joy. The artillery and light infantry corps-of this city paraded and at 12 o'clock a federal salute was fired. The congratulatory compliments of the members of the Legislature of the Union, the heads of the departments of the Union, foreign ministers, officers civil and military of the State, the reverend clergy and strangers and citizens of distinction were presented to the President on this auspicious occasion.

In 1793, however, when the Assembly ball was postponed from its usual date to February 22 in honor of Washington the political opponents of the President in the city criticised the managers of the ball severely for showing undue deference to him and the celebration was denounced as idolatrous. Notwithstanding these objections the ball was held on the appointed day, guns were fired and bells were rung and there was the usual parade of the militia, the officers of which called upon the President to pay their respects as in the past. In 1796, however, when the usual resolution for adjournment on the day was introduced in Congress it was defeated and Congress continued in session. The partisans of the congressional majority throughout the country omitted all notice of the anniversary and the celebrations arranged by the friends of the President were slimly attended.

When John Adams succeeded Washington to the presidency he took official notice of the anniversary and encouraged its celebration, but Thomas Jefferson ignored the day, and for a long time it was observed sporadically. The observance of February 22, instead of February 11, did not become general until after 1796.

The feeling that the celebration of the anniversary was intended as a partisan political demonstration did not disappear with the retirement of Washington from the presidency. Sharf and Westcott, in their *History of Philadelphia*, recounting the customs of the early nineteenth century, say:

Washington's birthday was an occasion for processions, orations and banquets, and it should have been a national holiday, in which all the people would have participated, were it not that the societies most prominently engaged in the celebration being entirely composed of Federalists, the Democrats came to consider the twenty-second of February as a political anniversary, and they abstained from participating in the ceremonies directed by their political opponents. This abstention extended even to the volunteer companies not in sympathy with the Federalists.

Political partisanship, however, did not seriously interfere with the first observance of his birthday following his death. He died on December 14, 1799. Philadelphia was then the national capital and Congress was in session there. One of its last acts before adjourning to meet in the District of Columbia was the adoption of a resolution recommending that February 22, 1800, he observed throughout the country with exercises intended to express the popular esteem for the first President. The suggestion was widely acted upon and such exercises were held in many cities. In Philadelphia the Freemasons and the Society of the Cincinnati arranged special observances. The Freemasons met at their hall in the State House and marched to Zion church where a eulogistic oration was delivered and odes in the German language were sung by a select choir. Another memorial oration was delivered in St. Mary's church, and at the German Reformed church, where the members of the Society of the Cincinnati gathered, another address was delivered by an officer of the army. The exercises at the church were preceded by a parade from the State House led by the First City Troop, followed by other military organizations. Preceding the members of the society a horse was led "caparisoned in full war-trappings, bearing a portmanteau, holsters, saddle, and having thrown across him a pair of military jack-boots, a uniform coat, a sword and a cocked hat." President John Adams, Vice President Thomas Jefferson, members of the Senate and the House of Representatives and the British minister to the United States were among those attending the services at the church. All business was suspended during the day and no unnecessary work was done.

The University of Pennsylvania has probably held exercises regularly in honor of the anniversary longer than any other institution. The faculty of the university marched in a body to the President's house in Philadelphia in 1794 to congratulate him on his birthday. In 1826 the trustees voted to make February 22 University Day and to celebrate it every year. In the catalogue for 1829 it is stated that "the twenty-second of February shall be devoted to some public exercises in the college chapel adapted in part to the day." For many years this celebration received only local attention, but since the latter part of the nineteenth century it has become national. In 1898 President McKinley was the orator. In succeeding years President Theodore Roosevelt, President Taft, Chief Justice Hughes of the Supreme Court and other distinguished men have been glad to take part in the annual celebration.

On the hundredth anniversary of his birth in 1832 communities which had hitherto taken no particular notice of the day held celebrations. It was the first official celebration in Boston. What happened in New York was described by Philip Hone in his diary. He wrote:

> This has been a jubilee in New York, the centennial anniversary of the birth of Washington. We had the firing of cannons and ringing of bells. At the new Dutch church two odes, composed by Samuel Woodworth, were sung, and an oration read by General Morgan Lewis. He was one of the small band remaining of the Revolutionary heroes. In the evening the City Hall, the theatres and several other public buildings were illuminated. A grand ball was given by the militia officers and other citizens in the City Hotel. It was like all holiday balls, crowded and mixed, dull and tiresome. I was glad to get home. Silas E. Burroughs brought with him from Virginia the tent of General Washington, his sword, pistols, and a piece of the coffin which covered the leader. The sword is that which was presented to Washington by the President of Congress when he resigned command of the army.

Another interesting contemporary account of a celebration occurs in the diary of Joseph Sill, a Philadelphia merchant, under the date of February 22, 1836:

> The day, made sacred by the birth of so great a man as Washington, passed by with but little attention or demonstration of feeling. On account of the snow in the streets the military did not turn out. What rare soldiers! And with the exception of the roasted bullock and the rather unusual throng in the streets, nothing testified the attachment of the people of this generation to him who was "first in war, first in peace and first in the hearts of his countrymen."

The celebration of the hundredth anniversary of the birth of Washington was pale and insignificant in comparison with the celebration of the two hundredth anniversary in 1932. Congress appointed a commission to make the necessary arrangements for a celebration to continue for many months. President Hoover issued a proclamation on February 2 in which he said:

> The happy opportunity has come to our generation to demonstrate our gratitude and obligation to George Washington by a fitting celebration of the two hundredth anniversary of his birth. To contemplate his unselfish devotion to duty, his courage, his patience, his genius, his statesmanship and his accomplishments for his country and the world, refreshes the spirit, the wisdom and the patriotism of our people. Therefore, I, Herbert Hoover, President of the United States, acting in accord with the purposes of Congress, do invite all our people to organize themselves throughout every community and every association to do honor to the memory of Washington during the period from February 22 to Thanksgiving Day.

The celebration began in Washington on February 22 with an address by the President before a joint session of the two houses of Congress. In the course of his address the President described the government of which Washington was the first head. He said:

It comprises a political system of self-government by the majority, resting upon the duties of individual men to the community and of the local communities to the Nation. It is a government designed in spirit to sustain a dual purpose— to protect our people among nations by a great national power and to preserve individual freedom by local self-government. It comprises a social system free of inherited position, based upon the ideal of equality of men before the law, the equal privilege of men to strive and to achieve and the responsibilities of men to their neighbors. It embraces an economic system based upon the largest degree of freedom and stimulation to initiative and enterprise which can be permitted and still maintain the ideal of equality of opportunity among men.

The address was followed by the singing of patriotic songs by massed choruses at the east front of the Capitol. The President then went to Alexandria, Va., where he reviewed a military parade and thence he went to Mount Vernon and laid a wreath on the tomb of Washington. A symbolic masque by Percy Mackaye was presented in the evening with chorus singing and tableaux representing historic events.

The Post Office Department issued a series of twelve memorial stamps, each showing a portrait of Washington taken from paintings by well known artists or from busts or statues by famous sculptors. The portrait on the half-cent stamp was from a miniature by Charles Wilson Peale and the Gilbert Stuart portrait of 1795 appeared on the ten-cent stamp. These were put on sale early in the year. In the succeeding months celebrations of various kinds were held in different parts of the country. An exhibition of paintings by American artists was held in Washington. Memorial trees were planted in parks and squares in different cities and on the grounds of public schools.

It was not in America alone that the anniversary year was noted. In forty foreign countries in Europe, Asia and South America there were special celebrations on the Fourth of July in honor of Washington. In many foreign cities streets and squares were renamed for him, and the heads of the governments attended meetings to celebrate his greatness. The official observances of the anniversary year were formally brought to an end on November 24 by the placing of a wreath at the base of the Washington monument in the national capital.

February 22 is now a legal holiday in every state of the Union, and in the District of Columbia and the territories.

LOWELL'S BIRTHDAY

The anniversary of the birth of James Russell Lowell, poet, essayist and diplomatist, is observed with more or less regularity in the public schools of many states. The celebration is voluntary and is arranged for the purpose of directing the attention of the pupils to the work of Lowell as a man of letters. Sometimes the principal of the school con-

141

tents himself with calling attention to the birth of Lowell on this date and conducts exercises in honor of the birth of Washington. At other times the classes in English literature prepare a program which includes essays on the poet. And in still other cases the whole morning or after-noon session of the school is devoted to a celebration.

The Superintendent of Schools of West Virginia, in order to en-courage the schools to observe the day, sent out a suggested program. It began with a sketch of Lowell's life and an outline of his writings. This was to be followed by recitations by the pupils of "The Fountain," "The Fatherland," "The Heritage," and the reading of the prelude to the first part of "The Vision of Sir Launfal." At the conclusion of the reading it was suggested that the teacher tell the story of the Holy Grail and call attention to Tennyson's poem on the same subject. Then some extracts from *The Biglow Papers* were to be read with an explanation of their place in American political history. The exercises were to close with a sketch of the anti-slavery movement in the promotion of which *The Biglow Papers* had a part.

James Russell Lowell was born in Cambridge, Mass., on February 22, 1819. He was graduated from Harvard College in 1838 and entered the law school of the college in the autumn. He was graduated from that school but never practiced law, preferring to devote himself to litera-ture. His first volume of poems was published in 1841. Two years later he joined with Robert Carter in editing *The Pioneer*, a literary and critical magazine which survived only a few months. Among the con-tributors to this magazine were Poe, Hawthorne, Whittier and Elizabeth Barrett who later became the wife of Robert Browning. He spent 1851 and 1852 in Europe studying Italian art and literature. In 1855 he was appointed Smith professor of modern languages in Harvard college, to succeed Henry Wadsworth Longfellow who had resigned. He held this post until 1877. In 1857 he became editor of the *Atlantic Monthly* and continued as its editor until 1862. From 1864 to 1872 he was joint editor of the *North American Review*. He wrote his "Commemoration Ode," regarded as probably his best poem, to be read at the exercises at Harvard in 1865, in memory of the students and graduates who had fallen in the Civil War. In 1877 President Hayes appointed Mr. Lowell as minister to Spain and three years later he was transferred to London. He remained in London until 1885. On his return to America he wrote much literary criticism of a high order. He died on August 12, 1891.

FEBRUARY TWENTY-THIRD

BIRTHDAY OF EMMA WILLARD

Emma Hart Willard, pioneer in education for women, was born February 23, 1787, in Berlin, Conn. She married Dr. John Willard in

1809, and in 1814 opened a boarding-school for girls in Middlebury, Conn. Her theories on the importance of female education were very advanced for her time, but the first teaching venture was sufficiently successful to enable her to secure the establishment of a seminary for girls at Waterford, N.Y., in 1819, which was partly supported by the state. The school was removed to Troy, N.Y., in 1821, and became celebrated as the Troy Female Academy. It is now known as the Emma Willard School. In 1830 she published a book of poems, of which the best known is "Rocked in the Cradle of the Deep." She died in 1870 and, in recognition of the importance of her life work, is represented in the Hall of Fame.

THE BATTLE OF BUENA VISTA

The most brilliant battle in the war between Mexico and the United States was fought at Buena Vista, a small settlement on the San Juan river, beginning with a skirmish on the afternoon of February 22, 1847, and ending with the complete victory of the Americans on the afternoon of February 23. General Zachary Taylor, in command of a force of about forty-eight hundred, had occupied a strong position on February 21 and awaited attack by General Santa Anna with twenty thousand Mexicans. Jefferson Davis, who was then a captain, distinguished himself for gallantry during the battle. When the fighting ended on February 23 Santa Anna knew he was defeated and he retreated southward the next morning. The victory weakened the Mexicans and thus contributed to the success of General Winfield Scott's campaign around Mexico City.

FEBRUARY TWENTY-FOURTH

FEAST OF ST. MATTHIAS

St. Matthias, whose feast is celebrated on February 24, is the Apostle selected to take the place of Judas who betrayed Jesus. The account of his selection is told in the first chapter of the Acts of the Apostles. Peter standing up "in the midst of the disciples" of whom there were about one hundred and twenty, explained the inevitability of the betrayal as in fulfillment of prophecy and said that a successor to Judas should be chosen. The record continues:

And they appointed two, Joseph, called Barsabas, who was surnamed Justus, and Matthias. And they prayed and said, "Thou Lord, which knowest the hearts of all men, show whether of these two thou has chosen that he may take part of this ministry and apostleship from which Judas, by transgression fell, that he might go to his own place." And they gave forth their lots and the lot fell upon Matthias; and he was numbered with the eleven apostles.

143

FEBRUARY 24

There is nothing authentic known about him beyond this account of his selection. There is a tradition that he preached in Judea and then in Colchis. This appears in an ancient document which reads:

Matthias preached the gospel to barbarians and cannibals in the interior of Ethiopia (Colchis) at the harbor of the sea of Hyssus, at the mouth of the river Phasis. He died at Sebastopolis and was buried there near the Temple of the Sun.

Another tradition is that he was stoned by the Jews at Jerusalem and then beheaded. The Greek church celebrates his feast on August 9.

BIRTHDAY OF CHESTER WILLIAM NIMITZ

Chester William Nimitz, who became commander in chief of the United States Pacific Fleet in World War II, was born February 24, 1885, in Fredericksburg, Tex., a German-American settlement which his grandfather, Captain Charles H. Nimitz, helped found about the middle of the nineteenth century. A few years after his birth his parents, Chester Bernhard and Anna Henke Nimitz, moved to Kerrville, Tex., where young Chester attended the public schools. He wanted to go to West Point, but lack of vacancies there and impending competitive examinations for Annapolis settled the problem for him, and in 1901 he was appointed to the Naval Academy. In 1905, having completed his four-year course, he was ordered to the "Ohio" at San Francisco with several members of his class and they had "a fine cruise to Manila." From there he went on to serve on various ships on the China station, including the "Panay," sailing home on the "Ranger" via Singapore and the Suez Canal in 1908. Meanwhile, he had been commissioned ensign in 1907 and, when he asked for duty on a battleship, was given a submarine assignment. This was at a time when "under-sea craft were regarded as a cross between a Jules Verne fantasy and a whale." Only four years out of Annapolis and still an ensign, he took command of the "Plunger." In 1910 he was promoted to lieutenant second grade, and then to lieutenant, and commanded the "Narwhal." In 1912 he commanded the "Skipjack" and while on this submarine won a Silver Life Saving Medal for rescuing a fireman from drowning. At the same time that he commanded the "Skipjack" he was also commander of the Atlantic Submarine Flotilla which comprised all the submarines in the Atlantic, together with the tenders "Castine" and "Tonapah." He then received a shore assignment visiting the diesel engine shops of Belgium and Germany, and thereafter spent about two and a half years at the Navy Yard in New York City. During this period he built the diesel engines for the oil tanker "Maumee" and, in the fall of 1916, was assigned as executive officer and chief engineer of the tanker with the rank of lieutenant commander. In August 1917 he was assigned to the staff of Admiral Robison, who commanded the submarine force in the Atlantic Fleet, and for his service during World War I Lieutenant Commander Nimitz was awarded a

144

special Letter of Commendation by the Navy Department. At the end of the war, after a short period in the Navy Department, he went to sea as executive officer of the "South Carolina." Again in 1920 he went to sea as commander of the "Chicago" with additional duty as commander of Submarine Division 14, and commanding officer of the submarine base at Pearl Harbor. For his service on the "Chicago" he received a Victory Medal with Escort Clasp and, in June 1922, reported for a course of instruction at the Naval War College. A year later he went to sea once more as aide on the staff of the commander in chief of the Battle Fleet with additional duty as assistant chief of staff. In October 1925 he reported as aide on the staff of the commander in chief of the United States Fleet, and the following year was ordered to the University of California to install a Naval Reserve Officers' Training Corps unit. He remained there three years, completing the work in June 1929, and was then ordered to command Submarine Division 20. While at the University he had become a captain, but in 1931 his title was changed to commander, Submarine Division 12, and in June he was given command of the U.S.S. "Rigel" and destroyers out of commission. From 1933 to 1935 he commanded the "Augusta" and next, from 1935 to 1938, served as assistant chief of the Bureau of Navigation in the Navy Department.

His first command as a rear admiral came in June 1938 when he was ordered to Cruiser Division 2, Battle Force. He was transferred to duty as commander of Battleship Division One, Battle Force, and remained there until June 15, 1939, when he assumed duty as Chief of the Bureau of Navigation. In this post Admiral Nimitz was rated in service circles as second only to Admiral Stark, Chief of Naval Operations. His job was to take full charge of personnel, including the setting up of a new officer-training program which proved so effective he was able to announce to the House Naval Affairs Committee that "probably many of the admirals of the future will never have been to Annapolis."

On December 17, 1941, he was promoted from rear admiral to admiral and ordered to replace Admiral Husband E. Kimmel, who had been relieved of his command pending the outcome of the investigation of the Pearl Harbor disaster. As commander in chief of the Pacific Fleet Admiral Nimitz returned to the scene of much of his early training and experience, immediately meeting with the other admirals in this theatre to plan the war strategy. Their plans were necessarily kept secret and to the question, "What is the Pacific Fleet doing?" the Admiral's only answer was the Hawaiian phrase "hoomana wa mu," which means, be patient. However, in June 1942, as the master strategist behind the heroic Battle of Midway, he announced that "a momentous victory is in the making—Pearl Harbor has now been partially avenged." Later he stated that Japanese personnel losses in the Coral Sea and Midway battles were at least ten times greater than those of the United States and that enemy plane losses were in the same proportion. He was awarded the Distinguished Service Medal in July 1942 for "exceptionally meritorious service as commander in chief of the Pacific Fleet." At a ceremony in which he decorated thirty-four heroes of the battle of the Solomon Islands, Admiral Nimitz told of his visit to the territory won by the Marines and commented on the fact that the United States forces learned very quickly to fight successful jungle warfare, going on to speak optimistically of the future course of the war. In December 1942, the anniversary of Pearl Harbor, he declared at a press conference that the United States forces would sweep the Japanese from the Aleutians and repeated his optimistic prophecies, but predicted a long struggle and increasing sacrifices. His predictions of ultimate victory were fulfilled September 2, 1945, when Japan formally surrendered, her home islands bombed and blockaded and her navy demolished.

FEBRUARY TWENTY-FIFTH

THE NATIONAL BANK ACT

The Civil War made it necessary for the government to borrow large amounts. Soon after the war began it was proposed to permit the banks to organize under a new law and issue circulating notes based on bonds. It was some time, however, before Congress was able to agree on a definite plan. Finally in February 1863, the National Bank Act was passed and signed by President Lincoln on February 25. This act with the amendments later adopted regulated the capital of the banks according to population with a minimum of $50,000 in cities with less than six thousand inhabitants. At least 30 per cent of the capital was to be invested in government bonds upon which the banks could issue circulation notes up to 90 per cent of the par value of the bonds, redeemable in lawful money on demand. It was hoped that a market for the bonds would thus be created. The plan did not work as well as was expected. But when an act was passed in March 1865, imposing a tax of 10 per cent on the circulating notes of state banks more than a thousand such banks took out national charters. One of the purposes of the tax was to force the notes of the state banks out of circulation, and it was effective.

THE SIXTEENTH AMENDMENT

The sixteenth amendment to the Constitution was proposed to the state legislatures by the 61st Congress in 1909, and was declared ratified by the Secretary of State on February 25, 1913. This amendment provided for a federal income tax, stating specifically that "the Congress shall have power to lay and collect taxes on incomes, from whatever sources derived, without apportionment among the several states, and without regard to any census or enumeration." It was the first constitutional amendment adopted in the twentieth century, the most recent previous amendment, the fifteenth which provides for equal rights for white and colored citizens, having been adopted in 1870.

FEBRUARY TWENTY-SIXTH

BIRTHDAY OF WILLIAM F. CODY

William F. Cody, better known as Buffalo Bill, who was born in Scott County, Iowa, on February 26, 1846, was noted in the West as a scout and Indian fighter before he became known in the East and in Europe as the proprietor of his Wild West Show. But before he organized that show his career had been used by Colonel Judson, who wrote under the name of Ned Buntline, in a series of Western adventure stories widely read by boys. His father moved to Salt Creek Valley, near Fort Leavenworth, Kansas, in 1854 and died in 1857. The son, then eleven years old, was employed as a mounted messenger by a freighting firm. In 1860, when only fourteen, he was hired as a pony express rider and in 1863 he served as a scout with the Ninth Kansas Cavalry Regiment in its operations against the Indians. He enlisted in the army in 1864 and served as a scout in Tennessee and in Missouri. In 1867 he was employed to provide buffalo meat for the builders of the Kansas Pacific Railroad and this occupation led to his being called Buffalo Bill. He was elected to the Nebraska Legislature in 1872 but declined to serve. In 1882 the citizens of North Platte, Neb., asked Cody to arrange their Fourth of July celebration. He gave a show lasting for three days in which wild buffalo were killed, bucking horses were ridden and Indians and cowboys performed. Its success led to the organization of his traveling show. He received a large grant of land from the State of Wyoming for a ranch. A town was laid out on part of it and named Cody. An equestrian statue of him has been erected there guarding the Wyoming Trail to Yellowstone Park. A Buffalo Bill Museum has been established in the town by the Buffalo Bill Memorial Association which celebrates the anniversary of his birth with appropriate ceremonies.

FEBRUARY TWENTY-SEVENTH

LONGFELLOW'S BIRTHDAY

The public schools throughout the country have for many years taken note of February 27, the anniversary of the birth of Henry Wadsworth Longfellow, one of the most popular American poets of the nineteenth century, a poet whose popularity in England during his life time rivaled

147

that of Lord Tennyson, the British poet laureate. It is impossible to discover in what school the first celebration was held. It was probably in some school named for the poet. There are many such in the United States. But the observance of the day has spread until the superintendents of schools in some states have officially recognized the anniversary by preparing suggestions for the guidance of teachers in the exercises of the day. As long ago as 1905 the Superintendent of Schools in West Virginia offered such suggestions in his biennial report. His program opened with the singing of "The Rainy Day," followed by an essay by a pupil on Longfellow's prose works. Then "The Children's Hour" and "The Village Blacksmith" were to be recited. There was to be a dramatization of a scene from "Hiawatha" and from "The Courtship of Miles Standish," and the singing of "Excelsior" and "The Arrow and the Song."

There was an elaborate celebration of the centenary of Longfellow's birth by the Historical Society of Cambridge, Mass, in 1907. Longfellow spent the greater part of his adult life in that city while serving on the faculty of Harvard University and afterward. Addresses were made by William Dean Howells, Charles W. Eliot, the president of Harvard University, Charles Eliot Norton of the university faculty, and Thomas Wentworth Higginson. Children from the public schools sang "The Village Blacksmith," arranged as a cantata.

Bowdoin College in Brunswick, Me., from which Longfellow was graduated, has always cherished his memory and frequently celebrated the anniversary of his birth. In 1910 the anniversary was observed by the Phi Beta Kappa Society of the college when William Winter delivered a memorial address on "Longfellow and American Letters." Visitors to Brunswick go to see the house in which he roomed while a student which is also the house in which Harriet Beecher Stowe wrote "Uncle Tom's Cabin." The house in which he lived as a boy in Portland now belongs to the Maine Historical Society and is preserved as a Longfellow Memorial and Museum. A reception is held there every year on February 27. The Craigie House in Cambridge, in which he lived, is also preserved in his memory. When he went to Harvard as a professor he applied for lodgings in the house which was then owned by a family that had fallen on evil days. He was youthful looking and the landlady mistook him for a student and was about to turn him away when he revealed his identity. Thereupon she gave him the best room in the house as she had read *Outre Mer* and was delighted with it. When he married his second wife—his first wife had died early—his father-in-law bought the house and gave it to the couple for a wedding present. There is a house in Pittsfield, Mass., which is also regarded as a sort of Longfellow shrine as it was of this house that he wrote "The Old Clock on the Stairs" while visiting in the town one summer.

Longfellow was born in Portland, Me., in 1807. His father, Stephen Longfellow, was a well-to-do lawyer, and his mother, Zilpah Wadsworth, was descended from John Alden and Priscilla Mullins whose story he told in "The Courtship of Miles Standish." When he was only thirteen years old he wrote poetry which was printed in the Portland *Gazette.* He was graduated from Bowdoin college in 1825, at the age of eighteen in the same class with Nathaniel Hawthorne and one class behind Franklin Pierce who later became President of the United States. He was at once elected professor of modern languages in Bowdoin, but received a leave of three years for study in Europe. He remained at Bowdoin until 1835, when he resigned and after another year of study in Europe became professor of modern languages and belles lettres at Harvard. He resigned his professorship in 1854 and devoted the remainder of his life to writing. He died on March 24, 1882. The greater part of his poetry was written after his retirement from his college professorship.

FEBRUARY TWENTY-EIGHT

EXPLOSION OF THE "PEACEMAKER"

The warship, "Princeton," lay in the Potomac in February 1844, and Captain Stockton, its commander, invited President Tyler, his Cabinet, and a large number of other guests to inspect the vessel and to take a trip for the day on the river. He especially wanted them to see a large gun called the "Peacemaker." The guests to the number of four hundred boarded the ship on February 28. The vessel steamed down the river below Fort Washington. During the passage the gun, carrying a ball weighing two hundred and twenty-five pounds, was fired several times. What a contemporary account calls "a sumptuous repast" was eaten by the guests in the dining saloon between decks. On the return trip, while most of the people were below, the captain was asked by some one who had gone above, to fire the gun again. A number of men gathered around the gun to note the effect of the shot. It was loaded with a smaller charge of powder than on the previous occasions but when the fuse was lighted the gun burst at a point three or four inches from the breach. Abel P. Upshur, Secretary of State; Thomas W. Gilmer, Secretary of the Navy; Commander Kenyon, one of the officers of the ship and Virgil Maxey, who had recently returned from The Hague as the American Minister, were instantly killed and seventeen seamen were wounded. Among those stunned by the explosion but not seriously injured were Captain Stockton himself, Senator Benton of Missouri, Lieutenant Hunt of the "Princeton," and a servant of the President's. The vessel anchored opposite Alexandria and the passengers were taken back to Washington by the steamer "Joseph Johnston." The bodies of the dead were carried to the White House and lay in state in the East room until the funeral. President Tyler sent a message to Congress concerning the disaster and the members of both houses attended the funeral. A

149

committee of investigation which was appointed exonerated Captain Stockton from blame.

FEBRUARY TWENTY-NINTH

BIRTHDAY OF ANN LEE

Ann Lee, the founder of the Shakers in America, was born in Manchester, England, on February 29, 1736. She never learned to read or write. In 1758 she joined a society called the Shaking Quakers which awaited the second coming of Christ. Four years later she married Abraham Standerin, known in Shaker history as Stanley or Standley. She bore him four children, and later became obsessed by a morbid repugnance to the marital relation. During an imprisonment in 1770 for "profanation of the Sabbath" she became impressed with the evil of marriage and when she was released preached openly against it. She had a vision in which she believed it was revealed to her that she was Christ on his second appearance. In 1774 she and her husband and several other Shakers came to America and founded a Shaker Community at what is now Watervliet, N.Y. Her husband, however, renounced the Shaker principles and went to live with another woman. Her followers called themselves "the first witnesses of the Gospel of Christ's Second Appearing," and after her death they organized a church which they called "The United Society of Believers in Christ's Second Appearing," or "The Millenial Church." They preached against war and during the Revolution Ann Lee and her elders were arrested, charged with being British sympathizers. She made a tour of New England in 1781 preaching to the small Shaker communities there. She died in 1783. The Shaker villages which she organized were communistic, the members holding all property in common. Although marriage was not forbidden, the men and women usually lived in separate houses. They built up a prosperous community at Mount Lebanon, N.Y., which farmed a large tract of ground and engaged in some small manufacturing enterprises. Similar communities were established in other parts of the country. In the course of time the membership dwindled and some of them were abandoned. One of their ablest leaders in the latter half of the nineteenth century was Frederick W. Evans of the Mount Lebanon community who wrote a history of the society and an account of its beliefs.

This account sets forth the theory that although marriage and the family must continue there is a possibility of attaining an angelic state of existence in which virginity will be essential. It is held that the virgin life is necessary in an organized communism as the family life implies private affections and economic interests which conflict with the demands of a communistic society to which all a person's interests should be devoted. They worship neither Christ nor Ann Lee nor any person but what is described as "the highest good wherever it may be found." They regard the Bible with respect but insist that it contains biographies and history which are purely secular. Their form of worship is described thus: "We sing and march to tunes of different measure and move our hands in a gathering form, expressive of one's desire to obtain the treasures of the spiritual realm. Sometimes we are led to go forth in the dance which seems to quicken the body and soul and kindle anew the fire of truth. We use some stronger means to banish the elements of worldly bondage by shaking, as an expression of our hatred of all evil; are bold in denouncing idolatry, pride, deceit, dishonesty and lust." Unlike outside churches all the members are free to speak their religious convictions and to exercise in any good gift.

LEAP YEAR

See Appendices. Calendar

St. Patrick in Ireland

MARCH

With rushing winds and gloomy skies
The dark and stubborn Winter dies;
Far-off, unseen, Spring faintly cries,
Bidding her earliest child arise;
March!

—BAYARD TAYLOR

March takes its name from Mars, an ancient Roman deity commonly regarded as the god of war, but according to some authorities, he was originally the god of vegetation. The old Saxon name was Hlyd-monath, meaning boisterous month. It was sometimes called Lencten-monath, meaning lengthening month, as the days are then perceptibly longer. The Dutch called it Lent-Maand, which refers to the same change in the length of the days. The old saying, "Mad as a March hare," alludes to the effect of the burgeoning of spring upon the temperament of the animal, as it is the mating season. March was the first month of the Roman year until the adoption of the Julian calendar in 41 B.C.. It continued to be the beginning of the legal year in England and its colonies until the eighteenth century. It was the first month of the year in France until 1564 when Charles IX, decreed that January should be the first month. England, by act of parliament, adopted the Gregorian calendar in 1752 changing the first month of the year from March to January. According to an old saying common in England and Scotland, based possibly on weather conditions, March borrowed from April the last three days in the month.

Some persons are unaware that in early colonial days the year began in March. They conclude that a transaction begun, for example, on February 27, 1720, and ending on April 2, 1721, was spread over thirteen months whereas it really lasted only a little more than a month.

MARCH FIRST

ST. DAVID'S DAY

The life of St. David, the patron saint of Wales, is commemorated on March. 1. The Welsh in America have observed the anniversary from very early times. There was a large migration of Welsh to Pennsylvania near Philadelphia at the beginning of the eighteenth century. They gave Welsh names to many settlements in that part of the state. On March 1, 1729, some Welsh citizens of Philadelphia formed the Society of Ancient Britons at a meeting at the Queen's Head Tavern. Thence they marched in procession with leeks in their hats to Christ Church where a sermon in Cymric was preached to them by the Reverend Dr. Weyman. After the sermon they returned to the tavern and dined ceremoniously with the chief men of the province as their guests. The society celebrated St. David's Day in this way for many years.

The first church in America to be named for St. David was erected in Radnor, near Philadelphia, in 1715. It was built of stone, but there is a tradition that a log church had once occupied the site. The Reverend John Chubb, a Welshman, who had been sent to America at his request by the English Society for the Propagation of the Gospel in Foreign Parts, was influential in building the church. In its early years it was used for worship by Baptists and Presbyterians as well as by members of the Church of England. But in the course of time it came under control of the Protestant Episcopal Church. The family of General Anthony Wayne has been connected with the parish almost from the beginning, and the general is supposed to be buried in its cemetery. A monument was erected over his grave by the Pennsylvania Chapter of the Society of the Cincinnati early in the nineteenth century.

The Society of Ancient Britons was succeeded in Philadelphia in 1797 by the Welsh Society, formed to aid distressed Welsh immigrants after the fashion of the Society of the Sons of St. George (see St. George's Day, April 23). Joseph Sill, a prominent Philadelphia merchant, made the following entry in his diary for March 1, 1836:

> St. David's Day. The Welsh Society gave their annual dinner which I was invited to address as an officer of the St. George's. The dinner was numerously attended and consisted of all the luxuries of the season. The toasts were heartily responded to and much good humor prevailed. After the cloth was removed we had some glees and excellent songs by amateur and professional singers and the night passed pleasantly away.

The annual dinners of this society and of the other St. David's Societies in different parts of the country, where there are persons of Welsh

153

descent, are enlivened by singing to this day. In the summer the Welsh hold singing festivals which they call Eisteddfods, a word meaning "sitting" or "session," at which there are contests in vocal and instrumental music. Whenever the Welsh assemble they always sing their national song, "Men of Harlech," or in Welsh, "Rhyfelgyrch gwyr Harlech." The song is in celebration of the defense of the castle of Harlech which Edward IV ordered the Earl of Pembroke to capture. When the earl's brother demanded that the defenders surrender the castle, Dafydd ap Jevan, the commander, replied, "I held a tower in France until all the old women in Wales heard of it, and now all the old women in France shall hear how I defend this castle." Hunger, however, forced him to surrender but he made honorable terms before opening the gate of the castle. The Welsh of the first four lines of the famous song reads:

> We le goelcerth wen yn fflamio,
> A thafodau tan yn bloeddio,
> Ar I'r dewrion ddod i daro,
> Unwaith et o'n un.

John Oxenford has turned the song into English and this is his version:

> Men of Harlech, march to glory,
> Victory is hovering o'er ye,
> Bright eyed freedom stands before ye,
> Hear ye not her call?
> At your sloth she seems to wonder,
> Rend the sluggish bonds asunder,
> Let the war-cry's deaf'ning thunder,
> Ev'ry foe appall.
> Echoes loudly waking,
> Hill and valley shaking;
> Till the sound spreads wide around,
> The Saxon's courage breaking;
> Your foes on ev'ry side assailing,
> Forward press with heart unfailing,
> Till the invaders learn with quailing,
> Cambria ne'er can yield.
>
> Thou who noble Cambria wrongest
> Know that freedom's cause is strongest,
> Freedom's courage lasts the longest,
> Ending but with death.
> Freedom countless hosts can scatter,
> Freedom stoutest mail can shatter,
> Freedom thickest walls can batter,
> Fate is in her breath.
> See they now are flying!
> Dead are heaped with dying!
> Over might hath triumphed right,
> Our land to foes denying;
>
> Upon their soil we never sought them,
> Love of conquest hither brought them,
> But this lesson we have taught them,
> "Cambria ne'er can yield."

Little more is known of St. David, the patron of Wales, than is known of St. George, the patron of England. St. David, however, was born in the British Isles and not in a foreign country. According to tradition his native place was Henvynwyv in Cardiganshire. He became bishop of the Roman port Menapia in Pembrokeshire, later known as St. David's. This at the time was the chief port of departure for Ireland. The earliest written mention of him is in a tenth century manuscript which reports that he died in 601. The earliest biography dates from the eleventh century. According to this he was the son of Sant ab Ceredig ab Cunedda, prince of Heretica, the ancient name for Cardiganshire, and either a nephew or uncle of King Arthur. His mother was a nun who had been violated by Sant. There is a legend that his birth had been foretold thirty years before it occurred. He spent ten years studying the Bible and was sent by St. Paulinus to evangelize the British. He founded or restored twelve monasteries, including those at Glastonbury and Bath. He settled in the vale of Ross and lived in great austerity. After a time he went to Jerusalem and was made a bishop by the patriarch there. When he returned to Britain he removed his see from Caerlon to Menapia with the consent of King Arthur, and died there at the reputed age of 147 years. Tradition says that his body was taken to Glastonbury in 966. He was canonized by Pope Callistus II in 1120.

His name is connected with the origin of the leek as the symbol of Wales. He was leading his people in a great battle against the Saxons, as the legend runs, and told them to wear a leek in their hats to distinguish them from the enemy. There is another and different legend which the Welsh themselves tell with a smile. The country was troubled with orang-outangs and the people could not oust them so they sent into England for help. The English, when they arrived, are said to have found it hard to tell the difference between the Welshmen and the orang-outangs and at last, after mistaking a Welshman for one of the apes several times, they asked the Welsh to wear the leek so that it might not happen again.

NEBRASKA STATE DAY

State Day in Nebraska is proclaimed annually by the governor, who designates March first for patriotic observance by the public schools and the citizens of the state. Exercises are held in the schools dealing with Nebraska's natural resources and history, with particular emphasis on the admission to the Union, March 1, 1867, which the observance commemorates. The day is also celebrated by Service Clubs, Kiwanis, Rotary, and Chamber of Commerce groups, usually with a prominent Nebraskan as speaker at the program or banquet. Mrs. G. H. Wentz, first state president of the Nebraska Congress of Parents and Teachers, originally conceived the idea of a State Day program and in 1926 a contest for the best program was sponsored by this congress with the cooperation of the State Historical Society. In 1931 a bill was passed by the State Legislature providing that the governor should proclaim the day each year, and thereafter the Parents and Teachers Association has continued to sponsor annual programs and essay contests.

The early history of Nebraska is typical of many western states. Various tribes of Indians, numbering about forty thousand, were found within the boundaries of the present state by early explorers, the first of whom are believed to have been Francesco Vasquez Coronado and a small party of Spaniards. This was in 1541 during Coronado's search for gold in the "seven cities of Cibola," when the expedition explored the regions adjacent to his route from Mexico to Cibola. It was not until the year 1700 that French fur traders and trappers began to venture up the Missouri River, but they were followed during the eighteenth century by both Spanish and French explorers. Spain, France, and England all claimed Nebraska at different times, but France finally ceded all her claims west of the Mississippi to Spain in 1769 at the end of the Seven Years' War. Nebraska was thus a part of the Spanish province of Louisiana until Napoleon bought it back in 1800. In 1803 it was acquired by the United States as part of the Louisiana Purchase. Nebraska was proposed as a political territory in 1844 by the Secretary of War, with an area much larger than the present state, but the Nebraska Act by which it finally became a territory ten years later greatly reduced its size. The creation of Colorado and the Dakotas in 1861 narrowed its boundaries once more. In 1866 Congress passed an enabling act for the admission of Nebraska to statehood, but the constitutional convention regarded statehood as too expensive and adjourned *sine die*, although the following year Nebraska was admitted to the Union. The state constitution drafted in 1875 was revised in 1920 by a convention and the significant change to a one-house legislature became effective in 1937. This legislature was organized in a nonpartisan fashion, adopted the name of Senate, and functioned very satisfactorily. Nebraska is primarily an agricultural state. It leads in the production of wild hay, cattle exceed three million, and there are nearly two million swine. In the prairie counties the soil is very fertile and three large power and irrigation projects make up for the lack of rainfall in some regions.

MARCH SECOND

TEXAS INDEPENDENCE DAY

This day is a legal holiday in Texas in commemoration of its declaration of independence from Mexico. Late in 1835 a conference of citizens of Texas drew up a "Declaration of causes for taking up arms against Mexico" in which it was stated that Texas would continue faithful to Mexico so long as that nation was governed by the constitution and laws "that were framed for the political association." This has sometimes been characterized as a declaration of independence because there were certain phrases in the document that might be interpreted in that way. But the conference by a large majority voted down a motion to secede. However, on March 2, 1836, while Santa Anna was besieging the Alamo, another conference was held which formally declared Texas to be independent of Mexico. This was signed by about sixty men, only two of whom were Mexicans. The declaration was made good by the Battle of San Jacinto on April 21 (See San Jacinto Day, April 21) in which Santa Anna was defeated by General Sam Houston. A constitution was drafted and General Houston was elected president of the new republic of Texas. Its independence was recognized by the United States on March 2, 1837.

FESTIVAL OF ST. JOHN MARO

The Maronite Catholics, a Syrian branch of the Roman Catholic church, celebrate on March 2, the festival of St. John Maro, the first Catholic patriarch of Antioch, who lived near the end of the seventh century. This branch of the church is very old and in the early days it entertained theological views not approved by Rome, but since the Lateran Council of 1516 it has been in close union with the Vatican. It is represented in the United States by the Church of Our Lady of the Cedar of Mt. Lebanon in Boston, Mass., and possibly by others. This church was the first of its kind to be erected in this country and the first in which the mass was said in the Syriac language. It has a relic of St. Anne which is exposed at the festival of St. John Maro and during a nine days devotion in her honor beginning with the festival.

Although the Maronites honor their saint some ecclesiastical scholars deny that any such person ever lived. Many other points in the history of this branch of the church are also in dispute. But the Syrians in the United States have brought their worship and their religious traditions with them undisturbed by the differences of historians.

MARCH THIRD

BIRTHDAY OF ALEXANDER GRAHAM BELL

Alexander Graham Bell, the inventor of the telephone, was born in Edinburgh, Scotland, on March 3, 1842, the son of Alexander Melville Bell who invented a system for teaching deaf-mutes to speak. The son was educated in Edinburgh and at London University, and in 1870 migrated to Canada with his father. In 1872 he became professor of vocal physiology in Boston University, where he applied his father's system. He was employed by Gardiner Greene Hubbard to teach his

MARCH 3

daughter, who was a deaf-mute and whom Bell later married. In the course of his efforts to make an electrical device which would improve the hearing of the young woman he invented the telephone. Mr. Hubbard promoted the invention and Bell, through his connection with the family, was able, unlike many inventors, to reap rich profits from the company which was formed. He became interested in geographical and aeronautical research and built several aeroplanes and encouraged experimentation by others. He was a member of the National Academy of Sciences and in 1881 he received the Volta prize from the French Government. He served as president of the American Association to Promote Teaching of Speech to the Deaf, as president of the National Geographic Society and as a regent of the Smithsonian Institution. He died on August 2, 1922.

HUNDREDTH NIGHT AT WEST POINT

One of the annual jollifications at the United States Military Academy at West Point is the celebration of the hundredth night before graduation. The celebration does not always occur precisely on that night. It was held on March 3 in 1945. The cadets usually give a dramatic performance of some kind. The origin of the celebration is uncertain, but it is known that it began before 1866. The program for 1884 is in existence and it shows that it consisted of an address and reading from *The Howitzer*, the cadet newspaper. In 1900 the cadets presented "The Amazons." Since then, however, the plays have been written at the academy. W. Irving Hancock in *Life at West Point* published in 1902, writes: "The Hundredth Night dramatic performance takes the form of a farce written by the cadets of the first class with all the roles acted by them. Even the feminine parts are played by cadets and great care and thought are expended upon the costuming to which work the young lady friends of the men are invited to give their aid and even to supply gowns. The West Point band is present and the audience is a brilliant one. The farce invariably abounds in witty hits on academy life. Formerly the cadets were allowed to pay their respects to their instructors in these hits, but of late years it has been considered that such thrusts at superiors were prejudicial to the best interests of discipline and now the farce must be censored by the authorities. It is still considered a good joke, however, to have passed in the farce some disguised allusion that will cause the initiated cadets to roar with laughter. Cadets are rigorously forbidden to use any alcoholic beverages. In the play, therefore, a bottle is apt to be introduced a few times simply because at any other time it would be punished—but the bottle contains nothing but cold tea, or some equally harmless beverage. And, probably because the use of tobacco is sternly forbidden cadets, one of the characters in the farce is sure to produce a cigarette and light it—a performance which always produces laughter."

The celebration is arranged by the Dialectic Society which claims to have presented the shows since 1824. It was in that year that the Dialectic Society was formed by the amalgamation of two older societies. During the Civil War the society ceased to function but in 1866 it was revived and it began publishing a year book called *The Howitzer* and its members began to present one-act plays on the Hundredth Night, thus changing the form of the celebration dating from a much earlier period. It has developed into one of the most important functions of the year.

MARCH FOURTH

VERMONT DAY

Vermont was admitted to the Union on March 4, 1791, as the fourteenth state, the first to join the original thirteen. For nearly fourteen years preceeding admission it had been an independent republic performing almost all the functions of a sovereign government; issuing bills of credit, coining money, regulating weights and measures, establishing post offices, naturalizing citizens of other countries, and corresponding with foreign governments. Although this period of independence was unsought, Vermont having applied in 1777 for admission to the confederation of states fighting Great Britain and been refused, such has always been the sturdy individualism of its citizens that critics assert this tendency to sovereignty is innate and has not changed in succeeding years. However, on the credit side, the same individualism made the early Vermonters strong exponents of the rights of man. Vermont was the first state expressly to prohibit human slavery, and also the first to grant universal suffrage; every other state, despite the proclamations of equality in the preambles, made the right to vote dependent upon property or upon a specified yearly income. President Washington, at one time, thought it might be necessary to subdue the then independent state by arms, so contentious were its relations with other states and with Congress. But after adopting the first constitution at Windsor in 1777, and later settling the dispute over land claims with New York, Vermont steadily gained the friendly confidence of her neighbors. She finally ratified the Constitution of the United States at Bennington in January 1791, and on March 4 Congress unanimously passed an act for admission of Vermont to the Union (see Vermont's Declaration of Independence, January 15).

BIRTHDAY OF PULASKI

See October 11, Pulaski Day

MARCH FIFTH

THE BOSTON MASSACRE

When British troops were quartered in Boston in 1768 the people of the city resented it, and there were frequent clashes between them and the soldiers. The trouble culminated on March 5, 1770, when seven soldiers under command of Captain Preston were pelted with stones and snowballs in King Street by a crowd of fifty or sixty persons. Captain Preston ordered his men to fire. Three of the crowd were killed outright, including Crispus Attucks, a Negro. This aroused the people, and a mass meeting, attended by three thousand, was held in Faneuil Hall at which speeches denouncing the outrage were made. It was demanded that the troops be removed from the city at once and a week later they were transferred to Castle Island in the harbor. In November the soldiers and their commander were tried for murder and were defended by John Adams and Josiah Quincy. Two were found guilty of manslaughter and received light sentences. The others were acquitted. Although Adams, as a lawyer, defended the soldiers, as a patriot he wrote in 1816: "Not the Battle of Lexington, not the surrender of Burgoyne or Cornwallis, were more important events in American history than the battle of King Street on March 5, 1770."

The people of Boston held this view at the time and on March 5, 1771, they held a meeting to commemorate the event with James Lovell as the orator. In the audience were the members of the General Court, as the state legislature is called, and many distinguished citizens. The meeting was held in a church where the pulpit was draped in black. Some of the survivors of the massacre were present and a collection was taken for their relief. This anniversary was observed until 1783 and in the town records it is described as being intended "to perpetuate the memory of the horrid massacre perpetrated on the evening of the fifth of March 1770, by a party of soldiers under the command of Captain Preston of the Twenty-ninth Regiment." In the meantime the Declaration of Independence had been adopted, and the Revolutionary War had been won. And the Bostonians thought the time had arrived to celebrate the Fourth of July. It was accordingly voted that the observance of the anniversary of the massacre should be combined with the observance of the day on which the declaration had been adopted (see the Fourth of July). In 1888 a monument to the memory of the victims of the massacre was erected on the Common, and the spot in the street where they fell was marked with a circle of paving stones. The Crispus Attucks Post of colored veterans of the American Legion of Philadelphia observes its anniversary.

MARCH SIXTH

ALAMO DAY

The anniversary of the fall of the Alamo is one of the historic days celebrated in various ways by the Texans. The Alamo was. a Franciscan mission built about 1722. After 1793 it was occasionally used as a fort. It consisted originally of a church, an inclosed convent yard about a hundred feet square, a convent and hospital building and a plaza of two and a half acres all surrounded by a wall eight feet high and thirty-three inches thick. It was garrisoned by the Texans in their war for independence in 1836. Santa Anna, the Mexican general, laid siege to it on February 23 and fired upon its walls for many days without making a breach in them. On March 1 thirty-two reinforcements for the besieged arrived, making a total of about one hunded and eighty men who defended the place. On March 6 Santa Anna assaulted in force. He and his men were driven back twice, but on the third attempt they succeeded and there followed a hand to hand fight until only five of the defenders remained alive. These, including Captain David Crockett, who had gone to Texas to aid the Texans in their efforts to gain independence, were shot in cold blood on the orders of Santa Anna. The Mexican loss during the siege and in the final assault has been put at five hundred. Santa Anna admitted a loss of seventy killed and three hundred wounded. The brutality of Santa Anna aroused the Texans to fury and they went into the battle of San Jacinto on April 21 with the cry "Remember the Alamo," defeated Santa Anna, took him prisoner and forced him to sign a treaty pledging the use of his influence to bring about a recognition of their independence. The historians of Texas call the Alamo the Thermopylae of America. The monastery was in ruins for many years but in 1913 the city of San Antonio restored it to its original condition and preserves it as a patriotic shrine.

MARCH SEVENTH

LUTHER BURBANK'S BIRTHDAY

California observes Arbor Day on the anniversary of the birth of Luther Burbank. It had celebrated the day by planting trees on various dates since 1886, but in 1909 the Legislature passed a bill the essential part of which follows:

March 7 of each year, being the anniversary of the birthday of Luther Burbank, is hereby set apart and designated Bird and Arbor Day. All public schools and educational institutions are directed to observe Bird and Arbor Day, not as a holiday, but by including in the school work of the day suitable exercises having for their object instruction as to the economic value of birds and trees, and the promotion of a spirit of protection toward them.

161

Luther Burbank was still alive when he was thus honored by the selection of the anniversary of his birth as the day on which the importance of trees and birds was to be impressed upon the minds of the public school children. He was born on a farm at Lancaster, Mass., on March 7, 1849, and was educated at the local academy. He began market gardening in a small way when a youth and developed a new variety of potato. At the age of twenty-six he established a nursery at Santa Rosa, Calif., where he experimented with the production of new varieties of flowers and vegetables. He abandoned the nursery in 1893 and devoted himself to a long series of plant experiments. He produced many new and valuable varieties of fruits, flowers and forage plants, through experimentation with countless numbers of seedlings (see Arbor Day, April 22).

MARCH EIGHTH

BIRTHDAY OF OLIVER WENDELL HOLMES

Oliver Wendell Holmes, celebrated American jurist, was born March 8, 1841, at Boston, Mass., son of the distinguished American writer of the same name (see August 29). He served in the Civil War, was wounded at Ball's Bluff, Antietam, and Fredericksburg, and was on the staff of General H. G. Wright. Admitted to the Massachusetts bar in 1867, he lectured on common law at the Lowell Institute in 1880, and became professor of law at the Harvard Law School in 1882. Subsequently he was associate justice and chief justice of the Supreme Court of Massachusetts, and thereafter, from 1902 to 1932, associate justice of the Supreme Court of the United States. He was generally conceded to be one of the few great jurists to serve in that capacity. He died, a few days short of his ninety-fourth year, in 1935.

BIRTHDAY OF SIMON CAMERON

Simon Cameron, one of the most powerful political "bosses" of his generation, was born in Lancaster County, Pa., on March 8, 1799. Early in life he was thrown on his own resources and became an apprentice in a printing office in Harrisburg. At the age of twenty-two he went to Doylestown to edit a Democratic newspaper and remained there about a year when he returned to Harrisburg as partner in the ownership of a newspaper. About two years later, after spending some time in Washington working at his trade, he again returned to Harrisburg and bought the Harrisburg *Republican*, the ownership of which gave him considerable political influence. In 1826 he was made adjutant general of the state. He abandoned the newspaper business when he had accumulated a little capital and became a canal contractor, a builder of railroads, and a banker. He was active in promoting the nomination of Jackson and in the election of James Buchanan to the Senate. He was elected to the Senate in 1845 by a coalition of Whigs, Native Americans and Protectionist Democrats to succeed Buchanan who had entered President Polk's Cabinet. He made two unsuccessful attempts for reelection to the Senate and succeeded in his third attempt in 1857 with the support of the new Republican party. He threw in his lot with that party, and agreed to the support of Lincoln by the Pennsylvania delegation in the Republican National Convention in 1860 for the promise of a position in Lincoln's Cabinet. Lincoln kept the promise made in his name but with considerable reluctance and when he became dissatisfied with Cameron's conduct as Secretary of War he sent him to Russia as the American Minister. Cameron returned to the United States in about a year and sought unsuccessfully for election to the Senate again. He succeeded, however, in 1867, and remained in the Senate until 1877 when he resigned and the Pennsylvania Legislature elected his son, J. David Cameron, as his successor. He had been the dominating power in Pennsylvania politics for many years and with the election of his son to the Senate he transferred that power to the son. The political dynasty which he established was controlled successively by Matthew Stanley Quay and Boies Penrose, each selected by his predecessor. Penrose left no successor. Simon Cameron lived until his ninety-first year, the latter period of his life being spent in retirement in the enjoyment of his wealth and in the society of his many friends. He died on June 26, 1889.

MARCH NINTH

EDWIN FORREST'S BIRTHDAY

The Edwin Forrest Home for Retired Actors in Philadelphia keeps alive the memory of its founder by periodic celebrations of the anniversary of his birth, March 9, 1806. On the hundredth anniversary in 1906 the celebration was elaborate. Some years later plans were made for an annual celebration.

Forrest was in his time the most famous American actor. He was born in Philadelphia of Scotch and German parentage. His first regular appearance on the stage was in 1820, when at the age of fourteen he acted in Home's "Douglas." When he was twenty he scored a brilliant success in New York in "Othello." Ten years later he appeared in the Drury Lane theatre in London in "The Gladiator." His success in England and in the United States was so great that he amassed a large fortune. He built a castle on the Hudson river which he called Fonthill, but later he bought an estate in the northern part of Philadelphia to which he transferred his large library and his art collections. He continued to act until 1871, when he retired from the stage. He died from a stroke of apoplexy on December 12, 1872. He left the greater part of his estate to found a home for retired actors (see April 23, Shakespeare's Birthday).

FAST OF ESTHER

The Fast of Esther occurs on the thirteenth day of the month Adar, which in 1944 corresponded to March 9. It is observed by the Jews on the day preceding the Feast of Purim. The first mention of it is in the eighth century, at which time it was explained that the fast was based on an arbitrary interpretation of Esther IX:18, which reads: "But the Jews that were at Shushan assembled together on the thirteenth day thereof (Adar) and on the fourteenth day thereof; and on the fifteenth day they rested and made it a day of feasting and gladness. The thirteenth is described as being a time of gathering which had for its purpose public prayer and fasting. When the thirteenth occurs on the Sabbath, the fast is observed on the preceding Thursday.

MARCH TENTH

ALBANY BECOMES THE CAPITAL OF NEW YORK

Following the defeat of Burgoyne at Saratoga in 1777, Albany was occupied as the seat of government of New York at intervals for the next twenty years. It was not until March 10, 1797, however, that it was definitely selected as the capital of the state and plans made for the erection of a State House. It is said by historians of the city that it is the second oldest permanent settlement within the limits of the thirteen colonies. In 1540 a French trading post was set up near the present site of the city but it was abandoned not long afterward. Henry Hudson explored the region in 1609 and in 1614 a Dutch trading post was established and called Fort Nassau. The first actual settlers were eighteen Walloon families sent out by the Dutch East India Company in 1623 and they built Fort Orange on the banks of the Hudson river. In 1630 Kiliaen Van Rensselaer bought an extensive tract of land surrounding Fort Orange and sent settlers from Holland who rented the land from him. The colony was known as Rensselaerswyck, but the name was later changed to Beverwyck. On the transfer of the New Netherlands from the Dutch to the English in 1664 the name of the village was changed to Albany in honor of the Duke of York and Albany who sat on the English throne as James II. The population was chiefly Dutch. It was not until 1714 that there were enough English inhabitants to warrant the erection of an English church. The first general Congress of the colonies met at Albany when plans for their federation were discussed.

FEAST OF PURIM

This feast is celebrated by the Jews on the fourteenth day of the month Adar. which fell on March 10, 1944. One of their great days

of rejoicing, it is observed in commemoration of the deliverance of the
Jews in Persia from the plot of Haman to exterminate them. The story
is told in the Book of Esther. Ahashuerus, commonly identified with
Xerxes, had deposed Vashti his queen because she refused to expose
her charms before the princes. Many beautiful maidens were presented
to the King that he might choose a successor to Vashti. Esther was among
them and he selected her as the most beautiful. She was an orphan
living with her cousin Mordecai. The grand vizier, Haman, commanded
Mordecai to bow before him or to do obeisance to the image of an idol
on his breastplate. Mordecai refused and thereupon Haman told the
King that the Jews were a useless people and disloyal and asked permission to exterminate them. The King consented and issued a proclamation
ordering the confiscation of all Jewish property and a general slaughter
of all the Jews, for which he fixed a date. Mordecai persuaded Esther
to undertake the deliverance of her people. After a fast of three days by
all the Jews, including Esther, she decided to go before the King, although
she was not supposed to appear before him unless she was summoned,
and ask that the order be rescinded. The King was delighted with her
appearance and received her graciously and promised to dine with her
in her own apartments on two successive nights. On the night after the
first banquet the King was sleepless and ordered that the national records
should be read to him. The part which was read told of the revelation
by Mordecai of a plot against the King's life by two of his chamberlains,
a service for which the man had not been rewarded. Esther in the meantime had invited Haman to the second banquet with the King. Pleased
by this honor he asked the King for permission to execute Mordecai at
once. The King asked him "What shall be done to the man whom the
King delighteth to honor?" Haman suggested a pageant at which one
of the great nobles should attend the man thus honored. Thereupon the
King ordered the pageant in honor of Mordecai and commanded Haman
to attend him. At the banquet Esther confessed that she was a Jewess
and asked that the order for the destruction of her people be withdrawn.
The King consented and ordered that Haman be hanged on the gallows
which he had prepared for the death of Mordecai. Then Mordecai
was made grand vizier and the King issued an order permitting the Jews
to slay their enemies. And they slew them in great numbers. Mordecai
wrote letters to all the Jews commanding that they celebrate their deliverance. The record says:

> And the Jews undertook to do as they had begun and as Mordecai had
> written unto them; because Haman, the son of Hammedatha, the Agagite, the
> enemy of all the Jews, had devised against the Jews to destroy them and had
> cast Pur, that is, the lot, to consume them and to destroy them; but when Esther
> came before the King he commanded by letters that his wicked device which he
> devised against the Jews should return upon his own head, and that he and his
> sons should be hanged on the gallows. Wherefore they called these days Purim
> after the name of Pur. . . . The Jews ordained and took upon them . . . that
> these days should be remembered and kept throughout every generation, every

family, every province and every city; and that these days of Purim should not fail from among the Jews, nor the memorial of them perish from their seed.

Whether the Book of Esther in which this story is told is history or historical romance is a question upon which critics disagree. John D. Prince, professor of Semitic languages in Columbia University, however, writing in the *Jewish Encyclopedia,* says that the vast majority of modern expositors have reached the conclusion that "the book is a piece of pure fiction." He says that "the object of Esther is undoubtedly to give an explanation of and to exalt the Feast of Purim, of whose real origin little or nothing is known." Some Semitic scholars regard the story of Esther as a Babylonian-Elamite myth. Esther is identified with Ishtar, or Aphrodite; Mordecai is said to be Marduk the tutelary deity of Babylon; and Haman is said to be Hamman or Humman, the chief god of the Elamites. And Vashti is also supposed to be a goddess of the Elamites. One of the scholars holding these views thinks that the Feast of Purim may have been adapted by the Jews from a similar festival celebrated by the Babylonians. But all this is a matter of conjecture.

The Feast of Purim differs from other Jewish holidays in that there is no rigid prohibition against working or doing business. In the account of its celebration in Esther there is no reference to religious ceremonies. It has however assumed certain religious features. At the services in the synagogues certain portions of the Book of Esther are read, and there have been regulations regarding the manner of reading. One feature of its observance which has persisted from the beginning is the giving of gifts to the poor. In the middle ages children dressed in fantastic costumes would go from house to house asking for food or money, very much as American children masquerade on Hallowe'en. The adults also masqueraded, taking over some of the customs of the Roman carnival. Plays especially written for the occasion were acted, and Haman was hissed and Esther was applauded. Indeed, when the story was read in the synagogue it was for a time customary for the people to berate Haman in loud tones and shake rattles in order to drown out the sound of his name. It is a day of feasting and rejoicing.

In addition to the Purim celebrated by all Jews there are many special Purims observed by Jews in different parts of the world to commemorate their deliverance from special peril.

MARCH ELEVENTH

THE BLIZZARD OF 1888

There have been worse snowstorms in the Eastern part of the country than that which began on March 11, 1888, but the heavier snow fall came when the country was less populous and when the population was not concentrated in large cities. The fall in 1888 was just short of twenty-one inches, but the wind blew it into deep drifts. Conditions were particularly bad in New York City where the snow was so deep that all methods of transportation were put out of service. Roscoe Conkling walked from his office in Wall Street to his house in Fourteenth Street and died about a month later from the effects of the exposure. The total loss of life in the East was four hundred. Not long after the storm an organization was formed in New York known as the Blizzard Men of 1888. It holds a meeting on the anniversary of the storm every year and its members recall their experiences. One of the members who was living in Philadelphia as a boy at the time said that the drifts reached the second story windows of his house and that twenty-eight horses were hitched to the snow plow on the streetcar tracks. Another member said that the wind blew at the rate of eighty-four miles an hour and that the thermometer registered four degrees below zero. A salesman in a shoe store said that he sold twelve hundred pairs of men's rubber boots. Not a year goes by without the newspapers in the large cities taking note of the anniversary.

MARCH TWELFTH

GIRL SCOUT DAY

On March 12, 1912, Daisy Gordon with ten other young girls gathered in an unused stable belonging to her aunt, Mrs. Juliette Low, in Savannah, Ga., and organized the first patrol of Girl Guides which later developed into the Girl Scouts. Mrs. Low, the daughter of General W. W. Gordon, had married William Low of Warwickshire, England, and maintained a home in London as well as in Savannah. She became acquainted with Sir Robert Baden-Powell, the founder of the Boy Scouts, and became interested in the Girl Guides, an organization founded in 1909 by his sister, intended to do for girls what the scouts did for boys. It was at her suggestion that her niece and her girl friends started the organization in Savannah. Other groups were formed in other cities and the headquarters were removed to Washington in 1915 and the name changed to Girl Scouts. The headquarters were later moved to New York. There were in 1946 about 1,147,700 active members, with troops in every state. The anniversary of the founding of the organization is observed with special ceremonies. On the occasion of the twenty-first anniversary exercises in Constitution Hall in Washington, Mrs. Roosevelt, the wife of the President, lighted twenty-one green candles on a birthday cake and made an address. Mrs. Herbert Hoover was actively interested in the scouts and entertained them at the White House during her residence there.

The Girl Scouts are organized on a plan similar to that of the Boy Scouts. Members are from ten to sixteen years old. A troop may be formed with eight girls. The usual number, however, varies from twenty-four to thirty-two. Each troop is divided into patrols with from four to eight members. Each patrol has its own name with special emblems and songs, and its own leader. The leaders of the patrol, with the captain and lieutenant of the troop, form the executive board called a Court of Honor. A girl must attend at least four meetings of the troop before she is eligible for membership. Then she becomes a Tenderfoot if she passes the test which includes a knowledge of the scout law, flag etiquette, four woodcraft signs, and the tying of knots. When she has qualified in nature study, sewing, first aid, cooking, thrift and care of health she may become a second class scout. To be promoted to the first class she must be able to make a map, to judge height, weight and distance, to send code messages, to swim, pitch a tent, and to supervise over-night hikes into the country. Special merit badges are awarded to girls who qualify in various activities, including archery, athletics, naming birds, playing the bugle, cooking, caring for children, dressmaking, life saving and the like. After a girl has earned twenty-one badges she is eligible for the Golden Eaglet, the highest award. She is expected to do a good turn for someone every day and to obey the scout law which requires that she be worthy of trust, loyal, useful and helpful to others, a friend to all and a sister to every other scout, courteous, a friend to animals, obedient, cheerful, thrifty, and clean in thought, word and deed.

MARCH THIRTEENTH

BIRTHDAY OF JOSEPH PRIESTLY

Joseph Priestly, the discoverer of oxygen, was born at Fieldhead, Yorkshire, England, on March 13, 1733. From 1752 to 1755 he attended the Nonconformist Academy at Daventry and mastered Latin, Greek, Hebrew, Italian, French, German, Chaldee and Syriac. While at this academy he joined in theological discussions, usually taking the unorthodox view. He was later appointed a teacher of languages and belles lettres at the academy, and the University of Edinburgh gave him an honorary degree in recognition of his literary attainments. He became a clergyman and while pastor of a chapel at Leeds interested himself in chemistry. He became librarian to Lord Shelburne in 1772 and two years later traveled with him on the continent. It was in 1774 that he discovered oxygen, a discovery which changed many of the accepted views of the chemists. He left Lord Shelburne's service in 1780 and became pastor of a dissenting chapel at Birmingham. He sympathized with the French revolutionists and was made a citizen of the French Republic, but his views incensed the people of Birmingham and in 1791 a mob burned his house and the chapel, destroying all his books and scientific instruments. He then went to London to preach and in 1794 he came to America, living in Philadelphia for a time. He was asked to become professor of chemistry in the University of Pennsylvania and to become its president. He declined both offers and settled at Northumberland, Pa., where he died on February 6, 1804. While living in Philadelphia he founded a Unitarian church, the second in the United States. The first was King's Chapel at Boston which, in 1784, removed the trinitarian references in its liturgy, thus withdrawing from the Church of England, and ordained James Freeman, a Unitarian, as its pastor.

MARCH FOURTEENTH

ELI WHITNEY PATENTS THE COTTON GIN

Eli Whitney, a native of Massachusetts, went to Georgia as a teacher after his graduation from Yale College in 1792 and lived on the estate of the widow of General Nathaniel Greene. Some of Mrs. Greene's neighbors asked him if he could invent a machine for separating the seed from the fiber of the cotton. Little cotton was then grown in the South because of the tedious process of freeing the fiber from the seed. It is said that it would take one person two years to turn out an average bale of cotton by the hand process. Whitney invented a device consisting of revolving circular saws which would extract the seed from fifteen bales in a day, and he obtained a patent for it on March 14, 1794. South Carolina voted him a reward of $50,000 in recognition of the importance of the invention. Following the invention of the gin the cultivation of cotton in the South expanded rapidly and made slave labor profitable. The great increase in the production of cotton led to the wide use of cotton fabrics which were still further cheapened by the general adoption of the power loom in the cotton mills.

MARCH FIFTEENTH

MAINE ADMITTED TO THE UNION

The coast of Maine was touched by several Spanish navigators in the sixteenth century. More than one of them sailed up the Penobscot river in search of the fabled city of Norumbega the buildings of which were said to be ornamented by columns of crystal and silver. In 1604 a colony was planted on an island in the St. Croix river by a French expedition, but it was soon abandoned. The region was within the grant to the Plymouth Company made in 1606. Various attempts at permanent settlement were made by the English, but it was not until 1625 that such a settlement was established at Pemaquid. In 1650 or thereabouts Massachusetts assumed authority over the region and in 1691 the rights of Massachusetts were confirmed. At the close of the Revolutionary War Massachusetts continued to exercise its authority over what had come to be known as the District of Maine. The people of the district, however, began agitation for separation. They did not succeed, however, until 1820, when the admission of Missouri led Congress to believe that a new Northern state should be set up to offset the admission of a Southern state and on March 15, 1820, Maine entered the Union as an independent state. Its citizens were so proud of their new state that they fell into the habit of referring to their place of residence as the State of Maine, to distinguish it from the old District of Maine, a dependency of Massachusetts.

BIRTHDAY OF ANDREW JACKSON

See January 8, Jackson Day

MARCH SIXTEENTH

BIRTHDAY OF JAMES MADISON

James Madison, fourth President of the United States, was born at the home of his maternal grandparents at Port Conway, Va., on March 16, 1751 (Old style, March 5, 1750). Soon afterward his mother took her young son to her husband's home, Montpelier, in Orange County. He began his formal schooling under a Scotch teacher at the age of twelve and studied the classics and French and Spanish. After further tutoring he entered the College of New Jersey, now Princeton University, at the age of nineteen. He was one of the founders of the American Whig Society, a debating club, which became famous in the history of the college. He was graduated in 1771 but remained at Princeton for another year studying Hebrew and ethics, and continued his theological studies after his return to Virginia. After a time he became interested in politics and in the controversy over religious toleration which was waging in the state. He argued in favor of religious freedom. He was a delegate to the state constitutional convention in 1776 and did his best to have inserted in the Constitution a declaration that the free exercise of religion was a matter of right. He was elected a member of the first Assembly under the new Constitution. He was elected to the Governor's Council in 1778, and in 1780 was sent as a delegate to the Continental Congress, and served until December 1783, when he returned home because of illness in his father's family. He began the study of law in order, as he wrote to Edmund Randolph, to have a profession in which he could "depend as little as possible on the labor of slaves." He wrote to Jefferson asking him to buy books for him occasionally and especially "whatever may throw light on the general constitution and droit public of the several confederacies which have existed." Not long after his return home he was elected by his county to the Virginia House of Delegates and served for three years. He opposed proposals for the issue of paper money, and defeated a project supported by Patrick Henry and others to impose a general tax for the support of religion. He was influential in bringing about a series of interstate conferences which ultimately led to the calling of the Constitutional Convention in Philadelphia in 1787. He was a member of the Continental Congress for the second time from February to May 1787, and then took his seat in the Constitutional Convention as a delegate from Virginia. In a series of letters written in March and April of that year he set forth his views on the various provisions that should be embodied in the proposed Constitution. He wrote that the large states should have more representatives in the national legislature than the small states, that the national government should have complete authority in all cases which require uniformity, that the national supremacy should extend to the judiciary departments, that the national legislature should be composed of two houses with differing terms of office, that there should be a national executive, and that the national government should guarantee the tranquility of the states against internal as well as external dangers. He immediately took a prominent part in the deliberations of the convention, attending every session and taking copious notes on the debate which have since been published. He has been described as the "master builder of the Constitution." He wrote a number of the papers in the *Federalist* urging its ratification by the states and when there appeared to be uncertainty in Virginia about its approval he successfully sought election to the ratifying convention and under his leadership, assisted by that of John Marshall, the opposition of Patrick Henry and others was overcome and the Constitution was ratified by a majority of ten. He aspired to election to the first United States Senate under the new Constitution, but Patrick Henry succeeded in preventing it. In spite of Henry's opposition, however, he was elected to the House of Representatives. He was active in framing the first ten amendments to the Constitution and in drafting the legislation setting up the executive departments, and he opposed the creation of the United States bank proposed by Hamilton. When he became President, however, he signed the charter for the first bank.

On September 15, 1784, he married Dolly Payne Todd, a young widow of Philadelphia whose mother kept a boarding house. He voluntarily retired from Congress at the expiration of his term on March 4, 1797, when the Federalists came into complete control of the government. He was bitterly opposed to the Alien and Sedition Acts and he and Jefferson wrote the resolutions adopted by the Virginia and Kentucky legislatures condemning them as unconstitutional and declaring that "in case of deliberate, palpable and dangerous exercise of other powers not granted by the said compact (the Constitution), the states, who are parties thereto, have the right and are in duty bound to interpose for arresting the progress of the evil, and for maintaining within their respective limits the authorities, rights and liberties appertaining to them." When this declaration was cited as justification for the South Carolina nullification resolutions Madison explained that he did not mean that a state could by its own action nullify an Act of Congress, but that if the states regarded such an act as unconstitutional they should either work for its repeal or for an amendment to the Constitution which would invalidate it. When Jefferson was elected President in 1800 he made Madison his Secretary of State. Madison refused to dismiss Federalist supporters from his department in order to put followers of the party of Jefferson in their places, and consequently won the hostility of the patronage mongers. As Secretary of State he had to deal with the issues arising out of the European war, issues which ultimately led to the War of 1812 with Great Britain, which arose after he succeeded Jefferson as President in 1809. He directed that war and brought it to a successful conclusion and retired to private life on March 4, 1817. He supported Jefferson in founding the University of Virginia in 1819 and became its rector on the death of Jefferson in 1829. He died at Montpelier on June 28, 1836, at the age of eighty-four, and is buried on the lawn of his estate.

FOUNDING OF THE UNITED STATES
MILITARY ACADEMY

The United States Military Academy at West Point, N. Y., was founded by Act of Congress approved on March 16, 1802. Graduates of the academy assemble every year in the various cities of the country on that date and celebrate the anniversary with a dinner or in some other appropriate manner.

The academy was opened on July 4, 1802, with a class of ten cadets. West Point, on the Hudson river fifty miles from New York City, had been a military post since January 20, 1778. General Knox in May 1776, urged the establishment of a military academy for the army and on October 1, 1776, Congress adopted a resolution appointing a committee to prepare plans for such an academy, with the approval of General Washington. On June 20, 1777, it was ordered that a Corps of Invalids, organized as "a military school for young gentlemen previous to their being appointed to marching regiments," be created. This was done at once, and in 1781, at the request of General Washington, the Corps of Invalids was marched from Philadelphia to join the garrison at West Point, where an engineering school, a laboratory and a library had already been opened. But this was not regarded as adequate, for two years later Washington discussed with his officers at Newburgh the plans for a military academy, and in his message to Congress on December 3, 1793, he called attention to the need for such an institution.

On May 9, 1793, Congress authorized the organization of a Corps of Artillerists and Engineers, with a school of instruction for them at West Point. The buildings that had been used for the school were burned in 1796 and the work of the academy was suspended until 1801. The faculty at that time consisted of four army officers and a civilian.

It was not until March 16, 1802, that the Military Academy as it is now known was formally organized. Provision was made for twenty officers and cadets who were to receive $16 a month. The next year the number was increased to forty and in 1808 the admission of one hundred and fifty-six was authorized. Congress, however, neglected to make provision for them and by March 1812, this neglect left the academy without a single instructor. The War of 1812 called attention to the need for trained officers and President Madison urged upon Congress the importance of making the academy a scientific as well as a military college, and on April 29, 1812, the academy was reorganized upon the general plan now followed. Cadets had been admitted without any mental or physical examination and it was not until 1818 that President Monroe approved rules requiring an examination before the cadets could be promoted in the corps. Colonel Sylvanus Thayer had been appointed as superintendent in the previous year and remained in charge for sixteen years during which time he made the academy famous among the military schools of the world. He resigned in 1833 because of differences with President Jackson over details of management. Five years later the superintendency was offered to him again, with the understanding that he should be virtually in absolute control, but he declined the offer. Many of the commanding generals on both sides in the Civil War received their training under him.

The academy occupies a reservation of 3294 acres, not including Constitution Island in the river with an area of 280 acres. Congress made large appropriations for new buildings early in the present century and this money has been spent so wisely that the physical plant is one of the finest in the world. Among the new structures is a magnificent Memorial Chapel in which famous battle flags are hung. Among the monuments on the grounds is an equestrian statue of General Washington, and a marble shaft surmounted by a figure of victory, erected in memory of the officers and men of the regular army who fell in the Civil War.

MARCH SEVENTEENTH

ST. PATRICK'S DAY

St. Patrick, the patron saint of Ireland, has been honored and the anniversary of his death, March 17, 493, has been celebrated in America from very early times. Celebrations outside of those in the church

began in Boston with the Charitable Irish Society, founded in 1737.
The Friendly Sons of St. Patrick, founded in Philadelphia in 1780,
observed the day and four years later in New York the Friendly Sons
of St. Patrick of that city took note of the anniversary. The New York
society, curiously enough, was organized by Irish Catholics and Presbyterians and its first president was a Presbyterian.

These societies, as well as similar organizations in other cities,
usually celebrate the day by giving a public dinner at which prominent
speakers respond to toasts. The Ancient Order of Hibernians celebrates
the day by a parade. At a celebration in Boston in the early years of
the present century Justice John W. Hammond of the Supreme Judicial
Court of the state, in responding to the toast "Massachusetts," said:
"You are of Irish ancestry and are proud of it. I am of the strongest
Pilgrim ancestry, and am equally proud of it. Neither of us would
be worthy of his ancestry if he were not proud of it. It is right, proper
and beneficial that each of us should maintain those memories which
are peculiar to ourselves. It is right for us to emulate the virtues of our
ancestors as it is right to criticise their faults and avoid them if we can. . . .
I clipped from the *Boston Herald* the other day something said by Archbishop O'Connell (he later was made a Cardinal) who is, I suppose a
pretty good authority with most of those assembled here. He urges the
election to office of honest men, of square-dealing men, though they be
non-Catholics, rather than the election of unworthy Catholics. That is
the language of an Irish Catholic speaking as an American citizen. It
shows the breadth of mind of the man who spoke it and the sense of
political duty under which he labored. And so far as I have the power
to represent anybody I send back as the echo of the remark that I prefer
a good, honest, square-dealing public official not of my race or creed to
anyone, no matter how puritanical his name or religion, who does not
possess those qualifications."

St. Patrick, according to the Roman Catholic authorities, was born
at Kilpatrick, near Dumbarton, Scotland, in the year 387. His father
was Calphurnius, a member of a Roman family of high rank. He
held the office of Decurio in Gaul, or Britain. When Patrick was sixteen
years old he was captured by Irish marauders and sold as a slave to a
chieftain, who was a high priest, in the territory of the present county
of Antrim. He remained in servitude for six years, learning meanwhile
to speak the Celtic language. When he escaped from his master he fled
to the west coast of Ireland where he found a ship ready to sail, was
allowed on board, and in a few days landed in Britain. He had decided
to devote himself to religious work and made his way to the monastery
of St. Martin at Tours, where he studied for a while. He remained on
the continent for more than eighteen years preparing himself for his
work. He was commended to Pope Celestine and visited Rome. The
Pope commissioned him to work in Ireland and probably in the summer
of 433 he landed there at the mouth of the Vantry river near Wicklow

Head. The Druids resented his arrival but he escaped from them and sought a more friendly territory. But he first went to his old master and paid the price of his freedom and, it is said, converted the man and his family to Christianity. He preached and taught in Ireland for many years, building churches and organizing parishes and performing miracles. He and his companions were taken captive twelve times by the Druids and once he was loaded with chains and condemned to death. He lived until March 17, 493, and was buried, in a shroud made for him by St. Brigid, in the place on which in later years the Cathedral of Down was built.

Many traditions have grown up about the life of St. Patrick. One which is regarded as authentic is that in an effort to explain to the Irish people the mystery of the Trinity he plucked a shamrock and said that the three leaves represented the three persons of the Trinity and that the stem on which they grew represented the godhead and was typical of the unity of three in one. Another tradition relates to the expulsion of snakes from Ireland. Cardinal Moran, who wrote the article on St. Patrick in the *Catholic Encyclopedia,* does not mention it although he does tell of the besetment of St. Patrick by a crowd of demons in the shape of vultures and the final drowning of the demons in the sea in answer to the prayers of the saint. The story of the snakes, however, is interesting. He had banished them all except one old serpent, which refused to leave. St. Patrick, according to the story, made a box and invited the serpent to enter it. The serpent objected on the ground that it was not big enough to hold him but St. Patrick insisted that it was large enough to be comfortable. After a long discussion the serpent finally agreed to enter the box to prove that it was too small. As soon as the serpent was safely inside the saint shut the lid, fastened it and threw it into the sea.

BIRTHDAY OF ROGER B. TANEY

Roger B. Taney, the fifth Chief Justice of the United States, was born in Calvert County, Md., on March 17, 1777. He was graduated from Dickinson College, Carlisle, Pa., in 1795, and was admitted to the bar in Calvert County in 1799. He was elected a delegate to the General Assembly of the state and in 1801 moved to Frederick. He was later elected to the State Senate in which he served four years. In 1823 he took up his residence in Baltimore and five years later was appointed Attorney General of the state. President Andrew Jackson took him into his Cabinet as Attorney General of the United States in 1831. He supported the President in his attacks upon the United States Bank and when Secretary of the Treasury Duane refused to remove the federal deposits from the bank the President removed Duane and, in September 1833, appointed Taney as his successor. Taney did as the President ordered. The Senate, however, postponed action on his appointment until June 1834, when it refused confirmation. In 1835 Jackson appointed him as an Associate Justice of the Supreme Court but the Senate refrained from acting on the appointment. When Chief Justice John Marshall died Jackson appointed Taney as his successor, and the Senate, the political complexion of which had changed, confirmed the appointment in March 1836. Taney took his seat on the bench in January 1837. He was an able Justice, but suffered somewhat in popular esteem because of the great distinction which his predecessor had won. He is remembered among laymen chiefly because of his connection with the Dred Scott case, in which the rights of Negroes were involved. His early views on slavery were expressed in 1818 when he was defending the Reverend Jacob Gruber from the charge of inciting Maryland slaves to disorder. He then said: "A hard necessity indeed compels us to endure the evils of slavery for a time. It was imposed on us by another nation, while we were yet in a state of colonial vassalage. . . . Every lover of freedom confidently hopes that it will be effectually, though it must be gradually, wiped away. . . . Until the time shall come when we can point without a blush to the language held in the Declaration of Independence, every friend of humanity will seek to lighten the galling chains of slavery, and better, to the utmost of his power, the wretched condition of the slave."

The technical legal point involved in the Dred Scott case was whether Scott, a Negro, had any standing as a citizen and could sue in the courts. Scott was a slave, owned by Dr. Emerson of Missouri, an officer in the army. Dr. Emerson had taken Scott into Illinois, in 1834, where slavery was prohibited, and two years later had taken him into what is now Minnesota, a part of the Louisiana Purchase in which there were to be no slaves under the terms of the Missouri Compromise. While in free territory he had been allowed to marry a wife who was also a slave belonging to Dr. Emerson. He was taken back to Missouri by Dr. Emerson in 1838 with his wife and child. Ten years later he decided to sue for his freedom and was assisted by anti-slavery lawyers. He contended that through residence in free territory he had obtained the status of a free man. The Supreme Court of Missouri, in 1852, decided that when he was taken back to Missouri where slavery was allowed he became a slave, whatever he might have been elsewhere, and had no standing in court. In 1854 his lawyers took the case to the Federal District Court in Missouri which decided that he was a citizen of Missouri and could be a party to a suit in a Federal court, but it refused to free him. The case went to the Supreme Court of the United States chiefly on the issue whether the Federal Court could assume jurisdiction in a case brought by a Negro held in slavery. The case was argued at length in 1855 and in 1856, and it was in March 1857, that the Supreme Court ruled, with two justices dissenting, that the lower court had erred in assuming jurisdiction in the case, as at the time of the adoption of the Constitution Negroes descended from Negro slaves were not and could not be citizens of any state. Justice Taney, in his opinion, discussed the status of the Negro at the time of the adoption of the Constitution, saying:

They had for more than a century been regarded as beings of an inferior order and altogether unfit to associate with the white race, either in social or political relations; and so far inferior that they had no rights which the white man was bound to respect, and that the Negro might justly and lawfully be reduced to slavery for his benefit. He was bought and sold and treated as an ordinary article of merchandise.

The decision, coming soon after the inauguration of President Buchanan, aroused the abolitionists and widened the breach between the North and the South, which a few years later led to the Civil War. Justice Taney remained on the bench until his death at the age of eighty-seven in 1864.

When Justice Taney died he was buried in Frederick where he began the practice of law, and a monument to his memory has been erected there. His house, built in 1799, is preserved as a museum in which many relics are preserved. In the drawing room is a painting showing the Chief Justice administering the oath to President Lincoln at the time of his inauguration in 1861. The desk on which he wrote the Dred Scott decision is also there. He administered the oath to seven Presidents—Van Buren, Harrison, Polk, Taylor, Pierce, Buchanan and Lincoln—and the portraits of these men are hanging on the wall. And there is also a bust of Taney himself in the room. In the dining room is a collection of portraits of the Chief Justice, including a miniature—his earliest known portrait—which he presented to Miss Anne Key, before she became his wife. She was a sister of Francis Scott Key, who wrote "The Star Spangled Banner." At the rear of the house are the slave quarters. Taney never approved of slavery and he freed the slaves which he owned. In the living room of the slave quarters is preserved the record of their freedom. One of the rooms in the house is dedicated to Francis Scott Key. It contains a collection of portraits and papers of the Key family, along with a magazine, dated 1814, containing the first printing in such form of "The Star Spangled Banner," which was then called "The Defence of Fort McHenry."

EVACUATION DAY

The anniversary of the evacuation of Boston, Mass., by the British on March 17, 1776, was made a legal holiday in Suffolk County, Mass., in 1941. Prior to that it was celebrated annually in Boston, and in 1901 there was an elaborate celebration on the one hundred and twenty-fifth anniversary. There were parades, public meetings, and dinners with much oratory. In ordinary years the celebration is arranged by the residents of the southern part of the city, although the city and state officials usually participate. In 1908 the celebration began with a dinner in Bethesda Hall on the evening of March 16. The chairman of the committee in charge said in the course of his address: "We will never rest content until the tramping of our local parades shall be heard in Washington and legislative enactment shall make March 17 a national holiday."

Major General Duval of the United States Army, another speaker, said: "Our army is the last guarantee of government. Sometimes we seem to forget that all free institutions require force for their preservation. Behind every great government the army must stand quiescent in times of peace, but giving force to the laws and the courts by its very existence."

At the outbreak of the Revolution Boston was occupied by the British troops and all attempts to dislodge them failed until Washington fortified Dorchester Heights. While the work was in progress early in March the American forces kept up a cannon fire on the British lines to distract attention from what was going on in the rear. On the evening of March 4 General Thomas with two thousand men took possession of Dorchester Heights. A train of three hundred wagons and carts followed in the darkness. The vehicles were filled with bales of hay and fascines. When day broke on the morning of March 5 the British saw two redoubts on the heights armed with cannon and commanding the city. General Howe, the British commander, was astounded and Admiral Shuldham, in command of the British ships, admitted that if the Americans could not be driven from their position he could not keep a single vessel in the harbor. Accordingly a picked company of twenty-four hundred soldiers under command of Lord Percy was sent in boats under cover of the darkness to dislodge the Americans. A sudden storm drove some of the boats ashore and it rained so hard in the morning that the troops could not move. General Howe called a council of war which decided that the city should be evacuated, and Howe agreed to leave the city with his forces if he were allowed to go without molestation. There was no formal assent to this plan but Washington maintained a watchful attitude and was ready to atack if any hostile move was made. The evacuation was delayed until Sunday, March 17, when the British troops were taken aboard the ships along with eleven hundred loyalist citizens and the fleet sailed for Nova Scotia. The Continental Congress thanked Washington for the delivery of the city from the British and voted him a gold medal.

MARCH EIGHTEENTH

BIRTHDAY OF GROVER CLEVELAND

Grover Cleveland, the twenty-second and twenty-fourth President of the United States, died on June 24, 1908. The National Democratic Club of New York celebrated the anniversary of his birth on March 18, 1910, by a dinner in his honor at which addresses were made dealing with his distinguished achievements. He had been the first Democratic President to be elected following the Civil War and was consequently enthusiastically received by the members of his party in the early days of his residence in the White House. After his death in Princeton, N.J., plans were made to honor him by erecting a tower to be known by his name on the main building of the new postgraduate school of Princeton University. A fund of $100,000 for this purpose was completed on his birthday in 1911. The tower was erected, and is the most conspicuous structure on the campus of the university. The Southern Club of New York, on the same day, formed an association to perpetuate his memory. About two weeks later the congregation of the Presbyterian Church at Caldwell, N.J., voted to sell the manse in which Cleveland was born to a memorial association. On the seventy-fifth anniversary of his birth, in 1912, a public meeting in his honor was held in City College in New York at which many of his political and official associates were present. William H. Taft, who was then President, wrote the following message which was read: "Grover Cleveland earned the sincere gratitude of his countrymen and justified recurring memorial occasions like this one in which we are taking part. He was a great President, not because he was a great lawyer, not because he was a brilliant orator, not because he was a statesman of profound learning, but because he was a patriot with the highest sense of public duty, because he was a statesman of clear perceptions, of the utmost courage of his convictions and of great plainness of speech, because he was a man of high character, father and husband of the best type, and because throughout his political life he showed these rugged virtues of the public servant and citizen, the emulation of which by those who follow him will render progress of our political life toward better things a certainty." The meeting was in charge of John H. Finley, then president of the City College, who for many years was active in the promotion of movements to keep alive the memory of Cleveland.

As March 18, 1933, approached it was found that $18,000, the money needed to pay for the Presbyterian manse in Caldwell had been raised and on that day the building was turned over to the Grover Cleveland Birthplace Memorial Association, with appropriate exercises. A large crowd assembled before the platform which had been erected in front of the house. Dr. Finley, president of the memorial association, began the exercises by addressing Mayor John Espy of the borough and informing him of the purpose of the gathering. Mr. Espy welcomed the visitors. William F. Day, president of the Equitable Life Assurance Society, who had assisted in raising the money to buy the house, said that those who had contributed "believe that Grover Cleveland in his life proved that fidelity to trust was the fundamental fact on which character was built; they believe that he stood for the highest standards of conduct in public affairs; and they believe in his unfaltering faith in the sufficiency of the Constitution of the United States in future years."

Then the deed to the property was delivered, and the key to the house was handed to Richard F. Cleveland, the son named for his grandfather, and with it he unlocked the door. A bouquet of flowers was given to Miss Esther Cleveland, the daughter born in the White House, and she carried it to the room in which her father was born. Addresses were made by men who had known the President intimately and had been associated with him, and a hymn by Fanny Crosby was sung. Cleveland, when a boy, had taught in the home for the blind in New York with which Miss Crosby was connected and she had remained his friend throughout his life.

Many public schools in different parts of the country are named for Cleveland. They take note every year of the anniversary of his birth. And in Caldwell special services are annually held in his honor on the Sunday nearest to March 18. In 1934, the memorial association turned the Caldwell house over to the state of New Jersey.

Grover Cleveland was born in Caldwell, N.J., on March 18, 1837, the son of the Reverend Richard Cleveland. While he was still a small boy the family moved to New York and it was at Fayetteville and Clinton that he received his elementary education. When his father died in 1853 he became a teacher in the New York Institution for the Blind, but soon removed to Buffalo at the suggestion of his uncle where he studied law and was admitted to the bar in 1859 at the age of twenty-two. He served as an assistant district attorney but was defeated when he ran as a candidate for district attorney. In 1870, however, he was elected sheriff. In 1881 he was elected as a reform Mayor of Buffalo and was so successful in his attacks upon political and social corruption that before he had served a year as Mayor the Democrats in the state nominated him for governor. He was elected by a large majority. As governor he attracted the attention of the country by his wisdom and independence so that in 1884 before his term was ended his party nominated him for the presidency. He was elected over James G. Blaine, the Republican candidate. His party renominated him in 1888, but he was defeated by Benjamin Harrison. He was nominated again in 1892 and won this time over Mr. Harrison who had been named for a second term by the Republicans. The free silver controversy was waging at the time but Cleveland opposed the proposals of the silver advocates and used all his power to protect the soundness of the currency. But his party, under the urging of William Jennings Bryan and other Westerners, had accepted the theory that prosperity could be restored by the free coinage of silver at the ratio of sixteen to one, and he left office under the impression that he was the most unpopular man in the country. He took up his residence in Princeton, N.J., and was elected a trustee of Princeton University. In the course of a few years he came to be regarded as one of the political sages of the country and the esteem in which he was held when he died is indicated by the message from President Taft already quoted.

DE MOLAY DAY

The Order of De Molay observes every year the anniversary of the martyrdom of Jacques De Molay, the last grand master of the Order of Knights Templars, who was burned to death at Paris on March 18, 1314.

The Knights Templars had obtained great wealth and influence in Europe and King Philip IV of France wanted to possess their property in his country. He summoned De Molay from Cyprus, the headquarters of the order, to attend the christening of his child. When De Molay arrived in Paris he was arrested and imprisoned and tried before the Inquisition. On the order of the King he was sentenced to death.

The Order of De Molay was founded in Kansas City, Mo., in March 1919, by Frank S. Land who was interested in the problems of a sixteen-year-old boy of his acquaintance. On his invitation this boy and eight others met in the Masonic Temple in Kansas City and planned a boys' club. A week later thirty boys gathered at the same place and the club was well on its way to a successful career. It had no name but when the boys were told of the martyrdom of De Molay they decided to name the organization for him. A constitution was adopted providing that the members should be boys between sixteen and twenty-one years old, that sons of members of the Masonic order and their friends should be eligible, that they would observe March 18 as Devotional Day, May 1 as Patriots' Day, Educational Day at a date in September and Parents' Day in November, and that they would observe a day in January as Comforting Day. The members were also required to pledge themselves to support the public school system, to live cleanly, to be good sons, to honor women and to offer a prayer every night for their fathers and mothers. From this small beginning the order has spread throughout the United States with chapters in other countries as well. It is not a Masonic order, but each chapter is under the patronage of a Masonic lodge with a Master Mason as its councillor. There is a Legion of Honor within the order composed of members who have distinguished themselves in some way. The badge of the order is a shield resting upon crossed swords and surmounted by a helmet with the visor down. The shield bears a cross with four arms of equal length and in the quarterings thus formed a star, a crescent and the initials D and M are placed.

MARCH NINETEENTH

BIRTHDAY OF WILLIAM JENNINGS BRYAN

William Jennings Bryan, who was the most popular leader of the Democratic party for many years, was born at Salem, Ill., on March 19, 1860. He was graduated from the Illinois College in 1881. During his college course he took a prize in an oratorical contest. He was graduated from the Union College of Law at Chicago in 1883 and began practice at Jacksonville, Ill. In 1887 he moved to Lincoln, Neb., and in 1890 he was elected to the national House of Representatives, serving two terms. He favored the free coinage of silver at the ratio of sixteen ounces of silver to one of gold and in a congressional debate on August

16, 1893, he spoke for three hours in defense of bimetallism. While he was still in the House he twice unsuccessfully sought election to the Senate. He was editor of the Omaha *World-Herald* from 1894 to 1896, resigning after he was nominated for President by the Democratic National Convention in the latter year. As a delegate to the convention, he mounted the platform on the third day and delivered the famous "Cross of Gold" speech in denunciation of the gold standard, ending with the declaration, "You shall not press down upon the brow of labor this crown of thorns—you shall not crucify mankind upon a cross of gold." He was enthusiastically applauded and on the next day he was nominated for President on the fifth roll call. The National Silver Party and the Populists also nominated him, but he was defeated by William McKinley, the Republican candidate. He was nominated by acclamation by his party convention in 1900 and again defeated by McKinley. He was nominated for the third time in 1908, but was defeated by William H. Taft. His influence in his party continued, however, and it was largely because of his efforts that Woodrow Wilson was nominated in 1912. Mr. Wilson took Mr. Bryan into his Cabinet as Secretary of State, an office which he resigned because of his opposition to the war policy of the President. As Secretary of State he had negotiated a large number of arbitration treaties which he hoped would make war impossible. He was a popular lecturer and on his retirement from the Cabinet, indeed while he was still Secretary of State, he lectured in many parts of the country. In 1925, when John T. Scopes, a teacher in the high school at Dayton, Tenn., was charged with teaching evolution in violation of a law forbidding it in the public schools of the state, Mr. Bryan volunteered to act as attorney for the enforcement of the law. Scopes was convicted and Mr. Bryan, weakened by his exertions in the heat of a southern summer, died suddenly on July 26, 1925. A college has been founded at Dayton named for him and committed to teaching the story of creation as told in Genesis literally interpreted. During the height of his career he was almost worshipped by millions of people in the West. A Presbyterian clergyman who occupied the house in which he had lived in Lincoln once said that visitors to the city were in the habit of driving to the house and stopping to look reverently at it. One day the clergyman saw a farmer in the yard at the rear taking a tin can from a pile there and asking if he might have it as a memento from the place where Bryan had lived.

MARCH TWENTIETH

BIRTHDAY OF NEAL DOW

Neal Dow, known as the father of prohibition in Maine, was born at Portland in that state on March 20, 1804, of Quaker parents. He was trained in the principles of peace, industry, thrift and temperance held by the Quakers and espoused them throughout his long life. He was dismissed from the Society of Friends, however, because he came to disagree with it on the propriety of using "carnal weapons." He was educated at the Friends' Academy at New Bedford, Mass., and then joined his father in the tanning business, accumulating a large fortune. He early began to advocate temperance. His first speech on the subject was made in opposition to serving liquor at a dinner of the Deluge Engine Company of Portland. His plea was successful and no liquor was served to the firemen at the dinner. He attended as a delegate the first temperance convention in Maine when the State Temperance Society was organized. This was in 1834. Four years later he joined with others in organizing another temperance union whose members were pledged to total abstinence. It was not until 1845, however, that he persuaded this society to favor legislation forbidding the sale of intoxicants in the state. The Legislature passed a prohibitory law the next year which was unsatisfactory. In 1851, Dow while Mayor of Portland, was made chairman of a committee to urge stringent liquor legislation. He drafted a bill passed by the Legislature and signed on June 2, 1851, which is generally regarded as the date when prohibition began in Maine. Dow became the colonel of a Maine regiment when the Civil War began and rose to the rank of brigadier general. He was the candidate of the Prohibition party for President in 1880. Four years later, due to his urging, the Constitution of Maine was amended so as to prohibit the sale of intoxicants in the state. He died on October 2, 1897.

MARCH TWENTY-FIRST

THE FIRST INDIAN TREATY

On March 21, 1621, Governor Carver of the Plymouth Colony, made a treaty with Massasoit, sachem of the Wampanoag or Pokanoket Indians, pledging friendship and alliance between the Indians and the colonists. This was the first treaty with the Indians made within the thirteen colonies. It remained in effect for fifty-four years during which it was respected by both parties. The territory over which Massasoit ruled as head of the tribe embraced nearly all of southeastern Massachusetts. The tribe at one time was very large, but on the arrival of the Plymouth colonists in 1620 it numbered only about three hundred. Massasoit took sixty warriors with him to Plymouth when the treaty was made which probably included about all the adult males in the tribe. It was more than sixty years later that William Penn made his treaty with the Indians in eastern Pennsylvania.

MARCH TWENTY-SECOND

SIGNING OF THE STAMP ACT

On March 22, 1765, King George III approved the Stamp Act without any realization of the consequences. It provided for raising revenue by the sale of stamps to be affixed to various documents and commercial papers in the American colonies. It had been passed by the House of Commons by a large majority and passed unanimously by the House of Lords. Several speeches in opposition to it, however, had been made in the House of Commons. The enforcement of the act was resisted by the colonies which resented the levying of internal taxes by a body in which they were not represented. It was repealed in about a year (see Repudiation of the Stamp Act, November 23).

MARCH TWENTY-THIRD

PATRICK HENRY'S SPEECH FOR THE REVOLUTION

When a provincial convention assembled in Virginia in March 1775, Patrick Henry introduced a resolution providing for the organization of the militia in order to put the colony in shape for defense. It was bitterly opposed by the loyalists. On March 23 Henry defended his resolution in one of his most famous speeches. It concluded in this way:

There is no retreat but in submission to slavery. Our chains are already forged. Their clanking may be heard on the plains of Boston. The next gale that sweeps from the North will bring the clash of resounding arms. Our brethren are already in the field. Why stand we here idle? What is it that the gentlemen wish? What would they have? Is life so dear or peace so sweet as to be purchased at the price of chains and slavery? Forbid it, Almighty God! I know not what course others may take, but as for me, give me liberty or give me death!

His prophecy of the "clash of arms" from the North was fulfilled within less than a month, for on April 19 the Battle of Concord and Lexington was fought. This speech has been a favorite declamation with school boys.

MARCH TWENTY-FOURTH

BIRTHDAY OF FANNY CROSBY

Fanny Crosby, notable for her success in overcoming the handicap of blindness, was born at Southeast, Putnam County, New York, on March 24, 1820. She lost her sight when she was six weeks old through the blunder of a doctor. When she was fifteen years old she became a pupil in the New York Institution for the Blind where she showed facility in writing rhymes and was encouraged in it. From 1847 until her marriage in 1858 to Alexander Van Alstyne, one of her blind pupils, she taught English and history at the institution. Her career as a teacher won fame for her and she lectured in all parts of the country and was invited to address both Houses of Congress on several occasions. She began to write hymns in 1864, after she had already written many secular poems. The words of the song "There's Music in the Air," are hers. Among her best known hymns are "Safe in the Arms of Jesus," and "Pass Me Not, O Gentle Savior." It is estimated that she wrote at least six thousand religious poems. Many of them were included by Moody and Sankey in their *Gospel Hymns*. About seventy were adopted by the churches in England and some have been translated into other languages. The Methodist Episcopal Church observed in her honor a "Fanny Crosby Day" for many years. She died in her ninety-fifth year at Bridgeport, Conn.

MARCH TWENTY-FIFTH

MARYLAND DAY

This day is a holiday in Maryland set apart for the celebration of the landing in 1634 on St. Clement's Island of the colonists sent over from England in the "Ark" and the "Dove" by Lord Baltimore under the leadership of his brother Leonard Calvert. It is observed generally throughout the state. The first Lord Baltimore had arranged for a charter for the colony which Charles I insisted should be called Terra Mariae or Maryland for his queen, Henrietta Maria. He died before the charter was issued and King Charles granted it to his son, Cecil, under date of June 20, 1632. It made the colony an independent principality under the government of Lord Baltimore and provided that as compensation Lord Baltimore, his heirs and successors, should yield "unto us, our heirs and successors, two Indian arrow heads of these parts to be delivered at the said Castle of Windsor every year on Tuesday in Easter week; and also the fifth part of all gold and silver ore which shall happen from time to time to be found within the aforesaid limits."

It took some time to collect the colonists and to assemble supplies so that it was not until November 22, 1633, that the expedition sailed from Cowes on the Isle of Wight. Two vessels carried the colonists, the "Dove" of fifty tons, belonging to Lord Baltimore, and the "Ark" of three hundred and fifty tons, which had been chartered. They carried Leonard Calvert and about two hundred others of various trades, professions and religions. They sailed by way of the Barbadoes, Martinique and St. Kitts and arrived at Point Comfort, Virginia, on February 14. On March 25 they landed on St. Clement's island in the Potomac river and held a religious service. Not many days later they sailed up St. Mary's river and founded the town of St. Mary's which became the capital. Religious freedom was guaranteed in the beginning, but in 1649 some Puritans, fleeing from the religious intolerance in Virginia where the Church of England was the state church, got possession of the government and practiced intolerance of their own. In 1660 they were ousted and there was religious freedom until 1689, when it was again restricted and remained so until the adoption of the Federal Constitution in 1788.

The tercentenary of the founding of the state was celebrated with elaborate ceremonies in 1933 and 1934. On November 22, 1933, there was a celebration at Cowes, from which the colonists had sailed three hundred years before. Addresses were made by Sir Timothy Eden, a descendant of Lord Baltimore, by Lord Fairfax, and by Robert W. Bingham, American Ambassador to England. President Roosevelt, who was at Warm Springs, Ga., spoke over the radio in honor of the anniversary. Among other things he said: "Lord Baltimore and his colonists sought in their charter liberty, not alone for members of the expedition, but for all later comers as well. It is a good thing to demand liberty for ourselves and for those who agree with us, but it is a better thing to give liberty to others whom we do not agree with." On Sunday, February 3, 1934, Governor Ritchie of Maryland presented to the Washington Cathedral a Maryland flag on behalf of the Colonial Dames. There were celebrations in different parts of the state between that date and June 16 when a three-day celebration took place at St. Mary's, the site of the first capital of the state.

A tract of land including a part of the site of the city had been deeded to the state by Mrs. James Milburn Bennett of Philadelphia and Mrs. J. Spencer Howard of Baltimore, the surviving daughters of a family which had owned it for years. The city itself had long since disappeared. In order to perpetuate its memory and make the site a shrine of patriotism a reproduction of the first state house, erected from the original plans, was dedicated during the celebration. A British ship of war was sent from Bermuda to take part in the celebration and American ships of war were also present. Reproductions of the "Ark" and the "Dove" sailed up the river and men and women landed from them dressed in the costumes of the seventeenth century. Other persons dressed as Indians watched the landing from the shore, and there were a parade and a pageant recounting in floats and tableaux the history of the settlement. A concrete cross was dedicated on St. Clement's island. There were also a dinner and a ball. At the dinner Governor Ritchie proposed a toast to King George V of Great Britain and Captain Fallowfield of the British sloop of war, "Dundee," proposed a toast to the President of the United States. An ode to Maryland was read by Nancy Byrd Turner, whose father was once the rector of the parish of St. Mary's.

PALM SUNDAY

Beginning in the tenth century, if not as early as the fifth, the Sunday before Easter has been observed as Palm Sunday. It fell on March 25 in 1945. It is in commemoration of the entry of Jesus into Jerusalem as described by Matthew. Jesus told two of his disciples, when he reached the Mount of Olives on his way to the city, to get him an ass. The record follows:

And the disciples went and did as Jesus commanded them and brought the ass and the colt and put on them their clothes and they set him theron. And a very great multitude spread their garments in the way; others cut down branches from the trees and strewed them in the way. And the multitudes that went before and that followed cried, saying, "Hosanna to the Son of David: Blessed is he that cometh in the name of the Lord; Hosanna in the highest." And when he was come into Jerusalem, all the city was moved, saying, "Who is this?" And the multitude said, "This is Jesus, the prophet of Nazareth of Galilee."

From very early days the church ordered that palm branches should be carried in procession on the day. The palms were blessed by the priests and distributed among the people. This custom survives to the present when palms are given to the worshipers. Sometimes two pieces are joined in the form of a cross and the men wear them in their hats. These palms were once supposed to have the power of warding off evil from their possessors. In countries where there are no palms or where their branches are not easily obtainable the branches of other trees are used. In Germany the day was known as Blossom Sunday and in England, where branches of the willow and other trees were used it was known as Olive or Branch Sunday, Sallow or Willow, Yew or Blossom Sunday, or Sunday of the Willow Boughs. The celebration was so popular that when Henry VIII broke with the church of Rome he ordered that the observance of the day in the usual manner should be continued although he forbade the practice of other Roman Catholic observances. In the early days it was customary to reproduce the entry of Jesus into Jerusalem with a priest riding an ass and carrying the host leading a procession through the town and back to the church while the people threw branches of trees in the street before him. Sometimes a wooden ass, mounted on wheels and carrying a wooden figure representing Jesus was used. These old customs, however, have died out for the most part in the Old World where they originated. They were never adopted in the United States.

Little note was taken of the day by the reformed churches after the time of Martin Luther, but with the growing breadth of vision nearly all of the Protestant churches observe it with special services and some of them even distribute palm branches to the congregation. Even in the least ritualistic of them a sermon appropriate to the occasion is usually preached.

MARCH 26

LADY DAY OR THE FEAST OF THE ANNUNCIATION

The supposed anniversary of the announcement to Mary that she would bear a son and that he would be called Jesus is celebrated by the Christian church on March 25. The celebration was mentioned as early as 430. The date was fixed after it had been decided that Jesus was born on December 25. The New Testament account of the annunciation follows:

In the sixth month the angel Gabriel was sent from God unto a city of Galilee named Nazareth, to a virgin espoused to a man whose name was Joseph of the house of David; and the virgin's name was Mary. And the angel came in unto her and said, "Hail, thou art highly favored, the Lord is with thee; blessed art thou among women." And when she saw him, she was troubled at his saying and cast in her mind what manner of salutation this should be. And the angel said unto her: "Fear not, Mary, for thou hast found favor with God, and behold thou shalt conceive in thy womb and bring forth a son, and shalt call his name Jesus. He shall be great and shall be called the Son of the Highest; and the Lord God shall give unto him the throne of his father David."

Lady Day was highly regarded in England for many centuries. It is now one of the days on which it is customary to pay rent and other bills.

MARCH TWENTY-SIXTH

BIRTHDAY OF COUNT RUMFORD

Benjamin Thompson, who became Count Rumford, a distinguished American physicist and loyalist during the Revolution, was born at Woburn, Mass., on March 26, 1753. He entered a merchant's office at Salem at the age of thirteen and spent his spare time studying medicine and physics. He later moved to Rumford, N.H., as Concord was then called, and at the age of nineteen he married a rich widow of the town and was made a major of militia by the English Governor. At the outbreak of the Revolution he went to Boston and when the British evacuated the city he was sent as their agent bearing despatches to London. He became Under Secretary of State there and because of his scientific investigations he was elected a fellow of the Royal Society. He is especially noted for his studies into the nature of heat. The prevailing theory was that it was due to "caloric," an elastic fluid which permeated all matter. He insisted that it was produced by motion, the theory now generally accepted. On the resignation of Lord North's ministry Thompson returned to America and fought with the British armies. At the close of the war he entered the military service of Bavaria, becoming a lieutenant general and Minister of War. He was made a count of the Holy Roman Empire and chose Rumford as his title after the New Hampshire town in which he had lived. He returned to London in 1799

188

and at his suggestion the Royal Institution was founded in 1800. He finally settled in France and died there on April 21, 1814. He had previously founded the Rumford medal of the Royal Society and was the first to receive it, and he founded a similar medal to be awarded by the American Academy of Arts and Sciences and he also endowed a chair at Harvard college. Like Franklin he was interested in practical things and discovered a way to build fireplaces and chimneys to prevent them from filling the rooms with smoke.

MARCH TWENTY-SEVENTH

REBUILDING THE NAVY

The United States had no navy worth mentioning from the close of the Revolutionary War until 1794. Such ships as the country had were either destroyed in battle or dismissed from the service. But the Barbary pirates were attacking American merchant vessels in the Mediterranean and it became necessary to build a navy to defend the vessels. President Washington, on March 3, 1794, sent a message to Congress calling attention to the action of the pirates. Congress thereupon passed an act providing for the purchase or construction of six frigates of not less than thirty-two guns. The President signed the act on March 27. Arrangements were immediately made for building the "Constitution," the "President," the "United States," the "Chesapeake," the "Constellation" and the "Congress." The act provided that if the trouble with the pirates should cease the construction of the vessels should be stopped. A treaty with the Dey of Algiers was signed in November 1795, and an order was issued stopping work. The President protested and Congress ordered the completion of three of the vessels. One of them was the "Constitution" which was launched on October 21, 1797. She made a brilliant record in the War of 1812 and in 1830 an order to dismantle her was issued. But Oliver Wendell Holmes protested in a stirring poem and the order was rescinded. The ship is preserved to this day, in South Boston Navy Yard, as one of the most interesting relics of the navy. (See also August 19, The "Constitution's" Great Victory.)

MARCH TWENTY-EIGHTH

PRESIDENT JACKSON CENSURED

One of the few resolutions of censure passed by the United States Senate was adopted on March 28, 1834, by a vote of twenty-six to twenty in condemnation of President Jackson for removing the deposits from the United States Bank. President Jackson's campaign against the bank began in his second term. He had decided to withdraw the deposits of money from the bank which had been the fiscal agent of the government, receiving its revenues and paying them out on the order of the proper official. The President appointed William J. Duane of Philadelphia as Secretary of the Treasury, with the expectation that he would obey orders. Duane, however, refused to withdraw the deposits and he was removed and Roger B. Taney of Virginia, the Attorney General, was appointed in his place and ceased making deposits in the bank and the money there was drawn to pay bills. The opponents of the President and the friends of the bank denounced the President in bitter terms and charged him with producing a financial panic. The President's friends charged the bank with causing the panic by reducing its circulation and restricting its loans. When Congress met, Senator Henry Clay introduced a resolution condemning the President for what he had done. He charged that all power had been concentrated in the hands of one man and that an "elective monarchy" was all but established, that the power over the purse had been lodged with the power over the sword, a combination fatal to freedom. The debate on the resolution continued for many weeks with Senator Benton of Missouri leading the defenders of the President.

DAFFODIL FESTIVAL IN WASHINGTON

The first Daffodil Festival was held on April 6, 1926, at the estate of Charles Orton, near Sumner, Wash., under the auspices of the Sumner Garden Club. It continued as an annual event and by 1934 had achieved national fame, attracting many thousands of visitors from all over the United States. The communities of Tacoma, Puyallup, and Sumner have joined forces in promoting the festival and selecting a royal court to preside over the ceremonies. The celebration lasts a week, usually beginning late in March when the daffodils are in full bloom. The festival in 1948 began on March 28th. An endless cavalcade of motorists tours the Puyallup valley past hundreds of acres of the golden flowers whose scenic beauty is enhanced by the white-capped head of Mt. Rainier against a springtime sky. A flower show is held at Sumner during the festival, exhibiting several hundred varieties of bulbs grown locally. There is a fifteen-mile-long floral parade in which the three communities participate, and picturesque coronation ceremonies for the festival queen and her royal court, as well as many other lesser events.

The Puyallup valley is one of the chief centers of bulb culture in the world. The local industry is valued in the neighborhood of eight million dollars, with annual shipments approximating three million dollars worth of bulbs. They are sent by carload lots to eastern markets where many are placed in hothouses and forced into early spring bloom. Ideal soil, moisture and other growing conditions, together with innovations in the use of machinery in the fields differing radically from the hand labor technique of Holland, have combined to foster the development of the industry. Small, experimental plantings were first made at Fox Island, Washington, in 1905. These and later plantings in 1915 were principally for the purpose of producing cut flowers, but by 1924 the favorable conditions for bulb growing led to the formation of the Northwest Bulb Growers Association, and subsequent successful expansion.

MARCH TWENTY-NINTH

BIRTHDAY OF JOHN TYLER

John Tyler, the tenth President of the United States, was born at Greenway, Charles City County, Va., on March 29, 1790. He was the son of Judge John Tyler, who was Speaker of the Virginia House of Delegates, Governor of Virginia and a judge of the state and federal courts. He was graduated from William and Mary College in 1807 and was admitted to the bar in 1809. At the age of twenty-one he was elected to the Virginia Legislature where he acted with the Republican party now known as the Democratic party. He served five terms and was then elected to the national House of Representatives. He served three terms in Washington, acting with the states-rights wing of his party, opposing the Missouri Compromise. In 1823 he was again elected to the state legislature. Two years later he was elected governor and at the end of his term was unanimously chosen to succeed himself. At the close of his second term he was elected to the United States Senate over John Randolph, taking his seat on December 3, 1827. He was elected for a second term, made a report censuring President Jackson for removing the deposits from the United States Bank and voted for Clay's resolution of censure. When the Virginia Legislature adopted a resolution calling on him to vote for expunging the resolution of censure from the record he refused to obey, resigned his seat in February 1836, and retired to private life. He was now affiliated with the Whig party and was an unsuccessful aspirant for the Whig nomination for Vice President in this year. But in 1840 he was nominated for Vice President by the Whigs on the ticket with General Harrison and was elected. It is said that the nomination had been arranged in the previous year when he had agreed not to become a candidate for reelection to the Senate at the request of the Whig leaders who then agreed to make him the candidate for vice president. General Harrison died one month after he entered office. This was the first time the presidency had become vacant since the adoption of the Constitution and there was much discussion about the manner in which the Vice President should function. Some authorities insisted that he did not become President by the death of the man elected to that office, but was only Acting President. Tyler settled the dispute by moving into the White House and by assuming the title by which its official occupant is known.

Tyler had been elected as a Whig but he broke with that party and worked with the Democrats. The Whigs had favored rechartering the Bank of the United States and as they controlled both houses of Congress they passed a charter. Tyler vetoed it. A new bill was drafted in an attempt to meet his objections and was passed, but he vetoed that also. He had retained the Cabinet appointed by Harrison, but in September 1841, all its members save Daniel Webster resigned. Webster remained to conclude the treaty with Great Britain fixing the northeastern boundary. When this task was finished he also resigned. Thereupon some of the Whig leaders issued a public address declaring that "all political connection with them and John Tyler was at an end from that day henceforth." He negotiated a treaty for the annexation of Texas, but it was rejected by the Senate. Texas was later annexed by a joint resolution, precipitating the Mexican War.

Tyler sought the presidential nomination in 1844, but the Whigs nominated Henry Clay. A small group of them, however, named Tyler, but when he saw that he had no popular following he withdrew and gave his support to Polk, the Democratic candidate. On the expiration of his term he retired to his estate in Charles City County. He remained there until he was called to Washington to preside over a futile Peace Convention in Washington in 1861. He then voted for secession in the Virginia convention, served in the Provisional Confederate Congress, and was elected to the Confederate House of Representatives. He died, however, on January 1862, before taking his seat.

MARCH THIRTIETH

GOOD FRIDAY

Good Friday falls on the Friday before Easter Sunday which is a movable celebration. It fell on March 30, 1945, as Easter was April 1 in that year. It is observed as a holiday in Arkansas, Connecticut, Delaware, Florida, Illinois, Indiana, Louisiana, Maryland, Minnesota, New Jersey, North Dakota, Pennsylvania, South Carolina, and Texas; also in five counties of Arizona. The day is known in the Greek Church as the Holy and Great Friday. The Anglo-Saxons called it Long Friday. It is called Holy Friday in the countries in which the Romance languages are spoken, and in English speaking countries it is Good Friday. Why it is called "good" is not definitely known. According to one theory it comes from "God's Friday," and according to another the word refers to the good which came to the world through the life and death of Jesus.

The day is observed in commemoration of the Crucifixion. It is customary to read the following account of the event from the Gospel of St. John during the services in the churches:

And it was the preparation of the passover, and about the sixth hour; and he (Pilate) saith unto the Jews, "Behold your King!" But they cried out, "Away with him, away with him, crucify him!" Pilate saith unto them, "Shall I crucify your King?" The chief priests answered, "We have no king but Caesar." Then delivered he him, therefore, unto them to be crucified. And they took Jesus and led him away. And he, bearing his cross, went forth into a place called the place of the skull, which is called in the Hebrew Golgotha; where they crucified him, and two others with him, on either side one, and Jesus in the midst. And Pilate wrote a title and put it on the cross. And the writing was "Jesus of Nazareth the King of the Jews." This title then read many of the Jews: for the place where Jesus was crucified was nigh to the city; and it was written in Hebrew, Greek and Latin. Then said the chief priests of the Jews to Pilate, "Write not, the King of the Jews; but that he said I am King of the Jews." Pilate answered, "What I have written I have written." Then the soldiers, when they had crucified Jesus, took his garments, and made four parts, to every soldier a part; also his coat: now the coat was without seam, woven from the top throughout. They said therefore among themselves, "Let us not rend it, but cast lots for it, whose it shall be": that the scripture might be fulfilled, which saith, "They parted my raiment among them, and for my vesture they did cast lots." These things, therefore, the soldiers did.

Now there stood by the cross of Jesus his mother, and his mother's sister, Mary the wife of Cleophas, and Mary Magdelene. When Jesus therefore saw his mother and the disciple standing by whom he loved, he saith unto his mother, "Woman, behold thy son!" Then saith he to the disciple, "Behold thy mother." And from that hour that disciple took her unto his own home.

After this, Jesus, knowing all things were now accomplished, that the scripture might be fulfilled, saith "I thirst." Now there was set a vessel full of vinegar: and they filled a sponge with vinegar, and put upon it hysop, and put it to his mouth. When Jesus therefore had received the vinegar, he said, "It is finished," and he bowed his head and gave up the ghost.

The Jews, therefore, because it was the preparation, that the bodies should not remain upon the cross on the Sabbath day, (for that Sabbath was an high day), besought Pilate that their legs might be broken, and that they might be taken away. Then came the soldiers and brake the legs of the first and of the other which was crucified with him. But when they came to Jesus, and saw that he was dead already, they brake not his legs; but one of the soldiers with a spear pierced his side, and forthwith came there out blood and water. And he that saw it bare record and his record is true; and he knoweth that he saith true, that ye might believe. For these things were done that the scripture might be fulfilled, "A bone of him shall not be broken." And again another scripture, "They shall look on him whom they pierced."

And after this Joseph of Arimathaea, being a disciple of Jesus, but secretly for fear of the Jews, besought Pilate that he might take away the body of Jesus, and Pilate gave him leave. He came therefore and took the body of Jesus. And there came also Nicodemus, which at first came to Jesus by night, and brought a mixture of myrrh and aloes, about an hundred pound weight. Then took they the body of Jesus, and wound it in linen clothes with the spices after the manner of the Jews, to bury. Now in the place where he was crucified there was a garden, and in the garden a new sepulchre wherein was never man laid. There laid they Jesus, therefore, because of the Jew's preparation day; for the sepulchre was nigh at hand.

The Good Friday services in the Roman Catholic churches are in accordance with an elaborate ritual, based on the services of the early Christian church. In the beginning every Friday was a fast day and every Sunday a feast day. But the Friday before Easter came to be observed with special rigors. The priests wear black vestments, the altar is bare at first and the candles are not lighted. In the course of the ceremonies the cross is adored and the body of Jesus is buried again symbolically in a tomb behind the altar.

With the gradual growth of an understanding that the great Christian anniversaries are the property of all Christendom, the Protestant churches now observe Good Friday with appropriate services as they observe Christmas and Easter.

The custom of eating hot cross buns on Good Friday was introduced in America from England. As is well known the bun is a small spiced confection marked on the top with a cross in white icing. In England they were sold on the street by venders who cried their wares in this way:

> One a penny, buns,
> Two a penny, buns,
> One a penny, two a penny
> Hot cross buns!

Another version of the street cry, frequently repeated by American children is:

> One a penny, two a penny,
>   Hot cross buns,
> If you have no daughters,
> Give them to your sons;
> But if you have none of these merry little elves,
> Then you may keep them all for yourselves.

The origin of the word "bun" is lost in the mists of antiquity. An attempt has been made to connect it with a species of sacred bread offered to the gods in the time of Cecrops, the mythological founder of Attica. This bread was called boun, which with the final letter changed to an "s" becomes bous, the Greek word for an ox. The cake was ornamented with the two horns of an ox, and, according to the theory, when the pagan custom was adopted by the early church, the horns were changed into a cross. This is an interesting theory based on the well known practice of the early church, but it is not accepted by the lexicographers. Writers on the early customs in England entertain the theory that the bakers, envious of the profits of the church, began to make the buns marked with the cross to increase their own revenues. At any rate it is known that in the early eighteenth century there was in London the Old Chelsea Bun-House, to which the people flocked on Good Friday morning to the number of fifty thousand at times to buy the buns and that as many as a hundred and fifty thousand of them were sold. A rival bun house arose and the competition was fierce. George III showed his preference for the Chelsea house by going there in person and buying his buns.

There are many Good Friday customs in Europe which have not found a footing in America. In Portugal it has been customary to hang Judas in effigy. In Spain the ladies appear in the street in black and sit in the churches and solicit alms for the poor. There have been processions of penitents in Palermo, Sicily, made up of persons masked with a hood containing two openings for the eyes. A crown of thorns rests upon the hood and each penitent wears a rope around his neck which reaches down to the hands that are tied with it. They march through the streets in charge of monks or priests. And in other places a mystery play is presented, preceded by a procession through the streets.

SEWARD DAY IN ALASKA

March 30 is a holiday in Alaska known as Seward Day, observed in commemoration of the signing by Secretary Seward on March 30, 1867, of the treaty with Russia under which the territory was ceded to the United States for $7,200,000. Alaska was for many years called "Seward's Folly," but with the discovery of gold the wisdom of the purchase was no longer questioned.

The northwestern part of North America came into the possession of Russia through the explorations of Bering for whom the Bering Sea and Bering Strait were named. The St. Petersburg government, however, was not particularly interested in the new land but the fur traders attracted attention to the possibilities of wealth there and when other countries began to look in that direction the fur traders appealed to the Empress Catherine for protection. She replied that she would "furnish neither men, nor ships, nor money," and renounced forever "all lands and possessions in the East Indies and America." But in spite of lack of official encouragement private adventurers made numerous expeditions to Alaska and accumulated considerable wealth. In 1788 the government granted a trading company a monopoly of trade in all Russian possessions on the shores of the North Pacific. This monopoly was renewed for another twenty years and the company was occupying most of the present area of Alaska when a third renewal was obtained, but when the time came for a fourth renewal the company was in financial trouble and the renewal was refused. In the late 1850's there was talk of a transfer of Alaska to the United States, but the outbreak of the Civil War prevented any definite negotiations. In 1864, the Secretary of State, on instructions from the President, invited the Tsar to send the Grand Duke Constantine to this country as a friendly commissioner to discuss the relations between the two countries, but the invitation was not accepted. The Legislature of Washington Territory sent a memorial to Washington, D.C. in 1866 setting forth the difficulties arising out of the relations of the fishing boats from the territory with the Russians to the north. Later in the same year Mr. de Stoeckl, the Russian Minister in Washington, went to St. Petersburg on a leave of absence and set forth to the government there the reasons for the surrender of Alaska to the United States. He returned in March 1867, with the assurance that the territory would be surrendered. On March 23 he received an offer of $7,200,000 on condition that the cessation be "free and unencumbered by any reservations, privileges, franchises, grants or possessions by any associated companies." On March 25 the Russian minister replied that he believed he was authorized to accept the offer. On March 29 a cable message from Russia confirmed this impression and at four o'clock on the morning of March 30 the treaty was signed. It was ratified in May, and on June 20 the President issued a proclamation annoucing the purchase. The formal transfer was made on October 18, 1867 (See Alaska Day, October 18.)

MARCH THIRTY-FIRST

WIDOWS OF THE PRESIDENTS PENSIONED

When President Garfield died in 1881 he left little property. Within a few months his friends suggested that his widow be pensioned by the government, and a bill for that purpose was introduced in Congress. It was soon learned that the widows of Presidents Polk and Tyler were still alive and the bill was amended so as to include them as the recipients of a pension of $5000 a year. It was passed on March 31, 1882. And it has been customary since then for Congress to vote a similar pension to the widows of other Presidents.

TRANSFER OF VIRGIN ISLANDS

The Virgin Islands, a group of islands about sixty miles east of Porto Rico and formerly known as the Dutch West Indies, was purchased from Denmark by the United States in 1917 for $25,000,000. The group consists mainly of the islands of St. Thomas, St. Croix, and St. John, with a total area of one hundred and thirty-two square miles. The capital is St. Thomas on the island of that name. It is the principal port, with coaling and oil fueling stations.

Columbus discovered the group in 1494, and its subsequent history was that of the New World; of colonial expansion by European powers and of exploitation of these colonies. The Danish Code of Laws, known as the Colonial Laws, remains in force. Civil, military, and judicial powers are vested in a governor who is appointed by the President of the United States with the consent of the Senate. The legislative council has twenty-four members elected by popular vote and nine nominated by the governor.

The chief industries were rum, bayrum and sugar refining, but prohibition and the decline of the sugar trade left the islands so destitute that Congress appropriated over four hundred thousand dollars for relief work in 1930. Meanwhile, United States citizenship had been conferred on the natives in 1927, and in recognition of these and other benefits Transfer Day is observed annually on March 31.

Ponce de Leon

APRIL

O April, welcome home! The stirring earth
Is scrubbed and scoured, fresh clean with rain;
You are the hope of beauty and the birth
Of life from death—come, welcome home again!

—ANNE MARY LAWLER

April was the second month in the ancient Roman year but when the calendar was revised it became the fourth month. The origin of its name is lost in the mists of antiquity. The most commonly accepted theory is that it is derived from the Latin verb asperie, meaning "to open," in allusion to the opening of the buds on the trees and plants at this season. This theory is supported by analogy with the modern Greek custom of calling the spring "anoixis," or "the opening." On the other hand, it was the Roman custom to name the months for divinities. As April was sacred to Venus and as the Festival of Venus was held on the first day of the month it has been conjectured that Aprilis, the Latin form of the word, was originally Aphrilis from the Greek, Aphrodite. Jacob Grimm, a distinguished German phi-lologist, however, suggested that the name is derived from a hypothetical god or hero, Aper or Aprus, thus rejecting the theory of its connection with Aphrodite, but seeking to find its origin in the name of a deity. The month was called Oster-monath or Eostur-monath by the Anglo-Saxons, from Eostre or Ostra, the goddess of the spring, from whom the Christian festi-val of Easter takes its name.

April has been a fateful month for the United States for it was in this month that the Revolutionary War began with the Battle of Concord and Lexington; that the Civil War began, with the firing on Fort Sumter; that the Spanish-American War started, with the ultimatum to Spain and that the declaration of war against Germany was made in 1917.

APRIL FIRST

ALL FOOLS' DAY

Many explanations have been offered for the custom of playing practical jokes on the first of April, but there is agreement on none of them. The impression prevails, however, that the custom has something to do with the observance of the spring equinox. In India the Feast of Huli, which occurs on March 31, has been celebrated for numberless centuries by sending people on foolish errands. One fantastic explanation is that the custom arose from a farcical celebration of the sending of Jesus from Annas to Caiphas, from Caiphas to Pilate, from Pilate to Herod and from Herod back to Pilate at the time of the trial and crucifixion. But this is not taken seriously. Another theory is that it is a relic of the Roman Cerealia, held at the beginning of April. According to the legend, Proserpina had filled her lap with daffodils in the Elysian meadows when Pluto found her and carried her screaming to the lower world. Ceres, her mother, heard the echo of the screams and went in search of the voice, but her search was like a fool's errand for it was impossible to find the echo.

April fooling became customary in France after the adoption of the reformed calendar by Charles IX in 1564, making the year begin on January 1. It had previously been common for the people to make new year's gifts and exchange calls on April 1 under the old calendar, and conservatives objected to the change. Wags accordingly sent to these persons mock gifts on April 1 and made calls of pretended ceremony. Nowadays the person fooled in France is called a *poisson d'avril*, that is an April fish. Whether this is because the sun is leaving the zodiacal sign of Pisces at the time or because April fish are easily caught no one knows. It was not until the beginning of the eighteenth century that April fooling became common in England. In Scotland the April fools are called April gowks, the gowk being a cuckoo. The early settlers of America brought the custom with them. It is observed here chiefly by small boys. They will write "Kick Me" on a piece of paper and pin it surreptitiously on the back of a companion, and await the result with ill suppressed glee. They will also pin a card with "April Fool" written on it on another's coat. They will tie a string to a purse, drop the purse on the sidewalk and then conceal themselves with the end of the string in their hands. When some one stoops to pick up the purse they pull it out of his reach. Sometimes they nail a purse to a board and fool the unsuspecting. Or they put a brick under an old hat and wait for some one to try to kick it out of his way. Balls of cotton covered with chocolate to look like candies are also prepared as well as balls of pepper and salt. Little children find delight in telling one of their elders that there is a hole in his sock or a thread on his coat or a black spot on his cheek and then laughing uproariously as the victim looks for it, and shouting "April fool!" Their elders are not immune to the temptation to play practical jokes on the day. It has been common in cities in which there is an aquarium or a zoological garden for a man to tell another in his office to call up such and such a telephone number, giving the number of the aquarium or the zoo, as "Mr. Fish" or "Mr. Camel" wished to speak to him. This custom became so annoying to those in charge of the Aquarium and the Zoological Garden in New York that they have their telephones disconnected on April 1. In towns without such natural history collections the butcher's telephone number is given to the victim and he is told that Mr. Lamb has a message for him.

EASTER

Easter is the principal feast of the ecclesiastical year. It is now celebrated on the Sunday after the first full moon following the spring equinox. In the early years of the Christian church there was a controversy over the proper date for the celebration. The resurrection occurred at the time of the Jewish Passover festival. This was on the fourteenth day of the month Nisan. Because of the peculiarities of the Jewish calendar this date did not fall on the same day of the week and was shifted about from year to year so that there was a variation of thirty days in the time of its celebration. Jesus rose from the dead on the first day of the week, that is, on Sunday. The Gentile Christians insisted that Easter should be celebrated on Sunday and the Christians who had been Jews observed the day on the date of the Passover, regardless of whether it was Sunday. The Council of Nicaea in 325, decided that the celebration should occur on the same day throughout the church. It was finally decided that the date should be the Sunday after the first full moon following the spring equinox. The date for the equinox was fixed as March 21, and it was provided that if the full moon appeared on that date Easter should be the next Sunday. Consequently Easter moves between March 22 and April 25. The day in 1945 fell on April 1. The event celebrated is described in St. Matthew's gospel in this way:

In the end of the Sabbath, as it began to dawn toward the first day of the week, came Mary Magdalene and the other Mary to see the sepulchre. And, behold, there was a great earthquake, for the angel of the Lord descended from heaven, and came and rolled back the stone from the door and sat upon it. His countenance was like lightning, and his raiment as white as snow. And for fear of him the keepers did shake and become as dead men. And the angel answered and said to the women, "Fear not ye; for I know that ye seek Jesus, which was crucified. He is not here, for he is risen, as he said. Come, see the place where the Lord lay. And go quickly and tell his disciples that he is risen from the dead; and behold, he goeth before you into Galilee; there ye shall see him. Lo, I have told you." And they departed quickly from the sepulchre with fear and great joy, and did run to bring his disciples word. And as they went to tell his disciples, behold, Jesus met them, saying, "All hail." And they came and held him by the feet and worshipped him. Then said Jesus unto them, "Be not afraid. Go tell my brethren that they go into Galilee, and there they shall see me."

The name of the feast, according to the Venerable Bede, comes from Eostre, a Teutonic goddess whose festival was celebrated in the spring. Her name was given to the Christian festival in celebration of the Resurrection. Eostre it was who, according to the legend, opened the portals of Valhalla to receive Baldur, called the White God, because of his purity and also the Sun God, because his brow supplied light to mankind. It was Baldur who, after he had been murdered by Utgard Loki, the enemy of goodness and truth, spent half the year in Valhalla and the other half with the pale goddess of the lower regions.

The French call the festival Pasque, from the Latin Festa Paschalia. The word paschalia comes from an Aramaic form of the Hebrew word meaning passover. There is no doubt that the Church in its early days adopted the old pagan customs and gave a Christian meaning to them. As the festival of Eostre was in celebration of the renewal of life in the spring it was easy to make it a celebration of the resurrection from the dead of Jesus, whose gospel they preached.

The Roman and the Greek churches have an elaborate ritual for the services on the day. With the rise of Puritanism in England and its abhorrence of religious ceremonial the Protestants for a long time took no notice of Easter, or of any other of the church festivals. At one time the celebration of Christmas was forbidden in New England. But within the past fifty years virtually all the Protestant denominations observe Easter, unusually with elaborate services including special music. And early in the present century many of the Protestant churches began to adopt the custom of the Catholic churches by holding sunrise services on Easter morning in commemoration of the resurrection at sunrise. There is a traditional belief that on Easter morning the sun dances and that those who rise in time can see it. Recently the custom has arisen of holding a sunrise service on a mountain top.

It was during the Civil War that the nonritualistic churches began to observe Easter. So many men were killed and so many homes were made desolate that the churches strove to bring all the consolations of religion to the bereaved. In the Presbyterian churches first, and in the others later, the Easter season was selected for reminding those in mourning, whether widow, mother or orphan, of the promise of resurrection in the story of the risen Christ. The custom of decorating the churches with flowers for the Easter service has become general and a Bermuda lily which blossoms in the spring is used so largely that it has come to be known as the Easter lily.

In ecclesiastical art the lion is a symbol of the resurrection. It was believed that the lioness brought forth her young dead, and that the lion brought them to life after three days by howling over them. Another resurrection symbol is the phoenix, a mythical Egyptian bird, which dies and lives again. The egg also came to be regarded as symbolical of the resurrection, as it holds the seed of a new life. But eggs came to be associated with Easter originally because it was forbidden to eat them during Lent and on Easter Sunday they were served. They were dyed red to suggest joyousness, but according to another theory the color was symbolic of the blood shed on Calvary. The egg, however, as a symbol of new life is much older than Christianity. And the coloring of it at the spring festival is also of very ancient origin. The Egyptians, the Persians, the Greeks and the Romans used it in this way. Eggs were eaten during the spring festival from very early times. In medieval England the priest blessed the Easter eggs in a form of benediction authorized by Pope Paul V in the course of which he said that they were eaten "in thankfulness on account of the resurrection of our Lord." The children are told that the rabbit lays the Easter eggs and the eggs are sometimes hidden in the garden for the children to find. This is an adaptation of the pagan custom of regarding the rabbit as an emblem of fertility, that is, of new life. Many American Catholics have a boiled ham for dinner on Easter without being aware of the origin of the custom. It is a survival of the ancient habit among the English of eating a gammon of bacon on that day to show their contempt for the Jewish custom of not eating pork. It was doubtless brought to this country by the English and Irish settlers.

APRIL SECOND

PASCH MONDAY

Easter Monday, which fell on April 2 in 1945, has been celebrated in various ways in Europe and some of the customs have been adopted in the United States, although with much of their original significance forgotten. The day is called Pasch Monday, the name coming to us from the Hebrew through the French. The Dutch form is Pass Monday. In early England the day was one of jubilation in which various sports were indulged in. One was the custom called "Lifting." The women would go about the villages and two of them would make a chair with their hands, lift a man in it, and carry him to the village green where he had to pay a forfeit the nature of which was decided by the people gathered there. On the next day the men carried the women in the same way. The connection of eggs with Easter Monday has been common for many centuries. The egg has long been regarded as the symbol of a new birth. The ancient Persians believed that the earth was hatched from an egg at the time of the spring equinox. The early Christians regarded the egg as a symbol of the resurrection and when dyed red the color represented the blood shed on the cross.

There is an ancient French superstition that the church bells, which were silent during Passion Week, went to Rome to receive the blessing of the Pope and that they returned on Easter eve, bringing with them eggs dyed scarlet like the cloak of a cardinal. These eggs were supposed to be given to the heads of families to be distributed among the children. In England and in some parts of Europe there were egg-rolling contests in which the children would roll the eggs, boiled hard, down a hill. The winner was the child who rolled the greatest number of eggs without cracking the shell. This custom has been adopted in Washington where the egg-rolling contest on the grounds of the White House is one of the pleasantest and most picturesque observances in the national capital. The custom is said to have been introduced by Dolly Madison, the wife of President Madison. At first the eggs were rolled down the terraces of the Capitol grounds. A contemporary description of the frolic follows:

At first the children sit sedately in long rows; each has brought a basket of gay-colored hard-boiled eggs, and those on the upper terrace send them rolling to the line next below, and those pass on the ribbon-like streams to other hundreds at the foot, who scramble for the hopping eggs and hurry panting to the top to start them down again. And as the sport warms, those on top who have rolled all the eggs they brought finally roll themselves, shrieking with laughter. Now comes a swirl of curls, ribbons and furbelows, somebody's dainty maid indifferent to bumps and grass stains. A set of boys who started in a line of six with joined hands are trying to come down in somersaults without breaking the chain. On all sides the older folks stand by to watch the games of this infant carnival.

When the guardians of the Capitol found that the sport injured the grass on the terraces, the egg-rolling was transferred to the larger grounds of the White House. The gates of the grounds were opened at nine o'clock in the morning and remained open until five o'clock in the afternoon. During this time thousands of children accompanied by adults rolled three hundred thousand eggs in the old time contest in which the children whose eggs were not cracked were declared the winners. As no adult was allowed in the grounds unless accompanied by a child some commercially minded boys escorted adults into the grounds for a fee of fifteen cents and then went outside to find others who wished to see the sport close at hand. It is customary to open the gates to the public, when the egg-rolling is over, to listen to a concert by the Marine Band. Mrs. Coolidge appeared among the children in 1926 with a pet raccoon in her arms to the delight of the youngsters, and Mrs. Hoover in 1929 had two May poles set up around which a group of Girl Scouts gave an exhibition dance.

The egg-rolling custom was observed except during and immediately following the Civil War and the two World Wars. The sport was revived during Harding's administration, in 1921, discontinued during the second World War, revived again in 1946 and again discontinued in 1947, because with food shortages throughout the world it seemed unsuitable.

ESTABLISHMENT OF THE MINT

As the Constitution conferred on Congress the power to coin money and to regulate its value it became necessary to make some provision to exercise this power. Alexander Hamilton, the first Secretary of the Treasury, made a report to Congress in May 1791, recommending the adoption of a coinage system with the dollar as 'the unit, consisting of twenty-four and three-fourths grains of pure gold or three hundred and seventy-one grains of pure silver, based on the relative value of the two metals at the time. On April 2, 1792, Congress passed an act establishing a mint for the coinage of money. The word "mint" is derived from a Latin term meaning "money." It had been adopted by the European nations several hundred years before it was used in this country. Hamilton recommended the coinage of ten-dollar and one-dollar gold pieces, one-dollar and ten-cent silver pieces and one-cent and half-cent copper pieces. The first coin which came from the mint was a copper cent, dated 1793. Silver dollars were first coined in 1794 and gold eagles in 1795.

The colonies in the early days had no coinage of their own. They used English money and the Spanish dollar, when they did not resort to tobacco or some other commodity as a medium of exchange. The New England colonies at one time used the Indian wampum. When they were hard put to it for currency they began to use paper money. After the colonies united to resist Great Britain the Continental Congress authorized an issue of paper money. Provision for its redemption within three years was made and each colony was held responsible for its proper proportion of the issue. As the first issue of three hundred thousand dollars was indaequate there were many subsequent issues and all pretense of redemption was abandoned. Its value depreciated until in 1782 it took five hundred Continental dollars to buy one Spanish silver dollar. Washington once said that it took a wagon load of money to buy a wagon load of provisions. The depreciation in value of this Continental currency was so great that the people got in the habit of saying of a useless thing that it was "not worth a Continental."

The first mint was opened at Philadelphia. In the course of time other mints were established at San Francisco, Calif.; New Orleans, La.; Carson City, Nev., and Denver, Colo. The Philadelphia mint is the most important. The designs of the coins are made there as well as the designs of the medals conferred by Congress. The New Orleans and Carson City mints have for many years been used only as assay offices.

MULE DAY IN COLUMBIA, TENNESSEE

Ever since the early settlers came to Tennessee from North Carolina and Virginia, Mule Day has been celebrated on the first Monday in April in Columbia with picturesque ceremonies. In 1945 this was on April 2. During World War II the festivities were necessarily curtailed in extent, but plans for elaborate programs similar to those of prewar years began to take shape as soon as peace was declared. Originally the event was known as Breeders Day. Shortly before the middle of the nineteenth century the settlers in the region started bringing their stallions, mares and work stock to town on the first Monday in April for showing and breeding, and the day was named accordingly.

The records attest that the mule stock in the United States began with a pair of donkeys shipped to President Washington from Spain. The work mares in this country were bred to the imported jack and an excellent strain of mules resulted. In 1880 Dr. W. P. Woldridge conceived the idea of elaborating the customary Breeders Day ceremonies in Columbia, which had heretofore been confined to a simple parade and inspection of the horses and mules. At his suggestion couple riding was introduced, with the ladies on side saddles in the current vogue, and prizes were offered for the best riding, the handsomest couple, and other distinctions. Not only was the occasion a gala event each year, but it encouraged scientific breeding and favorable results were noted in stock throughout that part of the country. However, after the first World War, the influx of power machinery for farming and automobiles for transportation led to the neglect of both horse and mule breeding. Although Breeders Day was never entirely abandoned, a government survey showed that the stock had deteriorated until there was scarcely a jack of the old strains in existence. Both Spain and France had sent agents to the United States to recover some of the famous strains of stock imported from those countries, but after a thorough canvas only six animals suitable for their purpose were found. This discovery led to the establishment of a donkey breeding farm at the Middle Tennessee Experiment Station.

Concurrently, W. D. Hastings of Columbia suggested to the Chamber of Commerce that premiums should be offered on Breeders Day in order to renew interest in breeding. At one time Columbia had been a famous mule market, train loads of mules, selling for as much as $700 to $1500 a pair, being shipped from the town following mule sale days. The suggestion was followed and Mule Day in 1934 attracted a large crowd. The next year the celebration was extensively advertised and attended by motion picture photographers from New York. This publicity aroused widespread interest in the event, which subsequently drew photographers and newspapermen from all parts of the country, as well as a large number of sightseers.

A typical celebration was that of 1940, when several hundred girls rode on as many mules, and thousands of persons came to Columbia to view the Mule Day ceremonies. James Farley, then Postmaster General, attended with his famous mule Queenie, which rode on a large, decorated log wagon drawn by a team of twenty-four picked mules. Mr. Farley and the local officials rode in an old-fashioned carriage, brought down from Quebec for the occasion, drawn by four mules driven by the late Colonel Jack Hanes of horse-breeding fame. The cornerstone of the Federal Building in Columbia was laid with due formalities, as a feature of the celebration. The parade, accompanied by numerous bands, was so long it took two hours to pass any given point; among the many animals participating were the miniature mules, small enough to be held in a man's arms without difficulty. However, the hero of the day was the mule crowned "king" of the festivities by a young lady especially selected for the honor. His Majesty looked somewhat silly in his tall crown, flanked by long ears, but drew more applause than the Governor of Tennessee presiding over the ceremonies. In the evening a Mule Ball was held and the Mule Trot, originated locally, danced. An annual celebration on a similar scale continued until World War II, when the program was greatly simplified. But after V-J Day projects for future spectacular Mule Days immediately got under way.

APRIL THIRD

BIRTHDAY OF WASHINGTON IRVING

Washington Irving, the first American literary man to attract attention in England, was born in New York City on April 3, 1783. At the age of sixteen he began the study of law, a profession which he never seriously followed. When he was twenty-one he went to Europe for his health, and remained two years. On his return he published his *Knickerbocker's History of New York*, intended to burlesque a pretentious guidebook. During the War of 1812 he was on the staff of Governor Tompkins of New York and wrote for a Philadelphia magazine. In 1815 he went to England to look after the business interests of his brothers' firm in which he was a partner and on its failure three years later he began to devote himself exclusively to literature. *The Sketch Book* was published in England and America in 1819 and was enthusiastically welcomed on both sides of the ocean. The fame of two of the tales which it contained has survived—"Rip Van Winkle" and "The Legend of Sleepy Hollow." He then wrote more sketches in the same manner and several books of history and travel. He was Secretary of the United States Legation in London from 1829 to 1831 and while there wrote *The Alhambra*. Ten years later he was appointed United States Minister to Spain and remained on duty there for three years. On his return he lived on the banks of the Hudson River near Tarrytown, N.Y., and continued to write. His last book published before his death on November 28, 1859, was *The Life of Washington*. His works have been published in forty volumes.

In 1933 the one hundred and fiftieth anniversary of his birth was celebrated, with appropriate ceremonies, by the school children of New York City and Tarrytown. At Christ Church in Tarrytown, the silver communion service which he bought in Europe and presented to the Church was used for the first time in many years. Later in the year three thousand persons attended a Spanish-American fiesta in his memory at Granada, Spain.

APRIL FOURTH

ADOPTION OF THE PRESENT FLAG

It was on June 14, 1777, that the Continental Congress voted that the flag of the United States should contain thirteen alternate red and white stripes and thirteen white stars on a blue field (See Flag Day, June 14). On January 13, 1794, as Vermont and Kentucky had been admitted to the Union, Congress voted that the flag should consist of fifteen stripes and fifteen stars, beginning with May 1, 1797. It was the evident intention to have a star and a stripe added for each new state. In 1818 there were twenty states but the flag had remained unchanged since 1797. Congress, in order to meet the issue, ordered on April 4, 1818, that the flag should be redesigned and that the number of stripes be reduced to the original thirteen and that there be twenty stars. And it further ordered that "on the admission of every new state into the Union one star be added to the union of the flag and that such addition shall take effect on the Fourth of July next succeeding such admission." The flag has been made in accordance with this design since that date and it now has forty-eight stars representing the forty-eight states and thirteen stripes representing the original states which formed the Union.

APRIL FIFTH

BIRTHDAY OF ELIHU YALE

Elihu Yale, one of the earliest benefactors of what is now Yale University, was born near Boston, Mass., on April 5, 1648. His father was David Yale, who had emigrated from Wales in 1638, lived for a time at New Haven, Conn., and then removed to Massachusetts. He returned to England in 1652, taking his family with him and settling in London. After receiving an education the son entered the service of the British East India Company in 1672 and went to India where in 1687 he become Governor of Madras. Five years later he returned to London with a large fortune and later became one of the governors of the company. He made many gifts for religious and educational purposes and became interested in the Collegiate School at Saybrook, Conn., which had been founded by ten of the principal ministers of the colony by the gift of books for a library . Between 1714 and 1721 Elihu Yale gave money and books to the school amounting to £900. The school was removed to New Haven in 1718 when the name was changed to Yale College, in honor of its benefactor. Yale spent the latter years of his life at Wrexham in North Wales where he died in 1721 and where his body now lies. His memory is kept green at the college named for him which in the intervening centuries has grown beyond his wildest imaginings.

FOUNDER'S DAY AT TUSKEGEE INSTITUTE

The birthday of Booker Taliaferro Washington is celebrated as Founder's Day at the Tuskegee Normal and Industrial Institute, a nonsectarian school for the higher education of Negro men and women in Tuskegee, Alabama. Founded in 1881 by Booker Washington, the Institute has prospered, now having an endowment of several million dollars and giving regular and systematic instruction to an average enrollment of between three and four thousand students.

The founder was born in 1858 on a plantation near Hale's Ford, Franklin County, Virginia, the son of a mulatto slave woman. His first education was obtained at a night school. In 1872 he traveled five hundred miles to the Hampton (Virginia) Normal and Agricultural Institute, where, during three years, he paid for his board and education by acting as janitor. After being graduated he taught at Malden, West Virginia, and then studied at the Wayland Seminary, Washington, D.C. Appointed as instructor at Hampton Institute he trained seventy-five Indians under General S. C. Armstrong, and developed a night school. Then, in 1881, he was appointed organizer and principal of a Negro school at Tuskegee, Alabama. In advancing the interests of this institution, Booker Washington became a well-known public speaker, and was recognized as the foremost exponent of the education and advancement of the Negro. Between 1899 and his death in 1915 he published a number of books dealing with the problems of his race, among them *The Future of the American Negro* and *Up From Slavery*.

APRIL SIXTH

ARMY DAY

In response to President Wilson's message, delivered in person on April 2, 1917, Congress, called in special session, adopted a resolution on April 6 setting forth that as the Imperial German Government had committed repeated acts of war against the government and the people of the United States, a state of war between the United States and that government was "hereby formally declared."

When peace came the Military Order of the World War was organized and in 1927, at a meeting of its general staff, it was voted to celebrate the anniversary of the declaration of war as Army Day, and arrangements were made accordingly. Since then the day has been observed every year by the organization. Other organizations soon began to participate in the celebration, including the Military Order of Foreign Wars and the American Legion. There are military parades in Washington, reviewed by the President, and parades of veterans and military organizations in other cities followed by luncheons or dinners addressed by officers of the army who usually discuss the need for preparedness, the lack of which hampered the United States in its prosecution of the World Wars. And the societies of pacifists usually protest against the celebration.

The President, in his message of April 2, explained that on February 3 he had informed Congress of the announcement of the German Government that after February 1 it was its purpose to put aside all restraints of law or humanity and use its submarines to sink every vessel that sought to approach either the ports of Great Britain and Ireland or the western coast of Europe or any of the ports of the Mediterranean controlled by the enemies of Germany. He said that in pursuance of this policy vessels of every kind, whatever their flag, their cargo, their destination or their errand had been sunk without warning and without help or mercy for those on board. Even hospital ships and ships carrying food for the relief of Belgium had been sunk. After explaining in much detail the reasons for accepting the "challenge of hostile purposes," as he described them, he said "We are now about to accept the gage of battle with the natural foe of liberty, and shall, if necessary, spend the whole force of the nation to check and nullify its pretensions and its power." The address concluded:

It is a fearful thing to lead this great, peaceful people into war, into the most terrible and disastrous of all wars, civilization itself seeming to be in the balance. But the right is more precious than peace, and we shall fight for the things which we have always carried nearest our hearts—for democracy, for the right of those who submit to authority to have a voice in their own governments, for the rights and liberties of small nations, for a universal dominion of right by such a concert of free people as shall bring peace and safety to all nations and make the world at last free. To such a task we dedicate our lives, our fortunes, everything that we are and everything that we have, with the pride of those who know that the day has come when America is privileged to spend her blood and her might for the principles that gave her birth and happiness and the peace which she has treasured. God helping us, she can do no other.

A draft bill was passed, training camps for officers and men were opened, and money was appropriated. About four million men were put in uniform, and about two million were sent to the scene of war in France before the Armistice of November 11, 1918. (See November 11, Armistice Day.)

FOUNDING OF THE MORMON CHURCH

The anniversary of the founding of the Mormon Church, April 6, 1830, is observed every year at the General Conference of the church held in Salt Lake City, Utah, during a period which includes this date. According to the account accepted by the church, John the Baptist appeared to Joseph Smith, Jr., and Oliver Cowdery while they were translating *The Book of Mormon* and made them priests after the order of Aaron. This was on May 25, 1829. Less than a year later the apostles Peter, James, and John appeared to them and made them priests after the order of Melchizedek. They soon began to preach and baptize converts into their church, but their organization had no legal standing. Under the laws of New York there must be at least six persons interested before a corporation can be formed. On April 6, 1830, Joseph Smith, Jr., Oliver Cowdery, Hyrum Smith, Samuel H. Smith, Peter Whitmer, Jr., and David Whitmer gathered at Fayette, N.Y., and perfected the organization which in 1834 began to be known as the Church of Jesus Christ of Latter-Day Saints. In 1831 the church removed to Kirtland, Ohio, where a temple costing about $40,000 was built. In 1835 the apostolate of twelve was established. In 1837 the first missionaries were sent to England, and in 1842 twelve ships were chartered to bring the Briitsh converts to America. After troublous times in Ohio, Missouri and Illinois the great body of the Mormons migrated to the Great Salt Lake Valley in Utah. The missionaries of the church have always been active in this and other countries. It had a membership in the United States in 1947 of close to a million.

GREEK INDEPENDENCE DAY

The Greeks in the United States, of whom there are several hundred thousand, celebrate the anniversary of the beginning of their war for independence. The date is April 6, according to the Gregorian calendar, but March 25 by the Old Style calendar. On this day in 1821 Alexander Ypsilanti, a Greek officer in the Russian army, invaded Greece from Moldavia with a small force. He was defeated, but the war to free the Greeks from the tyranny of the Turks which he began was finally successful and an independent government was set up which lasted until World War II.

The war for independence stirred the imagination of poets in Europe and America. Lord Byron, who went to Greece to help the Greeks in their fight and died there from exposure, wrote one of his most famous poems about the struggle, the first three stanzas of which run in this way:

> The isles of Greece; the isles of Greece!
>   Where burning Sappho loved and sung,
> Where grew the arts of war and peace,
>   Where Delos rose, and Phoebus sprung!
> Eternal summer gilds them yet,
> But all except their sun is set.
>
> The Scian and the Teian muse,
>   The hero's harp, the lover's lute,
> Have found the fame your shores refuse:
>   Their place of birth alone is mute

To sounds which echo further west
Than your sires' "Islands of the Blest."

The mountains look on Marathon—
    And Marathon looks on the sea;
And musing there an hour alone,
    I dreamed that Greece might still be free:
For standing on the Persians' grave.
I could not deem myself a slave.

    Fitz-Greene Halleck, stirred by the death of Marco Bozzaris, one of the heroes of the revolution which ended with the victory of the Greeks over the Turks, wrote the poem by which he is best known, a poem which used to be declaimed with zest by school boys at public exercises. It begins:

At midnight, in his guarded tent,
    The Turk was dreaming of the hour
When Greece, her knee in suppliance bent,
    Should tremble at his power:
In dreams through camp and court, he bore
The trophies of a conqueror;
    In dreams his song of truimph heard;
Then wore his monarch's signet ring:
Then pressed that monarch's throne—a king;
As wild his thoughts, and gay of wing,
    As Eden's garden bird.

At midnight, in the forest shades
    Bozzaris ranged his Suliote band,
True as the steel of their tried blades,
    Heroes in heart and hand.
There had the Persian's thousands stood,
There had the glad earth drunk their blood
    On old Plataea's day;
And now there breathed that haunted air
The sons of sires who conquered there,
With arm to strike, and soul to dare,
    As quick, as far as they.

    The celebration of the anniversary in the United States usually begins with appropriate services in the Greek Orthodox church. These are followed by athletic sports, dinners and balls. At a celebration in New York a company of uniformed Greeks mounted the stage in the hall and saluted the Stars and Stripes and the Greek flag. "The Star Spangled Banner" and the Greek national anthem were played while the audience rose out of respect to the two banners. Addresses were made celebrating the heroism of Ypsilanti and the progress of modern Greece. The fame of Ypsilanti is kept green in America as well as in Greece, for a city in southern Michigan is named for him.

APRIL SEVENTH

THE ALABAMA CLAIMS

It was on April 7, 1865, that correspondence began between Great Britain and the United States looking to a method of dealing with the question of damages done to shipping of the United States by Confederate privateers during the Civil War through the neglect of the British to enforce neutrality with sufficient rigidity. It is known in history as the Alabama Claims Dispute because a ship which came to be called the "Alabama" was built in a British port and was allowed to sail in spite of the protest of the American Minister in London. Privateering had been abolished by the Declaration of Paris in 1856 and both the United States and Great Britain had laws making it the duty of the government to prevent private citizens from operating against the commerce or territory of a friendly nation. The United States charged the British with failing in their duty in permitting their citizens to build a ship for the Confederates and in allowing it to sail. They also charged that the British had not exercised due care to prevent several other ships from operating from their West Indian ports. A treaty was made on May 8, 1871, which provided for submitting the question at issue to an arbitration commission. The commission met at Geneva, Switzerland, on December 15, and after many sittings and long investigation the arbitrators found that the United States was entitled to damages in the sum of $15,500,000 in settlement of all claims. Congress on June 23, 1874, created a court of claims to which American business men could submit proof of their losses from the privateers and collect their proper share of the amount paid by the British. It was many years before all the claims were settled. The verdict of the arbitration commission is regarded as important in the history of international law as it recognized the responsibility of a nation for the consequences when it fails to exercise due diligence in the enforcement of its neutrality between belligerents.

APRIL EIGHTH

PONCE DE LEON SEEKS THE FOUNTAIN OF YOUTH

The people of the Old World who had not been able to find there the magic cities and the life-giving springs of which their legends told, began to search for them in the New World discovered by Columbus. Less than twenty years after his discovery had been reported in Europe Ponce de Leon set sail from Porto Rico, of which he had been governor for several years, to discover a fabled fountain of youth said to be on an island or region called Bimini. He started on March 3, 1513, and on April 8 landed on the coast of Florida near the present site of St. Augustine. The date òf his landing is frequently celebrated by the people of the city. He searched in vain for the fountain and it was not until many centuries later that men and women from colder climes discovered that they could prolong their lives by spending the bleak months of winter in the balmy air of the state. The memory of the Spanish explorer is kept green there by enterprising business men aware of its value to them. Although Ponce de Leon did not die until he was sixty-one he would have lived longer in spite of his failure to find the fountain of youth, if ironically he had not, while in search of the fountain, been wounded by an Indian arrow which subsequently led to his death at Porto Rico in 1521.

APRIL NINTH

APPOMATTOX DAY

The anniversary of the surrender of the Army of Northern Virginia under General Lee to General Grant at Appomattox Court House, Va., on April 9, 1865, was observed for many years by Grand Army Posts, by organizations of veterans who served under General Grant in the campaign which led to the surrender, and by many civilian organizations in the North. The Hamilton Club of Chicago has been in the habit of observing the day and the Pilgrims, an organization of veterans in the Union League of Philadelphia which visited a battlefield of the Civil War every year, also arranged an annual celebration. Distinguished speakers always addressed those who attended these celebrations. The fiftieth anniversary in 1915 was observed widely throughout the North.

In 1930 Congress passed a bill providing for the erection of a monument at Appomattox Court House, to commemorate the restoration of the Union, but because of opposition from the South, the plan was abandoned.

Lee, with his starving army, had evacuated Richmond and was moving south when his retreat was cut off by General Sheridan on April 8, and he decided to surrender. April 9 was Palm Sunday in 1865. The news of the surrender reached the North in the evening of that day. Bells were rung, crowds of people gathered in public places and sang "Praise God from whom all blessings flow," and torch-light processions were improvised by the enthusiastic populace to show their thankfulness that the war was ended. General Grant in his *Memoirs* has told the story of the surrender. He wrote:

When I had left camp that morning I had not expected so soon the result that was taking place and consequently was in rough garb. I was without a sword, as I usually was when on horseback on the field, and wore a soldier's blouse for a coat with the shoulder straps of my rank to indicate to the army who I was. When I went into the house (the McLean house) I found General Lee.

We greeted each other, and after shaking hands took our seats. . . . General Lee was dressed in a full uniform which was entirely new, and was wearing a sword of considerable value—very likely the sword which had been presented to him by the State of Virginia; at all events it was entirely different from one that would ordinarily be worn in the field. . . . We soon fell into conversation about old army times. He remarked that he remembered me very well in the old army, and I told him that as a matter of course I remembered him perfectly.

General Grant then gave the terms of surrender, that the men lay down their arms and give their word not to take them up again until they were exchanged, and that the officers should retain their horses and side arms. Since the cavalry and artillery owned their own horses and were small farmers General Grant agreed that they should keep their horses also. And when General Lee explained that his men were starving, General Grant ordered that two out of every three rations for his own men should be sent to the surrendered army. General Lee himself returned to Richmond and was later pardoned by President Johnson. Congress, however, had deprived Johnson of the power of pardon before he acted.

APRIL TENTH

SALVATION ARMY FOUNDER'S DAY

William Booth, the founder of the Salvation Army, was born on April 10, 1829, and died on August 20, 1912. The anniversary of his birth is celebrated by the organization in the United States and throughout the world. Eulogistic addresses are made and the growth of the army is described.

William Booth was the son of an English contractor doing business in Nottingham. After a preliminary secular education he studied theology under a private tutor preparatory to entering the ministry of the Methodist Church. In 1852, at the age of twenty-three, he began an evangelistic career, preaching in all parts of England. After his marriage to Catherine Mumford he served several years as a settled pastor when he decided that religious teaching should be carried to those overlooked by the churches— the outcasts in the city slums. He proposed the plan to the Methodist New Connection Church, but failed to obtain its approval. Thereupon he set out independently and began preaching in an old tent in a disused Quaker burying ground in Mile End Waste in the East End of London. This was in 1865. Thirteen years later, in 1878, he organized a body of religious workers which he named the Salvation Army, and equipped them with uniforms, flags, drums and cornets. They preached in the streets and at first were greeted with riotous demonstrations. The police arrested them for obstructing traffic. In the course of time this hostility disappeared and the work was expanded from street preaching to the organization of social reforms, to the establishment of food and shelter depots, children's homes, and agencies for helping discharged criminals.

In 1889 George Scott Railton was sent from England to organize the Salvation Army in the United States. His efforts were received in this country very much as the efforts of William Booth had been first received in London. But in the course of time the value of the work in which he was engaged was appreciated, and he and his successors received valuable support from persons interested in helping the unfortunate and the under-privileged.

In the United States, the work is divided into two departments. The headquarters of one are in New York and of the other in Chicago. Relief of distress is extended to those who are unfortunate from any cause as was illustrated by its generous financial contribution in 1906 to the sufferers from the fire in San Francisco. It maintains day nurseries, fresh air camps in the country for women and children, employment bureaus, farm colonies, free coal and ice distribution, a missing friends bureau, an anti-suicide bureau, lawyers to serve those without money, and shops for the sale of discarded furniture and the like which is repaired and made usable. It is supported by voluntary contributions and by the proceeds from the sale of the articles in its shops. (See July 28, Founder's Day of the Volunteers of America.)

APRIL ELEVENTH

BIRTHDAY OF CHARLES EVANS HUGHES

Charles Evans Hughes, the eleventh Chief Justice of the United States, was born at Glens Falls, N.Y., on April 11, 1862. His father, the Reverend David C. Hughes, a Welshman, was pastor of the Baptist church in the village. He was a precocious youth and entered Madison, now Colgate University, in 1876 at the age of fourteen. He studied there for two years, when his father became pastor of a Baptist church in Providence, R.I., and took up his residence in that city. Young Hughes was then entered in Brown University from which he was graduated in 1881. He taught for a year in an academy at Delhi, N.Y., and in 1882 he entered the Columbia University Law School in New York City. He was graduated in 1884 and obtained a prize fellowship for three years. He was admitted to the bar soon after graduation and practiced until he was appointed professor of law at Cornell University in 1891. He remained at Cornell for two years when he resumed practice in New York, but he continued his connection with the university as a special lecturer. He was also a lecturer at the New York Law School from 1893 to 1900. In 1905 he was counsel to a state commission appointed to investigate the cost of gas and served so brilliantly that when the legislature ordered an investigation into the affairs of the life insurance companies operating under state charters he was made counsel for the commission appointed to conduct the inquiry. As a result of the investigation many abuses were corrected. While it was in progress an offer of the Republican nomination for mayor was made to him, but he declined it for he did not want his work to be complicated by partisan political issues. He was retained by the Federal Government in 1906 to investigate alleged violations of the antitrust laws by the coal carrying railroads. In the same year he was nominated for Governor of New York by the Republicans and elected and he was reelected in 1908. Through his influence many reforms were instituted in the conduct of public business.

He did not serve out his second term for on October 6, 1910, President Taft appointed him an Associate Justice of the United States Supreme Court. While he was governor there began to be talk of him as a possible Republican candidate for president and he made an address before the Republican Club in New York setting forth his views on national issues. Those who were opposed to the renomination of President Taft in 1912 began to consider him, and it is generally believed that he was in a receptive mood. But when President Taft definitely let it be known that he wanted a renomination, Justice Hughes announced that he was not an aspirant. He would not enter the race against the man who had put him on the bench of the Supreme Court. In 1916, however, he was nominated and immediately resigned from the bench to enter the campaign. He carried the large Eastern states and on election night it was believed that he had been successful. But when the returns from California came in he had lost that state by about four thousand votes and with it had lost the election.

He resumed the practice of his profession in New York. President Harding made him Secretary of State in his Cabinet, and he began service in that capacity on March 4, 1921. Attempts were made to persuade him to favor the recognition of Soviet Russia, but they were unsuccessful. With the authority of the President he invited representatives of the principal nations of the world to a conference on the limitation of armaments to be held in Washington. At its opening session he outlined a plan for limitation which was adopted in its general terms and embodied in a treaty to continue for fifteen years. On the death of President Harding he continued as the head of the Cabinet until March 4, 1925, with President Coolidge as his chief. President Coolidge named him as a member of the Permanent Court of Arbitration at The Hague on September 30, 1926, and he served until 1930. He was elected by the Council and Assembly of the League of Nations as a Judge of the Permanent Court of International Justice in 1928, but resigned in 1930 when President Hoover appointed him Chief Justice of the United States Supreme Court.

On June 2, 1941, Justice Hughes retired under the provisions of the Act of Congress of March 1, 1937. He wrote President Roosevelt that "considerations of age and health make it necessary that I be relieved of the duties which I have been discharging with increasing difficulty."

The President replied: "My every inclination is to beg you to remain; but my deep concern for your health and strength must be paramount." Thus, at the age seventy-nine the Justice, who has been described as "a great liberal" and "a deadly conservative," stepped down from the highest judicial position in the world. He died August 27, 1948.

APRIL TWELFTH

HALIFAX RESOLUTIONS DAY

This is a legal holiday in North Carolina in commemoration of the adoption in 1776 of resolutions favoring the independence of the colonies. It was the first colony to make a formal declaration in favor of separation from Great Britain. The congress of the colony had organized the militia and had created a provincial council in which was vested the public authority. It had also set up committees of safety for the various districts. A large portion of the inhabitants were loyalists, among them a considerable body of Scotch immigrants. The Royal Governor represented to the home government that if the loyalists were supported by a body of British troops the colony might be kept in line. In the winter of 1775-76 a force under Sir Henry Clinton was sent south with instructions to act first in North Carolina. Commissions were issued to influential men in the colony. These men, under the direction of the Royal Governor, enlisted about fifteen hundred loyalists. The patriots were aware of what was going on and the militia was called out and took the field under Colonel James Moore. When Sir Henry Clinton was expected at Cape Fear, General McDonald, in command of the loyalist force, moved to join him. Colonel Moore ordered parties of militia to post themselves at Moore's Creek Bridge, over which McDonald must pass. The patriots, under command of Colonel Richard Caswell, fought a decisive battle at this bridge on February 27, 1776, defeating the loyalists, taking seven hundred prisoners and capturing a large amount of military supplies. Inspired by this victory delegates elected to a provincial congress which met at Halifax on April 4 were ready to declare themselves. A committee appointed to learn the desires of the people about independence reported a resolution authorizing the delegates in the General Congress "to concur with the delegates in the other colonies in declaring independency, and forming foreign alliances, reserving to the colony the sole and exclusive right of forming a constitution and laws for it" and also "of appointing delegates in a general representation of the colonies for such purposes as might be agreed upon." This resolution was unanimously adopted on April 12, 1776. The example of North Carolina was largely influential in bringing about the adoption of the Declaration of Independence by the Continental Congress on July 4, 1776.

APRIL THIRTEENTH

JEFFERSON'S BIRTHDAY

Thomas Jefferson, when he became President, abandoned the custom of calling on the country to celebrate the anniversary of the birth of Washington which had been started by President Adams. But against his wishes the admirers of Jefferson celebrated informally the anniversary of his birth during his presidency. He was born on April 13 (old style April 2), 1743.

What the historians have called the first formal celebration occurred in Washington in 1830. The debate between Webster and Hayne earlier in the year had made the nation conscious of the gravity of the issue of state's rights. Webster had defended the view that this is an indissoluble union of sovereign states. The supporters of Calhoun of South Carolina, which had tried to nullify an act of Congress, planned the Jefferson celebration for the purpose of associating the distinguished leader of the party with the view that the states could do as they chose regardless of the action of the central government. It was to be a dinner at which the toasts proposed were to support the views of Calhoun. This was not known, however, save to the small group making the arrangements. An inkling of the truth reached Andrew Jackson, who was serving his first term as President. Jackson shared Webster's views, and after consultation with Martin Van Buren, it was decided that he should attend the dinner and propose a toast which would leave no doubt as to his position on this question.

On the night of the dinner the guests assembled and looked over the printed list of toasts. The Congressional delegation from Pennsylvania, when it discovered their tenor, left the hall before the dinner began and others followed their example. After the regular toasts were given volunteers were called for. President Jackson arose, drew himself to his full height and, looking straight at Calhoun, paused a moment. Then in the hush he proposed: "Our Federal Union: It must and shall be preserved." He lifted his glass as a sign that the toast was to be drunk standing. Calhoun rose with the rest and, according to an eye witness, "his glass trembled in his hand and a little of the fluid trickled down the side." When the toast had been drunk Jackson left his place at the table to talk with his secretary in another part of the room. As the guests took their seats Calhoun, who had remained standing, slowly and hesitatingly proposed the toast: "The Union: next to our liberty the most dear," and followed it by saying that the rights of the states must be respected. Everyone present knew that an issue had been drawn in a most dramatic manner and in the excitement all but thirty left the room within five minutes. Thus the first formal observance of the birthday of Jefferson was the occasion of one of the most dramatic incidents in American history. In Virginia Thomas Jefferson Day is now a legal holiday; in Nebraska it is observed by proclamation of the governor; and in Missouri and Oklahoma it is a public, although not a bank, holiday.

In the succeeding years the anniversary has been observed with more or less regularity by Democrats in different parts of the country. It is the occasion for glorifying the achievements of the party, in that respect resembling the celebration of the anniversary of the birth of Andrew Jackson. (See Jackson Day, January 8.) In 1910 the Democrats in Washington planned a dinner to which they invited all the men whose names had been discussed in connection with the nomination for the presidency in 1912, but when William J. Gaynor, Mayor of New York, declined the invitation due to press of business, the others also declined. The guests were chiefly Democratic members of Congress. Champ Clark of Missouri, the minority leader of the House of Representatives, who came near winning the presidential nomination, was present and made a speech in which he arraigned the Republicans for extravagance, charging them with appropriating $1,044,000,000 in the previous year and asserting that none of the worthy legislation could have been passed without the help of the Democrats. At the dinner in Indianapolis in the same year an attempt was made to promote the candidacy of Thomas R. Marshal, Governor of Indiana, who was finally nominated for the vice presidency on the ticket with Woodrow Wilson.

There is an annual non-political observance of the anniversary at the University of Virginia which Jefferson founded. In 1913, Woodrow Wilson, who was a graduate of the law school of the university, sent the following message to be read at the celebration:

> May I send to my alma mater, University of Virginia, my warmest greetings on Founder's Day, 1913, and express the hope that her prosperity and her fame may increase from decade to decade? Her sons all look to her to maintain the great place she has in the education of the country.

In 1919 on the hundredth anniversary of the founding of the university a delegation was sent to Paris to dedicate a tablet on the site of the house which Jefferson occupied during his residence in the French capital. It was at the corner of the Avenue Champs Elysées and Rue de Berri. Josephus Daniels, then Secretary of the Navy in the cabinet of President Wilson, made the dedicatory address. The first World War had been ended for only a few months. Mr. Daniels referred to it in this way:

> As the soldiers from our country, privileged to fight with the inter-allied heroes of all the allied nations, confident that right and justice will emerge and shine upon all the world free from absolutism, turn their faces to their own country, it is fitting that the patriotic overseas alumni of the University of Virginia should mark the place of abode of their illustrious founder.

Jefferson was born at Shadwell, Albemarle County, Va. His mother was Jane Randolph of the famous Randolph family. He entered the College of William and Mary at the age of seventeen and on leaving college studied law, but practiced his profession for only a few years as he was more interested in scientific farming. At the age of twenty-six he was elected to the Virginia House of Burgesses. In 1773 he sent to the House of Burgesses, the meeting of which he was prevented by illness from attending, the draft of a document which he hoped might be adopted as instructions to the delegates to the Continental Congress. It was printed in a pamphlet as *A Summary View of the Rights of British America.* He was elected to the Continental Congress in 1775 and while a member of that body drafted the Declaration of Independence. In 1779 he was elected Governor of Virginia. In May 1784, he was sent to France with Benjamin Franklin and John Adams to negotiate commercial treaties. He remained in France until 1789 when he returned and entered the cabinet of Washington as Secretary of State. He resigned before completing his term and when John Adams was elected President he became Vice President having received the second highest number of votes for President. He was elected President in 1800 and again in 1804 and on the expiration of his second term retired to his home, Monticello, in Virginia where he died on July 4, 1826.

HUGUENOT DAY

The Huguenot Society of America observes April 13, the anniversary of the Signing of the Edict of Nantes, by holding its annual meeting on that day. The society was organized in 1884 by descendants of the French Huguenots who had fled from France to America, and celebrated its semicentennial in 1934. Its founding was due to the suggestion of the Reverend Dr. Wittmeyer, rector of the French Church of St. Esprit in New York. The society observed the three hundredth anniversary of the signing of the edict by religious services in the churches and by receptions to foreign guests and delegates. An account of the celebration was printed in a volume of 425 pages embellished with portraits of distinguished descendants of those who had fled from France to obtain religious freedom. The American society cooperates with the French Huguenot Society known as L'Histoire du Protestantisme Français in preserving the records of the struggle for toleration. It has joined with that society in placing a tablet to mark the site of the grave of John Paul Jones in the Protestant Cemetery in Paris. The body of Jones now rests in the crypt of the chapel of the United States Naval Academy at Annapolis, Md. The society gave a communion table to the Huguenot Memorial Church at Huguenot, Staten Island, N.Y., on the occasion of its dedication during the celebration of the tercentennial of the famous edict. And it participated in the celebration of the two hundred and fiftieth anniversary of the landing of the Huguenots in South Carolina, arranged by the Huguenot Society of Charleston. Many distinguished Americans are descendants of the Huguenots. Among them is Thomas F. Bayard, Secretary of State in the first Administration of President

Cleveland. When the society was organized Mr. Bayard said of it: "Remember that our inheritance of honorable names and of the inestimable blessings of civil and religious liberty carry with them the obligation to keep them in honor and maintain and defend them; that we hold them in trust, to enjoy in our lifetime and transmit them untarnished and undiminished to posterity. We cherish these traditions, not for the glorification of family names, but for the honor and advancement of humanity, as incentives to those private and public virtues that constitute the true strength of a nation."

The Edict of Nantes, signed by Henry IV on April 13, 1598, gave peace to the French Protestants for a few years. It was in the first quarter of the sixteenth century that Lutheran Protestantism began to get a foothold in the country, and it was accepted by large numbers of the nobility and the middle classes, although they were not called Huguenots until about the year 1560. Within ten years after the Lutherans got a foothold persecutions began and many of the Protestants were burned. There were periods of toleration and persecution for more than fifty years, with civil wars between the Catholic and Protestant parties. The edict of toleration which Henry IV signed granted liberty of conscience, permitted the Huguenot chiefs and nobles to attend public religious exercises along with their families and dependents, allowed them to establish new churches except in Paris and the surrounding districts, and permitted them to maintain colleges and theological seminaries. The Huguenots were to be eligible to all civil offices, but they were obliged to observe the festivals of the Catholic Church and to pay tithes to the priests. The edict remained nominally in force until it was formally revoked by Louis XIV in October 1685.

The most notorious event in the series of persecutions which preceded the signing of the edict was the massacre of St. Bartholomew in 1572 when thousands of Huguenots were slain, among them some of the most distinguished men in France (see Feast of St. Bartholomew, August 24). Hundreds of thousands of Protestants left France to escape the persecutions, fleeing to Switzerland, the Netherlands, England, Germany, the West Indies, as well as to South Carolina, New York, Massachusetts, Pennsylvania and other American colonies. The number has been estimated at between 400,000 and 1,000,000. When in the middle of the eighteenth century an edict was issued declaring that marriages and baptisms by Huguenot ministers were null another flight of Protestants began and it became so serious that in a few years the edict was rescinded.

BIRD DAY

Bird Day, or Audubon Day, as it is sometimes called, is celebrated in some states on the same date as the celebration of Arbor Day. In New York that is the second Friday in April. This fell on April 13 in 1945. In many states the observance is arranged in cooperation with the National Association of Audubon Societies for the Protection of Wild Birds and Animals. This association grew out of the interest of George Bird Grinnell, editor of *Forest and Stream*, in the protection of wild life. It started on a small scale in 1886 and has expanded until now there are branches in many states. It has brought about the passage of laws against trapping or snaring non-game birds, and against the sale of aigrettes and the feathers of other native birds. It has been influential in the establishment of bird reservations and in the protection of migratory birds. In cooperation with the schools it organizes classes of children for the study of bird life.

It was many years after the Audubon Societies were organized that the observance of Bird Day every year began. The credit for arranging the first observance of the day is said to belong to Charles A. Babcock, Superintendent of Schools of Oil City, Pa. He noticed that the children in the nature study classes were deeply interested in describing the birds common in the city and surrounding country. So he wrote to a number of ornithologists asking them to write something about birds that would interest the children. They responded and what they wrote was read in the classes. Then he asked the ornithologists what they thought of setting apart a day to be known as Bird Day. They approved the plan. As a result in May 1894, Bird Day was observed in the schools of Oil City, for the first time in any community in the United States. The United States Department of Agriculture and the Audubon Societies were quick to see the benefits that would follow the adoption of the Oil City plan throughout the United States and they fostered it so successfully that Bird Day is observed generally.

Salt Lake City had a special observance of Bird Day on April 3, 1915, the anniversary of the birth of John Burroughs, a lover of birds, when it dedicated a bird sanctuary in Liberty Park. The sanctuary was marked by a sign enjoining the protection of birds. It began with the question "Do you prefer destruction by insects to the song of the birds?" The people of Utah have special reason for gratitude to birds for their first crops sowed in the spring of 1848, the year after they arrived, were attacked by black crickets and nearly destroyed. The same pest returned in 1849 and 1850, when large flocks of gulls appeared and feasted upon the insects and saved the crops. A monument, consisting of two bronze gulls, has been erected in Salt Lake City in commemoration of this event.

APRIL FOURTEENTH

PAN AMERICAN DAY

What is frequently called the first Pan American Conference, although there had been conferences between South American countries and the United States before it, opened in Washington on October 2, 1889, and remained in session until April 21, 1890. James G. Blaine, Secretary of State in the Cabinet of President Harrison, had called the conference and presided at its sessions. On April 14 a resolution was adopted forming the Pan American Union, composed of the republics in North, Central, and South America. A splendid building for the headquarters of the Union was built in Washington through the generosity of Andrew Carnegie.

The governing board of the union adopted a resolution on May 7, 1930, setting forth the desirability of observing a day to be known as Pan American Day in all the American republics and suggesting April 14, the date of the resolution creating the Pan American Union, as an appropriate time and recommending that all the governments represented in the union designate that day as Pan American Day and that the national flags be displayed then. The various governments acted on the recommendation. President Hoover issued a proclamation on March 7, 1931, ordering that the flag be displayed on all government buildings on April 14 and inviting the schools, civic associations and people of the United States generally to observe the day with appropriate ceremonies, "thereby giving expression to the spirit of continental solidarity and to the sentiments of cordiality and friendly feeling which the government and people of the United States entertain toward the peoples and governments of the other republics of the American continent."

Pan American Day was thus observed for the first time in 1931. The ceremonies in Washington were held in the Pan American Building, attended by the President of the United States and the members of his Cabinet and by the diplomatic representatives of the other American republics. Addresses were made by the President, the Secretary of State, the Mexican and Cuban Ambassadors, and by two students, one from Chile, attending Georgetown University, and the other from the Western High School at Washington. The day was observed by public ceremonies in other cities attended by the resident consular officers of the Latin-American countries, and appropriate exercises were held in many schools. It has been observed in the succeeding years in a similar manner in Washington and elsewhere in the United States as well as in the countries represented in the Pan American Union.

APRIL FIFTEENTH

EXPATRIATION TREATY WITH GREAT BRITAIN

The right of a person to change his allegiance from one country to another is not generally recognized. One of the causes of the War of 1812 with Great Britain was the denial of this right. The British seized seamen from American ships claiming that they were British subjects, as they had been born within British territory. The United States Government insisted that they were American citizens. As the population of the country was continually increased by immigration it was inevitable that the government should insist on the right of the new residents to become citizens. Congress declared that the right of expatriation, or of changing allegiance, was "a natural and inherent right of all people, indispensable to the enjoyment of the rights of life, liberty and the pursuit of happiness." Great Britain refused to recognize this right for many years and it was not until 1869 that she agreed to abandon her position. A treaty recognizing the right of British subjects to become American citizens with no obligation to their native country was negotiated, and was ratified by the United States Senate on April 15, in that year and later ratified in London. Most if not all the other European powers refuse to recognize the right of expatriation. Men of Italian birth living in this country who were summoned to the colors by Italy during World War I obeyed the summons for they feared that otherwise they would be imprisoned if they ever returned to Italy for a visit.

APRIL SIXTEENTH

ENDOWMENT OF A COLLEGE TEACHERS PENSION FUND

The unfortunate lot of college professors, who receive modest salaries, attracted the attention of Andrew Carnegie when he was disposing of his fortune. No adequate provision was made for their support after their years of usefulness ended. Therefore, on April 16, 1905, Mr. Carnegie put $10,000,000 in the hands of five distinguished men, the income from which was to be used in paying pensions to retired professors in the universities, colleges and technical schools of the country. He later increased the amount by $5,000,000. In 1906 the Carnegie Foundation for the Advancement of Teaching was chartered to administer the fund and to select the institutions to benefit by it. In 1918 on the initiative of the Foundation for the Advancement of Teaching, the Teachers Insurance and Annuity Association was organized to issue life insurance and annuity contracts to employees of colleges and universities. The Carnegie Corporation of New York endowed it initially with a million dollars and for a number of years all expenses were paid by them. In 1938 a further endowment of about six and a half million dollars was given them and the stock of the Association was transferred to a self-perpetuating, membership corporation. Its retirement annuity contracts are the basic instrument for providing retirement income for staff members of a large majority of the colleges and universities throughout the country.

APRIL SEVENTEENTH

CHARTERING OF THE AMERICAN ACADEMY OF ARTS AND LETTERS

After several years of effort the American Academy of Arts and Letters obtained a charter from Congress on April 17, 1916. The granting of the charter was at first opposed on the ground that the institution was not democratic, but this objection was finally overcome. The Academy is affiliated with the National Institute of Arts and Letters which was organized at a meeting of the American Social Science Association in 1898. It was thought desirable that there should be an independent association composed of artists and men of letters. The first president was Charles Dudley Warner. Its membership was fixed at two hundred and fifty and in the course of time that number of distinguished men were elected. In 1904, however, it was thought that a more select body should be organized composed of the outstanding men—a body which should encourage the best creative work and serve in the United States some of the purposes of the famous French Academy. Its members met on April 23 in that year and formed the American Academy of Arts and Sciences to consist of thirty members. These first seven members were elected by ballot: William Dean Howells, Augustus Saint-Gaudens, Edmund Clarence Stedman, John LaFarge, Samuel L. Clemens, John Hay, and Edward McDowell. They were directed to choose eight others and the resulting fifteen should choose five more and the twenty should select ten, making thirty, the number then thought large enough. It has since been raised to fifty. The members are now chosen by ballot in the American Institute of Arts and Letters from its own membership. The Academy and the Institute occupy a building in West One Hundred and Fifty-fifth Street, New York, where a library and art museum are maintained.

APRIL EIGHTEENTH

THE SAN FRANCISCO FIRE

Probably the most disastrous fire in the history of the United States started in San Francisco on April 18, 1906, following an earthquake which was severest at thirteen minutes after five o'clock in the morning. An area four hundred miles long and fifty miles wide was affected by the quake. Relatively more damage was caused by the quake outside of the city than within its borders. But the water mains were broken impeding the efforts of the fire department to extinguish the flames which had been caused by burning gas from the broken gas mains and by overturned stoves. The fire raged for three days throughout the business section. To prevent its spread buildings were blown up by dynamite and when the supply of dynamite was exhausted artillery was used in razing the structures. By the fourth day the water mains had been repaired and the fire was brought under control, but the greater part of the business district and large residential areas were in ruins. The property loss was estimated at $200,000,000 and about 250,000 persons were rendered homeless. Relief committees were immediately formed and because of their efficiency there was comparatively little suffering. Disorder was prevented by General Funston of the United States Army, who put the city under martial law which he enforced rigidly.

PASCH OR THE FEAST OF THE PASSOVER

The Feast of the Passover, regarded by the Jews as one of the most important celebrations of the year, begins on the fourteenth day of the month Nisan and continues for eight days. The beginning of the feast in 1934 fell on April 18. As the Jewish differs from the Gregorian calendar it falls on different dates from year to year (see Jewish New Year, September 10). The feast, which scholars believe to be derived from an ancient spring time festival, came to be regarded by the Jews as a celebration of the deliverance of their first born in Egypt from the doom which Moses predicted would overtake the first born of the Egyptians, a prediction the fulfilment of which led Pharaoh to allow the Children of Israel to leave the country. As it began early in the second millenium before the Christian era and continues to the present day it is one of the oldest festivals known to history. There are various explanations of the meaning of the word "passover," but an explanation widely accepted is that it refers to the Angel of Death who passed over the houses of the Jews in Egypt the doors of which had been sprinkled with the blood of a lamb. This sprinkling of blood was an ancient custom, followed when a pestilence prevailed, arising from the belief that the plague could not enter a house thus marked. The Jews, obeying the injunction of Moses, remained in their houses on the fatal night, dressed ready for a journey, and ate unleavened bread and the lamb that had been slain to provide the blood. The Last Supper which Jesus ate with his disciples before the Crucifixion was in celebration of the Passover.

Many of the rites of Biblical times have fallen into disuse but the orthodox Jews still observe the festival and retain some of the significant customs. They eat unleavened bread and before the beginning of the feast they remove all leaven from their houses and cleanse all their dishes to remove all possible traces of yeast. Many families have a special set of dishes used only at this time. In order that there may be no leaven in the house the head of the family on the eve of the feast puts a piece of leavened bread on a window sill and then lights a wax candle. Starting from the window he searches throughout the house for any traces of yeast which there may be, gathering it in a spoon until he returns to the starting place. He then puts in the spoon the piece of bread left there and everything is then tied in a bundle and suspended over a lamp to prevent mice from getting at it during the night and scattering it about. The master of the house then announces that all the leaven in the house which he may have overlooked is no more than dust.

On the first day of the feast the first-born son of the family, if he is more than thirteen years old, fasts in memory of the deliverance of the first born in Egypt. In the evening the male members of the family attend services in the synagogue and on their return home they find the house brilliantly lighted and the Paschal Table spread. All the members of the family, including the servants, sit around the table. The master of the house sits in an arm chair filled with cushions and pillows so that at the appropriate time he may recline on them in the ancient manner of freemen who reclined at table. Unleavened bread and bitter herbs and the shank bone of a lamb, typifying the sacrificial lamb, are on the table. These are eaten in accordance with a special ritual. There is wine on the table and a glass at each place with an extra glass for the prophet Elias. Four glasses of wine are drunk, each at a fixed point in the ceremonial meal. At the conclusion all wash their hands and after some further rites the real feast is served. At the end of the feast a grace after meat is said and wine is poured out in the cup set for Elias. Then there is silence for some time. Then in accordance with a custom introduced in the Middle Ages imprecations against unbelievers taken from the Psalms and the Lamentations are recited. Special services are held in the synagogues during the whole Passover season.

APRIL NINETEENTH

PATRIOTS' DAY

The anniversary of the Battle of Lexington and Concord is a legal holiday in Massachusetts and Maine, and is celebrated annually with more or less ceremony. It was of this battle, which was fought on April 19, 1775, that Emerson wrote in his poem at the dedication of a monument at Concord bridge:

> By the rude bridge that arched the flood,
> Their flag to April's breeze unfurl'd,
> Here once the embattled farmers stood,
> And fired the shot heard round the world.

In the spring of 1775, General Gage, the British commander in Boston, learned that the patriots of Massachusetts had assembled a quantity of ammunition and other munitions of war at Concord, sixteen miles away. He planned a secret expedition to seize and destroy these military stores, but the patriots learned of his purpose. Toward midnight on April 18 he sent a force of eight hundred men under Lieutenant Colonel Smith and Major Pitcairn to carry out his purpose. When this force set out Paul Revere, waiting across the Charles River for a signal from a church tower in Boston, saw the light in the tower and started on horseback to give the alarm to the patriots. The story of his ride has been made famous in a poem by Longfellow. Revere carried the news to the farmers and soon church bells were rung and guns were fired to rouse the people. When at dawn Pitcairn with his advance guard reached Lexington, six miles from Concord, he found seventy armed men, under command of Captain Jonas Parker, gathered on the village green to resist his advance. Pitcairn rode forward and shouted: "Disperse! disperse you rebels! Down with your arms and disperse!" But the men did not disperse. Thereupon he ordered his men to fire and the War for Independence was begun. Eight men were killed and several others were wounded and the survivors were forced to retreat. A horseman meanwhile had ridden on to Concord to give the alarm there and the military stores were hastily taken to a place of concealment and the patriots armed themselves to resist with guns and axes and every other conceivable kind of weapon. They were commanded by Major Buttrick and Adjutant Joseph Hosmer. When the British reached the North Bridge and began to destroy it they were met by Major Buttrick's force. The British fired upon the defenders and the fire was returned. Some of the British were killed and the others retreated. They succeeded, however, in destroying that part of the military stores which had not been hidden. On their way back toward Boston they were fired upon by the patriots from behind trees and stone walls and houses. They were reinforced by a thousand men under Lord Percy, near Lexington, otherwise all the survivors would have been killed or taken prisoners. Instead of attempting to renew the battle, the larger force, after resting at Lexington, retreated and was fired upon from ambush all the way back to Charlestown. The men rested there during the night and crossed the river to Boston under cover of the guns of the British warships the next morning. The British loss in killed, wounded and missing was two hundred and seventy-three men. The American loss was one hundred and three.

This battle aroused the people of the colonies. Those in New England resolved to confine the British army to Boston, New Hampshire voted to raise two thousand men, Connecticut raised six thousand, Rhode Island contributed fifteen hundred, and Massachusetts thirteen thousand six hundred. The city was soon encircled by patriot troops (see Bunker Hill Day, June 17). As the news spread from colony to colony, arms and ammunition were seized, provincial congresses were formed and before the end of the summer the power of the royal governors was completely destroyed.

APRIL TWENTIETH

GIFT OF THE HAGUE PEACE PALACE ·

There were rosy views of international peace when the first Peace Conference at The Hague adjourned in 1899. Shortly after its adjournment Professor von Martens, the Russian minister at Berlin, visited Andrew D. White, the American minister, at the legation, and said that there ought to be a palace of justice at The Hague for the use of the Arbitration Tribunal, and that there ought to be some American millionaire willing to build it. Mr. White replied that the only American millionaire he knew with vision broad enough to see the importance of it was Andrew Carnegie. He thereupon wrote to Mr. Carnegie and got little satisfaction from the reply. The correspondence continued for a long time. Finally Mr. White by invitation, visited Mr. Carnegie at his castle in Scotland, but found no opportunity to broach the subject until the last day of the visit when Mr. Carnegie agreed to finance the project. On April 20, 1903, he gave $1,500,000 to be used in building a suitable structure for The Hague Court and for a library of international law. It was more than ten years later, however, that the peace palace was dedicated. It is a splendid building, standing in its own grounds in the capital city of the Netherlands, the contribution of an American citizen to the cause of international peace.

APRIL TWENTY-FIRST

SAN JACINTO DAY

The anniversary of the Battle of San Jacinto, fought on April 21, 1836, is a holiday in Texas. It was by this battle that the Texans forced Mexico to recognize their independence. When the Mexican revolution, which resulted in driving Spain out of the country, began in 1810 the Texans, assisted by forces from the United States, decided to set up a government of their own. They proclaimed the country a republic with Nacogdoches as the capital. It did not last long for the Spanish forces broke up the new government. Moses Austin obtained from the Mexican Government the right to found a colony in Texas in 1821. He died soon afterward and his work was carried on by his son Stephen. The colony settled in the Brazos and Trinity valleys. By 1826 the American settlers, resenting the misrule of the Mexicans, proclaimed the eastern part of the state an independent republic, but it survived only a short time. There was another revolt against Mexican rule in 1832, followed by the calling of a convention which elected Stephen Austin president, but the authority of Mexico over the country continued. Austin was sent to Mexico to

229

demand reforms, but he was unable to get a hearing from those in authority and was made a prisoner. Armed revolt broke out in 1835 and in December the Texans captured San Antonio. A provisional government was formed with Henry Smith as governor and Sam Houston as major general of the armies. On February 23, 1836, Santa Anna, in command of a Mexican army, attacked the Alamo, a Franciscan mission at San Antonio, in which a company of Texans and Americans, including Colonel David Crockett, had taken refuge. The siege lasted until March 6, when a breach was made in the walls and what was left of the defending force was massacred. On March 2 the Texans again issued a declaration of independence and when Santa Anna had finished his work at the Alamo he marched eastward, and on April 21 met the Texas army under Houston at San Jacinto near Houston. Santa Anna was defeated and taken prisoner and was forced to sign a treaty by the provisions of which he pledged himself to do what he could to get the independence of Texas recognized with boundaries extending as far south as the Rio Grande. A constitution was drafted which was ratified in September. General Houston was made the first president of the new republic and Houston was made the capital.

The battlefield has been set aside as a state park. The anniversary is observed throughout the state with special exercises in the public schools and by elaborate pageants in the various cities. The people of Houston, aware of the importance of the victory, celebrated it in 1837, the first of a long series of celebrations there. An account of this first celebration by one who was present was printed in the *Hesperian or Western Magazine* of Columbus, Ohio, in 1838. The program, according to him, included the erection of a liberty pole upon which was to float the lone star flag of the republic. There was a speech by a distinguished orator and there was a dance in the evening. As there were not more than sixty or seventy women in Houston, young and old, married and single, it was necessary to scour the surrounding country to get partners for the men at the dance. The writer says:

After prayer the speaker ascended the rostrum. [The record does not tell who the speaker was.] It was so arranged that the speech should not only be delivered upon the day, but upon the very hour in which the battle was fought so that the speaker might be animated with the reflection that just one year from the very moment he was speaking he was engaged in the battle. During the remarks, which continued for an hour, the cheeks of the President [General Houston] colored for a moment as the speaker dropped an expression which seemed to imply doubt as to what portion of the honor of the day he was entitled. It may not be known to the world that the soldiers and officers are unwilling to divide with their general the laurels of San Jacinto. The speaker acquitted himself to his entire satisfaction. The multitude now adjourned to meet in the evening. Night came and with it the merry dancers; the president, dressed in a rich silk velvet suit, moved among the throng with a gallantry and grace which have always distinguished him when he chose to assume them. There was a separate dance for the heroes of San Jacinto, as there was for those present at the storming of Bexar. The evening passed off with much pleasure and satisfaction to all and without any disturbance.

The celebration of the anniversary, which began in Houston, has become more elaborate from year to year until it has developed into a gorgeous pageant there and in other cities of the state. In San Antonio it extended over Thursday, Friday and Saturday, April 19, 20 and 21, 1934. The development of Texas in material and cultural resources in the intervening years can be appreciated by comparing the foregoing descriptions by eye witnesses of the first celebration with the description of the San Antonio celebration by the writers for the San Antonio *Express*. The fiesta began on Thursday evening with the crowning of the queen of the occasion, and the presentation of a pageant based on Norse mythology. The coronation ceremony was conducted by the Order of the Alamo. The crown was placed on the head of Miss Olivia Nolte, and she was named Her majesty, Gerda, Asynia of the Aesir and Queen of the Court of the Midnight Sun. Her costume was "of sunset hued metal cloth. A wide collar reaching to the shoulders was of solid jewels, blue, green and gold predominating. The center was adorned with a dragon design in gold sequins. A jeweled belt and a panel of jewels extended to the hem which was elaborately ornamented with sparkling stones of all colors. From her shoulders fell the gorgeous train which bore the symbols of Norse mythology. The central design depicted in glowing gems the Midnight Sun with its rays extending to the shoulders and blazing with white, gold and amber rhinestones. At the foot of the train appeared the Midgard Serpent. His gleaming scales were wrought in blue and green sequins. The entire edge of the train was intricately embroidered in gold, green and blue jewels." The Queen had a numerous court composed of mythological characters each gorgeously costumed. An entertainment was provided beginning with a pageant called "The Gift of the Golden Apples of Eternal Youth" in which a company of young women participated. This was followed by a concert by Charles Hackett, tenor of the Metropolitan Opera Company of New York. The evening ended with a ball. Preceding the coronation ceremonies there had been a pilgrimage to the Alamo (see Alamo Day, March 6). Wreaths were laid in the historic mission by Boy Scouts, Reserve Officer Training Corps cadets and children from nearly all the public schools in the city. Friday was the great day of the celebration when what was called the Battle of the Flowers parade was held. The San Antonio *Express* described it in this way:

Glittering with military array and bright with vari-colored flowers decorating the elaborate floats, the three-mile procession wended its way down Broadway through the downtown section and to the reviewing stand at the historic Alamo through a sea of faces. Spectators were banked ten and twelve deep in some sections of the line of march. Others crowded out into the street until the motor cycle escort had difficulty in clearing a way for the floats. . . . Greater variety than ever was seen in the colorful procession from the small decorated cars of the individual entries to the spectacular floats bearing the attendants to Miss Olivia Nolte, Gerda, Asynja of the Aesir and Queen of the Court of the Midnight Sun. The historic and pioneer note was strong, represented in several floats entered by historical societies. One represented a family of early Texas settlers in a covered wagon with all the pioneering paraphernalia, and inscribed "Texas or Bust— 1835." Another recalled the Gonzales incident and another the unfurling of the Texas flag. One of the floats which drew applause from the spectators was probably the simplest, a woman clad in pioneer garb seated on a log and holding a child. Across her knees was a musket and in front of her a shepherd dog. A novel group of floats was entered by the San Antonio schools and displayed the leisure-time activities. Others were realistic even in minor details. On one depicting an outdoor scene a real fire was burning and a Boy Scout was frying a piece of bacon. The most elaborate group of floats bore the attendants of Her Divine Majesty, the Queen of the Court of the Midnight Sun. In keeping with the theme of the coronation ceremony, taken from Icelandic mythology, the floats were designed with the Northland severity of the goddesses the riders represented. The colorful simplicity of their flowing robes heightened the effect.

The celebration closed with the presentation of "Elijah" in the Municipal Auditorium on Saturday night. The anniversary is to Texas what the Fourth of July is to the older part of the country. The Texans remember with pride the message which General Houston sent to General Gaines on the Brazos five days after the battle:

Tell our friends the news, that we have beaten the enemy. . . . Tell them to come on and let the people plant corn.

APRIL TWENTY-SECOND

ARBOR DAY

The first formal observance of Arbor Day as a time for planting trees was on April 10, 1872, in Nebraska. It was in pursuance of a resolution adopted by the State Board of Agriculture on the motion of J. Sterling Morton, a member of the board. The resolution read:

Resolved, That April 10,1873, be and the same is hereby especially set apart and consecrated for tree planting in the State of Nebraska, and that the State Board of Agriculture hereby names it Arbor Day. And to urge upon the people of the state the vital importance of tree planting hereby offers a special premium of $100 to the Agricultural Society of that county in Nebraska which shall upon that day plant properly the largest number of trees, and a farm library of $25 worth of books to that person who on that day shall plant properly in Nebraska the greatest number of trees.

Nebraska at the time lacked trees. Mr. Morton believed that they would be useful as windbreaks and to conserve the moisture in the soil. On the first Arbor Day in the state a million trees were planted. Within sixteen years six hundred million had been planted and within twenty years a hundred thousand acres of waste land had been turned into forests. In succeeding years the governors of the state named the third Wednesday in April as Arbor Day. This continued until 1885. In that year the Legislature passed an act fixing the date as of April 22, the anniversary of the birth of Mr. Morton and made the day a legal holiday. The Arbor Day Memorial Association of the state has erected a monument in honor of Mr. Morton on the grounds of his old home, Arbor Lodge, near Nebraska City.

Mr. Morton was born in Adams, Jefferson County, N.Y., on April 22, 1832. His parents removed to Michigan in his early youth and he received his elementary education at the Methodist Episcopal Academy at Albion. In 1850 he entered the University of Michigan, but transferred to Union College from which he was graduated in the class of 1854. The next year he settled in Nebraska and founded the Nebraska City *News* after living a short time in Belleville. He served in the territorial legislature and was for a time territorial governor. He was defeated when he ran as the Democratic candidate for governor when the territory was admitted to the Union as a state. He was Secretary of Agriculture in President Cleveland's second Cabinet and President McKinley appointed him in 1901 as one of the United States Commissioners for the Louisiana Purchase Exposition. He died in 1902.

The belief in the desirability of planting trees did not originate with Mr. Morton. It is much older than he and was recognized in Europe long before it was admitted in America. In the early days in this country, especially in the East the trees had to be cut down to clear the land for agriculture. Dr. Birdsey Grant Northrup, born in Kent County, Conn., is credited with first directing attention to the subject. He was the founder and organizer of village improvement associations and urged the removal of the fences from the front lawns of the village houses and the planting of trees. He traveled in this country, in Europe and Asia advocating the beautification of the landscape with trees.

Arbor day is now generally observed with special exercises in the schools and with the planting of trees. John B. Peaslee, Superintendent of Schools at Cincinnati, Ohio, was one of the earliest supporters of the movement. On April 27, 1882, the school children planted in Eden Park an Authors' Grove. Each tree was named for a distinguished author, statesman or soldier and marked with the name of the man honored. The American Forestry Congress, meeting in Philadelphia in April 1889, planted an oak in Fairmount Park in that city in honor of Mr. Peaslee. It is known as Peaslee's Oak.

Rhode Island is the only state besides Nebraska in which Arbor Day is a legal holiday. It observes the day on the second Friday in May. In many states the date is fixed either by proclamation of the governor, by the State Board of Education or by the county school superintendents. In the following states there is a fixed date: Arizona, in northern counties, Friday following April 1; in southern counties, Friday following February 1; Arkansas, the first Saturday in December; California, March 7, Luther Burbank's birthday (see March 7); Colorado and District of Columbia, third Friday in April; Florida, first Friday in February; Geor-

APRIL 22

gia, first Friday in December; Indiana, second Friday in April; Louisiana, second Friday in January; Massachusetts, last Saturday in April; Mississippi, first Friday in February; Missouri, first Friday after the first Tuesday in April; Montana, second Tuesday in May; New Jersey, second Friday in April; New Mexico, second Friday in March; North Carolina, first Friday after March 15; Oklahoma, Friday after second Monday in March; Oregon, second Friday in February in the western part of the state and second Friday in April in the eastern part; South Carolina, third Friday in November; Tennessee, first Friday in April; Texas, February 22; Utah, April 15; Virginia; second Friday in March; Vermont, Washington, and Wisconsin, first Friday in May; West Virginia, second Friday in April. The Indiana law directing the observance of the day provides that "the exercises on Arbor Day shall give due honor to the conservers of forestry and the founders of the study and conservation of Indiana forestry, and particularly to the leading spirit of Indiana forestry conservation, Charles Warren Fairbanks."

THE OPENING OF OKLAHOMA TERRITORY

The anniversary of the opening of Oklahoma Territory is a legal holiday in Oklahoma. It is observed throughout the state on April 22 each year by parades, rodeos and patriotic speeches, but Guthrie in Logan County, the first capital of the State of Oklahoma, is declared by the statutes as the official city for celebrations, and the ceremonies there are more elaborate. This holiday commemorates the opening of the Unassigned Lands on April 22, 1889, and is generally referred to as "The Run" in Oklahoma history, although other land openings are similarly termed. On April 22 in Guthrie, the cobbled streets echo the rumble of hundreds of prairie schooners and buckboards drawn by teams of oxen or mules, while cowboys and Indians spur their horses through the crowd. A rodeo is a part of the program and, in accordance with Oklahoman tradition, the meanest horses are provided for the best rodeo performers in the United States to ride. In short, only the "gol-dangest best" of anything is acceptable. This criterion also applies to the parade which must be miles in length to satisfy the enthusiasm of the celebrants, both participants and spectators. Visitors are invited to try their luck at bulldogging, calf-roping, or spinning tall tales with the oldtimers.

Oklahoma came into the Union with a history of forty-four million acres of land thrown open to settlement by seven land openings and a Supreme Court Decision. The region was a part of the Louisiana Purchase and, except for a small strip of land north of Texas, was organized in 1834 as an Indian Territory. White people were barred as settlers, but, although there was a large influx of Indians from other parts of the country, a considerable area in the central part of the territory remained unoccupied. This section was purchased by the United States Government and opened to the public on April 22, 1889. More than fifty thousand persons entered in one day in a frantic rush to stake out claims. The scene was one of indescribable and picturesque confusion, making a fascinating page in American history which has subsequently been used to great effect in fiction. The No-Man's Land strip just north of the Texas panhandle was a narrow section of public land west of the Cherokee Strip in Indian Territory. Efforts were made to include it in Kansas and New Mexico without success. The people who lived there considered it a part of Indian Territory, in which it was finally included when opened to the public in 1889. It is now a part of the State of Oklahoma. (See September 16, Cherokee Strip Day, for another celebration commemorating a land opening in Oklahoma.)

APRIL TWENTY-THIRD

BIRTHDAY OF JAMES BUCHANAN

James Buchanan, the fifteenth President of the United States, was born near Mercersburg, Pa., on April 23, 1791. He was graduated from Dickinson College at Carlisle, Pa., at the age of eighteen. He was admitted to the bar in 1812 and began to practice law in Lancaster, Pa., where he made his home for the rest of his life. Two years later he was elected to the state legislature and in 1820 he was elected to Congress and served five terms in the House of Representatives, becoming chairman of the Judiciary Committee. As Minister to Russia, he negotiated the first commercial treaty between that country and the United States. He was elected to the United States Senate in 1833 and was twice reelected. While in Congress he upheld the right of the opponents of slavery to petition for its abolition but insisted that Congress had no control over slavery in the states. He obtained the Democratic nomination for President in 1856 and was elected over John C. Fremont, the first nominee of the newly organized Republican party. Buchanan has been charged with fostering the secession of the Southern states by arguing that while the states had no right to secede the Federal Government had no power to prevent it, as the Government could employ force in a state only at the demand of the lawful authorities in the state. South Carolina passed a secession ordinance on December 20, 1860, and sent a commission to Washington to demand the surrender to it of all public property in the state. He received the commissioners as "private gentlemen of high character" and told them that he could only refer their request to Congress. He did, however, refuse to remove the Federal troops from Charleston harbor. His attitude led to the resignation of Lewis Cass as Secretary of State and to the reorganization of the Cabinet. He then tried to reinforce the garrison at Charleston and announced his intention to protect Federal property in the state if it were attacked. He wrote to John A. Dix of New York after the inauguration of President Lincoln:

The present Administration had no alternative but to accept the war initiated by South Carolina or the Southern Confederacy. The North will sustain the Administration almost to a man, and it ought to sustain it at all hazards.

Buchanan was a man of exceptional ability. Within three years after he began to practice law in Lancaster his earnings were more than $11,000 a year, regarded as a large income at the time. He had mastered the law and he had developed skill as an orator. These qualities started him on his political career which led him to the highest office in the gift of the people. He and Grover Cleveland were the only bachelors ever elected to the presidency. Cleveland married while in office but Buchanan died unwed. His niece, Harriet Lane, was the mistress of the White House during his administration, as she had been the mistress of his house abroad during his diplomatic career. On his retirement from the presidency he returned to his home, Wheatland, in the suburbs of Lancaster, and died there on June 1, 1868.

SHAKESPEARE'S BIRTHDAY

The accepted date of the birth of William Shakespeare is April 23, 1564. The only available records show that he was baptized on April 26, and as it was the custom to have the baptism three days after birth the date is probably correct. The anniversary has been observed by the Shakespeare societies in America for many years. One of the earliest to be organized in this country was formed by admirers of the poet in 1851. One of the most notable annual celebrations is that in the Edwin Forrest Home for Retired Actors in Philadelphia. When Forrest died he left his home, Spring Brook, in the northern part of that city, as a home for actors and his will provided that there should be a celebration every year of the anniversary of the birth of Shakespeare. That provision has been respected to the present.

Forrest died in 1872, but it was 1876 before the complications in the settlement of the estate could be unraveled and the home opened to actors. In the course of years the property, including 106 acres, increased in value so that it was thought advisable to sell it. It was sold in 1925 for $600,000. About one fourth of this sum was used to build a new home in the Elizabethan style of architecture facing Fairmount Park on a plot of about two acres. It has a large hall in which the annual celebrations are held, participated in by distinguished actors and by persons interested in Shakespeare. This is a tribute by players to the greatest English playwright who through community of language belongs to America as much as to England. The Shakespearean societies in other cities, whose members are interested in the plays as literature, do not neglect the anniversary. The celebration at the Forrest Home in 1923 was particularly interesting as it was the three hundredth anniversary of the publication of the first folio edition of the plays.

So little is known about the life of Shakespeare that most of the biographies say that he "doubtless" did this or that at such a time. It is known that he was one of eight children of John Shakespeare and Mary Arden, that he was the eldest son, and that he was born at Stratford-on-Avon. At the age of twenty he went to London, having previously married Anne Hathaway. It is said that his first occupation in London was holding the horses outside a theater for those who attended the shows. He became an actor and appeared in some of his own plays, and after accumulating a fortune he retired and settled in Stratford where he died in 1616 on his birthday. Students have professed to find cryptograms in the plays which prove that Francis Bacon or some other person wrote them. It was the custom of the time to conceal names by cryptograms in what appeared to be straightforward writing. In this connection it is interesting to note that in the forty-sixth Psalm of the King James version the name of Shakespeare is skilfully concealed. This version was authorized on July 22, 1604, and was not completed and published until 1611. In 1610, the year before the version was published Shakespeare was forty-six years old. The forty-sixth word in the Psalm, counting from the beginning is "shake" and the forty-sixth word, counting from the end, omitting "Selah," is "spear." Whether this is sheer coincidence or whether Shakespeare was consulted in the translation of this poetic book of the Bible and deliberately inserted his name in the psalm numbered according to his age are questions which probably can never be answered. The Players Club of New York observes the anniversary of Shakespeare's birth as the annual Ladies Day, opening its doors to prominent actresses and other ladies invited as guests of the members.

ST. GEORGE'S DAY

St. George has been venerated in England since the eighth century and Englishmen, in whatever part of the world they may be, celebrate April 23 in his honor. The first St. George's Society in America was probably the one organized in Philadelphia by the Englishmen in the city in 1729. It held its first meeting at the Tun Tavern on April 23 in that year and for many years thereafter held an annual dinner either on St. George's Day or on some more convenient date. This society was succeeded in 1772 by an organization known as the "Society of the Sons of St. George established at Philadelphia for the Advice and Assistance of Englishmen in Distress." Membership was restricted to "natives of that part of Great Britain called England, or to the sons of such." Among the early members were Robert Morris, Benjamin Franklin and Governor Penn. It celebrated St. George's Day until the beginning of the Revolutionary War after which its meetings were suspended for some years. They were resumed in the latter part of the eighteenth century and the day of the saint has been observed by an annual dinner since that time, at which the British Ambassador in Washington has been a frequent guest.

There are St. George's Societies in many other American cities. The Philadelphia society was the host in 1902 to the North American St. George's Union on St. George's day. On April 23, 1910, St. George's Protestant Episcopal Church in New York celebrated St. George's Day with a pageant representing the slaying of the dragon by St. George in which the children of the parish participated. After the dragon was slain the children gave folk dances. The committee had borrowed for the occasion the dragon used in the presentation of "Rheingold" at the Metropolitan Opera House. The monster was so realistic that it frightened many of the smaller children.

Little is definitely known of St. George although there are many traditions about him. A decree attributed to Pope Gelacius in about 495 includes him among those saints "whose names are reverenced among men, but whose actions are known only to God." He is supposed to have been born in Cappadocia in the eastern part of Asia Minor. The stories about him represent him as a soldier. Gibbon identifies him with a disreputable bishop, George of Cappadocia, saying that "The infamous George of Cappadocia has been transformed into the renowned George of England, the patron of arms, of chivalry and the Garter." But the scholars say that the worship of St. George is too old to permit any such identification. Clovis built a monastery in his honor at Baralle about 515. His fame reached England in the eighth century and the story of his deeds was translated into Anglo Saxon. Churches were dedicated in his honor before the Norman Conquest. In 1284 the seal of Lyme Regis was a ship with a flag bearing the cross of St. George. In 1347 Edward III founded the Order of the Blue Garter, an order of knighthood of which St. George was the principal patron. As early as 1222 St. George's Day was set apart as a special holiday and in 1415 it was ordered that the day be celebrated as a great feast day after the manner of Christmas.

The best known form of the legend is that translated into English by Caxton. A terrible dragon had ravaged all the country about Selena, a city in Libya. Its lair was in a marsh. Its breath caused pestilence whenever it approached the town. The people gave it two sheep every day to satisfy its hunger and prevent it from leaving the marsh. But when there were no sheep a human victim was necessary. Lots were drawn to determine who should be the victim. On one occasion the lot fell to the King's young daughter. The King offered a great price to buy a substitute, but the people had agreed that no substitutes were to be allowed. Therefore, the maiden, dressed as a bride was led toward the marsh. St. George chanced to be riding by and asked the maiden where she was going. She told him and besought him to leave her lest he also should perish. St. George, however, refused to go and when the dragon appeared he made the sign of the cross and began to fight it. After a fierce struggle he transfixed it with his spear. Then he asked the maiden for her girdle and bound it around the neck of the helpless monster, and the maiden led it like a lamb back to the city. St. George told the people not to be afraid but only to be baptized and accept Christianity. The people were all converted. One story says that twenty thousand of them were baptized that day. Then St. George cut off the dragon's head. The King offered to give the saint half his kingdom but St. George refused to accept it, saying that he must ride on, but that the King must take good care of God's churches, honor the clergy and have pity on the poor.

According to the story, after slaying the dragon he continued his journey into Palestine and arrived there just when the edict of Diocletian against the Christians had been posted at the temple and in the market places. St. George is said to have torn it down in indignation and trampled it under his feet. He was arrested and condemned to cruel torture. A cup of poisonous wine was given to him, but he drank it without harm. Then he was bound to a wheel, but the wheel was broken by two angels who came to help him. He was taken to the temple and ordered to sacrifice to the heathen idols, but he prayed to God instead and the temple was destroyed by lightning. Thereupon the proconsul ordered him beheaded, and he bowed his neck to the executioner. His cross, which is red, is represented on the British flag on a white ground with the arms intersecting at right angles along with the cross of St. Andrew of Scotland the arms of which form the letter X.

APRIL TWENTY-FOURTH

THE BRITISH BURN WASHINGTON

On April 24, 1814, during the War of 1812, a British force of about five thousand under General Ross and Admiral Cockburn defeated an unorganized force of militia at Bladensburg, Md., and then advanced without resistance upon Washington. The President and other public officials fled, taking with them such important public treasures as they could. The British officers ordered their men to burn the public buildings and they lighted fires in the Capitol, the White House and other structures. The interior of the Capitol was burned out and serious damage was done to the White House. The smoke discolored the stone on the outside of the latter building making it necessary to paint it; it has been painted periodically ever since. The burning of the buildings was a wanton and unnecessary act accomplishing no military purpose.

239

APRIL TWENTY-FIFTH

ST. MARK'S DAY

The feast of St. Mark, the evangelist, is observed on April 25 by the Roman and the Protestant churches. St. Mark was a Jew converted to Christianity by Paul and became his favorite disciple. He accompanied Paul to Rome, and it is believed that he wrote his gospel while in that city. For twelve years or more he preached in Egypt, Libya and Thebaïs and finally went to Alexandria where he founded a church which became one of the most celebrated among the early Christians. The Alexandrians denounced him as a magician and when at Easter he condemned their idolatry in worshipping Serapis, they seized him, bound him with ropes and dragged him through the streets until he was dead. His followers rescued his body and put it in a sepulchre which became a shrine visited by the faithful. In 815 some Venetian merchants trading in Alexandria obtained possession of the relics and carried them to Venice where a church was built over them known as St. Mark's, famous in religious and architectural history. There is an old English superstition that the ghosts of those who are to die during the year can be seen entering the church on St. Mark's day. Many churches in the United States are named for the saint.

APRIL TWENTY-SIXTH

CONFEDERATE MEMORIAL DAY

On April 26, 1865, Mrs. Sue Landon Vaughn, a descendant of John Adams, the second President of the United States, led some women to the cemetery in Vicksburg, Miss., and decorated the graves of the soldiers buried there. This day is now a legal holiday in Mississippi, known as Confederate Memorial Day. The graves of the Confederate dead are decorated on the same day in Alabama, Florida and Georgia. The day set apart for this purpose in North Carolina and South Carolina is May 10. It is observed in Virginia on May 30 and in Kentucky, Louisiana, and Tennessee on June 3. In Winchester, Va., the graves in the Confederate cemetery are decorated on June 6 and in Petersburg on June 9. The people of Petersburg are in the habit of insisting that the setting apart of a day in the North for decorating the graves of the soldiers came about from a visit of General John A. Logan to that city in 1865 to look over the fortifications raised for its defense. He and his wife, while passing through Blandford Cemetery on June 9, saw some ladies decorating the graves of the Washington Artillery in the square south of the Blandford church. General Logan thought he might be intruding, but the ladies, members of a Confederate Memorial Association, welcomed him and explained what they were doing and why. As General Logan was Commander in Chief of the Grand Army of the Republic when the order was issued in 1868 that the Grand Army posts should decorate the graves of the soldier dead on May 30 it is reasonable to assume that he was influenced by what he had seen in Petersburg. (See Memorial Day, May 30.)

Louisiana, which observes June 3, combines the decoration of the graves with a celebration of the anniversary of the birth of Jefferson Davis. Colonel W. L. Goldsmith in the course of his address at the exercises in New Orleans on June 3, 1911, said:

> Memorial Day is exclusively a Southern legislative action. Seven Southern states have made the third of June (the anniversary of the birth of Jefferson Davis) Memorial Day and a legal holiday. Scores of cities hold memorial services on this sacred day. Memorial Day is quite different from Decoration Day. The triumphant Grand Army of the Republic has a Decoration Day, May 30. To decorate is to rejoice. We recall hallowed memories on this sad day. With bitter tears and sweet fragrant flowers we sanctify these sacred places where our dead sleep. The day was inaugurated in Columbus, Ga., in March 1866, and has been observed by more and more ever since, until today a great part of the South celebrates the day.

A plot in the Arlington National Cemetery, across the Potomac from Washington, has been set apart for the Confederate dead. This was done through the efforts of President McKinley in 1898. The bodies of many Southern soldiers, captured after being wounded and taken to the Washington hospitals where they died, were buried in different parts of the District of Columbia. They were disinterred and removed to Arlington. Special services are held for these dead on Confederate Memorial Day and a wreath is always placed on the monument of General Joseph Wheeler, who fought in the Confederate armies and who fought with the armies of the United States in the war with Spain in 1898.

FAST DAY IN NEW HAMPSHIRE

New Hampshire is the only state in which there is still a legal holiday known as Fast Day. The date is fixed by proclamation of the governor and it is customary for him to set apart the fourth Thursday in April for its observance. This fell on April 26, 1945. Maine and Massachusetts once had laws which directed their governors to proclaim a day of fasting and prayer in the spring, but these laws have been repealed. Good Friday, which is a day of fasting for those who observe it, is a holiday in the following states: Arkansas, Connecticut, Delaware, Florida, Illinois, Indiana, Louisiana, Maryland, Minnesota, New Jersey, North Dakota, Pennsylvania, South Carolina, and Texas; also in five counties in Arizona.

The Governor of New Hampshire issues his proclamation annually, but there is little fasting on the day. Governor H. Styles Bridges, in the course of an explanation of the custom in his state, said in 1935:

The fact that the season of outdoor sport is then opening in this latitude tends to secure a general observance of the day so far as ceasing from labor is concerned. I do not know personally of any instance of its observance by fasting. Some church services are held and the official proclamation usually recalls the original reason for establishing Fast Day, and the existing need for a continuance of the thought that inspired the first observance.

Massachusetts abolished Fast Day in 1895. Two years later Governor Ramsdell of New Hampshire, in a message to the Legislature, urged that the example of Massachusetts be followed, but his recommendation was not adopted.

The gradual abandonment of a religious observance of the day in Maine led to the repeal of the law setting it apart as a holiday. There is a tradition in that state that in one year the Governor, in the absence of his secretary, asked his messenger to draw up the usual Fast Day proclamation, expecting him to copy one that had been issued in a previous year. The messenger, however, who had little reverence in his constitution, wrote the following proclamation:

Having consulted my Council and learned that none of them has an engagement to dine on that day, and feeling fully assured that I shall receive no invitation to dine until the high school graduating exercises begin and field strawberries get down to eight cents a quart, I do hereby appoint Thursday, the seventeenth day of April, as a day of public humiliation, fasting and prayer. While the scoffers in our sister state (Massachusetts) are holding horse races, playing baseball and gorging themselves with forbidden food, let us thank our stars that we know when we have enough, and feel grateful for the empty stomach and clear heads we shall have the morning after. Though I am unable to say what the Council will do on that day, for myself I shall attend church if I can find a minister who will stay long enough to preach to me. Given in the Council Chamber, etc.

The messenger is said to have engrossed this in the proper form and submitted it to the Governor who signed it without reading. He then took it to the Secretary of State to be attested. That official began to write his name but the pen was bad and while looking for a better pen he noted the unusual wording of the document. He then read it carefully and rebuked the messenger for making light of Fast Day and trifling with the dignity of the governor. The messenger explained that it was nothing but an April fool joke and the Secretary of State, on looking at his calendar, noted that the day was April 1 and took back all the harsh things that he had said. A proper proclamation was then prepared.

BIRTHDAY OF JOHN JAMES AUDUBON

It was supposed for many years that John James Audubon, the naturalist, was born at Mandeville, La., in 1780 or thereabouts. The year and the day were unknown. It has been learned, however, by F. H. Herrick, his biographer, that he was born on April 26, 1785, at Les Cayes, in what is now the republic of Haiti. He was the son of Captain

Jean Audubon, a successful business man and officer in the French navy. The son, christened Jean Jacques, or in English, John James, was educated in France. He landed in New York in the autumn of 1803 and went to live on a farm near a village that was later named Audubon in his honor, not far from Philadelphia where he devoted ten years to collecting birds and making sketches of them. His farming was unprofitable and he made two or three unsuccessful attempts at a business career in Louisiana and Kentucky. After losing his property he supported himself by giving dancing lessons and painting portraits. In Kentucky he met Alexander Wilson, known as the father of American ornithology, who was soliciting subscriptions for a book which he was publishing describing the American birds. Wilson's drawings were crude and it is supposed that the sight of them suggested to Audubon the preparation of a work of his own. In 1826 he went to London to arrange for the publication of his book by subscription. By 1827 he had obtained enough subscriptions to warrant starting the publication of his *Birds of America,* and later his *Quadrupeds of America.*

He died in New York City on January 27, 1851, and was buried in Trinity Cemetery near which a park named for him has been laid out. His widow survived him for many years and in order to earn a living, conducted a school for little children. Among her pupils was George Bird Grinnell, who became editor of *Forest and Stream* and in 1886 organized a society for the study and protection of birds which he named the Audubon Society. Many branches of it were soon formed and a National Association of Audubon Societies was organized. The association maintains many sanctuaries for birds and organizes school children into bird study clubs. It is affiliated with Junior Audubon Clubs in this country, and with similar societies in foreign countries. The association arranged a national celebration of the one hundred and fiftieth anniversary of the birth of Audubon on April 26, 1935.

CAPE HENRY DAY

In Virginia the Governor annually proclaims April 26 as Cape Henry Day in commemoration of the first landing on American soil of the expedition that founded Jamestown. The sponsors of this observance have advanced the reasonable contention that, although Jamestown was destroyed during Bacon's Rebellion some seventy years after its founding, it was nevertheless the first English settlement in America that can properly be called permanent, and the landing of the colonists thus deserves equal, if not greater, fame and recognition than the much-publicized landing of the Pilgrim Fathers on Plymouth Rock. Since the landing at Cape Henry on April 26, 1607, marked the beginning of colonization in Virginia which continued uninterruptedly despite the burning of Jamestown, and since it antedated the Plymouth Rock landing by thirteen years, there is considerable to be said for the argument. In any event, celebration of the day has been fostered by the Assembly of Tidewater Virginia Women until it has become a noteworthy occasion in the state attended yearly by several thousand, including many distinguished persons.

The idea for a permanent memorial on the sand dunes and an annual Cape Henry Pilgrimage originated in 1920 when English members of the Sulgrave Committee came to America. The Committee, named for Sulgrave Manor, the ancestral home of the Washingtons, visited various historic sites, among them Cape Henry where a memorial service was held. Finally, in 1926, the first organized pilgrimage to Cape Henry was led by Governor Byrd of Virginia, with religious services and patriotic ceremonies marking the anniversary. The Association for the Preservation of Virginia Antiquities had placed a tablet marker on the old Lighthouse Hill in 1896, but in 1935 the Daughters of the American Colonists erected a granite cross on the so-called First Landing Dune with an inscription dedicating it as a permanent memorial to the landing of the English colonists who established at Jamestown the first permanent English settlement in America. The site was allocated by the War Department, and in 1938 Congress passed a bill for the inclusion of Cape Henry in the Colonial National Historical Park. In 1940 the Virginia Assembly designated April 26 as Cape Henry Day. Since then the governor has continued to issue a proclamation each year calling upon the people to observe it with appropriate ceremonies.

In 1946 the celebration occurred on Sunday, April 28, so that more people desirous of joining the Pilgrimage would be enabled to do so than if it took place on a week day. Otherwise the commemorative program was typical of ceremonies held on April 26 in preceding years. An estimated three thousand persons gathered in the vicinity of the Cape Henry lighthouses to listen to an address by Governor William Tuck of Virginia extolling the faith of the early settlers and calling for a renewal of such faith to meet our present world problems. The Right Reverend William A. Brown, Bishop of the Diocese of Southern Virginia, spoke of "the greatest of the liberties wrought by their [the colonists'] actions," that of worshipping God according to the dictates of conscience, termed by the late President Franklin D. Roosevelt as one of the Four Freedoms. A procession to the natural dune-amphitheatre where the memorial cross stands prefaced the exercises, which began with religious services followed by a patriotic program including songs and speeches. After the benediction by Bishop Brown, a salute to the cross was made by the crucifer and flag bearers who carried the flags of the church, the United States, Great Britain, and Virginia. In addition to this program, the governor's ball was held on the previous evening, and an official luncheon on Sunday preceded the exercises.

APRIL TWENTY-SEVENTH

GRANT'S BIRTHDAY

About eighteen months after his death, admirers of General Grant began to plan for the celebration of the anniversary of his birth. On March 5, 1887, the Americus Republican Club of Pittsburgh, Pa., appointed a committee to make suitable arrangements for a celebration. In accordance with the plans of the committee consisting of H. D. W. English, H. F. Davis, A. J. Logan and J. D. Littell, a dinner was held at the Monongahela House on April 27. John Dalzell was toastmaster. J. B. Foraker of Ohio responded to the toast:

> General Ulysses S. Grant: We cannot elevate him higher than he elevated himself. On the ladder of his fame there was not another round between that which he reached and the immortality of the third heaven.

Other speakers were Simon Cameron, Charles W. Stone, J. P. Foster, Charles E. Warwick and Major General Frederick Dent Grant, the eldest son of the General. William McKinley, Jr., who later became President of the United States, was one of the speakers on the program but his address was read by another. The Americus Club held a dinner on each anniversary of Grant's birth until it was disbanded more than a quarter of a century later.

While the celebration was in progress in Pittsburgh in 1887 the Army and Navy Club of Hartford, Conn., and the Metropolitan Methodist Episcopal Church in Washington, which General Grant attended during his presidency, were holding meetings in honor of the anniversary. At the Hartford celebration Mark Twain made a vigorous speech in praise of the beautiful English in which Grant had written his memoirs, an English which commanded the admiration of critics on both sides of the ocean for its simplicity and its purity.

The anniversary was not observed in New York City until 1888. But on April 27, 1887, a large number of friends of General Grant were gathered in a private parlor in the Fifth Avenue Hotel making plans for the next year. The meeting was called to order by General Charles H. T. Corliss, who stated its purpose and then asked General William T. Sherman to preside. Resolutions were adopted providing for the foundation of a permanent organization to be known as the Grant Birthday Association and a committee of thirteen was appointed to have charge of the celebration the next year and to confer with the authorities in New York and other states for the selection of April 27 for the spring parades of the militia. The suggestion for the spring militia parades did not bring forth fruit, and the birthday association was later merged with the Monument Association which had been chartered in 1886 to arrange for a permanent memorial in the city. But in 1888 the projected dinner was

245

given at Delmonico's in New York and was attended by a large company of men of all parties. General Sherman presided. There was only one toast, "The Day We Celebrate," proposed by General Sherman and responded to by Chauncey M. Depew, then the most popular after-dinner speaker in the country.

Among the things that Mr. Depew said was that:

The one hundred years of our national existence are crowded with an unusual number of men eminent in arms and statesmanship, but of all the illustrious list only one has his birthday a legal holiday—George Washington. Of the heroes and patriots who filled the niches in the temple of fame for the first century the birthdays of only two are of such wide significance that they receive wide celebrations—Lincoln's and Grant's. When the historian of the future calmly and impartially writes the story of this momentous period these two names will be inseparably linked together.

Then he said that while Grant was the greatest soldier of his time he could not be called the best of presidents and quoted the remark of Grant to a critic of his administration at the close of his second term:

In some cases you were right, in others wrong. I ask this of you in fairness and justice—that in summing up the results of my presidency you will only say that General Grant, having no preparation for civil office, performed his duties conscientiously and to the best of his ability.

The Massachusetts Club of Boston held its first celebration in 1888. Hannibal Hamlin of Maine, who was Vice President during Lincoln's first term, was one of the speakers. In the course of his address he remarked that the United States had fewer national holidays than any other Christianized nation and suggested that the number be increased by the birthdays of Lincoln and Grant (see Lincoln's Birthday, February 12). Although Grant's birthday has not been made a legal holiday by any state its observance by public meetings or dinners spread rapidly to various parts of the country.

APRIL TWENTY-EIGHTH

BIRTHDAY OF JAMES MONROE

James Monroe, the fifth President of the United States, whose place in history is assured because of his enunciation of what is known as the Monroe Doctrine, was born in Westmoreland County, Va., on April 28, 1758. At the age of sixteen he was sent to William and Mary College. He left college two years later, with the rank of lieutenant, to join the Third Virginia Regiment, engaged in the Revolutionary War. He took part in the battles of Harlem Heights, White Plains and Trenton. During the campaigns of 1777-78 he served on the staff of the Earl of Stirling with the rank of major, and took part in the battles of Brandywine, Germantown and Monmouth. In 1778 with the rank of lieutenant colonel he was commissioned to raise a regiment in Virginia. This was the virtual end of his active military career. He made the acquaintance of Thomas Jefferson, who was then Governor of Vriginia, and formed a friendship which continued as long as they lived. In 1782 he was elected to the Virginia legislature and the next year was elected to the Congress of the Confederation. He was again elected to the Virginia legislature in 1786 and in 1788 was a member of the convention called to ratify the Federal Constitution. He joined with Patrick Henry in opposing ratification, but through the efforts of John Marshall and James Madison the Constitution was ratified. He was elected to the United States Senate in 1790 where he opposed the administration of President Washington. The President, nevertheless, appointed him as Minister to France in 1794, as he was known to be friendly to that country. He did not succeed in easing the strained relations between the United States and France and was recalled within two years. He became Governor of Virginia in 1799 and served four years. Thomas Jefferson, who had become President in 1801, sent him to France with Robert R. Livingston, to negotiate for the purchase of Louisiana. On the completion of the negotiations he was sent as Minister to England and later as Minister to Spain. He was elected Governor of Virginia a second time in 1810, but served only a short time, resigning to become Secretary of State in the Cabinet of President Madison. He succeeded Madison as President in 1817 as the candidate of what is now known as the Democratic party, defeating the Federalist candidate by a majority of 149 electoral votes. During his first term the Federalist party went to pieces and he was reelected for a second term without serious opposition. He received every electoral vote but one, as one of the electors was unwilling that any succeeding President should be elected unanimously as Washington had been.

The Monroe Doctrine was promulgated in the annual message in 1823. It was in response to the resolutions of the Congress of Verona of November 1822, which were directed against the representative system of government and favored the restoration of the power of Spain in South America against which the people of that part of the world were rebelling. The pertinent part of the message follows:

We owe it, therefore, to candor and the amicable relations existing between the United States and those Powers [represented at the Congress of Verona], to declare that we shall consider any attempt on their part to extend their system to any portion of this hemisphere as dangerous to our peace and safety. With the existing colonies and dependencies of any European Power we have not interfered and we shall not interfere. But with the Governments who have declared their independence and maintained it, and whose independence we have, on great consideration and just principles, acknowledged, we could not view any interposition for the purpose of oppressing them, or controlling in any manner their destiny, by any European Power, in any other light than a manifestation of an unfriendly disposition towards the United States.

Monroe died on July 4, 1831, and the one hundredth anniversary of the event was observed in 1931.

APRIL TWENTY-NINTH

BIRTHDAY OF OLIVER ELLSWORTH

Oliver Ellsworth, the third Chief Justice of the United States, was born in Windsor, Conn., on April 29, 1745, the second son of Captain David Ellsworth. His father wanted him to become a clergyman and sent him to Yale College, which he entered in 1762. He remained at Yale for two years when he transferred to Princeton. The only information regarding the reason for this move is contained in the journal of the president of Yale, who wrote that Ellsworth and another youth were "dismissed from being members of this college" at the request of their parents. He was graduated from Princeton in 1766 and returned home to take up the study of theology with the Reverend John Smalley of New Britain. Within less than a year he decided to abandon theology and study law. He was admitted to the bar in 1771 and tried to practice his profession at Windsor, but he had so few clients that he had to support himself by farming and by wood chopping. He later said that his earnings from the law during the first three years amounted to three pounds a year in Connecticut currency. In 1775 he moved to Hartford where his practice improved rapidly. Four years later Noah Webster, who began the study of law in his office, said that he had from one thousand to fifteen hundred cases on his lists and that there was hardly a suit tried in the city in which Ellsworth did not appear on one side or the other. He was appointed State's Attorney for Hartford County in 1777 and became a member of the Governor's Council three years later. In 1781 he was made a judge of the Superior Court, an office which he held for four years. While holding the office of State's Attorney he was sent to the Continental Congress in 1777 as one of the delegates from Connecticut. He was reelected five times, when he declined to serve longer. He was active on important committees in the Congress and performed valuable service. When the convention was called to draft a Federal Constitution he was one of those chosen to represent his state. He took an active part in framing that instrument, and was influential in bringing about its ratification by Connecticut. He was chosen as one of the first two senators from his state. He remained in the Senate for seven years, resigning in 1796 to accept appointment as Chief Justice. He was sent to France in 1799 as a delegate to adjust the differences between that country and the United States. The hardships of the journey are said to have undermined his health and while in France he resigned the chief justiceship in 1790. He remained in England for a time on his way home, in an effort to recover his health. When he returned to America he took up his residence in Windsor, where he occupied himself with agriculture and the reading of theological books, and wrote a weekly column on agricultural topics for the Connecticut *Courant*. He died on November 26, 1807. The Ellsworth homestead in Windsor has been bought by the Ruth Wyllys Chapter of the Daughters of the American Revolution which maintains it as a memorial and a museum.

APRIL THIRTIETH

FEAST OF SAINT CATHERINE OF SIENA

There are six Saint Catherines noted in the catalog of saints. One of the most interesting of them is Catherine of Siena, in whose honor several Catholic churches in this country are named and in which her day is specially observed. She was born in Siena, Italy, on March 25, 1347, and died in Rome on April 29, 1380. She was canonized by Pope Pius II in 1461. Pope Urban VIII transferred the festival in her honor to April 30 in the seventeenth century.

Catherine was the youngest but one in a large family. Her father, Giacomo di Benincasa, was a dyer and her mother the daughter of a local poet. From her earliest childhood she was religiously inclined and at the age of seven took a vow of virginity. In her sixteenth year she took the habit of the Dominican Tertiaries and lived the life of an anchorite in a small room in her father's house. When she was nineteen she left her seclusion and devoted herself to caring for the poor and sick. When she was twenty-three she began to interest herself in the affairs of the church and wrote to Pope Gregory XI begging him to leave Avignon and return to Rome to reform the clergy and administer the affairs of the Papal States. She was later active in an effort to suppress an insurrection in the Papal States and visited the Pope at Avignon. It is said that through her influence, and in spite of the opposition of the French King, the Pope returned to Rome on January 17, 1377. Catherine thereafter devoted herself to reviving the religious life of the people in the rural regions of the Republic of Siena. When the schism broke out in the Church she supported the claims of Pope Urban VI, who summoned her to Rome in 1378. She spent the remainder of her life in that city, helping the destitute and writing letters in support of Urban to all who, she thought, might be able to use influence in his behalf. Before her death she succeeded in reconciling Pope Urban and the Roman Republic. She wrote much devotional literature and her works are described as among the classics of the Italian language of the fourteenth century. The emblems by which she is known in Christian art are the lily and book, the crown of thorns and sometimes a heart.

Memorial Day

MAY

Spring's last-born darling, clear-eyed, sweet,
Pauses a moment, with twinkling feet,
*   And golden locks in breezy play,*
Half teasing and half tender, to repeat
*   Her song of "May."*

—SUSAN COOLIDGE

     May, originally the third month of the ancient Roman calendar, became the fifth month in the revised calendar. The origin of the name is uncertain, but the theory most widely accepted is that it comes from Maia, the mother of Mercury, or Hermes. Maia was the eldest of the Pleiades, the seven daughters of Atlas and Pleione, the Oceanid. In a cave in Cyllene she became the mother of Hermes by Zeus. The Romans identified her with Maia Majesta, an old Italian goddess of spring to whom the priests of Vulcan made sacrifices on the first day of May. They regarded the month as unlucky for marriages because the festival of the unhappy dead and the festival of the goddess of chastity were celebrated in May. The latter is known as Bona Dea or the good goddess. She is described as the sister, wife or daughter of Faunus. Accordingly she was sometimes called Fauna. She was a prophetic goddess and revealed her oracles only to females as Faunus revealed his secrets only to males. Her festival was celebrated in the house of a consul or praetor when the sacrifices were offered in behalf of the whole Roman people. The services were conducted by the Vestals and no male person was allowed in the house while they were in progress. The belief that May is an unlucky month for marriage, which has survived among other races until the present, is supposed to account for the popularity of June as the month for weddings. The Anglo-Saxons called the month Thrimilce because then the cows could be milked three times a day.

MAY FIRST

MAY DAY

May Day observances in the United States have lost all the ritualistic and symbolical character of their Old World originals. They have become merry springtime sports participated in by girls in the schools and colleges. One of the beautiful customs observed by little girls in some parts of the East is the making of May baskets to be hung on the doors of their playmates. The baskets are made of paper or card board and filled with flowers. They must be hung on the door without the knowledge of the little girl living in the house. Sometimes when it happens that there is a girl baby in the neighborhood a tender-hearted child will hang a basket on her door that she may not be left out.

This custom probably has its origin in the May-dolls which used to be dressed and carried about in a small chair by the girls in various parts of England. Sometimes the doll had a smaller doll in its lap and both were decorated with ribbons and flowers. The May-doll in England was a survival from the images of Flora which were carried about in the Roman festival of Floralia in the spring which in Christian times became images of the Virgin and Child.

The older girls in the schools and colleges select a May Queen and crown her with appropriate ceremonies. It frequently happens that someone recites Tennyson's "The May Queen," which begins:

You must wake and call me early, call me early, mother dear;
To-morrow'll be the happiest time of all the glad New-year;
Of all the glad New-year, mother, the maddest, merriest day;
For I'm to be Queen o' the May, mother, I'm to be Queen o' the May.

There's many a black, black eye, they say, but none so bright as mine:
There's Margaret and Mary, there's Kate and Caroline;
But none so fair as little Alice in all the land they say,
So I'm to be Queen o' the May, mother, I'm to be Queen o' the May.

May Day celebrations vary in different schools and colleges but there is usually a May Queen. Sometimes they erect a May pole and dance around it. The girls in Wellesley College in Wellesley, Mass., have for years had a hoop rolling contest among the members of the senior class. The girl who wins is supposed to be the first one to be married. After the race the contestants stand in parallel lines with their hoops raised, making an arch through which the girls in the lower classes march into one of the college buildings. Occasionally some of the Wellesley girls don little boys' costumes and others short dresses such as those they wore when children. They play tag, "London bridge is falling down," hide and seek and other children's games.

251

MAY 1

There is a May festival at Bryn Mawr College at Bryn Mawr, Pa., every year, but every fourth year it is especially elaborate. Then a tall May pole is drawn on to the campus by a yoke of oxen and set up. From the top hang colored ribbons. A girl takes hold of each ribbon and they dance around the pole weaving in and out until the pole is completely wrapped about with a varicolored sheath. Then the girls engage in various gymnastic exercises. They have a jester, with a toy balloon on the end of a rod, dancing about the grounds and making merry quips. One year they had a Japanese girl, dressed in native costume, singing a quaint little oriental air and leading another girl clad in a bear skin. On various parts of the campus other girls were presenting acts from the plays of Shakespeare and a play about Robin Hood. This quadrennial celebration is so popular that alumni and friends of the college from different parts of the country hire special railroad trains to carry them to it.

At Vassar College near Poughkeepsie, N.Y., the May Day celebration has sometimes been joined with field sports before the dancing around the May pole and the crowning of the May Queen, and it occasionally happens that college records are broken in the fence vault, the running high jump, the seventy-five yard dash, and the hop, step and jump.

The California State Normal School at San Jose began to celebrate May Day in 1902 with games for the kindergarten department. These were so popular that the next year the children in the primary department were included. By 1910 the interest in the celebration had grown so that more than six thousand spectators were attracted to see the folk games, dances, Grecian floral games, and chariot races. These are all May Day celebrations although they do not all occur on May 1. The date is fixed to meet the convenience of each institution.

Students of folk customs have traced the May Day celebration back to the Floralia of the Romans, the festival in honor of Flora, the goddess of flowers, who is identified with the Greek goddess Chloris. The festival was instituted in Rome in 238 B.C., and was celebrated from April 28 to May 3. Tradition, however, gives Romulus credit for instituting it. Definite information dates from 173 B.C., when the edile Servilius, following the orders of the Senate, arranged for its celebration as the cold weather had seriously delayed the blossoming of the flowers. Undoubtedly the Romans, during their occupation of Great Britain for four or five centuries, introduced the festival there. There is also a theory that the May Day festivals find their origin in the phallic festivals of India and Egypt when the renewal of the fertility of nature in the spring was celebrated. The May pole is said to be a phallic symbol. The Druids had a custom of celebrating the feast of Bel on May 1. Bel is identified with Apollo and with Baal of the Old Testament. Among the Irish and the Scotch Highlanders the festival was known as Beltine, or the day of Bel's fire. Great fires were lighted in honor of Bel and various ancient rites were performed about them.

252

The festival of Floralia in Rome was accompanied by many acts of licentiousness, which also characterized the May Day celebrations in England for many years. In the course of time what is known as the morris or Moorish dance was introduced with the dancers dressed in fantastic costumes as they danced about the May pole. The May Day customs offended the Puritans and the Parliament of 1644 forbade the erection of May poles. This prohibition was repealed after the Restoration. In 1661, in celebration of the revival of the old customs a May pole 134 feet high was set up in London. It remained until 1717 when it was bought by Sir Isaac Newton and removed to Essex as a support for his great telescope.

The Puritans in New England objected to the May pole festivities, but before they made their objection effective Governor Endicott of Massachusetts in 1660 led a company of men to Merrymount where a pole had been erected and chopped it down and named the place Mount Dagon after the idol of the Philistines that fell before the ark.

The observance of May Day was gradually abandoned in England, but in recent years it has been revived. The manner of the celebration in London in the middle of the last century is thus described by F. C. Bernand in his *Reminiscences*:

I remember well May Day as celebrated by the small remnant of melancholy mummers going about the London streets. One was attired as a bedraggled clown, another as a dandy with whom came a fascinating Columbine in dirty book muslin kirts and soiled fleshings, "a thing of beauty" to me as a boy, but by no means "a joy forever." And the mysterious Jack in the Green himself who danced about within a bower of green leaves which he supported on his shoulders with only his legs from below the knee visible, while his face could just be seen through a small hole peering out like an owl in a bush. There were sweeps, too, accompanying it with shovel and broom, and a muffled man with Pandean pipes and a big drum was the peripatetic orchestra. It was poor Columbine's business to "smile and smile" as she presented a large silver ladle to such spectators as appeared at all likely to be generous toward art, whatever grotesque form it might take. The mummers are seen no more, "lost to sight, to memory dear!"

It used to be thought that there was a magic in certain rites performed on May Day as there was about the rites on Hallowe'en. Pepys in his diary tells of a trip to the country by his wife to wash her face in the dew as she had been told that it was good for her complexion. The ritual for this ceremony requires that the young woman should go into the fields and just as the sun rises wash her face in the fresh dew in a private place where no one can see her. This and other customs have been described by Anne Mary Lawler in the following verses:

Ever on the first of May did magic walk—the legends say—
Maidens rose at early dawn to find a dew-ensequined lawn,
And she who humbly bathed her face in dewdrops in the magic place,
She, they say, need never fear the curse of freckles for a year,
And, did she add a certain rune—lo! she would wed a lover soon!
Milkmaids garbed in gay array blithely gave their wares away;
And chimney sweeps in masquerade would dance the streets in mock parade—

And there were darker, wilder rites—black altars and unholy lights—
Men treading in silent fear—lest Evil Spirits hear—
For even the dullest souls must know on May Day Easter Witches go
To blight the cattle and the crop, and cause the budding trees to stop
Their growth—unless a man should seize whatever spells he can!
Goblins from the hills would come, a-step-step to a distant drum,
Leprechauns and faun-eared elves, chuckling gently to themselves—
The Little People, bad and good, from dell and tree and haunted wood—
Pray, do they find a city street a most unkinkly place to meet?
Or do they meet in grave amaze, and grieve for all the happy days?
Or do they even meet at all? Some claim to hear the bugle call
That even progress cannot drown, rippling through the noisy town.
I cannot say, I never hear, although I cock a waiting ear;
And if they meet, pray tell me where? A poet vowed he had met a pair
Of Little People in a park bewildered in the quiet dark.
I do not know, I never see, although I look most patiently.
The bells are swaying in the steeple—
Are there really Little People?

A modern May Day observance has grown up in the United States which is a reecho from Europe of the American Labor Day celebration. When Labor Day was established here the working men of Europe thought they ought to have a similar celebration and they fixed May 1 as the date. But in Europe Labor was engaged in politics and the day became the time for political demonstrations, and in the course of years it was utilized by the extreme radicals for demonstrations against the government. There were riots and the police and sometimes the army had to be called out to restore order. It was not uncommon for bombs to be thrown and for buildings to be burned. Radicals in the United States followed the example of their comrades in the Old World and made a demonstration on May Day. In some cities, notably New York, the demonstration takes the form of a parade of radical, labor and other organizations followed by mass meetings.

DEWEY DAY

The anniversary of the Battle of Manila Bay, May 1, 1898, is celebrated every year by the Dewey Congressional Medal Men's Association, composed of the officers and men who were engaged in the battle. Other organizations of war veterans usually take part in the celebration. The exercises were held for a number of years in the Philadelphia Navy Yard where the "Olympia," Admiral Dewey's flag ship, was tied up after it was put out of commission in 1922. It was customary to hold a parade of war veterans in one of the streets to the Navy Yard in advance of the formal exercises on board the "Olympia." At the celebration in 1934 Admiral Dewey's flag, which was shot down during the battle of May 1, was restored to the ship and hoisted to its proper place. It had been bought by a patriotic citizen at an auction sale of some of the household effects of the Admiral. The exercises on board the ship consisted of patriotic speeches by public officials and officers of the veterans organizations.

Congress declared war on Spain on April 24, 1898. The next day Secretary Long cabled to Dewey ordering him "to proceed to the Philippine Islands; commence operations at once against the Spanish fleet; capture vessels or destroy." The fleet immediately sailed for Manila arriving at the entrance to the bay late in the evening of April 31, with all lights masked. Just then a red flame belched from the smokestack of the "McCulloch" in which some soot had probably caught fire. A shot from the forts guarding the entrance was fired at the invading fleet which returned the fire without slowing its speed. When the fleet was out of range it slackened speed as Dewey wanted to reach the anchorage of the Spanish ships at daybreak. The distance was seventeen miles. At a little before five o'clock on May 1 the fleet was sighted by the Spaniards and they opened fire at a distance of four or five thousand yards. Dewey continued on his way, and when he was about a thousand yards nearer, he is said to have calmly remarked to the commander of his flag ship: "You may fire when you are ready, Gridley." Although doubt has since been thrown upon the accuracy of this report it is likely to remain part of the record for years to come. Gridley fired a broadside from the "Olympia" and sailed on, followed by the other ships in the fleet each of which fired a broadside. Then the "Olympia" turned and fired another broadside as she passed the Spanish ships. This maneuver was continued for three hours, when action was suspended for breakfast. After breakfast the fighting was renewed and in another hour or so the Spanish ships had been completely disabled or destroyed. The American casualties were four wounded men. When the news of the victory reached Washington Secretary Long cabled to Dewey promoting him to the rank of rear admiral. Congress later made him Admiral of the Navy, and awarded medals to the officers and men who had taken part in the battle.

CHILD HEALTH DAY

The importance of protecting the public health attracted more attention in the first third of the twentieth century than in any previous period. In 1921 the hospitals began to celebrate the anniversary of the birth of Florence Nightingale (see Hospital Day, May 12) and in May 1928, Congress passed a joint resolution requesting the President to issue a proclamation every year setting apart May 1 as Child Health Day. The first proclamation in response to this request was issued by President Hoover in 1929. At his invitation a large number of persons interested in the subject met in conference at the White House in Washington in February 1931, to discuss measures for the protection of the health of the children. They adopted what was described as a Children's Charter. In his address to the conference the President said that thirty-five million of the forty-five million children in the United States could be regarded as "reasonably normal," and that the only defect in six million of the remaining ten million was undernourishment. This left four million in

255

need of some form of medical treatment to restore them to normal health. In his proclamation for that year he urged that particular attention be given to the recommendations in the Children's Charter. Those recommendations were:

1. Spiritual and moral training for every child.
2. Understanding and guarding of the child's personality as his most precious right.
3. A home, with its love and security, for every child; for the foster child, the nearest possible substitute for his own home.
4. Full preparation for birth, with prenatal, natal and postnatal care for every mother, and protective measures to make child-bearing safer.
5. Health protection from birth through adolescence, including periodical health examinations with care of specialists and hospital treatment when necessary; regular dental examinations and care of the teeth; protection against communicable diseases; and pure food, milk, and water.
6. Promotion of health with health instruction and a health program, with physical and mental recreation under adequately trained teachers and leaders.
7. A safe, sanitary and wholesome dwelling place, with reasonable provisions for privacy.
8. Well equipped schools, with nursery and kindergarten to supplement home care for younger children.
9. For every child a community which plans for his needs, protects him from dangers and provides for play and recreation.
10. Education which develops the child for life through developing his individual abilities and vocationally prepares him for a livelihood yielding the maximum of satisfaction.
11. Training for children to prepare them for parenthood, home-making and citizenship, with supplementary training to parents for parenthood.
12. Education for safety and against accidents.
13. For the physically and mentally handicapped child, measures to train him to become a social asset rather than a liability. Expenses involved should be met publicly when they cannot be met privately.
14. For every child in conflict with society, intelligent dealing as society's ward, not society's outcast, in the attempt to return him to the normal stream of life.
15. For every child the right to grow up in a family with an adequate standard of living and the security of a stable income.
16. Protection against physical or mental labor which retards physical or mental growth, limits education, or prevents play, comradeship and joy.
17. Schooling and health facilities for the rural equal to those for the city child, with an extension of social, recreational and cultural facilities to rural families.

18. The encouragement of voluntary youth organizations to supplement the home and the school.

19. Properly conducted local organization for child health, education, and welfare with trained health officials, nurses, inspection and laboratory workers; available hospital beds; services for children in special need; and protection against abuse, neglect, exploitation or moral hazards.

In many cities Child Health Day is extended to Child Health Week with the health authorities urging parents to have their young children immunized to the ordinary communicable diseases while they are below school age.

FEASTS OF ST. JAMES THE LESS AND ST. PHILIP

These two Apostles are honored together on May 1. St. James the Less is so called, either because he was shorter than the other St. James or because he was younger. The ecclesiastical scholars, in spite of the Spanish tradition, believe that he was the first bishop of Jerusalem (see Feast of St. James the Greater, July 25). A Hebrew Christian, writing in the second century, says that he was called the "Just" and that he drank no wine or strong drink, ate no animal food, allowed no razor to touch his head, and was put to death by the Jews.

Little is known about St. Philip save that he preached in Phrygia after the Ascension. There are many legends about him. One of them is that while at Hieropolis in Phrygia he saw the people worshiping the god Mars in the form of a dragon. Philip held up the cross and commanded the dragon to disappear. It obeyed, gliding beneath the altar emitting such a foul odor that many persons, including the King's son, died from the stench. Philip restored the boy to life whereupon the priests who served the dragon seized Philip and crucified him on a cross in the form of the Greek letter tau, known as a T cross.

AMERICANISM DAY IN PENNSYLVANIA

The creation of Americanism Day was proposed to the Pennsylvania Legislature in 1939 due to the fact that communistic elements in the United States had adopted the date of the ancient and picturesque observance of May Day as a day for speeches and ceremonies in honor of their doctrines. Members of the Veterans of Foreign Wars and the American Legion had undertaken to counteract these demonstrations, and in 1932 an Americanism parade was staged in Uniontown, Pa. Subsequently, May first was unofficially celebrated in the western counties of Pennsylvania, by various patriotic organizations, as Americanism Day. It was suggested, therefore, that the day should be recognized in the entire state and the legislature accordingly adopted a resolution urging the governor to issue a proclamation inviting the people to join in "a real celebration of Americanism Day." This was described as a celebration which would bring to the citizens a full realization of the benefits and privileges that come to them through the continuance of our American form of government. The governor has continued to issue the proclamation each year, and numerous groups and organizations have joined in observing the day with parades and with patriotic speeches combatting all subversive doctrines opposed to the ideals of a democracy.

MAY SECOND

FIRST PAID FIRE DEPARTMENT IN NEW YORK

Until the latter half of the nineteenth century fires were extinguished in American cities by volunteer companies. There was intense rivalry among the companies and it occasionally happened that when two arrived at a fire at the same time the members would fight with one another for the right to turn on the water while the fire burned before them. And sometimes the firemen would loot the houses on fire instead of putting out the flames. The captains were frequently political leaders and rose to high office through the support of their organization. It was not until May 2, 1865, that the volunteer system in New York city was abolished by an act of the State Legislature which established a fire department in the city with paid firemen. Its validity was disputed by the volunteer companies but the courts sustained the law and the volunteer companies were disbanded. Some of their members were employed in the paid department. Volunteer companies still survive in the smaller communities of the country which are unable to maintain a paid force such as is now supported in all cities of any size. It was not until 1871 that the volunteer system was abolished in Philadelphia.

RURAL LIFE SUNDAY

Rural Life Sunday, the fifth Sunday after Easter, was first observed in 1929 at the suggestion of the International Association of Agricultural Missions, and according to plans adopted by the Home Missions Council and the Federated Council of the Churches of Christ in America. The intention was to set apart a day for the invocation of God's blessing upon the seed, the fruits of the soil, and the cultivators of the earth; for the consideration of justice for agriculture, and of the spiritual values of rural life. It is a nonsectarian observance, all Christian churches both city and rural being invited to celebrate the day with a special service designated by the Federated Council of Churches, which includes prayers and hymns suitable to the occasion. It is further suggested that parishes consisting of several churches should make it a parish day for all services with a dinner on the grounds; that country and city pastors should exchange pulpits; and that a rural play or pageant with an appropriate moral or spiritual theme should be given in the evening. Local agricultural organizations, such as 4-H Clubs, Future Farmers, Farm Bureau, and Grange and Farmer's Union, are encouraged to attend and share in the observances. Since its inception in 1929 Rural Life Sunday has been a regular annual observance by many churches of all Christian denominations throughout the United States, and in certain states the 4-H Clubs constitute themselves its special sponsor. In 1948 the day fell on May 2.

MAY THIRD

FIRST MEDICAL SCHOOL IN AMERICA

It was on May 3, 1765, that Dr. John Morgan and Dr. William Shippen, Jr., established a medical department in the College of Philadelphia, now the University of Pennsylvania. It was the first school for the training of physicians organized in America. After graduation from the college Morgan studied medicine with a Philadelphia physician for a while, then went abroad and was graduated from the University of Edinburgh with the degree of M.D. While abroad he conceived the idea of establishing a medical school in this country. On his return he suggested the plan to the trustees of the college in Philadelphia and they approved it. Dr. Morgan was the first professor of the theory and practice of medicine and William Shippen, Jr., who had been lecturing on anatomy in the city, became the first professor of anatomy and surgery. From this small beginning developed one of the great medical colleges of the country—the first of the professional schools now maintained by the University of Pennsylvania, and the first school for post graduate professional training established in America.

SHENANDOAH VALLEY APPLE BLOSSOM FESTIVAL

The Shenandoah Valley in Virginia is one of the principal apple growing regions in the eastern part of the United States. Hundreds of thousands of barrels of apples are shipped from the valley every year. In the blossoming season, motorists from neighboring states are in the habit of riding through the region to enjoy the beauty of the countryside. In 1924, W. A. Ryan of Winchester conceived the idea of holding an Apple Blossom Festival in the spring of each year. The plan appealed to the residents of the valley and the first festival was held in that year. Its purpose, in Mr. Ryan's mind, was to have the general public join with the people of the valley in a festival of rejoicing and thanksgiving for the gifts of nature bestowed upon the country and for the promise of bountiful crops contained in the blossoming orchards. The festival, beginning in a small way, has become more elaborate from year to year until that held on May 3 and 4, 1934, surpassed all that had preceded it. The number of visitors to Winchester, where it is always held, was estimated at 120,000.

On the first day the Queen of the Festival, known as Queen Shenandoah, was crowned. Because of rain the ceremony of the crowning which usually takes place in the open where it can be seen by more spectators, was performed in the Handley High School. A minister of the crown, impersonated by R. Gray Williams, administered the oath. The Queen swore to "govern my dominions with prudence and justice according to the laws and customs of the same and to discharge the duties of my office with fidelity." The key to the city was presented to her by Mayor C. R. Anderson of Winchester, and the coronation prayer was offered by the Rev. Robert B. Nelson, rector of Christ Episcopal Church. Cadets of the Staunton Military Academy acted as the military escort. Young women from about thirty schools and colleges formed the court of the queen, which included a crown bearer, train bearers and maids of honor.

The chief event of the second day was a parade described as "The Trail of the Pink Petals." Its historical section, over a mile in length, reviewed the history of the valley. It began with a group of horsemen led by a man impersonating Governor Alexander Spottiswood and his Knights of the Golden Horseshoe, showing their discovery of the Shenandoah Valley. This was followed by another group of horsemen representing Joist Hite and his companions entering the valley as its first settlers in 1732. Then came a company of surveyors impersonating Colonel James Wood and his assistants making a survey of a townsite called Opekon, in 1743. (This town was known as Frederickstown for a few years, but in 1752 was incorporated by the Virginia House of Burgesses as Winchester, so named from Colonel Wood's native city of Winchester, England.) The arrival of Lord Fairfax in 1749 accompanied by outriders and a herald bearing a placard, "Thomas, Lord Fairfax, Baron of Cameron in that part of England called Scotland and proprietor of the Northern Neck," was portrayed. For 1756 there was a float showing George Washington drafting plans for Fort Loudon, and for 1758 a float showing Colonel James Wood being "chaired" as a proxy for Washington on the latter's election to the House of Burgesses. Daniel Morgan and his riflemen starting for Quebec were represented on a float dated 1775. Then history made a jump to 1861-65 with General Robert E. Lee and "Stonewall" Jackson riding side by side followed by a band of Confederate cavalrymen. For 1865 there was a float showing the founders of the Stonewall Memorial Association, which originated the Confederate Memorial Day in Winchester on June 6 in that year by decorating the graves of the dead in the Confederate cemetery. The last float represented the decoration of the Confederate graves in 1885, the twentieth anniversary of the first dedication.

MAY FOURTH

RHODE ISLAND DECLARATION OF INDEPENDENCE

Early in the present century Rhode Island began to celebrate the anniversary of the Declaration of Independence made by the Colony on May 4, 1776, just two months before the Continental Congress in Philadelphia adopted its declaration. The document had been buried in the written archives of the state and almost forgotten. When it was brought to the attention of the General Assembly of the state that body voted to call upon the citizens to observe the anniversary. The observance then began by public meetings at which historical addresses were made, by the display of flags, and by exercises in the public schools.

The Rhode Island Declaration of Independence was in the form of an act entitled "An act repealing an act for the more effectually securing to His Majesty the allegiance of his subjects in the colony and dominions of Rhode Island and Providence Plantations, and altering the forms of all commissions, of all writs and processes in the courts and of the oaths prescribed by law." The preamble to the act relates that protection and allegiance are reciprocal and asserts that the King, in violation of the compact, had introduced fleets and armies into the colony to force upon the people a detestable tyranny. It further asserts that as under such circumstances it becomes the right and duty of a people to make use of the means at hand for their preservation, therefore, the act of allegiance is repealed. The act directs that in all writs and processes of law, wherever the name and authority of the King has been employed, there should be substituted "The Governor and Company of the English colony of Rhode Island and Providence Plantations." It was declared that the courts were to be no longer the King's courts and that written instruments should no longer bear the year of the King's reign.

The act not only repudiated the authority of the King, but formally substituted for it the authority of the government of the colony, differing in this respect from the more famous declaration of the Fourth of July which "out of a decent respect to the opinions of mankind" set forth the grievances of the colonies and asserted their independence, leaving the details for further action.

McDONOGH DAY IN NEW ORLEANS

John McDonogh, born in Maryland in 1779, accumulated a large fortune in Louisiana. He died on October 26, 1850, and in his will left one half of his fortune to found public schools in New Orleans, and requested that the school children might occsaionally place flowers on his grave. The money has been used to build new school houses. He was buried in McDonoghville, near New Orleans, and the children in

261

accordance with his request decorated his grave with flowers. His body was later removed to Maryland and a monument surmounted by his bust was erected in Lafayette Square in New Orleans in his honor. It was paid for by the school children who for years contributed a cent apiece until the amount needed was raised. On the first Friday in May—it fell on May 4 in 1945—the children from the kindergarten to the high schools march to Lafayette square and cover the monument with spring blossoms. As they approach the monument they raise the flowers above their heads forming a ribbon of color and they sing what is known as the McDonogh Ode to the tune of "Maryland, My Maryland," which runs in this way:

> He gave his wealth to educate,
> He lived that end to consummate.
> His memory then perpetuate,
> Praise to him, all praise to him!

Before marching to the square the children assemble in the schools where addresses are made in honor of McDonogh and of other benefactors of the educational system, including Frank T. Howard, Isaac Delgado and Rudolph Danneel.

WENATCHEE APPLE BLOSSOM FESTIVAL

The Apple Blossom Festival in Wenatchee, Wash., is one of the three largest annual festivals in the United States. The date varies from mid-April to early May and is set by a committee, known as the Three Wise Men, who forecast the time when the trees are expected to be in full bloom. In 1946 spring was late for the region and the festival was not held until May 3 and 4. The program was typical of this celebration, which has been observed each year since its origin in 1920 at the suggestion of Mrs. E. Wagner, who recalled with pleasure a similar blossom festival in her former home in New Zealand. A queen and two princesses, selected from the senior class of the Wenatchee High School, reign over the festivities, together with fifty or sixty other princesses representing communities throughout the Pacific Northwest, including Canada. Visitors come from near and far also, attracted not only by the pageant and parades and other gala events, but particularly by the beautiful scenic effect of the blossoming orchards against a dramatic background of mountains and spring sky. A legend is associated with the festival that Peter Pan visits the Wenatchee Valley at the foot of the Cascade Mountains each year and sweeps it clean in preparation for the lovely spectacle of the blooming trees.

In 1946 the school childrens' costume parade, the princesses' banquet, and the queen's ball, attended by the governor and other dignitaries, were held on the first day. On the morning of the second day, May 4, there was a festival parade, with bands and numerous beautifully decorated floats, which took two hours to pass the line of march. The coronation ceremony in the afternoon, when the young queen was crowned by Governor Mon C. Wallgren, was followed by a pageant at Memorial Park presented by the high school students and entitled "Year's at the Spring." The episodes covered widely varied subjects, starting with one called "In Roman Days" and proceeding chronologically with "Viking Spring," "A Pilgrimage to Canterbury," and "The Ireland of Witches and Elves" until, after the intervening periods of history were suitably commemorated, springtime in the twentieth century was epitomized by the final episode, "Blossom Time in Wenatchee." The evening entertainment was supplied by a baseball game and a fireworks display. There were also a track meet, a grange picnic, and a carnival during the festival.

Wenatchee is situated on the Columbia River about a hundred miles from the Grand Coulee Dam, in a valley between six and seven hundred feet above sea level. Apples were first shipped from the area in 1902, and Wenatchee now proudly calls itself "The Apple Capital of the World." In 1944 nearly twenty thousand carloads of apples were shipped and there were also smaller shipments of cherries, apricots and peaches.

MAY FIFTH

DERBY DAY

The Kentucky Derby, named from the famous racing family in England, and run every year in May on Churchill Downs, Louisville, has come to be regarded as the greatest racing event in the United States. It is usually run on May 5. The first Derby race was on May 17, 1875, on the opening day of a six-day meet. The distance was a mile and a half. The winner was Aristides, owned by Price McGrath. It was the second race of the day. Aristides had been entered as a pace maker for Chesapeake, also owned by Mr. McGrath. He ran so well that when the time came for him to let Chesapeake pass him Chesapeake was so far in the rear that there was no hope of his overtaking his pace-maker. Mr. McGrath saw what had happened and he waved to the jockey on Aristides to come on. He obeyed and reached the wire a winner with what was regarded as the remarkable speed of 2:37¾ minutes. The best record for the mile and a half course was made in 1889 when Spokane beat Proctor Knot, the favorite, by covering the distance in 2:34½ minutes. In 1896 the course was shortened to a mile and a quarter. The race is for three-year-olds, carrying weight not in excess of 126 pounds. Its popularity is so great that it attracts spectators from all parts of the country. A crowd of 100,000 is not unusual. The Earl of Derby himself came to the United States one year to be present. The purse in 1922 amounted to $50,000 with added money and a gold cup valued at $7000, the largest amount up to that time. It was won by Morvich, a colt bred in California and owned by Benjamin Block of

MAY 5

New York. Governor Morrow of Kentucky in presenting the cup to Mr. Block said:

Kentucky always has recognized courage; courage in man and woman and thoroughbred. Nothing that lives has more real, more true courage than the heart of a great race horse. Today, before the beauty and chivalry of Kentucky, courage was the quality which won the Kentucky Derby. Over a grueling distance, setting his own pace, out in the front from start to finish, there fled, like light, a gallant steed. Tried in bone and muscle and tried above all else in heart and spirit, he never faltered, never failed and would not be denied. California sent Mollie McCarthy in the days of old to try her mettle with Ten Broeck. Today California, defeated then, has with Morvich brought back the classic trophy of the turf to the state of the setting sun.

I congratulate the owner who bred the winner, the trainer who, with skill and enthusiasm, directed this thoroughbred, and the owner who brought him from a great distance to the soil of Kentucky, who entered him as a sportsman, raced him as a sportsman and won in a fashion worthy of the commendation of all. In the name of the Kentucky Jockey Club, and upon behalf of the people of Kentucky, with the good wishes of every true sportsman, I present you this cup. I congratulate you, Trainer Burlew; congratulate you, Owner Block. But, above all else, I congratulate, thank God, the horse.

The purse remained at about $50,000 for twelve years. In 1934 it was reduced to $30,000 plus the fees from the starters. In 1937 the purse was again about $50,000. It has increased steadily since 1940, and passed the million dollar mark in 1947. The winners, their time, and the amount of the purse won, follow:

Year	Horse	Time	Purse
1875	Aristides	2:37 3/4	$2,850
1876	Vagrant	2:38 1/4	2,950
1877	Baden Baden	2:38	3,300
1878	Day Star	2:37 1/4	4,050
1879	Lord Murphy	2:37	3,550
1880	Fonso	2:37 1/2	3,800
1881	Hindoo	2:40	4,410
1882	Apollo	2:40 1/4	4,560
1883	Leonatus	2:43	3,760
1884	Buchanan	2:40 1/4	3,990
1885	Joe Cotton	2:37 1/4	4,630
1886	Ben Ali	2:36 1/2	4,890
1887	Montrose	2:39 1/4	4,200
1888	Macbeth	2:38 1/4	4,740
1889	Spokane	2:34 1/2	4,970
1890	Riley	2:45	5,460
1891	Kingman	2:52 1/2	4,680
1892	Azra	2:41 1/2	4,230
1893	Lookout	2:39 1/4	4,090
1894	Chant	2:41	4,000
1895	Halma	2:37 1/2	2,970
1896	Ben Brush	2:07 3/4	4,850
1897	Typhoon II	2:12 1/2	4,850
1898	Plaudit	2:09	4,850
1899	Manuel	2:12	4,850
1900	Lieut. Gibson	2:06 1/4	4,850

264

Year	Horse	Time	Purse
1901	His Eminence	2:07 3/4	4,850
1902	Alan-a-Dale	2:08 3/4	6,000
1903	Judge Himes	2:09	6,000
1904	Elwood	2:08 1/2	6,000
1905	Agile	2:10 3/4	6,000
1906	Sir Huon	2:08 3/5	5,000
1907	Pink Star	2:12 3/5	5,000
1908	Stone Street	2:15 1/5	6,000
1909	Wintergreen	2:08 1/5	5,000
1910	Donau	2:06 2/5	6,000
1911	Meridian	2:05 2/5	6,000
1912	Worth	2:09 2/5	6,000
1913	Donerail	2:04 4/5	6,000
1914	Old Rosebud	2:03 2/5	13,350
1915	Regret	2:05 2/5	14,900
1916	George Smith	2:04	9,750
1917	Omar Kayyam	2:04 3/5	16,660
1918	Exterminator	2:10 4/5	15,000
1919	Sir Barton	2:09 4/5	20,825
1920	Paul Jones	2:09	30,375
1921	Behave Yourself	2:04 1/5	38,450
1922	Morvich	2:04 3/5	53,775
1923	Zev	2:05 2/5	53,625
1924	Black Gold	2:05 1/5	52,775
1925	Flying Ebony	2:07 3/5	52,950
1926	Bubbling Over	2:03 4/5	50,075
1927	Whiskery	2:06	51,000
1928	Reigh Count	2:10 2/5	55,375
1929	Clyde Van Dusen	2:10 4/5	53,950
1930	Gallant Fox	2:07 3/5	50,725
1931	Twenty Grand	2:01 4/5	48,725
1932	Burgoo King	2:05 1/5	52,350
1933	Broker's Tip	2:06 4/5	48,925
1934	Cavalcade	2:04	28,175
1935	Omaha	2:05	39,525
1936	Bold Venture	2:03 3/5	37,725
1937	War Admiral	2:03 1/5	52,050
1938	Lawrin	2:04 4/5	47,050
1939	Johnstown	2:03 2/5	46,350
1940	Galiahadion	2:05	60,150
1941	Whirlaway	2:01 2/5	61,275
1942	Shut Out	2:04 2/5	64,225
1943	Count Fleet	2:04	60,725
1944	Pensive	2:04 1/5	65,200
1945	Hoop	2:07	64,850
1946	Assault	2:06 3/5	96,400
1947	Jet Pilot	2:06 4/5	1,253,042

Horse racing has always been popular with Kentuckians. An advertisement in a Louisville newspaper in August 1789, announced that a purse race would take place in Lexington on the second Thursday of the following October, free for any horse, mare or gelding; weight for age; agreeable to the rules of Newmarket (three-mile heats), best two in three, each subscriber to pay one guinea including his subscription.

the horses to be entered the day before the running. In 1787, two years earlier, the practice of racing horses through the streets of Lexington became so common that the trustees of the town ordered it to be stopped. Thereupon the lovers of horses built the first race track in the state. The Louisville Jockey Club advertised in a newspaper of the city on October 3, 1823, that beginning on Monday, October 15, it would hold a race meet for three days, with three-mile heats the first day, two-mile heats the second day and one-mile heats the last day, with weights running from seventy-five to one hundred and twenty pounds, according to the age of the horse. This is the Jockey Club which in 1875 held the first Kentucky Derby.

CINCO DE MAYO

One of the great days in Mexican history, celebrated by Mexicans at home and in foreign countries is known as the Cinco de Mayo, or the Fifth of May. In Mexico City one of the streets is named for the day. In that city it is customary for the President of the Republic to review the troops which march through the streets between buildings gayly decorated with flags and banners, while the regimental bands play the national anthem. The day is observed by Mexicans living in the United States, particularly those in the Southwest. They have a great festal dinner in the afternoon, and in the evening there is a ball at which the dancing usually lasts until morning.

The day is the anniversary of the battle of Guadaloupe near Puebla, which was fought in 1862 by a Mexican force of about two thousand against a French force of six thousand which was repulsed. The battle was one of those fought in the campaign of the French to place Maximillian on a Mexican throne. Mexico had defaulted payments on her bonds. An arrangement was made by France, Spain and England at a conference in London in October 1861, to make a joint naval demonstration against Mexico in order to compel payment to the bondholders. Fleets of the three powers sailed for Vera Cruz and arrived there near the end of the year. It was announced that there was no intention of conquering Mexico and that nothing was desired but a settlement of just claims. A conference was arranged with Mexican representatives and a preliminary agreement was made. Thereupon the British and Spanish fleets sailed for home. The French remained, repudiated the agreement and started a war of conquest. The French army met the Mexicans under the command of Ignacio Zaragoza on May 5 and was driven back with serious losses. The battle itself was not of great importance, but the victory appealed to the imagination of the Mexicans as they had succeeded, even though temporarily, in resisting foreign invasion. The French ultimately conquered the country and put Maximillian on the throne only to have him deposed and shot by the Mexicans after a short and troubled reign. The city of Puebla, which had been known as Puebla de los Angeles, changed its name to Puebla de Zaragoza as a tribute to the general who defended it from the French. The body of the general lies in the Panteon de San Fernando in the Mexican capital.

MAY SIXTH

BIRTHDAY OF ROBERT E. PEARY

Robert E. Peary, the discoverer of the North Pole, was born at Cresson, Pa., on May 6, 1856, was graduated from Bowdoin College in 1877 and became an engineer in the United States Navy in 1881. He was engaged in surveys of a route for the Nicaragua canal for three or four years. His first expedition into the Arctic was in 1886 for an inspection of the Greenland icecap. He found that Greenland was an island. Thereafter he devoted himself almost exclusively to Arctic study and exploration. From one trip to the North he brought back a meteorite weighing ninety tons. After more than twenty years' experience in the Arctic he started on his final expedition on July 6, 1908, on the ship Roosevelt. He established winter quarters and when the Arctic dawn began he started on a dash for the pole. He made the last one hundred and twenty-five miles over the ice in five days, arriving within a short distance of his goal so exhausted that he had to rest. On the next day, April 7, 1909, he reached what he regarded as the pole itself, took astronomical observations to verify his position, remained there thirty hours, and returned to his base. In the meantime Dr. Frederick A. Cook, who had been in the North, had returned with the announcement that he had discovered the pole. Philip Gibbs, as the correspondent for a London paper, who had gone to Denmark to interview Dr. Cook, concluded that the man was an imposter and so wrote for his paper. When Peary's announcement was made there was much popular sympathy with him because of Dr. Cook's supposed prior discovery, a discovery which in spite of the scepticism of Philip Gibbs was generally credited. Considerable controversy arose and Peary made some bitter remarks which led a wit to say that Dr. Cook was a liar and a gentleman while Peary was neither. When it was proposed that Congress honor Peary for his discovery his claims were carefully examined and majority and minority reports were made by members of the committee, but each report held that the evidence indicated that he had reached the pole. He was then promoted to the rank of rear admiral and received the thanks of Congress. Many geographical societies awarded gold medals to him and he was made a Grand Officer of the Legion of Honor of France. He died on February 20, 1920, and is buried in Washington.

FEAST OF ST. JOHN BEFORE THE LATIN GATE

The special feast day of St. John the Evangelist is December 27, but a feast is celebrated on May 6 because of the legend concerning his deliverance from persecution by the Emperor Domitian. According to the story, when he arrived at Rome, John was taken outside the walls at the Latin Gate and cast into a caldron of boiling oil, but the oil instead of burning him refreshed him as though he had been in a bath of warm water. The emperor concluded that magic was responsible for this and he banished John to the isle of Patmos where he wrote the book of Revelations (see Feast of St. John the Evangelist, December 27).

MAY SEVENTH

SINKING OF THE LUSITANIA

As the Cunard liner, "Lusitania," on the way from New York to Liverpool, on May 7, 1915, was off the Old Head of Kinsdale on the coast of Ireland it was torpedoed without warning by a German submarine and so badly damaged that it sank with the loss of eleven hundred and fifty lives. Among those drowned were Charles Frohman, theatrical manager; Elbert Hubbard, author and lecturer, and Alfred G. Vanderbilt, capitalist, a member of the well known New York family. Germany had begun submarine warfare upon the shipping of the nations opposed to it in the first World War. The German Ambassador to the United States had printed an advertisement in the newspapers before the ship sailed warning passengers against traveling on it, but the warning was ignored as no one imagined that a great passenger vessel would be attacked. The action shocked the civilized world and so outraged sentiment in the United States that when the Government at Washington decided to make war upon Germany the people were ready to support its plans.

MAY EIGHTH

FEAST OF THE APPARITION OF ST. MICHAEL

The church observes May 8 in celebration of the many appearances to men of the Archangel Michael. He is believed to be the angel who cheered Hagar when she fled to the wilderness with Ishmael and who told her that the boy would found a great nation. And he is also supposed to be the angel who wrestled with Satan for the body of Moses. He is honored again on September 29 at the feast of St. Michael and All Angels (see Michaelmas Day, September 29).

V-E DAY

The end of World War II in the European theater actually occurred on May 6, 1945, when Germany surrendered unconditionally to the

Western Allies and the Soviet Union at Reims, France. The Act of
Military Surrender was signed in a little red schoolhouse, the headquarters of General Dwight D. Eisenhower, Supreme Commander of the
Allied Expeditionary Force, on that date. However, the surrender was
not formally ratified in Berlin until May 8, which was termed V-E Day.
From Washington, D.C., President Truman announced over the radio
the end of the war in Europe and issued a proclamation:

The Allied Armies, through sacrifice and devotion and with God's help, have
won from Germany a final and unconditional surrender. The Western World has
been freed of the civil forces which for five years and longer have imprisoned the
bodies and broken the lives of millions upon millions of free-born men. They
have violated their churches, destroyed their homes, corrupted their children and
murdered their loved ones. Our armies of liberation have restored freedom to
these suffering peoples, whose spirit and will the oppressors could never enslave.

Much remains to be done. The victory in the West must now be won in
the East. The whole world must be cleansed of the evil from which half the
world has been freed. United, the peace-loving nations have demonstrated in the
West that their arms are stronger by far than the might of dictators or the tyranny
of military cliques that once called us soft and weak. The power of our peoples
to defend themselves against all enemies will be proved in the Pacific as it has been
proved in Europe.

For the triumph of spirit and of arms we have won, and for its promise to
peoples everywhere who join us in the love of freedom, it is fitting that we, as a
nation, give thanks to Almighty God, who has strengthened us and given us this
victory.

Now, therefore, I, Harry S. Truman, President of the United States of
America, do hereby appoint Sunday, May 13, 1945, to be a day of prayer. I call
upon the people of the United States, whatever their faith, to unite in offering
joyful thanks to God for the victory we have won and to pray that He will support
us to the end of our present struggle and guide us into the way of peace. I also
call upon my countrymen to dedicate this day of prayer to the memory of those
who have given their lives to make possible our victory.

There was universal rejoicing throughout the United States on V-E
Day, but realization of the war in the Pacific still to be won tempered
the general relief, and public demonstrations were moderate as compared to the triumphant victory mood which was to sweep the nation on
V-J Day the following August. In New York and other large cities
crowds resembling those of New Year's Eve and election night gathered
to express their jubilation by tooting horns and staging impromptu
parades. On the other hand, business as usual was the rule in most
offices, factories and defense plants, where employees reported on their
shifts and went quietly about their work. Perhaps the most significant
indication of a prevailing spirit of intense but sober interest in the event
was the fact, revealed by the Hooper radio poll, that the largest radio
audience in history, comprising 64 per cent of all adult listeners, tuned
in on President Truman's address officially confirming the surrender.
The previous record was an audience of slightly over 59 per cent, who
heard the late President Franklin Roosevelt ask Congress to declare war
on Japan following the attack on Pearl Harbor.

BIRTHDAY OF HARRY S. TRUMAN

Harry S. Truman, the thirty-third President of the United States, was born May 8, 1884, on a farm near Lamar, Mo., the son of John Anderson and Martha Ellen Young Truman. The middle initial is an anonymous compromise referring presumably to his grandfather, Anderson Shippe Truman, who came from Shelby County, Ky., and also to a grandparent on the maternal side, Solomon Young. The presidential oath was administered to him as Harry Shippe Truman, but his response was Harry S. Truman. Mr. Truman was the seventh Vice President in the history of the country to succeed to the presidency upon the death of the President. President Franklin D. Roosevelt died April 12, 1945, and Mr. Truman took over the heavy responsibility of domestic and international postwar adjustments, saying to the correspondents assembled at a press conference: "Pray for me. I mean it."

It has been remarked that his later political career was not primarily of his seeking, since each step upward was mainly fortuitous rather than the result of determined ambition on his part. He was described as modest, conscientious in the performance of his duties and, when holding office as Democratic Senator from Missouri, was regarded as one of the best-informed members of the United States Senate. Also noteworthy was his diplomatic handling of political dynamite during his investigation of the National Defense Program; his conduct of this affair was highly regarded by Mr. Roosevelt and the acceptability of Mr. Truman to the President was one of the factors which led to his nomination as Vice President at the 1944 Democratic National Convention in Chicago, defeating Henry A. Wallace, candidate for renomination.

However, Mr. Truman was a dark horse at the Democratic Convention, his candidacy coming as a complete surprise to the country at large. Similarly, his earlier political advancement occurred as the result of several remarkable turns of chance. In 1924 he served two years as judge in the Jackson County, Mo., Court. He was defeated for reelection, although he was under the political sponsorship of Thomas Pendergast, Democratic boss of Missouri. Later Mr. Truman was elected presiding judge of the court which had supervision of the spending of sixty million dollars for road construction, accounting for every penny with scrupulous accuracy. He decided to run for the office of county collector, a more lucrative post, to the embarrassment of Mr. Pendergast who had promised the collectorship to another faithful adherent. He therefore offered Mr. Truman instead the seat in the United States Senate to which he was duly elected in 1934. The year 1939 found reform Governor Lloyd C. Stark and crusading Federal District Attorney Maurice Milligan both in office. In April of that year Tom Pendergast was indicted for evading the income tax and eventually sent to Leavenworth prison. Ruin fell on the Pendergast machine and apparently on Mr. Truman too for, although he was not personally involved in the scandal, he stood by

Mr. Pendergast to the end, refusing, as he said, to desert a sinking ship. After this political reversal for Mr. Truman it appeared probable that either Governor Stark or District Attorney Milligan, both of whom desired the United States senatorship, would win the nomination, since by the time they had removed all the dead men from Thomas Pendergast's Kansas City registration rolls, the Democratic vote in the senatorial primary was reduced by 42,479, and Mr. Truman's majority in the whole state had been 40,475. It was thus said in Missouri that he had first been elected, not by the Democrats of Missouri, but by Tom Pendergast's 40,000 ghosts! Any strong opponent should have been able to defeat a candidate so badly discredited by the downfall of his political associate, but when Governor Stark and District Attorney Milligan both came out against him, they split the vote, incidentally reelecting Mr. Truman. That he deserved his political survival was amply proved in 1940 when he drove between twenty and thirty thousand miles in his own car, visiting many scenes of heavy construction work and discovering that federal funds were being "poured down rat-holes in tremendous streams." Back in Washington he suggested to his colleagues that the mistakes of 1917 could be avoided by setting up an investigation committee immediately instead of awaiting our entry into the war which was regarded as an eventual certainty. Mr. Truman was made chairman of this committee whose findings saved the country large sums of money on war contracts.

His family background conforms to a pattern which has become the traditional ideal for Presidents of the United States since Lincoln's time, that of comparatively humble origin. His father was a farmer who paid his debts and kept his land but never got beyond the necessity of earning a living. As a young man Mr. Truman worked for a time on the farm and later held various unimportant jobs—in two banks and on the Kansas City *Star*. During World War I he commanded a battery composed largely of hard-fighting Irishmen from Kansas City and was discharged as a major. In 1919 he married his childhood playmate, Bess Wallace; they had one child, a daughter, Mary Margaret Truman.

His administration will probably be mentioned by historians chiefly for the assembly of the United Nations and their efforts to promote lasting peace in a world threatened with catastrophe by the development of the atomic bomb which marked the end of World War II.

MAY NINTH

BIRTHDAY OF JOHN BROWN

John Brown, an extremely radical advocate of the abolition of slavery, was born at Torrington, Conn., on May 9, 1800. He engaged in business of different kinds but was unsuccessful in all of them, and

271

pursued a roaming career for many years in Connecticut, New York and Ohio, and finally went to Kansas where he came into prominence during the free state controversy. In 1857 he made a heroic stand against an overwhelming force of invaders from Missouri at Osawatomie, after which he continued his activities in the border warfare. He won the support of many abolitionists in the North who regarded him as a hero. In an effort to free the slaves he led a band of less than twenty followers into Harpers Ferry, Va., on the night of October 16, 1859, and seized the national arsenal there. He intended this to be the signal to the slaves to rise and free themselves. Soldiers of the regular army under command of Robert E. Lee attacked the arsenal, killing several of the men inside and finally capturing Brown and the survivors. He was tried, convicted of "treason and of conspiring and advising with slaves and others to rebel, and of murder in the first degree," was sentenced to death and hanged at Charleston, Va., on December 2, 1859. He was buried at North Elba in northern New York on the farm which he had made a refuge for runaway slaves. As he lost his life in his efforts to free the slaves his death stirred the abolitionists to greater activity. He was called a martyr to the cause of human freedom. He is still regarded by the Negroes as one of the great heroes of America. They have organized a John Brown Memorial Association to perpetuate the memory of his deeds. In 1935, on the anniversary of his death, this association dedicated a monument to him at Lake Placid, N.Y., on the North Elba farm where he is buried. It is of heroic size and represents Brown with his arm about the shoulders of a Negro boy. The farm is in a state park reservation and the monument was accepted by a representative of the governor. On the same day another statue was unveiled in the John Brown Memorial Park at Osawatomie, Kan., which was dedicated in 1910 by Theodore Roosevelt. The base of the statue contains the inscription: "John Brown of Kansas: he dared begin; he lost, but losing, won."

MAY TENTH

THE FIRST TRANSCONTINENTAL RAILROAD

The first printed proposal for a transcontinental railroad appeared in the *Emigrant*, a weekly paper published at Ann Arbor, Mich., on February 6, 1832, at a time when there were only twenty-three miles of railroad in the United States. In 1849 Asa Whitney, a New York merchant, published a pamphlet in which he laid down a plan for building such a railroad. Its need was admitted but there was such acute rivalry among the eastern cities which wished its terminus to be within their borders that no definite plan could be agreed upon. With the outbreak of the Civil War, however, the importance of rail communication between the East and the West became so great that it was possible to reach a compromise. In 1862 Congress passed the first Pacific Railroad Act, alloting the construction of the transcontinental line to the Union Pacific and the Central Pacific Railroad Companies. The Central Pacific was to build from the West eastward and the Union Pacific from the East westward.

It was first planned that the two lines should meet at the western boundary of California, but it was finally arranged that the two should be joined wherever the construction crews should meet. Thereupon there was a race between the two companies. Th two lines met at Promontory Point, Utah, on May 10, 1869. The last tie laid was of polished California laurel to which a silver plate was fixed bearing the inscription: "The last tie laid in the completion of the Pacific Railroad, May 10, 1869." The rails were spiked to this with a silver spike supplied by Nevada, an iron-silver-and-gold spike provided by Utah, and a gold spike from California. The gold spike was driven with a silver sledge hammer by Leland Stanford, president of the Central Pacific, and Thomas C. Durant, vice president of the Union Pacific, striking it alternately. The report of each blow was telegraphed throughout the country. In San Francisco the strokes were repeated by peals of the bell in the City Hall tower and in New York the chimes of Trinity Church played "Old Hundred." The final stroke was hailed by a salvo of cannon in San Francisco, Omaha, and New York. There was an immense parade in Chicago and general rejoicing throughout the nation.

ASCENSION DAY

This is a movable holy day of the Latin, the Greek and the English churches. It occurs forty days after Easter and is sometimes called Holy Thursday. It commemorates the ascension of Christ into Heaven after His resurrection. It fell on May 10 in 1945. According to tradition it is one of the earliest festivals of the Christian church, dating from the year 68. No written record of its celebration, however, occurs before the fourth century. Special services for the day are arranged in the ritual of the churches. The Knights Templars are in the habit of attending religious services in the churches on this day.

The New Testament contains brief accounts of the Ascension in St. Mark, St. Luke and in the Acts of the Apostles. The account in the Acts, which is the fullest, appears in the first twelve verses of the first chapter. It follows:

The former treatise have I made, O Theophilus, of all that Jesus began both to do and teach, until the day on which he was taken up, after that he through the Holy Ghost had given commandments unto the apostles whom he had chosen; to whom also he showed himself alive after his passion by many infallible proofs, being seen of them forty days and speaking of the things pertaining to the kingdom of God; and, being assembled together with them, commanded them that they should not depart from Jerusalem, but wait for the promise of the Father, which, saith he, ye have heard of me, for John truly baptized with water; but ye shall be baptized with the Holy Ghost not many days hence. When they, therefore, were come together, they asked of him, saying, "Lord, wilt thou at this time restore again the kingdom of Israel?" And then he said unto them, "It is not for you to know the times or the seasons which the Father has put in his own power; but ye shall receive power, after that the Holy Ghost is come upon you: and ye shall be witnesses unto me both in Jerusalem and in all Judea and in Samaria and unto the uttermost parts of the earth." And when he had spoken these things, while they beheld, he was taken up and a cloud received him out of their sight. And while they looked steadfastly toward heaven as he went up, behold, two men stood by them in white apparel; which also said, "Ye men of Galilee, why stand ye gazing into heaven? This same Jesus which is taken up from you into heaven, shall so come in like manner as ye have seen him go to heaven." Then returned they unto Jerusalem from the mount called Olivet, which is from Jerusalem a Sabbath day's journey.

St. Helena built a church upon the Mount of Olives from which the ascension was made, but it was destroyed by the Persians. It was rebuilt and the Mohammedans destroyed the new church, leaving only an octagonal structure which forms an oratory in the church that now stands on the original site. This oratory contains a stone said to bear the imprint of the feet of Jesus.

The Feast of the Ascension has a vigil and an octave in the Latin church. Many curious customs grew up about the celebration of the feast including the blessing of beans and grapes, the blessing of first fruits, the blessing of a candle, the wearing of miters by deacons and sub-deacons, the triumphal processions with torches and banners outside the church to commemorate the entry of Christ into Heaven. In England it was customary to carry at the head of the procession a banner bearing the device of a lion and at the foot of the lion a dragon to symbolize the triumph of Christ over the devil. In some churches the figure of Christ was raised above the altar through an opening in the roof and in still others a figure of the devil was made to descend as Christ ascended.

PHILADELPHIA CENTENNIAL EXPOSITION

In 1872 the Congress passed an act creating a Centennial Board of Finance, a commission was formed of one delegate from each state and territory, and the President of the United States was authorized to invite other nations to participate in a Centennial Exposition at Philadelphia. Thirty-nine countries responded and the Exposition opened on May 10, 1876, attended by a vast throng which included many distinguished persons, chief among them President Grant and Dom Pedro II, Emperor of Brazil. Richard Wagner had sent a march and John Greenleaf Whittier composed a hymn; with an orchestra of preponderant brasses Theodore Thomas played, in alphabetical order, the airs of sixteen nations beginning with Argentina and ending with Turkey and our "Hail Columbia." President Grant addressed an estimated crowd of two hundred thousand and pulled a lever starting the great Corliss engine. This steam railway engine was furnished by George Hunt Corliss, an American engineer and inventor born in 1817, who established the Corliss

Steam Engine Company. He made and patented many improvements in steam engines, and the full-size 1400 horse power model exhibited at the fair was considered the finest, most modern railway engine in existence at that time. Due to its spectacular size and appearance it attracted a great deal of interest.

The Exposition closed on November 10 of the same year with a record attendance of 9,900,000 people, only exceeded up to that date by the international exhibit at Paris in 1867 which was open for a longer period. The success of the Exposition was particularly remarkable in view of the fact that it was held during a time of bad business conditions. However, the railroads offered greatly reduced rates and people poured into Philadelphia from all over the country. The total receipts were three million dollars and, although the stockholders were never repaid in full, the indirect financial benefit was considerable since, after viewing the progress made in one hundred years, Americans had renewed faith in the future of the United States.

The size of the fair was impressive. Numerous buildings occupied an enclosure of two hundred and thirty-six acres in Fairmount Park. The main building which covered twenty acres was devoted chiefly to manufactures and mining products of all nations. Machinery Hall housed the magnificent Corliss engine and other symbols of the triumphs of American industry. There were also an agricultural exhibit, an educational exhibit, and exhibits of art and architecture. England sent paintings by Gainsborough and Reynolds; France, Spain and Italy also lent their art treasures, and there were examples of arts and crafts from all over Europe and the Far East. Thus, the Exposition had a cultural and educational value, broadening the viewpoint of Americans at a time when there was a tendency toward narrow provincialism.

MAY ELEVENTH

THE CONNECTICUT CHARTER

Until John Winthrop, the younger, obtained a charter for Connecticut in 1663 there were two colonies, Connecticut and New Haven, in what is now the state of Connecticut. The Connecticut colony was founded by the Rev. Thomas Hooker, who objected to the Massachusetts laws which permitted no one but church members to vote. He took a company of the members of this church from Newtowne, as Cambridge was then known, to the Connecticut River valley and set up an independent government based on manhood suffrage. Other settlers had founded the New Haven colony which maintained its independence. Governor Winthrop, of the Connecticut colony, went to London and obtained the charter already referred to. The New Haven colonists objected to the surrender of their independence and negotiations were continued for three years before an agreement was reached on May 11, 1665, under which they joined the Connecticut colony but retained two capitals, New Haven and Hartford. This arrangement continued until late in the nineteenth century when Hartford was made the capital.

MAY TWELFTH

HOSPITAL DAY

This date, the anniversary of the birth of Florence Nightingale, has been observed as Hospital Day since 1921. In 1920 on the hundredth anniversary of her birth, Matthew O. Foley, the editor of a hosptial magazine in Chicago, decided that something should be done by the hospitals to honor the memory of this woman and he began to urge an annual observance of the date of her birth. He agitated so successfully that a few hospitals took note of the anniversary the next year. It has become customary for hospitals in cities to open their doors to the inspection of the public on this date and in many of them special exercises are held in honor of Miss Nightingale. Many hospital associations are in the habit of calling attention to the progress which has been made in the prevention and cure of disease since 1820.

Miss Nightingale was born at Florence, Italy, on May 12, 1820, the daughter of William Edward Nightingale of Embley Park, Hampshire, England. Through her mother, a woman of a philanthropic disposition, she became interested in the careless treatment of patients in the hospitals in England, which were popularly regarded as little better than alms-houses. She traveled on the continent to study conditions in hospitals there and took a course of training as a nurse with the Sisters of St. Vincent de Paul in Paris and at the Institute of Protestant Deaconesses at Kaiserswerth on the Rhine. She then decided to lift nursing into an honorable occupation for women. In 1853 she became superintendent of a hospital for governesses in London. Upon the outbreak of the Crimean War in 1854, after reports of the neglect of the wounded British soldiers reached England, she went to the front with thirty-eight nurses and organized nursing departments at Scutari and Balaklava. At the close of the war a testimonial fund of $250,000 was raised for her benefit. She turned it over to St. Thomas's Hospital in London for the founding of the Nightingale Home for the training of nurses. The Order of Merit was conferred on her in 1907, three years before her death at the age of ninety years.

The story of Miss Nightingale's efforts to ease the sufferings of the wounded soldiers in the Crimea stirred the imagination of humane people in all parts of the world. It inspired Henry Wadsworth Longfellow to write "Santa Filomena" published in the first number of the *Atlantic Monthly*, November 1857:

Whene'er noble deed is wrought,
Whene'er is spoken a noble thought,
    Our hearts in glad surprise,
    To higher levels rise.

The tidal wave of deeper souls
Into our inmost being rolls,
    And lifts us unawares
    Out of all meaner cares.

Honor to those whose words or deeds
Thus helps us in our daily needs,
    And by their overflow
    Raise us from what is low!

Thus thought I, as by night I read
Of the great army of the dead,
    The trenches cold and damp,
    The starved and frozen camp,—

The wounded from the battle-plain,
In dreary hospitals of pain,
    The cheerless corridors,
    The cold and stony floors.

Lo! in that house of misery
A lady with a lamp I see
    Pass through the glimmering gloom,
    And flit from room to room.

And slow, as in a dream of bliss,
The speechless sufferer turns to kiss
    Her shadow, as it falls
    Upon the darkening walls.

As if a door in heaven should be
Opened and then closed suddenly,
    The vision came and went,
    The light shone and was spent.

On England's annals, through the long
Hereafter of her speech and song,
    That light its rays shall cast
    From portals of the past.

A Lady with a Lamp shall stand
In the great history of the land,
    A noble type of good,
    Heroic womanhood.

Nor even shall be wanting here
The palm, the lily and the spear,
    The symbols that of yore
    Saint Filomena bore.

AMERICAN INDIAN DAY

It occurred to Dr. Arthur C. Parker, director of the Museum of Arts
and Sciences at Rochester, N.Y., in 1912, that a day should be set apart

for honoring the American Indian. He persuaded the Boy Scouts to adopt his suggestion and for three years they observed an American Indian Day. In 1915 the American Indian Association, at its annual congress at Lawrence, Kans., attended by twelve hundred and fifty Indians, formally approved the plan and directed its president, the Reverend Sherman Coolidge, an Arapahoe Indian, to call upon the country to observe such a day. He accordingly issued the following proclamation on September 28, 1915, which is the first formal appeal for definite recognition of the Indians as citizens:

> Know all men by these presents, That I, Sherman Coolidge, President of the Society of American Indians, by virtue of power vested in me by the Executive Council of the Society, do hereby declare the second Saturday in May each year henceforth American Indian Day, and call upon every person of American Indian ancestry to specially observe this day as one set apart as a memorial to the red race of America and to a wise consideration of its future. In the judgment of wise and impartial men the heroic struggle of our fathers against forces which they had no means of measuring or appreciating, yet which they fought against for homes, for family, for country and the preservation of native freedom, has no parallel in all history. Yet while we consider these things we are not unmindful that they made upon occasions the same mistakes that have been common to all human kind, of every race and age—and yet were virtuous men. Now that the glory and the shadows of the past have become a part of the historic record that has been written, we are not to forget the present and the future of our people, that we may henceforth live in greater fullness. Let us now move forward and acquire all those things that make races and nations more efficient and more noble; let us reach out for a larger life through brotherly love, purposeful action and constructive service to our country, not only for our own welfare, but in order that the American people and all humanity may be uplifted because we have performed, and strive to perform, our full duty as men. Let these things, and the means by which they may be accomplished, be considered upon American Indian Day. Likewise do we invite every American who loves his country and would uphold its honor and dignity to celebrate this day and to consider our early philosophy, our love of freedom, our social institutions and our history in the full light of truth and the balances of justice, in honest comparison with the annals of other races, and to draw therefrom those noble things that we believe are worthy of emulation. But we call upon our country not only to consider the past but to earnestly consider our present and our future as a part of the American people. To them we declare our needs now and tomorrow as those primarily of Americans struggling for enlightenment and that competency that is consistent with American citizenship. We do avow our hopes and our destiny inseparably united to that of the people of the United States of America and that our hearts and minds are now and forever loyal to our country, which we would serve in our fullest capacity as men and Americans.

The year before this proclamation was issued Red Fox James of the Blackfoot Nation of Montana rode his pony four thousand miles from state to state seeking approval of the celebration of a day in honor of the Indians. The governors of twenty-four states expressed their sympathy with the movement, and he presented their indorsements at the White House in Washington on December 14, 1914. The first American Indian Day was observed on the second Saturday in May 1916. The Governor of New York fixed that day for its observance in his state calling attention to the fact that the Confederacy of the Six Nations of Iroquois occupied the region before it passed into the hands of the white settlers and asking for consideration of the present and future needs of the five thousand Indians living on a reservation in the state. The day is observed in many states. In some, as in Illinois, the date is the fourth Friday in September, fixed by legislative enactment in 1919. In Massachusetts, in accordance with a law passed in 1935, the governor issues a proclamation naming the day to be observed. He named November 25 in that year and in 1936. In other states other dates are observed for the convenience of the people. The second Saturday fell on May 12, 1945.

There are Indians in nearly if not quite all the states. They are most numerous in the West with a population in excess of 10,000 in Arizona, California, Minnesota, Montana, New Mexico, North Carolina, North Dakota, Oklahoma, South Dakota, Washington, and Wisconsin. According to the census of 1940 there were 63,000 living in Oklahoma and 55,000 in Arizona. Many men with Indian blood have risen to distinction. Among them are Charles Curtis, of Kansas, who has been a United States Senator and Vice President; and Otis Skinner, the actor, who in his old age was the admitted dean of the American stage. There are many societies interested in the Indians. Among them are the Indian Rights Association, the National Indian Association, the Mohonk Indian Conference and the Carlisle Alumni Association. There is a large Indian Museum in New York. Indian relics are preserved in many museums in other parts of the country, and archaeological societies are engaged in tracing the origin of the Indians on this continent. One theory is that their ancestors crossed over from Asia to Alaska and moved south and in the course of centuries spread over the continent. Another theory is that they came from islands in the Pacific. No indisputable proof of either theory, however, has yet been found.

MAY THIRTEENTH

MOTHER'S DAY

The observance of Mother's Day dates from May 1907. It began under the inspiration of Miss Anna M. Jarvis, of Philadelphia, who thought that at least once a year sons and daughters should pay a tribute to their mothers. She arranged for a special mother's service in one of the churches and asked that white carnations be worn by those attending the service. The plan appealed to the imagination of others and services were held in more churches the next year, and the second Sunday in May was agreed upon as the suitable date. This fell on May 13 in 1945. By 1911 the observance had spread so widely that there was not a state in the United States in which special exercises were not held. The day was also observed that year in Canada, Mexico, South America, Africa, China, Japan and some of the islands of the sea. Leaflets suggesting programs for the exercises were printed in ten different languages and distributed in the different countries. Following is a passage from one of the leaflets:

A day that has shown that it has heart and living interest for all classes, races, creeds, native and foreign-born, high and low, rich and poor, scoffer and churchman, man, woman and child, is Mother's Day, observed the second Sunday in May. The common possession of the living world is a mother. Everyone has —or has had—a mother. The marvelous growth of Mother's Day in a few years to a national and international day can be attributed to the heart and living interest it possesses for almost every home and every person of a mother-loving heart in this and other countries.

In December 1912, a Mother's Day International Association was incorporated to encourage a greater observance of the day. In May of the next year the House of Representatives by unanimous vote adopted a resolution calling upon the President, his Cabinet, the Senators and Representatives and all officials of the Federal Government to wear a white carnation on the second Sunday of the month in observance of the day. Congress itself, in 1914, designated the day as Mother's Day and requested the President to issue a proclamation calling upon government officials to display the national flag on all public buildings. President Wilson, on May 9, issued such a proclamation asking the people also to display the flag on their homes as "a public expression of our love and reverence for the mothers of the country." Similar proclamations are issued each year by his successors.

The custom of wearing a white carnation was modified so that a distinction might be made between those whose mothers were still alive and those whose mothers were dead. White flowers are worn by the motherless and red flowers by the others. Sons and daughters soon got into the habit of making little gifts to their mothers on this day. The most popular has been a reproduction in colors of Whistler's portrait of his mother, probably the most popular mother painting of modern times. It is estimated that more than 5,000,000 reproductions of it have been made. The painting was first exhibited in London in 1872 at the Royal Academy under the title of "An Arrangement in Grey and Black." It was exhibited in the Paris Salon in 1883 and received a third-class medal. It was sold to the French Government in 1891 for $600 with the proviso that it was to be hung in the Louvre ten years after the painter's death. It did not reach the Louvre, however, until Whistler had been dead for twenty years. It was brought to America in 1933 to be exhibited at the Century of Progress Fair in Chicago, after which it was exhibited in several large cities. In 1934 a three-cent stamp was issued showing a reproduction of the Whistler painting.

Various organizations engaged in the protection of the health of mothers have taken advantage of the interest aroused by the celebration

of Mother's Day to ask for support of their enterprises. The Maternity
Center Association of New York, for example, called attention in 1931
to the fact that of the sixteen thousand women who die every year from
childbirth fully ten thousand could be saved if they had proper medical
care. It noted many ignorant superstitions entertained by midwives in
some parts of the country. Among them is the belief that wild boar's
teeth, fried rats, and hog's foot oil will charm away evil spirits at the
time of childbirth; that running water, fire and smoke will also make
the demons which lie in wait powerless; that three nails driven in the
door will prevent the evil spirits from entering; that mustard seed thrown
on the threshold helps as the evil spirit must pick up all the seeds before
he can enter; that gunpowder given to the woman eases pain and that
a hornet's nest hung in one corner of the room is also helpful. The stork
as a symbol of maternity originated in Sweden and Germany where the
bird builds its nest on the roofs of houses. It was a popular belief that
the stork brought good luck and thus the folk lore myth developed that
babies were brought by the stork.

The custom of holding a festival in honor of motherhood is very
old. It dates back in the Western world to the times of the ancient Greeks
who worshipped Cybele, the mother of the gods, and honored her with
rites in woods and caves. The custom was introduced into Rome from
Greece about 250 B.C., and on the Ides of March the festival of Hilaria
in honor of Cybele was begun and continued for three days. But these
celebrations were entirely different from that in honor of mothers on the
second Sunday in May.

FIRST PERMANENT ENGLISH SETTLEMENT

Early in the seventeenth century the British Government adopted the
policy of colonizing America. In 1606 a joint-stock company was formed
for setting up two colonies. The company had headquarters at London
and at Plymouth in Devonshire and the two branches were known respectively as the London Company, sometimes called the Virginia company, and the Plymouth company. It was the London company which
sent out one hundred and five colonists from England who landed at
what is now Jamestown, Va., on May 13, 1607. They built a small fort
and a few huts, and quarrelled among themselves. Largely through the
valor of Captain John Smith they succeeded in resisting the attacks of
the Indians and in establishing the first permanent English settlement in
what is now the United States. The settlement was almost completely
destroyed during Bacon's rebellion against the Royal Governor in 1676.
It was the capital of Virginia until 1698, when Williamsburg was chosen
as the seat of government. The three hundredth anniversary of the
founding of the settlement was celebrated by a great exposition at Hampton Roads in 1907.

MAY FOURTEENTH

THE ROCKEFELLER FOUNDATION CHARTERED

Probably the largest single benefaction in the history of the world was that of John D. Rockefeller when he gave $100,000,000 to a group of trustees chartered by the legislature of New York on May 14, 1913, as the Rockefeller Foundation. The trustees are empowered to use the funds for "promoting the well-being of mankind throughout the world," through charitable, religious, missionary and educational activities as well as through research. They are engaged in a wide variety of enterprises. Through research in different parts of the world the cause of hookworm has been discovered and a method of prevention explained. A medical school in China was endowed. The Red Cross, in efforts to check the ravages of typhus fever in Serbia, received assistance, and many colleges are benefitted by contributions of money to enable them to carry on their work. The Rockefeller Institute for Medical Research, a separate organization, is supported by large gifts from the fund.

MAY FIFTEENTH

FESTIVAL OF ST. PETER AND HIS COMPANIONS

In the calendar of the saints May 15 is set apart to honor Peter, Paul, Andrew and Nichomachus of Lampsacus, a city near the Hellespont, who were martyred by Decius the proconsul. It was known that Peter was a Christian and Decius had him arrested and broken on the wheel. Paul, Andrew and Nicomachus were then brought before him and they confessed that they also were Christians. They were ordered to offer sacrifice to Venus and when they refused were condemned to the rack. Nicomachus recanted but according to the legend no sooner had he done so than "the devil seized him and beat his head upon the ground" until he was dead. Andrew and Paul were beheaded as they continued steadfast in the faith.

MAY SIXTEENTH

THE MEMPHIS COTTON CARNIVAL

The Cotton Carnival at Memphis, Tenn., first held in 1931, has developed into a demonstration which rivals if it does not surpass the Mardi Gras Carnival in that city which was held from 1872 until it was finally abandoned after 1892. The Cotton Carnival grew out of a suggestion by Herbert Jennings, manager of Loew's Theater in Memphis, that a cotton week celebration be arranged with displays of cotton goods in the stores and the lobbies of the theaters. Everett R. Cook, the president of the Memphis Cotton Exchange, was asked to cooperate. He thought that the proposed plan was inadequate and at his suggestion the Memphis Cotton Carnival Association was organized and a carnival was planned. It began on March 1 and continued four days. The theme, which was "The Old South" was illustrated by a parade of eighty-six floats. A king and queen of the carnival, arriving at the city by boat on the Mississippi, were escorted to the court house, welcomed by the mayor, and the keys of the city were presented to them at a formal ceremony. In addition to the parade illustrating life in the old South there were floral and children's parades, a style show exhibiting cotton fabrics, and parties and balls at various clubs.

The life of Washington was the theme of the second carnival which attracted larger crowds than the first. Because of weather conditions the date of the celebration has been moved forward to May. The carnival in 1934 began on May 16 and continued for four days. Its theme was Egyptian based on the ancient city of Memphis. It began with a parade of Arab horsemen through the streets announcing its opening. The king and queen of the carnival had boarded the royal barge, five miles south of the city before the parade of the horsemen, and were escorted up the river by a multitude of gaily decorated craft. As the flotilla moved forward it was saluted by exploding bombs from the shore and tooting whistles from the boats. The royal party was welcomed at the landing and escorted to Jefferson Davis Park where a pageant in pantomime was presented showing Memphis on the Nile in the time of Menes, its first prince. The king and queen were then escorted to the Cotton Exchange where they were formally crowned. After this ceremony they were taken to the main reviewing stand where the presidents of all the organizations participating in the carnival were assembled, along with the city and county officers. The key to the city was presented to King Cotton and he issued a proclamation dedicating the city to joy and gaiety for four days.

Among the events of the second day were a flower show, a floral parade with fifty floats, a beauty contest, a horse show and a ball. On the third day there was a children's parade of thirteen divisions presided over by the children's king and queen, selected by lot from among the children in the schools. The parade illustrated the enchanted world of childhood showing the children's games and festivals, Mother Goose tales, famous children and famous stories about children and girl and boy athletes. The last division was a parade of children's pets, dogs, cats, goats, ponies, rabbits, squirrels and the like including even ducks, snails and snakes. This was followed by a children's ball.

On the afternoon of the last day there was a mummers' and maskers' parade with paraders in comic costumes. And in the evening the Grand

Carnival Parade was held, the climax of the whole celebration. The king and queen led the parade and at its close returned the keys of the city to the mayor and declared the carnival officially ended. After two floats, carrying the ladies and gentlemen of the court of the king and queen, came a float with Menes, the Prince of Memphis, upon it. This was followed by five floats carrying members of the Memphi, a secret organization of promoters of the carnival, the successor of a similar organization of the same name which had promoted the Mardi Gras Carnival until it was abandoned. Other floats showed the gods and animals of Egypt, the sacred scarab, cotton raising on the Nile, an oasis, ancient Memphis, the god Thoth, mummies, palms, the sphinx, the temple of Ptah, the sacred ibis, Apis, Ra, the asp, the phoenix, Osiris, crocodiles, obelisks, Isis, Pharaoh's daughter, the pyramids, Ammon, Anubis, hippopotami, Queen Hatsheput, the colossus of Memnon, Cleopatra and Anthony, and the last float represented the death of Cleopatra from the sting of an asp.

During the carnival there was dancing in the streets, lawn parties were given, and there was an exhibition of the streets of Cairo as well as many other incidental entertaining features.

MAY SEVENTEENTH

NORWEGIAN INDEPENDENCE DAY

The Norwegians in America and elsewhere celebrate May 17 as the anniversary of the independence of their country. This is the date of the adoption in 1814 of their constitution. Norway, Sweden and Denmark had been one kingdom for a century or two. Sweden became independent in the first quarter of the sixteenth century. By the treaty of January 14, 1814, Norway was ceded to the King of Sweden by Denmark, but the Norwegians declared themselves independent, elected Prince Christian Frederick of Denmark as their king, and adopted a constitution for their country on May 17 of that year. The powers declined to recognize the election of Prince Frederick Christian and on August 14 an agreement was made under which Norway should be an independent kingdom united with Sweden under a common king. This arrangement was dissolved on October 26, 1905, when Norway separated herself entirely from Sweden and elected a king of her own.

As the Norwegian settlements in America have been chiefly in the West the celebration of the anniversary there is more elaborate than in other parts of the country. Amalie Hofer, in an article in the Year Book of the American Playgrounds Association for 1908, has described a Chicago celebration in this way:

The great Norwegian natal day, Frihesdag, is May 17 and is celebrated wherever Norwegians are settled. Outside of thousand-year old Norway the most extensive festival is held in Chicago and is participated in by seventy thousand Norwegian-Americans who on that day are again descendants of vikings and explorers as well as immigrants in a foreign country. On that day there has been in Chicago for twenty years singing and dancing and merrymaking because Norway secured a constitution and government of her own. This independence day, which has so long been an end in itself on the other side becomes here the day for reviving Norwegian traditions and renewing the characteristic folk nature which made of Norsemen a nation. On this day it is proudly recalled that the first occupants of Ireland were Norwegians and that the best English blood of today is Norman-Norse descent and that Lief Erikson was the first discoverer of America. At daybreak on May 17 the Norwegian colony of Chicago was awakened by the music of national hymn and choral as the band wagon carried the musicians from street to street. In the fatherland this same custom prevails, however, with far more stirring music of the ringing chimes and the maennerchor and instruments sounding throughout the realm from the high towers in the early morning. At once preparations are made for the chief event of Frihesdag—the morning procession of children. Three thousand Norwegian boys and girls assembled at Humboldt Park, costumed to represent the various provinces of Norway, children from six to youths of seventeen in this historical procession, each carrying the flag of his choice. In the recent parade it was found that 80 per cent chose the Norwegian flag, the rest chose the American or both. This assembling of the youth was witnessed by representative citizens whose care it now is to keep the younger generation from becoming less and less Norwegian. In the Fiorland each school has its banner or pennant and the entire younger generation (for education is compulsory) marches school by school after the respective flags. When the national hymn was sung, "Ja, vi elkser dette laudet" the entire assemblage arose; every head was uncovered to the sun. The afternoon was given to patriotic speaking, national games, athletic sports, folk singing and dancing. Three Norse maennerchore assisted the singing, carrying the anthems and folk songs with a timbre and artistic power worthy of the fatherland of Grieg. I asked a young Norwegian whether any proclamation had ordered the day to be celebrated. He said, with great warmth of feeling, "Every child and every adult looks for this day to come as you do to your Fourth of July. It is like the sun coming up—just so—like the sun. It can never be kept back any more."

The Norwegians of Boston observe the day by decorating the statue of Lief Ericson which stands in Commonwealth Avenue, and by holding a ball in the evening. Lief Ericson is probably a historic character. In the Icelandic sagas he is represented as the son of Eric the Red and it is said that he sailed westward and discovered a country which he called Vineland. There is no agreement on the location of this country, but there is an ancient stone tower at Newport, R.I., which is believed by some students to have been built by the early Norse explorers.

The hundredth anniversary of the independence of Norway was celebrated in 1914 much more elaborately than usual. In 1934 Norwegians from all parts of the country gathered in the latter part of June at Norway, Ill., to celebrate the centennial anniversary of the founding of the first settlement of Norwegians in the United States at that place. A stone was set up, marked by a bronze tablet containing an appropriate inscription. This memorial was provided by the descendants of the first settlers. William Morgenstierne, the Norwegian Minister to the United States, was present at the unveiling of the tablet.

MAY EIGHTEENTH

FEAST OF PENTECOST

The Jewish feast of Pentecost, occurring fifty days after the feast of the Passover, as the Christian festival of Whitsunday falls fifty days after Easter, was observed on May 18, 1945. Like Easter it is a movable feast. The name is Greek, meaning "fiftieth" with the word "day" understood. It was given to the festival by the Greek-speaking Jews. The day is referred to by various names in the Old Testament where it is called the Feast of Harvest, the Feast of Weeks and the Day of First Fruits. It was observed at the end of the wheat harvest. The regulations for its observance directed the faithful to take offerings of the first fruits of the harvest to the sanctuary and "rejoice before the Lord thy God, thou and thy son and thy daughter, . . . the Levite within thy gates, and the stranger and the fatherless and the widow." Many of the ancient ceremonies have fallen into disuse but the day remains one of the great feasts of modern Jews.

MAY NINETEENTH

I AM AN AMERICAN DAY

In 1940 Congress passed a resolution providing that the third Sunday in May each year should be set aside as Citizenship Day, and authorizing the President to issue an annual proclamation urging civil and educational authorities throughout the United States to arrange for its observance. The statute describes the day as a public occasion for the recognition of all who, by coming of age or naturalization, have attained the status of citizenship. It provides that the observance shall be designated as "I Am an American" Day. In 1946, the third Sunday in May was the 19th.

Many communities have adopted this celebration enthusiastically, variously employing pageantry, music, dancing, and speeches of welcome to emphasize the importance and significance of the occasion. Boston, Seattle, Greater New York, San Diego, Philadelphia, Chicago, Cincinnati, Cleveland, South Bend, Ind., and Miami, Fla., are but a few that hold public exercises designed to impress upon the new citizens the privileges and responsibilities of their status. Rochester, N.Y., holds citizenship suppers, while Portland, Ore., has been featuring the induction of her citizens for nearly a quarter of a century and is thus a notable contributor to the education in democracy and patriotism which the day is designed to foster. Manitowoc, Wis., takes a careful census of new voters throughout the state, in accordance with the "Manitowoc Plan," evolved by a group of men and women largely composed of city and county officials. This project was started in 1939, is now known as "The Manitowoc Plan for Citizenship Training and Induction of New Voters," and has become a regular part of the educational program of the state of Wisconsin. The new voters are organized in each community for the purpose of conducting forums on good government and kindred subjects, and to arrange a program of celebration for "I Am an American" Day. Other states soon became interested, and the plan was largely responsible for the introduction of the resolution before Congress.

THE FIRST AMERICAN CONFEDERATION

That confederation of the colonies which ultimately resulted in the establishment of the United States of America began on May 19, 1643. It was on that date that there was formed what was described in its articles of agreement as "a confederacy, to be known as the United Colonies of New England—between delegates from Plymouth, Connecticut, and New Haven, on the one hand, and the General Court of Massachusetts, on the other." It was planned that two delegates from each colony should meet at least once a year to consider the common problems of all. Each delegate was to be a church member and no war was to be declared without the consent of these delegates who were also to supervise all Indian affairs and all foreign relations. With the change of the boundaries of the colonies and the consolidation of others the confederacy gradually broke up to be superseded in 1686 by the Territory and Dominion of New England under a royal governor-general. King James commissioned Colonel Sir Edmund Andros to be captain-general and governor-in-chief over his "territory and Dominion of New England in America," and two companies of Irish soldiers were sent over with him to defend his title to the office.

MAY TWENTIETH

MECKLENBURG DECLARATION OF INDEPENDENCE

In 1831 the Legislature of North Carolina made May 20 a legal holiday to be observed in celebration of the adoption on that date in 1775 by a convention in Charlotte, Mecklenburg County, of a Declaration of Independence renouncing allegiance to Great Britain. Whether such a declaration was adopted on that date is a subject on which historians differ. Washington Irving, in his life of Washington, and George Bancroft, in his history of the United States, refer to the event without any suggestion of doubt that it occurred. President James K. Polk, whose great uncle is said to have been one of the signers of the declaration, wrote to the Governor of North Carolina on February 21, 1847, sending him copies of documents which had been sent to England by the colonial governors of Georgia and North Carolina in June 1775, and discovered by Mr. Bancroft in the British archives. President Polk wrote:

These official papers . . . confirm and establish beyond all question (if, indeed, there could before have been any doubt) the fact that the County of Mecklenburg formally and solemnly renounced all allegiance to the British Crown and established a Provisional Government for themselves in the month of May 1775.

Mecklenburg County was settled by Scotch-Irish Presbyterians from Pennsylvania and Germans from the Palatinate. It was named for the home of Queen Charlotte, the daughter of the Duke of Mecklenburg and the wife of George III, and the county seat was named for the Queen herself. The settlers objected to the oppressive measures of Josiah Martin, the Provincial Governor. In the spring of 1775 Thomas Polk, colonel commanding the militia in the county, after consultation with the leaders of the community ordered each militia company to elect two delegates and send them to a convention at Charlotte. They met on May 19 with the intention of setting up a local government, as the British government had declared the colonies to be in a state of rebellion. A set of resolutions was drafted and during the discussion of them a messenger arrived with the news of the fighting at Concord and Lexington a month earlier. This stirred their enthusiasm and they began to perfect their resolutions of independence, sitting until two o'clock in the morning of May 20, when they were finally adopted.

Governor Martin had tried to prevent North Carolina from sending delegates to the Continental Congress in 1774, but a provincial congress met in defiance of him and elected delegates. This is said to be the first legislative body to meet in America without royal authority. After the news of the Battle of Lexington reached North Carolina Governor Martin was virtually a prisoner in his palace at Newburn. He finally fled to Wilmington and later returned to England. His last proclamation as governor, dated August 8, 1775, contained the following which is regarded as a reference to the Mecklenburg Declaration:

And, whereas, I have also seen a most infamous publication in the Cape Fear *Mercury*, importing to be a resolve of a set of people styling themselves a Committee for the County of Mecklenburg, most traitorously declaring the entire dissolution of the laws, governments and constitution of this country and setting up a system of rules and regulations repugnant to the laws and subversive to His Majesty's Government.

The North Carolina delegates to the Continental Congress were instructed to submit the declaration to that body. But it is said that the President of the Congress did not think it expedient to receive them, as an appeal for reconciliation was about to be drafted and submitted to the British Government. That Congress was not unaware of the conditions existing in North Carolina is indicated by the following entry in the Journal of the Continental Congress for June 26, 1775:

The state of North Carolina being taken into consideration, the Congress came to the following resolutions:

Whereas, it is represented to this Congress that the enemies of the liberties of America are pursuing measures to divide the good people of North Carolina and to defeat the American Association:

Resolved, That it be recommended to all in that colony who wish well to the liberties of America, to associate for the defence of American liberty, and to embody themselves as militia, under proper officers.

Resolved, That in case the Assembly or Convention of that Colony shall think it absolutely necessary, for the support of the American Association and safety of the Colony, to raise a body of forces not exceeding one thousand, this Congress will consider them as an American army and provide for their pay.

The temper of the people of Mecklenburg County is indicated by the remark of Lord Cornwallis that Charlotte was "the hornet's nest of North Carolina," a description of which the people of the city are so proud that the hornet's nest appears on its coat of arms and one of its military companies is known as the Hornet's Nest Riflemen, popularly called the Hornets.

No copy of the Declaration has survived. What was believed to be a copy was destroyed when the house of one of its signers was burned. In 1819 or thereabouts he wrote it out from memory. In his version there are five paragraphs, the first of which declares that whoever aids or abets invasion of American rights is an enemy to this country; the second declares that all political bonds between England and those passing the resolutions are dissolved; the third declares that they are free and independent and are and of right ought to be a self-governing association; the fourth declares that they adopt their former laws so far as they do not recognize the authority of the crown; and the fifth announces that all military officers are retained in their former command and that every member of the convention is a civil officer with power to issue processes and to hear and determine matters in controversy.

There are phrases in the full text which resemble those in the Declaration of Independence adopted in Philadelphia on July 4, 1776. It has been said that the document written out from memory never existed and that the man who wrote it was paraphrasing the more famous Declaration. It has also been said that there was no meeting in Charlotte on May 20, but that there was a meeting on May 31, at which resolutions were adopted which do not resemble the version just summarized. Books have been written on both sides of the controversy. Nevertheless the people of North Carolina insist on the authenticity of the Declaration of May 20, 1775, and celebrate the anniversary every year.

On May 20, 1875, a monument to the Declaration was dedicated in Charlotte, and Adlai E. Stevenson, then a member of the National House of Representatives, and later Vice President of the United States, made the dedicatory address. Andrew Jackson, who lived in Mecklenburg County at one time, had a copy of the Declaration hanging in the Hermitage, his house near Nashville, Tenn., and showed it with pride to his visitors. President Woodrow Wilson spoke at the celebration of the anniversary in 1916, but his address dealt with war issues. President Theodore Roosevelt, a few years earlier, in the course of an address in North Carolina, referred to the Declaration without any suggestion of doubt about its genuineness. But Thomas Jefferson, in a letter to John Adams, expressed the opinion that no such declaration had ever been adopted. He said that if it had reached Philadelphia and the Continental Congress he would have known of it, but the defenders of the Declaration charge him with jealousy of the men of North Carolina who, more than a year before he drafted the Declaration adopted by the Congress, had asserted their independence of the British crown in vigorous language.

DOLLY MADISON DAY

On May 20, 1912, about five hundred women, wives of Democrats in public life—the equal suffrage amendment to the Constitution had not yet been adopted—met at a breakfast in Washington to do honor to the memory of Dolly Madicon, the famous wife of the second Democratic President, on the anniversary of her birth. Mrs. Champ Clark, wife of the Speaker of the House of Representatives, presided at the guest table. One table was set apart for the women who were lineal descendants of Democratic Presidents and Vice Presidents. No men were present save the waiters and the members of the Marine Band. Mrs. Henry D. Clayton, of Alabama, wife of the chairman of the Judiciary Committee of the House of Representatives, welcomed the guests. Among other things she said:

Ladies, this is a patriotic gathering. If the observance of the birthdays of George Washington, Thomas Jefferson or James Madison or any other renowned American soldier or statesman serves a wise purpose, surely a tribute to the life, the character and conspicuous virtues of a good and distinguished woman is equally as wise and is of equal public benefit. All honor to Dolly Madison and this occasion, and again heartiest greetings to our guests.

Mrs. Madison was born in what is now Guildford County, North Carolina, where her parents, Virginians, were spending a year with an uncle. She was the eldest daughter of John Payne and Mary Coles, a cousin of Patrick Henry. The family returned to Virginia while Dolly—she was named Dorothea—was still an infant and lived at Scotchtown in Hanover County. Her father, wishing to find better schools for his children, freed his slaves and moved to Philadelphia in 1783, where he engaged unsuccessfully in business, and died in 1792. His widow then supported herself by keeping a boarding house for gentlemen. Dolly was married on January 7, 1790, to John Todd, Jr., a lawyer of the city and a member of the Society of Friends, to which her own family belonged. She had two sons, John Payne Todd, born on February 29, 1792, and another who died in early infancy. Her husband died during the yellow fever epidemic on October 24, 1793, after which she lived with her mother.

James Madison, then a Representative in Congress from Virginia, was introduced to her by Aaron Burr, and on September 15, 1794, she was married to Madison at the home of her sister, Mrs. George Steptoe Washington, at Harewood, Jefferson County, Va. When President Jefferson made Madison Secretary of State in 1801, she was invited to act as hostess at the White House social affairs as Jefferson was a widower with no ladies in his family who could serve in that capacity. When her husband was inaugurated in 1809 she became mistress of the White House in her own right and the leader in the social life of the Capital. She is described as a woman of great friendliness, with a remarkable memory for names and faces and with unfailing tact in dealing with people. When the British invaded the city in August 1814, she saved many state papers from the White House as well as a portrait of Washington. When Madison's term expired in 1817 she went with him to Montpelier, his estate in Virginia, and presided gracefully over his house and his plantation until his death in 1836. She returned to Washington in 1837 with her niece Anna Payne, whom she had adopted, and again became a notable social figure. Her last public appearance was at a reception in the White house in February 1849, when she passed through the rooms on the arm of President Polk. She died on July 12 of the same year.

FOUNDER'S DAY AT GIRARD COLLEGE

The anniversary of the birth of Stephen Girard is observed with appropriate exercises on May 20 of every year at the college which he founded in Philadelphia. From five to ten thousand persons gather in the grounds of the college to do honor to his memory. One of the most notable celebrations was that held in 1911 when Jules Jusserand, French Ambassador to the United States, was the principal speaker. The presiding officer, in introducing him said:

Stephen Girard, born in Bordeaux, bequeathed to his adopted country one of the noblest and most enduring of charities. It is, therefore, fitting that on this the anniversary of his birth another distinguished Frenchman, born in Lyons, should in the name of France, their common country, here place a wreath of love to the memory of the founder of this great American institution.

M. Jusserand, in an address praising the wisdom and foresight of Stephen Girard in his plans for the institution, said:

Time out of mind people of a superior morality have created establishments to serve as a refuge for their brethren, as fortresses which would protect them against the storms and perils of ordinary life. Such were in the Middle Ages those great abbeys and monasteries whose impressive ruins are an ornament for the earth. The saints who founded them are venerated for their deeds. Scarcely less venerated should be the lay saint who, in this very modern world of ours, devised this institution. Some say he had faults; most probably he had; saints, too, being men, had faults. This lay saint of yours, who was such a shrewd man of business, devised this institution with so much wisdom that there was but to follow the rules laid down by him for the work to grow and prosper.

291

The college was founded for the education of orphan boys. Preference was to be given, first, to boys born in the City of Philadelphia as it was bounded in 1831 at the time of the death of Mr. Girard; next, to those born in any other part of Pennsylvania; third, to those born in the city of New York, "that being the first port on the continent of North America at which I arrived" as the will explains; and, fourth, to those born in the city of New Orleans, "being" as the will explains, "the first port on the said continent at which I first traded, in the first instance as first officer, and subsequently as master and part owner of a vessel and cargo."

It is interesting to note the directions laid down for the care and the instruction of the students. Admission was to be granted to boys between the ages of six and ten years and they were to remain in the school until they were not more than eighteen years old. The section of the will dealing with the conduct of the college reads:

The orphans admitted into the college shall be there fed with plain but wholesome food, clothed with plain but decent apparel (no distinctive dress ever to be worn) and lodged in a plain but safe manner. Due regard shall be paid to their health, and to this end their person and clothes shall be kept clean, and they shall have suitable and rational exercise and recreation. They shall be instructed in the various branches of a sound education, comprehending reading, writing, grammar, arithmetic, geography, navigation, surveying and experimental philosophy, the French and Spanish languages (I do not forbid, but I do not recommend, the Greek and Latin languages)—and such other learning and science, as the capacities of the several scholars merit or may warrant. I would have them taught facts and things, rather than words and signs. And especially, I desire, that by every proper means a pure attachment to our republican institutions, and to the sacred rights of conscience, as guaranteed by our happy constitutions, shall be formed and fostered in the minds of the scholars.

Regarding religious instruction the will required that the college be non-sectarian and the provision has been strictly obeyed. No clergyman of any church has ever been allowed within the grounds of the institution, but religious exercises are held regularly and a blessing is asked on each meal. Chapel services are held every day and on every Sunday there are services in the chapel with a religious address by a layman. In 1933 a new chapel was completed at a cost of $1,000,000 and it was dedicated with prayer, Scripture reading and religious hymns.

The college occupies a tract of forty-five acres in the city of Philadelphia, bought by Mr. Girard in the year preceding his death. Although he died on December 26, 1831, the first building for the college was not completed until 1847, a few months before the college was opened on January 1, 1848. This building, modeled on the Parthenon in Athens, is one of the finest structures of the kind in the United States. It is 152 feet wide and 202 feet long and is surrounded by a colonnade of thirty-four Corinthian columns each one of which cost $12,994. The original bequest amounted to about $7,000,000. It consisted largely of real estate which the trustees were forbidden to sell. It has increased in value so that by the end of the first third of the twentieth century it was worth more than $88,000,000. The number of orphans for which original provision was made was three hundred, but Mr. Girard foresaw the increase in the value of his bequest and directed that the number should be increased as the income justified. In 1934 the college was teaching about fifteen hundred and was engaged in a building program to enable it to take care of two thousand.

Stephen Girard, as already indicated, was born at Bordeaux, France, on May 20, 1750. He was the son of a sea captain and became a sailor himself at the age of fourteen. By the time he was twenty-three he was a captain and part owner of a ship engaged in the West Indian and American coastwise trade. He sailed up the Delaware river to Philadelphia in 1776, engaged in business there and made that city his home for the remainder of his life, never returning to France even for a brief visit to his relatives in Bordeaux. He engaged extensively in the West Indian trade and accumulated a considerable fortune. In 1810 he became interested in the first United States Bank and when its charter lapsed he bought a majority of its stock and its building in Philadelphia. He gave financial support to the government during the war of 1812 and in 1814 he subscribed for nearly all of a loan of $5,000,000 which the government floated. When the second United States Bank was chartered in 1816 he became one of its principal stockholders and directed its policies for many years.

WHITSUNDAY

This is a movable feast, celebrated fifty days after Easter. In 1945 it fell on May 20. It is observed in commemoration of the events on the day of the Jewish Pentecost fifty days after the Resurrection. The story is told in the second chapter of the Acts of the Apostles in this way:

And when the day of Pentecost was fully come they [that is, the followers of Jesus] were all with one accord in one place. And suddenly there came a sound from heaven, as of a rushing mighty wind, and it filled all the house in which they were sitting. And there appeared unto them cloven tongues, like as of fire, and it sat upon each of them: and they were all filled with the Holy Ghost, and began to speak with other tongues, as the Spirit gave them utterance. And there were dwelling in Jerusalem, Jews, devout men, out of every nation under heaven. Now when this was noised abroad, the multitude came together and were confounded, because that every man heard them speak in his own language. And they were all amazed, and marvelled, saying one to another, "Behold, are not all these which speak Galilaeans? And how hear we every man in our own tongue, wherein we were born?". . . And they were all amazed, and were in doubt, saying one to another, "What meaneth this?" Others said, "These men are full of new wine." But Peter, standing up with the eleven, lifted up his voice, and said unto them, "Ye men of Judaea, and all ye that dwell at Jerusalem, be this known unto you and hearken to my words; for these are not drunken, as ye suppose, seeing it is but the third hour of the day. But this is that which was spoken by the prophet Joel, "And it shall come to pass in the last days, saith God, I will pour out my spirit upon all flesh, and your sons and your daughters shall prophesy, and your young men shall see visions, and your old men shall dream dreams."

293

Peter continued at length and as a result of his sermon three thousand professed belief in Jesus and were baptized.

Records are lacking to show when the day began to be observed annually by the early Christians, but it is supposed that it was some time in the first century. There grew up a custom in Italy of scattering red rose leaves from the ceilings of the churches to represent the tongues of fire and in France it was once the custom to blow trumpets during the services on the day to recall the sound of the mighty wind. In England the day was observed by merrymakings after the church services. Whitsunday, as the day is known among English speaking people, is supposed to be a contraction from "white Sunday" a term used to refer to the white robes worn by those who were baptized on that day.

MAY TWENTY-FIRST

LINDBERGH LANDS AT PARIS

Charles Augustus Lindbergh, a professional aviator, took off from Roosevelt Field, New York, on May 20, 1927, on a non-stop flight to Paris to win a prize of $25,000 offered for the first successful flight of this kind. He landed at Paris on the evening of May 21, having covered an estimated distance of three thousand six hundred miles in thirty-three and a half hours. He was welcomed by an enthusiastic crowd and was officially received by the French Government which made him a Chevalier of the Legion of Honor. Before he returned to the United States he visited Brussels and London where he was officially welcomed.

His first flight in an airplane was made in company with a pilot on April 9, 1922. His first flight alone was in April 1923. He enlisted as a cadet in the United States Air Service Reserve at San Antonio, Tex., on March 19, 1924, and, after the New York to Paris flight, was advanced to colonel of the Air Corps Reserve.

In 1926 he was an air mail pilot, having made his first flight as such from Chicago to St. Louis on April 15, 1926. When the prize for a non-stop flight to Paris was offered he went to San Diego, Calif., backed by a group of St. Louis men, to superintend the building of an airplane to be called the "Spirit of St. Louis," in which to make the flight. On May 10, 1927, when the airplane was completed he flew in it to St. Louis and thence to Roosevelt Field, New York, in twenty-one hours and twenty minutes. This was the fastest flight across the continent that had been made up to that time. His Paris flight stirred the imagination of the world and while it was in progress the people in Europe and America waited anxiously for news and the flying field at Paris where he landed and all the streets and roads leading to it were crowded with people eager to get a glimpse of him, much to his surprise. He had expected to land quietly and after a rest present some letters of introduction to a few people in the city. As it turned out he needed no letters of introduction.

On May 20, 1935, the eighth anniversary of his famous flight was commemorated by the unveiling of a bronze plaque at St. Louis.

MAY TWENTY-SECOND

NATIONAL MARITIME DAY

May 22, the anniversary of the sailing of the steamship "Savannah," was designated as National Maritime Day by resolution of Congress, adopted in May 1933. President Franklin D. Roosevelt, in accordance with the instructions of the resolution, issued the following proclamation on May 2, 1933.

Whereas in Public Resolution 7, approved May 1933, it is stated that on May 22, 1819, the steamship "The Savannah" departed from Savannah, Georgia, on the first successful transoceanic voyage under steam propulsion, thus making a material contribution to the advancement of ocean transportation; and

Whereas by said resolution the President of the United States is authorized and requested annually to issue a proclamation calling upon the people of the United States to observe May 22 of each year as National Maritime Day;

Now, therefore, I, Franklin D. Roosevelt, President of the United States of America, by virtue of the authority vested in me do hereby issue my proclamation calling upon the people of the United States to observe May 22, 1933, as National Maritime Day by displaying the flag at their homes or other suitable places, and I hereby direct that government officials display the flag on all government buildings on that day.

Because of the shortness of the notice the day was not very widely observed in 1933. It was observed in New York City, however, at a public meeting at which the principal speaker was Alfred E. Smith, former Governor of the State and the Democratic candidate for the presidency in 1928. Mr. Smith made a plea for the patronage of the American merchant marine by American travellers and shippers. And there were celebrations in Georgia, particularly in Savannah. In 1934 the day was observed in more than fifty cities by organizations interested in shipping, and in that year the celebration was broadened to include the one hundredth anniversary of the launching of the "Randolph," the first iron ship to be built in the United States. At New London, Conn., special services were held at the grave of Steven Rogers, navigating officer of the "Savannah," a brother-in-law of Moses Rogers, its sailing master. In New York arrangements were made to place a tablet in Corlears Hook Park on the East River, the site of the shipyard where the "Savannah" was built.

Fourteen years before Congress took cognizance of the anniversary the city of Savannah celebrated the centenary of the sailing of the ship, including it in a series of observances celebrated by pageants and parades. One was the centenary of the founding of the first Presbyterian church in Georgia; another the centenary of the Savannah Theatre, one of the oldest in the United States and the last was the anniversary of the founding of the Bethesda Orphans Home, the cornerstone of which was laid by George Whitefield on March 25, 1740.

The "Savannah" was built for a transoceanic steamship company incorporated by the Georgia Legislature in 1818. The builders were Feckett & Crockett of New York under the supervision of Moses Rogers of New London, Conn., who had commanded the "Clermont," the steamship which Robert Fulton sailed on the Hudson river. The registry dimensions of the vessel, according to the records in the Bureau of Navigation and Steamboat Inspection of the United States Department of Commerce, were: Length 98.5 feet; beam, 25.8 feet; depth, 12.9 feet; gross tonnage, 319.7. The ship was fitted with an inclined engine built by Stephen Vail of Speedwell, N.J. The boiler was made by Daniel Dodd of Elizabeth, N.J. The paddle wheels were of wrought iron with eight radial arms constructed so as to be folded up like a fan. They were sixteen feet in diameter and when not in use were raised to the deck. In addition to the engine the ship carried a full complement of masts and sails. The total cost was $50,000.

The log book of the ship, now preserved in the United States National Museum, tells the story of the first voyage. It reports that the ship got under way in the East River with a full crew on board at 10 A.M. on Sunday, March 28, 1819, and that the pilot left the ship three hours later at Sandy Hook. It got under steam an hour after starting, but as a stiff wind came up the wheels were folded up and hauled on deck. The vessel came to anchor in Savannah harbor at 4 A.M. on April 6, eight days and fifteen hours after leaving Sandy Hook during which the engine was used only forty-one and a half hours. The *Republican*, a Savannah newspaper, announced in its issue of April 7 that:

> The steamship Savannah arrived at our port last evening after a boisterous passage of seven days from New York. On her approach to the city hundreds of citizens flocked to the banks of the river and while she ascended saluted with long and loud huzzas! The utmost confidence is placed in her security. It redounds much to the honor of Savannah when it is said that it was owing to the enterprise of her spirited citizens that the first attempt was made to cross the Atlantic ocean in a vessel propelled by steam. We sincerely hope the owners may reap a rich reward for their splendid and laudable undertaking.

On May 19 the same newspaper contained an advertisement of the sailing of the ship on May 20 and announcing that there were ample accommodations for passengers. None appeared and when the ship sailed it was without either passengers or cargo. James Monroe, President of the United States, was in Savannah on May 11 and he was taken for a sail on the ship. He asked that it be taken to Washington on its return from Europe. On Thursday, May 20, the date set for sailing, a member of the crew coming aboard at 2 o'clock in the morning fell off the plank and was drowned. The inquiry into his death delayed the sailing until May 22. The entry in the log for that date reads: "At 7 A.M. got steam up, winded ship, and hove up the anchor, and at 9 A.M. started with steam from Savannah."

The "Savannah" was sighted at sea on May 29 by the captain of an American schooner. It was headed eastward with large volumes of smoke pouring out so that the captain thought that the vessel was on fire. He stood by in order to give relief, but soon discovered that it was a steamboat as he said, "crossing the ocean, laying her course, as we judge, for Europe, a proud monument of Yankee skill." The arrival of the ship was reported in the London *Times* of June 30, 1819, in the following brief item: "The 'Savannah,' a steam vessel, recently arrived at Liverpool from America—the first vessel of the kind which ever crossed the Atlantic—was chased the whole day off the coast of Ireland by the 'Kite,' revenue cruiser on the Cork station, which mistook her for a ship on fire." Steven Rogers, the navigating officer, described this incident some time later in a letter to a Connecticut newspaper. He wrote:

She [the "Savannah"] was seen from the station at Cape Clear, on the southern coast of Ireland and reported as a ship on fire. The admiral, who lay in the Cove of Cork, dispatched one of the King's cutters to her relief; but great was their wonder at their inability, with all sail set, in a fast vessel, to come up with a ship under bare poles. After several shots were fired from the cutter the engine was stopped and the surprise of her crew at the mistake they had made, as well as their curiosity to see the singular Yankee craft, can easily be imagined. They asked permission to go on board and were much gratified by the inspection of this novelty.

As she approached Liverpool the piers and the roofs of houses on the waterfront were crowded with people anxious to see her. She remained at Liverpool for twenty-five days and was visited by many naval officers and London merchants. The authorities, however, kept a careful watch over her as she was suspected of seeking to win the large reward offered by Jerome Bonaparte to anyone who would rescue his brother, Napoleon, from St. Helena. Richard Rush, the American minister to Great Britain, thought the arrival of the ship was of enough importance to send a report about it to John Quincy Adams, who was then Secretary of State. Among other things he wrote:

She excited admiration and astonishment as she entered port under the power of her steam. She is a fine ship, and exhibits in her construction no less than in her navigation across the Atlantic a signal triumph of American enterprise and skill upon the ocean.

In accordance with the original plan to visit Russia the "Savannah" left Liverpool on July 21 and on August 9 arrived at Elsinore where she was held in quarantine until August 14. On that day she sailed for Stockholm, arriving there on August 22. On August 28, according to

297

the log, H.R.H. Prince of Sweden and Norway visited the ship and on September 1 she took many members of the royal family, Russian nobles and officers and foreign ministers to the Swedish court on an excursion to let them see how the ship was operated.

On September 5 she started for St. Petersburg, arriving there on September 13. She was maneuvered about the harbor for three days for the benefit of the members of the Russian royal family and other distinguished persons. She was operated by steam for ten of the thirty-three days of the voyage from Liverpool to St. Petersburg. On the return voyage, which began on October 10 she was operated under sail until the arrival in the Savannah river on November 30 when with the tide at flood she moved under steam to her anchorage. Her owners were compelled to sell her because of losses in the fire in Savannah in 1820. The engine was removed from her and she was used as a sailing packet between Savannah and New York. She was finally wrecked in a storm off the coast of Long Island. But her fame survives as the first ship in which steam was used in crossing the Atlantic ocean.

The "Randolph," the centenary of whose launching was joined with the anniversary of the sailing of the "Savannah," was built of boiler plate a quarter of an inch thick. This plate was rolled by John Laird in Birkenhead, England, as there was no mill in the United States which could do the work. It was brought to the United States in a sailing ship. The Randolph was 110 feet long, with a beam of twenty-two feet and a depth of about ten feet. Her engines were thirty-six horse power and were built by Fawcette, Preston & Company of Liverpool. She was intended for use in the Savannah river between Savannah and Augusta. Her owner was Gazaway B. Lamar, a Georgia banker and cotton merchant.

MAY TWENTY-THIRD

THE HANGING OF CAPTAIN KIDD

Captain William Kidd, whose career as a pirate has stirred the imagination of boys for generations and for whose supposed buried treasure many men have hunted along the Atlantic coast, was hanged at Execution Dock at London on May 23, 1701. Kidd was the son of a Calvinist clergyman of Scotland and was born at Greenock about 1650. He went to sea at an early age and prospered, and by 1690 was a shipowner and sea captain with headquarters in New York City. At about this time he married a rich New York widow and he and his wife came to own considerable property in the city. He lived in a large house at the corner of Pearl and Hanover Streets and had a country estate in Harlem. He was employed in running down the French privateers, and in 1691 the Provincial Council of New York voted to give him £150 as a special reward for his services. Pirates were troubling merchant shipping in the Indian ocean and in 1695, at the suggestion of Colonel Robert Livingston, the Earl of Bellomont who was Governor of New York, employed Captain Kidd to wage war on them. The expedition was financed by several British noblemen. Under the agreement Bellomont was to receive four fifths of the profits of the expedition. On April 23, 1696, Kidd sailed from Plymouth, England, for New York in the galley "Adventure" carrying thirty-four guns. On the way to New York he captured a small French vessel and with the money obtained from it he bought supplies. He sailed from New York on September 6, headed for the Indian Ocean. He had taken no prizes and had not paid his crew and when off the East African coast his crew mutinied and he hit one of them with a bucket and injured him so that he died. Thereafter, instead of seeking to capture the pirates he became a pirate himself.

Early in 1698 he captured an Armenian merchantman, the "Quedagh Merchant," with a rich treasure. He divided it among his crew and after capturing other ships he sailed for home, arriving in the West Indies in September of 1698. He then heard that he had been denounced as a pirate and he sailed for Boston to learn the truth. It is said that he turned over to the Earl of Bellomont 1,111 ounces of gold, 2,353 ounces of silver and various commodities which he had taken. It was not until July 1699, that he was arrested, not however, on the charge of piracy but on the charge of murdering a seaman. He was sent to England and tried in April 1700, and found guilty both of murder and of piracy and was hanged on May 23, 1701, protesting his innocence. After his death it was reported that he had buried immense treasure at various places along the Atlantic coast and its adjacent islands.

MAY TWENTY-FOURTH

BRITISH EMPIRE DAY

Empire Day, the anniversary of the birth of Queen Victoria, is observed in the United States by British citizens and persons of British ancestry. The celebration originated in Canada through the activities of Mrs. Clementina Fessenden. She had attended a meeting of the Wentworth Historical Society in 1897, accompanied by her eight-year-old granddaughter, who showed great interest in the historical discussions. Mrs. Fessenden said to herself: "If one child is capable of such enthusiasm in what its leaders in their presumption decide is quite above its level, why not another? Why should not hundreds and thousands find a similar delight in learning the history of their own and their mother land, that land from which their forebears came, it may be, centuries before?" She thereupon wrote to the Canadian Minister of Education suggesting that May 24 be observed in the schools, and that when May 24 fell on Saturday or Sunday it should be observed on the last school day before that date. She appeared before the school boards in the various provinces urging the plan upon them. At the meeting of the Dominion Teachers Association at Halifax, Nova Scotia, on August 24, 1898, a resolution was unanimously adopted approving the annual celebration. The idea had been previously commended by Queen Victoria, herself. The first wide celebration of the day in Canada was in 1899, and it has been celebrated annually ever since.

The Earl of Meath, apparently unaware of what was happening in Canada, began early in the twentieth century to urge the celebration of Empire Day throughout all the British possessions. In an address in Exeter Hall, London, on May 24, 1905, he said that the day was celebrated for the first time in the British isles in the previous year and that Australia, which was the last of the self-governing colonies to join the movement, had through its premier signified its intention of observing the day.

The Earl's motive in interesting himself in the movement was to arouse the patriotism of school children who would have to take up the burden of governing the empire when their elders passed on. In his Exeter Hall speech he said:

> I would scarcely have labored as I have, to promote the movement had it not contained an inner spiritual meaning, of which I trust all who hear me today are conscious. This inner meaning it is difficult to express in a few words, but it may partially be translated as the subordination of selfish or class interests to those of the state and of the community, and the inculcation on the minds of all British subjects of the honorable obligation which rests upon themselves, each in his or her own sphere, for the fulfilment of the duties and responsibilities attached to the high privilege of being subjects of the mightiest Empire the world has ever known.

He issued a series of leaflets intended to arouse an interest in the movement in the schools of the empire. The title page of each contained the watchwords, "Responsibility, Duty, Sympathy, Self-sacrifice," and the motto, "One King, One Flag, One Fleet, One Empire." And it was stated that British citizens should love and fear God, honor the King, obey the laws, prepare to advance the highest interests of the empire in peace and war, cherish patriotism, regard the rights and duties of other nations, learn citizenship, follow duty, consider duties before rights, acquire knowledge, think broadly, practise discipline, subdue self, work for others and consider the poor and suffering. As early as 1912 the day was celebrated in 61,400 schools in the empire and in many churches and by many other organizations of adults. In 1913, however, Prime Minister Asquith explained in answer to a question in the House of Commons, that he would not order the flag to be displayed on the public buildings on Empire Day as it "is not officially celebrated in this country where we keep officially the King's birthday."

In the course of time the official English attitude toward the day changed so that by 1929 it was observed by a monster massmeeting in the evening at Hyde Park in London addressed by Stanley Baldwin, the Prime Minister. Massed surpliced choirs from the London churches assembled in the park and sang "Land of Hope and Glory." During the evening messages were received from all parts of the Empire reporting that similar celebrations were in progress there. In the course of his address the Prince Minister said:

Imperial power has declared itself in many forms in the course of the world's history, but often empire has meant the loss of dominion. Governments built on the foundations of tyranny and oppression have flourished, decayed and perished. The British Empire has shown that the lessons of the fate of empires have not been lost. We have loosened the formal bonds of unity with the great dominions. The destinies of their peoples are guided by their own governments. No rigid framework cramps our conversations with one another or with the world outside the family circle. When we meet together in equal freedom we are united by common allegiance to the Crown. In that model unity lies our strength. It is a bond of service and it summons us to active cooperation and friendly rivalry in every sphere of life, and we hold together and work together not only or merely for our own material prosperity but for the promotion of peace and the advancement of knowledge throughout the world.

It is customary for the British Ambassador to attend one of the many celebrations of the day in the United States.

MAY TWENTY-FIFTH

EMERSON'S BIRTHDAY

The anniversary of the birth of Ralph Waldo Emerson, which occurred in Boston, Mass., on May 25, 1803, is one of many such anniversaries observed in the public schools. The Superintendent of Schools of West Virginia in one of his annual reports said: "The pleasing custom of observing the birthdays of eminent statesmen and leading authors in our schools has become a very popular and efficient means of bringing before the youth of our state the life, character and writings of some of our greatest Americans." The hundredth anniversary of Emerson's birth was celebrated widely in England and the United States in 1903, when distinguished men paid tributes to his genius. The celebrations in Boston, where he was born, and in Concord, where he died, were particularly notable. The house in which he lived in Concord has long been a shrine to which literary pilgrimages are made. It stands on the same street and not far from the homes of Nathaniel Hawthorne and Louisa M. Alcott. It is only a short walk from the famous bridge of which Emerson wrote in his hymn sung at the dedication of the battle monument:

Here once the embattl'd farmers stood
And fired the shot heard round the world.

301

A program for the observance of the anniversary, suggested by the school authorities in one state, opens with a recitation of the "Concord Hymn" (from which these lines are taken), "Each and All" and "The Fable." After a song other pupils would recite selections from "Representative Men" and "Compensation." And then each pupil would be asked to respond, when the roll was called, with a short quotation from Emerson and the exercises would close with an address by a prominent citizen on the life and works of the poet and philosopher.

Ralph Waldo Emerson was the son of the Reverend William Emerson, a Unitarian clergyman. He was graduated from Harvard College at the age of twenty, and taught school for a time. He then decided to study for the ministry and on the completion of his course he was ordained on March 11, 1829, and became the assistant pastor of the Second Unitarian Church in Boston, one of the most important of the denomination in New England. He soon succeeded to the pastorate, but on September 9, 1832, he resigned, as he explained in his farewell sermon, because he had ceased to regard the Lord's Supper as a necessary rite and was no longer willing to administer it. He visited Europe in 1833, meeting Carlyle and Landor. In the winters of 1835, 1836 and 1837 he delivered a series of literary and philosophical lectures in Boston. In 1836 his first book, *Nature*, was published anonymously. In 1837 he delivered the Phi Beta Kappa address at Harvard College on "The American Scholar" which was described by one listener as the "Intellectual declaration of independence" of America. It was a plea for men to do their own thinking, in which he set them an example. He continued to write and was in demand throughout the country as a lecturer. He wrote for the *Dial*, started by Margaret Fuller in 1840, and succeeded her as editor. His first volume of poems appeared in 1847. He died at Concord, on April 27, 1882.

MAY TWENTY-SIXTH

FEAST OF ST. AUGUSTINE OF CANTERBURY

The feast of St. Augustine of Canterbury is observed on May 26 by the Roman Catholic Church with a mass which is designated in the Catholic missal. St. Augustine, the first Archbishop of Canterbury, was sent to England in the sixth century by Pope Gregory the Great with a company of monks to convert the heathen Anglo-Saxons to Christianity. When the embassy reached Aix in Provence they were so terrified by reports of the savage islanders that Augustine returned to Rome for permission to give up the attempt, but Gregory refused. A favorable circumstance, of which they were in ignorance, was the fact that Bertha, the wife of the Saxon king, Ethelbert, and daughter of Charibert, king of Paris, was a Christian.

They landed at Thanet in Kent in 597, where Ethelbert received them, listened to Augustine's sermon, and promised shelter and protection. The little band went to Canterbury, where a residence was assigned to them. On June 2, 597, Ethelbert himself was baptized. Thereafter the new faith spread rapidly among the Anglo-Saxons. The acceptance of Christianity and the influence of its teachings opened to them the history and literature of the ancient world, and brought them into communication with the great Christian nations of Europe. As a reward for his labors Augustine was made Archbishop of Canterbury, which has ever since been the highest office in the Church of England.

Augustine died on May 26, 604, but his fame was such that a rule was deduced from his saint's writings and adopted by several religious bodies in the Roman Catholic Church. These bodies are known collectively as Augustinians and include monastic fraternities and an order of nuns; also the Hermits of St. Augustine, one of the most noted mendicant orders, which still flourishes throughout the Christian world to this day.

MAY TWENTY-SEVENTH

FIESTA DE LA SEÑORA CONQUISTADORA

When the Spaniards sent Don Diego de Vargas from Mexico to recapture Santa Fe from the Indians in 1692 (see Santa Fe Fiesta, September 1) he took with him three hundred mounted men and a statue of the Virgin Mary together with the statues of seven other saints. When he reached the outskirts of the town he halted and built an altar and called his men to prayer. After a high mass they vowed that if the Virgin would give them victory they would build a chapel on the site of the altar and they and their children's children would celebrate the anniversary forever with proper ceremonies. They were victorious, slaying the Indians without mercy. Then they built the chapel and called it El Rosario and their descendants have kept the vow. The original chapel was burned early in the nineteenth century, and the head of the Virgin was lost. A new one was obtained from France and the statue was placed in the cathedral in Santa Fe and kept there until the Sunday following Corpus Christi Day. As Corpus Christi Day is the Thursday after Whitsunday, a movable festival, the date changes from year to year. It fell on May 27 in 1945. On that day the statue is escorted by a religious procession from the cathedral to the chapel of El Rosario, where is it venerated by the worshippers for a week and then escorted back to the cathedral by a similar religious procession. The Virgin is called la Señora Conquistadora, or the Conquering Virgin, and the annual transfer of the statue from the cathedral and back is known as the Fiesta de la Señora Conquistadora.

MAY 27

ST. BEDE'S DAY

Bede, or Baeda, as he wrote his name in Latin, known as the Venerable, was one of the most learned figures in the early Anglo-Saxon church. The Catholic chapel of the University of Pennsylvania is named St. Bede's in his honor and on May 27, 1934, St. Bede's day, a reception was given to the Rev. Father John W. Keogh, the priest in charge of the chapel in celebration of the twenty-fifth anniversary of his ordination.

St. Bede was born in 672 or 673, the exact date is not definitely known. Virtually all that is known about his life appears in the last chapter of his *Ecclesiastical History of the English People*. He wrote:

Thus much concerning the ecclesiastical history of Britain and especially of the race of the English, I, Baeda, a servant of Christ and priest of the monastery of the blessed apostles St. Peter and St. Paul, which is in Wearmouth at Jarrow [in Northumberland], have with the Lord's help composed so far as I could gather it from ancient documents or from traditions of the elders, or from my own knowledge. I was born in the territory of the said monastery, and at the age of seven I was, by the care of my relations, given to the most reverend Abbot Benedict [St. Benedict Biscop], and afterwards to Coolfrid, to be educated. From that time I have spent the whole of my life within that monastery, devoting all my pains to the study of the Scriptures, and ᾽ amid the observance of monastic discipline and the daily charge of singing in the Church, it has been ever my delight to teach or write. In my nineteenth year I was admitted to the diaconate, in my thirtieth to the priesthood, both by the hands of the most reverend bishop John [St. John of Beverley], and at the bidding of Abbot Ceolfrid. From the time of my admission to the priesthood to my present fifty-ninth year, I have endeavored for my own use and that of my brethren, to make brief notes upon the holy Scriptures, either out of the works of the venerable Fathers or in conformity with their meaning and interpretation.

He then gave a list of thirty-four books which he had written and concluded: "And I pray Thee, loving Jesus, that as Thou hast graciously given me to drink in with delight the words of Thy knowledge, so Thou wouldst mercifully grant me to attain one day to Thee, the fountain of all wisdom and to appear forever before Thy face."

He died on May 26, 735, just as he had completed a translation of the Gospel of St. John. The boy to whom he was dictating told him that one sentence still remained to be translated and when he had made the translation and the boy had written it down and had told him that the work was finished St. Bede said: "Thou has spoken truth. It is finished. Take my head in thy hands for it much delights me to sit opposite any holy place where I used to pray that so sitting I may call upon my Father." Thus sitting on the floor of his cell and singing the Gloria he peacefully passed away.

He was the most learned man of his time and had a great influence upon the scholars of England and of foreign countries. He pursued his studies diligently in order the more accurately to interpret the Scriptures which he placed above all other books, not only because of their divine authority but also for their antiquity and literary form. His ecclesiastical

304

history is regarded as his great work. He also wrote summaries of the general history of the world from the creation to his own times. He also wrote on church music, as well as a book of hymns. He holds a very high place in the history of British scholarship.

The origin of his title "Venerable" is in dispute. There is no contemporary authority for the tradition about the inscription on his tomb. According to it the monk wrote in Latin

> Hac sunt in fossa
> Bedae ——— ossa

and left it that way until he could think of a suitable word to describe the holy man. When he awoke the next morning he found that the angels had written the word "venerabilis" in the vacant space. He was called venerable by Alcuin and at the Council of Aachen in 835 he was described as both venerable and admirable, a characterization which succeeding generations have decided was deserved.

Cardinal Wiseman and the English bishops petitioned the Holy See in 1859, praying that Bede might be declared a Doctor of the Church, a distinction the propriety of which had been discussed before that time. It was not until November 13, 1899, however, that Leo XIII decreed that the feast of Venerable Bede with the title of Doctor Ecclesiae, should be celebrated on May 27 each year throughout the church.

MAY TWENTY-EIGHTH

BIRTHDAY OF LOUIS AGASSIZ

Louis Agassiz, who won lasting fame as an American naturalist and as an inspiring teacher of science, was born at Motier in the Canton of Frieburg, Switzerland, on May 28, 1807. He early became interested in zoology and studied medicine and natural history at Zurich and Heidelberg as well as at Erlangen and Munich. After graduating in medicine and taking a degree in philosophy he studied under Cuvier at Paris. From 1832 to 1846 he was professor of natural history at Neuchatel, and spent his summers studying the Swiss glaciers. He was invited to the United States to give a series of lectures in the Lowell Institute at Boston and in 1848 he was appointed professor of natural history in the Lawrence Scientific School of Harvard University, a chair which he held until his death. He studied and wrote on the fishes of the Lake Superior region and the coral reefs of Florida. He traveled extensively throughout the country lecturing to large and interested audiences on scientific subjects. He founded the Museum of Comparative Zoology at Harvard and conducted the first summer scientific school in the United States. He died on December 14, 1873, and was buried in Mount Auburn Cemetery where a boulder from the glacier of the Aar in Switzerland was placed over his grave as a monument.

MAY TWENTY-NINTH

BIRTHDAY OF CHARLES II

The English colonies in America were in the habit of observing the anniversary of the birth of whatever king might be reigning in England. But the action of Virginia after the restoration to the throne of Charles II is particularly noteworthy. On the same day in 1662 on which it had made the anniversary of the beheading of Charles I a fast day, it also set apart May 29, the anniversary of the birth of Charles II, as a holiday. Charles had been recognized as King on May 29, 1660, two years earlier, but it was a long time before the news reached Virginia. When the news did reach the colony there was great rejoicing. Philiip A. Bruce in his *Institutional History of Virginia in the Seventeenth Century,* writes:

The proclamation issued in Surry county announcing the restoration of Charles II to the English throne was a duplicate of all those publicly read at the same time throughout Virginia. It declared that immediately on the decease of Charles I the English Crown and the whole of the English dominions had descended to his son as the next heir of royal blood, and that his subjects in Surry faithfully submitted themselves to him as their lawful King. This proclamation was made in the presence of a large part of the population of the county assembled at the county seat in anticipation of the event; and we learn from the contemporary records that it was received with loud and joyful acclamations. In York, the same happy occasion was celebrated by the expenditure of one barrel of powder in repeated volleys. The big guns used for this purpose belonged to Captain Fox who was paid a liberal fee for lending them to the county. The trumpeters must have preceded and followed up the proclamation with a long and lively fanfare, for they were allowed for their services so large a sum as eight hundred pounds of tobacco. One hundred and seventy-five gallons of cider were provided for the people's consumption in drinking the health of the King. Nor were the authorities content to furnish fusillades, music and liquor alone for the crowd in attendance: they also employed Reverend Philip Mallory to deliver a sermon in which the popular gratitude to God for the restoration of their rightful sovereign should be voiced with pious gravity and dignity worthy of so memorable an event.

Charles II, one of the most dissolute kings in the history of England, was born in St. James's Palace in London, on May 29, 1630, the second but eldest surviving son of Charles I. While still a young boy he accompanied the royal army in campaigns in the Civil War. After the defeat at Naseby he escaped to France where he visited his mother in Paris. In July 1648, he sailed up the Thames with a small fleet, took several prizes, and returned to The Hague on the continent. During the trial of his father he exerted himself to the utmost to save him. On his father's death on January 30, 1649, he assumed the title of king and was proclaimed as such in Scotland, Ireland, the Channel Islands and in one or two places in England. He landed in Scotland on June 24, 1650, and on September 3, a Scottish force fighting under him was defeated.

He escaped, however, and was crowned at Scone on January 1, 1651. He invaded England in the following August with a force of ten thousand men and in advance of his arrival was proclaimed King at Carlisle and two or three other places. Cromwell's army defeated him at Worcester on September 3, 1651, and a price was put on his head. He succeeded in evading his pursuers and on October 15 escaped to the coast of Normandy. He lived on the continent for eight years supported by a pension from the King of France. He spent these years chiefly in idleness and dissipation. On the death of Oliver Cromwell plans for his restoration to the throne were perfected. He was proclaimed King at Westminster on May 8, 1660, landed at Dover on May 26, and was welcomed at Whitehall by the two houses of Parliament on May 29, after a triumphant progress through the city of London. He was formally crowned on April 23, 1661. As King he sought to exercise the powers which his father insisted belonged to the monarch. He was tyrannical and capricious and stopped at nothing in his efforts to accomplish his purposes. He had not been on the throne long before the people began to regret the passing of Cromwell, but an unsuccessful plot against his life a few years later restored his popularity. He was affable and gracious and it was said of him that those whose requests he had denied left him better pleased than those who left his father after having their wishes granted. He married Catherine of Braganza, the daughter of the King of Portugal, two years after his restoration to the throne, but had no children by her. He had several children by his mistresses. He ennobled them and their descendants bear the titles he gave to their ancestors. He made the five children of the Countess Castlemaine, the Duke of Southampton and Cleveland, Duke of Grafton, Duke of Northumberland, Countess of Sussex, and Countess of Lichfield. The son of the Duchess of Portsmouth was made Duke of Richmond. Lucy Walter's son became the Duke of Monmouth and Buccleuch, and Nell Gwynn's son received the title of Duke of St. Albans. The son of Catherine Peg became the Earl of Plymouth, Lady Shannon's daughter, the Countess of Yarmouth, and Mary Davis's daughter the Countess of Derwentwater.

The Restoration era is known as one of the most licentious and dissolute in English history. Whether this was because of the habits of the King or because of a reaction from the strictness of the Puritan regime under Cromwell is a matter of opinion. It was Charles who made the grant of Pennsylvania to William Penn in payment of a debt of £16,000 owed to Admiral Penn by the crown, permitting him to set up a free government in America. His subjects in America as well as in England were monarchists and were therefore loyal to him as the head of the monarchy. It was in tribute to him as such that the General Assembly of Virginia made the anniversary of his birth a holiday by special enactment (see A Royalist Fast in Virginia, January 30).

MAY THIRTIETH

MEMORIAL DAY

The formal observance of Memorial Day, or Decoration Day, as it was popularly called for many years, dates from 1868. The graves of the soldiers killed in the Civil War had been decorated with flowers before that year, especially in the South. The women of Columbus, Miss., for example, laid flowers on the graves of both Union and Confederate dead in 1863. On April 26, 1865, Mrs. Sue Landon Vaughn, a descendant of John Adams, the second President, led some women to the cemetery in Vicksburg and decorated the soldiers' graves there. And in May of the same year some women in Winchester, Va., formed the Stonewall Jackson Memorial Association. On June 6, 1865, they went to the Confederate Cemetery in Winchester, said to be the first cemetery laid out especially for the soldier dead in the South, and decorated the graves with flowers.

Early in May 1865, Adjutant General Chipman of the Grand Army of the Republic, the organization of Union veterans, suggested to General John A. Logan, the commander in chief, that arrangements be made for the organization to decorate the graves of the Union soldiers on a uniform date throughout the country. General Logan approved the plan and issued a general order to all the Grand Army posts in part as follows:

The thirtieth day of May 1868, is designated for the purpose of strewing with flowers or otherwise decorating the graves of comrades who died in defense of their country during the late rebellion, and whose bodies now lie in almost every city, village and hamlet churchyard in the land. In this observance no form of ceremony is prescribed, but posts and comrades will in their own way arrange such fitting services and testimonials of respect as circumstances may permit.

It is the purpose of the commander in chief to inaugurate this observance with the hope that it will be kept up from year to year while a survivor of the war remains to honor the memory of his departed comrades. He earnestly desires the public press to call attention to this order and lend its friendly aid in bringing it to the notice of comrades in all parts of the country in time for simultaneous compliance therewith.

Department commanders will use every effort to make this order effective.

This order was generally obeyed, especially in the smaller communities. Special exercises were held in the National Cemetery at Arlington, Va., across the Potomac River from Washington, constituting the first formal and official observance of the day.

General James A. Garfield, a member of the House of Representatives and later President of the United States, was the orator of the occasion. He was known as one of the most eloquent speakers of the time. Following are some of the significant passages from his address:

I am oppressed with a sense of the impropriety of uttering words on this occasion. If silence is ever golden, it must be here beside the graves of fifteen thousand men whose lives were more significant than speech and whose death was a poem the music of which can never be sung. With words we make promises, plight faith, praise virtue. Promises may not be kept; plighted faith may be broken; and vaunted virtue be only the cunning mask of vice. We do not know one promise these men made, one pledge they gave, one word they spoke; but we do know they summed up and perfected, by one supreme act, the highest virtues of men and citizens. For love of country they accepted death, and thus resolved all doubts, and made immortal their patriotism and virtue. For the noblest man that lives, there still remains a conflict. He must still withstand the assaults of time and fortune, must still be assailed by temptations, before which lofty natures have fallen; but with these the conflict ended, the victory was won when death stamped on them the great seal of heroic character, and closed a record which years can never blot. I know of nothing more appropriate on this occasion than to inquire what brought these men here; what high motive led them to condense life into an hour and to crown that hour by joyfully welcoming death. Let us consider. Eight years ago this was the most unwarlike nation of the earth. For nearly fifty years no spot in any of these states had been the scene of battle. Thirty millions of people had an army of less than ten thousand men. The faith of our people in the stability and permanence of their institutions was like their faith in the eternal courses of nature. Peace, liberty and personal security were blessings as common and universal as sunshine and showers and fruitful seasons; and all sprang from a single source, the old American principle that all owe due submission and obedience to the lawfully expressed will of the majority. This is not one of the doctrines of our political system—it is the sytsem itself. It is our political firmament, in which all other truths are set, as stars in heaven. It is the encasing air, the breath of the nation's life. Against this principle the whole weight of the rebellion was thrown. Its overthrow would have brought such ruin as might follow in the physical universe if the power of gravitation were destroyed. . . . As a flash of lightning in a midnight tempest reveals the abysmal horrors of the sea, so did the flash of the first gun disclose the awful abyss into which rebellion was ready to plunge us. In a moment we were the most warlike nation on earth. In a moment we were not merely a people with an army—we were a people in arms. The nation was in column—not all at the front, but all in array. I love to believe that no heroic sacrifice is ever lost; that the characters of men are molded and inspired by what their fathers have done; that treasured up in American souls are all the unconscious influences of the great deeds of the Anglo-Saxon race, from Agincourt to Bunker Hill. It was such an influence that led a young Greek, two thousand years ago, when musing on the battlefield of Marathon, to exclaim, "The trophies of Miltiades will not let me sleep!" Could these men be silent in 1861; these whose ancestors had felt the inspiration of battle on every field where civilization had fought in the last thousand years? Read their answer in this green turf. Each for himself gathered up the cherished purposes of life—its aims and ambitions, its dearest affections—and flung all, with life itself, into the scale of battle. And now consider this silent assembly of the dead. What does it represent? Nay, rather, what does it not represent? It is an epitome of the war. Here are sheaves reaped in the harvest of death from every battlefield of Virginia. If each grave had a voice to tell us what its silent tenant last saw and heard on earth we might stand, with uncovered heads, and hear the whole story of the war. . . . What other spot so fitting for their last resting place as this, under the shadow of the Capitol saved by their valor? Here, where the grim edge of battle joined; here, where all the hope and fear and agony of their country centered; here let them rest, asleep on the nation's heart, entombed in the nation's love.

Memorial Day was not yet a legal holiday in any of the states. The veterans in New York succeeded in persuading the legislature to pass an act in 1873 designating "the thirtieth day of May, known as Decoration

Day," as one of the "public holidays for all purposes whatsover as regards the transaction of business in the public offices of the state." Rhode Island made the day a legal holiday in 1874, Vermont in 1876, New Hampshire in 1877, Wisconsin in 1879, Massachusetts and Ohio in 1881, and it is now a legal holiday in all the Northern states and in the territories.

In the course of time regulations were adopted by the army and the navy for the observance of the day. Article 516 of the Army Regulation reads:

On Memorial Day, May 30, at all army posts and stations the national flag will be displayed at half mast from sunrise till midday and immediately before noon the band or field music will play a dirge, "Departed Days," or some appropriate air and the national salute of twenty-one guns will be fired at 12 M. at all posts and stations provided with artillery. At the ceremonies of this memorial tribute, at noon, the flag will be hoisted to the top of the staff and will remain there until sunset. When hoisted to the top of the staff the flag will be saluted by playing one or more national airs. In this way fitting testimonial of respect for the heroic dead and honor to their patriotic devotion will be appropriately rendered.

The naval regulations provide for a suspension of all drills and exercises on the day and the firing at noon of a salute of twenty-one guns by all ships in commission and at all naval stations during which the ensign is to be at half mast.

As it is impossible to decorate the graves of the men of the navy who died in battle at sea it has become the custom to construct little ships of flowers and set them afloat on the water at the chief ports of the country in order that the tide may carry them out on the great waters and strew the blossoms on the bosom of the deep so that perchance they may rest over the spot where the dead went down.

In the smaller communities the day is observed with a reverence which is lacking in the larger cities. A man who spent many years in a Kansas village, writing in 1934 of the celebration there, said:

And so my mind turns back to it and I see it again on every recurring Memorial Day. I can see its people moving along its clean streets in groups to converge upon the "opera house," where the exercises of the day will be held and the orator of the occasion will hold forth. And I can see the procession setting out for East Hill Cemetery, the graves which it will presently garland with flowers, the names cut upon the stones reared above them. And it comes to me as I write that I knew in the flesh nearly all those who lie there—that I have taken them by the hand and given them greeting.

For many years the celebration in the North was devoted to an oratorical glorification of the victory of the Northern armies. But as the years passed the hearts of men were mellowed and the note of triumph died out from the Memorial Day oratory. The feeling was well expressed by Thomas Bailey Aldrich in an essay in *Ponkapog Papers* when he **wrote:**

The earlier sorrow has faded out of the hour, leaving a softened solemnity. It quickly ceased to be a local commemoration. While the sequestered country churchyards and burial-places near our great Northern cities were being hung with May garlands, the thought could not but come to us that there were graves lying southward above which bent a grief as tender and sacred as our own. Invisibly we dropped unseen flowers upon these mounds.

As the day was originally set apart for decorating the graves of the soldiers with flowers it was called Decoration Day for many years. As late as 1882 the Grand Army was protesting against this name and insisting in the use of the term Memorial Day. But the other name survives in popular usage. This usage was without doubt fostered by the custom for many years of having some one read Will Carleton's poem, "Cover Them Over with Beautiful Flowers," during the Memorial Day exercises. Its appropriateness to the occasion was such that there was hardly a celebration in any part of the country at which it did not appear on the program. It consists of eight twelve-line stanzas. An abridgment was made for use in exercises in the schools, the first stanza and chorus of which follow:

> Cover them over with beautiful flowers,
> Deck them with garlands, those brothers of ours,
> Lying so silent by night and by day,
> Sleeping the years of their manhood away.
> Give them the meed they have won in the past;
> Give them the honors their future forecast;
> Give them the chaplets they won in the strife;
> Give them the laurels they lost with their life.
> *Chorus*—Cover them over, yes, cover them over,
>   Parent and husband, brother and lover,
>   Crown in your hearts those dead heroes of ours,
>   Cover them over with beautiful flowers.

In many states the public school authorities prepared programs for the observance of the day by the pupils. They sent out booklets containing poems and extracts from notable patriotic addresses for the children to learn and recite. In Wisconsin, for example, from which there were 91,379 enlistments in the Civil War armies, with a fatality record of 10,868, it was suggested in one of the booklets that the children be taught to salute the flag and pledge allegiance to it. Directions for the salute were given and this form of a pledge was offered: "I pledge my allegiance to my flag and to the Republic for which it stands—one nation, indivisible with liberty and justice for all."

The day established to honor the memory of those who died in the Civil War has come to be observed in memory of the dead in the succeeding wars. The Spanish War Veterans and the veterans of the two World Wars participate in the exercises with the few survivors from the war of 1861-65.

Reference has been made to the gradual disappearance of the note of triumph over the South in the Memorial Day oratory in the North.

The annual ceremonies in the National Cemetery on the Gettysburg battle-field have come to be a celebration of national unity. Five Presidents have spoken there on the day since Lincoln, whose Gettysburg address was delivered on November 19, 1863. The first was Rutherford B. Hayes, less than fifteen years after the close of the Civil War. Theodore Roosevelt spoke of national unity in his address in 1905. Calvin Coolidge was the orator of the day in 1928 and spoke of the importance of inter-national peace. Herbert Hoover, in the course of his address there, said:

> The Union has become not merely a physical union of states, but rather a spiritual union in common ideals of our people. Within it is room for every variety of opinion, every possible experiment in social progress. Out of such variety comes growth, but only if we preserve and maintain our spiritual solidarity.

Franklin D. Roosevelt, in the course of his address on the battlefield in 1934, said:

> On these hills of Gettysburg two brave armies of Americans met in combat. Not far from here in a valley likewise consecrated to American valor, a ragged Continental army survived a bitter winter to keep alive the expiring hope of a new nation; and near to the battlefield and that valley stands the invincible city where the Declaration of Independence was born and the Constitution of the United States was written by the fathers. Surely, all this is holy ground. It was in Philadelphia, too, that Washington spoke his solemn, tender, wise words of farewell—a farewell not alone to his generation but to the generation of those who laid down their lives here and to our generation and to the America of to-morrow. Perhaps if our fathers and grandfathers had truly heeded those words we should have had no family quarrels, no battle of Gettysburg, no Appomattox. As a Virginian, President Washington had a natural pride in Virginia; but as an American, in his stately phrase, "The name of American, which belongs to you in your national capacity, must always exalt the just pride of patriotism, more than any appellation derived from local discrimination." . . . It was an inspired prophet of the South who said: "My brethren, if we know one another, we will love one another." The tragedy of the nation was that the people did not know one another because they had not the necessary means of visiting one another. Two subsequent wars, both with foreign nations, measurably allayed and softened the ancient passions. It has been left to us of this generation to see the healing made permanent. We are all brothers now in a new understanding.

One of the most significant gestures of national unity was made in May 1934, when Congress formally accepted the statues of George Wash-ington and Robert E. Lee presented to the National Capitol by Virginia to be placed in Statuary Hall. The statues had been presented twenty-five years earlier, but because General Lee was represented in a Confederate uniform opposition to their acceptance was raised. The statues, however, were finally put in place. Senator Carter Glass of Virginia opened the formal ceremonies following the Congressional vote of acceptance, by saying:

> We come, not to pay tribute to George Washington and Robert E. Lee, but to perform belated formalities in doing honor to Statuary Hall.

The custom of decorating the graves of the dead with flowers is of great antiquity, and it was adopted as a matter of course for Memorial Day. In Greece, when a person died, the nearest female relatives concluded their last offices by crowning the head with flowers. The Romans used flowers more freely, for they covered the couch of the dead with leaves and blossoms. Wreaths of flowers were carried to the house of mourning by friends and wreaths were put on the grave. Ovid, writing to his wife, said:

But do you perform the funeral rites for me when dead and offer chaplets with your tears. Although the fire shall have changed my body to ashes, yet the sad dust will be sensible of your pious affection.

FESTIVAL OF ST. JOAN OF ARC

The anniversary of the death of Joan of Arc, which occurred on May 30, 1431, is observed as her feast day by the Latin church. In New Orleans, however, her feast is observed on May 9. She was beatified by Pope Pius X on April 11, 1909, and a few years later was canonized and included among the saints of the church. She is honored throughout the Christian world and statues of her have been erected in several American cities.

She was one of the most remarkable young women in history. Her birthplace was the village of Domremy, near Vaucouleurs, France, and the date of her birth was sometime between 1410 and 1412, the exact month and day are not known. Her parents were prosperous peasants. When she was thirteen years old she began to hear what she described as an angel's voice. It said to her, "Be good, Jeannette, and God will aid thee." As the years went on the voices came to her with increasing frequency and finally one of them said, "Daughter of God, thou shalt lead the Dauphin to Rheims, that he may there receive worthily his anointing." Henry VI of England had been crowned King of France at Paris in 1422 and the Dauphin, Charles VII, was making a feeble effort to recover his throne. Joan was troubled over the sad state of her country and toward the end of 1428, while the English were besieging Orleans, her voices were insisting that she go to the relief of the city. She communicated with the French commander at Vaucouleurs who rejected her help. She went a second time and obtained an escort to Charles VII to whom she made her offer. She was examined by a committee of theologians who accepted her story and the Dauphin employed her. A suit of armor was made for her, and a white banner which she later carried in every battle. She went to Orleans, arriving there on April 29, 1429. Through her efforts the English were compelled to raise the siege on May 8. Thereafter she was known as the Maid of Orleans. The victory aroused the drooping spirits of the French and in June, under her leadership, they won several notable victories. On June 17, 1429, she conducted the Dauphin to the cathedral in Rheims where he was crowned.

313

Her fortunes waned after this and she was captured by the Burgundians on May 23, 1430, and sold six months later to the English. They took her to Rouen in chains where she was tried by an ecclesiastical court on the charge of sorcery. She was found guilty and condemned to be burned at the stake. She was afraid of the fire and recanted what was called her heresies and the sentence of death was commuted to imprisonment for life. At the instigation of the English this commutation was rescinded and she was finally burned at the stake on May 30, 1431. The French have erected a large mounted statue of her before the cathedral at Rheims. She is in armor and carrying her famous banner. For a century or more she was virtually forgotten, but her fame has grown with the passing years.

MAY THIRTY-FIRST

WALT WHITMAN'S BIRTHDAY

The observance of the anniversary of the birth of Walt Whitman, May 31, 1819, began while the poet was still alive. A group of his friends gathered at his house in Mickle Street, Camden, N.J., every year to congratulate him. In 1887 the Walt Whitman Fellowship was formed and it celebrated the anniversary. In the course of time it became an international fellowship through the efforts of Horace Traubel who was a Boswell to Whitman's Johnson. Whitman clubs were organized in various American cities and one was formed in England. The Fellowship held an annual dinner on May 31 in Philadelphia for some years and then moved the dinner to New York where it was largely attended. Dinners were held by Whitman admirers in other cities on the same day. The Fellowship was an informal organization, with dues paid by its members in its early days. These were soon abolished, and members were admitted in accordance with the following simple formula: "I announce myself to be a member of the Walt Whitman Fellowship International. The withdrawal of this announcement terminates my membership." Whitman died in 1892 and was buried in an elaborate tomb in Harleigh Cemetery in Camden. The house in which he lived is preserved and maintained as a memorial. The celebration of the birthday continues. In Camden it is in charge of the Whitman Foundation.

Whitman was born at West Hills, Long Island, N.Y. The Colonial Society of Huntington marked the place with a bronze tablet on a rough boulder in 1905. The inscription reads: "To mark the birthplace of Walt Whitman, The Good Gray Poet. Born May 31, 1819." Whitman was educated in the public schools of rural Long Island and Brooklyn. When he was seventeen he taught school in a village near his birthplace. He learned the carpenter's trade and also the trade of printer.

He worked as a printer on the Brooklyn *Times* and while there he wrote his *Leaves of Grass*, put it in type himself and printed it. There was for many years a copy of this first edition with many penciled changes in the library of that newspaper. It was not the first draft, for that draft he had taken with him to the eastern end of Long Island where, hidden out of sight in a cave, he read it and decided that it was worthless. He then threw the manuscript to the winds and returned to his work and his writing. For a year he was editor of the Brooklyn *Daily Eagle*. After wandering about the country for some years, going as far south as New Orleans, he returned to Brooklyn in 1850 and started a Free Soil newspaper which had a short life. Then he became a builder, working at his trade as a carpenter and making workmen's houses which he sold. In the second year of the Civil War his brother, who had enlisted, was wounded and he went to Washington to nurse him in the army hospital there. While in Washington he wrote frequently for the New York *Times*. He was a clerk in the Treasury Department from 1865 to 1871, after he had lost his employment in the Interior Department because its head disapproved of his *Leaves of Grass*. He suffered a paralytic stroke in 1873 from which he never completely recovered. At this time he moved to Camden where his brother was living and spent the remainder of his life there.

It is generally admitted that the influence of Whitman on American poetry is greater than that of any other poet of the country. His admirers sought for many years to persuade the jury of selection to admit his bust to the Hall of Fame of New York University to stand beside the busts of Longfellow and Lowell, Emerson and Whittier, Poe and Cooper. They succeeded at last in 1930 when he received sixty-four votes out of the hundred and two which were cast.

THE SEVENTEENTH AMENDMENT

The seventeenth amendment to the Constitution transferred the election of United States Senators from the state legislatures to direct popular vote. It was proposed to the states by the 62nd Congress in 1912 and ratified on May 31, 1913, after being adopted by thirty-seven states. The political events leading up to the adoption of this amendment are an interesting example of the power of our democratic form of government to express the will of the people. Public opinion gradually came to believe that too often a state legislature, in choosing a senator, was controlled by special and selfish interests. For more than fifty years there had been agitation for reform. Repeatedly the House of Representatives passed an amendment by the necessary two-thirds majority, providing for popular election of senators, but the senate refused its assent. At length the states began to apply the direct primary for nominating candidates, and Oregon passed a law to compel the legislature to accept the nominee of the people. By 1910 three quarters of the states nominated their senators by means of the primary. Thus the senate was forced to yield and in 1911 passed the amendment. Had it not done so, it is more than probable that the state legislatures would have become as impotent in choosing senators as the electoral college is in choosing a president.

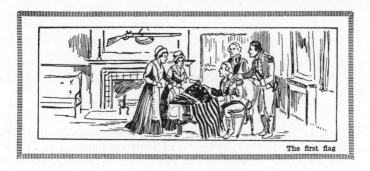
The first flag

JUNE

There is all of beauty in these few things—
A new-born child—and a new-born moon—
A tree a-bud in the flush of spring—
A ship at sea—and a bride in June—
Ivy and bittersweet in fall—
But the bride is the loveliest of all!

—Anne Mary Lawler

There are so many theories about the origin of the name by which the month of June is known that all tastes should be satisfied. Ovid in one place makes Juno assert that the month was named in her honor, but in another place he derives it from *juniores*, the name by which the lower branch of the ancient Roman legislature was known. As Ovid disagrees with himself other authorities also hold different views. One group insists that the name comes from the gentile name Junius and others that it is associated with the consulate of Junius Brutus. The Saxons, however, were not troubled with such matters. They called June Sere-Monath, or dry month, and also Lida-Oerra, or joy time. June is the month of the summer solstice, the time when apparently the sun has moved to the point farthest north from the equator and seems to stand still before moving south again. The word "solstice" is of Latin origin and means "the sun stops." Juno was regarded by the ancient Romans as the protective genius of women. Accordingly, following the theory of Ovid that the month is named for her, the Roman women believed that June was the most favorable month for marrying. It is probable that this view arose in part from the belief that May marriages were unlucky. However this may be, the popularity of June as a marriage month has survived through the centuries to the present and it is the ambition of many young women to be June brides.

JUNE FIRST

STATEHOOD DAY IN KENTUCKY

Kentucky, originally a part of Virginia, was admitted to the Union as a state on June 1, 1792, by an Act of Congress approved on February 4 of the same year. Following the passage of the act a constitutional convention met in Danville on April 2 and completed its work on April 19. The constitution drafted by the convention went into effect on June 1 without being first submitted to the people for ratification. The anniversary of statehood has been observed in various ways in the intervening years.

In 1931 and 1932 the celebration took the form of a Mountain Laurel Festival at Clear Creek Mountain Springs in the Cumberland Mountains. Beside taking note of the anniversary of statehood the festival was arranged to celebrate the arrival within the territory included within the state of a party of explorers headed by Dr. Thomas Walker. He entered the region in 1750 through the Cumberland Gap and named the mountain range and the river for the Duke of Cumberland. Dr. Walker erected a hut near Pineville, said to be the first habitation for a white man built within the state. This festival has become an annual event. In 1934 it was held in a natural amphitheater in Laurel Cove, in Pine Mountain State Park, a reservation of twenty-five hundred acres near Pineville. Governor Ruby Laffoon and about a hundred members of the General Assembly were present along with thousands of spectators. The program included concerts by bands from high schools in that part of the state, the singing of mountain ballads by choirs of school children, the singing of Indian songs by Mrs. L. L. Dantzler of Lexington, an address by Mrs. Emma Guy Cromwell, Secretary of the State Park Commission, and an address by Desha Breckenridge, editor of the Lexington *Herald*. Following this part of the program Governor Laffoon placed a crown of laurel leaves and blossoms on the head of Miss Mary Evelyn Walton, a junior in the Western State Teachers College at Bowling Green, and named her Queen of the Festival. The queen was selected by a committee of judges from a group of eighteen candidates who marched to the stage to the strains of "Beautiful Lady." When they had been presented to the governor by the master of ceremonies, they took their places among the ladies of the court. When the selection of Miss Walton was announced the royal procession marched to the stage. It was headed by two jesters clad in purple. Following them were twenty-four little maids-in-waiting wearing pink organdie gowns and carrying laurel blossoms. Then came twenty-four ladies-in-waiting similarly gowned. The pillow bearer followed with two standard bearers, two heralds and the crown bearer. The queen, wearing a white chiffon gown with a long silver train and carrying a bouquet of mountain blossoms, came next. She was followed by a special court of honor consisting of seventeen young women. She knelt on the pillow before the governor and when he had adjusted the crown she sat on the throne beside him. The festival ended with a ball in the evening.

Desha Breckinridge, in the course of his address, said:

Dr. Walker's coming marked the very beginning of the conquest of the West, the Southwest, the Northwest and the South. From that day on until 1769, when Daniel Boone and four companions left Yadkin to explore the land that the vision of Richard Henderson beheld as a great empire, there were a number driven by the zest of adventure, impelled by the quest for land, who penetrated the forests and braved the dangers of the Indians. Christopher Gist in 1750, John Finley in 1752 and 1757; Henry Skaggs in 1764, James Smith and his companions under Isaac Lindsey, James Harrod and Michael Stoner are some who during these years explored the hunting grounds of Kentucky. But the real exploration of Kentucky came after the Stanwix treaty of 1786 by which the Six Nations ceded to Virginia their claims to the country between the Ohio and Tennessee rivers and gave to Virginia the nominal right to the Kentucky country. With the coming of Boone and the long hunters there began a migration that is among the most remarkable in all the annals of the world. The settlement of Kentucky was in defiance of royal edict. In 1763 a royal proclamation expressly forbade the granting of warrants of survey or patents beyond the heads or sources of any of the rivers which fell into the Atlantic ocean, or further west. There were already then mutterings of the storm that found its expression in the American Revolution so that the King desired to limit the growth of the colonies west of the Alleghenies and to confine the increase to the narrow slope between the mountain range and the seacoast that was accessible by navigable rivers and could, therefore, be controlled from the seacoast and those rivers. Kentucky is the only state whose very existence was created in express disobedience of all governmental authority. Before the Revolution broke in 1774 when the merchants of the Bay Colony were preparing for Bunker Hill, when Henry was thundering in Williamsburg and Franklin leading toward revolution, a house was built where this state now exists—a log cabin, it is true, yet it consecrated all this state to that Anglo-Saxon civilization which founds the state on the family and was proof that they who came as adventurers were settlers and builders of states.

STATEHOOD DAY IN TENNESSEE

The Legislature in 1929 passed an act designating June 1, the anniversary of the admission of Tennessee to the Union as Statehood Day, and calling on all loyal citizens to observe it with pride. Since then the governor of the state has annually issued a proclamation appealing to the people to celebrate the day. In 1934 the anniversary was ushered in by the firing of a salute of nineteen guns in Nashville. Governor McAlister, in his proclamation said:

Not only Tennesseans, but all Americans, are sensitive to the fact some of the greatest statesmen that have been produced in this democracy of ours own Tennessee as their birthplace. Into these years of Tennessee's history as a state there have been crowded events that stand out in American history to mark it as one of the great commonwealths of the United States.

319

JUNE 1

Thirty-two years before the legislature set apart the anniversary as a day for special observance there was a statewide celebration. It took the form of a Centennial Exposition, held in Nashville from May 1 to October 30, 1897. Although the state was admitted to the Union in 1796 it was not possible to complete arrangements for the centennial celebration in that year. A plot of two hundred acres was occupied by the exposition and more than a hundred buildings were erected to hold the exhibits. The total attendance was 1,786,714. The receipts were $1,101,285 and the expenditures were $1,101,246, leaving a net balance of $39 above expenses.

In an editorial article on Statehood Day in 1934 the Knoxville *Journal* said:

> The history of Tennessee goes a long way back, as the New World counts time, with the five flags here thrown to the air since the reckoning began, symbols, as we well may feel, of such varied impulses and emotions as make her people what they are. First there was the flag of Spain planted by de Soto on the bluffs of the Mississippi where Memphis now stands. Then the French flag, first the lilies and then the tri-color brought by adventurous traders and voyageurs into the middle reaches of the virgin land on which a great state one day would be builded. Then came the British flag, with the gallant and tragic fall of Fort Loudon and the massacre that followed, a part of its story. And then the flag of the American Republic, with life, liberty and the pursuit of happiness among the beautiful promises this star-spangled banner brought. Years later, after a fruitful time of growth, Tennessee adding her full share of great men and great deeds to the country's story, the state of Jackson and of Polk, gave its allegiance to the fateful flag of the Confederacy, blood-red when stripped for battle, and blazoned with a blue saltire set with silver stars. Now, again, at the last, and forever as we trust, the flag we call Old Glory is that to which we lift our hearts.

Dr. Thomas Walker with a party of Virginians whose arrival within the present territory of Kentucky is celebrated in that state, passed through the region that is now Tennessee in 1750 on his exploring expedition. The first English settlement, however, was at Fort Loudon in 1756. Various settlements were made later by immigrants from Virginia who thought that the territory was part of that colony. When it was learned that it belonged to North Carolina the people formed a government known as the Wautega Association which survived for several years. In 1775 or 1776 the settlers changed the name of their colony to the Washington District and in 1776 it was formally annexed to North Carolina. In 1784, however, North Carolina ceded all the territory within the state to the central government on condition that it be accepted within two years. The people, thinking they had been abandoned, met at Jonesboro on August 23, 1784, and formed the State of Franklin and chose John Sevier as governor. He served until 1788, when the status of the territory was in confusion. Finally arrangements were made for its admission to the Union as a state on an equal footing with the other states. A constitutional convention met in January 1796, and drafted a constitution which went into effect without submission to a popular vote and on June 1 of that year Tennessee became the sixteenth state in the Union.

PERE MARQUETTE DAY

June 1, 1937, was the three hundredth anniversary of the birth of Jacques Marquette. Arrangements were made to celebrate it with elaborate ceremonies both in the United States, parts of which he explored and where he worked as a missionary, and in France where he was born. A bronze statue of him cast from coins contributed by the school children of his native province was erected in Laon his birthplace. Catholics and Protestants joined in the arrangements and particular stress was laid on his exploration of an unknown region in America. The State of Michigan had several years before sent a statue of Marquette to the national capital in Washington thus honoring him as one of its most distinguished citizens. There is also a statue of him in Chicago. A city, a river, a college and a railroad have been named in his honor.

In 1943 Mayor Edward J. Kelly of Chicago issued a proclamation designating December 4 of that year as Marquette Day in Chicago, marking the two hundred and fiftieth anniversary of Pere Marquette's arrival at the Chicago River, and the establishment of the first white man's settlement there.

Marquette was a member of a distinguished French family. His mother was Rose de la Salle, and from her he inherited a disposition to the religious life. At the age of seventeen he became a Jesuit novice and when his education was completed he taught for several years, but he hoped to imitate Francis Xavier and become a missionary. His wish was gratified in 1666 when he was sent to Canada, landing at Quebec on September 20. Within less than a month he was sent to Three Rivers where he spent nearly two years studying the language of the Indians. Then he was sent to work among the Ottawa Indians on Lake Huron. Soon after he went to Sault Ste Marie working there for several months, making many converts. Because of the hostility of neighboring Indian tribes he fled to Lake Michigan, and in 1671 founded the mission of St. Ignace on the Straits of Mackinac.

Louis Jolliet went to St. Ignace in 1672 and told Marquette that he had been commissioned to find the great river of which the Illinois Indians had told him and that he had been ordered to take Marquette with him. The two made preparations for their journey during the winter and in May of the next year started by way of Green Bay and the Fox River. On June 17, 1673, their canoes shot out into the Mississippi and they headed southward going as far as the mouth of the Arkansas. There they learned that the Spaniards were on the lower river and turned back.

They reached Lake Michigan by way of the Illinois River and by portage to the Chicago River and the lake, and arrived at the mission of St. Francis Xavier at De Pere. Marquette was ill and remained there for more than a year. Then he set out to found a mission among the Illinois Indians but when he reached the mouth of the Chicago River he was too ill to go on. After a time he decided to return to the mission of St. Ignace but he became so weak that his companions had to carry him ashore at the mouth of the river now known as the Pere Marquette where he died on May 18, 1675. Two years later some of his converts carried his remains to St. Ignace where they were buried in the chapel. In 1877 what were thought to be his bones were found. They were reburied save for some fragments which were given to Marquette University. Marquette and Jolliet were the first white men to follow the course of the Mississippi, an achievement which gives them fame as explorers. Marquette is honored by his church, by the country of his birth and by the country which he explored and in which he worked for the civilization of the Indians.

JUNE SECOND

BIRTHDAY OF JOHN RANDOLPH OF ROANOKE

John Randolph of Roanoke, one of the most picturesque Virginians of his time, was born June 2, 1773, in Cawsons, Va., now part of the city of Hopewell. He was a member of a prominent family and claimed Pocahontas as one of his ancestors. He was educated at the College of New Jersey, later known as Princeton, and at Columbia College in New York. He was elected to Congress at the age of twenty-six and soon became the leader of the Democratic-Republican party in the House of Representatives. He introduced the resolution calling for the impeachment of Samuel Chase, an associate justice of the United States Supreme Court. Eight charges were made against Justice Chase. He was acquitted of all of them. Randolph opposed the Missouri Compromise and called the Northern members who voted for it "doughfaces." He entered the Senate in 1825, serving for two years. In speaking of the relations between Henry Clay and John Quincy Adams, Randolph characterized them as "a combination of a Puritan and a blackleg." Clay thereupon challenged him to a duel. It was fought with pistols and neither was wounded by the first shot. Randolph refused to fire a second time and the men separated. He served a short time as Minister to Russia and died on June 24, 1833. By his will he freed his slaves of whom he owned more than three hundred. He was a man of brilliant intellect noted for his gift of vituperation which made him many enemies. Many stories are told of his eccentricities.

JUNE THIRD

BIRTHDAY OF JEFFERSON DAVIS

The anniversary of the birth of Jefferson Davis, the President of the Confederacy, was made a legal holiday by Florida in 1891 and observed for the first time in 1892. The example was followed by other Southern states and the day is now a holiday in Alabama, Arkansas, Georgia, Louisiana, Mississippi, South Carolina, Texas and Virginia as well as in Florida. The day is observed in other states in which it has not been made a holiday. There was in 1934 the usual celebration in Lexington, Ky., the capital of the state in which Davis was born. The exercises were held in the Confederate section of the Lexington cemetery under the auspices of the Lexington Chapter of the United Daughters of the Confederacy, assisted by the Philip Johnston Camp of Sons of the Confederacy and the Captain Richard W. Shurr Chapter of the Children of the Confederacy. An address was delivered by the Reverend Dr. J. W. Porter, pastor of the Immanuel Baptist Church of Lexington, and the pastors of other churches took part in the exercises.

Davis was born in Christian (now Todd) County, Ky., on June 3, 1808, the tenth child of Samuel Davis who had migrated from Georgia. Samuel Davis was the son of Evan Davis, a Welshman who had landed in Philadelphia and moved southward to Georgia. While Davis was still a small boy the family moved to Mississippi and lived on a small plantation near Woodville, Wilkinson County. The eldest son, Joseph, became the richest man in Mississippi and assisted Jefferson in many ways. When Jefferson was only seven years old he rode many hundred miles northward to become a student in the Roman Catholic Seminary in Washington County, Ky., which his Baptist parents had permitted him to enter. He remained there two years and became so fond of his teachers that for a time he wanted to join their church. On his return home he studied in the local schools and entered Transylvania University at Lexington, Ky., in 1821, at the age of thirteen. He did not finish his course there, for in 1824, when he was sixteen the Congressman from his district appointed him to the Military Academy at West Point. He was graduated in 1828 and was commissioned a second lieutenant in the United States army. Robert E. Lee was a cadet in the class below him. Davis spent seven years in army posts in Wisconsin and Illinois. He saw service in the Black Hawk War in which Abraham Lincoln was an officer of volunteers.

While stationed at Fort Crawford, Wis., commanded by Colonel Zachary Taylor, he met Taylor's daughter, fell in love with her, and married her in 1835 against her father's will. He had resigned from the army before the marriage, and returned to his home in Mississippi. His wife died within three months of her marriage. During the next ten years he lived on his plantation, Brierfield, developing it, working at times in the field with his slaves. He married his second wife, Varina Howell, on February 26, 1845, and in December of that year took his seat in the House of Representatives to which he had been elected as a Democrat. He defended slavery and the right of the states to regulate their own internal affairs.

He resigned from Congress in June 1846, accepted command of a regiment known as the Mississippi Rifles, and joined General Taylor in time to take part in the attack on Monterey in the Mexican war. The next year his conduct at the Battle of Buena Vista was so gallant that he was praised highly as a military genius, an opinion which his biographers say he also held. He withdrew from the army in 1847 and Mississippi sent him to the United States Senate where he supported President Polk in his Mexican policy. When the proposal was made to organize the territory of Oregon without a provision for slavery he denied that there was any power in Congress or in the people of the territory to interrupt the slave system or to prevent a slave owner from taking his property there. He opposed the admission of California as a free state. He resigned from the Senate in 1851 to run for governor of Mississippi as a candidate of the Southern extremists, but was defeated. Franklin Pierce made him Secretary of War in 1853. He is said to have been responsible for the acquisition from Mexico of the strip of territory in the Southwest known as the Gadsden Purchase. He wanted that territory so that a railroad to the Pacific coast might be built through it to bring the South into closer connection with the West for political reasons. At the close of his term as Secretary of War he was again sent to the Senate by Mississippi, and resigned from it a second time in 1861, when the Southern states had decided to secede from the Union.

His state immediately made him commander of its troops, but a convention of the seceding states elected him President of the new Confederacy and he was inaugurated as provisional president at Montgomery on February 18, 1861. He was formally elected in October of that year and formally inaugurated on February 22, 1862. He sought to direct the military operations of the war, confident of his own military genius, and had considerable trouble with his generals as a result. His conduct of the war was criticized as bitterly in the South as Lincoln's course was criticized in the North. He was confident of victory for the South even to the end. When Richmond was taken he fled from the city and was captured at Irwinville, Ga., on May 10, 1865, by Federal cavalry. He was imprisoned at Fortress Monroe for two years, but was never brought to trial. He was released under bond on May 13, 1867, Horace Greeley and Gerritt Smith becoming his bondsmen. The war had impoverished him and Mrs. Sarah A. Dorsey, a friend of his wife's, bequeathed to him the estate of Beauvoir on the Gulf of Mexico, where he spent the remaining years of his life, dying on December 6, 1889. In his retirement he wrote *The Rise and Fall of the Confederate Govern-*

ment. In his prime he was a man of many social graces and during his service as Secretary of War under President Pierce his home in Washington was the center of social life, visited by men of all parties.

JUNE FOURTH

JACKSONVILLE, TEXAS, TOMATO FESTIVAL

According to what is regarded as a well authenticated tradition it was not until 1834 that tomatoes were eaten in the United States. They had been regarded as poisonous and in remote sections of the country there are people who still believe that they cause cancer when eaten. Yet they had been an article of diet in Europe for a hundred years after their discovery and importation from South America. It is said that an Italian emigrant, in 1834, persuaded his American neighbors to eat tomatoes, which they called love apples and raised for ornament but had not considered edible.

Tomatoes have been raised on the farms around Jacksonville since 1897. The cultivation of the crop has expanded until the city is the center of one of the largest tomato growing areas in the country.

In 1934, the hundredth anniversary of the first consumption of tomatoes as food in the United States, the people of Jacksonville, Tex., decided to hold a Tomato Festival in celebration. The governor of the state by proclamation made Tuesday, June 5th, State Tomato Day. The 1934 festival in Jacksonville lasted two days beginning on Monday, June 4th. On the first day there was a luncheon to the visiting mayors and officers of the chambers of commerce of other cities of Texas who had gone to Jacksonville to take part in the celebration. An address was made by one of the officers of a Dallas national bank. In the afternoon there was a golf tournament and a parade through the streets of the city with decorated and symbolic floats. In the evening, the queen of the festival, Miss Billye Sue Hackney, was crowned in Ragsdale Park, attended by her ladies in waiting. Following the coronation there was a ball, presided over by the queen. On the second day there was a barbecue in the City Park for the tomato growers who were addressed by the State Commissioner of Agriculture. The queen of the festival had been elected in the previous week and she at once sent telegraphic greetings to all the tomato growing sections in the country expressing her wishes for their prosperity and contentment and she received many replies inviting her to visit the regions where tomatoes are grown. The festival has been held every year since 1934, except for the war years, becoming more elaborate each year. In 1935 it extended over three days with a pageant "The Romance of the Love Apple." The queen of the festival was crowned by the governor of the state.

JACK JOUETT DAY

In Virginia Jack Jouett Day is observed annually on June 4 by proclamation of the governor who "calls upon the citizens of the Commonwealth, and particularly all civic, veteran and patriotic societies in the state" to celebrate the anniversary of the hazardous ride of Jack Jouett from Cuckoo Tavern to Charlottesville. The event commemorated occurred during the Revolutionary War when Thomas Jefferson and the Virginia Legislature had been forced to flee, first from Williamsburg to Richmond, then to Charlottesville in May 1871. Governor Jefferson was in residence at Monticello, his home in the mountains, and Charlottesville was the temporary capital of the state. Earlier in the year the British had pursued Lafayette, who was in command of the Continental Troops in Virginia, to the Rapidan, where he was compelled to fall back, crossing at Ely's Ford on the bank of the North Anna River. In May Arnold, the traitor, was reinforced by two thousand men and occupied Manchester, threatening but not taking Richmond. They pushed up the North Anna River to Hanover County, and Lieutenant-Colonel Tarleton with one hundred and eighty dragoons and seventy infantry was sent to seize Mr. Jefferson and the legislature at Charlottesville.

Captain Jack Jouett, Jr., an officer of the Virginia State Militia, happened to be in the vicinity—it is supposed because his father owned a farm six miles east of Louisa—and he concealed himself in the shrubbery as the British swept by Cuckoo Tavern in Louisa County. So rapidly had Tarleton approached that the raid was not suspected, although the Tavern was only twenty-four hours ride from Charlottesville. Guessing their intentions, Captain Jouett saddled his throughbred mare and galloped at great speed to Charlottesville by way of an abandoned road nearly impassable in places. Several times he narrowly escaped capture, but by dawn of June 4 he had accomplished the forty-five miles and rode through the town crying, "The British are coming!"

Warned in time, Mr. Jefferson and most of the members of the legislature made their escape. Had the gallant captain failed in his mission and the governor been captured he would undoubtedly have been tried by the British as a traitor and taken in chains to England. Thus, there would have been no grave on the mountain near Monticello with the inscription: "Here was buried Thomas Jefferson, author of the Declaration of Independence, of the Virginia Statute for Religious Freedom, and the Father of the University of Virginia."

JUNE FIFTH

REPEAL OF THE GOLD CLAUSE

President Franklin D. Roosevelt, on June 5, 1933, signed the resolution of Congress providing that government bonds and bonds of private corporations should be paid in whatever currency was legal tender notwithstanding provisions in the bonds that they should be paid in gold. The resolution declared that these provisions for gold payment obstructed "the power of Congress to regulate the value of the money of the United States." Following the signing of the resolution the President ordered that all gold coin and all gold certificates should be surrendered by their owners in exchange for other forms of currency, with penalties for disobedience. The constitutionality of the resolution was disputed and the issue was taken to the Supreme Court. That court held that Congress had power to invalidate the gold clause in private bonds but that the invalidation in government bonds was unconstitutional.

The resolution changed the policy of the government laid down after the free-silver presidential campaign of 1896 when Congress provided that all national currency should be redeemable in specie, that is, in gold. There was no question about the payment of Government bonds in gold. The gold content of the dollar had been the same for about a hundred years. The same Congress which repealed the gold clause in bonds authorized the President to reduce the gold content of the dollar by not more than 50 per cent. In accordance with this authority he reduced it a fraction more than 40 per cent.

JUNE SIXTH

D-DAY

On June 6, 1944, the greatest amphibious force in history, composed of American, British, Canadian and Allied troops, landed in Normandy, starting the final campaign against Germany in World War II which led to her unconditional surrender on May 8, 1945. Thousands of troops from an armada of warships and parachutes covered a stretch of more than a hundred miles of beaches from Le Havre to Cherbourg. The main landings were made in the Bay of Cherbourg, at Bernieres, north of Caen, and near Le Havre on the Seine estuary. The first forty-nine days were passed in securing and enlarging the beachhead, prior to the smashing offensives which later swept across France to the Westwall and on to Berlin, the whole operation of the invasion being an extraordinary and spectacular military feat.

The first report of the long-awaited event reached the United States through the German news agency Transocean, in a broadcast announcing that the Allies were landing at Havre and a naval battle was in progress in the English Channel. There was no Allied confirmation, but the New York *Times* of June 6 departed from its usual conservative format with a three-line, eight-column display of "scareheads" repeating the Transocean broadcast. The national radio networks stood by to confirm the report, all programs, even those sponsoring the highest-paid comedians and other performers, being subject to interruption without warning. Throughout America people talked of little else, in the homes, on the street, in stores, and in offices, where business was disrupted by the day-long suspense. Led by President Roosevelt over the radio at ten that evening, the entire country joined in a solemn prayer for the success of the invasion. General Dwight D. Eisenhower's communique from London was the first official announcement and gave the brief facts of the landings with no details, but it was greeted with a triumphant burst of sirens and whistles, and a general public demonstration. The Liberty Bell in Philadelphia was rung six times, and the New York *Times* of June 7 again displayed scareheads proclaiming that Hitler's seawall had been breached and the invaders were fighting inland while the Nazis expected still further landings.

More than four thousand ships, exclusive of smaller landing craft, participated in the tremendous undertaking, and the largest airborne force ever employed was landed with remarkably low losses. Radar was used by the Allies to counterfeit the approach of ships and planes at false locations and the Germans were thus confused, the actual landings taking them completely by surprise. Allied short wave radio stations in the United States, England, North Africa and Italy were coordinated early on the morning of June 6 for an unprecedented propaganda campaign directed at Germany and the occupied countries. At the hour of invasion the broadcasting facilities were linked together in an international chain to insure a maximum audience for General Eisenhower's statement to the people of Western Europe. Subsequently transmissions were made in twenty-two languages on a twenty-four-hour basis.

In comparison with the D-Day invasion, Philip of Spain's armada, which struck terror to the hearts of Elizabethan Englishmen before its destruction by a providential storm, was a puny force. The operation by which the continent of Europe was successfully invaded in the teeth of a formidable and strongly entrenched enemy will probably remain unique in the annals of history for a long time to come.

JUNE SEVENTH

BOONE DAY

The Kentucky State Historical Society has for many years celebrated June 7, the anniversary of the day when Daniel Boone "first saw the beautiful level of Kentucky" in 1769. He had been preceded by Dr. Thomas Walker (see Kentucky Statehood Day, June 1). He entered the state by the Cumberland Gap which Dr. Walker had named for the Duke of Cumberland.

At the celebration in 1934 of the two hundredth anniversary of Boone's birth, the speaker at the exercises in Frankfort was Dr. Louise Phelps Kellogg of the University of Wisconsin, a student of the frontier history of the country. She quoted from Byron's "Don Juan" which described Boone as the "happiest among mortals anywhere," and gave him an international reputation. Here, in part, is what Byron wrote:

Of all men, saving Sylla the man-slayer,
    Who passes for in life and death most lucky,
Of the great names which in our faces stare,
    The General Boon, back-woodsman of Kentucky,
Was happiest among mortals anywhere;
    For killing nothing but a bear or buck, he
Enjoy'd the lonely, vigorous, harmless days
Of his old age in wilds of deepest maze.

Crime came not near him—she is not the child
    Of solitude; Health shrank not from him—for
Her home is in the rarely trodden wild,
    Where if men seek her not, and death be no more
Their choice than life, forgive them, as beguiled
    By habit to what their own hearts abhor—
In cities caged. The present case in point I
Cite is, that Boon lived hunting up to ninety.

And what's still stranger, left behind a name
    For which men vainly decimate the throng,
Not only famous, but of that good fame,
    Without which glory's but a tavern song—
Simple, serene, the antipodes of shame,
    Which hate nor envy e'er could tinge with wrong;
An active hermit, even in his age the child
Of Nature, or the man of Ross run wild.

'Tis true he shrank from men even of his nation,
    When they built into his darling trees,—
He moved some hundred miles off, for a station
    Where there were fewer houses and more ease;
The inconvenience of civilization
Is, that you neither can be pleased nor please;
But where he met the individual man,
He show'd himself as kind as mortal can.

He was not all alone; around him grew
    A sylvan tribe of children of the chase,
Whose young, unawaken'd world was ever new,
    Nor sword nor sorrow yet had left a trace
On her unwrinkled brow, nor could you view
    A frown on Nature's or on human face;
The free-born forest found and kept them free,
And fresh as is a torrent or a tree.

And tall, and strong, and swift of foot were they,
    Beyond the dwarfing city's pale abortions,
Because their thoughts had never been the prey
    Of care or gain; the green woods were their portions;

No sinking spirits told them they grew grey,
    No fashion made them apes of distortions;
Simple they were, not savage; and their rifles,
Though very true, were not used for trifles.

Motion was in their days, rest in their slumbers,
    And cheerfulness the handmaid of their toil;
Nor yet too many nor too few their numbers;
    Corruption could not make their hearts her soil;
The lust which stings, the splendor which encumbers,
    With the free foresters divide no spoil;
Serene, not sullen, were the solitudes
Of this unsighing people of the woods.

Dr. Kellogg's address was on "The Fame of Daniel Boone." She expressed the opinion that fame grew out of the qualities of his character rather than out of his prowess as a hunter and fighter. His delight was in a good gun, a good horse and a good wife. She said that he found pleasure in beauty "with terror looking over his shoulder." His reputation as a killer of Indians was exaggerated, for he did not wantonly take life. As a hunter he was supreme for even when afflicted with rheumatism so that his wife had to carry his gun he was able to kill more deer than any of his companions.

The bicentennial of Boone's birth was celebrated under the direction of a commission authorized by the General Assembly of the state and appointed by Governor Laffoon. Congress authorized the coining of a fifty-cent piece in honor of Boone to be circulated in the bicentennial year.

Daniel Boone was born on November 2, 1734, about eleven miles from Reading, Pa., of a Quaker father and mother. His grandfather came to America from near Exeter, England, in 1717. His father was a farmer and a blacksmith, and Daniel helped him from his early youth. When he was twelve years old his father gave him a rifle and he became an expert hunter. In 1750, when he was fifteen years old, the family started for North Carolina, but remained on the way in the Shenandoah valley for about a year, not arriving at their destination till the spring of 1751. Boone, as a teamster and blacksmith, joined a contingent from North Carolina in the Braddock campaign. In 1756 he married Rebeccah Bryan, the daughter of a neighbor. A few years later he visited Florida and planned to settle there, but abandoned the project because of the objections of his wife.

In 1767 he set out for Kentucky with some companions, but they turned back before they reached their destination. On May 1, 1769, he and four others started once more for Kentucky and this time they continued their journey until they passed through the Cumberland Gap on June 7 and made a camp in what is now Estill County. They returned home in the spring of 1771 and in March 1775, Boone led a company of settlers into the new country, and on April 1 began to build a fort on the present site of Boonesborough. Some months later he took his family to Kentucky. He was made a lieutenant and then a captain of militia and later a lieutenant colonel. He was elected to the legislature and also served as sheriff of his county. He took up many tracts of land but lost them because of defective titles. When he lost the last tract he moved to the region now known as Missouri and obtained a land grant there. His title was voided by the United States land commissioners but was finally confirmed by Act of Congress on February 18, 1814. He died on September 26, 1820. Many legends have grown up about him, few of which are authentic, but the record of his life shows that he was a man of distinction in the communities in which he lived.

ROYAL POINCIANA FESTIVAL IN MIAMI

In 1937 the Coral Gables, Fla., Chamber of Commerce became interested in a plan sponsored by several public-spirited citizens for planting royal poincianas, and one hundred of the trees were actually set out during June of that year. The Miami Chamber of Commerce cooperated in the project, Mayor E. G. Sewell of Miami proclaiming July 20, 1937, as the first Royal Poinciana Planting Day. In 1940 the idea of a festival, which had grown out of the earlier scheme, first came to fruition. A queen was chosen by the University of Miami from among the students and a coronation ceremony was held in Miami's Bayfront Park. The festival continued as an annual observance in early June throughout World War II. In 1945 there was a typical program in the Park on June 7, which included music by a concert band and vocal soloists, exhibition dancing, public addresses, and the coronation of the Royal Poinciana Festival queen, who was attended by six ladies-in-waiting with escorts from the various service branches. During the festival week a number of private estates with extensive and beautiful plantings of royal poincianas are open to the public, and there is always a banquet and a ball. Otherwise, the ceremonies vary from year to year. In 1941 there was a pageant; in 1946 a city-sponsored art show in the Park auditorium was incorporated with the festival. A large number of canvases portraying poincianas were included in the exhibits, the first prize being awarded for the most realistic painting of the tree.

In 1940 it was estimated that there were some fifty thousand royal poincianas in the Greater Miami area. Due to interest aroused by the yearly festival, the plantings have continued, constantly increasing this figure. Dr. John C. Gifford, professor of forestry at the University of Miami, delivered an address during the 1945 celebration on the history of the trees. Their origin in the United States is not positively known, but the most credible theory attributes their source to Madagascar. It is believed that the seed was carried to this and other countries in the straw bedding of slave ships. Royal poinciana is only one of several names by which the tree is popularly known. It is said to have been so named in honor of an early Spanish governor of the West Indies. The trees are

331

referred to as royal poincianas in Miami, Key West, and in Brownsville, Texas, these cities being among the few localities in the United States with the subtropical climate necessary for their growth. In Latin America they are known as the peacock flower, flamboyant, or flame tree, and in India as the guli-mohur. The tree is umbrella-like in shape and the horizontally spreading branches are covered with a lacy foliage of small, clustered leaves. In the United States it blooms in the spring or early summer. The blossoms are a brilliant flame color and appear in great profusion, giving the effect of a tree on fire.

JUNE EIGHTH

THE YOAKUM, TEXAS, TOMATO TOM-TOM

Beginning in 1928 the city of Yoakum, Tex., has held an anuual Tomato Festival which it calls a "Tomato Tom-Tom." It lasts for two days during which there are parades and balls and festivities of various kinds. It was held on June 8 and 9 in 1934. The first festival was not very elaborate, but in 1929 plans were made to crown a queen of the festival and a queen is now crowned every year. The first to be enthroned as Queen Ceres was Miss Dorothy May. In the course of time a king, known as King Tom-Tom, was crowned along with the queen. The festival had grown to such proportions in 1935 that the governor of the state attended it and made an address on the opening day.

In that year the festival began with a parade of floats by various organizations through the streets of the city, followed by the address by the governor. Then the firemen from Yoakum and neighboring cities contested in races. The queen and king were crowned in the evening in the open air stadium of the high school, and there was dancing in the streets. There was a ball at which the queen presided along with a court of "duchesses" representing more than forty towns in South Texas. On the second day a terrapin race was arranged followed by a parade of the school children dressed in fantastic costumes. There was street dancing in the early evening followed by another ball. During the two days there was a tomato and industrial exhibition. In the district of which Yoakum is the center about 35,000 acres are devoted to raising tomatoes, producing a crop worth from $200 to $500 an acre, varying with the market price and the skill of the cultivators.

JUNE NINTH

FEAST OF ST. COLUMBA

This day, the anniversary of the death of St. Columba in 597, is observed as a feast day especially in Ireland and Scotland and by the

Roman Catholic churches in the United States named for the saint. He was born at Cartan, County Donegal, Ireland, on December 7, 521, and belonged to the clan O'Donnell. He was a great-great-grandson of Niall, an Irish king of the fourth century. He was named Colum at his baptism, a word meaning a dove which was Latinized as Columba. He was also known as Columb-cille and Columb Kill, the word "cille" meaning "of the churches." He entered the monastic school at Moville and after embracing the monastic life was made a deacon. He studied in other places and became known in subsequent history as one of the Twelve Apostles of Ireland. He was raised to the priesthood by the bishop of Clonfad. In the course of time he returned to Ulster, his native province. He planned a trip to Rome and Jerusalem, but he got no farther than Tours from which it is said that he took back to Ireland a copy of the gospels which was deposited in Kerry.

In 563 he left Ireland for Scotland. There are various explanations for his departure. One of the most interesting, which the scholars of the Church regard as unfounded, is that he admired fine manuscripts and had asked the abbot of Moville to let him copy a manuscript of the Psalter which he had. The abbot, who prized it highly, would not let it out of his possession. But when Columba was visiting the monastery in 560 he surreptitiously got possession of it. When Finnian, the abbot, discovered his loss and traced the manuscript to Columba and demanded its return Columba refused to give it up. Thereupon King Diarmid undertook to recover it and the battle of Guildreme resulted. A synod of the saints of Ireland was called to consider the matter. It decided that Columba was responsible for the loss of life in the battle and it was ordered that he should rescue as many souls from paganism as lives had been lost in the fight.

Although there is disagreement among the scholars over the reason for his leaving Ireland, it is agreed that he did set sail with twelve companions in a currach, a wickerwork frame covered with hides, similar to the crude boats used even to this day on some parts of the Irish coast. The company landed on Iona island on May 12, 563. They built a church, a refectory, and huts in which to live, of wattles and rough planks. Columba then began to preach to the inhabitants of the island. After a time he crossed to the mainland of Scotland and preached to the northern Picts. He and two other monks visited King Brude, at his castle in Inverness. The gates were closed against them, but according to tradition, Columba made the sign of the cross and the gates flew open. The monks entered and preached to the king, who accepted Christianity and his followers also professed belief. Columba organized many churches in Scotland and, in spite of the opposition of the Druids, spread Christianity throughout the country. He made his home in the monastery on Iona island, and spent much time there in transcribing ancient manuscripts. He wrote three hundred books, two of which have been preserved. One, a psalter called "The Cathach" was carried into battle by the O'Donnell clan as a talisman to insure victory.

When the bell sounded for the midnight service on June 8, 597, he was the first to enter the church, but he was so weak from age and illness that he soon fell to the floor before the altar and died early in the morning of June 9. He was buried within the monastic inclosure on the island where he had begun his missionary work.

PETERSBURG MEMORIAL DAY

The city of Petersburg, Va., observes June 9 as Confederate Memorial Day in commemoration of the successful defense of the city on that day in 1864. Petersburg, twenty-two miles south of Richmond, commanded the approach to the Confederate capital and General Grant set out to capture it. A week before the siege of the city began it was menaced by Union troops. It was successfully defended by men too old and boys too young to enter the army, and held until reinforcements arrived. Although there were other notable incidents in connection with the defense of the city this is the one of which its residents are proudest. (See also Crater Day, July 30.) On its first anniversary in 1865 a company of women went to a graveyard south of the old Blandford church and decorated the graves of the dead of the Washington Artillery Regiment buried there. Every year since then the graves of the Confederate dead in the section of Blandford Cemetery set apart for them have been decorated on June 9, although Confederate Memorial Day in Virginia is observed on May 30.

BIRTHDAY OF JENNIE CASSEDAY

The anniversary of the birth of Miss Jennie Casseday is observed by the Woman's Christian Temperance Union as Flower Mission Day when flowers and religious tracts are sent to the inmates of prisons. It had its inspiration in the work of Miss Casseday in Louisville, Ky. From the age of twenty, when it was learned that she would never be able to walk again, until her death more than thirty years later, she devoted herself to good works. Under her inspiration the Jennie Casseday Infirmary for women was opened in Louisville with accommodations for forty patients. Miss Casseday was also in the habit of sending flowers to prisoners. In writing of her years ago Frances Willard, of the Woman's Christian Temperance Union, said:

> In Boston, newcomers are told that they must see Bunker Hill monument and the State House; in New York, Central Park and the Pulitzer building; in Philadelphia, Liberty Bell and City Hall; but in Louisville they point out the statue of George D. Prentice and the white window from which smiles the loving face of our white ribbon worker. . . . With an earnest prayer for guidance I sought her sacred presence. Never shall I forget the kindling smile, the soft and tender handclasp, the Bible on the snowy counterpane, the fresh flowers on

the pretty shelf between the bed and window. We talked of the ministry of those winsome heralds of good will, with the beautiful mission with which Miss Casseday was already connected, and I asked if she would accept the superintendency of such a department should it be established by the convention. To this she consented, not without reluctance, having already much Christian work on hand, but from that day to this—well nigh ten years—she has been our faithful and beloved leader in the most lovely line of Christian endeavor among all our forty-six "branchings out." This department aims to graft our gospel work upon a beautiful form of philanthropy. Bouquets are tied with white ribbon and a Scripture verse and selection relative to temperance is attached. Our literature is circulated to accompany the flowers and the total abstinence pledge is offered at appropriate times in prison, hospital and other centers of sin and sorrow. . . . June 9 is the anniversary of Miss Casseday's birth, and it has become known as Prisoner's Day throughout our borders.

Miss Casseday died on February 8, 1893, but the work which she started is carried on in her memory.

JUNE TENTH

CHILDREN'S DAY

The observance of the second Sunday in June as Children's Day by the Protestant churches began in the middle of the last century. It fell on June 10 in 1945. The earliest observance of which any record has been found was arranged by the Rev. Dr. Charles H. Leonard, pastor of the Universalist Church of the Redeemer in Chelsea, Mass. It was on the second Sunday in June 1856, when a special service was held for the children and when those who had not been baptized were christened. Dr. Leonard called the day Rose Sunday. The day was later called Flower Sunday, but in the course of a few years it came to be known as Children's Day. The Methodist Episcopal Church was the first denomination formally to recognize the day. Its adoption was recommended in 1865, and in 1868 the general conference voted that the second Sunday in June be observed in honor of the children. A children's service was held in Camden, N.J., on that day in 1866 and in 1867 the general convention of the Universalist Church recommended that this day be adopted as the time for the baptism of children.

Like many American customs the observance of Children's Day has its roots in the Old World. May Day was the day on which children were confirmed in the Roman and the Lutheran churches. The children carried flowers in a procession to the churches. This is probably why Children's Day here was first called Rose Day or Flower Day. The change from May Day to June is a natural shifting of the date to conform to the season of flowers, especially in the northern part of the country.

ROSE DAY AT MANHEIM, PENNSYLVANIA

Baron Henry William Stiegel, born in Manheim, Germany, in 1730, came to America in 1750 at the age of twenty and settled in Philadelphia. He brought with him a fortune valued at 40,000 English pounds. In 1753 he married the daughter of Jacob Huber, an ironmaster of Lancaster County, Pennsylvania. He bought his father-in-law's furnace, moved to Lancaster County, and took title to a large tract of land on which he laid out a town which he named Manheim after his native place. He built a glass factory there, and imported workmen to make the glass, while his American workmen made stoves in the iron foundry. The glassware from his factory is highly prized by collectors.

He was religiously disposed and organized and built a Lutheran church in 1772. As the people were poor he deeded the property to them on condition that the church pay "therefor unto the said Henry William Stiegel his heirs or assigns, at the said town of Manheim, in the month of June yearly forever hereafter, the rent of one red rose if the same shall be demanded." The rent was paid for two years, but when the baron got in financial difficulties in the depression of 1774, the payment was abandoned, and the condition laid down in the deed forgotten for more than a century. In 1891, however, when the old church was torn down to make way for a new one, the deed was found in a vault in the basement by Dr. J. W. Seiling, the treasurer, and he decided that arrangements should be made to fulfill its terms. Announcement was published that the rental would be paid on the second Sunday in June of the next year. When the new church was finished it contained a window in memory of Baron Stiegel in which the principal object is a large red rose. J. C. Stiegel, of Harrisonburg, Va., a direct descendant of the baron, was invited to receive the rose in June 1892.

The ceremonies attending the payment of the rental have developed into a festival of roses. A descendant of the baron has been present every year since 1892 until very recent years to receive the single rose. The members of the congregation take roses to the church and deposit them in the chancel. They are afterwards distributed among the hospitals. The beautifully poetic ceremony of the payment of the rental attracts visitors from far and near every June. At the ceremony on June 10, 1934, the presentation of the rose was made by Owen J. Roberts, Associate Justice of the United States Supreme Court. The recipient was Mrs. John Robertson, the oldest living descendant of Baron Stiegel.

JUNE ELEVENTH

KAMEHAMEHA DAY IN HAWAII

The birthday of King Kamehameha I is celebrated in Hawaii on June 11 each year. Many towns and villages throughout the Islands observe the traditional ceremonies, but those in Honolulu are somewhat more elaborate. Outrigger canoe, surfboard, and swimming races are customary early in the day. Later there is a luau, or native feast, usually held on the capitol grounds. Whole pigs are roasted in deep pits, fish wrapped in leaves are cooked in similar pits; there are wooden calabashes of poi, also great quantities of small crabs seasoned with native condiments, and cocoanut pudding. Originally the luau was served to groups seated in a circle about a thick mat of ti and banana leaves; nowadays, however, the feast is eaten at long trestle tables. Ceremonial native dancing and singing follow the feast, but often a song is started to the accompaniment of guitar or ukelele in the midst of the feasting. The crowd joins in, or occasionally someone starts an antiphonal.

Often there is a torchlight procession which is usually led by a Hawaiian man chosen for his impressive physique. He wears a yellow feather cloak and helmet to represent King Kamehameha. He is surrounded by native young men, also wearing feather capes, and carrying torches made of kukui nuts on long poles. Behind them march the various civic organizations and clubs, men and women alike wearing leis. Frequently Chinese, Japanese and Korean organizations take part, dressed in their native costumes. When this torchlight parade is a part of the ceremonies it ends at the capitol grounds with the luau, or feast, which has been in preparation for the greater part of the day.

Kamehameha I, founder of the dynasty of that name, is the king who conquered Oahu, Mauai and Kauai early in the nineteenth century and united them to his original kingdom of the island of Hawaii. He was responsible for many reforms in custom and religion; he abolished restricting and purely superstitious tabus and somewhat elevated the lot of women. He also arranged for the coming of the American missionaries, who later accomplished great educational reforms among the docile and teachable natives, but Kamehameha died before their arrival. It is recounted on reliable authority that he was a magnificent physical specimen. As evidence of this, his surfboard in the Bishop Museum in Honolulu is extraordinarily long and heavy, his spears of great length, and his feather capes too long to be worn by any but a man well over six feet.

FEAST OF ST. BARNABAS

St. Charles Borromeo in 1582 appointed June 11 as the feast day of St. Barnabas. It has been observed annually since then. Barnabas was a Jew of the tribe of Levi, born in the island of Cyprus early in the Christian era. He studied in Jerusalem and lived there near his cousin Mark, the evangelist. He is said to have owned land near the

337

city and to have been a man of considerable wealth. He was probably converted to Christianity soon after the Pentecost for it is recorded in Acts that "Joses (or Joseph) who by the apostles was surnamed Barnabas, which being interpreted is, the son of consolation, a Levite and of the country of Cyprus, having land, sold it and laid it at the apostles' feet." Barnabas stood sponsor for Paul when he went to Jerusalem after his conversion and was regarded with suspicion by the Christians because of his record as a persecutor. Paul and Barnabas went on many missionary journeys together. At Lystra, after Paul had cured a lame man, the people took them for gods from heaven and called Barnabas Jupiter and Paul they called Mercury "because he was the chief speaker." The two men had great difficulty in preventing the sacrifice of a bull in their honor. There was later a disagreement between Paul and Barnabas and they separated, Paul taking Silas with him on a tour of the churches and Barnabas going with his cousin Mark.

There are various traditions about Barnabas which the authorities do not regard as well founded. One is that he always preached from the gospel of St. Matthew, which he carried with him, and that it was buried with him. When his remains were found the manuscript was still in his hands. The remains and the body were taken to Constantinople where a church was built in his honor. Another tradition is that he was the first bishop of Milan, a tradition which St. Charles Borromeo seems to have accepted when he set apart June 11 as the feast day for the saint. The tradition regarding his use of the gospel of St. Matthew survives in the representations of him in Christian art for he is shown with the gospel in one hand and with a pilgrim's staff in the other. The staff symbolized his missionary journeyings.

There is in the Protestant Episcopal church a Guild of St. Barnabas for Nurses, named from a religious order founded in 1535 and associated originally with the church of St. Barnabas in Milan.

JUNE TWELFTH

THE PORTLAND ROSE FESTIVAL

In early June of every year since 1907, with a few exceptions, the rose season has been celebrated in Portland, Ore., by a Rose Festival. It lasts from two days to a week. The festival in 1934 continued for four days, beginning on June 11 and ending on June 14. The celebration originated with the Portland Rose Society which held its first exhibition in 1889. The Rose Society, to supplement its annual exhibition, arranged a floral parade on June 10, 1904, with decorated carriages, bicycles and automobiles moving through the streets. There were only four automobiles and they moved so slowly and with so many stops that they were

ridiculed in the newspaper reports, and the owners of automobiles, determined to prove that their cars would run, arranged a special floral parade
on the following Sunday with twenty in line. It was three years before
there was another floral parade. Frederick Holman, president of the Rose
Society, called together some of the leading citizens in the spring of 1907
and proposed that a Rose Festival be held in conjunction with the annual
rose show. A plan was agreed upon and on June 20 and 21 there was
such a festival. It included in its features the usual exhibition of roses
and other flowers in the Forestry building, a "human rosebud" parade of
two thousand school children, and a parade of automobiles and horse-
drawn carriages decorated with flowers. It was so brilliantly successful
that within a week of its close enthusiastic citizens incorporated the Rose
Festival Association with the declared purpose of holding an annual floral
fete. The second festival, in 1908, lasted for a week, beginning on
June 1. It was presided over by a ruler called Rex Oregonus, and by
Queen Flora, impersonated by Miss Carrie Lee Chamberlain, daughter of
the governor of the state. Two United States cruisers and five torpedo
boats under command of Rear Admiral Swinburne, were anchored in the
harbor to do honor to the festival. As in the first year there was an exhibition of flowers and a parade of school children as well as a parade
of decorated vehicles. In addition there was a night electrical parade of
allegorical floats depicting "The Spirit of the Golden West." The festival continued for a week until 1914 when it was shortened to four days.
The automobile had increased in popularity and efficiency by 1910 so that
at the festival in that year there was a procession five miles long of
decorated cars, from runabouts to heavy trucks. A train of six trolley
cars was loaded with roses and on one of the days of the festival these
flowers were thrown from the cars to the spectators lining the sidewalks.

Rex Oregonus was deposed in 1914 and a queen ruled over the
festival in his stead. The first was Miss Thelma Hollingsworth, known
as Queen Thelma. The queens in the succeeding years have been called
by their own Christian names. The coronation of the queen as Ruler of
Rosaria is accompanied by elaborate ceremonies. In 1930 the queen and
her seven attendants were chosen from the graduating classes of the
eight high schools in the city instead of being named by a special committee or chosen in a contest. The first high school queen was Miss
Caroline Hahm. By 1922 the festival had become so popular that floats
were entered in the parade not only from Portland, but from McMin-
ville, Salem, Sandy, Newberg, Prineville and Albany in Oregon and also
from Vancouver, British Columbia; San Francisco, Oakland and Los
Angeles, Calif.; and Seattle, Wash. And in 1923 the Portland section
of the Oregon Trail was dedicated during the festival. A pageant called
"Rosaria" was introduced in 1925 and in 1933 the play "Alice in
Wonderland" was presented by the Portland Theater School and there
was a marine pageant. The festival in 1934 was arranged for the time
of the meeting of the convention of the Canadian Legion in the city

and for the first convention of the American Rose Society to be held west of the Mississippi river. These conventions drew many visitors attracted by the Rose Festival as well as by the conventions which they were attending officially. The festival has become one of the notable events of the year on the Pacific coast.

JUNE THIRTEENTH

FEAST OF ST. ANTHONY OF PADUA

St. Anthony of Padua shares with St. Anthony the Great the distinction of being listed among the most notable Christian teachers of his time (see Feast of St. Anthony the Great, January 17). He was born at Lisbon in 1195 and died at Vercelli on June 13, 1231. There is an unverified tradition that he was a descendant of Godfrey de Bouillon, commander of the First Crusade. It is known, however, that his parents were of noble lineage and were living near the cathedral at Lisbon at the time of his birth. He was christened Ferdinand, and when he was old enough entered the cathedral school. At the age of fifteen he joined the Canons Regular of St. Augustine, in the monastery of St. Vincent, just outside of the walls of Lisbon. Two years later he entered the monastery of Santa Croce at Coimbra where he remained for eight years devoting himself to prayer and study. On seeing the bodies of the first Franciscan martyrs, slain in Morocco, being carried into the church of the monastery on January 16, 1220, he decided to seek martyrdom and became a Friar Minor with the intention of going to Morocco to preach to the Saracens. He took the name of Anthony, doubtless in memory of Anthony the Great, and started for Africa, but illness compelled him to abandon the journey.

When he applied to the provincial of his new order for a place where he could live in solitude and penance he was sent to the hermitage of Montepaolo, near Forli, to celebrate mass for the lay brethren. While there a number of Franciscan and Dominican friars arrived to be ordained. When it was learned that no one had been selected to preach the ordination sermon, Anthony, of whose learning his associates were ignorant, was called upon to officiate and to speak whatever the spirit of God might inspire him to say. He began timidly and modestly but as he gained confidence he astounded everyone by his knowledge of the Scriptures and his erudition. From that day he become noted as a preacher and teacher. He lived and preached in France for a while and on October 3, 1226, he returned to Italy and was elected Minister Provincial of Emilia. But on May 30, 1230, he resigned the office and retired to the monastery at Padua which he had founded, and died a little more than a year later.

Within less than a year of his death his name was placed in the calendar of saints by Pope Gregory IX, who had known him and had called him the "Ark of the Covenant." Many miracles are ascribed to him, so that he is known as the Thaumaturgist. In discussing the miracles the article on him in the *Catholic Encyclopedia* says:

It may be that some of the miracles attributed to St. Anthony are legendary, but others come to us on such high authority that it is impossible to eliminate them . . . without doing violence to the facts of history.

After his death the people of Padua built a splendid church in his honor in which his relics are preserved. Many churches in the United States are named for him and in these churches his feast day is observed with special ceremonies. The memory of his miracles survives and he is especially invoked for the recovery of things that have been lost. The children of Catholic families in the United States have a little rhyming prayer which they say when they need his help. It is as follows:

Dear St. Anthony, please come around,
Something is lost and must be found.

JUNE FOURTEENTH

FLAG DAY

On June 14, 1777, the Continental Congress, sitting in Philadelphia, adopted a resolution declaring:

That the flag of the United States shall be of thirteen stripes of alternate red and white, with a union of thirteen stars of white in a blue field, representing the new constellation.

The resolution was adopted following the reception of the report of a special committee appointed to suggest a design for the flag. A contemporary description of the design follows:

The stars of the flag represent a new constellation rising in the West. The idea is taken from the great constellation Lyra, which in the hands of Orpheus, signifies harmony. The blue in the field is taken from the edge of the Covenanters Banner of Scotland, significant of the covenant of the United States against oppression. The stars are disposed in a circle, symbolizing the perpetuity of the Union, the ring signifying eternity. The thirteen stars show the number of the united colonies and denote subordination of the States of the Union as well as equality among themselves. The red, the color which in the Roman days was a symbol of defiance, denotes daring, and the white purity.

The resolution was not promulgated by the Secretary of the Congress until September 3, 1777. The flag made according to this design was first carried in the Battle of the Brandywine, on September 11, 1777. There is a tradition that the first flag with these stars and stripes was made by Mrs. John Ross, better known as Betsy Ross, of 239 Arch Street, Philadelphia, at the request of General Washington. There is also a tradition that there was some discussion about the number of points which the stars should have. A star with six points had been made. According to one version General Washington did not like this and he folded a piece of paper and cut across it with the shears making a five-pointed star. According to another version the five-pointed star was cut by Mrs. Ross. In any event the star with five points was adopted.

Flags of different designs had been in use before the adoption of the Congressional resolution of June 14 and continued in use for some time afterward. As the Washington coat of arms contained stars and stripes it has been suggested that the national flag drew its inspiration from this, but the report of the Congressional committee on the design for the flag does not support this view. The new flag was hoisted on the naval vessels of the United States and it was first saluted by a foregin power when the "Ranger," in command of Captain John Paul Jones, arrived in a French port on February 14, 1778, with the flag flying.

The popular observance of the anniversary of the adoption of the flag was of slow growth. In 1889 George Bolch, principal of a free kindergarten for the poor in New York City, decided to hold patriotic exercises on that day. They attracted considerable attention and the State Department of Education arranged to have the day observed in all the public schools. Not long afterward the State Legislature passed a law providing that:

It shall be the duty of the State Superintendent of Public Schools to prepare a program making special provision for observance in the public schools of Lincoln's Birthday, Washington's Birthday, Memorial Day and Flag Day.

In obedience to this law the superintendent ordered that the flag should be displayed on every public school building at 9 o'clock in the morning and that there should be patriotic exercises with a history of the flag and the singing of songs. In 1897 the Governor of New York issued a proclamation ordering the display of the flag over all the public buildings in the state. This is sometimes called the first official recognition of the anniversary outside of the schools. But four years earlier the Mayor of Philadelphia, in response to a resolution of the Society of Colonial Dames of Pennsylvania, ordered the display of the flag on the public buildings in the city. The resolution was offered by Mrs. Elizabeth Duane Gillespie, a direct descendant of Benjamin Franklin, then president of the Colonial Dames of the state, and it proposed that the day be known thereafter as Flag Day and that the flag be displayed by all citizens on their residences and on all business places as well as on the public buildings.

President Wilson, on June 14, 1917, took advantage of the celebration of Flag Day to justify the declaration of war against Germany made on April 6. In his introduction to an eloquent address, he said:

We meet to celebrate Flag Day because this flag which we honor and under which we serve is the emblem of our unity, our power, our thought and purpose as a nation. It has no other character than that which we give it from generation to generation. The choice is ours. It floats in majestic silence above the hosts that execute those choices whether in peace or war. And yet, though silent, it speaks to us of the past, of the men and women who went before us and of the records they wrote upon it. We celebrate the day of its birth, and from its birth until now it has witnessed a great history, has floated on high the symbol of great events, of a great plan of life worked out by a great people. We are about to carry it into battle, to lift it where it will draw the fire of our enemies. We are about to bid thousands, hundreds of thousands, it may be millions, of our men, the young, the strong, the capable men of the Nation, to go forth and die beneath it on fields of blood far away— for what? For some unaccustomed thing? For something for which it has never sought the fire before? American armies were never before sent across the seas. Why are they sent now? For some new purpose, for which this great flag has never been carried before, or for some old, familiar, heroic purpose for which it has seen men, its own men, die on every battlefield upon which Americans have borne arms since the Revolution?

He then explained the reasons which had made it imperative that the United States should join the other nations engaged in resisting German aggression.

Although the anniversary is not a legal holiday in any of the states it has come to be observed in one way or another throughout the country. Special exercises are held in the public schools when the children are asked to pledge allegiance to the flag. Patriotic songs are sung and patriotic poems recited. It is customary to hold a celebration in the Betsy Ross House in Philadelphia, and the Patriotic Order of the Sons of America are in the habit of placing a wreath on the grave of Betsy Ross in Mount Moriah Cemetery in Philadelphia. The Daughters of the American Revolution observe the day with exercises of some kind. One chapter of this order presented flags to thirty-six newly organized Boy Scout Troops in 1934. The Sons of the American Revolution, not to be outdone by the Daughters, also hold exercises. The increasing observance of the day with the passing years has brought about a more lively appreciation of the significance of the varicolored bit of bunting as the banner of a free people.

JUNE FIFTEENTH

ASHEVILLE RHODODENDRON FESTIVAL

The blossoming of the rhododendrons in the mountains surrounding Asheville, N.C., has been celebrated by a festival since 1928. The celebration occurs in the middle of June, when the blossoms are at their best. It was in November 1927, that the directors of the Asheville Chamber of Commerce began to consider the project, and in February of the next year plans were perfected. At the first festival held in the following June, ten beautiful young women from the colleges in ten neighboring states were invited as guests of the city. A floral parade was held and there was a water carnival with decorated boats on Lake Craig. There was a rhododendron ball and a pageant, and a king and queen of the festival were selected from the young people of the city and crowned with elaborate ceremonies. There was also a baby parade and a night carnival with frolicking paraders. Visitors were taken on tours through the mountains to see the blossoms. The water carnival was abandoned and a "mutt" dog parade took its place in which the boys of the city and the surrounding towns entered their pets for prizes. Boys who owned thoroughbred dogs were allowed to join the parade but they could not compete for the prizes.

The festival in 1934 began on June 12 and ended on June 15, although tours of the mountains to see the blossoms were continued on June 16. A circus which started the festival on June 11, gave performances every day. On the second day there was a military ball given by the Rhododendron Brigade of Guards, organized in 1934 for the first time. At this ball Henley Richbourg, the king of the festival in 1933, called King Henley of the House of Richbourg, turned over the rule of the mythical Kingdom of Rhododendron to his successor, Grove Seely, called King Grove of the House of Seely and the candidates for investiture with a fantastic Order of Knighthood presented themselves to receive the honor. They were those who had been active in promoting the festival. There are three divisions in the order for men and one for women— the Civil Order of the Laurel, the Military Order of the Laurel and the Gentlemen at Arms. The branch for the women was the Order of the Azalea. There were three degrees in each order. The lowest was that of Knight, followed by Knight Commander, and the highest was that of Knight Grand Cross. A College of Heralds was also established the members of which were to have general charge of the details of the celebration.

The third day began with a floral parade in which beautifully decorated floats moved through the streets and in the evening there was a Rhododendron Pageant at which the king and queen were formally crowned. The king, as already indicated, was Grove Seely. The queen, known as Queen Myra of the House of Lynch, was Miss Myra Peyton Lynch. The pageant told the story of the imaginary Princess Rhodora "who calls the magic kingdom of Rhododendron into being." The baby parade opened the fourth day and in the evening there was a rhododendron ball at which the ten sponsors from the ten adjoining states were presented. There was a "mutt" dog parade in the morning of the fifth day at the close of which prizes were awarded to the best and worst dogs. Every boy with just a common dog who could get in line appeared with his pet. In the evening there was a carnival parade with burlesque floats and paraders in fantastic and ridiculous costumes, followed by a burlesque coronation of the King and Queen of Mirth. The formal celebration ended with a sponsors' ball at which the young women delegates from the ten states were guests of honor.

The visitors to the city were entertained not only by tours through the mountains but they were admitted to Biltmore House, the French chateau which the late George W. Vanderbilt erected a few miles from Asheville. The lower rooms were opened and a pamphlet was given to each visitor describing the rooms and their contents including historic furniture, tapestries and paintings.

IDAHO PIONEER DAY

What is regarded as the first permanent white settlement in Idaho was made at Franklin, in the southeastern corner of the state, on June 15, 1860. Governor James H. Brady issued a proclamation on April 26, 1910, fixing June 15 as Idaho Day to be observed in commemoration of the founding of Franklin. The next year the legislature changed the name to Idaho Pioneer Day and made it a legal holiday. All public offices are closed on the day and the pioneer societies in all parts of the state celebrate it with picnics, pioneer reunions, and in other ways.

White men had entered the region that is now Idaho long before the founding of Franklin. Lewis and Clark, during their explorations in 1804 and 1805, passed through the region and traced the sources of several rivers. In 1810 the Missouri Fur Company made an unsuccessful attempt to establish a trading post and the next year William P. Hunt, representing John Jacob Astor's Pacific Fur Company, made some explorations along the Snake River. Captain Bonneville's expedition entered the region in 1834 and a fort was built by Nathaniel Worth on the east bank of the Snake River north of Point Neuf. The Rev. Henry Spaulding and Dr. Marcus Whitman were active as missionaries within the territory from their station near Walla Walla, Washington. The Jesuit Fathers founded a missionary settlement on the Coeur d'Alene River in 1853 and in 1855 the Mormon missionaries extended their activities northward. But none of these made what is regarded as a permanent settlement, the honor for this achievement going to the men who founded Franklin.

Idaho was part of the great Northwest Territory. When it was organized as a territory by the act of March 3, 1863, it included the whole of Montana and nearly all of Wyoming. The act provided that nothing in it should be construed so as to prevent the Government of the United States "from attaching any portion of said territory to any other state or territory." A year later Montana was separated from Idaho and in 1868 Wyoming also was taken away leaving the boundaries of Idaho as at present. It was admitted to the Union as a state by the Act of July 3, 1890. In the early days there had been large migrations of Mormons into the region and in 1883 laws were passed providing that no polygamist might vote and the law was sustained by the United States

345

Supreme Court. When the heads of the Mormon church ruled that polygamy was not an essential article of faith the anti-Mormon restrictions were removed.

MAGNA CHARTA DAY

The anniversary of the signing of the Great Charter by King John of England in 1215 is observed by the Baronial Order of Runnemede, an American organization of descendants of the barons who met the King at Runnemede (other spellings of the name are Runnimede and Runnymede) and forced him to grant their demands. It was organized in the latter part of the nineteenth century with the object of fostering Anglo-American friendship. The descendants of the barons belonging to the order live in many different places and hold their celebrations sometimes in one city and sometimes in another.

The story of the granting of the charter is one of the most romantic in English history. King Henry I, on his accession in 1100, had signed a charter of liberties, but his successors had ignored its provisions from time to time until they disregarded them almost altogether. King John followed the example of his predecessors, trespassing upon the rights of the knights and the barons, diverting the courts from administering justice to serving his own ends and levying oppressive taxes to finance the wars waged to retain possession of his French provinces. When he was defeated in his attempt to win back Normandy by the battle at Bouvines in 1214 the barons decided to revolt. In January 1215, they met and demanded redress of their grievances, but John procrastinated. Later they marched in force upon London, which opened its gates to them. Other cities were equally friendly. Finally the King agreed to meet the barons on the bank of the Thames, about twenty miles from London and not far from Windsor, on June 15. The King rode to the meeting place from Windsor with a few attendants, and found the barons assembled on a meadow on the opposite bank of the river. They met the King on an island and presented him with a document which they demanded that he sign. He demurred at first, but the barons were insistent and threatening. He finally signed it and affixed his seal at the first meeting, on Monday, June 15. There were forty-eight demands made upon the King, and the next three days were occupied with the task of formulating them into a charter. On June 19 the work was completed and several copies which had been made were formally sealed. Then all swore to observe its provisions, and orders were issued to the sheriffs to publish it. The existing copies of the charter, however, all bear the date June 15. The conference did not adjourn until June 23, the time being occupied with arrangements for carrying out the reforms to which the King had agreed.

The essential clauses of the charter are those which protect the personal liberty and property of all freemen, by giving security from arbitrary imprisonment and spoliation. Although it is in its essentials a restatement of the rights granted by Henry I a hundred and fifteen years earlier it came to be regarded as the charter of English liberties and the basis of the British Constitution. It foreshadowed by more than five hundred years the Declaration of Independence and asserted against the King the rights of a privileged class, rights which the Declaration maintains belong to all men equally.

JUNE SIXTEENTH

FATHER'S DAY

The setting apart of a day on which to honor fathers by special services in the churches and in other ways, originated independently in different parts of the country in different years. And different days were chosen before there came to be general agreement on the third Sunday in June. It fell on June 16 in 1946.

The credit for making the first suggestion probably belongs to Mrs. John Bruce Dodd of Spokane, Wash. The idea occurred to Mrs. Dodd in 1909 as a suitable tribute to her own father who had successfully reared a family of children after the death of their mother. She wrote to the Rev. Conrad Bluhm, president of the Spokane Ministerial Association, proposing that the third Sunday in June be set apart for honoring fathers. The association approved the proposal and the first celebration of the day was held in Spokane in June 1910. Sons and daughters were asked to wear a red rose in honor of a living father and a white rose if the father was dead. Knowledge of the celebration did not spread far, for in 1911 the observance of Father's Day was discussed in Chicago as though it were something new. Miss Jane Addams approved it, saying, "Poor father has been left out in the cold. He doesn't get much recognition. But regardless of his bread-earning proclivities it would be a good thing if he had a day that would mean recognition of him." The discussion produced no general observance of the day.

A despatch from Vancouver, Wash., in the Portland *Oregonian,* for May 18, 1913, gives the impression that the people of Vancouver believed that the celebration of Father's Day originated there. The despatch states that a suggestion made in the *Oregonian* by the Rev. J. H. Berringer, pastor of the Irvington Methodist Church of Vancouver, in the previous year, that fathers be honored, was followed by special father's services in his church, thus establishing a custom which might "become a national one."

In 1920 Harry C. Meek, president of the Uptown Lions Club of Chicago was able to bring about the observance of a day in honor of fathers on the third Sunday in October. And in 1924 President Coolidge wrote to Mr. Meek: "As I have indicated heretofore, the widespread

347

observance of this occasion is calculated to establish more intimate relations between fathers and their children, and also to impress upon fathers the full measure of their obligations." President Wilson had antedated President Coolidge in recognizing Father's Day, for he pressed a button in Washington unfurling a flag on the platform at a celebration in Spokane. Mrs. Dodd, proud of her connection with the celebration, had already organized a Father's Day Association. Ten years after the first celebration in Spokane, Mrs. Walter Hamlet Burgess of Cheltenham, Pa., who was then a girl in Drewry's Bluff, Va., had taken out a charter for National Father's Day, incorporated, and registered the name in the United States Patent Office. She had then never heard of any observance of Father's Day. When she learned of Mrs. Dodd's activities she withdrew her claims to priority in establishing the day.

Before there was any widespread observance of the day Mrs. Charlotte Kirkbride and Mrs. D. Carrie Sternberg of Philadelphia induced J. Hampton Moore, a representative in Congress from that city, to introduce a resolution in the House of Representatives designating the first Sunday in June as Father's Day. This resolution did not pass; neither did a similar resolution introduced by Representative Bertrand H. Snell of New York.

A Father's Day of a different kind was observed on November 24, 1918, when at the suggestion of the *Stars and Stripes*, the official newspaper of the American Expeditionary Force in France, the fathers at home wrote to their sons in the field and the sons in the field wrote home. Arrangements were made for the delivery of the letters without delay. The war was over then and delivery was possible without risk.

While the rose is recognized as the appropriate flower for the day a white lilac with a green leaf was worn at first at the celebration in Vancouver, Wash. The members of the Martin W. Callener Bible Class of Wilkinsburg, Pa., selected the dandelion in 1924, as "the more it is trampled on the more it grows," but its use did not become general.

The confectioners have made Mother's Day profitable by offering candy specially wrapped as a gift. The tobacconists and haberdashers have likewise found profit in Father's Day from special sales of tobacco, cigars and neckties to be presented to fathers.

ORGANIZATION OF THE WORLD COURT

Although the United States was not affiliated with the League of Nations, Americans were actively engaged in the organization of the Permanent Court of International Justice and sat on its bench. The creation of a world court had been urged by American advocates of peace for many years. At the invitation of the League of Nations a conference of jurists met at The Hague to organize a court. Elihu Root who had been Secretary of State under Theodore Roosevelt was active in the organization. Popularly known in America as the World Court, it was commissioned to pass on juridical disputes between nations. It differed from the Arbitration Court at The Hague in that it was a permanent body of judges, while the Arbitration Court is a panel of judges from which disputants may select arbitrators.

The Permanent Court of International Justice has been superseded by the International Court of Justice under the United Nations organization.

JUNE SEVENTEENTH

BUNKER HILL DAY

The anniversary of the Battle of Bunker Hill, fought on June 17, 1775, is observed in Boston. Although it is not a legal holiday the banks are usually closed. The Battle of Bunker Hill was the second armed conflict between the colonists and the British forces in America. The first was the Battle of Lexington and Concord on April 19, 1775. The American army assembled around Boston was about sixteen thousand strong in May 1775. It surrounded the city, completely imprisoning the British on the land side. General Gage, reinforced by troops from England under Generals William Howe, Sir Henry Clinton and John Burgoyne, had an army of ten thousand.

On June 12 General Gage declared martial law and offered pardon to all who would return to their allegiance to England, excepting Samuel Adams and John Hancock. The Committee of Safety learned that he had decided to take possession of and fortify Bunker Hill and Dorchester Heights on the night of June 18. Colonel William Prescott was immediately ordered to march on the evening of June 16 with a thousand men, including a company of artillery, to take possession of and fortify Bunker Hill before General Gage could act. Instead of stopping at Bunker Hill Colonel Prescott moved on to Breed's Hill which was nearer Boston and commanded the city and the shipping in the harbor. The men worked all night building a redoubt and a flanking breastwork, and the British were astonished on the morning of June 17 to see the new fortification. The guns of the ships immediately opened fire on the redoubt, awakening the people of the city. The work of perfecting their defenses was continued by the American force until eleven o'clock in spite of the shower of shot and shell falling about them. At noon General Putnam, who was with Colonel Prescott's force, moved with a company of men to Bunker Hill to throw up fortifications there. A picked corps of three thousand men, led by Generals Howe and Pigot, crossed the Charles River to make an attack, and landed on the eastern base of Breed's Hill. In the meantime Colonel Prescott had received reinforcements. A little after three o'clock in the afternoon General Howe moved his guns toward the redoubt and opened fire, and the guns of the British ships and a battery on Copp's Hill in Boston bombarded the Americans. Colonel Prescott's men withheld their fire until the attacking force, moving on their works, were so near that they could see the whites of their eyes, then they fired volley after volley wreaking destruction upon the enemy and forcing it to retreat. Some shots had been fired at the British as they moved through Charlestown toward Breed's Hill and General Gage after their repulse ordered that the town should be burned. The British made a second attack but were again repulsed. The ammunition of the Americans was now exhausted and they were no longer able to resist and the redoubt was carried at the point of the bayonet after the battle had lasted for two hours. Of the three thousand British troops engaged a thousand and fifty-four were killed or wounded. The American loss was four hundred and fifty. Among the Americans killed was General Warren who had gone to the redoubt to give what aid he could. Although the Americans were defeated the gallantry with which they defended their position aroused enthusiasm throughout the country. The British ministry, dissatisfied with General Gage's conduct of the battle, removed him from command and appointed General Howe in his place.

On the fiftieth anniversary of the battle, June 17, 1825, the cornerstone of a monument to commemorate it was laid on Breed's Hill by Lafayette who was revisiting the country for the independence of which he had fought in his youth. The oration was delivered by Daniel Webster in the presence of a vast multitude which had assembled for the occasion. The monument is thirty feet square at its base and rises to a height of two hundred and twenty-one feet. The chamber at the top is reached by a flight of two hundred and ninety-five stone steps. Although the monument was begun in 1825 it was not completed until 1843. It was dedicated on June 17 on that year in the presence of President Tyler, his Cabinet, and a great company of interested citizens.

BLESSING THE BERRIES

It is customary in some of the agricultural regions of Europe for the people to gather on a fixed day at a religious ceremony in which the blessing of God upon the crops is asked. This custom was introduced in Boyle County, Ky., in 1930, at the suggestion of C. E. Miller, the county farm demonstrator. Berries are one of the principal crops of the county. On the third Sunday in June, beginning with 1930, a special service has been held in one of the churches in the county at which the people express their gratitude for the bountifulness of the crop. The service is always largely attended. In 1934 it was held in the Parksville Baptist Church on June 17. Officers of the Associated Fruit Growers Association of the county carried two crates of berries to the pulpit, representing the crop. The Rev. Dr. T. E. Cochran, pastor of the church, presided at the services. The invocation was offered by The Rev. E. L. Jorgenson, pastor of the Parksville Christian Church. The principal address was delivered by the Rev. A. E. Smith, pastor of the Perryville

Methodist Church, who dwelt on the debt of the people to the Giver of all good for the bounties of nature which they enjoyed and the duty of gratitude for their blessings. The benediction was pronounced by the Rev. Dr. William E. Phifer, pastor of the First Presbyterian Church of Danville. Among those present was a representative of the State College of Agriculture at Lexington. This annual ceremony of blessing the berries attracts attention throughout the state.

JUNE EIGHTEENTH

SUSAN B. ANTHONY FINED FOR VOTING

Susan B. Anthony, one of the most militant of the advocates of equal suffrage, insisted on voting at an election in Rochester, N. Y., in 1873. She was arrested, tried, convicted and on June 18 of that year was sentenced to pay a fine. Miss Anthony was born of Quaker parents in South Adams, Mass., in 1820, taught school for fifteen years and after the Civil War devoted herself wholly to the equal suffrage movement. She published a woman's rights paper, called *The Revolution*, for two years, and lectured throughout the country. She was for many years the president of the American Women Suffrage Association, relinquishing that office in 1901. She died in 1906, honored by those who had been associated with her. Because of her advocacy several states granted the privilege of voting to women but it was not until 1920 that the privilege was granted to women throughout the nation by the adoption of the Nineteenth Amendment to the Federal Constitution.

JUNE NINETEENTH

NEW CHURCH DAY

Emanuel Swedenborg, whose followers organized themselves into the Church of the New Jerusalem, commonly called the New Church, attached the following memorandum to *The True Christian Religion*:

After this work was finished the Lord called together his twelve disciples, who followed him in this world; and the next day He sent them all out into the spiritual world, to preach the Gospel that the Lord God Jesus reigns, whose reign will be for ages of ages, according to the prediction of Daniel, VII: 13-14; and in Revelation XI: 15 and that they are blessed who come to the wedding supper of the Lamb, XIX, 9. This was done on the nineteenth of June in the year 1770.

In the New Church Annals, which quotes this passage, it is stated that "from this date, therefore, may be counted the actual beginning of the New Church in the spiritual world."

351

JUNE 20

The significance of this date in the history of their church was not at first appreciated by the followers of Swedenborg. In the course of time, however, they noted that they were holding important meetings on June 19 and soon afterward they began consciously to fix that date for their meetings and to hold services appropriate to the celebration of the anniversary notable in the history of their organization. Swedenborgians in various parts of the United States and in other countries who adopted the custom of taking note of the day send congratulatory telegrams and cablegrams to one another.

The Rev. Gilbert H. Smith, in the course of an explanation of the significance of the day, said that it was celebrated as the anniversary of the second coming of Jesus as Christmas was the anniversary of His first coming. He explained that in 1757 there was a great judgment in the spiritual world called the Last Judgment when the evil spirits were separated from the good, and a New Heaven was set up. Then Swedenborg wrote the doctrines of the New Church and as it was necessary that there should be someone to preach them to the spirits in the New Heaven Jesus called his disciples together on June 19, 1770, and commissioned them to preach them in the spiritual world, and the next day sent them forth. Mr. Smith explains:

And this is the reason why the nineteenth and twentieth of June are such important days to us, because that was the very first beginning of the New Church when Peter and James and John and the rest of the twelve disciples, were sent by the Lord everywhere in the spiritual world to teach the Doctrine of the New Church and to tell them that the Lord God Jesus Christ reigns.

(See January 29, Swedenborg's Birthday.)

JUNE TWENTIETH

WEST VIRGINIA DAY

In December 1862 Congress passed an act providing for the admission of West Virginia to the Union as an independent state on condition that certain changes were made in its proposed Constitution. Those changes were made and on April 20, 1863, President Lincoln issued a proclamation that admission should take effect sixty days later. Thus West Virginia entered the Union on June 20. This day is a legal holiday in the state, observed by the display of flags and in other ways. Special note of the day is taken in those public schools which are then in session.

West Virginia was originally part of the old State of Virginia. Its economic life, however, was different from that in the eastern part of the state. The region is mountainous and it was settled by woodsmen and small farmers who owned few slaves. Its citizens frequently complained of unfair representation in the State Legislature as representation was based in part on the slave population of the eastern end of the state. When the Civil War began and Virginia passed its ordinance of secession there was much dissatisfaction in the west. Meetings of protest were held and on May 13, 1861, delegates from twenty-five counties met at Wheeling and called a convention to meet on June 11. Representatives from forty counties attended the convention and declared their independence of Virginia and elected Francis H. Pierpont as provisional governor. A legislature, which had been elected, met on July 2 and chose two United States Senators who went to Washington and were admitted to the Senate. A constitution was adopted on May 3, 1862, and what was called the Legislature of the "Restored Government of Virginia" gave formal assent to the separation of West Virginia. This was followed by the Act of Congress admitting the new state.

Virginia in 1907 brought suit in the United States Supreme Court to collect from West Virginia its proper share of the debt of the state incurred before the separation. The court decided that West Virginia must assume responsibility for about $12,000,000 of the debt and for about $8,000,000 in interest which had been paid by Virginia, but it also decided that there should be offset against this to the credit of West Virginia about $3,000,000, its share of the assets arising from the original debt.

JUNE TWENTY-FIRST

THE CONSTITUTION RATIFIED

The last article in the Constitution of the United States provides that "the ratification of the conventions of nine states shall be sufficient for the establishment of this Constitution between the states so ratifying the same." The Constitutional Convention ended its work on September 17, 1787. It was not until June 21, 1788, that New Hampshire, the ninth state, ratified it. The United States Government formed by the Constitution began on that date. The conventions of the following states, in the order named, had ratified it before June 21: Delaware, Pennsylvania, New Jersey, Georgia, Connecticut, Massachusetts, Maryland and South Carolina. Rhode Island was the last of the thirteen States to approve the Constitution and it did not act until May 29, 1790.

RIOT OF UNPAID REVOLUTIONARY SOLDIERS

In June 1783, a large body of soldiers and non-commissioned officers stationed at Lancaster, Pa., angry because they had not been paid, decided to march on Philadelphia to demand from the Executive Council of the state the settlement of their grievances. Although the Executive Council asked that the militia be called out to stop the men before they reached Philadelphia, nothing was done. Upon their arrival they were quartered in the barracks and on Saturday, June 21, about thirty of them, fully armed, marched to the State House, now known as Independence Hall, where the Executive Council was in session. They presented their demands which they insisted should be granted within twenty minutes. The Council rejected the demands; in the meantime the number of soldiers had increased to about three hundred. A special meeting of Congress was called, but a quorum did not appear. Those members present arranged to meet later in the day at Carpenters' Hall, when a quorum was present and a resolution was adopted calling on the Executive Council to use "effectual measures" to compel the obedience of the soldiers to their officers. The Council took no "effectual measures" and Congress adjourned to meet at Princeton, N.J. The trouble was adjusted in a few days and the rebellious men returned to Lancaster. Congress was asked to resume its sitting in Philadelphia and proper protection was promised, but instead of accepting the invitation it voted to meet at Annapolis, Md.

BIRTHDAY OF DANIEL CARTER BEARD

Daniel Carter Beard, American artist, author, and naturalist was born in Cincinnati, Ohio, in 1850. For many years he was a successful magazine illustrator, and he also illustrated numerous books, of which the most notable is Mark Twain's *Connecticut Yankee at the Court of King Arthur*. In 1905 and 1906 he was the editor of a magazine known as *Recreation*. An enthusiast of outdoor life, he instituted what later became an international movement when he founded the first Boy Scouts' Society in the United States. The Boy Scouts of America, an outgrowth of the early organization, chose Beard as its national commissioner. He was awarded the gold eagle badge, the only one ever awarded; and the Roosevelt gold medal for distinguished service in 1927. Mt. Beard, the peak adjoining Mt. McKinley, discovered by the Browne and Parker expedition, was named for him. Fifty thousand Boy Scouts assembled in the Court of Peace at the New York World's Fair on June 21, 1940, to honor his ninetieth birthday. He died in 1941.

The Boy Scouts of America was incorporated in 1910 and chartered by Congress in 1916, its aim being to develop the character of boys and train them for the duties of adult life by influence brought to bear in their work and play. Its national constitution declares the intention to "promote the ability of the boys to do things for themselves and others, to train them in scout craft, and to teach them patriotism, courage, self-reliance, and kindred virtues." Each boy, on joining the organization, takes the scout oath promising to keep himself "physically strong, mentally awake, and morally straight." The movement is nonsectarian and without military or political connection. The Boy Scouts cooperate with the Forestry Department in its various activities, work with the Red Cross in aiding local campaigns, and are usually organized in troops connected with churches or schools, although boys living beyond the reach of a regular organization may join the movement as Lone Scouts. It is note-worthy that scouting as a modern art is almost wholly American in origin. It was carried to perfection by the Indian fighters and backwoods-men of pioneer days who developed a technique and tradition admirably adaptable as training for boys between the ages of twelve and eighteen.

JUNE TWENTY-SECOND

THE BEGINNING OF OSTEOPATHY

Dr. Andrew Taylor Still, a Kansas physician, not satisfied with the accepted theories of his profession, decided that the cause of disease could be found "in the limited or excited action of the nerves which control the fluids of part or the whole of the body," and, as he writes in his *Autobiography*, "on June 22, 1874, I flung to the breeze the banner of osteopathy." Through his efforts a College of Osteopathy was opened at Kirksville, Mo., in 1892, and he became its first president. Since that date several other similar colleges have been established and the practice of osteopathy has been legalized on the same basis as the practice of other medical systems. The American Osteopathic Associa-tion was organized in 1897. Its headquarters are in Chicago where it publishes four periodicals.

JUNE TWENTY-THIRD

THE PENN TREATY WITH THE INDIANS

A tradition which survives with great persistence is that William Penn made a treaty with the Lenni Lenapi or Delaware Indians at Shacka-maxon on the Delaware river, now part of Philadelphia, soon after his arrival in America. A picture of Penn and the Indians under a tree has been painted. There is a small park on the site marked by a monument bearing the inscription. "Treaty Ground of William Penn and the Indian Nation. 1862. Unbroken Faith." Penn made several treaties of one kind or another with the Indians. It is known that he made one on June 23, 1683, at the head of Chesapeake Bay for he referred to in it his letters. A committee of the Pennsylvania Historical Society, appointed in 1835 to inquire into the historical evidence of the Shackamaxon treaty, found that Penn did have a conference with the Indians under an elm tree at that place in November 1682. No reference to such a conference, how-ever, has been found in Penn's correspondence. June 23 is also the birth-day of William Penn.

355

JUNE TWENTY-FOURTH

ST. JOHN'S DAY

The feast of St. John the Baptist is said to be one of the oldest if not the oldest introduced into the liturgies of the Greek and Latin churches in honor of a saint. It is celebrated on the day of his birth instead of on the day of his death, which is customary with other saints. This is because he was sanctified before his birth.

He was the son of Zachary, a priest, and Elizabeth, a cousin of Mary, the mother of Jesus. His birth was foretold to Zachary by an angel while he was burning incense at the altar in the temple in Jerusalem. Zachary, who was childless, doubted the prediction and as a punishment he was stricken with dumbness which continued until the child was born. The exact date of the birth is unknown, but it has been agreed to accept June 24, as he was born about six months before Jesus and as December 25 is celebrated as the date of the birth of the Savior. But that date has been fixed arbitrarily in the absence of exact information. Nothing is known of the early life of John, but when he was about thirty years old he is found living as an anchorite in the wilderness beyond Jordan and preaching repentance and baptism. He was asked whether he was the Messiah, but he denied it and said that there was one coming after him the latchet of whose shoes he was unworthy to unloose. Jesus went to him to be baptized; John at first objected but finally consented. As they were coming out of the water a voice from heaven proclaimed "This is my beloved Son in whom I am well pleased."

John continued to preach and there arose disputes between the followers of Jesus and those of John. When they were taken to John he explained that Jesus "must increase but I must decrease," a saying which has been used to explain the celebration of midsummer day on June 24, when the days begin to grow shorter, and the celebration of Christmas on December 25, when the days have begun to grow longer.

John preached within the tetrarchy of Herod Antipas and when Herod, after marrying the daughter of the king of the Nabathaeans, went to Rome, fell in love with Herodias, the wife of his half-brother, and took her back with him, John denounced him for his offense. On the demand of Herodias he had John arrested and imprisoned. According to Josephus, however, Herod was afraid that John, because of his influence over the people would incite them to rebellion, and "thought it wiser, so as to prevent possible happenings, to take away the dangerous preacher . . . and he imprisoned him in the fortress of Machaerus." He remained in prison for a long time, but finally Herodias persuaded her daughter Salome, to whom Herod had promised anything she wished because he was pleased with her dancing, to ask for the head of John on a dish.

Herod reluctantly kept his promise and John was beheaded. (See Decollation of John Baptist, August 29.)

There are various traditions about his burial place and about the final disposal of his body. One tradition is that he was buried at Sebaste. In the fourth century his tomb there was honored. It is said to have been desecrated by Julian the Apostate about 362. Part of the remains were said to have been carried to Jerusalem and then to Alexandria where on May 27, 395, they were deposited in the basilica of St. John which had recently been dedicated on the site of a temple of Serapis. Many churches of the old world claim possession of some of the bones of the saint.

As already indicated St. John's Day was long associated in Europe with the midsummer festivities. These survive in the United States among the descendants of immigrants from that part of the world. The summer solstice was associated with the rites of sun worship long before the Christian era. Many of these survived for centuries among the Christians. On St. John's Eve fires were built on every hill, a survival of the old custom of Burning Beltane fires, or fires to the god Bel or Baal. Bathing was a pagan custom on St. John's Eve, and this was forbidden by the church, as well as round dances on the anniversary. An old Druid custom survived at Magdalen College, Oxford, for many years when a stone pulpit in an inner court was covered with green branches and turned into a bower. A clergyman mounted this pulpit and preached a sermon on the life of St. John. The students used to explain the custom by saying "This is St. John in the wilderness."

The Irish used to believe, and some of them may still do so, that on St. John's Eve the soul of every person left his body, found the place where death would overcome the body and then returned to its owner. An old English superstition is that a person sitting all night fasting on a church porch would see passing before him all the persons in the parish who would die during the year.

SWEDISH MIDSUMMER FESTIVAL

The Swedes have brought their midsummer celebration to the United States. The manner of it is described by Amalie Hofer in the Year Book of the Playground Association of America for 1908. She says:

One of the oldest festivals of the present time is the midsummer national merrymaking of the Swedish people, set for June 24. Again, no gathering outside of the native country on this day is so large as that held in some of the Chicago parks. Owing to the unavoidable thrift of the hardworking middle class making up the 175,000 Chicago Swedes St. John's Day is celebrated on the Sunday nearest to the 24th. In the old country where industrial interests are homogeneous the entire population is set free for whatever day of the week the day may fall upon. In this country no united recognition has as yet been secured for the day, and while Sunday is free many American and Swedish Methodists withhold their cooperation. Nevertheless the European out of door Sunday custom prevails to draw 30,000 or more to this most completely reproduced of old world festivals. Family groups are everywhere conspicuous and intoxicants and vulgarities are entirely prohibited. The fifteenth annual midsummer day celebration for Chicago was held last June 21, (1908) and promptly at one o'clock the customary raising of the majestic Maypole took place. The pole, seventy feet high, was bound with garlands and dressed in streamers. Great wreaths decorated the upper end.

In the old country each province has a different arrangement of pole decorations, various local emblems and souvenirs being utilized. The Chicago audience, being made up from many different provinces, has adopted a decorative scheme of its own. One great wreath is bound around the top of the pole and two others like the arms of a cross on either side. These are intertwined with the Swedish and American colors. As the pole was raised into place the "Star Spangled Banner" was played with a potpourri of Swedish national and folk songs. Then followed a carefully planned program of athletics, singing and dancing by various organizations occupying different platforms that the eager thousands might be accommodated. Sixteen folk dances representing the traditional dances and costumes of the different provinces of Sweden were a highly applauded feature. Some of the dancers were from the old country. Others were Chicago business men and their wives, notably members of the Philochorus Society of Chicago, organized fifteen years ago for the definite purpose of preserving in full detail the folk games and dances of the old time. Many of the dances were pantomime figures telling of courting, attracting and repelling, winning and losing, and compelling against odds, and carrying off the bride. In it all there was a clearness of good story telling and purity of natural feeling and straightforward exhibition of the old law that the fittest shall be the victor. It was on a level with epic poetry and bold saga. . . . The crowning and closing of the Midsommarbrud was carried out in all the traditional detail and proved to be more than a merely pretty affair, one that had a uniquely democratic fair play purpose. Out of the great assembly six men were named, men of family, each of whom was responsible, to nominate two married women, who each selected two of the most beautiful young women present, making twenty-four, probably all strangers to each other, possibly never having met until the afternoon of the festival. These selected from their own number the loveliest of all and proclaimed her the Midsommarbrud. Standing in all her beauty, tall and calm, surrounded by her generous peers, all wreathed and decorated, she was crowned and garlanded and formally presented with the customary gold medal, this medal of handsome and elaborate workmanship, having from time immemorial the same design of the Swedish arms—the Chicago medal having added the Stars and Stripes. This annual crowning took place at four o'clock and thousands in historical as well as in modern costumes gathered to witness the brilliant spectacle.

JUNE TWENTY-FIFTH

THE CUSTER MASSACRE

It was on June 25, 1876, that Lieutenant Colonel George A. Custer and his force of two hundred and eight men were slain by a much larger force of Indians on the Little Big Horn river in Montana. He was engaged in one of three expeditions, commanded by General Crook, General Terry and General Gibbon, sent out by General Sherman against the Indians under Sitting Bull. Lieutenant Colonel Custer with his regiment formed part of General Terry's force. After General Crook had fought an indecisive engagement, General Terry, unaware of Crook's failure to overcome the Indians, sent Custer with the Seventh Cavalry up the Rosebud river to locate the enemy. On June 24 Custer's scouts reported that the Indians were on the west bank of the Little Big Horn. He divided his men planning to take the Indians by strategy without knowing how large a force was assembled against him. He made the attack the next day but was driven back and completely surrounded and in an engagement lasting not more than twenty minutes he and all his men were slain. Their bodies were found on the next day stripped of clothing and all were scalped except Custer. General Sherman in his report of the campaign said that it had been planned on wrong premises as there was nothing to indicate that any detachment would meet more than six or eight hundred Indians.

Custer was born at New Rumley, Harrison County, Ohio, on December 5, 1839, the great-grandson of a Hessian officer named Kuster who served with Burgoyne and after Burgoyne's defeat settled in Pennsylvania. Custer served brilliantly as a cavalry leader in the Civil War and was brevetted a major general of volunteers. After the war he served in the Indian wars in the West and wrote of his experiences.

JUNE TWENTY-SIXTH

AMERICAN TROOPS LAND IN FRANCE

The United States declared War against Germany on April 6, 1917 (see Army Day, April 6) and as soon as possible a small body of troops was sent to France as a guarantee of good faith. The first contingent landed on the continent on June 26 and was welcomed enthusiastically by the French people and the French Government. As they marched through the streets of Paris they were cheered to the echo and emotional men and women wept tears of gratitude. These were the first troops which had ever left the United States to engage in a foreign war on the continent of Europe. It was not until the next year, however, that any considerable number of soldiers were sent across the ocean. Before the close of the first World War about two million men had been sent, with immense stores of ammunition and other military supplies.

JUNE TWENTY-SEVENTH

BIRTHDAY OF HELEN KELLER

Helen Adams Keller, probably the most notable blind deaf mute in the history of education, was born a normal child at Tuscumbia, Ala., on June 27, 1880. Her family on her father's side was connected with the Spottiswoods and Lees of Virginia and on her mother's side with the Adamses and Everetts of Massachusetts. When she was nineteen months old she had scarlet fever which left her without the sense of sight or hearing and consequently unable to learn to talk. No attempt was made to educate her until she was eight years old. She was then put under the care of Miss Anne M. Sullivan, who had been trained at the Perkins Institution for the Blind at Boston. With infinite patience Miss Sullivan taught her to communicate through her hands. She then taught her to read Braille. When she had learned to read Miss Keller was determined to learn to talk and was taught by Miss Sarah Fuller of the Horace Mann School in New York. She prepared for college and was graduated from Radcliffe in 1904. She was then appointed to the Massachusetts Commission for the Blind and served on many committees interested in the relief of the sightless. While still in college she wrote a book which she called *Optimism*; later she wrote several other books and lectured widely.

JUNE TWENTY-EIGHTH

WORLD WAR I

By a coincidence, the international incident which precipitated World War I, and the signing of the Treaty of Versailles which marked its end, both occurred on June 28. The World War of 1914-18, in which the United States became involved in 1917, started with the assassination at Sarajevo, Bosnia, of the Archduke Franz Ferdinand, heir to the throne of Austro-Hungary. The archduke had left Vienna, accompanied by his wife, the archduchess, on June 24, to attend the military maneuvers in Bosnia as commander of the Austro-Hungarian armies. On Sunday, June 28, 1914, they paid a visit of ceremony to Sarajevo, narrowly escaping death from a bomb thrown at their carriage as they entered the town. Later in the day both were shot and killed while they were returning from a reception at the town hall. The Serbian minister at Vienna had warned the Austrian Government against the visit since it was known there was a plot against the archduke's life. However, the Austrian Government held the Serbian Government responsible for the crime and made various demands upon it, that were not met, and the conflicting interests of the European Powers in the Balkan Peninsula led to an outbreak of hostilities which spread till they involved the continent of Europe and the United States.

After four years of savage conflict which devastated large areas of France, Germany surrendered unconditionally to the Allies, and on June 28, 1919, the Treaty of Versailles was signed. By its terms, Germany lost her navy, her merchant marine, all of her overseas possessions and about

13 per cent of her European domain. She was required to abolish compulsory universal military service, her army was reduced in size until it was impotent, all importation and exportation, and nearly all production, of war material was prohibited; and as a final humiliation she was forced to permit the trial of her ex-emperor, Kaiser Wilhelm, by an international high court on the charge of "a supreme offense against international morality."

JUNE TWENTY-NINTH

ST. PETER'S DAY

The exact date of the birth or the death of St. Peter is unknown. Since the third or fourth century, however, June 29 has been observed as the chief feast day in his honor and as the day of his death. According to the traditions of the Church he met his death as a martyr in Rome under Nero. Origen says that he "was crucified with his head downward, as he himself had desired to suffer." Tradition says that he made this request as he was unworthy to suffer as Jesus had suffered. The martyrdom is supposed to have taken place perhaps in A.D. 64 in the gardens of Nero at the foot of the Vatican Hill, where, according to Tacitus, Nero had his victims tortured. He was buried there, but later his body was removed to a vault on the Appian Way. And, again, according to tradition, it was restored to its original resting place where Constantine the Great erected a basilica over it. This was replaced by the present St. Peter's church in the sixteenth century under the altar of which the body now rests.

Peter, whose name was originally Simon, was a fisherman of Capernaum on the Sea of Galilee. He and his brother Andrew became followers of John the Baptist. Later they met Jesus and became followers of his. On one occasion Jesus asked his disciples who men said that he was. After they had answered he asked them who they thought he was and Simon replied: "Thou art Christ, the Son of the living God." Thereupon Jesus said: "Blessed art thou, Simon Bar-Jonah; because flesh and blood hath not revealed it to thee, but my Father who is in heaven. And I say to thee: That thou art Peter and upon this rock I will build my church and the gates of hell shall not prevail against it." He was recognized as the chief of the disciples. After the crucifixion he traveled about Asia Minor preaching to the Jews and to the Gentiles, baptizing Cornelius the centurion and his family and eating meat with them, contrary to the custom of the Jews who refrained from eating with Gentiles. Such evidence as there is that he went as far West as Rome is contained in the conclusion of his first epistle in which he wrote "The church that is at Babylon, elected together with you, saluteth you." Biblical scholars in both the Protestant and Roman Catholic churches assume that Rome is meant by Babylon, as ancient Babylon was then in ruins and as the city which had taken its place was known by a different name.

Many legends grew up about St. Peter. One is that the Gentiles shaved his head to make him an object of derision and that from this the tonsure originated. In Christian art he is usually represented with the tonsure when he is not shown wearing the papal tiara and carrying the keys—a golden key to unlock the gates of heaven and an iron key to open the gates of hell. It was not until the eighth century, however, that he was shown with the keys. According to one tradition regarding his death he started to flee from Rome after Nero had burned the city and accused the Christians of the crime, but he had a vision of Jesus who told him to return to the city. He was then seized by the soldiers of Nero and, with St. Paul, thrown into the Mamertine prison, from which he was taken to his death.

JUNE THIRTIETH

ST. PAUL'S DAY

Although, according to the traditions of the Roman Church St. Peter and St. Paul suffered martyrdom on the same day, June 30 is observed as the festival of St. Paul. While St. Peter was crucified in a public place, St. Paul, who was a Roman citizen, was beheaded in private. The accepted tradition is that he was executed two miles from Rome at a place now known as the Three Fountains. This name was given to the place because, according to the tradition, his head as it fell to the ground struck the earth three times before coming to rest and at each spot a fountain burst forth. On his way to the place of execution it is said that a Roman matron who was a Christian stood on the Ostian way to look upon him for the last time. St. Paul asked for her veil that he might bind his eyes so that he should not see the sword used by the executioner. He promised to return it to her. As the story goes he did appear to the woman with the veil stained with his blood thus keeping his promise. Cardinal Aldobrandini built the Church of St. Paul of the Three Fountains on the spot in 1590. This church is said to contain the marble pillar to which St. Paul was bound by his executioners.

The story of the life of St. Paul is told more fully in the New Testament than that of any of the other followers of Jesus. It is a romantic tale, full of perils by land and by sea, of miraculous escapes and of eloquent preaching of the gospel in which he believed. He was a Jew, born in Tarsus, educated in the doctrines of the Pharisees in Jerusalem and a persecutor of the new sect of Christians. He was a party to the stoning of Stephen the first martyr. On his way to Damascus to continue his persecutions he was stricken blind by a great light and heard a voice from heaven rebuking him and calling on him to change his course. This was in the year 34 or 35. He was led to Damascus by his companions and was blind for three days when his sight was restored to him by a follower of Jesus who baptized him after his conversion to the new faith. He did not immediately begin to preach the new doctrines, but retired to Arabia for nearly three years. When he did begin his ministry the Christians were afraid of him for they knew his record, but he finally convinced them of the sincerity of his conversion. He traveled throughout Asia Minor, visited Macedonia and Athens and Corinth. When he returned to Jerusalem the Jews entered into a plot to kill him, but the Roman authorities learned of the plot and sent him under the escort of a large company of soldiers to Caesarea to be tried on the charges which the Jews made against him. He appealed to Rome as he was a Roman citizen and was sent there by ship in the autumn of 57 or 58. The ship was wrecked on the island of Malta, but no lives were lost. St. Paul finally reached Rome where for two years he lived in his own hired house preaching to the Christians there. As the charges against him related to Jewish customs there was reluctance to bring him to trial in Rome. There is a tradition that he was allowed to visit Spain where he preached to the Christians and organized churches. It was not until Nero charged the Christians with burning Rome that the authorities decided to do away with him. The story of his adventures is told quite fully in the Acts of the Apostles.

Declaration of Independence

JULY

The linden, in the fervors of July,
Hums with a louder concert. When the wind
Sweeps the broad forest in its summer prime.
As when some master hand exulting sweeps
The keys of some great organ, ye give forth
The music of the woodland depths, a hymn
Of gladness and of thanks.

—BRYANT

July, originally the fifth month of the Roman year, was known as Quintilis, but when the calendar was changed it became the seventh month and was named July for Julius Caesar. The change was made by order of Marcus Antoninus, better known as Mark Antony, during his consulship. He was a kinsman of Caesar's through his mother. He unsuccessfully tried to persuade the Romans to make Caesar emperor. The best that he could do was to have a month named for him, the month in which he was born. The new name came into use in 44 B.C., the year of Caesar's death at the hand of Brutus. Mark Antony is the man who had the affair with Cleopatra and in whose mouth Shakespeare puts an oration over the dead body of Caesar. The Anglo-Saxons called the month Litha se oefterra, meaning lithe or mild. The old Saxon name for it was Maed-monath because the meadows were in bloom and the cattle were then turned out to feed. It was also called Lida oeftevr by them, meaning the genial month. Until the end of the eighteenth century the name of the month was pronounced with the accent in the first syllable, thus recalling its origin from Julius. Wordsworth, writing in 1798, rhymed it with "truly," and Suckling, writing in 1646, rhymed it with "newly." It is noted in American history because the Declaration of Independence was adopted in its first week.

JULY FIRST

THE BATTLE OF GETTYSBURG

The most important and hotly contested battle of the Civil War began at Gettysburg, Pa., on July 1, 1863, and continued for three days. The Federal Army of the Potomac, commanded by General Meade, numbered about eighty-two thousand men, and the Confederate Army of Northern Virginia, commanded by General Lee, contained about seventy-three thousand. Lee's plans, after the Battle of Chancellorsville, had been to cross the Susquehanna at Harrisburg and march on Philadelphia. When he learned that the Army of the Potomac was in Maryland he changed his plans. He hoped to defeat that army and to march on Baltimore and Washington. On June 30, General Meade concluded that General Lee intended to give battle at once and he prepared for the attack. Buford's cavalry, six thousand strong, met the van of Lee's army near Seminary Ridge on the morning of July 1, when a sharp skirmish followed. General Reynolds with his army heard the firing and hastened to the relief of Buford. While he was placing his men on the Chambersburg road the Confederates made an attack which was answered by a volley of musketry from the Fifty-sixth Pennsylvania Regiment, led by Colonel J. W. Hoffman. Thus began the famous battle. General Reynolds was killed not long afterward by the bullet from a sharpshooter's rifle and his place was taken by General Doubleday. The fighting increased in fury as the day advanced and it continued with the advantage first on one side and then on the other for the next two days. On the third day occurred the memorable and heroic charge of Pickett's brigade upon Cemetery Ridge. The Confederates had been concentrating their artillery fire on the ridge and had been answered by the Federal batteries stationed there. After about an hour and a half the Federal batteries ceased firing to save ammunition. The Confederates misconstrued this and Pickett was ordered to take the ridge by assault. He moved forward with five thousand men, only to be met by a withering artillery fire. It is said that two thirds of his command were killed or wounded or captured. Fighting ceased on the fourth day, and during the night following Lee began his retreat, leaving the Federals victorious and the invasion of the North definitely checked.

Will Henry Thompson, in his stirring poem, "High Tide at Gettysburg," tells the story of Pickett's charge. The concluding stanzas follow:

> God lives! He forged the iron will
> That clutched and held that trembling hill!
> God lives and reigns! He built and lent
> The heights for Freedom's battlement,
> Where floats her flag in triumph still!

Fold up the banners! Smelt the guns!
Love rules. Her gentler purpose runs.
A mighty mother turns in tears
The pages of the battle years,
Lamenting all her sons.

The anniversary of the battle is observed locally each year, usually in connection with exercises on July 4. Important anniversaries have been marked by more elaborate celebrations.

In 1913 the observance of the fiftieth anniversary lasted for four days. It was attended by both G.A.R. and Confederate veterans. Mrs. Helen D. Longstreet, the widow of General James Longstreet, who, after the death of "Stonewall" Jackson, became General Lee's principal advisor, was the guest of honor. Special exercises commemorated the arrival of General Buford's men, the appearance of the Texas troops, and Pickett's charge. An address by President Wilson on July 4 brought the celebration to a close.

The sixtieth anniversary in 1923 was marked by the re-enactment on July 2 of Little Round Top Battle by modern artillery.

JULY SECOND

FIRST EXHIBITION OF HUSSEY'S REAPER

Obed Hussey of Maryland obtained a patent for a reaper in 1833, and on July 2 of that year he exhibited it in public for the first time on the grounds of the Hamilton County Agricultural Society in New York. There had been reaping machines before Hussey's. Pliny, writing in 23 A.D. mentions one used in the lowlands of Gaul. It consisted of a cart carrying a box on the front edge of which were sharp projecting teeth. Pushed through the grain by an ox, it caught the heads of the grain, and a man sitting in the box raked them in. During the latter part of the eighteenth century and the first part of the nineteenth century a number of reapers were invented but they were not satisfactory. Hussey's machine contained pointed knives which vibrated through a bar cutting the grain which fell on a platform from which it was raked by a man riding on the machine. C. H. McCormick of Virginia patented a machine in 1834, similar in many respects to Hussey's. These two machines formed the basis on which the modern reaper has been built, a device which made possible the development of the great wheat fields of the West. The machine has been improved until it has been combined with a threshing machine, so that with a single process the grain is reaped, threshed and put in sacks as the enormous machine moves through the field. With the old hand process it would have been impossible to harvest grain enough to feed the people in this country.

366

JULY THIRD

BIRTHDAY OF JOHN SINGLETON COPLEY

John Singleton Copley, one of the most important American painters of his time, was born at Boston, Mass., of Irish parents, on July 3, 1737. He received his early artistic instruction from his stepfather, Peter Pelham, a mezzotint engraver. He showed great skill and at the age of seventeen he was recognized as a painter of merit. In 1769 he married the daughter of a rich Boston merchant and bought a stately house on Beacon Hill and was soon commissioned by the society people of the city to paint their portraits. Many of them are preserved in public museums. His paintings were exhibited at the Royal Academy in London, and in 1774, on the invitation of Benjamin West, he went to that city where he painted the portraits of Lord North and of the King and Queen. He made his residence thereafter in London and was elected to the Royal Academy in 1779. His son, named for him, born at Boston in 1772, grew up in England, became a lawyer, entered Parliament, was knighted in 1818, and in 1827 was promoted to the House of Lords as Baron Lyndhurst and became Lord Chief Baron of the Exchequer.

IDAHO ADMITTED TO UNION

See Idaho Pioneer Day, June 15.

JULY FOURTH

INDEPENDENCE DAY

John Adams guessed wrong when he wrote to his wife on July 3, 1776, of the adoption by the Continental Congress on the day before of the resolution offered by Richard Henry Lee of Virginia that "these United Colonies are, and of right ought to be, free and independent." He said in his letter:

The Second of July, 1776, will be the most memorable epoch in the history of America. I am apt to believe that it will be celebrated by succeeding generations as the great anniversary festival. It ought to be commemorated as the day of deliverance, by solemn acts of devotion to God Almighty. It ought to be solemnized with pomp and parade, with shows, games and sports, guns, bells, bonfires and illuminations, from one end of this continent to the other, from this time forward, forevermore. You will think me transported with enthusiasm, but I am not. I am well aware of the toil and blood and treasure that it will cost us to maintain this Declaration and support and defend these States. Yet, through all the gloom, I can see rays of ravishing light and glory. I can see that the end is more than worth all the means. And that posterity will triumph in that day's transactions, even although we should rue it, which I trust God we shall not.

JULY 4

It is July 4, the anniversary of the adoption of a declaration justifying and explaining itself out of "a decent respect to the opinions of mankind" and not July 2, that is celebrated with pomp and parade. The story of the adoption of the Lee resolution and of what is known in history as the Declaration of Independence is told in the *Journal of the Continental Congress* for 1776. The entry for Friday, June 7, notes that the following resolutions had been moved and seconded:

Resolved, That these United Colonies are, and of right ought to be, free and independent states, that they are absolved from all allegiance to the British Crown, and that all political connection between them and the State of Great Britain is, and ought to be, totally dissolved.

That it is expedient forthwith to take the most effectual measures for forming foreign Alliances.

That a plan of confederation be prepared and transmitted to the respective colonies for their consideration and approbation.

Consideration of these resolutions was postponed until the next day and all the members were "enjoined" to be present. The resolutions were debated in committee of the whole, but no action was taken and arrangements were made to continue the consideration on Monday, June 10. The committee of the whole resumed the debate on Monday and at its conclusion arose and submitted to the Congress the following resolution:

Resolved, That the consideration of the first resolution be postponed to this day, three weeks, and in the meanwhile that no time be lost, in case the Congress agree thereto, that a committee be appointed to prepare a declaration to the effect of the first of said resolutions, which is in these words: "that these United Colonies are, and of right ought to be, free and independent states; that they are absolved from all allegiance to the British Crown; and that all political connections between them and the state of Great Britain is, and ought to be, totally dissolved."

On the following day a committee of five members was appointed to draft the proposed declaration. Thomas Jefferson was the chairman. His associates were John Adams, Benjamin Franklin, Roger Sherman and Robert Livingston. Seventeen days later, on Friday, June 28, the committee submitted a draft of what has come to be known as the Declaration of Independence. It was read and laid on the table. On Monday, July 1, the Congress took up the resolution of June 7, consideration of which had been postponed on June 10 for three weeks. The resolution was debated in the committee of the whole, but action was postponed for a day. The next day, July 2, it adopted the Lee resolution, the one which stirred John Adams to write the rhapsodical letter to his wife already quoted. Then the committee of the whole began to consider the Declaration reported by the committee of five on June 28, and resumed consideration of it on July 3, and again on July 4. Following is the official record of its adoption:

Agreeable to the order of the day the Congress resolved itself into a committee of the whole to take into further consideration the Declaration. The presi-

dent resumed the chair. Mr. Harrison reported that the committee of the whole
Congress have agreed to a Declaration which he delivered in.

The Declaration being again read, was agreed to as follows:

"THE UNANIMOUS DECLARATION OF THE THIRTEEN UNITED STATES OF AMERICA.

"When in the course of human events it becomes necessary for one people
to dissolve the political bands which have connected them with another, and to
assume among the Powers of the earth, the separate and equal station to which the
Laws of Nature and of Nature's God entitle them, a decent respect to the opinions
of mankind requires that they should declare the causes which impel them to the
separation. . . ."

The adoption of this historic statement was celebrated by the people
of Philadelphia on the following Monday, July 8, by a mass meeting in
Independence Square, or the State House Yard, as it was then called.
It was read by John Nixon from a platform which had been erected by
the American Philosophical Society in 1769 from which to observe the
transit of Venus, and had not been removed. According to a description
of the event by John Adams a great crowd of people assembled. "Three
cheers rended the welkin," he wrote. "The battalions paraded on the
Common and gave us the *feu de joie*, notwithstanding the scarcity of
powder. The bells rang all day and almost all night. Even the chimes
chimed away." The chimes referred to were probably those in the tower
of Christ Church the rector of which was a well known royalist. Other
contemporary accounts are interesting. Charles Biddle, in his autobiography, says: "I was in the old State House Yard when the Declaration of Independence was read. There were few respectable persons
present." And Mrs. Deborah Logan, who lived in a house facing the
square on the east, wrote that "the first audience of the Declaration was
neither very numerous nor composed of the most respectable class of
citizens."

The Declaration was promulgated to the army in general orders by
General Washington on July 9. After announcing that the Continental
Congress had voted to dissolve the connection between the colonies and
Great Britain, the order continued:

The several brigades are to be drawn up this evening on their respective
parades at six o'clock, when the declaration of Congress, showing the grounds and
reasons of this measure, is to be read in an audible voice. The general hopes
this important event will serve as fresh incentive to every officer and soldier to
act with fidelity and courage, as knowing now that the peace and safety of his
country depends, under God, solely on the success of our arms, and that he is
now in the service of a state possessed of sufficient power to reward his merit and
advance him to the highest honors of a free country.

It occurred to someone in Philadelphia on July 2, 1777, that the
anniversary of the adoption of the Declaration should be celebrated.
The time was short, but arrangements for a dinner were made and Congress adjourned for the day. John Adams, in a letter to his young

daughter, described what was done. He said that the bells rang all day, that there were bonfires in the streets and fireworks in the evening. The war ships in the river were dressed with flags and at one o'clock the men on the ships were ordered aloft on "the tops, yards and shrouds, making a striking appearance . . . of companies of men drawn up in order in the air." He went on board the "Delaware" with the President of the Council and other gentlemen and they were greeted by a salute of thirteen guns from each ship in succession. The dinner which had been arranged was served at three o'clock with music furnished by "a band of Hessians taken at Trenton." Between the toasts a company of soldiers stationed outside the city tavern where the diners had assembled fired continual volleys. After the dinner there was a parade of the soldiers in the city. Mr. Adams says that in the evening he took a walk for exercise and "was surprised to find the whole city lighting up their candles at the windows. I walked most of the evening and I think it was the most splendid illumination I ever saw; a few surly houses were dark, but the lights were very universal. Considering the lateness of the design and the suddenness of the execution I was amazed at the universal joy and alacrity that was discovered and the brilliancy and splendor of every part of this joyful exhibition." Mr. Adams did not tell his daughter that the patriots broke the windows in the houses which were not illuminated, but this is noted by another contemporary authority.

There was a more elaborate celebration of the anniversary in Philadelphia in 1788 when it was known that the Constitution had been adopted by the requisite number of states. The last article of that document provided that "The ratification of the conventions of nine states shall be sufficient for the establishment of this Constitution between the states so ratifying the same." The people of the city, which was the capital of the country at the time, followed the action of the various states with deep interest. As the conventions in state after state expressed their approval the Federals were exultant and in June a company of them met in Eppley's tavern and decided that as soon as the ninth state ratified, the event should be properly celebrated. New Hampshire became the ninth state on June 21 and arrangements were at once made for a celebration on the Fourth of July in honor of the establishment of the new federal union. Virginia became the tenth state to ratify before the celebration was held. An official report of the occasion was prepared and published on July 8 by Francis Hopkinson, the chairman of the committee of arrangements. Mr. Hopkinson, in the introduction to his report, wrote:

The rising sun was saluted with a full peal from Christ Church steeple and a discharge of cannon from the ship "Rising Sun," commanded by Captain Philip Brown, anchored off Market Street, and superbly decorated with the flags of various nations. Ten vessels in honor of the ten States of the Union, were dressed and arranged through the whole length of the harbor, each bearing a broad white flag at the masthead, inscribed with the names of the States, respectively in broad gold letters. . . . The ships at the wharves were also dressed for the occasion,

and as a brisk south wind prevailed through the whole day, the flags and pendants
were kept in full display, and exhibited a most pleasing and animating prospect.
According to the orders issued the day before, the several parts which were to
compose the grand procession began to assemble at eight o'clock in the morning
at the intersection of South and Third Streets. Nine gentlemen, distinguished by
white plumes in their hats and furnished with speaking trumpets, were superintendents of the procession, viz.: General Mifflin, General Stewart, Colonel Proctor,
Colonel Gurney, Colonel Will, Colonel Marsh, Major Moore, Major Lenox and
Mr. Peter Brown.

The streets had been swept and the trees trimmed over the line of
march and all obstacles removed so that the parade might move freely.
The procession extended over a mile and a half and it took it three
hours to march over a route three miles long to Bush Hill, the residence
of William Hamilton, Esq., where it disbanded. It was led by twelve
axemen, dressed in white frocks, with black girdles around their waists
and wearing ornamental caps. The First City Troop of Light Dragoons,
commanded by Captain Miles, came next. This troop was followed by
five symbolical groups. The first was "Independence," led by John
Nixon, Esq., mounted and carrying a flag with the inscription, "Fourth
of July, 1776." The second was "French Alliance," led by Thomas
Fitzsimmons, Esq., carrying a flag of white silk adorned with three
fleurs-de-lis and thirteen stars and the date, "Sixth of February, 1778."
The third was the "Definitive Treaty of Peace," led by George Clymer,
Esq., carrying a staff ornamented with olive and laurel from which hung
a banner containing the words, "Third of September, 1783." Peter
Muhlenberg, Esq., led the fourth group called the "Convention of the
States." He carried a blue flag with the inscription, "Seventeenth of
September, 1787." The last symbolic group was "The Constitution."
Chief Justice McKean, Judge Atlee and Judge Rush, in their robes of
office, rode on a lofty ornamented car in the form of an eagle, drawn
by six horses, bearing the Constitution, framed and fixed on a staff
crowned with the cap of Liberty and the words "The People" in gold
letters on the staff immediately under the Constitution. Then came
ten gentlemen representing the states, the consuls and diplomatic representatives of foreign countries in alliance with the United States, public
officials, and representatives of various organizations. This was followed
by a float bearing what was described as a Federal Edifice. It consisted
of a dome supported by thirteen Corinthian columns, with a frieze decorated with thirteen stars. Ten of the columns were completed and three
left unfinished. There was a cupola on top of the dome surmounted
by a figure of Plenty and around the base of the structure was the inscription, "In union the fabric stands firm." There were eighty-eight
divisions in the parade, the greater part of them made up of members
of the various trades and occupations in the city including cordwainers,
coach makers, blacksmiths, tanners, sugar refiners and stay makers.
Tables with a cold collation had been arranged in a circle on the
grounds of Bush Hill and when the last division of the parade arrived

the Federal Edifice was set up in the center of the circle. James Wilson mounted the float and delivered what Mr. Hopkinson describes as "an eloquent oration." Then several companies of soldiers "fired a *feu de joie* of three rounds, also three volleys, followed by three cheers, to testify their satisfaction on this joyful occasion." Mr. Hopkinson concludes his report in this way:

After the oration the company went to dinner. No spirit or wines of any kind were introduced. American porter, beer and cider were the only liquors. With these were drunk the following toasts, announced by the trumpet, and answered by a discharge of artillary, a round of ten to each toast, and these in like manner were answered by a discharge from the ship "Rising Sun," at her moorings. The Toasts: The People of the United States; Honor and Immortality to the Members of the Late Federal Convention; General Washington; The King of France; The United Netherlands; The Foreign Powers in Alliance with the United States; The Agriculture, Manufactures and Commerce of the United States; The Heroes Who Have Fallen in Defense of Our Liberties; May Reason, and Not the Sword, Hereafter Decide All National Disputes; The Whole Family of Mankind. . . . As the system of government (now fully ratified) has been the occasion of much present joy, so may it prove a source of future blessing to our country, and the glory of our rising empire.

The celebration of the Fourth of July gradually spread throughout the country and into the new states and territories as they were admitted to the Union or as they were created, until the day is a holiday in every state and territory. Particular attention has been given to the anniversary in Philadelphia. There was a special celebration there and elsewhere on the fiftieth anniversary and on the one hundredth anniversary an international exposition was held in that city. And another international exposition was held there on the one hundred and fiftieth anniversary. In 1914, George W. Ochs, then editor of the *Public Ledger*, convinced that a national celebration of the day should be held every year at Independence Hall, started a movement which resulted in bringing President Woodrow Wilson to the city to make an Independence Day address, but the succeeding presidents have not found it convenient to make an annual visit to the scene of the adoption of the Declaration.

The first celebration in Boston did not occur until 1783. That city had been in the habit of celebrating March 5, the anniversary of the Boston Massacre. (See the Boston Massacre, March 5.) At the celebration in 1783, at which James Otis presided, a resolution was adopted declaring that the observance of the anniversary of the massacre should cease and that "instead thereof the anniversary of the Fourth Day of July, 1776—a day ever memorable in the annals of this country for the Declaration of Independence—shall be constantly celebrated by the delivery of a public oration in such place as the town shall determine most convenient for the purpose." In May a town meeting was held at which Samuel Adams presided, and a committee was appointed to make needful arrangements. The committee chose as orator Dr. John Warren, whose brother, General Joseph Warren, had been killed at the Battle of

Bunker Hill, and decided that as Fanueil Hall was not large enough to hold the celebration it should be held in Dr. Cooper's church in Brattle Street.

The report of the celebration in the Boston *Gazette* says, "The joy of the day was announced by the ringing of bells and the discharge of cannon." Governor Hancock was unable to attend because of illness, but at eleven o'clock a procession was formed at the old State House headed by Lieutenant Governor Thomas Cushing, who with the Honorable Council, the Senate and the House of Representatives and a long line of citizens under the escort of a train of artillery marched to the church. The Rev. Dr. Cooper, it is said, made a "polite and elegant address and at its conclusion returned thanks to Almighty God for His goodness to these American States and for the glory and success which had crowned their exertions; and the solemnity was concluded by a most eloquent and ingenious oration by Dr. John Warren." After the exercises in the church there was a military parade in State Street and then the Lieutenant Governor, the Council, the members of the Senate and the House had a "private sit-down" in the Senate Chamber at which thirteen patriotic toasts were drunk, one of which was "May the spirit of union prevail in this country."

By 1810 the Boston celebration had grown more elaborate and was participated in by a larger number of organizations. The official celebration was held in the morning at the Old South Meeting House, preceded by a military parade from the State House through the principal streets. The address was delivered by the Reverend William Ellery Channing. There was another parade in the afternoon preceding a dinner served to six hundred persons in Fanueil Hall. The Bunker Hill Association joined by the Young Republicans who had celebrated at the Exchange Coffee House, marched under a military escort to Bunker Hill in the afternoon where a dinner was eaten and many toasts were drunk. And in the evening there was a display of fireworks on the Common viewed by at least ten thousand persons.

Accounts of the celebration in other cities in 1810 have been preserved. In New York, by order of the city government, salutes were fired and the bells of the churches were rung at sunrise, at noon and at sunset. The masters of the ships in the harbor displayed their flags at the mastheads during the day, and the flag was also displayed on all public buildings. There was a military parade and review at the Battery at seven o'clock in the morning. At noon the Washington Benevolent Society, gathered on College Green, was joined by the Hamilton Society and paraded with banners bearing the names of deceased Revolutionary patriots. In the evening there were fireworks and "a grand operatic melodrama" entitled "Free Knights, or the Edict of Charlemagne," followed by the afterpiece, "The Caravan, or the Driver and His Dog."

In Washington salutes were fired at dawn and at intervals during the day. At ten o'clock an oration was delivered by Robert Polk in the Baptist church near the White House. The exercises were attended by President Madison and the heads of the various departments of the government. At noon the President held a reception. Later a dinner was served at Long's Hotel, attended by public officials and by Count Pahlen, the Russian minister. Twenty toasts were drunk. At another dinner at Lindsay's Hotel, consisting entirely of American fare, thirty toasts were proposed and drunk.

In Richmond, Va., the formal celebration was limited to a parade and dinner by the militia. The Richmond *Enquirer* observed that "there was no civic celebration of the day in this city, no orations, and no public rehearsal of the Declaration of Independence; omissions which were regretted by the more patriotic citizens."

The use of fireworks in the celebration of the anniversary became general in the course of the years. The day was filled with the noise of their explosions from early morning until late at night and many persons inexperienced in handling them were killed or injured. The number became so great that early in the present century the Chicago *Tribune* began to collect the statistics every year and to demand that a saner way of celebration be devised. As the result of the early years of its campaign the loss of life fell from 466 in 1903 to 215 in 1909 but about 5000 were injured by fireworks. In 1903 Springfield, Mass., forbade the sale of fireworks and arranged a quiet and orderly observance of the day. As a result there were no fires and no one was injured. In the intervening years many cities have followed the example of Springfield and have forbidden the sale of fireworks and such displays as have been allowed have been arranged by responsible organizations and in charge of men who understand the danger.

The day has been selected for starting many important undertakings. Governor DeWitt Clinton of New York turned the first sod for the digging of the Erie Canal on July 4, 1817. Charles Carroll, the last surviving signer of the Declaration of Independence, turned the first sod for the building of the Baltimore and Ohio Railroad, the first railroad in the country, on July 4, 1828. He said: "I consider this among the most important acts of my life, second only to that of signing the Declaration of Independence, if, indeed, second to that." To the Blacksmiths' Association, which presented to him the tools used, Carroll wrote:

You observe that republics can exist and that the people under that form of government can be happier than any other; that the republic created by the Declaration of Independence will continue to the end of time is my fervent prayer. That protracted existence, however, will depend on the morality, sobriety and industry of the people, and on no part more than on the mechanics, forming in our cities, the greatest number of their most useful citizens.

The cornerstone of the Washington monument in the National Capital was appropriately laid on July 4, 1850.

In 1919 the foreign governments with which the United States had been associated in the first World War arranged a celebration in Washington as an expression of their appreciation of the part this country had taken in winning the victory, and the governments which had taken no part in the war joined with them in the demonstration. It began at five o'clock in the afternoon with a series of tableaux arranged on the steps of the buildings surrounding the grounds of the Washington monument. They represented "Bugle Call to World Service," "Call of Labor," "Call of Liberty," "Call of Commerce, Business and the Professions," "Call of Children," "Call of Art," "Call of the Land" and "Offering of Peace." This was followed by a parade of floats from the Treasury Building to the Capitol by way of Pennsylvania Avenue. Lieutenant General Robert L. Bullard was the grand marshal of the parade and Colonel Roy H. Glen, honorary attaché of the British embassy, was the chief marshall. General Bullard's staff of aides included representatives of many foreign countries.

As one of the purposes of the demonstration was to celebrate the return of peace the first float contained figures representing the return of the soldiers to their ordinary vocations. This was followed by the French float to which this place of honor was given as a tribute to the valor with which she had defended herself for more than four years in the war which had ended in the previous November. It contained a figure representing the Spirit of Advancement seated on an elevated dais, while below it were two figures, one representing Alsace and the other Lorraine, joined to the upper figure by wreaths of laurel. Brazil was represented by twenty sailors taken to Washington from a Brazilian battleship anchored in New York harbor. The Spanish float, described as "A joyous shower of flowers from sunny Spain in tribute of peace," carried figures dressed in seventeenth century Spanish costumes. The Italians had a reproduction of "Il Carrochia," or the chariot, associated with the battle of Legano in 1176, when the Italians defeated Frederick Barbarossa and their cities ultimately obtained their liberty. The float carried a bell and figures of warriors of various centuries of Italian history.

A company of Russians, opposed to the rule of the Bolsheviks, carried the Russian imperial flag and the naval ensign. The British float had a figure of Britannia seated on a throne, while before her was a miniature garden with a maypole surrounded by dancing children. A miniature Fujiyama appeared on the Japanese float on which were seated figures representing Peace and Independence. Five young women representing the five chief products of the country sat on the Chilean float. Peru presented a series of tableaux on her float showing life in that country. Portugal was represented by a man in native costume carrying the national flag. Bolivia showed a bust of Samuel Bolivar and Norway provided a reproduction of a Viking ship with Lief Ericson in command. Guatemala exhibited a temple of Minerva and a modern locomotive to remind the spectators that she was the first Central American country to build a transcontinental railroad. Sweden showed a smallpox and bubonic plague were wiped out, the population increased four geniuses of history along with figures of Gustavus Adolphus, Swedenborg, Linnaeus and Charles XII. Denmark, like Norway, presented a Viking ship manned by a Viking along with a figure of Peace. The floats of Venezuela, Ecuador, Colombia, Uruguay and Salvador contained the national coats of arms. China offered a pavillion of peace surmounted by a golden phoenix. Panama had a miniature canal and called her float "The Kiss of the Oceans." Belgium was represented by seven young women, mounted, and carrying flags for the seven battles on Belgian soil. William Tell appeared on the Swiss float standing with his son near a cottage on the slopes of the Matterhorn. Greece showed the Parthenon and Athena surrounded by maidens posed with urns on their shoulders. The agricultural industries of Honduras were represented by that country. The Netherlands showed the negotiations between them and the Indians on the bow of the Half Moon in which Henry Hudson sailed up the Hudson river in 1609. Jugoslavia showed arms stacked beside a plow to indicate that the people were ready for peace or war. A palm tree surmounted by a liberty cap was the contribution of Haiti. The Rumanian float was similar to that of Jugoslavia. Persia presented Omar Kayyam seated among Persian rugs. Czechoslovakia, which had obtained its independence as a result of the war, presented a float representing the fulfillment of an ancient prophecy. Poland presented a figure of Freedom rising out of the rack of war and Lithuania also showed figures typifying the union of her people.

Following the parade there was a pageant at the east front of the Capitol symbolizing the return of peace to the world, and the victory of love and justice over hatred and jealousy. A chorus of a thousand voices assisted and the Marine Band played.

This was the most elaborate and impressive celebration of the anniversary ever held in Washington, particularly because of its international character.

It was long the custom in many towns throughout the East to celebrate the Fourth of July with two parades. In the morning there was a burlesque parade of Horribles, as they were called. Men and boys dressed in fantastic costumes anticked through the streets making a noise with all sorts of devices to the delight of the spectators save those who had no sense of humor. In the afternoon there would be a parade of military veterans and the members of various local organizations followed by a patriotic address.

One of the unusual celebrations of the day occurred for several years in Greeley, Colo. Beginning in 1922 it held what it called an Annual Greeley Spud Rodeo and Fourth of July Celebration, which attracted visitors from Weld County of which it is the county seat, and from neighboring counties. There were the usual rodeo contests among riders of bucking horses, expert ropers of steers, together with races, cow milking contests, and similar sports. Money prizes were paid to the winners, varying from $5 to $200 for the first prize.

PHILIPPINE INDEPENDENCE

On March 22, 1934, the Tydings-McDuffie Act was passed by Congress granting the Philippine Islands independence from the United States after a ten-year transitional commonwealth government under a Filipino executive. World War II was in progress at the expiration of the ten-year period and formal recognition of Philippine Independence did not occur, therefore, until July 4, 1946. In Manila, on that date, there was an official celebration of the event with speeches, flag raisings, planes circling overhead, a twenty-one gun salute, and a parade led by crack troops of the Philippine Army which the United States had returned to Philippine command on June 30. Paul McNutt, retiring United States Commissioner, appointed as the first United States ambassador to the Philippine Republic, read the formal proclamation from President Truman which transformed the Commonwealth into a Republic. Manuel Acuna Roxas, the Republic's first President, delivered a public address, as did General Douglas MacArthur who, when ordered out of the Philippines just before the fall of Bataan and Corregidor, had promised to return and had kept his promise.

The United States originally obtained control of the Philippine Islands during the war with Spain in 1898, as a logical outgrowth of the protest against Spanish misrule in Cuba. Assistant Secretary of the Navy Theodore Roosevelt ordered Commodore George Dewey to attack with his Pacific Fleet if war came. Dewey obeyed and won an overwhelming victory which gave the Philippines to the United States, although Spain was eventually paid twenty-two million dollars. Magellan had discovered the Islands for Spain in 1521 and, as with Cuba, they had endured a long history of Spanish abuse. Under American rule the Philippines prospered, enjoying the best health in the Orient. Cholera, small pox and bubonic plague were wiped out, the population increased from seven to sixteen millions, and the average height of the citizens from four feet, eleven inches to five feet, four inches. After World War II the United States promised six hundred and twenty million dollars in war damages, reparations and public works. The Bell Act, passed by the Congress of the United States on April 30, 1946, gave to the Philippine Republic eight years free trade with this country, followed by twenty years during which tariffs will be raised gradually until they are in line with the rest of the United States tariff policy.

BIRTHDAY OF CALVIN COOLIDGE

Calvin Coolidge, the thirtieth President of the United States, was born at Plymouth, Vt., on July 4, 1872. He was named John Calvin for his father, but when he grew to manhood he dropped "John," as Grover

Cleveland and Woodrow Wilson, respectively, dropped "Stephen" and "Thomas" from the names which their parents gave to them. His father was a farmer and country storekeeper, descended from John Coolidge, born in Cambridge, England, in 1604, who came to America in 1630, and settled at Watertown, Mass. In 1780 one of John Coolidge's descendants moved to Plymouth, Vt., where that branch of the family continued to live. President Coolidge's father was one of the substantial citizens of the state, serving two terms in the State Legislature and holding the rank of colonel on the military staff of Governor W. W. Stickney, from 1900 to 1902.

After attending the district school at Plymouth the son, at the age of thirteen, entered the academy at Ludlow, ten miles from his home. He completed his preparation for college at St. Johnsbury Academy, and entered Amherst College, at Amherst, Mass., in 1891, and was graduated in 1895. In the autumn of 1895 Coolidge began to study law in the office of Hammond & Field in Northampton, Mass., and in due course was admitted to the bar. While he was a senior in college, he wrote an essay on "The Causes of the American Revolution" for which he was awarded by the American Historical Society a gold medal valued at $150 for the best essay on a historical subject by a senior in any American college. He served on the City Council of Northampton during 1899, although he had been a resident for only four years. He served as City Solicitor for the next two years and was the clerk of the courts in 1904. He served two terms as a member of the lower house of the Massachusetts Legislature in 1907-1908, was Mayor of Northampton in 1910-1911 and a member of the State Senate from 1912 to 1915, and president of that body in 1914-1915. In his address on taking the chair he stated his conception of the nature of law when he said:

Men do not make laws. They do but discover them. Laws must be justified by something more than the will of the majority. They must rest on the eternal foundation of righteousness. That state is the most fortunate which has the aptest instruments for the discovery of laws.

He served three one-year terms as lieutenant governor and was governor in 1919 and 1920. The strike of the Boston police occurred in September of his first term. The police were not satisfied with their pay and formed a union affiliated with the American Federation of Labor in the course of their campaign for better pay. Permission to affiliate with that body, however, had been denied by the police commissioner and nineteen members of the force were put on trial on the charge of violating the commissioner's ruling. The outcome of the dispute was a strike and rioting in the streets. The mayor ordered out the militia in Boston and called on the governor for more troops from other parts of the state. This was in accordance with the procedure laid down in the law. Samuel Gompers, president of the Federation of Labor, intervened in the controversy and Governor Coolidge replied to him in a long letter in the course of which he defended what had been done and said: "There is no right to strike against the public safety by anybody, anywhere, anytime." This raised him into national prominence and he was asked to tour the country with a series of addresses but he declined. He was reelected governor, by a much greater majority than he had received the first time.

There was talk of nominating him for the presidency on the Republican ticket but he did not encourage it. After the Chicago convention had nominated Warren G. Harding for President, Judge Wallace McCammant of Portland, Ore., mounted the platform and announced that his "delegation had been instructed to vote for Senator Lodge . . . but there is another citizen of Massachusetts . . ." and before he could finish the delegates were shouting the name of "Coolidge." The nomination for vice president was seconded by many states and Coolidge was nominated on the first ballot by six hundred and seventy-four and one-half votes. The Republican ticket was elected and Coolidge began his national career on March 4, 1921, as the presiding officer of the United States Senate. President Harding went to visit Alaska in the summer of 1923. On his way back he was taken ill and died in San Francisco at half past seven o'clock on the evening of August 2. The news was telegraphed east and, a little before midnight, reached Mr. Coolidge, who was visiting his father at Plymouth. At half past two on the morning of August 3, he took the oath of office by the light of a kerosene lamp in the sitting room of the house. It was administered by his father who was a justice of the peace. After his arrival in Washington, where he went immediately, the oath was again administered by a Judge of the District of Columbia Courts and he assumed the responsible duties of the office.

In his first message to Congress, in December, he made many recommendations, but his declaration, in ten words, of opposition to the immediate payment of a bonus to the veterans of the first World War was hailed as an exhibition of political courage which commanded much admiration. It was largely responsible for his nomination to succeed himself by the Republican National Convention in 1924. He was elected in November. In 1928, there was talk of nominating him again, but before it crystallized he announced from the place in the West where he was spending his vacation, "I do not choose to run." Many of his supporters professed to regard this as an indefinite statement and they discussed plans for forcing the nomination upon him, but when the convention met in 1928 he had instructed a personal representative to check any efforts to nominate him. The convention named Herbert Hoover, who had served eight years as Secretary of Commerce.

On his retirement from the presidency Coolidge returned to Northampton, Mass., bought a house and planned to spend the remainder of his life in his law office and with his books. His health failed, however.

and he died suddenly on January 5, 1933, and was buried at Plymouth where he was born. In 1934, on the anniversary of his death, a large company of people went to Plymouth and held memorial exercises at the grave in the rural cemetery in the Vermont hills ten miles from a railroad.

JULY FIFTH

BIRTHDAY OF ADMIRAL FARRAGUT

David G. Farragut, the first admiral in the navy of the United States, was born near Knoxville, Tenn., on July 5, 1801. His father was a native of the island of Minorca who had emigrated to the United States in 1776 and took an active part in the Revolutionary War. The son was adopted by Commodore Porter in 1808 and two years later entered the navy as a midshipman. He was assigned to the ship commanded by his foster father, and accompanied it on its cruise in the Pacific, distinguishing himself in a battle with two British ships in the War of 1812. He served in various subordinate capacities until 1838 when he was placed in command of the sloop "Erie" and three years later was raised to the rank of commander. He served brilliantly in the Mexican War after which he established the Mare Island Navy Yard in San Francisco Bay. He was stationed at the Norfolk Navy Yard when the Civil War began and when Virginia seceded he left the state and offered his services to the Federal Government. He forced the Confederate forts commanding the mouth of the Mississippi in April 1862, and captured New Orleans; and conducted a brilliant attack at Mobile Bay in 1864. He was raised to the rank of rear admiral in 1862 and in 1864 was made vice admiral and, in 1866, Congress, which had created the grades of rear admiral and vice admiral in order to honor him, created the rank of admiral for the first time and promoted him to it. He died in 1870.

JULY SIXTH

THE FOUNDING OF THE REPUBLICAN PARTY

The anniversary of the founding of the Republican party at Jackson, Mich., on July 6, 1854, is observed periodically at that place by members of the party. There was an especially notable celebration in 1934 on the eightieth anniversary, at which "keynote" speeches were made in preparation for the approaching election campaign.

The party arose because of the demoralization of the old Whig Party and the dissatisfaction of many Northerners with the attitude of the Democrats toward the slavery issue. It had been assumed that the issue had been settled by the adoption of the Missouri Compromise which forbade the introduction of slavery in any part of the Louisiana territory north of the southern boundary of Missouri, while permitting slavery in Missouri. But it did not stay settled. The passage of the Kansas-Nebraska Bill on May 27, 1854, which permitted new states to decide whether they were to be free or slave, repealed the Missouri Compromise and aroused the opponents of slavery. On February 28 a mass meeting of Whigs, Democrats and Free Soilers, held in Ripon, Wis., had resolved that if the bill should pass they would "throw old party organizations to the winds and organize a new party on the sole issue of the nonextension of slavery." A local organization was effected three weeks later and the name Republican suggested for the new party. The Michigan opponents of slavery gathered at Jackson on July 6, organized a party, adopted the name Republican, and arranged for the nomination of candidates for all offices to be filled. Other opponents of slavery met in other parts of the country at various times and organized themselves as Republicans. Within less than a year the new party had elected eleven United States Senators and a large number of members of the national House of Representatives.

The first national convention was held in Philadelphia on June 17, 1856, the anniversary of the battle of Bunker Hill. A preliminary convention had been held in Pittsburgh, on Washington's Birthday, called by the chairmen of the Republican state committees of several Eastern and Western states. Twenty-three states were represented. The delegates present voted to call a national convention to nominate candidates for President and Vice President in Philadelphia on the date already mentioned. All the Northern states were represented as well as Maryland, Virginia, Kentucky and the territories of Minnesota, Nebraska, Kansas and the District of Columbia. Robert Emmet of New York, formerly a Democrat, was the temporary chairman and Colonel Henry S. Lane of Indiana, the permanent presiding officer.

The selection of a candidate for President gave the delegates much trouble. William H. Seward of New York, although in sympathy with the new party, declined to accept the nomination. Salmon P. Chase, United States Senator from Ohio, withdrew his name as he had been closely identified with the Democratic party and it was thought he could not carry his state. John McLean of Ohio, a Justice of the Supreme Court and a former Postmaster General under Monroe and Adams, was considered but his name was withdrawn. Colonel John C. Fremont, whose political experience was confined to a brief service as Senator from California, remained. He had a wide reputation as a soldier and explorer, however. It was urged against him that he could not carry Pennsylvania and the name of Judge McLean was revived. On an informal ballot, however, Fremont received 359 votes and Judge McLean 196. The nomination of Fremont was thereupon made unanimous. In the election he received 114 electoral votes to 174 cast for James Buchanan, the

Democratic candidate. In the election of 1860, however, the Republicans won with Abraham Lincoln in a three-cornered contest, and won every succeeding national election until that of 1884, when Grover Cleveland, the Democratic candidate, defeated James G. Blaine, the Republican nominee.

JULY SEVENTH

THE OPENING OF COLUMBIA UNIVERSITY

King's College, in New York city, the name of which was changed to Columbia College in 1784, opened on July 7, 1754, with eight students and Dr. Samuel Johnson, its president, as the only instructor. The need of a college in the Province of New York had been discussed for a long time and when a fund of £3500 had been raised, chiefly by lottery, a royal charter was obtained from King George II and the school was opened. A medical school was opened in 1767. The Committee of Safety seized its buildings in 1776 and all exercises were practically suspended until the end of the Revolutionary War. When they were resumed the name was changed to Columbia College. Because of insufficient endowment its growth was slow but by the middle of the nineteenth century the land which it owned had increased in value with the growth of the city and the institution began to expand. By 1896, a number of graduate schools had been added and the name was changed to Columbia University. It has grown to be one of the largest universities in the country and includes such special departments as schools of law, medicine, journalism, engineering, and a teachers college.

ANNEXATION OF HAWAII

Hawaii was annexed to the United States in 1898, and since then its history has been American history. In the eighteenth century the islands were in a stage of civilization barely past savagery. There were many kings, and the land was held in military tenure when it was discovered by Captain Cook in 1778. Cook named the group the Sandwich Islands after the fourth Earl of Sandwich. A half century later the American Board of Foreign Missions dispatched seven missionaries and their wives to convert the inhabitants to Christianity. Then, in 1843, Captain Paulet, a British naval officer, demanded that Hawaii declare her allegiance to Great Britain, and when this was done England acknowledged Hawaiian independence.

Meanwhile, the missionaries were well received. In less than forty years they taught the Hawaiian people to read and write, to cipher and sew. Kamehameha II and his queen visited England, doubtless as a result of curiosity aroused by this contact with another civilization, and both died in London in 1824. Kamehameha IV (1854-63) was succeeded by his brother, Kamehameha V, with whose death in 1873 the line of the Kamehamehas became extinct.

In January 1893 Queen Liliuokalani, sister of Kalakaua I, who had reigned for two years, was dethroned. When annexation to the United States failed through the opposition of President Cleveland, a Republic was inaugurated in 1894. In 1898, however, the islands were formally annexed to the United States, and in 1900 the Territory of Hawaii was organized.

JULY EIGHTH

BIRTHDAY OF JOHN D. ROCKEFELLER

John Davison Rockefeller, organizer of the Standard Oil Company, founder of philanthropic institutions and benefactor of colleges, was born at Richford, Tioga County, N.Y., on July 8, 1839. His parents moved to Cleveland, Ohio, when he was twelve years old and at the age of sixteen he became a clerk in a commission house at low wages of which he saved a little every week. When he was nineteen he engaged in the commission business with a partner named Clark, and was successful. When he was twenty-three he and his partner became associated with Samuel Andrews in the business of refining oil. His brother, William Rockefeller, was admitted to the partnership and a new company was formed known as William Rockefeller & Co., which built a large refinery at Cleveland in 1865. An eastern branch was established at New York with Henry M. Flagler as an additional partner. In 1870 the several firms were united under the name of the Standard Oil Company, with a capital of $1,000,000, which sought to control the oil business of the country. One of the methods used was to obtain from the railroad companies preferential freight rates denied to competitors. It was the custom then for the railroads to grant freight rebates to favored shippers, an arrangement which ultimately led to the creation of the Interstate Commerce Commission with authority to fix freight rates with penalties for granting rebates. This necessary reform opened the railroads on equal terms to all shippers. The Standard Oil Trust was organized in 1882, but it was dissolved by order of the court ten years later. The companies composing it, however, continued in business, with practical control of the oil business until the discovery of new oil fields led to the organization of competing companies. Mr. Rockefeller was bitterly denounced for his business methods and was charged with the use of unfair means in driving competitors out of business when they would not join with him. He retired from active connection with his enterprises in 1911. He accumulated a large fortune, said at one time to be the largest in the world, and used it for philanthropic purposes. One of his earliest large benefactions was the gift of $23,000,000 to revive the University of Chicago in 1892. He gave $50,000,000 to the General Education Board; in 1913 established the Rockefeller Foundation with an endowment of $100,000,000; built and endowed the Rockefeller Institute for Medical Research with $4,000,000; subsidized medical research all over the world, and gave millions for the restoration of places of historic interest after the first World War.

JULY NINTH

BRADDOCK'S DEFEAT

General Edward Braddock, who had served for forty-three years in the Coldstream Guards, was sent to America in 1754 as a major general in command of all the British troops here. He landed at Hampton, Va., in February 1755, with two regiments of infantry and soon after began preparations to attack the French at Fort Duquesne on the present site of Pittsburgh, Pa. He had no wagons to use in transport and Benjamin Franklin obtained them for him from the Pennsylvania farmers. Colonel George Washington, whom he met in Virginia, was taken along as a member of his staff. There were no roads and he began cutting a highway through the wilderness and built the first road across the Alleghanies. At Little Meadows, about fifty miles from his destination, he divided his force and pushed on with fourteen hundred men for the Monongahela River. On July 9, his advance guard encountered a force of about nine hundred French, Canadians and Indians eight miles east of Fort Duquesne. Ten minutes later General Braddock came up with his men in column formation. Instead of ordering the men to fight from behind trees in the manner of frontier warfare he followed the method with which he was familiar. The battle lasted for three hours. More than half his men were killed, sixty-three of his eighty-nine officers fell, and Braddock himself was shot through the lung. Colonel Washington rallied the survivors and conducted a safe retreat. Braddock died four days later at Great Meadow, the victim of his unwillingness to follow the advice of his American associates familiar with the methods of warfare in a new country.

JULY TENTH

THE WHISTLER CENTENARY

James Abbott McNeil Whistler, a distinguished artist who lived in Europe during nearly the whole of his adult life and won his fame there, was born in Lowell, Mass., on July 10, 1834. The hundredth anniversary of his birth was celebrated by the Lowell Art Association in 1934 by a reception and addresses in the house at 243 Worthen Street in which he was born, and by a popular concert in the Memorial Auditorium. The house was built in 1824 for the chief engineer of the canal system for the mills in Lowell. It was occupied by the Whistler family for four or five years. In the course of time it fell into disrepair and was used as a boarding house. The Lowell Art Association bought it in 1908, restored it, and maintain it as a social and art center. It is only incidentally a Whistler museum although it has a good collection of the artist's etchings and some reproductions of his paintings.

The speakers at the centenary celebration in the house were Walter S. Brewster, a trustee of the Chicago Art Institute, and Frederic Allen Whiting, president of the American Federation of Arts. Mr. Brewster presented to the house one of Whistler's earliest drawings done while he was a West Point cadet to illustrate a class song. It was received in behalf of the Art Association by Philip S. Marden, its president. The Memorial Auditorium was crowded in the evening by people who gathered to listen to the concert by the Philharmonic Orchestral Society, under the leadership of Julius Woessner, arranged by the Art Association in honor of Whistler.

Whistler was the son of Major George Washington Whistler of the United States army. When the boy was four years old the family moved to Stonington, Conn., and in 1843 they went to St. Petersburg, Russia, as Major Whistler had been commissioned by the Tsar to build a railroad from that city to Moscow. While in Russia the boy studied at the Imperial Art Academy. After the father's death in 1849 the family returned to America and settled at Pomfret, Conn., where the boy was sent to school to prepare for entrance to West Point. He entered the military academy in 1851, but he neglected his studies and was expelled at the end of three years. He once said that if silicon had been a gas he would have been a Major General. He was assigned to the United States Coast Survey, but was dismissed because he made caricatures on the margin of the maps which he engraved. At the age of twenty-two he found himself in Paris studying art. His paintings were rejected by the Salon for several years, but in 1863 "The Little White Girl" attracted a great deal of attention in the Salon des Refuses. In the meantime he had won considerable reputation as an etcher. He took up his residence in London in 1859 and lived there the greater part of the time until his death. He had numerous disputes with the art critics. When John Ruskin in *Fors Clavigera* wrote in 1877 of one of Whistler's nocturnes: "I have seen and heard much of cockney impudence, but never expected to hear a coxcomb ask two hundred guineas for flinging a pot of paint in the public's face," Whistler sued him for damages and obtained a verdict of one farthing. He wore the coin thereafter as a charm on his watch chain. He was an American and he wished to be recognized in America. This wish has been gratified as more of his paintings are exhibited in collections here than in any other country. The collection made by Charles L. Freer of Detroit, was bequeathed to the National Gallery in Washington. His portrait of his mother, bought by France for $600, hangs in the Louvre in Paris. It was used as the design for a United States postage stamp issued in honor of Mother's Day in 1934, and thus constituted a national tribute to the artist on the one hundredth anniversary of his birth.

AMERICAN TROOPS LAND IN SICILY

The Allied invasion of Europe in World War II really opened with the attack on Sicily July 10, 1943, by General Dwight D. Eisenhower's American and British forces. On July 19 Rome was raided by the United States Air Force and on July 25 King Victor Emmanuel of Italy announced the resignation of Premier Benito Mussolini and the appointment of Pietro Badoglio as his successor. This was the first serious break in the war structure of the Axis. The successful campaign in Sicily ended September 3 when a secret military armistice was signed by representatives of the Badoglio administration, effective September 8. On September 3, the Allies also invaded the mainland of Italy. British and Canadian troops from Sicily crossed Messina Strait landing on the west coast of the Province of Calabria. The American Fifth Army of General Mark W. Clark landed at Salerno, below Naples, and after a costly battle with the Germans established a beachhead six days later, almost simultaneously with the announcement that the government of Marshall Badoglio had surrendered. Italy was out of the war, but the Germans fought bitterly against the Allied advance. The Americans and their Allies made slow progress from Naples, fought the bloody battle of Casino, established a beachhead at Anzio, below Rome, and finally on May 11, 1944, launched an offensive that carried them to Rome on June 4.

The invasion of Sicily and the Italian mainland had been made possible by the successful completion of the campaign in northern Africa in which American troops under General Eisenhower had participated. With the decisive defeat of the Germans and Italians at Cape Bon, May 12, 1943, the Mediterranean was controlled by the Allies and the Italian campaign followed. Immediately after the fall of Rome came D-Day, June 6, 1944, and again American troops made good their beachheads in the tremendous landing operations in Normandy, the beginning of the great Allied invasion of Europe which came to a victorious conclusion on V-E Day, May 8, 1945.

WYOMING ADMITTED TO UNION

See Wyoming Day, December 10.

JULY ELEVENTH

BIRTHDAY OF JOHN QUINCY ADAMS

John Quincy Adams, the sixth President of the United States, was born in Braintree, now Quincy, Mass., on July 11, 1767, the son of John Adams. (See Birthday of John Adams, October 11.) His father took him on his mission to France in 1778 when he was only ten years old. The boy was put in school at Passy where he studied French and Latin. The next year, while his father was engaged on a diplomatic mission in Amsterdam, he attended the Latin School in that city, and entered Leyden University in January 1781, when he was only thirteen years old. Soon after, however, Francis Dana, appointed minister to Russia, took him to St. Petersburg as his secretary. Two years later he returned to Holland and resumed the study of the classics at The Hague. When his father was appointed minister to England he returned to the United States and entered Harvard University as a junior sophister and was graduated in 1787. He studied law and was admitted to the bar three years later. Like his father he gave much time in the early years of his practice to writing political articles. A few months before he was twenty-seven years old, President Washington sent him as minister to the Netherlands, but the French had taken the country in the meantime and he was made minister to Berlin. He remained in Berlin until 1801 when he resumed the practice of law in Boston. He was elected to the Massachusetts Senate in April of the next year and was an unsuccessful candidate for the national House of Representatives in November. The next year, however, the Massachusetts legislature elected him to the United States Senate, where he questioned the constitutionality of the Louisiana Purchase and proposed an amendment which would make it valid. But he voted for the appropriation of funds for the purchase. While he was serving in the Senate he had been appointed to the chair of rhetoric and oratory in Harvard College, a position which he accepted and filled for some time. He resigned from the Senate in 1808, and in 1809 President Madison appointed him as minister to St. Petersburg where he remained until 1814, conducting important negotiations. He was then made minister to England and assisted in the negotiations leading to the settlement of the issues of the War of 1812. President Monroe appointed him Secretary of State in 1817, an office which he filled with ability and distinction. He shares with Monroe the honor of formulating the Monroe Doctrine. He remained at the head of Monroe's Cabinet for eight years and in 1824 was a candidate for President. He received eighty-four electoral votes. Jackson received ninety-nine and Crawford and Clay received forty-one and thirty-seven respectively. As no candidate had a majority the election was thrown into the House of Representatives with each state having one vote, and thirteen states needed to elect. On the eve of the first vote Adams had the support of only twelve states, with the vote of New York going to Jackson. The friends of Adams worked upon Stephen van Rensselaer, a rich patroon of New York, seeking to convince him that a failure to elect would precipitate a long contest which would be injurious to the country, and to persuade him to vote for Adams so that the New York vote might decide the issue. Van Rensselaer was a pious man and when he entered the chamber of the House the next morning he bowed his head in prayer asking for guidance in the crisis. When he opened his eyes he saw on the floor before him a ballot with the name of Adams upon it and he took this for the answer to his prayer. Accordingly he voted for Adams and gave the election to him. This is the explanation of the result by Martin Van Buren in his autobiography. Adams had never been a political partisan and he did not remove his political opponents from office, even though they were known to be hostile to him. The friends of Jackson were bitter against him, charging that he had been elected because of a deal with Clay, a charge since disproved. But as Adams made Clay Secretary of State the charge was believed by many and when the next presidential election came around it was one of the chief arguments against keeping Adams in office. The administration of Adams was so unpopular that in the congressional election in the middle of his term a large hostile majority was elected for the first time in the history of the country. The campaign of 1828, marred with bitter personalities, resulted in the election of Jackson. Adams retired to Quincy with the detestation of the Federalist Party which had supported him in 1824. But a year after his retirement he was elected to the House of Representatives by a Massachusetts district and reelected every two years for the remainder of his long life. He was what might be called a free lance in Congress as he supported and opposed measures according to what he regarded as their merits regardless of the party or person proposing them. He fought for years for the right of petition when the House was refusing to allow petitions against slavery to be read or debated. He was a firm believer in the natural rights of man, which constitutions might recognize but could not create and believed that the American Constitution could be defended only so far as it recognized those rights. He was stricken with paralysis while walking in Boston in the autumn of 1846 when he was seventy-nine years old. He recovered sufficiently to take his seat in Congress in the following February. Just after responding to the roll call in the House on February 21, 1848, he had another stroke. He was carried to the Speaker's room where he died on February 23. He was buried beside his father in the crypt of the First Congregational Church in Quincy. Beside the pulpit there is an appropriate inscription on a marble tablet surmounted by his bust, opposite a similar memorial to his father.

JULY TWELFTH

ORANGE DAY

The anniversary of the Battle of the Boyne, fought on July 1, 1690, old style, is observed by the Orangemen in the United States on July 12. The battle was fought between the forces of James II, who had been deposed as King of England, and the forces of William of Orange, who had succeeded him as King. James had tried to restore Catholicism as the state religion. He was opposed by the Protestant leaders. They invited William of Orange, who had married Mary, the daughter of James, to invade England from the Netherlands. He accepted the invitation. A Convention Parliament declared William and Mary joint sovereigns in 1689 after they had accepted the requirements set forth in the Bill of Rights. Among the provisions were that no Roman Catholic could be King of England nor anyone who had married a Catholic. Catholic Ireland was loyal to James and arose in his defence. An army of 30,000 supporting the cause of James met an army of about the same size committed to the cause of William some three miles west of Drogheda on the banks of the River Boyne and was defeated with the loss of 1500 men. William's army lost only about 500. An obelisk 150 feet high has been erected on the site of the battle.

The Irish Catholics, because of their support of James, were oppressed by the English and began to form semi-revolutionary societies. The Irish Protestants, to counteract the effect of these organizations formed the Loyal Orange Institution, so named from William's title as Prince of Orange. The institution was committed to maintain the union between England and Ireland and the Protestant succession to the throne. The organization was not definitely established in Protestant Ulster until more than a hundred years after the battle. It was responsible for much turbulence and the British Parliament ordered its suppression in Ireland in 1813, an order which remained in force until 1828. Lodges of Orangemen were formed in England, Canada and the United States as well as in Ireland. In Ireland, however, they long ago ceased to exercise any political influence. The numerous lodges in the United States are maintained as centers of fellowship for the Protestant Irishmen. They usually celebrate the anniversary of the Battle of the Boyne with a parade on July 12, followed by a picnic and games.

JULY THIRTEENTH

BIRTHDAY OF NATHAN B. FORREST

The anniversary of the birth of Nathan Bedford Forrest, who won fame as a cavalry leader in the Confederate army during the Civil

War, is a legal holiday in Tennessee. Forrest, who was the eldest son of William Forrest, a blacksmith, was born in what is now Marshall County, Tenn., on July 13, 1821. The family moved to Mississippi in 1834 and William Forrest died three years later leaving Nathan, then sixteen years old, as its chief support. He had no formal education and worked at first as a farm laborer and as he grew older he dealt in a small way in horses and cattle and traded in slaves and real estate. In the course of time he accumulated a little capital and bought cotton plantations in Alabama and Mississippi which ultimately made him a rich man. He took up his residence in Memphis in 1849 and was elected alderman of the city. When the Civil War began he raised a battalion of cavalry and equipped it at his own expense, enlisting in it as a private. He was made lieutenant colonel within three months. He took part in the defense of Fort Donelson in 1862 and opposed the decision to surrender, insisting that it would be possible for a great part of the garrison to cut its way out through the Union lines. With the permission of the commanding general he did escape with his own command through a gap in the besieging line. He was made a brigadier general in June 1862, and began a series of raids on the Union lines of communication. In the spring of 1863 a junior officer, who did not like the duty to which he had been assigned, shot him, inflicting what was thought to be a fatal wound. Forrest killed his assailant and recovered from the injury. He, like the junior officer, did not like the duty to which General Bragg assigned him and had a fierce quarrel with his superior. Jefferson Davis transferred him from Bragg's division and made him a major general. He was wounded in battle at Tupelo in July 1864, but continued to lead his troops while riding in a carriage, until his wound healed. He was in command of the Confederate cavalry in the Nashville campaign, and was made a lieutenant general in February 1865. At the close of the war he returned to his cotton plantations and died in Memphis on October 29, 1877. As a soldier he was daring and venturesome, at times fighting in the ranks. It is said that twenty-nine horses were shot under him. He was the kind of man about whom traditions grow and who in the course of time becomes a romantic hero.

JULY FOURTEENTH

BASTILLE DAY

The celebration of the destruction of the Bastille in Paris on July 14, 1789, began in the United States on the first anniversary of the event. The Americans were in sympathy with the efforts of the French to obtain relief from the oppressions of the monarchial government and had hailed the destruction of the Bastile with joy. On July 14, 1790, a public celebration of the anniversary was held in Philadelphia, then the chief city of the country. The shipping along the river front was decorated with flags and salutes were fired from the French vessels of which there were several anchored in the harbor. There was a dinner at Oeller's Hotel at which toasts were drunk to the French king and the French people for what they had won. Another dinner by the officers of the Fourth Philadelphia Regiment to celebrate the anniversary was held on the same day at Ogden's Hotel. The record of the celebration of the day in Philadelphia in 1793 reports that it was arranged by the officers of the Second Regiment of militia in the form of a dinner at Weed's Ferry. Citizen Genet, the French minister, and Governor Mifflin of Pennsylvania, were among the guests. Scharf and Westcott, in their history of Philadelphia, say, "It was probably at this dinner that the head of a pig was severed from its body and being recognized as an emblem of the head of the murdered King of France, was carried around among the guests. Each one, placing the cap of liberty on his head, pronounced the word 'tyrant' and proceeded to mangle with his knife the head of the luckless creature doomed to be served to so unworthy a company."

As the Americans grew more accustomed to the heady draught of liberty the observance by them of Bastille Day was gradually abandoned as a separate event. It is now celebrated chiefly by French societies in the United States in cooperation with Americans interested in France and the French language. In 1918, however, when the United States was associated with France in the prosecution of the war against Germany a nationwide celebration of the day was arranged by a general committee of which William H. Taft was the chairman, with local committees in the different cities. One of the most notable celebrations was that at Independence Hall in Philadelphia, a building noted as the symbol of liberty as the Bastille came to be regarded by the French as the symbol of tyranny. The French residents of the city gathered at the French consulate and marched to Independence Hall where they were addressed by Lieutenant Paul Perigord of the French High Commission in the United States, a hero of Verdun, and by others. The "Marseillaise" and the "Star Spangled Banner" were sung. A meeting was also held in Fairmont Park attended by all the consuls of the Allied Governments in the city and by Governor Brumbaugh of Pennsylvania and Mayor Smith of Philadelphia. Secretary Baker of the War Department detailed a guard of honor of soldiers equipped for overseas service. In the evening the Four-Minute-Men of the Pennsylvania Council of National Defense, who were assigned to make patriotic speeches in the theaters, submitted a message to the French for the approval of the audiences they addressed which voted that it be delivered through the French Ambassador to the people in France. This message declared:

France stands erect today, unconquered and unconquerable. America stands beside her—our boys in khaki shoulder to shoulder with the horizon blue of France's brave men. . . . Today we ask for France nothing but the privilege of repaying the debt we owe. We, too, celebrate the fall of the Bastille, the first stronghold of absolutism to go down before the rising power of free men. We shall stand beside her till the last stronghold of autocracy falls in ruins about the Hohenzollern dynasty.

As Bastille Day fell on Sunday in 1918 these exercises were held on Saturday. In New York a military parade was arranged, reviewed by Lord Reading, the British High Commissioner; Jules Jusserand, the French Ambassador, and Count de Cellere, the Italian Ambassador. Charles Evans Hughes, later to become Chief Justice of the United States, presided over the exercises. On Sunday, however, the "Marseillaise" was sung in many churches in the morning and there was a mass meeting in the Metropolitan Opera House in the afternoon.

The word "bastille" means "fortress," and was originally applied to any stone building with towers or bastions for defense. The Bastille at first consisted of two towers one on each side of the road entering Paris from the Faubourg Saint-Antoine. It was later developed into a castle with four towers connected by thick walls, the whole surrounded by a moat twenty-five feet deep. Its construction was begun in 1370. During its whole history it was used as a prison and came to be regarded by the French as the symbol of oppression. It had accommodations, such as they were, for eighty prisoners. Stories were abroad that many of the prisoners were treated with inhuman cruelty. It is known that many political prisoners were sent there without trial in order to get them out of the way. When the Parisians began to revolt in 1789 they launched their first attack upon the famous prison. They took it by storm and killed the governor and seven of his men. The archives were seized and thrown to the winds and the prisoners were released. There were only seven of them at the time, but they were carried through the streets of the city and acclaimed as victims of tyranny. The building was torn down and Thomas Paine, who was in Paris at the time, obtained the key and sent it to George Washington. A duplicate of the key rests in Independence Hall in Philadelphia.

JULY FIFTEENTH

ST. SWITHIN'S DAY

St. Swithin (also called Swithun), whose festival on July 15 is retained in the calendar of the Anglical Church, is associated in the popular mind with weather signs very much like Candlemas or Groundhog Day (see Groundhog Day, February 2). The old rhyme associating the saint with the weather runs in this way:

> St. Swithin's Day, if thou dost rain,
> For forty days it will remain;
> St. Swithin's Day, if thou be fair,
> For forty days it will rain nae mair.

The saint, who was Bishop of Winchester, asked those with him when he was about to die that they bury him outside of the cathedral instead of in the chancel, "where the feet of passersby might tread and the rain of heaven fall" on his tomb. He died on July 2, 862, and was buried as he desired. His body was removed and buried within the cathedral on July 15, 971, when the weather was pleasant. In the course of time however, a tradition grew up that it rained on that day and for forty days thereafter and that the removal of the body had to be postponed. His body was again removed in 1094 to the new cathedral where it now lies.

Little was written about Swithin by his contemporaries. The biographies of him were compiled long after his death. They are filled with legends for which there is no known historical foundation. It is known, however, that he was one of the counsellors of Egbert, King of the West Saxons. It is assumed that he assisted in the education of Egbert's son and that Egbert brought about his election as Bishop of Winchester. He was consecrated as bishop by the Archbishop of Canterbury on October 30, 852. He is reported to have performed many miracles during his life and it is said that many miraculous cures resulted from visits to his grave, and that he was canonized by popular acclamation two centuries before the Popes began formally to canonize saints of the church. This canonization came about because for centuries Swithin was the most popular healing saint in England. It is not known when the weather tradition connected with him originated. Ben Jonson refers to it in *Every Man Out of His Humor*, written in 1599, as though it were well known then. An English almanac for 1697 contains the following rhymes for July suggestive of what had then become the feeling of the people about the legends concerning the saint:

> In this month is St. Swithin's Day,
> On which if that it rain, they say
> Full forty days after it will,
> Or more or less, some rain distill.

> This Swithin was a saint, I trow,
> And Winchester's bishop also,
> Who in his time did many a feat,
> As Popish legends do repeat;
> A woman, having broke her eggs,
> By stumbling at another's legs,
> For which she made a woful cry,
> St. Swithin chanced for to come by,
> Who made them all as sound or more
> Than ever they were before.
> But whether this were so or no
> 'Tis more than you or I do know.

> Better it is to rise betime,
> And to make hay while sun doth shine,
> Than to believe in tales and lies
> Which idle monks and friars devise.

The weather legend has kept the memory of the saint alive in spite of the fact that it has rarely happened that there have been either forty days of rain or forty days of sunshine following July 15. It is possible that a French priest, serving in England, adapted the St. Medard tradition to St. Swithin. The French saint, who lived about three hundred years earlier than St. Swithin, is supposed to have an irresistible influence over the weather. The French have a rhyme for this day similar to the English rhyme:

> Quand il pleut à la St. Médard,
> Il pleut quarante jours plus tard,
> À moins que le St. Barnabe
> Ne lui vienne couper le nez.

That is, if it rains on June 8 (St. Medard's Day) it will rain for forty days thereafter, unless it is pleasant on St. Barnabas's Day, which is June 11. St. Medard was bishop of Noyon and Tournai early in the sixth century.

JULY SIXTEENTH

BIRTHDAY OF MARY BAKER EDDY

Mary Baker Eddy, the founder of the Church of Christ, Scientist, was born at Bow, N.H., on July 16, 1821. The family moved to Tilton where at the age of seventeen she joined the Congregational church in the village. In December 1843, she married George W. Glover of Charleston, S.C., a friend of her brother's, and went South with him. He died in July 1844, leaving her without money. With the help of the local Masons she returned to New Hampshire where in September she gave birth to her only son, George Glover. Her mother died in 1849 and in 1850 her father married again. In 1853 she married a second time. Her husband was a dentist, Dr. Daniel Patterson, a relative of her stepmother's. She lived with him in various places where he practiced his profession. In 1862 he visited the Bull Run battlefield and was taken prisoner and sent to Libby prison. His wife returned again to New Hampshire to live with her sister. On the release of her husband she went with him to Lynn, Mass., where he opened an office. She separated from Dr. Patterson in 1866 and in 1873 divorced him on the ground of desertion, resumed the name of her first husband, and supported herself by teaching school. She was still living in Lynn, and in 1870, before she divorced Dr. Patterson, she and Richard Kennedy had begun to work together. He practiced medicine and she devoted herself to writing and to teaching her method of curing disease. She published the first version of *Science and Health* in 1875 of which one thousand copies were printed. She wrote that Eternal Mind is the source of all being, that there is no such thing as matter and that disease is caused by the mind alone. This continued to be the basis of all her teaching.

She married a third time in 1877, her husband being Asa G. Eddy, one of her disciples. Eddy died on June 2, 1882, from an organic disease of the heart as shown by the autopsy.

Her students began to call themselves Christian Scientists and in 1876 formed the Christian Students' Association. With her support they obtained a charter as "The Church of Christ, Scientist" on August 23, 1879. She organized in Lynn the Massachusetts Metaphysical College in 1881 for training Christian Science practitioners. When she moved to Boston in 1882 she took the college with her where it remained in operation for several years. In order to promote the interests of the new church and to combat attacks upon it she founded the *Journal of Christian Science* in 1883. The National Christian Science Association was organized in January 1886 and held its first convention in New York in the following February. In 1908, the *Christian Science Monitor*, a daily newspaper, was founded. She had moved to Concord, N.H., in 1888, to be freed from the details of management of the organization which she had created and remained there for ten years when she took up her residence in a fine mansion in Chestnut Hill, a suburb of Boston. Here she occupied herself in promoting the cause to which she had devoted her mature life. She survived until December 10, 1910. At her death her church had grown until there were 100,000 members who had bought 400,000 copies of *Science and Health*. She left an estate of the estimated value of $2,500,000, the greater part of which her will set apart for the promotion of the cause in which she was interested. According to the religious census of 1936 there were 2,113 Christian Science churches in the United States with a membership of 268,915. Figures for later years are not available for publication. Free reading rooms are maintained by the churches in which Christian Science literature is kept for the instruction of the faithful.

FEAST OF OUR LADY OF MT. CARMEL

This is the principal feast of the Order of Our Lady of Mount Carmel, traditionally the oldest mendicant order in the Roman Catholic Church. It is celebrated every year by Italians who parade the streets carrying candles and figures of the saint to which the spectators pin money as contributions to the church. In the Italian district of New York there is usually a four-day fiesta ending with the feast day. The church of Our Lady of Mount Carmel held services continuously from two o'clock in the morning of July 15, 1934, until midnight of July 16 and the entire block on which the church stands was crowded with worshippers seeking admittance. Each one carried a candle, some of them weighing as much as 200 pounds. It had been customary in the past for those suffering illness to present to the church wax models of the part of the body affected, but this was forbidden by the parish priest in 1934. During the four days of the fiesta there had been processions through the streets arranged by the Brotherhood of the order. The last one was on the afternoon of the feast day with the banner of the order carried at its head. Many of the faithful followed it barefoot in penance and others broke through the crowds of spectators and pinned dollar bills to its folds.

In Hammonton, N.J., the center of a large Italian population, the day was celebrated with special services in St. Joseph's Church and a procession two miles long made up of women and children carrying candles and men carrying statues of the saints. It was estimated that 20,000 people watched the procession. Special police officers from Camden and Atlantic City were enlisted to help in directing the automobile traffic. There were similar celebrations in other places where there are large Italian communities.

According to the tradition of the Order of Our Lady of Mount Carmel, it dates from the time of the prophet Elias who built an altar on Mount Carmel. It is said that he had a prophetic vision of the Virgin Mary. In an ancient history of the Carmelites written in the thirteenth century it is stated that "from the days of Elias and Eliseus the holy fathers of the Old and New Dispensation dwelt on Mount Carmel, and that their successors after the Incarnation built there a chapel in honor of Our Lady, for which reason they were called in papal bulls 'Friars of Blessed Mary and Mount Carmel.'" There is historical warrant for the belief that an Italian crusader, Berthold of Calabria, became a monk in fulfillment of a vow made on the eve of a battle in which he was victorious and in 1156 established himself with ten companions on Mount Carmel. The feast of Our Lady on July 16 was instituted sometime between 1376 and 1386. It was made a "scapular feast" and the principal feast of the order in 1609 and extended to the whole Church in 1726. The scapular of the Order in miniature is presented to the faithful who appear at the altars of the churches on the feast day. It is of cloth and contains a shield from the center of which rises Mount Carmel with three stars which represent the three epochs in the history of the mountain. The first, as if in a grotto of the mountain, typifies the prophetic era of Elias; the second and third stars rising over the mountain signify respectively the Greek and Latin eras when the order spread throughout the East and West. In the sixteenth century a cross was put on the shield as the distinctive sign of the barefoot Carmelites. In memory of the prophet Elias the monks added a crest consisting of an arm with a flaming sword and the motto in Latin, "With zeal have I been zealous for the Lord God of Hosts."

JULY SEVENTEENTH

FLORIDA CEDED TO THE UNITED STATES

Florida was discovered on Easter Day (Pascua Florida), 1512, by
Juan Ponce de Leon, and was explored by De Soto in 1539. In 1565 a
body of French Calvinists, who had established a settlement there years
earlier, were driven out by the Spaniards. The latter held possession
until 1763, when Florida was ceded to England in exchange for Cuba.
The Spanish regained the country in 1781, and two years later their
occupation was confirmed by the Peace of Versailles. Eventually, in 1819,
Florida was ceded to the United States by Spain, received a constitution
in 1833, and was admitted into the Union as a state in 1845. Between
1835-42 severe warfare with the Seminole Indians by the white settlers
was waged, but the Indians were gradually exterminated or driven back
into the swamps. Florida passed an ordinance of secession in 1861, sid-
ing with the Confederacy, although the battle of Olustee, in 1864, was
the only important one fought within its boundaries. One of the first
states to return to the Union, it framed a new constitution in 1865, and
was readmitted in June 1868.

BIRTHDAY OF JOHN JACOB ASTOR

John Jacob Astor, founder of the American family of Astor, was
born in the village of Waldorf, in the Duchy of Baden, Germany, on
July 17, 1763, the son of a butcher. His brother George left home at
an early age and opened a musical instrument store in London and his
brother Henry migrated to New York where he had a butcher shop.
In 1780 John decided to join his brother in London and set out on foot
for the Rhine. He worked his way down the river on a timber raft
earning enough to pay his passage to England. He was employed by
his brother for about three years. After the Revolutionary War in America had ended he decided to come to this country and in November 1783
he embarked for New York with twenty-five dollars and seven flutes.
The vessel entered Chesapeake Bay in January 1784, and was frozen in
for two months. While waiting for the vessel to be freed he talked with
another passenger who had been a successful fur trader and decided to
engage in that business. He reached New York in March and lived with
his brother, the butcher. He opened a musical instrument store but soon
engaged in the fur trade, making trips as far west as Mackinaw buying
furs. As early as 1800 he had amassed a fortune of $250,000 and was
the leading fur trader in the country. In order to have a station for
collecting furs in the Northwest he founded Astoria, at the mouth of the
Columbia River, in the spring of 1811, but the experiment was not successful. With Stephen Girard of Philadelphia he assisted in financing

the War of 1812. He sold his fur business in 1834 and devoted the remainder of his life to looking after his real estate in New York. He had early begun to buy land there and the increase in its value added greatly to his fortune. At his death on March 29, 1848, the estate was valued at $20,000,000, the greater part of which he left to his son, William B. Astor. Among his bequests was one of $400,000 for founding a library.

JULY EIGHTEENTH

BIRTHDAY OF JOHN PAUL JONES

John Paul Jones, a distinguished American naval commander in the Revolutionary War, was born in the parish of Kirkbean, Kirkcudbrightshire, Scotland, on July 18, 1747 (July 6, old style). His father was John Paul, the gardener of William Craik, a member of Parliament, and the son was born in the gardener's cottage on Craik's estate. When he was old enough he attended the parish school and at the age of twelve he entered the service of a shipowner at Whitehaven as an apprentice. He made his first voyage in the "Friendship" which took him to Fredericksburg, Va., at the head of navigation on the Rappahannock river. His elder brother William was working there as a tailor. When the shipowner suffered financial reverses his apprenticeship was terminated and he lived with his brother studying navigation. When he was nineteen he was made third mate on the slaver, "King George," and at the age of nineteen he became first mate of the "Two Friends," another slave ship. He made several voyages to the West Indies in these ships. He was made commander of the merchant ship, "John of Dumfries," in 1769 and held the post for two years, making two voyages to the West Indies. While his ship was at Tobago, on the second voyage he flogged the carpenter for neglect of duty and the man died at sea a few weeks later. When the ship returned to Scotland the carpenter's father charged Captain Paul with the murder of his son. Paul was imprisoned, but was soon released on bail when he obtained affidavits attesting his innocence of the charge. He became master of the "Betsy" of London and was again in the West Indies at Tobago in 1773 when his crew mutinied. The ring leader was killed by the master's sword. John Paul insisted that the man rushed upon the weapon and killed himself in that way. As the men who had seen the event were hostile, Paul was advised by his friends to go to America incognito to await the assembling of a court at Tobago to try him. Accordingly he went to Fredericksburg where his brother lived. While there he took the name of Jones and was thereafter known as John Paul Jones, instead of as John Paul. The probability is that he took this name to conceal his identity, although there is a tradition in the family of Willie Jones of

North Carolina that he took it out of gratitude for the Jones family's hospitality to him at their estate on the Roanoke river.

He was out of employment when the Revolutionary War began and went to Philadelphia and offered his services to the Continental Congress. On December 7, 1775, he was commissioned as a lieutenant and assigned to the "Alfred" which he had been engaged in fitting out. He hoisted the Continental flag on this ship on December 3, the first naval vessel to fly the flag. In 1776 he was put in command of the "Providence" and made captain. On his first cruise he captured sixteen prize ships and on his second he took the transport "Mellish" with a cargo of military supplies. He also took a privateer of ten guns and several smaller British vessels. He was appointed to the command of the sloop "Ranger" on June 10, 1777, and was sent to France to report to the American commissioners in Paris. He was told that command of the frigate "Indien," building at Amsterdam, would be given to him, but the American commissioners transferred the "Indien" to France for political reasons. He remained in France with the "Ranger" and on April 10, 1778, sailed from Brest, entered the harbor of Whitehaven, spiked the guns in the forts and made an unsuccessful attempt to burn the shipping. Then he visited the Scottish coast with the intention of seizing the Earl of Selkirk as a hostage. The earl was not at home, but the men sent to seize him stole part of the family silver. Jones later bought this from the men and returned it to the family. Then he captured the British naval sloop "Drake," after a battle of an hour and returned to Brest after an absence of twenty-eight days with many prisoners and seven prize ships. This cruise led the British to denounce him as a pirate and convinced the French that he was an able naval commander. He was summoned to Paris, and put in command of the French ship "Duras," an old East Indiaman of forty guns. Jones changed its name to the "Bonhomme Richard," in compliment to Franklin. The summer of 1779 was spent in fitting out a fleet of five naval vessels and two privateers under command of Jones, which sailed for the British coast on August 14, taking seventeen ships on the way. On September 23 he fell in with a fleet of forty-one British merchant ships from the Baltic as they approached Flamborough Head, convoyed by the "Serapis" with forty-four guns, and the "Countess of Scarborough" with twenty guns. Only three of Jones's ships took part in the ensuing battle. Jones with the "Bonhomme Richard" attacked the "Serapis" and by skilful maneuvering brought the two ships together. He lashed them fast and he and his men fought desperately. When the commander of the "Serapis" called on him to surrender he replied, "I have not yet begun to fight." When the "Serapis" finally surrendered, the "Bonhomme Richard" was so badly injured that Jones barely had time to transfer his wounded to the "Serapis" before she sank.

In April he went to Paris where he was welcomed as a hero and many honors accorded him, among them the cross of the Institution of

Military Merit. After his return to America in February 1781, he was formally thanked by Congress. His last visit to America was in the summer and autumn of 1787. Congress then by unanimous vote awarded a gold medal to him and directed Thomas Jefferson, then American minister in Paris, to have it made in that city. He returned to Paris in December and received an offer from the Empress Catherine of Russia to enter her navy and fight in the war with the Turks. He was made a rear admiral in the Russian service, but wrote to Jefferson that he could "never renounce the glorious title of citizen of the United States." He took command of a Russian squadron on the Black Sea on May 26, 1788, but because of the jealousy among the Russian officers he was deprived of his command. Catherine, however, conferred on him the cross of the Order of St. Anne. He returned to Paris in June 1790, where he spent the remainder of his life, dying there on July 18, 1792. He was buried in the Protestant Cemetery in that city in a leaden coffin. His estate was estimated at $40,000.

It was proposed in 1845 that his remains be brought to the United States, but the relatives of Jones in Scotland interfered and the plan was dropped. However, in the summer of 1905 the body was brought to America by a naval squadron escorted by a French cruiser and deposited at the Naval Academy at Annapolis. Memorial exercises were held in the armory of the Academy, addressed by President Theodore Roosevelt and Jules Jusserand, the French Ambassador. When the chapel at the Academy was built the body was placed in a marble sarcophagus in the crypt, and in 1912 a monument to Jones was erected in Potomac Park in Washington. His memory is kept green by periodical exercises at the Naval Academy and at other places. He was undoubtedly the most brilliant naval commander of his time. Lord Nelson, although engaged in the Revolutionary War, did not display his abilities until several years after the death of Jones.

JULY NINETEENTH

THE NATIONAL CHERRY FESTIVAL

It has been said that Michigan raises half of the cherries in the world and that half of the Michigan crop is grown in the region of which Traverse City, on Great Traverse Bay, is the center. The first cherry orchard in that region was set out early in the present century by B. J. Morgan who picked his first crop in 1905 and sold it at a good price to the astonishment of his neighbors. From this beginning the industry has developed to its present proportions. The business men of Traverse City, gratified by the prosperity which had come to the region, arranged what they called a National Cherry Festival in 1928 which was so successful that it has been held every year since. The date is fixed to correspond with the ripening of the cherries, usually in the third week in July. The festival in 1934 was held on July 18, 19 and 20. It is preceded by a religious ceremony of blessing the blossoms in the spring. Karl W. Detzer has described the ceremony:

Almost without warning the whole region bursts into blossom. And the next Sunday morning sees a religious ceremony as picturesque as those which accompany the sailing of the fishing fleet from Brittany. From farms and hamlets, cities and towns, the people trudge out to the orchards, all in their Sunday best. They follow their ministers and priests, a solemn and revent procession, with hope in their hearts and prayers on their lips. Then at eleven o'clock, along the whole length of cherry land, the ministers perform the ceremony of Blessing the Blossoms. They pray for a bountiful harvest, for gentle south winds, for protection from blight. Then soberly the men and women march back to their homes."

Then, when the cherries are about ready to be picked, they flock to Traverse City to attend the Cherry Festival.

The program for the festival of 1931 is typical. The celebration began at daybreak on the morning of the first day with a bombardment of the city from the air. The naval fleet of the Great Lakes dropped anchor in the harbor a few hours later and was welcomed in an address by Charles Wells, the Mayor, and by Miss Maxine Weaver, the Queen of the Festival. After these ceremonies were over the guests of the city were taken on a tour of inspection of the cherry orchards. One party went as far as Old Mission on the Great Traverse Bay peninsula and the other to Northport on Leelanau county peninsula. In the afternoon there were addresses, a shuffleboard match between the new Queen and the Queen of the previous year, the dedication of the municipal zoo to house wild animals native to the state, and a land parade of companies from the Great Lakes Training Fleet. In the evening there was a Cherryland Jubilee at the Northwestern Michigan Fairgrounds when the cherry harvest was greeted by Herbert E. Powell, the Michigan Commissioner of Agriculture, and a prayer of thanksgiving for the crop was offered by the Right Reverend C. E. Woodcock, Protestant Episcopal Bishop of the diocese of Kentucky. Then Queen Maxine and her court were formally presented to the people and there was an address by the Mayor and a display of fireworks and a band concert.

The second day began with ceremonies attending the departure of the first trainload of cherries for market. There were speeches and the train moved out of the station with Queen Maxine at the throttle of the engine. Following this ceremony Richard Freethy and Doris Jean Skiver were crowned Prince and Princess of the festival at the Court House where a fairyland pantomime was presented. It showed Prince Richard and Princess Doris Jean wandering in the woods and unmindful of their kingdom until they heard the blare of bugles which recalled their duties. In the afternoon there was a parade of children with Prince Richard and Princess Doris Jean riding in state, races by naval crews on Great Traverse Bay and horse races at the fairgrounds, followed by maneuvers at the airport by the Army Air Service Squadron from Selfridge Field. In the evening there was the Governor's ball at the Country Club, and an American Legion boxing contest at the fairgrounds. The third day began with the coronation of Queen Maxine at the Court House in the morning. The crown was placed on her head by Governor Wilber M. Brucker. In the afternoon there was a floral parade, a Coast Guard drill, more horse races and maneuvers at the airport by the Michigan National Guard Air Squadron. The festival ended in the evening with a Mummers' Parade and the selection and crowning of the Mummers' King. Every visitor was asked to don a grotesque or comical costume and join in the sport. After the paraders disbanded they engaged in street revels and every parader was provided with a noise-making device of some kind. While the street revels were in progress there was a Mummers' ball in a hotel and a display of fireworks on the bay.

The program for the festival in 1931 contained the following tribute to it from Arthur H. Vandenberg, United States Senator from Michigan:

The National Cherry Festival in Northwestern Michigan is one of the important events in our national life. The country as a whole will come to acknowledge this fact as time goes on. In the Japanese empire the cherry festival has long possessed the imaginations of the people and has become one of their great and useful symbolisms. In the course of a semi-official journey to the Orient this spring I passed through Japan at the time of their celebration. It is a very beautiful and thrilling thing to observe the universal enthusiasm with which the Japanese empire greets its cherry blossoms. But they are blossoms without fruit. Here in our own cherryland we have not only the beauty and the inspiration and idealism which flower with a fully equivalent display of blossoms: we also have the utility which comes with a great contribution to the wholesome and delectable food supply of the American people. In other words, we have even more to celebrate and more to praise and more to be thankful for than our great neighbors across the Pacific who enjoy a worldwide fame upon this score.

The managers of the Cherry Festival recalled, in 1935, the apochryphal story of Washington and the cherry tree, told by Weems in his life of the first President. So they had a tree dug from one of the Michigan orchards and transported to the grounds of the boyhood home of Washington, where it was transplanted on February 22 by George Steptoe Washington of Philadelphia, a collateral descendant of the father of his country, assisted by Miss Anna May York of Traverse City, the Festival Queen for 1934.

FIRST WOMAN'S RIGHTS CONVENTION

The movement which culminated on August 26, 1920, in the ratification of the Nineteenth Amendment to the Constitution granting to women the privilege of voting began formally at Seneca Falls, N.Y., on July 19, 1848, when the first woman's suffrage convention was held in that village. It was called by Lucretia Mott, Martha C. Wright, Elizabeth Cady Stanton and Mary McClintock. As the call appeared in the *Seneca County Courier*, published in the village, those who attended the convention came from that part of the state. A Declaration of Sentiments was drafted and signed by a hundred men and women. It asserted that woman was the equal of man and was entitled to all the rights and privileges of citizenship, including the right to hold property, to control her wages, to have a voice in the management of her children as well as the "right to vote." The women of Ohio held a similar convention at Salem in 1850, and soon after it had adjourned some women attending an anti-slavery meeting in Boston, Mass., arranged for a national woman's rights convention to be held at Worcester in the autumn. Two hundred and fifty delegates were present at Worcester representing eleven states. Conventions were held every year with one exception until the beginning of the Civil War. The agitation, begun in 1848, led Kentucky in 1852 to provide by law that any widow with children of school age might vote for the election of trustees of a school district. At the end of the war the women renewed their agitation and the annual conventions became a fixture in their program. Laws were passed by many states permitting women to vote, but this did not satisfy the leaders. They finally brought about the adoption of the amendment to the Federal Constitution which reads: "The right of citizens of the United States to vote shall not be denied or abridged by the United States or by any state on account of sex." (See Nineteenth Amendment, August 26.)

FEAST OF ST. VINCENT DE PAUL

St. Vincent de Paul, a distinguished French priest, was canonized by Clement XII in 1737, and his festival is celebrated by the Roman Catholic Church on July 19, the day of his canonization, by a mass designated in the Catholic missal. He is the patron saint of works of charity. Born about 1580 in Gascony, his life was devoted to the organization of works of charity and benevolence, with the exception of an adventurous interlude when he was captured by corsairs. He was voyaging from Marseilles to Narbonne when his ship was taken by the pirates; sold into slavery at Tunis, he managed to escape after several months, and returned to France. At Chatillon les Dombes, where he was curé, he founded the order of Mission Priests which later was established at St. Lazare, Paris, and became known as the Lazarist Fathers. To him Paris owes the establishment of the foundling hospital. The Sisters of Charity were founded under his direction, and he was intrusted by St. Francis of Sales with the direction of the newly founded Order of Sisters of the Visitation. He died at St. Lazare on September 27, 1660.

JULY TWENTIETH

ITALIANS LYNCHED IN LOUISIANA

The lynching of five Italians at Talulah, La., on July 20, 1899, was followed by a protest from the Italian Government and a demand for redress from the Government of the United States. The trouble leading to the lynching arose because Frank Defatta, an Italian, would not keep his goats from wandering about the neighborhood. They were in the habit of sleeping on the gallery of Dr. J. Ford Hodge's house. The doctor had protested on many occasions but Defatta ignored the protests. On the night of July 19, the doctor shot one of the goats. On the next evening Defatta and four other Italians waylaid the doctor and shot him, mortally wounding him. They were arrested by the sheriff but taken from him by a mob and hanged. Two of the men had been charged with similar killings in the past but had escaped punishment. An investigation was made by the Italian embassy in Washington which alleged that Dr. Hodge had been shot in self defense as he had drawn a gun first. The report of the Governor of Louisiana exonerated Dr. Hodge and charged the men with wanton killing. There was a long diplomatic correspondence over the incident during which it was pointed out that the Federal Government had no jurisdiction over crimes committed in one of the states and that if redress were sought it should be sought from Louisiana.

JULY TWENTY-FIRST

THE DESTRUCTION OF JERUSALEM

The Jews throughout the world observe by fasting the ninth day of the month Ab, corresponding in 1934 to July 21, in commemoration of the destruction of Jerusalem by Titus and his Roman legions. The city was taken after a terrible siege, which began on the fourteenth day of the month Nisan, A.D. 70, or April 28, and ended on the eighth day of the month Elul, or September 8, after having continued for one hundred and thirty-four days. On the fifteenth day of the siege the wall of Agrippa fell; on the eighty-fourth day sacrifices in the Temple were suspended; on the ninety-fifth day the cloisters of the Temple were destroyed and on the one hundred and fifth day the Temple was set on fire by the besiegers. According to Josephus 600,000 bodies of the dead had been thrown out of the gates of the city during the siege. When the city was taken many of the inhabitants were sold as slaves.

As part of the observance of the fast day in 1934, which marked the eighteen hundred and sixty-fourth anniversary of the fall of the city, an edict signed by more than three hundred rabbis was read in the synagogues explaining the significance of the day of mourning and calling upon Jews of all shades of belief to support the plan for repatriating the Jews in their ancient home. In New York Dr. Israel Goldstein, rabbi of Congregation B'nai Jeshurun and president of the Jewish National Fund, issued an appeal for contributions to the fund for acquiring land in

Palestine for Jewish settlement. In view of the persecution of the Jews in Germany under the Hitler regime he dwelt on the importance of using Palestine as an asylum for the people of his race. In Brooklyn and other cities the agencies included in the Federation of Jewish charities cooperated with the synagogues in observing the fast. The services in the synagogues began on the evening of July 20 and continued for a week. The Lamentations of Jeremiah over the sad state of Jerusalem in his time were read in many of the synagogues.

LOYAL TEMPERANCE UNION DAY

This day is known in the Woman's Christian Temperance Union as Loyal Temperance Union Day in memory of Miss Anna Adams Gordon, who was influential in organizing the Loyal Temperance Union among young people. Miss Gordon was elected president of the W.C.T.U. at the Atlanta Convention in 1914, following the death of Mrs. L. M. N. Stevens, who had been president for sixteen years.

Miss Gordon was born in Boston in 1853, the daughter of James M. Gordon, the treasurer for many years of the American Board of Commissioners for Foreign Missions. The family moved to Auburndale, a suburb of Boston, while she was still a little girl, and she grew up in rural surroundings. In 1877, when she was twenty years old, Dwight L. Moody was conducting a series of meetings in Boston and had asked Miss Frances Willard to take charge of the meetings for women. Miss Gordon had attended Mr. Moody's noon meeting at which he spoke from the text "Whatsoever He saith unto you do it." In the afternoon she attended the meeting conducted by Miss Willard. There was no one to play the cabinet organ which stood on the platform. In describing what happened Miss Willard wrote:

An earnest appeal was made and after a painful pause and waiting a slight figure in black with a little music roll in her hand came shyly along the aisle of the Berkeley Street Church and Anna Gordon gently whispered, "As no one volunteers I will do the best I can."

That was the first time the two met. They became lifelong companions and workers for temperance. Miss Gordon was made Loyal Temperance Legion secretary of the World's W.C.T.U. after she had worked successfully in the national legion. She was vice president of the national W.C.T.U. before she was elected president and she resigned the presidency of the national union to accept the presidency of the world union. She visited Europe, Asia and South America to promote the work for temperance. When the prohibition amendment to the Constitution was pending she exerted herself to the utmost to bring about its ratification and when it was ratified she wrote a song of triumph. This was only one of many songs which she wrote. She conducted her campaigns with so much courtesy and consideration that even those who

did not agree with her were forced to admire her. After the amendment
went into effect, Michael Kenna, a former Chicago alderman, familiarly
known as "Hinky Dink," sent to her in Evanston, the headquarters of
the W.C.T.U., a beer schooner from his saloon, and Alderman John J.
Coughlin composed the following lines to go with it:

> Dear, gentle, gracious, efficient president of the W.C.T.U.,
> This souvenir of pre-Volsteadean days I beg to present to you.
> My compliments go with it, as you gaze upon it filled with flowers sweet,
> Prithee remember that it oft contained Manhattan suds on Clark Street.

Miss Gordon died on June 15, 1931, but the W.C.T.U. did not wait
until that event to celebrate her birthday. In a biographical sketch it is
noted that the birthday "has for many years been observed all over the
United States as Loyal Temperance Legion Day. Perhaps the most significant birthday celebration she ever had was in 1923, at the close of the
membership drive, when her white ribbon comrades in every state surprised her with the presentation of a unique bouquet of 25,000 blossoms,
each flower representing a new member of the organization and incidentally a one-dollar membership."

JULY TWENTY-SECOND

FEAST OF ST. MARY MAGDALEN

The church observes the feast of Mary of Magdala on July 22.
There is disagreement among ecclesiastical authorities about her identity.
One group, regards her as the sister of Lazarus and Martha, the one of
whom Jesus said she had chosen the better part while her sister Martha
was busy with domestic duties instead of visiting with Him and learning
from His wisdom. She is supposed to be the woman who annointed the
feet of Jesus with precious ointment from an alabaster box causing Him
to say that she had annointed Him for His burial. She was present at
the crucifixion and at the resurrection. As there is difference of opinion
about her identity so there is lack of agreement on what became of her
after the Ascension. The Greek church holds that she retired to Ephesus
with Mary, the mother of Jesus, and died there and that her body was
transferred to Constantinople in 866 and is preserved there. There is a
French tradition, however, that she and her sister Martha went with
Lazarus to Marseilles and converted to Christianity the whole of Provence.
She retired to the hill of La Sainte-Baume near by and spent thirty years
in a life of penance. When the time of her death came she was carried
by angels to Aix and into the oratory of St. Maximus, where she received
the final offices of the church and her body was laid in an oratory at
Villa Latta. In 745 her remains were said to have been taken to Vezelay
and hidden through fear of the Saracens. No record of their return to

La Sainte-Baume exists but when Charles II of Naples erected a convent
there her shrine was found intact with an inscription explaining why the
body had been hidden. The remains were placed in a sarcophagus sent
to the monastery by Pope Clement VIII in 1600, and are now in the
church of La Sainte-Baume.

JULY TWENTY-THIRD

DEATH OF JOHN RUTLEDGE

John Rutledge, the second Chief Justice of the United States, died
on July 23, 1800. He was born in Charleston, S.C., in 1739, but the
month and day are not known. His father, John Rutledge, came to this
country from England in 1735 and settled in Charleston. He married
Sarah Hext, an heiress of great beauty, by whom he had seven children.
John, the eldest, was born when his mother was fifteen years old. Her
husband died when she was twenty-six. After completing his preliminary
education in this country John was sent to London to study law. He
finished his course at the Temple and returned to Charleston in 1761
where he began to practice and won distinction by the conduct of his
first case. The next year he was elected to the provincial assembly and
was Attorney General of South Carolina in 1764 and 1765. In the
latter year he was a delegate to the Colonial Congress called to protest
against the Stamp Act, and was made chairman of the committee to
draft the memorial against the act to be sent to the House of Lords.
He was a delegate to the first Continental Congress in 1774 and in 1775
was one of those who advocated the independence of the colonies. In
March 1776, he was chosen president of South Carolina and on the
approach of British forces he erected Fort Moultrie and defended it
successfully against a British attack on June 28. He resigned in March
1778, but was recalled in February 1779 and vested with plenary powers.
He held the army together and was present at the Battle of Eutaw
Springs when the British were finally driven from the colony. He was
sent to the Continental Congress again in 1782 and supported the policy
of the commissioners making the treaty of peace with Great Britain.
After retiring from Congress he became Chancellor of South Carolina in
1784. He was a member of the Constitutional Convention in 1787
where he opposed the proposal to forbid the importation of slaves and
was influential in bringing about the adoption of the provision that "the
migration or importation of such persons as any of the states now existing shall think proper to admit shall not be prohibited by the Congress
prior to the year 1808." When the new government was organized
President Washington appointed him as the first of the five Associate
Justices of the Supreme Court, with John Jay as Chief Justice. He re-

signed from the Supreme Court, however, in 1791 to become Chief Justice of South Carolina. When Chief Justice Jay retired Washington appointed Rutledge as Chief Justice on July 1, 1795, and he was sworn in and presided at the sittings of the court. He had opposed the ratification of the Jay treaty with England and when the Senate met in December and received his appointment from the President he was not confirmed. According to some authorities the appointment was rejected because of his opposition to the treaty and according to others confirmation was withheld because his mind had begun to fail. At any rate his mind did fail completely soon after he left the bench. He died in 1800 and was buried in St. Michael's churchyard at Charleston. He was a man of fine presence, a brilliant orator and one of the ablest and most active of the revolutionary fathers.

JULY TWENTY-FOURTH

PIONEER DAY IN UTAH

The history of Utah as a political community dates from the arrival of Brigham Young and his followers in the Great Salt Lake Valley on July 24, 1847. After the murder of Joseph Smith by a mob at Carthage, Ill., on June 27, 1844, the members of the Church of Jesus Christ of Latter-day Saints, which he had founded, decided to seek a region where they could practice their religion and manage their affairs without interference. A company of one hundred and forty-four men was organized to search in the unsettled regions of the West for such a place, but before the start was made in 1847 the wives of three of the men and two boys, Perry Decker and Lorenzo S. Young, a nephew of Brigham Young who had succeeded Joseph Smith as the president of the Church, were added. After many weeks on the march Brigham Young became ill with what was then called mountain fever. In order that they might reach the land they sought without delay the company was divided into two parties. One in command of Orson Pratt pushed forward and on July 22, 1847, he and his companions reached the Great Salt Lake Valley. On July 23, Brigham Young, riding in a carriage, was driven from the trail to an elevation from which he could see the surrounding country. The great basin in which the lake lies was spread out before him and he gazed upon it with content.

"Enough," he said. "This is the place. Drive on."

He reached the present site of Salt Lake City on July 24 and pitched camp, and the embryo city was laid out with solemn ceremonies and consecrated with prayers. The original company was enlarged by later arrivals when word was sent back that the promised land had been found.

The immigrants suffered great hardships for the first year or more but the westward movement of gold seekers to California soon made them prosperous. The new city was on one of the routes to the coast and thousands of immigrants passed through the valley. The crops of 1849 were so good that a great celebration was planned for the anniversary of the founding of the city, the first of many succeeding celebrations. At daybreak on July 24 a salute of cannon was fired and bands of musicians marched through the streets arousing the citizens for the great event of the day. After the people had eaten breakfast a procession was formed headed by a mounted marshal in military uniform, followed by a band. Then came twelve bishops of the church bearing the banners of their wards followed by twenty-four young men dressed in white with white scarfs across their right shoulders and coronets on their heads. Each carried in his right hand a copy of the Declaration of Independence and the Constitution of the United States, and in his left a sheathed sword. One of them held aloft a banner with the inscription "The Zion of the Lord." Twenty-four young women came next dressed in white with white scarfs over their right shoulders and wreaths of roses on their heads. A Bible and the Book of Mormon were carried by each and one bore a banner inscribed, "Hail to Our Chieftain." The leaders of the church came next, escorting Brigham Young. He was followed by twelve bishops carrying the flags of their wards and twenty-four Mormons brought up the rear each carrying a staff the upper end of which was painted red and ornamented with a bunch of white ribbon. One of them carried the stars and stripes on which was inscribed "Liberty and Truth." When the procession reached a building described as the bowery, a temporary structure sixty by one hundred feet and made still larger by a canopy one hundred feet wide on each side, it was received with shouts of "Hosanna to God and the Lamb" by the people assembled there.

After several patriotic addresses the procession reformed and marched to the feast prepared for the occasion, served on tables fourteen hundred feet long, spread, as Young himself said, "with all the luxuries of field and garden and with nearly all the vegetables of the world." The seats were filled and refilled by men and women who had been deprived of even some of the necessities for many months. The transient stranger within their gates was also fed, as well as a large number of Indians who had been attracted to the city by the celebration. Twenty-four formal toasts were proposed and many informal ones. In describing the affair a local newspaper said that "everybody was satisfied and not an oath was uttered, not a man intoxicated, not a jar or disturbance to mar the union, peace and harmony of the day."

This anniversary, which has been celebrated every year since 1849, was made a legal holiday by the territorial legislature in 1882.

Since its first settlement Utah has grown into a populous state and Salt Lake City has expanded from a forty-acre group of log houses protected by a stockade into a great modern city. The manner of celebrating Pioneer Day has changed with the changing resources of the people. One of the twentieth century celebrations in Salt Lake City was in the form of an elaborate pageant in which four thousand persons participated. The story was told by a series of floats drawn through the streets. The first float "The Desert Enchanted," represented the region as it was when Indians were its only inhabitants. It was portrayed by a young woman in chains on a barren heap of rocks surrounded by sand. The next was called "The Quest of Souls" and showed the early Spanish missionaries who encamped on the shores of the Great Salt Lake as early as 1776. They were represented as seeking the trail into Mexico and California. Then the arrival of the trappers called "The Quest of Wealth," was shown with white men trading blankets and other wares with the Indians for furs. This was followed by a pioneer train made up of descendants of the original settlers. A plow hung from the side of the wagon, dogs were running with the horses, chickens in coops were fluttering about restlessly, and water kegs to supply the needs of the immigrants over the arid plains were held in place by ropes. The second division representing the reclaiming of the desert was led by a float carrying figures of Faith and Labor with another figure, representing the Desert, pointing out the promise of the future. Another float showed the beginning of the irrigation project in the region; a third showed the raising of the national flag; another represented the building of the home and the church. The first church, called the "bowery," in which the first celebration of the anniversary was held in 1849, appeared on another float. Religious services were in progress within it. There were floats representing education and the early amusements of the people, showing the white men feeding the Indians and trading with them and also showing how the sea gulls in the spring of 1848 saved the crops of the settlers by eating the crickets which threatened to destroy them. And there were floats showing the arrival of immigrants from other nations. The Norwegians, for example, represented the discovery of America by the Norsemen.

The last division "The Fulfillment of the Promise," was devoted to glorifying the resources of the state in manufacture, mining and agriculture. The last float showed the sego lily, the state flower. Seated within a giant representation of the blossom were scores of small girls singing patriotic songs.

The two boys, Lorenzo S. Young and Perry Decker, who were members of the first company of Mormons to enter Utah, attended the Pioneer Day celebration in Salt Lake City in 1913.

MORMON PIONEER DAY IN IDAHO

The Mormons who arrived in the Salt Lake Valley on July 24, 1847, spread in the course of time to the neighboring states. In these states they observe the anniversary although not quite so elaborately as it is observed in Salt Lake City. On Pioneer Day in Idaho in 1934, there was a celebration at St. Anthony at which William E. Borah, United

States Senator from the state, was the orator. Senator Borah, in the course of his address, paid the following tribute to the pioneers:

> I have often wondered if the story of the movement which brought the Mormon people into the beautiful valley of the Great Salt Lake, eighty-seven years ago today would ever be adequately told. While much has been written, and ably written, no writer has, it seems to me, ever risen "to the height of this great argument." It was one of the great and marvelous treks of history. Perhaps even now we are too close to the event to fully weigh its significance or fairly and faithfully depict its outlines. The Mormon people naturally view the events with a deeper feeling of respect and reverence than others experience. These events are wrought into the moral and spiritual fibre of their very being. But while it is a day set apart by the Mormon people peculiar to the growth and development of the Mormon faith and people, yet everyone capable of being moved by deeds of great daring, by patient suffering, by a spirit of devotion which never failed, a leadership which never faltered, readily join with the Mormon people in paying tribute to those pioneer men and women who, rather than surrender their faith, faced the perils and privations of the wilderness, and in doing so planted the seeds of an empire. We all feel a just pride in the work they did. We all feel that in the achievement of the pioneer of whatever faith or political creed, there is glory enough for us all. We are all beneficiaries of their years of sacrifice and patient building. Few figures in history are more worthy of our emulation than the pioneer—sturdy, self-reliant, resourceful, unshaken by adversity, modest in success, he was truly the architect of his own fortunes, the builder of great commonwealths. If you would know his full stature and grasp the full force of his genius, contrast him with the cowed, whipped, fear-smitten, spineless, dependent creatures with whom nazi-ism, fascism and communism fill the world. In the wake of the one we find forests and deserts conquered and subdued, great states erected, law and order established and personal liberty preserved. With the other, violence and terror hold sway over a sorrow-stricken, harassed, tortured and enslaved people—millions of broken hearts and blasted souls. We can pay no higher tribute to the brave pioneer than to highly resolve that no such creeds shall ever find lodgment under the American flag.

July 24 is also observed by the Mormons in Wyoming and in the other states in which there is a considerable Mormon population.

JULY TWENTY-FIFTH

FRONTIER DAY IN CHEYENNE

Beginning in 1897, Cheyenne, the capital of Wyoming, arranged an annual Frontier Day celebration to keep alive the sports and customs of the early days of the state. It is estimated that more than a million visitors have attended the celebrations which attract larger crowds each year. They grew out of the attendance by a group of Cheyenne business men at the annual Potato Day celebration at Greeley, Colo., in August 1897. These men decided that Cheyenne should have an annual festival of some kind and on August 30 a meeting was held attended by the leading citizens to consider an exhibition of cowboy and range sports. A committee was selected to arrange for the sports made up of Warren

Richardson, chairman, J. A. Martin, E. W. Stone, J. H. Arp, G. R. Palmer, J. D. Freeborn and D. H. Holliday. This committee fixed the date for the first celebration on September 23 and the place as the fair grounds. The program consisted of cowboy races, a pony express battle, riding pitching and bucking horses, and a scene from the Overland Trail including an ox train and vigilantes fighting highwaymen trying to hold up a stage. The people in the crowds lining the fence around the race track carried umbrellas and when a wild steer or a horse approached the fence the umbrellas were immediately raised and pointed toward the animal to frighten it away.

The celebration has grown more elaborate from year to year until in 1934 four days were needed to complete all the contests and sports. It began on Wednesday, July 25, and continued until the afternoon of the following Saturday. Three hundred contestants, expert horsemen and cowboys and cowgirls took part in the sports. The program began each day with a parade around the half mile track at the Frontier Park, participated in by mounted cowboys and cowgirls, Indians in native costume, covered wagons and other vehicles reminiscent of the Overland Trail. This was followed by bronco riding, steer roping, calf roping, bulldogging, bareback riding, and relay races, as well as by potato races and similar sports. Enthusiastic visitors from the East who have attended the celebration have said that "Unless you have seen Frontier Days you have not seen America."

Bulldogging takes its name from the manner in which Will Pickett of Taylor, Texas, threw a steer during a rodeo in August 1904. He leaped from his horse to the horns of a running steer, sank his teeth into the under lip of the animal and threw his shoulder against its neck and strained and twisted until it sank slowly to the ground. It was the bulldog grip of the man's teeth on the lip of the animal which led the frontiersmen to describe the feat as "bulldogging." But the sport is conducted somewhat differently at the Cheyenne festival.

The winners in the roping and bulldogging contests take no more than twenty or twenty-five seconds. In the contest among riders of Brahma steers a circingle is the only harness allowed and the contestant must stay on the animal for ten seconds. In the races between wild horses, the rider must take the horse assigned to him but may have one assistant in putting on the saddle; he must mount the saddled animal and ride it around the track in the proper direction. The relay races of the cowboys and the cowgirls are under similar conditions, save that the horses of the cowgirls may be saddled before the start. Each has three horses and must change horses every half mile until a mile and a half has been covered.

In addition to these contests members of the Burnt Thigh tribe of the Sioux Indians participated in the celebration with native dances and the like. These Indians received their name from an experience in a foray against the Arapahoes in the course of which they were caught in a prairie fire and severely burned. When they returned home those not engaged in the foray called them Sichangues, or "Burnt Thighs" in ridicule and the name clung to them. The Seventy-sixth Field Artillery of the United States Army, stationed at Fort Francis E. Warren in the outskirts of Cheyenne, paraded every day at the Frontier Park and engaged in various military maneuvers.

There are similar exhibitions of cowboy sports at other cities in the West, but the people of Cheyenne insist that theirs is, in their own language, "The daddy of them all." It is the oldest and probably the best known. As is the custom at the festivals of other kinds a queen is chosen annually to preside over the celebration, called Miss Frontier.

FEAST OF ST. JAMES THE GREATER

The feast of St. James, the first of the Apostles to suffer martyrdom, is celebrated on July 25. St. James was the son of Zebedee and the brother of John. His father was a prosperous fisherman on the lake of Galilee, employing several men as well as his sons. His mother was Salome, said by the ecclesiastical scholars to have been a sister of Mary, the mother of Jesus. He and his brother John were called "sons of thunder" because of their fiery temper. After the Crucifixion James was active in the infant church, making many converts. Herod Agrippa I, the grandson of Herod the Great, anxious to please the Jews, ordered that he be slain and he was killed by the sword. According to tradition the person who accused him to Herod and led him to the judgment seat was moved to confess his faith in Jesus by the defense of his course made by James and he was beheaded at the same time with the Apostle. This was in the year 44.

There is an interesting Spanish tradition dealing with the supposed preaching by James in Spain. According to it, after his mission in Spain he returned to Palestine and was the first Bishop of Jerusalem and while preaching there was thrown from the battlements of the temple and killed. This story does not agree with the record in Acts which reports that James and his brother John were killed by the sword by Herod. The Spanish tradition further says his body was miraculously recovered and taken by ship from Joppa through the Pillars of Hercules to Iria Flavia in the northwest of Spain where it was laid upon a stone. This stone became soft and the body sank into it and was enclosed by it, when it hardened again. The location of the stone was revealed to a priest in a vision in 800 and the remains were removed to Compostela where a church was built to which pilgrims resorted. It is said that as many as a hundred thousand visited the church every year for many years. There is no historical evidence, however, that James ever visited Spain. Nevertheless, a knightly order of St. James of Compostela was founded in his honor in the twelfth century.

JULY 25

FEAST OF ST. CHRISTOPHER

St. Christopher, an early Christian martyr, is a saint of both the Roman Catholic and Greek churches, the popular patron of travelers against accidents. In World War II many men in the services, Catholics and other sects as well, carried small medallions or figurines of him for protection. The Greek Church celebrates his festival on May 9, the Roman Catholic on July 25, with a mass designated in the Catholic missal.

In pious imagination he became twelve feet high, and of prodigious strength; and in the pride of his strength would serve only the mightiest on earth. Said to have lived in Syria, and suffered martyrdom under Emperor Decius in the third century, he entered the service of a king. Because of this king's dread of the devil, St. Christopher became the devil's servant, but one day he saw Satan trembling before the image of Christ, and he resolved to serve Christ only. To carry out this resolution he undertook to bear pilgrims across a river. Then Christ came to him in the form of a child, requesting to be borne across the river upon St. Christopher's shoulders. Strangely, the burden of the child grew more and more heavy until the phenomenal strength of the saint was taxed to its utmost and he was barely able to reach the farther shore. "Marvel not, Christopher," said the Child, "for with me thou hast borne the sins of all the world."

St. Christopher, from the Greek "Christ-bearer," is usually represented with the infant Christ upon his shoulders, leaning on a great staff, and straining his mighty muscles to support the weight.

PONY PENNING ON CHINCOTEAGUE ISLAND

The annual penning and auction of wild ponies on Chincoteague Island goes back so many years that no record exists of its origin. It usually occurs during the last week in July; in 1946 the date was July 25. The event was sponsored by the Chincoteague Volunteer Fire Company, to whom the ponies belong, as the climax of a two-week carnival. The Volunteers had staged the round-up for twenty-odd years prior to 1946, and Fire Chief E. L. Jones reported that their original capital of four dollars and sixteen cents had grown to two hundred thousand dollars. The profit accruing from the Carnival Grounds, which also belong to the Company, is augmented yearly by the auction of the ponies who sell like hot cakes at prices up to one hundred and seventy-five dollars. The Island's inhabitants and thousands of visitors, from northern cities as well as Virginia, attend the carnival and auction each year. In 1946 there was a record crowd who rode the ferris wheel and merry-go-round, watched pony and bicycle races, and ate Irish stew and chicken dinners prepared by the Ladies Auxilliary of the Fire Company. The previous day the ponies swam through the Narrows from Assateague and Wallops Islands, where they roam wild in the piney woods and eat the salt marsh grass.

414

On July 25 about two hundred and fifty of the shaggy little beasts were herded through the main street to the corrals and auctioned off, some to pony dealers, but many to private buyers, the parents of enthusiastic youngsters. After the auction a prize of ten dollars was offered to anyone who could remain on the back of a pony for three minutes. Several young men attempted the feat, but only one, a Chincoteague truck driver, managed to stay on a wildly plunging and bucking little mare for the required time.

The origin of these wild ponies on the small islands off the Virginia coast is a matter of dispute. They are known to have roamed there since the seventeenth century and various theories account for their presence. One explanation is that they are the descendants of the survivors of a shipwreck in 1635; another claims their ancestors were small Spanish mustangs left in America by Ponce de Leon after he failed in his search for the Fountain of Youth; still another, that they are descended from horses "fenced in" on the islands when a colonial law ordered horse owners to confine their animals in 1662. The animals are larger than Shetland ponies and distinguished from them by long manes and flowing tails.

JULY TWENTY-SIXTH

FESTIVAL OF ST. ANNE

Saint Anne, or Hannah, in the Hebrew form, is traditionally the mother of Mary, the mother of Jesus. All that is known of her is gained from apochryphal writings dating from about 150. According to the account in these writings a rich and pious couple named Joachim and Hannah lived in Nazareth. They were childless. When Joachim presented himself at the temple with an offering he was repulsed and told that men without children were unworthy to enter. Thereupon he went into the mountains to pray for a child. His wife heard of what he had done and she besought the removal of her sterility and vowed to dedicate her child to God. Not long afterward an angel appeared to her and told her that she would give birth to a child who would be blessed by all the world. In due time a child was born and named Mary. The scholars doubt the authenticity of this account as it is apparently based on the story of the birth of Samuel in the Old Testament. Nevertheless the Greek and Latin churches observe the feast day of St. Anne.

The first record of it in the Latin church is found in an account of its celebration at Douai on July 26, 1291, where a foot of Anne was venerated. Urban VI introduced it in England in 1378 and in 1584 it was extended to the universal Latin church. What are regarded as relics of the saint are widely distributed and are said to have miraculous power. There is a famous church dedicated to her at Beaupré in Canada. The chapel which preceded it was begun on March 13, 1658. Louis Guimont,

415

who had great faith in the power of the saint, laid three stones in the foundation, and immediately reported that he was cured of the rheumatism from which he had suffered a long time. Ever since then many afflicted persons have made pilgrimages to the place and have announced that they have been cured in answer to their prayers. A large basilica has been erected in place of the early chapel, paid for by contributions from the faithful in all parts of Canada. Scores of thousands of persons visit it every year.

The observance of the feast is usually preceded by a novena, or nine days of devotions. At the church of St. Jean Baptiste, in New York, there is a relic of the saint, and the crippled and the ill in great numbers visit the church during the novena when the relic is exposed.

St. Anne is the patroness of miners and of the home and home life.

JULY TWENTY-SEVENTH

FIRST SUCCESSFUL ATLANTIC CABLE

It was on July 27, 1866, that the persistent efforts of Cyrus W. Field to connect Europe and America by electric telegraph were finally successful. In May 1854, he had organized the New York, Newfoundland and London Telegraph Company to lay a cable across the Atlantic. The Federal Government made deep sea soundings in 1856 and discovered a plateau in the bed of the ocean on which the cable could rest. In August 1857, and in June 1858, unsuccessful attempts were made to lay the cable starting from Valentia on the Irish coast, but each time the cable broke. In July 1858, another attempt was made and the cable was stretched from Ireland to Newfoundland, and on August 16, Queen Victoria sent a message over it to President Buchanan, but while England and America were celebrating the success of the undertaking this cable broke. Mr. Field, involved in the financial panic of 1857, had to go into bankruptcy and the Civil War began in 1861 forcing postponement of any further efforts. In 1865, the "Great Eastern" the largest steamship afloat, was chartered to lay another and heavier cable. It started westward on July 25 but the cable broke after six hundred miles of it had been laid. On July 13, 1866, another attempt was made and the cable was successfully landed on the shore of Newfoundland on July 27. It had been made strong enough so that it did not break.

JULY TWENTY-EIGHTH

THE FOURTEENTH AMENDMENT

The second of the Civil War amendments to the Constitution was approved by the Senate on June 8, 1866, submitted to the legislatures

of the states on June 16, and declared ratified by the Secretary of State
July 28, 1868. It is known as the Fourteenth amendment. The Thirteenth amendment abolished slavery. The Fourteenth granted to all persons born or naturalized in the United States equal protection of the
laws. Its primary purpose was to guarantee to the Negroes the rights of
citizens. Its terms are general, however; the last clause of the first section,
forbidding the states to deprive any person of "life, liberty or property
without due process of law," has been cited in litigation having nothing
to do with the rights of the Negroes. There are five sections in the
amendment, three of which deal with special issues growing out of the
war and the fifth empowers Congress to enforce its provisions by appropriate legislation.

FOUNDER'S DAY OF THE VOLUNTEERS OF AMERICA

Ballington Booth, second son of William Booth, founder of the
Salvation Army, was sent to the United States in 1887 with his wife,
Maud, to take charge of the work in this country. In 1896 he disagreed
with his father on the methods of operation in the United States and
Canada and withdrew from the organization. He then organized a body
with similar purposes which he named the Volunteers of America. It
expanded rapidly and conducts its work in most of the states of the
Union.

Ballington Booth was born in England on July 28, 1859. The anniversary of his birth is celebrated as Founder's Day by the organization
which he founded. Special services are held in the cities where the
organization is engaged in its work. (See April 10, Salvation Army
Founder's Day.)

JULY TWENTY-NINTH

FEAST OF ST. MARTHA

The church honors St. Martha, the sister of Lazarus and Mary
Magdelen, on July 22. Little is known of her with definiteness beyond
what is told in the New Testament, but there are many traditions about
her life after the Ascension. In the gospel story she was busy with her
domestic duties while her sister Mary sat at the feet of Jesus. She is
accordingly the patroness of housewives and cooks. One of the traditions
about her has her going with Lazarus and Mary (see Feast of St. Mary
Magdelen, July 22) to Marseilles. She is said to have been the first
person to found a convent for women. It was at Aix. This tradition
also relates that she subdued a dragon which lay concealed in the river
Rhone during the day and ravaged the country at night. After rendering
the beast powerless by sprinkling holy water upon him she bound him

417

with her girdle and slew him. A church was built at Tarascon where she is said to have had her encounter with the dragon and Louis XI endowed the church and presented to it a gold bust of Martha which is said to contain her head.

DAYS OF EZRA MEEKER

In 1939 Puyallup, Wash., joined with many other communities in the state in commemorating the fiftieth anniversary of the admission of Washington to the Union in 1889, by staging a pioneer celebration known as the Days of Ezra Meeker, in honor of an outstanding pioneer whom Puyallup claimed as a distinguished citizen, and who had achieved national recognition at the end of a long life by his efforts to have the Old Oregon Trail marked. During the years immediately preceding his death in 1928 at the age of ninety-eight, he made two transcontinental trips by ox wagon along the old trail and published voluminous material on the subject, in an attempt to awaken interest in the project. This resulted in the formation of the Oregon Trail Association and the American Trails Association. Although the festivities were greatly curtailed during World War II, the observance had been so successful that it was resumed on an ambitious scale following the war. In 1946 the Days of Ezra Meeker began on July 29 and continued through August 3. A varied program, enthusiastically promoted, undoubtedly accounted for its success. A kangaroo court was held daily; there was a pie-eating contest and a whisker contest; a minstrel-variety show and two horse shows; costume parades, street dances and carnivals; and, in short, entertainment for every taste so that all comers enjoyed themselves thoroughly.

Since most pioneer celebrations in the United States commemorate a date of historical significance, Puyallup is unusual in honoring an individual. However, Ezra Meeker unquestionably merits the tribute. His life span of ninety-eight years covered the entire period of the opening up of the West, and he included in his personal experience nearly every adventure traditionally attributed to the pioneers, with the exception of losing his scalp to the Indians. He was born in Ohio on December 29, 1830. In 1851 he travelled the Old Oregon Trail in a prairie schooner drawn by oxen with his young wife and baby daughter. They survived a trek that brought three hundred thousand settlers to the Pacific Northwest at a cost of twenty thousand dead along a two-thousand-mile wilderness trail. He first saw the Puyallup Valley in 1853 after a hazardous trip up the Puyallup River, but was discouraged by the rank forest growth and returned to lay out a farm and operate a general store at Steilacoom. The death of his brother in a shipwreck, while on a buying trip to San Francisco, took all his cash and ruined his credit, so that he was forced out of business. Shortly thereafter, penniless except for some livestock, Ezra Meeker went back to the Puyallup Valley with his wife and four children and took over a squatter's claim. On this farm he planted a few hop roots obtained from Olympia, as an experiment. In the ensuing twenty-six years he expanded the enterprise until he eventually owned five hundred acres of hops and a substantial interest in the greater part of the hop acreage in the valley, made trips to Europe to market the crop, and became known as "The Hop King of the World." It was estimated that his annual shipment of hops for peak years was worth half a million dollars. His achievement was particularly remarkable in view of the pioneer hardships he overcame, which included an exclusive diet of potatoes for himself and his family in lean times, and a narrow escape from an Indian massacre. But his later fame was due more to his civic activities than to his success in amassing a fortune. He planned the town of Puyallup and became its first mayor in 1890, sponsoring and aiding, over many years, the building of schools, churches, railroads, bridges, libraries, and institutions for the care of unfortunates. In addition, during this long and full career he resorted from necessity to numerous other activities, working at intervals as a farmer, longshoreman, millworker, merchant, banker, and as a miner in the Alaska goldrush. After his vast hop fortune was dissipated through losses caused by the infestation of the hop fields by aphis, and various other reverses, he turned at the age of seventy-six to writing. His promotional enthusiasm was apparently unquenched by years and adversity, and he undertook to interest the nation in marking the great westward trails of migration and empire.

JULY THIRTIETH

CRATER DAY

Among the interesting anniversaries occasionally observed in Virginia is Crater Day in commemoration of the unsuccessful attempt of the Union troops to take Petersburg by assault after blowing up one of the forts and its defenders by a mine. A tunnel had been dug five hundred feet long from the Union lines and extending under the fort with lateral branches extending forty feet each way at its termination. These were filled with powder which was exploded on the morning of July 30, 1864. Where the fort had been there was a crater two hundred feet long, fifty feet wide and from twenty to thirty feet deep. The defenders, three hundred strong, with all their weapons and supplies were blown to oms. The other defenders of the city immediately opened a cannonade on the spot and prevented the Union forces from passing through the opening which they had made. Various organizations of Confederate veterans and sons of veterans have observed the anniversary from time to time and in the first decade of the present century they held an elaborate celebration in honor of the superior military genius of the defenders.

419

JULY THIRTY-FIRST

FEAST OF ST. IGNATIUS DE LOYOLA

When the feast of St. Ignatius de Loyola, founder of the Society of Jesus, commonly called the Jesuits, was first observed in America it would be difficult to discover. But it is probable that as soon as the Jesuit missionaries here learned that he had been canonized they arranged to observe the anniversary of his death. He died in Rome on July 31, 1556, was beatified by Pope Paul V in 1609 and canonized by Gregory XV in 1622. The bull of canonization was published in 1623 by Pope Urban VIII. News traveled slowly in those days and it probably was not until 1624 at the earliest that the new saint's day could have been observed here.

The Jesuit missionaries had been on this continent several years then. They first arrived in Florida in 1566, only ten years after the death of Ignatius. A school for the Florida Indians was opened in Havana in 1568. Father Segura, the vice provincial went from Florida to the Chesapeake Bay Region, on the invitation of an Indian chief called Don Luis by the Spaniards, and with seven members of the order and some Indian youths who had been educated at Havana, tried to establish a mission there. Don Luis proved treacherous and Father Segura and all his companions save one were murdered in 1570. The Jesuits then left Florida for Mexico. They established a mission in California under Father Kuhn or Kino in 1583 and gradually built sixteen stations each in charge of one missionary. In 1611 they began to work in the French possessions in America with Quebec as their headquarters. It is probable that it was in Quebec if not in Mexico that the feast day was first observed when news of the canonization of the saint reached this continent. The work of the society was interrupted in 1629 when the English carried off the missionaries in Quebec, but was resumed again in 1633. Among the missionaries sent out from France was Jacques Marquette who came to America in 1666 and in 1668 founded the mission of Sault Sainte Marie. His zeal in the work cost him his life, for while on a mission to the Illinois Indians he was taken ill and died on May 18, 1675, before he could reach his friends and was buried on the banks of a small stream entering Lake Michigan a little south of the Marquette River. The next year a party of converts from Ottawa dug up the remains and took them to the mission of St. Ignace, north of Mackinaw and buried them beneath the floor of the chapel.

The Society or Company of Jesus was founded on August 15, 1534, by Inigo Lopez de Recalde, more commonly known as Ignatius de Loyola, and five other young men, including Francis Xavier. Its members took vows of chastity, poverty and obedience to the Pope and pledged themselves to go as missionaries wherever they might be sent. They were first called Jesuits by Calvin in his "Institutes." Ignatius was probably born in 1491, the year before Columbus discovered America. Some authorities, however, say he was born in 1495. His father was a nobleman and lived in the castle of Loyola in Guipuzcoa, Spain. The boy served as a page at the court of Ferdinand V and later became a soldier. He was badly wounded in the defense of Pampeluna against the French in 1521 when his leg was broken by a cannon ball. The injury was so unskilfully treated that he was permanently lame. During his convalescence he amused himself by reading religious books, the only ones available, and as a result he repented of all his misdeeds and decided to live a holy life. He made a pilgrimage to Jerusalem and on his return went to Paris where he studied to complete his neglected education. It was there that he met the five young men who joined him on August 15, 1534, in vows of chastity, poverty and the devotion of their lives to the conversion of infidels and to the defense of the Holy Church. The society was not completely organized until the Feast of the Assumption, January 25, 1537, when the men had completed their studies. Paul III granted a constitution to the society on September 27, 1540. Since then the society has been banned by the Pope only to have the ban removed at a later date and it has been expelled from most of the countries of Europe and then readmitted to many of them. It is distinguished for its missionary and educational work. Francis Xavier worked with considerable success in India and in Japan. One of his successors in the East converted the Chinese emperor to Christianity and it is said that the emperor was ready to make Christianity the state religion if he could do so without offending his ancestors. The Jesuits found a way, according to tradition, but the Pope refused to approve it. Yet as the result of the work which these missionaries began there are more than two million Chinese Catholics.

BRETTON WOODS AGREEMENTS

The United States led the way in ratifying the Bretton Woods Agreements when President Roosevelt signed, on July 31, 1945, the Bretton Woods Agreements Act which accepted membership in the International Monetary Fund and the International Bank for Reconstruction and Development. The year 1945 marked the beginning of international monetary reconstruction following the drastic disruption of foreign exchanges and monetary systems produced by World War II. Several countries took steps to reconstruct their own monetary systems, and to regulate their relations with other countries. Secondly, international cooperation to stabilize currencies and to finance reconstruction was assured by the adoption of the Agreements, the Fund and Bank set up by these pacts providing machinery for the solution of future foreign exchange problems. The Fund was to be operated as a pool of world currencies and gold, from which member countries might draw when temporarily short of another member's currency. It was designed to tide members over short-term trade difficulties when otherwise they might have to curtail imports, subsidize exports, impose exchange controls, or take other restrictive action. It was provided by the Act that the Governor of the Fund, appointed by the President of the United States, would also serve as Governor of the International Bank, a step expected to assure that nations needing longer-term credits would be directed to the Bank so that they would not freeze the resources of the International Monetary Fund. With the same end in view, the Act set up a National Advisory Council on international monetary problems, which was to be composed of the Secretary of the Treasury as Chairman, the Secretary of State, the Secretary of Commerce, the Chairman of the Board of Governors of the Federal Reserve System, and the Chairman of the Board of Trustees of the Export-Import Bank. This Council was required to recommend general policy directives for the guidance of the United States on the Fund and the Bank, and to advise on major problems arising in the administration of both institutions. The legislation amended the Johnson Act of 1934 which prohibited loans to foreign governments in default on obligations due the United States Government, by exempting foreign governments holding membership in the Fund and Bank.

Constitution and Guerriere

AUGUST

The flowers withered on their stems,
The leaves hung limp and wan,
Within the trees a wistful breeze
Whispered and was gone;
The sky reached down a sweating hand
And pressed upon the wearied land.

—ANNE MARY LAWLER

In the ancient Roman calendar August was called Sextilis, or the sixth month, and it had only thirty days. Mark Anthony had the name of the fifth month of the year changed from Quintilis to July in honor of Caesar. Caesar had adopted his nephew, Gaius Julius Caesar Octavianus, and made him his heir. Octavianus finally succeeded to the power which his uncle had held and was made emperor. The Senate gave to him the title of Augustus, meaning venerable or revered, a title which the succeeding emperors assumed. As July had been named for his uncle, Augustus decided that a month should bear his name also. Although he was born in September he chose the month following July and decreed that it should be called August, because it was then that he had been admitted to the consulate, had celebrated a triumph three times, had received the allegiance of the soldiers stationed in Rome, had ended all the civil wars and had conquered Egypt. The Anglo-Saxon name for the month was Weod-monath, or the month when the weeds flourished; the word "weed" is supposed to signify vegetation in general, although in its early form its derivation is unknown.

AUGUST FIRST

COLORADO DAY

August 1, the anniversary of the admission of Colorado to the Union, is a legal holiday in the state, known as Colorado Day, and is observed at least by the display of the state and national flags on all public buildings. Occasionally the governor makes a speech setting forth the glories of the state. The proclamation of President Grant admitting the Territory to the Union was signed on August 1, 1876, so Colorado is known as the Centennial State, as it was admitted one hundred years after the Declaration of Independence.

The Act of Congress, passed March 3, 1875, providing for the admission of the territory as a state contained some unusual provisions. It directed as a condition of admission that the Constitution should provide by ordinance, irrevocable without the consent of the United States and the people of the state the following provisions: That perfect religious toleration should be secured; that the people should disclaim all right to the unappropriated public lands; that the lands should remain at the sole disposition of the United States; that the land in Colorado belonging to citizens of the United States living outside the state should not be taxed at a higher rate than the lands belonging to residents; and that no tax should be levied on lands or property of the United States. As the people of the territory had adopted a constitution conforming to the Act of Congress in these particulars President Grant issued his proclamation.

The region that is now Colorado was first explored by the Spaniards in the second half of the eighteenth century, but Spain made no attempt to send settlers into it. Part of the region was in the territory that came into the possession of the United States by the Louisiana Purchase in 1803; the remainder was in territory ceded by Mexico.

Captain Zebulon M. Pike entered the territory in 1806-07 and saw the mountain which has been named for him. John C. Fremont explored part of the region in 1842 and 1844. Emigrants from Georgia and Kansas, including some prospectors for gold, entered Colorado in 1858. When gold was discovered near Boulder and Idaho Springs in 1859 emigrants from various parts of the country flocked there and the mining towns of Denver and Boulder sprang up. A territorial government was set up on February 28, 1861. In 1862 and 1864 unsuccessful attempts were made to organize a state government finally culminating in success in 1876.

424

SWISS INDEPENDENCE DAY

It was on August 1, 1291, that the cantons of Uri, Schwyz and Unterwalden in Switzerland formed a permanent confederation for defense. This was the beginning of the present Swiss Confederation, the oldest government with a continuous existence in the western world. The anniversary is celebrated with festivities in Switzerland. In the United States the Swiss emigrants and their descendants, led by the consuls of their country, observe the day in various ways. Switzerland is represented by consuls in twelve cities and by a minister in Washington. There are in the country about 293,973 persons born in Switzerland; counting the descendants of Swiss stock however the number who look with pride to the action of their ancestors more than six hundred years ago is several hundred thousand.

AUGUST SECOND

THE FIRST STREET LETTER BOXES

Prior to August 2, 1858, writers of letters in cities as well as in villages had to take them to the postoffice to be mailed. On that date, however, street boxes were set up in Boston in which letters could be deposited to be collected by men from the postoffice. This innovation was soon adopted in other cities. It was not until 1863 that the postoffices began to deliver mail to houses or offices in the large cities. In 1865 free delivery was extended to all cities with a population of at least 50,000. In 1873 it was extended to cities of 20,000 and in 1887 to those with 10,000 population, and since then it has been extended to smaller communities. In 1896 an experiment was made with free delivery to families living outside of the towns and villages which proved so satisfactory that it has been extended to cover practically the whole of rural America.

The present postal system has developed from that set up by the Continental Congress on July 26, 1775, when Benjamin Franklin was made postmaster general with authority to establish a line of postoffices from Falmouth, Me., to Savannah, Ga. The postal rates fixed in 1792 remained unchanged for nearly fifty years. The charge for letters was then six cents for thirty miles or less, eight cents for between thirty and sixty miles, gradually increasing until the rate was twenty-five cents for distances in excess of four hundred and fifty miles. In 1845 the rates were reduced but varied with the distance. It was not until 1851 that a uniform rate for not to exceed three thousand miles was fixed, and in 1863 the matter of distance was eliminated from the rate schedule.

AUGUST THIRD

COLUMBUS SAILS

Christopher Columbus sailed from Palos, Spain, on August 3, 1492, on his first voyage westward in search of a route to China and the Far East. He was authorized to search for certain islands west of the Sargasso Sea and when he reached the islands off the coast of the American continent he thought he had reached India. (See Columbus Day, October 12.) The consequences of the voyage which began on August 3 were greater than those of any other event in the Christian era for they broadened the human outlook and revolutionized the thinking of the world in more than the geographical field.

AUGUST FOURTH

FEAST OF ST. DOMINIC

St. Dominic, the founder of the Dominicans, or the Order of Preaching Friars, was born at Carlaroga, in the north of Spain in 1170. It is generally believed that he was a member of the famous Guzman family. He studied theology and in 1195 became a canon of Osma in Satile. With his bishop he traveled extensively, journeying as far north as Denmark. On his return he found some officials of his church at Montpellier discussing ways to counteract the disposition of the people to abandon the Catholic faith, and he joined in a movement to keep the people loyal. In 1215 he founded the order of preaching friars and while in Rome seeking approval of it from the Pope he met St. Francis of Assisi and the two became friends. As a result of this friendship the Franciscans and the Dominicans each celebrate the feast day of the other. Dominic died in 1221 and was canonized in 1224. The order spread rapidly until in the eighteenth century it maintained a thousand houses in various parts of the world. It was introduced into the United States in 1805 where there are a score of Dominican houses. Many churches are named for the saint and he is as highly esteemed by the Anglican as by his own church. One of the interesting observances of his feast day is at the San Domingo Pueblo in New Mexico when the Indians hold their great Corn Dance. This dance is in reality an animated prayer for rain, a survival of an ancient rite added to a Christian festival. The men paint their bodies gray or a bright blue and wear fringes of evergreen, and the women wear headdresses of carved wood painted blue. The dance lasts from dawn to sunset when the dancers drop from exhaustion.

426

ACQUITTAL OF JOHN PETER ZENGER

The anniversary of the acquittal of John Peter Zenger of New York of the charge of libel on August 4, 1735, is one of the most important dates in the history of the freedom of the press in America. Zenger landed in New York, a young boy, in 1710. He learned the printer's trade with William Bradford, publisher of the New York *Weekly Gazette*. As a reporter for the *Gazette*, he went to East Chester to report a special election for a member of the Assembly. Lewis Morris, who had been removed as Chief Justice of the Supreme Court by Governor William S. Cosby because he decided against the Governor in a case involving the fees of his office, was the candidate of the party opposed to the Governor. The Governor called the election for October 29, 1733, and had one of his lieutenants enter the race against Judge Morris. Zenger wrote a report of the election which was held in St. Paul's Episcopal Church, which still stands in what is now the city of Mount Vernon. He wrote that thirty-eight Quakers were not allowed to vote as they asked to affirm instead of swearing, that the sheriff tried to intimidate the voters, and that Cosby's agents tried to vote a group of nonresident sailors from the waterfront in New York. Bradford declined to print the report in his newspaper. Thereupon Judge Morris and two lawyers who had been disbarred by the Governor because they refused to do his bidding arranged to finance a new paper to be called the New York *Weekly Journal* and made Zenger editor. He printed his report of the election in the first number of the new paper and then in later issues printed exposures of graft and malfeasance by Governor Cosby and his associates. In November 1734, Zenger was arrested on orders from the Governor, charged with "publishing several seditious libels" and bail was fixed so high that Zenger could not raise the money. The Governor had assigned one of his ablest legal supporters to conduct the prosecution. The two disbarred lawyers supporting the cause of Zenger had obtained the assistance of Andrew Hamilton of Philadelphia, one of the ablest attorneys in the colonies. His appearance in court surprised the prosecution for his legal reputation was well known in New York. In the defense he admitted that Zenger had printed the accounts as charged, but he insisted that they were true. He denied the validity of the old legal maxim, "The greater the truth the greater the libel," and argued that if free government were to exist the people must be allowed to criticize their public officials and to be exempt from punishment if the charges against those officials were true. In his concluding appeal he said:

> The question before the court and you, gentlemen of the jury, is not of small or private concern. It is not the cause of a poor printer, nor of New York alone, which you are trying. No. It may in its consequences affect every freeman that lives under British government on the main of America. It is the best cause. It is the cause of liberty. And I make no doubt but your upright conduct, this day, will not only entitle you to the love and esteem of your fellow citizens, but every man who prefers freedom to a life of slavery will bless and honor you as

men who have baffled the attempt at tyranny and who, by an impartial and un-corrupt verdict, have laid a noble foundation for securing to ourselves and our posterity and our neighbors that to which nature and the laws of our country have given us a right—the liberty both of exposing and opposing arbitrary power by speaking and writing the truth.

The jury retired and in a short time returned with a verdict of acquittal, at which the crowd in the court room burst into cheers taken up by the crowd outside awaiting the outcome.

AUGUST FIFTH

BIRTHDAY OF JOHN ELIOT

John Eliot, known as the "Apostle to the Indians," was born at Widford, Hertfordshire, England, on August 5, 1604. He was educated at Jesus College, Cambridge University, came under the influence of Thomas Hooker, and left the Church of England. He sailed for America and arrived at Boston in 1631. Thomas Hooker followed him two years later. Eliot preached in Boston for two years and then became the "teacher" of a church at Roxbury, now part of Boston, and remained there for the rest of his life. He learned the language of the Pequot Indians from an Indian prisoner in 1637. It was not until 1646, however, that he began his active work among the Indians, preaching his first sermon to them at Nonantum, now part of the city of Newton in the suburbs of Boston, on October 26 of that year. He traveled through-out eastern Massachusetts, preaching to the Indians and organizing the Christians into separate communities. Through his influence a Society for the Propagation of the Gospel among the Indians, which was organized in London, sent him money every year to supplement the small salary which he received from the Roxbury church. His *Catechism*, the first book printed in the Indian language, appeared in 1653. He completed his translation of the Bible for the Indians in 1663; it was the first Bible printed in America. He also published an Indian Primer and an Indian Grammar. He died on May 21, 1690, after a long and useful life.

FIRST USE OF THE ATOMIC BOMB

The first atomic bomb used in warfare was dropped on Hiroshima, Japan, August 5, 1945, from an American superfortress called Enola Gay, piloted by Colonel Paul W. Tibbets, Jr. The city of 343,000 population was 60 per cent obliterated, only 2.8 square miles of its total 6.9 square miles remaining undemolished. Announcement from Washington, D.C., of the spectacular success of this new secret weapon was made August 6, and so great had been the psychological force of the demonstration that

428

Japan speedily sued for peace, surrendering within a matter of days. Thus the atomic bomb was the coup de grace which brought to an end World War II. A second bomb was dropped on Nagasaki five days later and it was reported one third destroyed; it had an area of twelve square miles. Domei, an official Japanese news agency, issued a statement August 22 that 70,000 had been killed outright and 120,000 made homeless in the two atomic blasts. On June 30, 1946, an experimental bomb was dropped on a fleet of seventy-three obsolete ships assembled at Bikini Atoll in the Pacific. Considerable damage was wrought, but the chief value of the experiment was in furnishing data for scientific study. It was planned to continue the experiments at intervals as a basis for extensive research in the field of atomic energy.

The history of the development of atomic energy is marked by four important dates: January 26, 1929, when American physicists learned of European experiments showing that one of the uranium isotopes underwent fission with release of nuclear energy when bombarded with slow neutrons; December 2, 1942, when the first self-maintaining nuclear chain reaction was initiated in a uranium-graphite pile at Stagg Field Stadium, Chicago; July 16, 1945, when the first atomic explosion created by man was released in the New Mexico desert; and August 5, 1946, when the first atomic bomb used in warfare was dropped on Hiroshima, Japan, wreaking unprecedented destruction.

In the announcement of the successful bombing of Hiroshima, President Truman stated that "we have spent two billion dollars on the greatest scientific gamble in history—and won." However, the development and use of the bomb, in addition to hastening the surrender of Japan, raised a serious issue in international diplomacy which complicated the peace conferences following World War II. Although it was expected that the scientists of other nations would eventually discover the secret of the bomb, meanwhile those nations not "in the know" regarded the situation with extreme distrust. After a conference in Washington, D.C., President Truman, Prime Minister Atlee of Great Britain, and W. L. Mackenzie King of Canada issued a statement, November 15, 1945, that the secret of the manufacture of the bomb was to be retained for the present by the United States, Canada and Great Britain, but would be shared with other powers after adequate international controls had been established over the use of atomic energy.

Aside from its unique capacity for destruction, as exemplified by the atomic bomb, scientific understanding of atomic energy revealed the fact that it is capable of introducing about five thousand new or improved products and procedures into American industry. Especially important were the improvements in pumps, since it was estimated that in twenty years the benefits accruing from this source alone will probably be worth the outlay of two billion dollars by the government for the whole atomic project. In the field of medicine, the development of atomic energy led to the discovery of a method for treating skin cancer, more

promising than anything except surgery which has been found in many
years of research.

AUGUST SIXTH

FEAST OF THE TRANSFIGURATION

The Feast of the Transfiguration is observed by all branches of the
Christian church. The event which it commemorates is described in the
seventeenth chapter of St. Matthew in this way:

After six days Jesus taketh Peter, James and John his brother, and bringeth
them up into a high mountain apart and was transfigured before them; and his
face did shine as the sun, and his raiment was white with light. And, behold,
there appeared unto them Moses and Elias talking with him. Then answered
Peter, and said unto Jesus, "Lord, it is good for us to be here; if thou wilt, let
us make here three tabernacles; one for thee, and one for Moses and one for
Elias." While he yet spoke, behold, a bright cloud overshadowed them; and
behold a voice out of the cloud which said "This is my beloved son in whom I
am well pleased; hear ye him." And when the disciples heard it they fell on
their faces and were sore afraid. And Jesus came and touched them and said,
"Arise, be not afraid." And when they had lifted up their eyes, they saw no
man, save Jesus only. And as they came down from the mountain Jesus charged
them, saying, "Tell the vision to no man, until the Son of man be risen again
from the dead."

The "high mountain" has been identified as Mount Tabor. Peter
in his Second Epistle calls it "the holy mountain." The Transfiguration
is described by the theologians as "the culminating point of His public
life, as His baptism is its starting point and His ascension its end." It is
uncertain when the Church first began to celebrate the event. An Armenian bishop writing near the end of the seventh century says that St.
Gregory the Illuminator, who lived in the first half of the fourth century,
was the first to observe it and that he substituted it for a pagan feast
of Aphrodite called Vatavarh, or Roseflame, and that he retained the old
name as Christ opened His glory like a rose in the presence of His disciples. The ecclesiastical authorities conjecture that the celebration began
in the fourth or fifth century in the highlands of Asia in place of some
nature feast. In the Armenian church it is kept for three days as one of
the five great feasts. It is not mentioned among the feasts of the Latin
church until 850. It found a place in the liturgy in the tenth century
and was celebrated on August 6. In Gaul and England it was observed
on July 27. In 1456 Pope Calixtus III extended its observance to the universal church in memory of a victory over the Turks gained by Hunyady
at Belgrade on August 6 of that year. It is the titular feast of the Lateran
Basilica at Rome, and on November 1, 1911, it was raised to the rank
of a double second class feast for the whole church. On that day the
Pope uses new wine at Mass or presses a bunch of ripe grapes into the
chalice, and he also blesses raisins. The Greeks and the Russians are

accustomed to bless grapes and other fruits on that day. (See Blessing the Berries, June 17.)

AUGUST SEVENTH

CREATION OF THE WAR DEPARTMENT

The War Department, the second of the executive departments of the Federal Government to be set up, was created by the Act of August 7, 1789, passed at the first session of the First Congress. The first was the State Department, established by the Act of July 27, 1789, and it was described as "an executive department to be denominated the Department of Foreign Affairs." The War Department originally had jurisdiction over the navy as well as the army. It was not until 1798 that the Navy Department was separated from the War Department. The heads of the executive departments were early spoken of as the Cabinet, although there is no provision in the Constitution for such a body. There was no mention of the Cabinet in any law until the Act of February 26, 1907, increasing the salaries of its members from $8,000 to $12,000 a year, in which reference is made to "the heads of the executive departments who are members of the President's Cabinet."

CHAUTAUQUA DAY

On the first Tuesday in August every year—it fell on August 7 in 1945—the Chautauqua Institution on Chautauqua Lake, N.Y., celebrates the anniversary of its founding. On August 4, 1874, a Sunday school camp meeting opened on the shores of the lake and continued in session for two weeks. It was planned by Lewis Miller of Akron, Ohio, and the Rev. John H. Vincent of New York. They were interested in improving the character of the Sunday schools and the quality of the teaching in them, and they arranged lectures and courses of study with this end in view. They also provided lectures on secular topics and various forms of amusement for the relaxation of those attending. A large relief map of Palestine was built on the shores of the lake and the students were conducted over it by guides who pointed out the various places mentioned in the Bible story.

The plan was broadened from year to year, and the length of the session increased. Courses were offered in subjects taught in colleges and a correspondence school was maintained for some years. Besides these exercises of particular interest to habitual Chautauquans, those who spend the summer or only a week or two there are entertained by symphony concerts, operas and plays as well as by lectures by noted laymen and clergymen. The tent city has given place to a community containing many substantial buildings for the use of the various schools, a large

431

auditorium, and many hotels and cottages. Dr. William R. Harper, who was president of the University of Chicago when he died, taught Hebrew there for several seasons. Fourteen or fifteen different schools are maintained during the summer. Dr. George E. Vincent, son of the founder, was president of the institution from 1907 to 1915. He was succeeded by Dr. Arthur E. Bestor, who served until his death on February 2, 1944. Since that time there has been an acting president. The anniversary of the founding is known as Old First Night and is celebrated by special exercises and frequently by a display of fireworks not only on the grounds but all around Chautauqua Lake itself.

AUGUST EIGHTH

BIRTHDAY OF CHARLES A. DANA

Charles A. Dana, who won fame as the editor of the New York *Sun*, was born at Hinsdale, N.H., on August 8, 1819. He studied at Harvard College, but had to abandon his course because of defective eyesight. He joined the Brook Farm Association in Massachusetts in 1841 and edited its paper. On the failure of this experiment he was employed by the New York *Tribune* and became its managing editor at a salary of $50 a week. While connected with the *Tribune* he planned the *New American Encyclopedia* and edited it in association with George Ripley. He was Assistant Secretary of War in 1863 and 1864. At the close of the war he edited the Chicago *Republican* and on its failure he returned to New York as part owner and editor of the *Sun* in 1868, which he conducted with great vigor and independence until his death in 1897.

AUGUST NINTH

BIRTHDAY OF IZAAK WALTON

The memory of Izaak Walton is kept green in America by a large number of fishing clubs named in his honor. He was born on August 9, 1593, in the parish of St. Mary, Stafford, England, and went to London when he was about eighteen years old where he became an ironmonger. From 1628 to 1644 he lived in Chancery Lane, a neighbor to Dr. John Donne. He became the intimate friend of other clergymen and visited them frequently in various parts of England. When Dr. Donne's sermons were published in 1640, the book contained a life of the clergyman written by Walton. The first complete edition of *The Compleat Angler, or the Contemplative Man's Recreation*, appeared in 1653. It was so popular that five editions of it were published during his life and since his death it has been republished more than one hundred times. The fame of this great classic of angling in English literature has led fishermen to call themselves disciples of Izaak Walton. Modern American fishermen, however, instead of imitating the simplicity and truthfulness of Walton, often offer prizes for the man who can tell the biggest and most incredible fishing yarn.

AUGUST TENTH

BIRTHDAY OF HERBERT CLARK HOOVER

Herbert Clark Hoover, thirty-first President of the United States, was born at West Branch, Iowa, on August 10, 1874. West Branch had been founded by his family as a Quaker settlement in 1853. His ancestors had been Quakers for many generations. The first American member of the family settled in Maryland about 1740, and like many other families its members made many migrations westward until some of them reached the Pacific coast. It was in West Branch, however, that Hoover spent his boyhood. When his father and mother died he went to Oregon to live with an uncle engaged in the real estate business. After talking with an engineer he decided to adopt that profession and at the age of seventeen, entered the first class in the new Leland Stanford, Junior, University at Palo Alto, Calif. He worked his way through college and was graduated in 1895. During his vacations he had worked upon the Arkansas and United States Geological Surveys thus obtaining much valuable training. Soon after his graduation he went to Nevada City hoping to find employment at his profession, but as there was no opening he accepted a job as a laborer in the mines. In 1896 he heard of Louis Janin of San Francisco who had large interests in mining, and left Nevada City for the coast to ask Janin for work. Janin at first hired him as a handy man about his office and as he proved his ability gave him more and more responsible work. When gold was discovered in Australia an English company which wished to use American methods in developing its Australian mines asked Janin to recommend an engineer to them. He recommended Hoover who accepted. So when he was not yet twenty-four years old he went to Australia at a salary of $7500 a year and opened and equipped a mine for his employers to their satisfaction. He remained in Australia for about two years when he went to China to superintend mining and transportation for the government of Sun Yat-sen. He was there during the Boxer insurrection and assisted the white population in resisting the attacks of the Chinese. Until 1914 he was engaged in mining operations in various parts of the world, while retaining his citizenship in the United States.

When the first World War broke out he was living in London and at once decided to devote himself to such tasks as the crisis presented.

433

At first he assisted Americans stranded in London to get passage home. Then he was occupied with feeding the starving people in Belgium and when the war ended he directed relief work in Germany. For a time he was at the head of the Food Administration in the United States. His fame by this time was worldwide and in 1920 there was a demand that he be nominated for President of the United States. But the politicians had decreed otherwise and Warren G. Harding was nominated by the Republicans. Mr. Harding was elected and took Hoover into his Cabinet as Secretary of Commerce, a post which he held until he was nominated for President by the Republican National Convention in 1928. He was elected over Alfred E. Smith of New York, the Democratic candidate, and was nominated to succeed himself in 1932. During his first year as President, in the autumn of 1929, there was a financial panic bringing disaster to tens of thousands. At his suggestion the Reconstruction Finance Corporation was created to relieve financial institutions and the railroads and save them from bankruptcy. It did not suffice and many banks failed. He was defeated for reelection as Martin VanBuren had been defeated more than seventy-five years before because of the financial panic which occurred during his term of office.

FEAST OF ST. LAWRENCE

St. Lawrence, one of the distinguished Christian martyrs, was noted for piety in his youth. According to the traditions about him Pope Sixtus II made him his archdeacon and put in his charge the treasures of the Church, including the vessels of gold and silver and the embroidered vestments of the priests. The Emperor Valerian, at the beginning of August 258, ordered that all Christian bishops, priests and deacons be put to death. On August 6 Sixtus was taken in the catacombs and summarily put to death. Before he died he predicted that Lawrence would die within three days and would suffer greatly. Lawrence in the meantime had distributed the treasures of the Church among the poor Christians in Rome and when Valerian demanded that he surrender the treasures he presented the poor to him with the remark, "Here they are." He was then put to torture in the hope that he would reveal the hiding place of the things which it was thought he had concealed. Then it was ordered that he be put to death by being placed on a grate of iron bars arranged like a gridiron and that a fire be lighted under it and kept burning until he died. This was on August 10, the day that is observed by the Roman and Anglican church as his feast day. On the night of this day the Perseids appear in the heavens and they were traditionally described for years as the sparks from St. Lawrence's gridiron. The Irish call them the tears of St. Lawrence.

The scholars of the Church discredit the legends about him, but they are confident that he was a real person. Whether he was a native of the kingdom of Aragon in Spain is not known with any definiteness although that is said to have been his birthplace. A church was built in Rome in his honor and there are many churches in the United States dedicated to him. He is usually represented in art with a gridiron. There is a thirteenth century manuscript in the library of Lambeth Palace in London, the official residence of the Archbishop of Canterbury, showing him in this way. And there is a painting in the Vatican by Fra Angelico representing him kneeling at the feet of Pope Sixtus who is ordaining him as a deacon.

The St. Lawrence River is named for this martyr. Jacques Cartier, on his second voyage of exploration, entered the gulf at the mouth of the river on August 10, 1536, and named it the Bay of St. Lawrence. In the course of time this name was extended to the whole river.

Philip II of Spain built the Escorial in honor of the saint. During the battle of San Quentin in which the Spaniards defeated the French on St. Lawrence's Day in 1557 a church dedicated to the saint was destroyed. In fulfillment of a vow of gratitude Philip built the Escorial on a bleak eminence called by the same name, a word which means "slag" or "scoria." It was begun in 1563 and completed in 1574. It covers a rectangle 750 by 580 feet and is built roughly in the shape of the gridiron on which St. Lawrence, according to tradition, was martyred. It is known as the Royal Monastery of San Lorenzo of Escorial. Included in it besides the monastery are a magnificent church and a royal palace. The Kings of Spain were buried in the church, the west portal of which was opened only to receive the King on his first visit after ascending the throne and to receive his body to be buried.

AUGUST ELEVENTH

FULTON'S STEAMBOAT SAILS

Although he did not invent the steamboat, Robert Fulton has the distinction of making steam navigation commercially successful. The "Clermont," built in 1807, sailed up the Hudson River from New York City on August 11 of that year. Within a month it was making regular trips between New York and Albany. The first steamboat in America was built by John Fitch of Philadelphia who operated it on the Delaware River for several weeks in the summer of 1788, but his enterprise failed because of lack of financial support. Fulton was born at Little Britain, Pa., in 1765, and as a youth he was apprenticed to a jeweller in Philadelphia. He added to his income by painting portraits and landscapes. In 1789 he went to London and studied painting under Benjamin West. But his mechanical genius asserted itself and he abandoned art for invention. In 1795 he went to Paris where he lived several years. While there he invented a submarine boat for use in naval warfare but could not persuade the French to buy it. In 1803 he built a small steamboat which he operated on the Seine. He received the support of Robert Livingston, the American minister in Paris, whose niece he later married, and on his return to America in 1806, he began to carry out his plans for steam navigation. In 1814 he built a steam frigate for the navy. He died in 1815.

JOHN ALDEN DAY

The descendants of John Alden and Priscilla Mullens (or Molines) gather in Duxbury, Mass., on the second Saturday in August every year to commemorate their first American ancestor. This fell on August 11 in 1945. They began an organized celebration in 1901 when the Alden Kindred of America was incorporated in Massachusetts. Branches of the kindred have since then been organized in various cities including Chicago, Los Angeles, Binghamton, N.Y., and New York City. It is in Duxbury that John Alden had a farm on which he built a house. Near its original site there stands a house built in early colonial days that was occupied by his descendants until it was bought by the Alden Kindred. According to some authorities it is the original Alden home. A log cabin has been built on the grounds in which the members of the association meet annually, eat an old-fashioned shore dinner, and listen to speeches in honor of the first American Alden.

The exact date of the birth of John Alden is not known, but it is supposed to have been in the year 1599. And nothing definite is known about his family although the name is not uncommon in the eastern counties of England. He was one of the passengers on the "Mayflower," and when Bradford drew up the Mayflower Compact, after the ship had arrived at Plymouth, Mass., in December 1620, Alden was one of those who signed it. He proved to be one of the responsible men in the new colony for in 1627 he was one of eight men who assumed the colonial debt. In that year or thereabouts he left Plymouth for a farm of 169 acres which he had acquired in Duxbury, not far from Plymouth. Miles Standish was one of his Duxbury neighbors. Alden held a number of important offices in the colony. He was surveyor of highways, a deputy representing Duxbury in the Colonial Council, treasurer, assistant governor and deputy governor. He died in 1667, the last surviving signer of the Mayflower Compact, and was buried in South Duxbury. The site of his grave, however, is not known. He married Priscilla Mullens, whether in 1621 or 1623 is not definitely known. She had come to America with her parents and a brother. According to some historians she was a French Huguenot. It is said that her father's name on the passenger list of the "Speedwell," when it left Delfthaven to meet the "Mayflower" at Southampton, appeared as Guillaume Molines, and that it was corrupted to Mullens by the English. At any rate the family was known as Mullens when the "Mayflower" landed. During the first winter the father, mother and brother died, leaving Priscilla an orphan. John

Alden courted and won her and Governor Bradford married them. Long-fellow's poem "The Courtship of Miles Standish" preserves a tradition for which there is doubtful historical basis. But there is not the slightest doubt that Alden married Priscilla. And Governor Bradford is authority for the statement that they had eleven children. It is estimated that their descendants number more than three million. Longfellow, himself, was one of the descendants on his mother's side and it may be that the story of the courtship came down to him as a tradition in the family. When John died at the age of eighty-eight years he left an estate valued at £80 of which half consisted of boots and shoes, indicating that he must have been a merchant of some kind. Their first home in Plymouth was a one-room log house with a roof of swamp grass. The house standing in Duxbury, assuming that it was occupied by them, is said to be the third which they built. It is a one-story frame building with an attic, similar to many houses that were built in the early days of the colony as well as in later years.

AUGUST TWELFTH

FEAST OF ST. CLARE

Saint Clare founded the order of Franciscan nuns sometimes called "Poor Clares," and was canonized by Pope Alexander IV in 1255, two years after her death. Her feast is observed on August 12. She was the daughter of Phavirino Sciffo of Assisi and attended the first great gathering of the Franciscan order on Palm Sunday, 1212, with her father and mother and two sisters. She was deeply impressed by the sermon of St. Francis who explained his theory of poverty and devotion, and decided to follow his example. That night she went to the Portiuncula where Francis was living in poverty and asked him to allow her to serve in any humble manner. She gave him her jewels and rich garments as proof of her sincerity. He was impressed by her devotion and took her to the Benedictine convent until he could prepare a place for her. He built a simple hut near those occupied by his followers where other devoted women joined her. Out of this group came the order of Franciscan nuns of which Clare became the head in October 1212. Its members are pledged to poverty and good works.

AUGUST THIRTEENTH

FEAST OF ST. HIPPOLYTUS

The feast of St. Hippolytus is observed on August 13, three days after the feast of St. Lawrence with whom he is connected in tradition. (See Feast of St. Lawrence, August 10.) According to this tradition

437

Hippolytus, a Roman officer and his family were converted to Christianity by the refusal of St. Lawrence to recant, and when he and his family remained steadfast in the faith his nurse was scourged to death and nineteen other members of his family were beheaded. He said that rather than recant he would prefer to be tied to the tails of wild horses. He was so tied and met his death in that way. This legend probably has its origin in the story of Hippolytus, the son of Theseus who was dragged to his death when his horses ran away. The ecclesiastical scholars, however, identify the saint whose feast is observed on August 13 with a bishop of Rome who died in 236 or thereabouts. He held views of his own and when Callistus was elected Pope in 207 or 208, he left the church of Rome and had himself elected antipope by a group of followers. He remained in opposition during the reigns of two other popes and was banished to the island of Sardinia where he died. His remains were taken back to Rome on August 13, probably immediately after his death. It is supposed that he had withdrawn his opposition before his death, as his name is in the calendar of saints.

AUGUST FOURTEENTH

V-J DAY

Although President Truman proclaimed September 2 as V-J Day, following the formal ratification of surrender by Japan to the Allies on September 1, 1945, aboard the battleship Missouri in Tokyo Bay, the Japanese capitulation and the end of World War II had been officially announced by the President on August 14, 1945, and this was the date on which the nation celebrated its great victory. Since then, the anniversary has been observed by the army and navy and other services, with appropriate ceremonies, at various posts and bases throughout the world. Michigan has made August 14 a legal holiday, calling it Victory Day. But it is certain no observance of the anniversary will ever approach the unrehearsed display that took place on the day itself. At 7 P.M., Eastern War Time, August 14, 1945, the moving electric sign on the Times Tower in New York City flashed the words, "Official—Truman announces Japanese surrender," and set off an unparalleled demonstration which was typical on a lesser scale of every city, town and village in the United States. The terriffic roar that greeted the announcement on the Times Tower lasted for twenty minutes and literally deafened the participants. Those in the streets tossed hats and flags into the air, and from those in the windows of adjacent hotels and office buildings came the shower of confetti streamers invariably cast upon the city by New Yorkers in celebration of major events. People began pouring into Times Square, from the subways and busses and on foot, and in a short time they were packed so solidly individual movement was impossible. By 10 P.M. the Manhattan police estimated that two million persons were in the Times Square area from 40th to 52nd Streets between Sixth and Eighth Avenues, making an all-time record. The rest of the city displayed equal enthusiasm; Greenwich Village was a madhouse and in Queens thousands staged impromptu parades; Emperor Hirohito was hanged in effigy from electric light poles in the Bronx and other boroughs; everywhere automobiles, taxis and trucks ran through the streets with passengers on the running boards and perched on the hoods, as well as two deep inside, their passage accompanied by shouting and horn blowing. The sacred dragon, reserved for the Chinese New Year and considered a symbol of peace, was called out in the narrow, crooked streets of Chinatown and there were four ritualistic, dragon-led processions through Mott, Doyer and Pell Streets. The metropolitan fire departments were run ragged answering both real and false alarms turned in by exhuberant citizens. Even those who stayed off the streets exhibited similar unrestraint by throwing "victory parties" for their friends lasting far into the night. Other cities expressed their joy and relief with the same extravagance; a victory bonfire was started on busy Market Street in San Francisco; servicemen and civilians, men and women, old and young, joined in a conga line on the grass of Lafayette Square across from the White House in Washington, D.C. Needless to add, the whole country, urban, suburban and rural, rejoiced in their hearts, whether or not they took part in the public demonstrations.

Prior to the surrender of Japan, in a joint proclamation issued at Potsdam, July 26, 1945, President Truman and retiring Prime Minister Winston Churchill of Great Britain, with the concurrence of Generalissimo Chiang Kai-shek, had called upon the Japanese Government to surrender unconditionally or face "prompt and utter destruction." It was promised that the Japanese people would be neither "enslaved as a race nor destroyed as a nation," but Japan's sovereignty was to be limited to her home islands, and she was to be stripped of the power to wage war. Following the proclamation American warships entered Tokyo Bay and smashed the remnants of the Japanese navy. Along a four-hundred-mile arc of coast, fliers wrought the same wholesale destruction which brought the fall of Germany; and still Tokyo ignored the surrender ultimatum. However, on August 5 the first atomic bomb used in warfare was dropped on Hiroshima, very nearly wiping out the munitions city. This was apparently the final blow needed to bring home realization of their defeat and Japan capitulated, with the provision that Emperor Hirohito might remain on the throne. The Allies agreed, but stipulated that the Emperor should submit to the authority of the Supreme Allied Command in Japan, and that his future should depend on a free election by the Japanese people. After some delay the Tokyo radio announced the decision of the Japanese Government to surrender. On September 1, 1945, the formal articles were ratified aboard the "Missouri" in Tokyo Bay, with General Douglas MacArthur, Supreme Commander in Chief, signing in behalf of the Allies, and Admiral Chester W. Nimitz for the United States. Altogether, twelve signatures were affixed to the historic document, including those of representatives of each of the Allies, as well as the two Japanese representatives. On September 7 the Stars and Stripes were raised over General MacArthur's headquarters in Tokyo, marking formal occupation of the city. Incidentally, the flag used was the one that flew over the Capitol in Washington, D.C., on December 7, 1941, when the Japanese attacked Pearl Harbor. This flag also flew over conquered Algiers, Rome, Berlin, and the battleship "Missouri" during the ratification ceremonies, the latter being a unique event since Japan had never before admitted total defeat in the two thousand years of her recorded history.

THE ATLANTIC CHARTER

President Franklin D. Roosevelt and Prime Minister Winston Churchill met "somewhere on the Atlantic" early in August 1941 and issued a joint declaration of the peace aims of the United States and Great Britain, which was termed the Atlantic Charter. The official statement covering the meeting was issued in Washington, D.C., on August 14. The whole problem of the supply of munitions of war, as provided by the Lend-Lease Act, for the armed forces of the United States and all other countries actively engaged in resisting aggression, was examined by the President and Mr. Churchill, who were accompanied by officials of their two countries, including high ranking officers of their military, naval and air services. They also particularly considered "the dangers to world civilization arising from the policies of military domination by conquest upon which the Hitlerite government of Germany and other governments associated therewith have embarked," and came to certain agreements.

Both countries disclaimed any territorial ambitions, and, further, desired no territorial changes anywhere in the world that did not accord with the freely expressed wishes of the people. Belief in the rights and privileges of a democratic form of government for all nations was strongly expressed, including a world economic policy that would enable every nation to prosper. Establishment of a lasting peace, affording security to all, was hoped for and such a peace must guarantee the freedom of the seas. Lastly, it was agreed that the "use of force" must be abandoned by the nations of the world and, as a first step, the disarmament of any nation actually or potentially threatening aggression was believed essential.

AUGUST FIFTEENTH

FEAST OF THE ASSUMPTION OF THE VIRGIN

The Feast of the Assumption of the Virgin Mary is celebrated on August 15 by the Roman Catholic Church with a mass designated in the

Catholic missal. From early times the Assumption, or taking up into heaven, of the Virgin Mary has been venerated as the greatest of her feasts and one of the chief solemnities of the Church year. The tradition of the Church claims that the Mother of Jesus "departed from this life" and was taken body and soul into heaven.

Few particulars are recorded in Scripture concerning the life of Mary. The apocryphal books tell of her birth, childhood, and betrothal to Joseph, while the Gospel narratives introduce her as the spouse of Joseph at the time the Angel Gabriel announced to her that the Son of God, conceived by the Holy Ghost, would be born of her, a Virgin. The narratives of the life of Jesus mention her in several places, most movingly when she stands on Calvary and her crucified Son commends her to the care of John. The date of her death is commonly fixed as the year 48 and the place, Jerusalem. The belief that her body was "assumed" into heaven is based on the tradition that the apostles, coming to her tomb on the third day after her interment, found the tomb empty, but exhaling an "exceedingly sweet fragrance."

AUGUST SIXTEENTH

BATTLE OF BENNINGTON

The anniversary of the Battle of Bennington is a legal holiday in the State of Vermont. The cities are decorated with flags on that day and there are parades and patriotic addresses and various organizations take advantage of the holiday to arrange picnics and athletic contests. Appropriate exercises are usually held at the base of the battle monument in Bennington. This monument rises to the height of 306 feet and four inches and is said to be the tallest memorial in New England. It stands in a park on the site of the battlefield.

The battle, fought on August 16, 1777, was largely influential in frustrating the plans of the British to separate New England from the rest of the colonies. General Burgoyne started from Canada early in May with a force of 10,000 with the hope of meeting Lord Howe with an army at Albany. Howe's army was delayed by its efforts to take Philadelphia and by Washington's tactics in the retreat after his defeat at the Battle of Brandywine. On August 13 General Burgoyne had sent a force of about seven hundred Hessians, British Loyalists and Indians under Colonel Baum to capture a depot of supplies at Bennington. On August 15 he sent reinforcements of six-hundred and forty Hessians under Colonel Breyman. But on August 16, before the reinforcements arrived, Colonel Baum's force was attacked by a force of New Hampshire

Militia under Colonel John Stark who had served at Bunker Hill, and in the battles of Trenton and Princeton. Nearly the whole of Baum's force was killed, wounded or captured. Colonel Stark, with his own army reinforced by five-hundred men under Seth Warner, then turned on Colonel Breyman's army and before night had almost annihilated it. This victory so weakened the army of General Burgoyne, by the loss of men in battle and by desertions following the defeat, that it impaired his ability to resist the attack of the patriot army at Saratoga. The victory also heartened the patriots so that many of them enlisted to serve under General Gates. Congress formally thanked Colonel Stark for his achievement and he was promoted to the rank of brigadier general.

FESTIVAL OF ST. ROCH

St. Roch, or Rocco, as the Italians call him, was a Frenchman, born in Montpellier in about 1295. His father was the governor of the city. According to tradition he was born with a red cross marked upon his breast. When he was about twenty years old his father died. Soon afterward Roch distributed his inheritance among the poor and set out for Italy as a mendicant pilgrim. When he had traveled as far as Aquapendente he found the people of the city stricken with the plague and devoted himself to their care and cure. He visited other plague-stricken cities before arriving at Rome and, according to the stories of his life, cured the sick by making the sign of the cross over them. He himself fell ill with the disease at Piacenza and hid himself in a hut in a neighboring forest. According to one version he was fed by a dog and, according to another, a gentleman, who learned by a miracle of his whereabouts, supplied his wants till he recovered. When he was able to travel he returned to Montpellier. As he refused to disclose his identity he was imprisoned as a spy and died in prison five years later, in 1327. At his death his identity became known and a public funeral was arranged for him.

During the Council of Constance in 1414 the plague broke out in the city, and it was ordered that there should be public prayers and processions in St. Roch's honor as his work in curing the disease was remembered. His remains were removed to Venice in 1485 where they are venerated to this day. His feast day was fixed for August 16. A confraternity in his honor was instituted by Pope Paul III which grew so rapidly that Pope Paul IV raised it to an archfraternity which still flourishes. The feast day is observed in the United States by the Italian Catholics with processions through the streets of the cities. The paraders carry candles and the image of the saint. In New York, St. Joachim's Church, the first exclusively Italian parish in America, is the shrine of annual pilgrimages participated in by thousands of persons.

AUGUST SEVENTEENTH

BIRTHDAY OF DAVID CROCKETT

David Crockett, picturesque frontiersman and politician, was born in Hawkins County, Tennessee, on August 17, 1786, the son of a Revolutionary soldier of Irish descent who kept a tavern. The boy ran away at the age of thirteen to escape a threatened whipping and spent the next three years wandering about the country. While he was courting a girl when he was eighteen he began to go to school in the hope that it would make her better disposed toward him. But in about six months, when she jilted him, he left school and never attended it again. He served as a scout in the Creek Indian war of 1813-14 under Andrew Jackson. In 1815 or thereabouts he was made a justice of the peace in the newly organized Giles county. And in 1821 he was elected a member of the State Legislature. He was a farmer but preferred hunting when he was not occupied with his legislative or other duties. According to his own story he killed one hundred and five bears in eight months. He was again elected to the Legislature in 1823 and a few years later some one made the jocular suggestion that he run for Congress. He acted on the suggestion and went about the district telling humorous stories and ridiculing his opponents and he was elected to the Twentieth Congress and re-elected to the Twenty-first, but was defeated when he ran a third time, yet he was elected to the Twenty-third Congress. He was opposed to Jackson and when he sought election for the fouth time the supporters of Jackson defeated him. Discouraged he went to Texas to assist the Texans in their war for independence and took part in the defense of the Alamo in 1836 and was killed along with the other defenders. He was uneducated, but a man of considerable natural ability. Many stories are told of him. One of the best known is about the 'coon which agreed to come down from the tree when it discovered that it was Crockett who was aiming his gun at him. What purports to be an autobiography of Crockett was published years ago, but it was probably written by someone who had talked with him and not by Crockett himself.

JOUSTING TOURNAMENT IN VIRGINIA

The jousting, or ring, tournament held at Natural Chimneys, eighteen miles from Staunton, Va., has been an annual event since 1821. On August 17, 1946, the tournament was staged for the hundred and twenty-fifth time, its sponsors claiming that it quite possibly has the distinction of being America's oldest continuous sporting event. In 1821 the first steam railway was still ten years in the future, and the first Kentucky Derby not destined to be run until fifty-four years later; the United States was a young nation and most of her traditional observances

443

were yet unborn. Therefore, the claim may well be true. In any case, the jousting tournament at Natural Chimneys boasts a long and picturesque tradition. The story goes that the hand of one of the local belles was sought by two ardent swains in the year 1821. The lady was unable to make up her mind and finally her schoolmaster-uncle suggested that she bestow her favor, as in the days of King Arthur's knights, upon the winner of a jousting contest. It was to be a bout proving skill and horsemanship, without the mortal danger of the old English tournaments when each rider sought to unseat the other, and as such aroused the sporting interest of the whole countryside. On the fateful day the two young "knights" met in the Valley of Virginia at a place called Natural Chimneys, where seven curious rock formations tower more than a hundred feet in the air from a level plain. At the end of the contest there was food and drink for the crowd who had witnessed the affair, and the winner lifted his betrothed to his saddle, escorting her home amid cheers and good wishes. Thereafter, it was decided to hold an annual tournament. On the same date in 1822, the third Saturday in August, the young men of the community all competed and the winner crowned his "Queen of Love and Beauty." Every year since then a tournament has been held at the same place, on the third Saturday in August. During the decade prior to 1946 the attendance averaged six thousand persons yearly.

The dictionary defines jousting as a form of combat between two knights on horseback armed with lances. From the beginning the tournaments at Natural Chimneys have been a modification of the lethal affairs of the days of chivalry. Old-timers state that the present rules are identical with those under which their grandfathers competed. The marshall's command is still the traditional, "Charge, Sir Knight!" Many contestants still wear costumes and sashes, and some of the lances used are heirlooms more than a hundred years old. The field is invariably set up in the same manner. Three posts with projecting arms are placed at thirty-yard intervals. From each post-arm a ring is suspended six and a half feet from the ground, the rings graduated from two-inch size to one-half-inch for the last objective. The lances are nine feet long and must be grasped at a designated point. The riders approach at a gallop and are allowed eight seconds to complete the course, any who miss all the rings being eliminated. Occasionally remarkable skill is exhibited, as in 1936 when a contestant rode the course seven times and won with twenty-one rings.

The competitors always assume fanciful names, calling themselves Knight of the Golden Horseshoe, Knight of the Stardust Trail, or whatever picturesque title they are able to invent. A brass band is present and strikes up whenever a knight spears all three rings. Various other field-day contests are held, but the jousting is the chief attraction. An old-fashioned flowery oration is always delivered and in the evening there is dancing and a coronation. In 1945, despite the war, twenty-seven horsemen entered the field. However, in 1946, with many young men released from the services, there was a much larger entry and a correspondingly large crowd who viewed the 125th consecutive jousting tournament at Natural Chimneys with enthusiastic enjoyment.

AUGUST EIGHTEENTH

THE FIRST GOVERNMENT EXPLORING
EXPEDITION SAILS

Congress on May 18, 1836, authorized the fitting out of an expedition to explore the Southern ocean. Captain John Wilkes of the navy was made its commander. He had been in charge of the division of instruments and charts and was regarded as well qualified for surveying and mapping the regions which he was to explore. This first exploring expedition under the auspices of the government consisted of a fleet of six ships and carried, besides the crews, a company of naturalists, botanists, a mineralogist and a philologist. It set out from Norfolk, Va., on August 18, 1838. After sailing into the Pacific ocean and visiting Chile, Peru, the Samoan and other island groups it entered the harbor of Sydney, Australia, and from that port sailed into the Antarctic ocean in December 1839, and reported the discovery of an Antarctic continent. The part which it touched was named Wilkes Land. Subsequent explorers unable to break through the ice barrier doubted the discovery. But Sir Ernest Shackleton and Sir Douglas Mawson confirmed the discovery so that the credit for the discovery of the southern continent belongs to the United States navy. The report of the expedition was published in nineteen volumes.

AUGUST NINETEENTH

NATIONAL AVIATION DAY

In 1939 Congress passed a resolution authorizing the President to designate August 19 of each year as National Aviation Day, and to issue a proclamation calling upon officials of the Government to display the flag of the United States on all Government buildings, and inviting the people of the United States to observe the day with appropriate exercises designed to stimulate interest in aviation in this country. The resolution further states, as the reason for this observance, that the rapid development of aviation has made it a profound influence in world affairs and that American initiative and industry, having greatly contributed to this development, should be encouraged in order that the United States may retain its outstanding position in the field of aeronautics.

445

AUGUST 19

The Aviation Defense Association claims to have originated and sponsored the celebration, with the intent of honoring the Wright brothers, "the fathers of flight," and also all our air heroes. August 19 is the birthday of Orville Wright. In accordance with the presidential proclamation, the day has been observed annually, both by the services and the general public. The Air Force particularly takes cognizance of it, making massed flights followed by suitable addresses and other ceremonies. In 1946 National Aviation Day was the theme of the Exhibit of the Week at the Library of Congress, August 17 to August 23. However, probably due to the fact that it is not so well established, the day is not so widely and generally celebrated as the other service days, Army Day and Navy Day. Further, it has been customary to honor the Wright brothers in particular and aviation in general on December 17, the anniversary of their first heavier-than-air flight at Kitty Hawk. (See December 17.)

THE "CONSTITUTION'S" GREAT VICTORY

It was on August 19, 1812, that the American frigate "Constitution" fought its famous battle with the British frigate "Guerrière," winning a decisive victory. The British newspapers had written in contempt of the American navy and had referred to the "Constitution" as "a bundle of pine boards sailing under a bit of striped bunting," and had said that "a few broadsides from England's wooden walls would drive the paltry striped bunting from the ocean." Captain Isaac Hull, in command of the "Constitution," was eager to show the British what the American navy could do and he sailed from Boston on August 12, cruising in search of British ships. Eastward of Nova Scotia he captured a number of merchant vessels and on the afternoon of August 19 he fell in with the "Guerrière" which showed a willingness to fight. It began firing at long range, but Captain Hull withheld his fire. It was not until he got close to the enemy that he gave the order, "Now, boys, pour it into them." The first broadside shot away the mizzen mast and did serious damage to the hull, spars and rigging. Not long afterward the main mast fell into the sea and the vessel was rolling like a log, out of control of its helmsman. Captain Hull sent his compliments to Captain Dacre, the British commander, and asked if he had struck his flag. Captain Dacre replied: "Well, I don't know; our mizzen mast is gone; our main mast is gone; upon the whole you may say we have struck our flag." The battle had lasted only thirty minutes with a loss of three hundred British killed and wounded and an American loss of thirty-four. The survivors were taken on board the "Constitution" and the "Guerrière" was set on fire and sunk. Captain Hull sailed for Boston with his prisoners and on his arrival was welcomed with great enthusiasm. A dinner attended by six hundred citizens was given in his honor. The authorities of New York gave him the freedom of the city and a gold box and Congress thanked him, voted him a gold medal and appropriated $50,000 to be distributed among his officers and crew. And the victory silenced the sneers of the British at the American navy.

In 1830 Oliver Wendell Holmes' stirring poem, "Old Ironsides," saved the "Constitution" from the junkyard by awakening public sentiment. In 1833 she was rebuilt, finally going out of commission in 1855 at Portsmouth, N.H., and being used as a training ship. Again in 1877 she was partially rebuilt, but by 1897 her use was no longer practicable and she was stored at the Navy Yard in Charlestown, Mass. In 1947 the one hundred and fiftieth anniversary of "Old Ironsides" launching on October 21, 1797, was celebrated with suitable ceremonies and considerable newspaper and magazine publicity, indicating that popular sentiment for the picturesque, broad-beamed old sailing ship is still alive. Carefully preserved, she is now at the South Boston Navy Yard side by side with her sister ship, the "Constellation," whose superstructure has been dismantled, and which is destined for scrap.

AUGUST TWENTIETH

BIRTHDAY OF BENJAMIN HARRISON

Benjamin Harrison, twenty-third President of the United States, was born at North Bend, Ohio, on August 20, 1833, on his father's farm, adjoining the farm of his grandfather, William Henry Harrison, the ninth President. His father was John Scott Harrison, who served two terms in the national House of Representatives, and his greatgrandfather was Benjamin Harrison, one of the signers of the Declaration of Independence. He was seven years old when his grandfather was elected President in 1840. (See birthday of William Henry Harrison, February 9.) He was graduated from Miami University in 1852 and for the next two years read law in the offices of Storer & Gwynee in Cincinnati. He settled in Indianapolis, Ind., in 1854 and began the practice of law, and soon obtained a large number of profitable clients. He joined the newly organized Republican party and became one of its most useful campaign speakers. In 1857 he was elected city attorney of Indianapolis. In 1862 Governor Morton appointed him colonel of the Seventieth Indiana Infantry Regiment, which he had assisted in raising. He rose to the rank of brigadier general and he was with General Sherman in the Atlanta campaign.

At the request of Governor Morton he returned to Indiana in 1864 to assist in the political campaign in that year. At the close of the war he resumed the practice of law and was soon recognized as one of the leading lawyers in the state. It was not long before he had an income of $10,000, which was unusually large for a lawyer in Indiana at the time.

When the greenback issue loomed large in the 'seventies he was one of the Republican leaders who prevented Indiana from supporting the theory of fiat money. He was nominated for governor in 1876, but was defeated by the Democratic candidate. He ran so far ahead of his ticket, however, that his availability for high office began to be seriously considered by party leaders in the nation. He was chairman of the Indiana delegation to the Republican National Convention in 1880 which nominated Garfield. Garfield, when elected, offered a Cabinet post to him, but he declined it as he had just been elected to the United States Senate.

There was talk of presenting him as a "dark horse" candidate to the Republican National Convention in 1884, but he declined to cooperate. He was nominated for President, however, in 1888 and elected with two hundred and thirty-three electoral votes to one hundred and sixty-nine for President Cleveland, who was running to succeed himself. As President he made a good record, but alienated many by the coldness of his manner. When he was renominated in 1892, he received lukewarm support from prominent party leaders, and as the country was on the verge of a financial crisis he was defeated by Cleveland, who had been nominated for the third time by the Democrats.

On his retirement he once more resumed the practice of law in Indianapolis. In addition he did considerable writing. At the solicitation of Edward Bok, editor of the *Ladies' Home Journal*, he wrote for that periodical a series of articles on the nature of the Federal Government. These were later revised and published as a book *This Country of Ours*, which was used for many years as a standard reference work for schools and colleges. It was republished in England and the Carnegie Endowment for International Peace had it translated into Spanish and distributed among influential leaders in Latin America. He was senior counsel for Venezuela in its boundary dispute with England before an arbitration tribunal in Paris. Before his argument was half finished the British counsel admitted defeat. Mr. Harrison was an elder in the Presbyterian church, taught a men's Bible class, was superintendent of the Sunday school and was several times a delegate to the General Assembly of the Presbyterian Church. He died on March 13, 1901, and was buried in Crown Hill Cemetery in Indianapolis.

AUGUST TWENTY-FIRST

FEAST OF ST. JANE FRANCES DE CHANTAL

The church honors, on August 21, St. Jane Frances de Chantal, the founder of the Sisters of the Visitation. She was born in 1572, the daughter of Benigne Freymot, president of the parliament of Burgundy. In her twentieth year she married Baron de Chantal at her father's wish, but vowed that if she should become a widow she would devote herself to the religious life. She bore four children, one of whom was the grandmother of Madame de Sévigné. After eight years of married life her husband was killed while hunting. She waited until her children no longer needed her care and then in 1610, at the suggestion of Francis de Sales, she and two other women joined in a community to care for the needy and visit the sick. The order was called the Sisters of the Visitation from the visit paid by Elizabeth, the mother of John the Baptist, to Mary, the mother of Jesus. She died on December 13, 1641, was canonized on September 2, 1769, and August 21 was set as her feast day. The order was introduced in the United States in 1799. Its members in this country devote themselves principally to teaching.

AUGUST TWENTY-SECOND

THE "AMERICA" WINS THE CUP

In 1850 an English merchant wrote to friends in New York suggesting that one of the pilot boats in use in the harbor be sent to England to take part in a yacht race during the international exhibition in London in 1851. A syndicate of members of the New York Yacht Club, acting on the suggestion, built the schooner "America" of one hundred and seventy tons displacement and entered it for the race. The boat arrived in England on July 31, 1851, and on August 22 sailed against fourteen yachts belonging to the Royal Yacht Squadron in a race around the Isle of Wight. The English boats were cutters and schooners and varied from forty-seven to three hundred and ninety-two tons. The "America" won the race and the prize, an ornate silver cup valued at £100. The owners of the boat presented the cup to the New York Yacht Club in 1857. There was no challenge from England for a race to recover the cup until 1870 when the "Cambria," a British boat, raced a fleet of twenty-three New York Yacht Club boats and lost. Since then there have been several challenges, the most persistent seeker of the cup being Sir Thomas Lipton. But an American yacht has won every race and the cup is still in the possession of the New York club.

AUGUST TWENTY-THIRD

BIRTHDAY OF OLIVER HAZARD PERRY

Oliver Hazard Perry, whose despatch from Lake Erie, "We have met the enemy and they are ours," made him famous, was born at South Kensington, R.I., on August 23, 1785. He entered the navy as a midshipman in 1799 and served in the war against Tripoli. In 1807 he was commissioned a lieutenant. Early in the War of 1812 he was sent to

Lake Erie with instructions to superintend the construction of a fleet to wrest control of the lake from the British. By the end of the summer of 1813 he had built nine vessels and on September 16 he fought the Battle of Lake Erie the result of which he announced in the famous despatch. Perry received a gold medal and a vote of thanks from Congress for the victory and was raised to the rank of captain. In 1819 he was sent to the West Indies with a small squadron to protect American commerce from pirates and while there he died of yellow fever on the anniversary of his birth. His body was buried at Port of Spain, Trinidad, but in 1826 was removed by order of Congress to Newport, R.I. The state erected a granite monument over his grave. The centennial anniversary of the Battle of Lake Erie was celebrated in 1913 and an elaborate memorial structure was unveiled at Put-in-Bay.

AUGUST TWENTY-FOURTH

FESTIVAL OF ST. BARTHOLOMEW

St. Bartholomew was one of the twelve apostles. The name is Hebrew and means "son of Talmai" (or Tholmai). Some biblical authorities believe that his name was Nathaniel and that in the list of the apostles given in the gospels of St. Matthew, St. Mark and St. Luke, and in the Acts he is described as the son of his father. The only mention of him in the New Testament as Bartholomew is in the lists of the apostles. His name does not appear in ecclesiastical literature before the time of Eusebius who lived in the third and fourth centuries. Eusebius, known as the father of ecclesiastical literature, writes that the master of Origen while preaching in India was told that Bartholomew had preached there before him and had given to his converts a copy of the gospel of St. Matthew written in Hebrew. India at that time was a loose term used to designate much of Asia not now known by that name. The traditions about him represent him as preaching in Mesopotamia, Persia, Egypt, Armenia and along the shores of the Black Sea. The legends concerning the manner of his death are untrustworthy. According to one he was beheaded. The most generally accepted story adopted by the ecclesiastical artists is that he was flayed alive and then crucified head downwards at Albanopolis in Armenia under orders from Astyages who resented the conversion of his brother Polymius, king of Albania. In Michelangelo's painting of the Last Judgment, Bartholomew is shown holding his skin in his left hand. In other paintings he appears as holding a knife used in flaying. His feast day is August 24.

It was on the night of St. Bartholomew's day in 1572 that the massacre of the Huguenots in France began, on the order of Charles IX incited by Catherine de Medici, with the murder of Coligny who was charged with a conspiracy against the King. It is estimated that 2000 victims were slain in Paris alone. How many were slain in the rest of

France is not known, but the number was undoubtedly very large. The massacre continued for several days and in Paris the mobs broke into the houses of the rich and plundered them, killing their owners, regardless of whether they were Huguenots or not.

AUGUST TWENTY-FIFTH

FEAST OF ST. LOUIS

St. Louis, as Louis IX of France was known after he was canonized, was one of the greatest monarchs of his time. He and his career are of particular interest to the United States as it was for him that the city of St. Louis, Mo., was named. In 1764 Auguste Chouteau, acting under orders from Pierre Laclede Ligueste, established a fur trading station on the present site of St. Louis. Ligueste arrived the next year and laid out a town, predicting that it would become one of he great cities of America. It was at first called Laclede's Village, but the name was soon changed to St. Louis.

St. Louis inherited the throne of France from his father in 1226, when he was only twelve years old. His mother, Blanche of Castile, was made regent and ruled in his stead until he was eighteen in 1234. She was a pious woman and reared her son carefully, giving him a thorough religious education. She said to him on one occasion, "I had rather see you dead at my feet than guilty of a mortal sin." It was under his patronage that Robert of Sorbonne founded the College of the Sorbonne which became the seat of the theological faculty in Paris. He fed beggars from his table and washed their feet and ministered to lepers. He was stricken with a severe illness in 1244 and vowed, if he should recover, to lead a crusade to take the holy places in Palestine from the Turcomans. He led two crusades, one in 1248-49 and the second in 1270. It was while on the second crusade that he was stricken with the plague and died in Tunis on August 25, 1270. He had lived such a holy life that within three years of his death it was proposed that he be canonized. The inquiries into his worthiness continued until 1297, when Pope Boniface VIII ordered the canonization and fixed August 25, the day of his death, as his feast day. His relics rest in the church of St. Denis in Paris, and there is an equestrian statue of him as a crusader in St. Louis, the American city named for him.

AUGUST TWENTY-SIXTH

SOLDIERS' HOSPITAL DAY

In honor of Mrs. Annie Wittenmyer, the first president of the national Woman's Christian Temperance Union, and in recognition of her

451

work in behalf of soldiers the union observes August 26 the anniversary of her birth as Soldiers' Hospital Day. The members visit hospitals and do what they can to relieve the inmates.

Mrs. Wittenmyer, nee Turner, was born in Ohio and spent her early life in Kentucky. She was educated at a ladies seminary in Ohio and married at the age of twenty-one, making her home in Iowa. At the beginning of the Civil War she was appointed sanitary agent for the state. She obtained a pass through the lines of the army from Secretary Stanton and carried supplies for the relief of the soldiers. She continued in work of this kind throughout the war, acting after a time with the Christian Commission. She set up diet kitchens for the sick and disabled. The first was in Nashville, Tenn., where food was prepared for eight hundred soldiers. As the war drew to a close she decided that there should be homes for soldiers' orphans and through her influence the army barracks at Davenport, Iowa, were turned over to the managers of the Iowa Home. Again, through her influence, the Methodist Church organized a Woman's Home Missionary Society to minister to the needs of strangers and the poor. She was made its corresponding secretary in 1871. At about this time she took up her residence in Philadelphia and started a paper which she called *The Christian Woman,* and a juvenile publication called *The Christian Child.* When the Woman's Christian Temperance Union was organized she was elected as its first president and held that office for a number of years. In February 1875, she presented to Congress a petition for the prohibition of the liquor traffic and appeared before a committee to urge its importance.

THE NINETEENTH AMENDMENT

On August 26, 1920, the Secretary of State proclaimed the Nineteenth Amendment to the Constitution in effect after its adoption by three quarters of the states, and the friends of women's suffrage rejoiced in the successful outcome of nearly a century of endeavor. The wording of the amendment is simple and direct: "The right of citizens of the United States to vote shall not be denied or abridged by the United States or by any State on account of sex." Thus, in November of that year, for the first time in the history of the United States women throughout the country were enabled to vote in a presidential election.

The organized campaign for women's suffrage in the United States started in 1848, although the cause had been agitated by isolated reformers for a long time. The Territory of Wyoming, in 1869, passed the first law to be found anywhere in legislative history granting the franchise to women, but it was twenty-four years before any other state followed suit. Colorado was the next, in 1893, and gradually all the western states came into line. However, when the question was submitted to a vote of the people in various states east of the Mississippi it was defeated in every one. The women themselves organized against it, opposition being particularly strong in the southern states, and not until 1917 did the movement make any real headway in the East. In that year the State of New York was captured in a popular election and, thereafter, events moved rapidly, culminating in the adoption of the amendment in 1920 which made Susan B. Anthony's dream a reality.

AUGUST TWENTY-SEVENTH

PETROLEUM DAY

On August 27, 1859, petroleum began to flow from a well which Colonel E. L. Drake had been drilling for many days near Titusville, Pa. This marked the beginning of the commercial development of the petroleum industry in the United States. The anniversary has been celebrated periodically in the oil region of western Pennsylvania for many years. In 1934, however, seventy-five years after the oil first began to flow, an elaborate celebration, extending over three days and culminating on August 27, was arranged. Among those participating were Governor George White of Ohio; Harold Ickes, Secretary of the Interior; a representative of Governor Pinchot of Pennsylvania, and Axtell J. Byles, president of the American Petroleum Institute. The celebration opened with a pageant descriptive of the discovery and use of petroleum. On the last day Drake Memorial Park, which includes the site of the first oil well, was presented to the state.

It was because the commercial possibilities in petroleum were known, provided it could be found in sufficient quantities, that Colonel Drake had been sent to Titusville by a group of Connecticut speculators. Professor Benjamin Silliman, Jr., of Yale College, had made a scientific study of crude oil and published his findings in 1855. He reported that an illuminant could be made from it, better and more economical than any then in use, that candles could be made from the paraffin which it contained and that a lubricant which did not gum could also be obtained. This did not exhaust its possibilities as modern chemists employed by the oil companies have succeeded in developing many hundred different commodities of commercial value from crude oil. A group of gentlemen in Hartford, Conn., familiar with Professor Silliman's report, formed the Seneca Oil Company, in 1858, and sent Colonel Drake into northwestern Pennsylvania to prospect for oil in the hope that he might be able to find it in commercial quantities. Colonel Drake had a theory that the oil lay in pools below the rock. His plan was to dig through the earth till he reached bed rock and then drill through that. After looking about for a long time he found near Titusville what he thought was a likely spot. The people of the neighborhood laughed at him. He hired a blacksmith and his two sons to help him and started digging. They struck solid rock at thirty-six feet and then started drilling, sinking the

drill about three feet a day. On Saturday, August 27, 1859, they stopped
work with the drill sixty-nine feet below the surface. On Sunday morning
one of the blacksmith's sons went to the well and peered into the pipe.
"Oil!" he shouted. "We've struck it!"

There was immediate excitement and, as the news spread, men
flocked from all parts of the country into Titusville and the surrounding
region as they had flocked into California in the gold rush. In 1859 two
thousand barrels of oil were produced. In 1860 the production was
500,000 barrels. The discovery in Pennsylvania led to prospecting for
oil in other parts of the country with satisfactory results. In 1910 the
country's production was more than 200,000,000 barrels and in 1945 it
was about 1,711,103,000. Oil has made multi-millionaires of hundreds
of men and thousands have become rich because of their investment in it,
but Colonel Drake, who proved that it could be drawn from its hiding
place, died a poor man, dependent in his later years on a pension of $1500
from the state.

AUGUST TWENTY-EIGHTH

FESTIVAL OF ST. AUGUSTINE

On August 28, 1565, Don Pedro Menendez de Aviles, sent by
Philip II of Spain to expel a colony of French Hugenots which had
settled on St. John's River near the coast of what is now Florida, landed
and built a fort which he called St. Augustine in honor of the saint on
whose feast day he had touched land. After massacring the French he
returned to the fort and established a settlement, the oldest within the
present limits of the United States. Thus early was the memory of this
great father of the Church associated with the history of America. Of him
Philip Schaff in his *History of the Christian Church* has said:

Compared with the great philosophers of past centuries and modern times
he is the equal of them all; among theologians he is undeniably the first, and
such has been his influence that none of the Fathers, Scholastics or Reformers
has surpassed it.

Many religious institutions have been named for him in the United
States and his feast day is widely observed.

Augustine was born in Tagaste, now Souk-Ahras, in Numidia,
Africa, on November 13, 354. His father, Patricius, was an official of the
city and a pagan. His mother, Monica, was a Christian and gave him
religious instruction in his youth. The boy's brilliant record in school
led his father to plan to have him trained as a lawyer in the schools in
Carthage. He lived in idleness at home during his sixteenth year while
his father accumulated money enough to send him away to study. He
indulged in all sorts of licentious excesses and continued this kind of
life in Carthage. But he had a brilliant career in the schools there and
qualified himself to plead in the forum. He preferred the academic

life and returned to Tagaste to "teach grammar." About 383 he went to Rome, but stayed there only a short time, leaving for Milan where he taught rhetoric. Four years later he resolved to become a Christian and was baptized on Easter eve, 387. He returned to Africa and was made bishop of Hippo in 395, an office which he held until his death on August 28, 430. He left a great mass of writings. The best known are his *Confessions* in which he tells the story of his religious life, and *The City of God,* in which he seeks to interpret the meaning of the past and to foretell the future, when the city of God, which is the Christian church, will supersede the city of this world.

AUGUST TWENTY-NINTH

BIRTHDAY OF OLIVER WENDELL HOLMES

The anniversary of the birth of Oliver Wendell Holmes, who was one of the group of famous men of letters produced by New England in the nineteenth century, is made the occasion of special exercises in many public schools. The purpose of these exercises, as of those in commemoration of other writers, is to impress upon the mind of the pupils some facts about the life and work of the men celebrated. The program suggested for use in the schools of West Virginia is well adapted to this end. It begins with a paper on the education and avocations of Dr. Holmes, followed by recitation of "The Chambered Nautilus" and "The Last Leaf," one of the most perfect poems of its kind in the English language. Then a pupil tells the story of how Dr. Holmes, while still a very young man, saved the old warship "Constitution," and another pupil recites "Old Ironsides," the poem that stirred the nation to protest against sending the famous ship to the junk heap. (See August 16, the Constitution's Great Victory.)

Dr. Holmes was born at Cambridge, Mass., on August 29, 1809, and was graduated from Harvard College in 1829. He entered the Harvard Law School with the intention of becoming a lawyer, but he abandoned law for medicine. After three years in the Harvard Medical School and two years of study in Europe he began to practice in Boston. He was professor of anatomy in Dartmouth College from 1838 to 1840 and from 1847 to 1882 he was Parkman professor of anatomy and physiology in the Harvard Medical School. Although he had published several volumes of verse previously his reputation was local until the *Autocrat of the Breakfast Table,* which appeared serially in the *Atlantic Monthly* in 1857, was published in book form in 1858. His great fame came to him after he was fifty years old. He lived to the age of eighty-five, dying in Boston, on October 7, 1894. He was the father of Oliver Wendell Holmes, who served for thirty years as an Associate Justice of the Supreme Court of the United States and won a wide reputation for the breadth and humanity of his views of the law and the Constitution, dying in his turn a few days short of his ninety-fourth year in 1935.

DECOLLATION OF ST. JOHN THE BAPTIST

The anniversary of the beheading of John the Baptist began to be observed at Sebaste, where he was supposed to be buried, as early as the fourth century. The traditional anniversary of the day of his birth was observed many years earlier. (See June 24, St. John's Day.)

The story of the beheading is one of the most dramatic in the New Testament. Herod Antipas, the tetrarch of Judea, had brought Herodias, the wife of his half-brother, from Rome, although he already had a wife. John denounced him for the offense and Herodias vowed vengeance. According to the New Testament story she persuaded Herod to arrest John and imprison him. According to Josephus, Herod had John arrested because he was afraid the man would stir the people to revolt. In any event John was arrested and imprisoned, and was held for a long time. Finally Herodias saw her opportunity at Herod's birthday celebration when he gave a feast to the chief men and princes of the country. Her daughter Salome entertained them with a dance which so pleased Herod that he told her that he would give her anything she wished. Her mother told her to ask for the head of John on a dish which she did and John was beheaded in prison and the bleeding head was brought to her.

Oscar Wilde wrote a play in French around this story which he embroidered with many unhistorical details. An English version, with illustrations by Aubrey Beardsley, was published in 1893. The licenser of plays forbade its representation in England, but Sarah Bernhardt played the French version in Paris in 1894, and in 1905 Richard Strauss used the play as the book for an opera. The opera has been sung and the play presented in the United States with Salome dancing before Herod as the climax in each.

AUGUST THIRTIETH

INTER-TRIBAL INDIAN CEREMONIAL

For many years Gallup, N. M., the trading center for the Navajo and Zuñi Reservations, has arranged an Inter-Tribal Indian Ceremonial during the last three days in August. It is in charge of a Ceremonial Association organized to help the Indian help himself. It offers cash prizes for Indian work in arts and crafts and thus stirs the spirit of emulation, and by the exhibition of such work by the members of different tribes it gives them all an opportunity to see what is being done. It perpetuates the traditional Indian customs by having them reproduced. And it arranges competitive sports to develop group play and the spirit of good sportsmanship. The Pueblo and Plains Indians participate in the ceremonial. Among the Plains Indians are the Navajos, the Kiowas and the Apaches, and the Pueblo Indians are represented by the Zuñi, the Hopi, the Taos, the Acoma, the San Idelfonso and the Zia.

On the morning of each of the three days there is a parade through the streets of the city, described in this way by the Ceremonial Association:

Thousands of Indians in native costume walk dignified and unconcerned before a multitude of onlookers. There is a wide variety of costume, varying from nakedness painted bright blue, black or ghostly white and combinations of nude torsos painted in stripes, to elaborate and beautiful feathered and beaded apparel. The Plains tribes in their striking headdresses of eagle feathers are superb. The Pueblo Indians from Taos, with their whirls of feathers, rows of tinkling bells and flashing mirrors are brilliant as they move with bird-like swiftness on feet that seem to barely touch the ground. The Zuñi women, bearing great ollas on their heads, walk with a poise that is almost monumental. Their costumes are beautiful. Then come the Navajos with more sedate garb, except the Fire Dancers who wear nothing but loin cloths and have their bodies painted a deadly white. And so the parade goes, a long panorama of amazing sights leaving the spectators almost breathless.

The afternoon is devoted to sports, games and races with a few Indian dances. Hopi and Zuñi runners compete for prizes in distance races. Navajos exhibit their horsemanship on bucking animals and in races. There are tugs of war and Indian clowns amuse the spectators. According to the description by the Ceremonial Association:

The evening performances open with a full review of the dancers in their finest costumes, led by an all-Indian band from one of the Indian schools. Large bonfires and a full harvest moon provide the only illumination. It's beyond description. The parade ended, the dancers form in line opposite the grandstand. Silence falls and as the band plays "The Star Spangled Banner," it is poignantly borne in upon one that, white or red, we are all one. Visitors are struck by this fact; natives of the Southwest take it for granted. Enthusiasm and applause increase as the audience hears the Acoma trio chant, sees the graceful movements of the Taos, gasps at the world headdresses of the Apache Devil Dancers. Navajos chant their mountain songs and make the feather dance in a basket. Zuñi Margaret thrills all when accompanied by a group of Zuñi maidens, she sings "The Zuñi Lullaby." The Zia Crow Dance, Hopi Butterfly Dance, Acoma Bow and Arrow Dance, all are applauded warmly. Each seems to outdo the other. But such is not the case for each dance is sacred and symbolic to the Indian. The finale, by popular request, is invariably the Navajo Fire Dance. Naked Indians, painted white, leap through hot fires and brandish and strike one another with burning embers.

During the three days of the ceremonial celebration there is an exhibit of Indian arts and crafts such as ceremonial rugs, gorgeous Hopi wedding robes, sacred Zuñi sashes, vivid Navajo fabrics and delicate silver work by Navajo and Zuñi artists. The Navajos are said to be the finest Indian silversmiths, using silver Mexican coins as their material. They make rings and bracelets set with turquoise and have even made a full table service of silver. The black pottery of San Ildefonso and Santa Clara, the orange and red of the Hopi and the fine types of the

Zuñi, Acoma and Zia are also shown along with the baskets and bead work of the Hopi and Apache. Thousands of visitors are attracted every year to this exhibition of Indian customs and Indian handiwork.

BANISHMENT OF ANNE HUTCHINSON

The case of Anne Hutchinson affords one of the most flagrant illustrations of the religious intolerance of the Massachusetts Bay Colony in its early days. Mrs. Hutchinson was born in England in July 1591, the daughter of the Reverend Francis Marbury, a clergyman of the Established Church with Puritan leanings. In 1612 she was married to William Hutchinson, the son of a well-to-do merchant. For twenty-two years she lived with her husband in England and bore him fourteen children. The eldest son migrated to Massachusetts in 1633 and the next year the whole family joined the son. Mrs. Hutchinson had been accustomed to listen to religious discussions in her home and she began to hold informal meetings of women in Boston at which she talked about the sermon of the previous Sunday. She argued that religion consisted of more than obedience to the laws of the church and the state, the theory on which the Massachusetts government was based. She was accused of advocating a religion which absolved its adherents from observing the moral law. She was defended, however, by Henry Vane and the Reverend John Wheelwright, her brother-in-law. Her views were condemned by a synod of the churches, and Wheelwright was banished from the colony. On August 30, 1637, she was tried on the charge of "traducing the ministers and the ministry" and sentenced to banishment. She was allowed to remain in the colony until the following spring when she and her family emigrated to Rhode Island, to which Roger Williams had fled two years earlier, where she was free to express her religious views without molestation. After the death of her husband in 1642 she moved to Long Island and then to Pelham Bay on the mainland shore of Long Island Sound. Here she and all but one of the members of her household were massacred by the Indians in 1643.

BIRTHDAY OF HUEY P. LONG

The birthday of Huey Pierce Long, United States Senator and politician, has been observed in Louisiana since 1937, shortly after his death from an assassin's bullet. It is a legal holiday and the banks and state offices are closed. Huey Long was born August 30, 1893, in Winfield, La., where he attended the local school and worked on his father's farm. At the age of sixteen he started selling books and other goods throughout the rural sections of the state. Thereafter he attended the University of Oklahoma for a short time, and in 1914 entered the Tulane University law school. He completed the three-year course in seven months, took a special examination for admittance to the bar, and was sworn in on May 15, 1915. He first practiced at Winfield and then, in 1918, settled at Shreveport, specializing in constitutional law. His first political office was as a State Railroad Commissioner and, as plaintiff, witness and counsel, he was successful in his case of Long vs. The City of Shreveport in a suit to reduce the transit fare to five cents. Thus began his long warfare against public utilities.

In 1921 he was elected to the State Public Service Commission, and two years later became its chairman. In 1924 he ran for governor of the state, but was defeated. However, in 1928 he ran again and was elected, his administration immediately becoming so chaotic that he was impeached in 1929 on charges of bribery and misappropriation of state funds. When brought to trial his forces moved for an adjournment of the senate *sine die* and, as the anti-Long group was unable to rally quickly enough, the forced adjournment ended the trial and in six months proceedings were *nolle prossed*. Cleared of these charges, Governor Long entrenched himself in Louisiana by the establishment of a strong political machine. His influence with the rural voters was considerable, both because of his early contacts with them when selling during his boyhood and because of his emphasis on legislation in their favour, and their votes kept his machine in power. Under his rule numerous public improvements were made, although the state's indebtedness was increased by eighty-five million dollars. New roads were built; illiteracy was reduced by the establishment of night schools and free text books for children; a new state capitol was built; Louisiana University was provided with a new medical building; and funds were obtained for a bridge across the Mississippi at New Orleans.

In 1930 he was nominated and elected to the United States Senate and after his election, in order to prevent the lieutenant-governor, Paul Cyr, a political opponent, from becoming the governor, Governor Long refused to relinquish his seat and appointed Alvin O. King as his successor. To enforce this appointment he called out the National Guard and not until January 1932, when his candidate was elected, did he take his seat in the United States Senate. In national politics he was in open rebellion against the administration, and his strength in his own state and his White House aspirations made him a power to be reckoned with on the eve of the 1936 elections. Meanwhile, in 1935, he called out the Guard again to protect himself against threats of assassination, established martial law and, when it was finally lifted, had obtained a virtual dictatorship over Louisiana. Upon the adjournment of the 74th Congress, he returned to attend a special session of the Louisiana legislature. On September 8, 1935, as he was leaving the state capitol where the legislature was in session, he was shot by Dr. Carl A. Weiss, Jr., a political enemy, who in turn was slain by Senator Long's bodyguards. On September 10 he died from the bullet wounds and was buried in the grounds of the capitol with public ceremonies which drew some hundred thousand people.

AUGUST THIRTY-FIRST

THE CHARLESTON EARTHQUAKE

On the night of August 31, 1886, occurred the most disastrous earthquake known east of the Mississippi River, if not the most disastrous in the history of the country. Its violence was greatest at Charleston, S.C. About three fourths of the buildings in the city were wrecked or badly injured and fifty-seven persons were killed. Many persons died from exposure as they took refuge in the parks for fear their houses would fall on their heads. The money damage amounted to many millions of dollars. The shock was felt as far north as Toronto, Canada, as far south as Jacksonville, Fla., as far west as Dubuque, Iowa and as far east as New Haven, Conn. There have been other earthquakes felt over a large part of the east, but they occurred when the country was less populous than it is now. In 1811, for example, there was an earthquake which was felt from New York to New Orleans and from Savannah, Ga., to St. Louis, Mo. Earthquakes have been frequent since America was settled. The first on record in New England occurred on June 1, 1638, old style, not quite eighteen years after the landing of the Pilgrims. The most disastrous earthquake west of the Mississippi was in San Francisco in 1906. (See April 18, San Francisco Fire.)

Cornerstone of the Capitol

SEPTEMBER

The morrow was a bright September morn;
The earth was beautiful as if new-born;
There was that nameless splendor everywhere,
That wild exhilaration in the air,
Which makes the passers in the city street
Congratulate each other as they meet.

—Longfellow

September was the seventh month in the ancient Roman calendar and became the ninth when the calendar was revised by Julius Caesar but its name was not changed. Caesar gave the month thirty-one days, but when the emperor Augustus changed the name of the month Sextilis to August he took a day from September and added it to his month so that it might have the same number of days as July, the month named for his uncle. In Charlemagne's calendar it was known as the harvest month. The old Saxon name for it was Gerst-monath, or barley month, as barley was harvested then. After the introduction of Christianity it was sometimes called Halig-monath, or holy month in allusion to the birth of Mary, the mother of Jesus, on the eighth. It corresponds in part to the Fructidor and in part to the Vendémiaire of the calendar of the first French republic. It is still called Herbst-monat, harvest month, in Switzerland. It is the month in which agricultural fairs are held when farmers exhibit for prizes their animals and their produce and the farmers' wives show their skill in cookery and needlework. It is also the month of what is known as the harvest moon. This is the moon which rises nearest to the autumnal equinox. It appears above the horizon at about sunset for several days giving light enough for the farmers to continue their harvesting.

SEPTEMBER FIRST

THE SANTA FE FIESTA

The celebration of the anniversary of the reconquest of New Mexico from the Indians in 1692, which was formally begun in September 1712, was renewed by the city of Santa Fe in 1919, and is known as the Santa Fe Fiesta. It usually continues for several days. The historical background of the celebration starts in 1528 when the expedition of Narvaez came to grief off the southeastern part of what is now the United States. Esteban, the Moor, and three other survivors started on foot across the continent finally arriving at a Spanish settlement in the western part of Mexico. In the latter part of 1530 Fray Marcos de Niza, accompanied by Esteban, the Moor, hearing of a land of fabulous wealth, went north into what is now the western part of New Mexico to find the seven cities of Cibola. The Indians killed Esteban but Fray Marcos escaped and returned to Mexico. In 1540 Coronado at the head of a military expedition subdued the Indians in the region and continued his explorations as far east as the southern part of what is now Kansas. In 1598 Don Juan de Onate fitted out a company of colonists at his own expense and settled at a point thirty miles north of the present site of Santa Fe.

The colony remained there several years, or until the Viceroy of Mexico ordered its new governor, Miguel de Peralta, to move it farther south. At some time between 1610 and 1614—the exact date is not known—the city of Santa Fe was founded and the governor's palace, still standing, was built from materials imported from Spain. This palace, extending along one side of the plaza, is now occupied by the museums of the historical society. The Spaniards and the Indians lived in comparative harmony for seventy-five years, but as some of the Indians were enslaved and compelled to work in the mines and others were slain by religious zealots because they did not accept their teachings, the Indians revolted and in 1680 killed all the Spaniards they could find, and the others fled from the country. In 1692 Don Diego de Vargas was appointed governor, was sent into New Mexico and reconquered it for the Spaniards.

In 1712 the Marquis de la Penuela, then governor of New Mexico, ordered that a fiesta should be held every year "in honor of the redemption of the province from the Indians." It is not known how long this order was obeyed, but in the course of time the fiesta was abandoned. For several years prior to 1911, the Woman's Board of Trade of Santa Fe had been holding an annual festival on the plaza to raise money for the library. Early in that year the Reverend James Mythen, at one time rector of the Protestant Episcopal church, suggested a celebration of the

462

important events in the history of the city, and on July 4, 1911, the women arranged a pageant representing the entry of de Vargas into the city, with more than a hundred Indians taking part. It was repeated two or three times in succeeding years, but abandoned because of the first World War. It was not until 1919, however, that the city began seriously to arrange for an annual celebration of the historic event.

In 1934 it began on Saturday, September 1, with the burning of an effigy of Zozobra, called Old Man Gloom, to indicate that joy was to be unconfined, followed by a band concert and the grand ball of the Conquistadores, at which men in costume representing de Vargas and his army arrived to lead the grand march. On Sunday morning there was a fiesta high mass at the Cathedral of St. Francis. In the afternoon there was a band concert in the plaza followed by a proclamation from the Alcalde announcing the two hundred and twenty-second fiesta. Then de Vargas and his soldiers made a formal re-entry into the city, representing the reconquest of New Mexico and were welcomed at the old Palace of the Governor. There was a vesper service at the cathedral in the early evening followed by a religious procession from the cathedral to the Cross of the Martyrs on the Heights of Cuma, with a sermon at the cross. At nine o'clock a play "The Coming of the Americans," was given at the Art Museum. Monday was devoted to sports and contests of various kinds and Pueblo Indian dances. The celebration reached its climax on Tuesday morning with what was described as a "Grand Hysterical Pageant of el Pasatiempo," with a parade through the principal streets, and ended with a street carnival in the evening.

The peculiar charm of Santa Fe and the celebration is described by Fleta Campbell Springer in *Harper's Magazine* for April 1935:

> We arrived in the midst of the Fiesta, an occasion I had not anticipated with too much enthusiasm, since nothing is so bad and disheartening as a serious communal festivity. I had foreseen that I should have the religious ceremonials explained to me. I had expected to be shown about, to have things pointed out to me, to listen to conversations about the culture of the American Indians. But I was wrong. The Fiesta was merely going on, and in half an hour we were part of it; for the people were the Fiesta, and nobody was taking either it or themselves in the least seriously. Even the Indians in the sunlit court danced with a consciously ironical stateliness and style. This I had expected to be the saddest spectacle of all; but to see them moving easily and naturally in this absurd and heterogeneous milieu, without the slightest loss of their native humor and dignity, recalled to me how for the last three hundred years and more the history of the New Mexican Indians has been their repeated discovery by aliens and the attempted imposition upon them of alien religions and cultures. . . . One has only to visit the Pueblos to see how successfully they have withstood it. . . . There were, to be sure, various formal and prearranged events, exhibitions of native handicrafts, the religious procession to the Cross of the Martyrs, rituals, races, a play "The Bad Man" given by local amateurs. But nobody went anywhere they had said they would go; they stayed where they were or went somewhere else, which made a sufficient if unexpected attendance at all the events. And I was so much relieved by this sense of freedom from duty as an observer that I managed to miss them all except the parade which closes the fourth day—an absurd, happily amateurish parade, given over entirely to mockery. No elaborate symbolical adver-

tising floats, no attempt at "the beautiful" (there had been the procession to the graves of the Martyrs for authentic beauty and symbolism) but everything as spontaneous as a party thought up yesterday, everybody a little tired but still a little more than gay, and a funny air of the old West about it all. There was a battered old Ford marked "Santa Fe or Bust" with its mechanism so inspirationally deranged that its occupants, a half dozen young natives, were violently jounced and bounced from the seat and seemed about to fly entirely out with every turn of the wheels.

SEPTEMBER SECOND

BIRTHDAY OF EUGENE FIELD

Eugene Field, poet, essayist, and translator, was born at St. Louis, Mo., on September 2, 1850. He sometimes said that he was born on September 3, but the earlier date is probably the correct one. His father, Roswell Martin Field, born in Vermont, migrated to Missouri in 1839, and was the counsel for Dred Scott in the fight of that Negro for freedom. When Mrs. Field died in 1856, Eugene and his brother were sent to Amherst, Mass., to be cared for by a cousin. He entered Williams College and spent part of a year there. Then he spent a year at Knox College, after the death of his father, and another year at the University of Missouri. In 1872 he went to Europe on the money which he had inherited. On his return from Europe he married and entered newspaper work, holding editorial positions in St. Joseph, St. Louis, Kansas City and Denver. In 1883 he joined the staff of the Chicago *Morning News* with which in its various changes of name he remained until his death on November 4, 1895. He conducted a column in that newspaper which he called "Sharps and Flats" and printed in it most if not all his poetry and short sketches and his travesties of the poems of Horace. After his death a public school in Chicago was named for him and a collected edition of his works in ten volumes was published. Several of his poems were set to music and are in the repertoire of concert singers.

LABOR SUNDAY

At the suggestion of the Reverend Charles Stelzle, superintendent of the Presbyterian Bureau of Social Service, in 1905 the Presbyterian churches began to observe the Sunday before Labor Day as Labor Sunday. It fell on September 2 in 1945. The services on Labor Sunday are arranged with special reference to labor and the members of labor organizations are invited to be present. In 1909 the arrangements for Labor Sunday were transferred from the Presbyterian Bureau of Social Service to the Commission on Church and Social Service of the Federal Council of Churches of Christ in America. In 1910 the convention of the American Federation of Labor, in session in Toronto, adopted the following resolution:

That the Sunday preceding the first Monday in September be designated by the American Federation of Labor as Labor Sunday, and that the churches of America be requested to devote some part of the day to a presentation of the labor question.

The officers of the Federation issued an appeal to the ministers of all denominations to arrange for the observance of the day and the labor organizations in the various cities were asked to cooperate with the churches. As a result the day was observed more generally than in any previous year. In 1912 the Commission on Church and Social Service of the Federal Council of Churches issued a leaflet with suggestions for making the special services successful and it prepared a program for the services, including suggested scripture readings and hymn. Among the suggestions in the leaflet was that "the regular morning service should be used to impress the congregation with the serious business before the church of meeting and of solving by the gospel the great and pressing questions of the social order, the heart of all these problems being industrial."

SEPTEMBER THIRD

LABOR DAY

Labor Day, observed on the first Monday in September, has come to be one of the most generally celebrated holidays in the United States, ranking with Washington's Birthday, Independence Day and Thanksgiving Day. It fell on September 3 in 1945. The propriety of setting apart one day in the year in honor of labor was first suggested by Peter J. McGuire in 1882. He was then president of the United Brotherhood of Carpenters and Joiners of America, and was an active leader in the Knights of Labor. In May of that year he submitted a proposal to the recently organized Central Labor Union in New York, that labor should select a day for a parade to show the strength and the esprit de corps of the trade and labor organizations," and that the parade be followed by a picnic or festival, the proceeds from which should be divided among the organizations taking part. It was argued that there were other holidays representative of the religious, civil and military spirit, but none "representative of the industrial spirit, the great vital force of the nation." Mr. McGuire thought that the first Monday in September was the most desirable date for it came about half way between Independence Day and Thanksgiving Day.

His proposal was adopted by the Central Labor Union and the first Labor Day celebration occurred on September 5, 1882, when the union held its parade in the streets of New York City. The General Assembly of the Knights of Labor voted for an annual celebration not long after this first parade. On October 9, 1884, the Federation of Organized Trades and Labor Unions of the United States and Canada which later became the American Federation of Labor, meeting in convention in Chicago, voted to make the celebration national. About two and a half years later the Legislature of Oregon, on February 21, 1887, set apart the first Monday in September as a state holiday in honor of labor. Within three months similar action had been taken by the legislatures of Colorado, Massachusetts, New Jersey and New York. Before the middle of 1894 the day had been made a legal holiday in thirty states and on June 28 of that year Congress passed an act making it a legal holiday in the District of Columbia and in the territories. The day is now observed in every state.

Samuel Gompers, for many years president of the American Federation of Labor, wrote an article for Labor Day, 1910, in which he discussed the importance of organization to improve the lot of the workers. He said, among other things:

> There is only one danger of the failure of constant and peaceful evolution for the elimination of all abnormal conditions under which workers are compelled to toil, and this danger is the possible failure of the wage earners to realize the necessity of more general and thorough organization in the unions of their respective trades. Such a failure beyond doubt would be taken advantage of by all the elements which prey upon and take advantage of the weak. And it is a source of great gratification that the workers have organized and federated so largely and comprehensively that there is little fear of a step backward. On the contrary, every evidence is shown that the toilers have awakened to the new found power of organized effort. Never before in the history of our country have they been so well organized as they are today.

SEPTEMBER FOURTH

LOS ANGELES BIRTHDAY CELEBRATION

The city of Los Angeles, Calif., holds an annual birthday celebration on September 4 with a program that varies from year to year, but is always interesting and picturesque. Often there is a parade led by the governor on horseback, followed by soldiers and other persons representing the early settlers. Many of the spectators, as well as those participating in the parade, are in costume and attempt to recreate a picture of Spanish and pioneer days. Usually a program is held at the Plaza, supposed to be the founding site of the city. The descendants of old Spanish families, others who cherish historical traditions, and city officials, deliver appropriate addresses interspersed with musical numbers, often played by some well-known orchestra. Sometimes a barbecue dinner is served in the evening; the mayor and various public officials and distinguished visitors speak, and the orchestra contributes song and dance music. Occasionally the celebration takes place on Olvera Street, the oldest street in Los Angeles. The speakers stand on the steps of the Avila Adode, said to be one of the oldest buildings in the city and famous as headquarters of General Fremont during the 1840's.

Los Angeles was founded by decree on September 4, 1781, when Filipe de Neve, who was Governor of California at the time, came from San Gabriel Mission with a small group of followers, under direct order of Carlos III of Spain. He called the city "El Pueblo de Nuestra Señora La Reina de Los Angeles de Porciuncula." It inevitably followed that this resounding name was shortened by common usage until it eventually became Los Angeles. At the southern end of Olvera Street, just north of the Plaza, stands a hand-carved cross in commemoration of the site upon which it is believed Governor de Neve read the proclamation founding the new pueblo.

Until 1847 the city alternated with Monterey as the seat of government for the entire region known as the Mexican Province of California. In 1850 the population was 1610. After the Spanish were ousted and California admitted to the Union as a state in 1850, the population increased with phenomenal rapidity, augmented by the gold rush to California, and later by the completion of the transcontinental railroad. In 1900 it was over one hundred thousand. During the early years of the twentieth century the city continued its mushroom growth, numbering well over a million and a half by 1940.

SEPTEMBER FIFTH

FIRST CONTINENTAL CONGRESS

The Journal of the First Continental Congress for Monday, September 5, 1774, begins with the statement:

A number of delegates chosen and appointed by the several colonies and provinces in North America to meet and hold a Congress at Philadelphia assembled at Carpenters' Hall.

Then follows a list of the delegates including John and Samuel Adams from Massachusetts, Roger Sherman from Connecticut, John Jay from New York, and Colonel Richard Henry Lee, George Washington, Patrick Henry and Benjamin Harrison from Virginia. Each group of delegates presented its credentials. Some of them merely set forth that the delegates had been properly selected. Others, notably those of the Pennsylvania delegates, preceded the names with a declaration that

there is an absolute necessity that a Congress of deputies from the several colonies be held, as soon as conveniently may be, to consult together upon the present unhappy state of the colonies and to form and adopt a plan for the purposes of obtaining redress of American grievances, ascertaining American rights upon the most solid and constitutional principles, and for establishing that union and harmony between Great Britain and the colonies which is indispensably necessary to the welfare and happiness of both.

467

After the credentials had been received the Congress adjourned. It met the next day, adopted rules of order and elected a chaplain after some debate. John Jay objected to opening the proceedings with prayer on the ground of differences in religious views among the members. Samuel Adams, however, according to the account of the proceedings by John Adams, said that he was no bigot and could hear a prayer from any gentleman of piety and virtue who was at the same time a friend to his country, and he mentioned the Reverend Mr. Duche, who was elected. Mr. Duche opened the session with prayer the next day to the great satisfaction of John Adams, who wrote to his wife that "it has had an excellent effect upon everybody here."

SEPTEMBER SIXTH

LAFAYETTE'S BIRTHDAY

The gratitude of the people of the United States to Lafayette for his assistance during the Revolutionary War was enthusiatically expressed when he revisited this country in 1824-25 at the invitation of Congress. His tour of the country resembled a triumphal procession. He was feted wherever he appeared and Congress voted $200,000 and a township of land to him. Cities and towns were named for him in all parts of the country and a college just founded at Easton, Pa., honored the name of Lafayette. His statue has been erected in many cities and monuments in his honor have been raised. One of the most interesting is in Monument Cemetery in Philadelphia, which is dedicated to the memory of Washington and Lafayette. The cemetery was originally named Père le Chaise, for the celebrated cemetery in Paris, but when the Washington-Lafayette monument was dedicated on May 29, 1869, its name was changed. The pedestal has a cubic content of seventy-seven and one-half yards intended to represent the seventy-seven years and five months of Lafayette's life. The height of the monument from the pedestal is sixty-seven feet and ten inches, corresponding with the length of the life of Washington who lived sixty-seven years and ten months. There are thirteen steps representing the original thirteen states and there are thirty-two vertical grooves in the sub-shaft, one for each of the states in the Union when the monument was erected.

The anniversary of the birth of Lafayette, on September 6, 1757, was observed without any regularity for many years. But beginning with 1916 there has been an annual celebration of the event. The first World War was in progress and there was much sympathy in the United States for the heroic efforts which France was making to defend herself against the German invasion. This sympathy took the form of a tribute to the Frenchman who had come to the relief of the colonies in their fight for independence. In announcing the plans for the celebration William D. Guthrie of the committee on arrangements, wrote:

As Washington declared, the generosity of France to America during the War of the Revolution "must inspire every citizen of the states with sentiments of the most unalterable gratitude." During the course of our history since 1783 the remembrance of that feeling of gratitude has undoubtedly seemed to be dim at times, but there are many evidences of its revival in our own day. The heroism and fortitude and the misfortune and sacrifices of the French people during the past two years have reawakened in every section of the United States, East and West, North and South, the old feeling of sympathy, affection and gratitude. . . . The celebration by Americans on Wednesday, September 6, of the anniversary of the birth of Lafayette is indeed singularly fitting and appropriate and should be looked upon as a sacred duty.

The day was observed in the city of New York with a dinner at which Jules Jusserand, the French Ambassador, was the principal speaker. A bust of Lafayette was unveiled in New Orleans on that day and there were special exercises in the hotel in that city at which he had been entertained when he revisited this country. Two days earlier the French Ambassador had unveiled an equestrian statue of Lafayette at Fall River, Mass. The anniversary was observed at Philadelphia, Boston, Washington, St. Louis, Providence, Louisville, St. Joseph, Iowa City and other places. The United States joined with the Allies in resisting the German advance early in the next year and the Lafayette anniversary was again widely observed. A monument to Lafayette was unveiled at one of the entrances to Prospect Park in Brooklyn, N.Y., and there was a meeting in the city of New York addressed by André Tardieu, the French High Commissioner to the United States. Theodore Roosevelt and Elihu Root were honorary presidents of the committee of arrangements.

In 1918, when the war was drawing to a close, the governors of seven states issued proclamations calling upon the people to observe the day. The French victory at the river Marne, which was won on the same day, was celebrated with Lafayette's birthday. Ambassador Jusserand was again the guest of honor in New York, and an address was made by Theodore Roosevelt. Admiral Grout represented the French navy, accompanied by his aid, Captain de Mandat-Grancey, a descendant of Lafayette. The French army was represented by General Vignal, who fought at the Marne, and Brigadier General Brigham represented the American Army. At the celebration in Washington, Count de Chambrun, a descendant of Lafayette, was one of the speakers at the exercises at the foot of the Lafayette monument near the White House, and Josephus Daniels, the Secretary of the Navy, spoke in behalf of the government. The Lafayette Society of California with headquarters in Los Angeles observed the day. In Philadelphia there was a celebration at Independence Square when a flag duplicating the one under which Lafayette fought here was raised over Independence Hall. On the same day a similar flag sent to France for the purpose was raised over the Hotel de Ville in Paris. The day has been observed every year since 1918. The flag raising in Philadelphia is an annual event. Lafayette College decorates its buildings with flags on the anniversary and special exercises are held at the United States Military Academy at West Point, N. Y.

The anniversary was selected in 1924 as the date for the dedication of a statue of Lafayette in Baltimore. President Coolidge made the dedicatory address in the course of which he said:

> On this anniversary of his birth we are gathered about this statue in this proud city which he loved, almost in the shadow of the stately monument reared to his great friend Washington, to rededicate ourselves to the inspiring memory of a true son of world freedom. This is not only his birthday, but the anniverasry of the farewell reception extended to him at the White House by President Adams during his last visit to our country. . . . He served the cause of ordered liberty in America; he was unwilling to serve any other in France. . . . We have come here today to honor the memory of Lafayette, because long ago he came to this country as a private citizen at his own expense and joined us in fighting for the maintenance and extension of our institutions. It was not so much to acquire new rights as to maintain old rights that the men of that day put their fortune to the hazard of war. They were resisting usurpations; they were combating unlawful tyrannies. No doubt they wanted to be Americans, but they wanted most of all to be free. They believed in individual liberty, safeguarded by constitutional guarantees. This principle to them was dearer than life itself. What they fought to preserve and extend we ought to be ready to fight to maintain. . . . No president, however powerful, and no majority of the Congress, however large, can take from any individual, no matter how humble, that freedom and those rights which are guaranteed to him by the Constitution. The Supreme Court has final authority to determine all questions arising under the Constitution and laws of the United States.

Marie Jean Paul Yves Roch Gilbert du Motier, Marquis de Lafayette, was born in France on September 6, 1757, in the castle of Chavagnac in the Department of Haute-Loire. He married at the age of seventeen and entered the army. When the news of the revolt of the American colonies reached France he decided to help them. He fitted out a ship at his own expense, sailed from a Spanish port, and arrived at Georgetown, S.C., on April 24, 1777, with eleven companions including the Baron deKalb, who were eager to join in the fight for independence. Lafayette was then only nineteen years old. About three months after his arrival Congress made him a major general and not long afterward he was attached to the staff of General Washington. On September 11, five days after his twentieth birthday, he was wounded in the Battle of Brandywine, while rallying the American troops. There is a monument on the battlefield marking the spot where he fell. In December he was put in command of an army intended for the invasion of Canada, but the expedition was abandoned for lack of supplies and he joined Washington at Valley Forge in April 1778. He fought under Lee at Monmouth on June 28, and in August he was one of the commanders of a land force sent to cooperate with the French fleet in an attack on Newport.

When war broke out between France and England Lafayette returned to France, sailing in January 1779. He persuaded the French King to send a land and naval force to help the Americans and in May he returned to this country. He was a member of the court martial which sentenced Major André to death. In February 1781 he was sent to Virginia with twelve hundred New England troops to operate against the British. The British received reinforcements and on May 24 Cornwallis set out in pursuit of Lafayette who was stationed at Richmond, saying, "The boy cannot escape me." But Lafayette, who retreated to the Rappahannock, joined with a thousand Pennsylvanian troops under Wayne and strengthened by local militia, offered battle to Cornwallis. The British retreated to Yorktown with Lafayette in pursuit. On the day after the surrender of Cornwallis Lafayette was publicly thanked by Washington. In December 1781 he sailed for home from Boston, and his direct connection with American affairs ended.

SEPTEMBER SEVENTH

BIRTHDAY OF JAMES FENIMORE COOPER

James Fenimore Cooper, the greatest American novelist of the first half of the nineteenth century, was born at Burlington, N.J., on September 7, 1789, the eleventh of twelve children, of Quaker parents. He was christened James Cooper, but when he was thirty-seven years old he changed his name to James Fenimore-Cooper, with a hyphen, adding his mother's maiden name to please his grandmother. He soon dropped the hyphen because it was criticized as an affectation. When he was two years old his father moved from Burlington to Cooperstown, N.Y., on the shore of Otsego lake, where he had obtained a large estate. The family lived at first in a log house, but later built a fine mansion known as Otsego Hall. The elder Cooper represented his district in Congress for two terms and was the first county judge.

There were many Indians in the region and the boy learned much about them. He entered Yale College in 1803, but because he was unwilling to submit to discipline he was expelled in his third year. He then took service in the merchant marine to fit himself for the navy and received a midshipman's commission in 1808, serving until 1811, when he married a daughter of John Peter DeLancy, a prominent resident of New York city. For the next ten years he lived in Westchester County devoting himself to farming.

In 1820 or thereabouts he had been reading an English novel which disgusted him and remarked to his wife that he could write a better one. When she asked him why he did not do it, he wrote *Precaution,* a novel of English life with which he was not familiar. It was a failure.. Then he wrote *The Spy,* with its scene laid in Westchester County, which became more popular than any previous American novel. In 1823 he began the publication of the Leatherstocking series of novels of Indians and the frontier on which his fame rests. *The Last of the Mohicans,* regarded as the best of the series, was published in 1826 and is still read. He went to Europe following its publication and remained there for

471

seven years. He wrote many other novels besides those in the Leather-stocking series including the *History of the Navy of the United States* and some books of travel. He took up his permanent residence in the family mansion at Cooperstown soon after his return from Europe and died there on September 14, 1851, and is buried in the Episcopal church yard.

SEPTEMBER EIGHTH

THE GALVESTON TORNADO

A West Indian tornado or hurricane, on September 8, 1900, blew the waters of the Gulf of Mexico inland in Southern Texas wreaking the greatest destruction upon Galveston, although for many miles east and west of that city great damage was done to the farms and villages. The water flooded the low-lying city and thousands of buildings were de-stroyed, either by the water or by the fierce wind. It is estimated that seven thousand persons lost their lives and the destruction of property amounted to millions of dollars. At first vandals robbed the bodies of the dead and looted the houses. But order was soon restored and the work of rebuilding begun. In order to prevent a repetition of the disaster the level of the city was raised nineteen feet by pumping sand from the gulf. A sea wall seventeen feet high on the gulf front was built with its base protected by riprap. A two-mile steel reinforced concrete cause-way was built across Galveston bay, connecting the city with the main-land, with railroad tracks and a roadway. While the work of raising the grade was in progress houses left standing were propped up on stilts, an elevated structure was built to carry the street car lines and the sidewalks were planks supported by tall poles. When the work was completed the sidewalks, street car tracks and paved streets were relaid and trees and shrubbery planted and the last state of the city was better than the first.

FEAST OF THE NATIVITY OF THE VIRGIN MARY

The feast of the nativity of Mary, the mother of Jesus, is observed on September 8 by the Greek, Roman and English churches. Its celebra-tion is mentioned as early as the seventh century when a special service was prescribed with prayers and collects. There are many legends con-nected with her birth. One is that a host of angels hovered over the mother and child singing songs of praise and strewing flowers over them.

SEPTEMBER NINTH

ADMISSION DAY IN CALIFORNIA

The anniversary of the passage of the Act of Congress admitting California to the Union is a public holiday in the state observed with appropriate exercises every year. The act was passed on September 9, 1850, but the news did not reach the Pacific coast until late in October. A jubilant celebration of Admission Day was belatedly arranged in San Francisco on October 26 with a military and civic parade through the streets of the city. This was the first of a long succession of celebrations.

California had been a Mexican province. Its population in 1840 consisted of 200,000 Indians, 5,000 Mexicans and about 200 Americans. In 1846 there were rumors that the Mexican Government intended to expel the Americans. On June 14 of that year a party of Americans appeared at Sonoma, captured the place, raised the Bear Flag and proclaimed the independence of the province. The flag was a piece of white cotton to the bottom of which a piece of red flannel, torn from a woman's petticoat, was sewed as a stripe. A star was painted in the upper left-hand corner and to the right of it the crude figure of a grizzly bear. The animal looked so little like a bear that the Mexicans thought it was a hog and called the banner the "Hog Flag." It is preserved in the rooms of the Pioneer Society in San Francisco.

As General John C. Fremont was about to attack the small Mexican force in the neighborhood word came that the United States was at war with Mexico. Thereupon the Bear Flag was hauled down and the Stars and Stripes raised in its place. The Treaty of Guadalupe-Hidalgo of 1848 arranged for the cession of California to the United States. Bills were introduced in Congress setting up a territorial government but none of them was passed. A convention sitting in 1849 adopted a state constitution, and California became a state on September 9, 1850.

The celebration is ususally arranged by the societies known as the Native Sons and the Native Daughters of the Golden West, which have branches known as "parlors" in a large number of towns and cities. They arrange the chief celebration sometimes in one city and sometimes in another. In 1913 it was in Oakland and lasted for four days, culminating with a pageant on the last day. It was estimated that 40,000 persons were in the line of march and 300,000 spectators watched the parade. One division carried the first American flag made on the Pacific coast. It was composed of silk and satin scraps assembled at the order of Ernest Haskell, manager of the Adams Express Company in San Francisco, to be carried in the first Admission Day parade. There were fifty floats carrying symbolic figures or famous relics. One of the relics was the old stage coach used by General Vallejo. Another had a representation of the old steamer "Oregon." There were prairie schooners and ox teams and men and women dressed in the costumes of pioneer days.

The celebration in Sacramento, the state capital, was the most notable in 1934. The date fell at the time when the state fair was in progress in the city. The managers of the fair arranged a special celebration not connected with the celebration by the Native Sons and Native Daughters. One of its features was a parade illustrating the evolution of transportation from pack mules and oxen to the aircraft of the present, made up

SEPTEMBER 10

of thirteen divisions, each with a band and symbolic or historic floats. One of the floats commemorated the one hundred and fiftieth anniversary of Fra Junipero Serra, the famous Franciscan missionary to the Indians of California, who died in 1784. Another contained a miniature reproduction of the bell tower on the campus of the University of California. In addition the day was made notable by the planting of a tree in Capital Park in memory of Governor James Rolph, Jr., who from 1896, when he became a member of the Native Sons, until his death in 1934, had not missed an Admission Day parade.

There were celebrations in many other parts of the state including Pasadena, San Diego and Ventura. In Los Angeles, for example, the one hundred and sixty-third anniversary of the founding of the mission of San Gabriel was celebrated together with Admission Day and the sesquicentennial of the death of Fra Junipero Serra, founder of San Gabriel.

SEPTEMBER TENTH

JOHN SMITH ELECTED PRESIDENT OF COUNCIL

When John Smith sailed for Virginia in 1606 with a company of settlers he was named in a secret list as a member of the Council for the new community. But during the voyage he was charged with sedition and imprisoned, and when the ship landed and the secret instructions containing his name were opened it was decided that he had forfeited his right to sit in the Council. Yet he went out on various expeditions foraging for supplies and exploring the country and dealing with the Indians. He was so successful that in 1607 he was permitted to take his seat in the Council and on September 8, 1608, he was elected its president. When a new charter for the Jamestown colony was granted in 1609 and the government was reorganized, he was left out and returned to England and set out on voyages of discovery exploring the New England coast from the Penobscot river to Cape Cod. He died in 1631. The tradition of the saving of his life by Pocahontas, when he had been condemned to death by Powhatan, is generally regarded as a fanciful exaggeration of what really happened.

JEWISH NEW YEAR

The Jewish New Year, or Rosh Hashana, which is the first of ten penitential days ending with the Day of Atonement (see Day of Atonement, September 19) falls on the first day of the month Tishri, which in 1934 corresponded to September 10. The Jewish year is divided into twelve lunar months with an additional month every two or three years. The twelve-month year contains 354 days and the year with thirteen months has 383 days. The beginning of the new year, therefore, moves from September 5 to October 5 and the Jewish feasts and festivals also fall on different dates from year to year because of the peculiarities of the calendar. New Year's Day and the day following are observed as holy days.

New Year's Day is described by the Jewish authorities as the "annual day of judgment when all creatures pass in review before the searching eye of Omniscience." According to the *Targum*, God on that day receives the report of Satan, the accuser in heaven. The other angels, presumably friendly to the accused, plead their cause. The shofar is sounded in an effort to confuse Satan. There is said to be a book in which the deeds of every human being are recorded. A Jewish writer has described the scene in heaven in this way:

God, seated on his throne to judge the world, at the same time, Judge, Pleader, Expert and Witness, openeth the Book of Records; it is read, every man's signature being found therein. The great trumpet is sounded; a still small voice is heard; the angels shudder, saying, this is the day of judgment; for his very ministers are not pure before God. As a shepherd mustereth his flock, causing them to pass under his rod, so doth God cause every living soul to pass before him to fix the limit of every creature's life and to foreordain its destiny. On New Year's Day the decree is written; on the Day of Atonement it is sealed who shall live and who shall die. But penitence, prayer and charity may avert the evil decree.

The customary salutation of the day "May you be inscribed for a Happy New Year" contains an allusion to the Book of Life, in which the name of every living creature is entered.

SEPTEMBER ELEVENTH

BATTLE OF BRANDYWINE

At the Battle of Brandywine, fought at Chadd's Ford, Pa., on the Brandywine creek on September 11, 1777, General Howe made his third and successful attempt to reach and take Philadelphia, the capital of the colonies. His first attempt was checked by the Battle of Trenton. He made a second attempt to reach the city by way of the Delaware River, but his way was blocked. His third attempt was by way of Chesapeake Bay. He landed his troops at the head of the bay and marched northward with a force of about eighteen thousand. General Washington, with about eleven thousand men, met him at Chadd's Ford where he fought a losing battle against a superior force, but succeeded in delaying the capture of Philadelphia for two weeks and preventing the consummation of the British plans to send troops north to unite with those moving south from Canada.

The sesquicentennial of the battle was celebrated in September 1927. Representatives of Great Britain, France and the United States, and of the states of Delaware and Pennsylvania took part in the celebration.

SEPTEMBER TWELFTH

MARYLAND DEFENDERS' DAY

This day is the anniversary of the Battle of North Point in the War of 1812. It was fought the day before the bombardment of Fort McHenry, the failure of which inspired Francis Scott Key to write "The Star Spangled Banner." The anniversary is a bank holiday in Baltimore and is observed periodically by special exercises in that city and in other parts of Maryland.

The British had captured Washington and set fire to many of the public buildings earlier in the year. Admiral Cockburn, in command of the British naval forces, had threatened to burn Baltimore. The fleet sailed up Chesapeake Bay and on September 11, 1814, arrived off Patapsco Bay at the mouth of the Patapsco River. He landed 9000 troops the next morning at North Point, twelve miles from Baltimore and then sailed into the bay preparatory to bombarding Fort McHenry, which was held by a garrison of 1000 troops under Major George Armistead. General Samuel Smith was in command of the militia which had been assembled to defend the city. When the news of the landing at North Point reached him he sent General Stricker with a force of 3200 to watch the movements of the British and to act as conditions required. General Stricker sent about 150 men accompanied by sharpshooters ahead to reconnoiter. General Ross in command of the British troops was riding ahead of his men in company with Admiral Cochrane when the sharpshooters fired upon them from concealment killing General Ross. The British force moved forward under the next in command and met the first line of General Stricker's army. They fought for two hours when the Americans fell back and were joined by reinforcements. The British halted and camped on the field for the night. The next morning the British ships began the bombardment of Fort McHenry from a distance of two miles (they could not get nearer because of the shallow water) and continued until three o'clock on the morning of the 15th, when they withdrew.

The citizens of Baltimore were so grateful to Major Armistead that they presented to him a service of silver, the principal piece of which was a vase in the form of a bomb shell. And in 1815 they erected a battle monument in Calvert Street to commemorate the delivery of the city from the British. It is fifty-six feet high and consists of a tall base surmounted by Roman fasces as a pedestal for a female figure representing the city.

This unsuccessful attack upon Baltimore is popularly remembered because it inspired Francis Scott Key to write "The Star Spangled Banner." He was on board a ship in Patapsco Bay watching the bombardment. When the firing ceased before daylight they did not know whether the fort had surrendered and they anxiously waited for the dawn. In the faint light of early morning of September 14, they saw through their glasses that the flag was still flying. Then Key, with the back of an old letter as his only paper, wrote a rough draft of the song which has become the National Anthem, beginning:

O, say can you see by the dawn's early light,
What so proudly we hailed at the twilight's last gleaming,
Whose broad stripes and bright stars, through the perilous night,
O'er the ramparts we watched were so gallantly streaming?

On the night after landing Key wrote the song out in full and read it to his uncle, Judge Nicholson, who had been one of the defenders of the fort. The judge liked it so well that he took it to the printing office of Captain Benjamin Edes and had it printed on a single sheet like a handbill and distributed it to the people. It was first sung, to the air of "Anacreon in Heaven," by Charles Durang in a restaurant next door to the Holliday Street Theater in the presence of a large company of those who had defended the city. Thereafter for a long time it was sung every night in the theater.

In 1914 a celebration of the Star Spangled Banner Centennial was held at Baltimore. It began with the unveiling of a tablet on the U.S. Frigate "Constellation" on September 8, and closed with an address on "The Flag" by Secretary of State William Jennings Bryan, whom President Wilson had appointed to speak for him at the exercises.

FRANCIS E. CLARK RECOGNITION DAY

The Board of Trustees of the Christian Endeavor movement, at the suggestion of the Canadian Christian Endeavor Union, voted in 1934 to observe September 12 as Francis E. Clark Recognition Day. This is the anniversary of the birth of Dr. Clark, at Aylmer, Quebec, in 1851, where his father, Charles Carey Symmes, an American engineer, was employed at the time. Both his father and his mother died before he was eight years old and he was adopted by his mother's brother, the Reverend Edward W. Clark, then pastor of a Congregational Church at Auburndale, Mass. His name was legally changed to Clark. He was graduated from Dartmouth College in 1873, from the Andover Theological Seminary in 1876 and became pastor of the Williston Congregational Church in Portland, Me.

In an effort to increase the interest of the young people in religious work he organized, on February 2, 1881, the Williston Young People's Society of Christian Endeavor, with about fifty members. They pledged themselves to read the Bible every day and to attend and to take some part, aside from singing, in the religious meetings. His plan succeeded so well that it attracted attention in other churches and in other cities. In August 1881, he contributed to the *Congregationalist*, a weekly paper of his denomination, an article describing what he had done, and the next year published a pamphlet giving a detailed account of the plan. He left Portland in 1883 and became pastor of the Phillips Church in Boston where he served for four years. But the Christian Endeavor movement was expanding so rapidly that he resigned his pastorate in 1887 to devote his whole time to it.

The United Society of Christian Endeavor had been incorporated in Maine in 1885, but was reincorporated in Massachusetts in 1887. Aided by a group of friends, Dr. Clark bought the *Golden Rule,* a religious weekly, and became its editor and made it the organ of the society. Its name was changed to *Christian Endeavor World* in 1897. His income from the paper and from his other writings was large enough to enable him to give his time without salary to supervising the work of the society and to organizing new branches throughout the country. He was made president of the Society in 1887 and held that office for thirty-eight years. He went to England in 1888 to explain the movement to the British Sunday School Union, and in 1895 the World Christian Endeavor Union was organized, and incorporated in 1902. He was its first president. In 1919 he resigned as editor of the *Christian Endeavor World* and was made its honorary editor. He presided at the convention of the World Christian Endeavor Union in London in 1926 at which delegates from forty nations were present. He wrote many books dealing with the work of the society and describing his travels about the world. He died on May 26, 1927.

No one was more surprised than he at the growth of the movement which he started. At the celebration of its fiftieth anniversary in 1931 it was reported that there were more than four million members of eighty thousand local societies in eighty different Christian denominations in one hundred and five different countries, dominions and island groups. The International Society of Christian Endeavor includes the united societies of North America, and the World Christian Endeavor Union is a federation of all the unions throughout the world.

SEPTEMBER THIRTEENTH

ANNIVERSARY OF THE DEATH OF COMMODORE JOHN BARRY

Americans of Irish descent keep alive the memory of John Barry, popularly known as the father of the American Navy, and they cooperate with the Navy itself in honoring him. When a statue of him was dedicated in Franklin Square in Washington on May 16, 1914, they gathered there by the thousands together with five thousand sailors and marines and a brigade of midshipmen from the Military Academy at Annapolis. His statue in Independence Square, Philadelphia, the gift to the city by the Friendly Sons of St. Patrick, and dedicated on March 16, 1907, is decorated with a wreath on Memorial Day. And on the anniversary of his death on September 13, 1803, they lay flowers on his tomb in

478

St. Mary's churchyard in Philadelphia. On the one hundred and twenty-fifth anniversary of his death delegations from Irish societies in various parts of the country went to Philadelphia and held memorial exercises at the tomb, followed by religious services in the church. A bill was passed in Pennsylvania in 1941 setting September 13 of each year as a day of tribute to Commodore Barry, the governor to recommend such observance on this day as he may see fit. The anniversary of his death is also observed in schools in Rhode Island.

Barry was born at Tacumshane, County Wexford, Ireland, in 1745, but the month and day of his birth are not known. He was interested in the sea and while he was still a young boy his father found a place for him on a merchantship. When he was only fourteen he came to America and found employment on a ship trading from Philadelphia. At the age of twenty-one he was master of a schooner and during the next ten years he commanded many fine trading vessels. At the outbreak of the Revolution he offered his services to the Continental Congress and in 1776 he was employed to fit out the first fleet which sailed from Philadelphia and was authorized by the Council of Safety to build a ship for Pennsylvania.

On April 17, 1776, while in command of the brig "Lexington" he captured the British tender "Edward," said to be the first capture in battle of a British warship by a regularly commissioned officer. In October of that year he was placed seventh in the list of naval captains and was put in command of the "Effingham" but the occupation of Philadelphia by the British prevented the ship from putting out to sea. Barry, however, busied himself on the lower Delaware river and with four small boats he cut out an armed British schooner without the loss of a man and captured several transports with military supplies. When the ice in the river made naval operations difficult he obtained command of a company of volunteers and took part in the Battle of Trenton and remained with the army during the winter campaign. He was appointed to the command of the "Raleigh," lying at Boston, and on September 25, 1778, went to sea but lost the vessel in an engagement with two British ships. He was then put in command of the "Alliance" and ordered to take Colonel Henry Laurens to France as a special envoy. On his return voyage he encountered two British warships, the "Atlanta" and the "Trepassy." In the ensuing battle he was wounded and the flag of the "Alliance" was shot away. But he continued to fight and forced the enemy to surrender. The captain of one of the ships had been killed but the captain of the other, when taken aboard the "Alliance," surrendered his sword. Barry took it and then returned it saying: "You have merited it, sir. Your King ought to give you a better ship." In the succeeding fall he was ordered to take the Marquis de Lafayette and Count Noailles to France.

Barry continued in the public service after the end of the war and made many suggestions for the improvement of the navy. President Washington, under an Act of March 27, 1794, appointed him senior

479

captain of the United States Navy. The rank of Commodore had not then been created, but the officer in command of more than one ship was popularly known by that title. J. Fenimore Cooper, in his *History of the Navy of the United States*, ranks Barry next to John Paul Jones as the most efficient and brilliant officer in the navy of that period.

THE PENDLETON ROUND-UP

Throughout the West rodeos are held each year in many localities. The annual rodeo and parade in Pendleton, Ore., is among the best known and is more or less typical of these celebrations. It dates back to the early pioneer days and since 1910 has been a regular event during the last four days of the second or third week in September. In 1946 the dates were the 11th through the 14th of that month. A so-called "Westward Ho! Parade," which is one of the most interesting and picturesque features of the occasion, was staged on the morning of September 13, preceding the afternoon rodeo program. This parade commemorates the pioneers and is named after their traditional slogan. Between four and five thousand people participate, including real Indians, and there is a correspondingly large crowd of spectators who come from far and near, taxing accommodations in the hotels and private homes of Pendleton to the limit. The 1946 parade was patterned on the same style as those of previous years. Each entry was historically correct, original equipment being used in many cases, and where this was not available, exact duplicates had been fashioned. Every pioneer vehicle known was represented; stage coaches, hacks, buckboards, surreys, buggies, the Indian travois, the Red River cart, covered wagons, Mormon carts, aparajo outfits, miners' pack outfits, squaw men's carts, and twelve-mule freighters thronged the streets of Pendleton. The colorful assemblage, accompanied by drivers and riders in appropriate costumes, traversed the town in a seemingly endless procession, raising as much dust and hullaballoo as might have been found in one of the goldrush towns of the Old West.

The rodeo, whose events are spread out over the four days, attracts cowboy and cowgirl talent from the entire West. Purses are awarded for the various features. These include bulldogging seven-hundred-pound steers and roping agile, bawling calves, bronco busting, and Brahma bull riding. The winner is determined by a point system in accordance with the rules of the Rodeo Association of America.

The Pendleton Round-up, as the combined rodeo and parade is termed, was organized in 1910 by a group of citizens as a non-profit affair. It has continued on that basis, governed by a board of directors who serve without remuneration, the proceeds each year going into a fund for the next year's show.

SEPTEMBER FOURTEENTH

FEAST OF THE EXALTATION OF THE CROSS

The feast of the Exaltation of the Cross, observed on September 14, commemorates a number of events in connection with the true cross. It is especially in honor of the recovery of the cross from the Persians who captured and sacked Jerusalem in the seventh century. St. Helena, according to the traditions of the church, had found the true cross at Jerusalem and she and Constantine, after his conversion, had built a shrine on the spot. The cross was carried away by the Persians and recovered by the Emperor Heraclius II who carried it to Constantinople and thence to Jerusalem. It was in the seventh century that the Feast of the Exaltation began to be celebrated at Rome. The story of Constantine's vision of the cross in the sky before his defeat of the Roman Emperor Maxentius is usually told in connection with this feast. Beside the cross in the vision were the Greek words "In this conquer." He placed the cross upon his battle standards and conquered.

SEPTEMBER FIFTEENTH

BIRTHDAY OF WILLIAM H. TAFT

William Howard Taft is the only man in the history of the country who has held the highest executive and the highest judicial office in the government. His record is remarkable in other respects for he held public office almost continuously from his early manhood until a few weeks before his death.

He was born in Cincinnati, Ohio, on September 15, 1857, the son of Alphonso Taft, who was Attorney General in the Cabinet of President Grant during the last nine months of his second term. He was graduated from Yale College in 1878, the second in his class. He then entered the Law School of Cincinnati College, and was graduated in 1880, sharing with another man the first prize for scholarship. He was at once admitted to the bar, but spent the next year as law reporter of the Cincinnati *Times* and the Cincinnati *Chronicle*. In 1881 he was appointed assistant prosecuting attorney for Hamilton County of which Cincinnati is the county seat. The next year he was appointed Collector of Internal Revenue for the first district of Ohio, serving for about a year, when he resumed the practice of law. But he was out of office only two years for in 1885 he was appointed Assistant Solicitor for Hamilton County. In 1887 he was made Judge of the Superior Court of Ohio to fill a vacancy and in 1888 he was elected to complete the term. He resigned in 1890 to accept the office of Solicitor General of the United States under President Harrison. Two years later the President appointed him United States Circuit Judge for the Sixth Circuit. He served as dean and professor in the law department of the University of Cincinnati from 1896 to 1900 while still on the bench. President McKinley took him from the bench in 1900 and made him president of the Philippine Commission. When civil government was established in the islands he became ex officio Governor General. The status of the church lands in the islands was uncertain and in 1902, in a personal interview with Pope Leo XIII, Taft arranged a satisfactory settlement under which $7,239,000 was paid for the lands. He was recalled to the United States by President Theodore Roosevelt in 1904 to serve as Secretary of War in his Cabinet. As Secretary of War he had supervision over the construction of the Panama Canal, and was influential in the selection of Colonel George W. Goethals to take charge of the work and complete the canal. In 1908 President Roosevelt used his influence to bring about the nomination of Mr. Taft as his successor and he was elected by a majority of one hundred and fifty-nine electoral votes over William Jennings Bryan, the Democratic candidate.

As President he recommended the adoption of an amendment to the Constitution which would permit the levying of income taxes. He urged upon Congress the importance of arranging for a national budget apportioning expenditures within the anticipated national revenues. He negotiated treaties with Great Britain and France providing for arbitration of disputes which could not be settled by the ordinary diplomatic means, but when the Senate began to modify them he withdrew the treaties. During his term there was a controversy over the conservation of natural resources, which resulted in the removal of Gifford Pinchot, the Chief Forester, and the resignation of Secretary Ballinger from the Department of the Interior.

Mr. Taft ran for reelection, but a section of his party which called itself "progressive," opposed him on the ground that he was too conservative and reactionary. When the Republican National Convention met in 1912 and gave him the nomination, the "progressives" held an independent convention and nominated Theodore Roosevelt, who had broken with Taft early in his term. Because of the divided opposition the Democrats elected their candidate, Woodrow Wilson.

On his retirement from the presidency Mr. Taft became Kent professor of law at Yale University. As his professorial duties did not occupy all his time he lectured frequently and for a year or more wrote editorial articles for the Philadelphia Public Ledger. He was elected president of the American Bar Association in 1913 and in 1914 became the first president of the American Institute of Jurisprudence, an organization formed to improve the administration of the law. He favored the ratification of the Versailles Treaty in 1919, regarding the Covenant of the League of Nations as its most important part. On the death of Chief Justice White in 1921, President Harding appointed Mr. Taft as Chief Justice of the United States, an office which he held until February 3, 1930. He then resigned because of ill health, dying on March 8, of the same year. As Chief Justice he revised the rules of the court and expedited business so that long delays in litigation were done away with.

SEPTEMBER SIXTEENTH

CHEROKEE STRIP DAY IN OKLAHOMA

The anniversary of the opening of the Cherokee Strip in 1893 is observed in some parts of Oklahoma on September 16 each year, principally in Hennessey, where the land office was located, and in Enid, Garber, and Ponca City. There is usually an elaborate parade witnessed by thousands of spectators who assemble both from the towns and the surrounding counties. The forty-sixth anniversary, in 1939, was celebrated on an even larger scale than is customary. Preparations were started weeks in advance. Nearly every adult male in the various localities allowed his whiskers to grow that he might exhibit a luxuriant beard and mustache on the great day, in imitation of the hirsute adornments of the pioneers. Authentic costumes of pioneer days, either copies or genuine heirlooms, were made ready, and the same was true of equipages. Old-fashioned horse and ox drawn vehicles were produced from barns and sheds and the cobwebs dusted off. The parade in Ponca City was two and a half miles in length, a colorful pageant of pioneer life, with the illusion of other days enhanced by the attending crowd, many of whom were also in costume. The unusually large celebration on this anniversary was inspired by the European war clouds, and was an attempt to express faith in American principles of democracy as opposed to Nazi doctrines. Many patriotic speeches were delivered during the ceremonies, all of them touching on this sentiment.

During World War II the celebration was reduced to an Old Settlers' Picnic, but in 1946 festivities were resumed on a prewar scale. An estimated forty thousand persons were on hand for the pioneer parade in Ponca City on the fifty-third anniversary. Prairie schooners, conestoga wagons, buggies, floats of all descriptions, and several hundred people on horseback proceeded down Grand Avenue past suitably decorated store fronts. Among the most interesting floats was one displaying an old-style derrick from which oil flowed into a tank. Many genuine pioneer rifles were carried by the participants who wore a motley array of costumes. Probably the most picturesque entry was that of four "coon dog" men, dressed in coonskins, smoking corncob pipes, carrying a gallon jug and accompanied by two hounds.

The opening of the Cherokee Strip occurred on September 16, 1893, when that part of the population of the surrounding states who were victims of the severe depression of the early nineties lined up around the border of a vast virgin area, the Cherokee Strip, in what is now the State of Oklahoma. At high noon signals were fired and the race began. By sunset seven counties had been staked out, farms of one hundred and sixty acres having been claimed throughout the twelve thousand square mile tract except on the sites allocated for towns, and hundreds of thousands of people were established in tents or wagon boxes on their own land. Ponca City was conceived in the minds of certain far-sighted pioneers prior to the Run, a site selected adjacent to the Arkansas River, a fresh water spring, and the railroad, and within two or three weeks of the opening of the Strip it was a full-fledged town. Unfortunately, in addition to the honest settlers there were numbers of dishonest characters, shysters, landrunners and crooks of various sorts, who attempted to exploit the inevitable confusion of events to their own advantage. In spite of this, and of some miscarriage of justice, the greater part of the area was claimed by the needy and worthy citizens for whom it was intended.

The Strip had previously been surveyed by government engineers and each quarter section marked at the corners. To obtain a claim the sole legal requisite was to be first comer to the spot and to plant a flag stake. Thus speed was essential in securing the best farms and every available means of conveyance was employed. The railroads ran special trains, but many made the race in lumber wagons, spring wagons, buckboards, on horseback, or even on bicycles. No harvest was possible until the following year and the intervening winter was one of bitter poverty, but most of the settlers survived and many eventually prospered, true to the tradition of the earlier pioneers who first came to America.

SEPTEMBER SEVENTEENTH

CONSTITUTION DAY

The Constitution of the United States, universally regarded as the finest expression of the determination of a free people to govern themthemselves and to protect their liberty, was signed on September 17, 1787, by the delegates to the convention called to draft it. The delegates had met in Independence Hall, Philadelphia, in the preceding May and had deliberated in secret for four months before agreeing on the final draft of the document. George Washington was president of the convention and Benjamin Franklin, James Madison, James Wilson, Alexander Hamilton, Gouveneur Morris and other distinguished men of the time were among the delegates. When the Constitution had been ratified by the required number of states it was taken to New York, which was the first seat of government. When Philadelphia became the capital it was taken to that city and after Congress had fixed upon Washington as the permanent capital it was removed there. It has always been at the seat of government save for a short time after the British captured Washington during the War of 1812. It was then removed to Virginia far enough from Washington to be safe. President Harding, in 1921, ordered that it be taken from the State Department, where it had been kept in a safe, and deposited in the Congressional Library.

Constitution Day is observed by proclamation of the Governor of Pennsylvania and the anniversary of the completion of the work of the Constitutional Convention has been observed with greater regularity in Philadelphia than in any other part of the country, because of the distinction conferred upon it by the drafting of the Declaration of Independence and the national Constitution in the famous building which houses the Liberty Bell.

The anniversary began to attract general attention throughout the country in the twentieth century. Various small but noisy radical groups had begun to agitate for the overthrow of American institutions. Public spirited men decided that the citizens should be more fully instructed in the nature of the Constitution and in its guarantees of their freedom.

In 1914, therefore, they organized the National Security League, one of the objects of which was to promote this instruction. It prepared *A Catechism of the Constitution* and circulated thousands of copies of it. The schools were urged to devote more time to teaching the Constitution and elaborate preparations were made for the celebration of the anniversary. By 1919 it had active committees at work in forty-one different states with distinguished citizens as chairmen. Under its guidance the day was observed in at least twenty-two states and one hundred cities in that year. The American Bar Association approved the celebration in the report of a committee in the course of which it declared:

> The Constitution, which provides a plan of government for the enforcement of the rights proclaimed by the Declaration of Independence, is of equal value with the incomparable Declaration itself. Both documents should be well known by all American citizens. Any plan leading to a better knowledge, particularly of the rights and benefits of the Constitution, should meet the approval of all good citizens, and especially lawyers.

The National Security League sought to counteract the effect of attacks upon the Constitution by radicals out of office. In 1934, it was charged that in disregard of the Constitution, the Democratic President and Congress were engaged in setting up the kind of government which the radicals of previous years had advocated. This was through measures adopted in an effort to overcome the effects of the financial panic of the autumn of 1929 and the consequent business depression. The American Liberty League was formed with prominent Republicans and Democrats as its organizers. Among these were John W. Davis and Alfred E. Smith each of whom had been a Democratic candidate for the presidency. The stated purpose of this League was to use all means in its power to prevent the destruction of those liberties guaranteed by the Constitution. The anniversary was widely observed in 1934. Distinguished orators of both parties characterized the legislation for the relief of business depressions as subversive of the Constitution. Meetings were held under the auspices of the Sons of the American Revolution, the Daughters of the American Revolution, the Young Men's Christian Association, the American Legion and many other organizations. A few speakers at the celebrations in some parts of the country defended the recovery legislation and insisted that it was constitutional. They professed to have as profound respect for the Constitution as the critics of the legislation. This difference of opinion on fundamental issues made the celebration in 1934 more notable than any which had preceded it. This was because Congress had delegated to the President and his appointees a control over industry and agriculture which it had hitherto been supposed Congress itself had no constitutional authority to exercise.

A national celebration of the one hundredth anniversary of the completion of the Constitution was held in Philadelphia on September 15, 16 and 17, 1887. It was arranged by a Constitutional Centennial Commission, of which John A. Kasson was president, composed of representatives from each of the states and territories, appointed by the governors. The President with his Cabinet, the governors and other officers of the states and territories and the members of the diplomatic corps went to Philadelphia to attend the celebration. It began with an industrial parade intended to show the progress made in a century. More than 12,000 persons took part in this demonstration. In the evening Governor Beaver of Pennsylvania held a reception in honor of the official guests. There was a parade of 30,000 members of the Federal and state military organizations on the second day, reviewed by President Cleveland. In the evening President Cleveland held a public reception in the Academy of Music attended by thousands.

The third day, which was the anniversary, was devoted to exercises in Independence Square before the building in which the Constitution was drafted. Mr. Kasson presided and delivered the opening address, followed by President Cleveland who concluded his address in these words:

> As we look down the past century to the origin of our Constitution, as we contemplate its trials and triumphs, as we realize how completely the principles upon which it is based have met every national peril and every national need, how devoutly should we confess with Franklin, "God governs in the affairs of men"; and how solemn should be the reflection that to our hands is committed this ark of the people's covenant, and that ours is the duty to shield it from impious hands. We received it sealed with the tests of a century. It has been found sufficient in the past; and in all the future years it will be found sufficient, if the American people are true to their sacred trust. Another centennial day will come, and millions yet unborn will inquire concerning our stewardship and the safety of their Constitution. God grant that they may find it unimpaired; and as we rejoice in the patriotism and devotion of those who lived a hundred years ago, so may others who follow us rejoice in our fidelity and in our jealous love of constitutional liberty.

BIRTHDAY OF BARON VON STEUBEN

Interest in the services of Baron von Steuben to the American colonies in their fight for independence was revived when preparations were made for the observance in 1930 of the two hundredth anniversary of his birth on September 17, 1730. In 1919, the Steuben Society of America, the members of which are American citizens of German birth or ancestry, had been founded for the purpose of keeping his memory alive. It now has chapters in several states. Its National Council has issued a standing order that the various branches should observe the anniversary with patriotic exercises in conjunction, wherever possible, with other patriotic organizations and the officials of the community.

Steuben's memory, however, had been honored long before the formation of the Steuben Society. In 1871 a monument was erected over his grave in Oneida County, New York, and dedicated by Horatio Seymour. Congress voted a large sum to pay for a statue of him to be erected in Washington. It was dedicated in Lafayette Square in December 7, 1910, in the presence of President Taft, his Cabinet and the diplomatic corps. Count von Bernstorff made an address and the statue was unveiled by Miss Helen Taft, the daughter of the President. Congress also voted that a copy of the statue be presented to the German Emperor in recognition of his gift to the United States of a statue of Frederick the Great. On September 2, 1911, the statue was presented to William II at Potsdam by Richard Bertholdt of St. Louis, the member of the House of Representatives through whose influence Steuben had been honored by a monument in the national capital. On August 3, 1914, a statue of Steuben was unveiled in Utica, N.Y., the largest city near the site of Steuben's home. It was paid for by popular subscription through the German-American Alliance.

The one hundred and fiftieth anniversary of Steuben's landing in America was celebrated on December 1, 1927, by dinners in New York and Philadelphia at which addresses were made in praise of his services to this country. On the same day the anniversary was observed in Berlin under the auspices of the Carl Schurz Society. Many of the baron's kinsfolk were present. Probably the most interesting celebration of the bicentenary of his birth occurred at Valley Forge. It was held on September 28, 1930, as it was not convenient to hold it on September 17. The exercises were held at the foot of the statue of the baron erected by the German American Alliance in 1915 on a hill at the site of the famous winter camp of Washington's army. Addresses were made by distinguished persons and Miss Maud von Steuben, of New York, a grand niece of the baron sang "The Star Spangled Banner." The Postoffice Department issued a two-cent stamp with a portrait of Steuben. The State of New York honored Steuben in 1931 by buying a tract of fifty acres in the township of Steuben, including the grave and monument, and on September 12 dedicated it as the Steuben Memorial Park. Addresses were made by Governor Franklin D. Roosevelt and by the German Ambassador, Dr. W. von Prittzwitz-Gaffon.

It was for a long time supposed that Steuben was born on November 15, 1730. The record of his baptism, however, discovered in recent years, shows that he was born on September 17 and that he was named Friedrich Wilhelm Rudloph Gerhard Augustin von Steuben. His birthplace was the fortress in the city of Madgeburg, Prussia. His father was an engineer in the Prussian army, his ancestors having been soldiers since the thirteenth century. They became Protestants during the Reformation. He received his early education in the Jesuit college at Breslau. At the age of fourteen he served as a volunteer with his father in the War of the Austrian Succession, and was present at the siege of Prague. When he was twenty-five he was a lieutenant of infantry and soon after was appointed to the staff of Frederick the Great and served on it during the Seven Years war. Frederick instructed him in the various branches of the military art. At the end of the war Frederick appointed him to a position which gave him a comfortable income. In 1777 he decided to go to England to visit his friend the Earl of Warwick. On his way he stopped in Paris in May 1777, and communicated with his friend the Count de St. Germain who had recently been made Minister of War. The count sent for him and showed him a map of America and said:

> Here is your field of battle. Here is a republic which you must serve. You are the man she needs most.

He explained that France would soon make an alliance with the colonies, that the American army was not properly organized and was wastefully maintained. Steuben raised objections, but he was finally persuaded to see Benjamin Franklin and Silas Deane, the American Commissioners in Paris. No agreement was reached, but at last Steuben consented to go as a volunteer and offer his services to Congress.

The French fitted out a ship for him, "Le Flamand," loaded among other things with seventeen hundred pounds of gunpowder, twenty-two tons of sulphur, fifty-two brass cannon, nineteen mortars and a large number of smaller pieces including muskets and pistols. The ship sailed from Marseilles late in September 1777, and arrived at Portsmouth on December 1. Steuben at once wrote to Congress saying:

> I have made no conditions with your deputies in France nor shall I make any with you. My only ambition is to serve you as a volunteer, to deserve the confidence of your general-in-chief and to follow him in all his operations, as I have during seven campaigns with the King of Prussia.

Following his letter he presented himself before Congress then sitting at York, Pa. He was received with distinction but Congress delayed voting a commission.

He then went to Valley Forge, arriving on February 23, 1778. Washington rode out to meet him and appointed an officer and twenty-five men as a guard of honor at his quarters. In March, Washington appointed him Inspector General and he immediately began to bring order out of the chaos which prevailed. He drilled the men in military maneuvers. He insisted on a record of all equipment. Under his regulations the men whose enlistment had expired were no longer allowed to carry their muskets away with them. It is estimated that he saved the army as much as half a million dollars by this rule. He taught the soldiers the use of the bayonet. On April 30, 1778, Washington urged Congress to commission him as a Major General, but Congress still delayed. Yet he served with distinction at the Battle of Monmouth. As the delay continued he visited Congress and said that he would resign unless they voted his commission, after which he went to Philadelphia and wrote his book *Regulations for Order and Discipline of the Troops of the United States.* This became the official drill book. When Congress finally confirmed his appointment as Inspector General with the rank of Major General he returned to the army and renewed his teaching. He organized a body of riflemen for quick movement, an organization that was copied by Frederick the Great and later by Napoleon. He served with distinction in the Virginia campaign and was present at Yorktown when Cornwallis surrendered. Washington thanked him, with Lafayette, for his services in that campaign.

Congress was dilatory in paying him and in reimbursing him for expenses paid out of his own funds. An appropriation of $50,000 failed to pass. Finally in April 1790, Congress did vote an annuity of $2500 and tracts of land were given to him by the states of Virginia, Pennsylvania, New Jersey and New York. The New York tract, lying twelve miles north of Utica, was laid out as the town of Steuben. After he received his annuity Steuben built a three-room log house upon it in which he spent his summers, and cleared about fifty acres which he cultivated as a farm. He died there on November 24, 1794, of a stroke of apoplexy, and was buried in his military cloak under a hemlock tree near his home. The grave was not marked and in later years a road was laid out over it. When this was learned the body was removed and buried near by and a stone was set up to mark it.

SEPTEMBER EIGHTEENTH

LAYING THE CORNERSTONE OF THE CAPITOL

When the District of Columbia was selected as the site of the national capital arrangements were made for the erection of the necessary public buildings. On September 18, 1793, the cornerstone of the new Capitol was laid by President Washington with Masonic ceremonies. A procession with two bands, Virginia artillery and the Masonic lodges marched from the President's square to the site of the Capitol. No streets had been opened and when the procession reached a brook at the foot of Capitol Hill the paraders had to break ranks and cross the stream on a log. Washington, acting in the dual capacity of Mason and President, tapped the stone with a gavel which is still preserved and declared the stone to be properly laid. It contained a silver plate upon which was engraved the statement that the stone was laid in the thirteenth year of the new nation, in the first year of the second term of President Washington and in the year 5793 of Masonry. The building erected at this time was only a small part of the present Capitol, with neither the present Senate or House wing and without the dome. After it was burned by the British it was rebuilt and another cornerstone was laid by President Madison on August 24, 1818. When it was enlarged in 1851 President Fillmore laid still a third cornerstone on July 4 of that year, and Daniel Webster made the dedicatory address.

SEPTEMBER NINETEENTH

FEAST OF ST. JANUARIUS

Italians born in Naples and their descendants in America celebrate the feast of St. Januarius, or St. Gennaro, every year. He is the patron saint of Naples and his relics are preserved in the cathedral in that city. He was the Bishop of Beneventum and it is supposed that he suffered martyrdom under Diocletian in about the year 305. There is little authentic information either about him or about his martyrdom, but there are many traditions. According to one of them Timotheus, president of Campania, the official who condemned the martyrs, ordered Januarius thrown into a fiery furnace, but the flames did not touch him. Then he and his camponions were exposed in the amphitheater to wild beasts but the beasts ignored them. Timotheus, declaring that this was due to magic, ordered the victims to be beheaded but he was stricken with blindness. Januarius restored his sight, and five thousand persons accepted Christianity because of the miracle, but Januarius and his companions were finally beheaded. His remains were taken to Naples and deposited in the cathedral there. Among them was a bottle said to contain his blood. A silver bust, said to inclose his head, is exhibited at stated periods during the year and, when the bottle containing his blood is placed near it the blood, which is apparently solid, liquefies. How and why this happens has been the subject of controversy for many years. But that it does happen is not disputed.

The manner of the celebration of the feast day by the Italians in New York in 1934 was described in a picturesque manner by the *Herald Tribune* of that city:

The staccato strains of the Fascist anthem burst into the travel agency of Raffaelo Prisco, 64 Mulberry street, just before five o'clock yesterday afternoon. Crowds, cameras and religious banners on the street could be seen through the plate glass windows.

"Cavaliere Prisco!" a delegation hurried into the office. It was time to go. The genial Cavaliere, alto patrono of the Festa San Gennaro and presidente della Società San Gennaro Napoli e Dintorni, Inc., jumped up from his huge mahogany desk and slipped over his shoulders a silk ribbon embroidered with the word "Auspice." Then he stepped to the door, smiled upon the throngs at the foot of the wrought iron stairs, and raised his hand in the Fascist salute.

Cavaliere Prisco's appearance set in motion the parade through Little Italy which takes place at this time every year in homage to Saint Gennaro, one time Bishop of Benevento, patron and protector of the City of Naples. In the Naples cathedral, according to tradition, the blood of Saint Gennaro should now be transferred from a coagulated to a liquid state and remain so until tomorrow morning. . . . The music started. The procession moved on. Past the files of pushcarts loaded with melons, clams, peppers, sausages, pastry, nuts and cheeses the parade advanced while the band ran through a sequence of Sousa's marches.

In front of a crumbling tenement between Canal and Hester streets the column came to a halt. Cavaliere Prisco took off his hat and faced a black doorway. There was a moment's silence. Then the band burst into the Fascist hymn. The crowds craned their necks, while two or three grinning Irish policemen flicked the cords of their night sticks against the bare legs of the pushing children. From the narrow doorway emerged the first of the principessine of the festa—a slender, dark-eyed Italian girl, clad in a tan lace evening gown, her hair clasped in a silver coronet with a star directly above her forehead, her full lips moist with crimson lipstick. Smilingly she took her place beside the Cavaliere and the parade moved on. Before another tenement a little farther on was another halt and the second princess stepped forth. She too wore the starred coronet and over the puddles of Mulberry street she daintily lifted the heavy folds of a red velvet gown. Then came two more principessine, one in silk, the other in green lace. Finally the parade called for the Regina della Festa, Miss Nancy Masucci, who emerged from a tenement on Baxter street, her white train upheld by two little girls.

For two hours Cavaliere Prisco, the band and the princesses led the procession through the narrow streets until the sun sank behind the gray clouds. Then the festoons of lights which arched overhead burst into red, green and white brilliance. The illuminated cross above the open-air shrine of San Gennaro, at Hester and Mulberry streets, sparkled in the gray twilight. The saint's upraised eyes stared over the fire escapes and clothes lines to the darkening lane of sky overhead. His two fingers pointing aloft, blessed the crowds, which, in passing, dropped contributions upon the altar at his feet. Despite the dampness under foot hundreds closed on the parade at every crossing. But hunger finally got the better of the marchers. They adjourned with Cavaliere Prisco for some fine Chianti and "an exquisite dinner of spaghetti." Last night, however, the celebration was resumed in the illuminated streets. Bands played on decorated floats at every corner. Couples danced on the wet pavement. Pushcarts did a thriving business far into the night. This evening San Gennaro will be returned to his niche in the Church of the Most Precious Blood, 113 Baxter street, and the feast will be over for another year.

DAY OF ATONEMENT

The Day of Atonement, or Yom Kippur, is the last of the ten penitential days which mark the beginning of the Jewish New Year. It is observed on the tenth day of Tishri, which fell on September 19 in 1934. No other Jewish fast day or feast day is observed so generally or with such reverent devotion. The day, according to Biblical tradition, was set apart by Moses. An elaborate ceremonial was prepared for its observance which was followed until the offering of sacrifices was abandoned after the destruction of the Temple in Jerusalem in 70 A.D. The high priest in the early morning offered the daily sacrifice. This was followed by the festival sacrifice of a bullock and seven lambs. Then the atone-

491

ment ceremonies began with the high priest dressed in a special vestment. He placed his hands on the head of a bullock and confessed his sins and those of his household. Two goats, contributed by the people, were placed before him, one designated by lot as a sin offering for the Lord and the other to be sent away into the wilderness.. The high priest again made confession of his sins and the sins of his brother priests over the head of the bullock which was sacrificed with ceremonies, including the burning of incense and the sprinkling of blood on the altar and on the Ark of the Covenant. Then he killed the goat chosen for sacrifice and repeated the ceremonies of sprinkling the blood of the animal. Thus the holy places were cleansed from all impurities. The blood of the goat and the bullock were then mixed and sprinkled on the altar. After this ceremony the live goat was brought forward and the priest laid his hands on its head and confessed "all the iniquities of the Israelites and all their transgressions and all their sins" and then sent the animal away into the wilderness. This is the origin of the term scape goat. There were other ceremonies of a similar character during the day.

The day is observed in modern times by services in the synagogues beginning in the evening of the preceding day and continuing until the evening of the day itself. The importance of repentance is stressed in the services. The souls of the dead are included in the community of those pardoned on the Day of Atonement and it is customary for children to have public mention made of their dead parents and to make charitable gifts on behalf of their souls. Commenting on this day of prayer and fasting, a writer in the *Jewish Encyclopedia* says:

No matter how much else has fallen into desuetude, so strong is its hold upon the Jewish conscience that no Jew, unless he has cut himself entirely loose from the synagogue, will fail to observe the Day of Atonement by resting from his daily pursuits and attending service in the synagogue. With few exceptions, the service even in the Reformed synagogues is continuous throughout the day.

SEPTEMBER TWENTIETH

PANIC OF 1873

The financial panic of 1873 reached a climax on September 20 when the New York Stock Exchange closed its doors. The trouble arose because of the failure of the new railroads to pay the interest on their bonds. In the five years preceding September 1873, at least $1,700,000,-000 had been spent on railroad expansion. The money was raised by the issue of bonds which were bought largely by the banks. As the roads defaulted in the payment of interest it was no longer possible to sell any more bonds. The roads had borrowed money for short periods in the hope that they could repay the loans by an issue of new bonds. When this became impossible the banks were in trouble.

The first symptom of serious trouble came with the failure of a bank which had made advances on the bonds of the Missouri, Kansas

& Texas Railroad. Then on September 13 another bank failed because
of loans to the Canadian Southern Railroad. Again on September 18
the bank of Jay Cooke & Company of Philadelphia, one of the largest
in the country, closed its doors. It had lent $15,000,000 to the Northern
Pacific Railroad and it had deposits of $4,000,000 from all parts of
of nation. Railroad shares were immediately offered on the Stock
Exchange for whatever they would bring and broker after broker
failed. On September 19 the banking house of Fitch & Hatch of New
York went under, and a run was started on the Union Trust Company,
and on the Fourth National Bank; three large banks closed their doors.
Then on the morning of September 20 the Stock Exchange shut its
doors to prevent trading. This was the first time in its history that such
a thing had happened. To ease the situation the Clearing House voted
to issue certificates secured by proper collateral to be used in settling
daily balances. President Grant went to New York with his Secretary
of the Treasury to offer his assistance and announced his intention to buy
Government bonds to the amount of $13,000,000. The Stock Exchange
was closed for ten days and when it reopened there was a general feeling
that there would be a rush to sell stocks and the prudent offered none
for sale. As a result the market was steady and in the course of time
the feeling of panic disappeared and normal trading was resumed.

SEPTEMBER TWENTY-FIRST

FEAST OF ST. MATTHEW

The feast of St. Matthew, one of the Twelve Disciples and the
author of the first book of the New Testament, is observed on September 21. He was a Galilean known as Levi until he was summoned
to the service of Jesus. He is described in the New Testament as a
publican, that is, he was a collector of customs duties at Capernaum for
Herod Antipas. As a tax gatherer he was hated by those who had to
pay the taxes. He gave a feast in honor of Jesus and invited to it other
"publicans and sinners." When the Pharisees protested Jesus rebuked
them, saying, "I came not to call the just, but sinners, to repentance."
He was present at the Last Supper and was one of the witnesses of the
Resurrection and the Ascension. The meager record of his life in the
New Testament is supplemented by tradition, much of which is of
doubtful value. It is said that he preached to the Hebrews for fifteen
years and that he wrote his gospel for them in their own language. He
is said to have preached in other countries, including Ethiopia or Colchis
to the south of the Caspian Sea, Persia, Macedonia and Syria. According
to Clement of Alexandria he died a natural death, but other authorities
say that he was martyred. There is a disagreement, moreover, on the manner and place of his martyrdom. One tradition has it that he was buried

honorably at Hieropolis in Parthia. What purported to be his bones were removed and, according to Pope Gregory VII, who mentioned them in 1080, they were kept in a church of St. Matthew at Salerno.

SEPTEMBER TWENTY-SECOND

HANGING OF NATHAN HALE

Nathan Hale, who has a secure place in American history, was hanged as a spy by the British in New York on September 22, 1776. His last words on the scaffold were "I only regret that I have but one life to give for my country." He was born at Coventry, Conn., on June 6, 1755, and was graduated from Yale College in 1773. He taught school until 1775 when he became a lieutenant in a Connecticut regiment and was promoted to the rank of captain on January 1, 1776. In March of that year he started for New York with Heath's brigade and was engaged in harrassing operations about the city. Early in September he volunteered to enter the city to get some needed information about the British force there. Disguised as a Dutch schoolmaster he entered the British lines, obtained the information and was about to return when on the night of September 21 he was recognized and arrested. He was hanged as a spy on the following morning. A bronze statue of Hale by Macmonnies stands in City Hall Park, New York, and there is another statue at Hartford, Conn., where the 150th anniversary of his execution was commemorated on September 22, 1926.

SEPTEMBER TWENTY-THIRD

BIRTHDAY OF WILLIAM H. McGUFFEY

William H. McGuffey, whose series of Eclectic Readers for use in the schools made him famous, was born near Claysville, Pa., on September 23, 1800. When the Connecticut Reserve in Ohio was opened to settlement his father moved to Ohio and settled near Youngstown in 1802. He prepared for college at the Old Stone Academy at Darlington, Pa., and was graduated from Washington College in 1826. He immediately became professor of languages in Miami University at Oxford, Ohio, and served on the faculty until 1836 when he was elected president of Cincinnati College. In the meantime he had been licensed to preach by the Presbyterian church but he never held a pastorate. After three years at Cincinnati College he became president of Ohio University at Athens, and later served on the faculty of Woodward College at Cincinnati and the University of Virginia. It was while he was a professor in Miami University that a firm of Cincinnati publishers asked him to edit a series of school readers. This series, begun in 1836 and finished in 1857, became immediately popular and before it was superseded by other text books about 122,000,000 copies were sold. The selections in the readers for the lower grades always contained a moral, and extracts from the best English writers appeared in readers for the older pupils. Millions of Americans formed their literary taste on these books.

SEPTEMBER TWENTY-FOURTH

JOHN MARSHALL'S BIRTHDAY

John Marshall, the fourth Chief Justice of the United States, whose memory is kept green by the bench and bar, was born in Fauquier County, Virginia, on September 24, 1755. When the Revolutionary War began he suspended the study of the law and enlisted as a volunteer. He rose to the rank of captain in 1777. He took part in the battles of Brandywine, Germantown and Monmouth and was at Valley Forge during the winter of 1777-78. He was without a command in 1780 and spent most of the year studying law at William and Mary College, and was admitted to the bar the next year. He served three terms in the Virginia Legislature and in 1788 was delegate to the Constitutional Convention. The arguments advanced in favor of ratification by him and by James Madison were effective. In 1795 he was elected to the Virginia Legislature for a fourth time.

Washington offered him the post of Attorney General in his Cabinet, but he declined it. He consented, however, to go to Paris in 1797 with C. C. Pinckney and Elbridge Gerry to try to persuade the French to remove the restrictions which they had laid on American commerce. A seat on the Supreme Court bench as the successor to James Wilson was offered to him in 1798, but he declined that also. In the same year, at the solicitation of Washington, he became a candidate for election to the national House of Representatives and won. President Adams asked him to enter his cabinet as Secretary of War, but he refused. He did, however, serve as Secretary of State for a short time.

On January 31, 1801, President Adams commissioned him as Chief Justice of the United States, a position which he held until his death on July 6, 1835, in Philadelphia, where he had gone for medical treatment. The Liberty Bell in the tower of Independence Hall was cracked while it was tolled to announce his death. During his service as Chief Justice he did much to clarify and interpret the Constitution. He insisted that it was the function of the Supreme Court to interpret the Constitution and to decide whether the acts of Congress and of the state legislatures exceeded the powers delegated to these bodies. His view was that unless it was admitted that the Supreme Court had the power to decide whether an act of Congress was constitutional or not the Constitution itsel. would

495

become a dead letter and Congress could pass any law that pleased it regardless of whether the people had delegated to it the right to legislate on the subject.

SCHWENKFELDER THANKSGIVING DAY

Many small sects grew out of the flux of religious theories that accompanied the Protestant Reformation. Some lasted a few years and others continue to the present. Among the latter is the Schwenkfelder society, composed of followers of Caspar von Schwenkfeld of Ossig in Lower Silesia. Von Schwenkfeld was born in 1490 and was educated at Cologne and at other universities where the writings of the Church Fathers interested him. While a young man he entered the service of Carl, Duke of Munsterberg, a grandson of the King of Bohemia, a follower of John Huss. The young man was in sympathy with the beliefs of Huss. Later he became counsellor to Frederick II, Duke of Liegnitz, and there he became acquainted with many theologians who were drifting away from the doctrines of the Church of Rome. He withdrew from the ducal court and became Canon of St. John's Church in Liegnitz. The preaching of Luther, who had withdrawn from the Church of Rome, attracted his attention. Finding that his conscience would no longer permit him to hold his position in St. John's Church he resigned and devoted the next thirty-six years of his life to evangelistic preaching, attracting a large following. He died at Ulm on December 10, 1562.

After his death his followers were persecuted and driven from place to place. They received the protection of Count Zinzendorf for a time, but when he could protect them no longer two families set sail for the New World, arriving in Philadelphia on September 18, 1733. They reported to their friends who had taken refuge in Holland that there was religious freedom in Pennsylvania and on June 19, 1734, a company numbering a hundred and eighty-four set sail from Rotterdam on the English ship "St. Andrew," and arrived in Philadelphia on September 22. Christopher Heydrick, in his historical sketch of the sect writes:

On the next day all male persons over the age of sixteen years proceeded to the State House and there subscribed allegiance to King George II, King of Great Britain, and his successors, and of fidelity to the proprietor of the province. They spent the 24th in thanksgiving to Almighty God for delivering them out of the hands of their persecutors, for raising up friends in the times of their greatest need, and for leading them to a land of freedom where they might worship Him unmolested by civil or ecclesiastical power. This day, the 24th of September, was thenceforth set apart to be observed by them and their descendants, through all time, as a day of Thanksgiving commemorative of the Divine goodness manifested in their deliverance from the persecutions of the Fatherland. To this day it is so observed.

These immigrants settled in Montgomery, Lehigh, Berks and Bucks counties in Pennsylvania where their descendants now live. In 1934 they celebrated the two hundredth anniversary of the arrival of their ancestors by a series of meetings and pageants beginning in May and culminating in the annual thanksgiving service in the Towamencin Church on September 24. The sect is small, but it maintains a religious paper and the Perkiomen Seminary at Pennsburg, Pa., an excellent college preparatory school with a good plant.

FEAST OF THE TABERNACLES

This Jewish feast begins on the fifteenth day of the month Tishri, which in 1934 fell on September 24. It is generally believed that its observance began after the Jews had ended their wanderings in the wilderness and had entered the promised land. There is a tradition, however, that it was observed by Abraham. Whether it was originally a Jewish feast or was adopted by the Jews from a custom of the Canaanites is uncertain. It is referred to in the Bible as the Feast of Ingathering and the Feast of Kings as well as the Feast of the Tabernacles.

As it occurred at the end of the harvest season the feast was undoubtedly observed in celebration of the gathering of the crops. In the early days the maidens danced in the vineyards and the families lived in booths in the fields until the harvest was completed. These booths, or tabernacles, gave the name to the feast. It was one of the great festivals during which all males were required to make a pilgrimage to the Temple in Jerusalem.

An elaborate ritual with sacrifices was prepared for the Temple services. The custom arose of living in booths during the eight days of the feast and in the course of time the theory was evolved that these booths were typical of the tents in which the Jews lived during their wanderings in the wilderness, thus giving a historical significance to the festival. After their return from the Captivity the Jews, according to the account in Nehemiah, "made themselves booths, every one upon the roof of his house, and in their courts, and in the courts of the house of God, and in the broad place of the water gate, and in the broad place of the gate of Ephraim." The booth was to be especially built for the festival, thatched so as to be a protection against the sun while allowing the stars to shine through at night. It was to serve as a permanent dwelling place for seven days and all males were compelled to live in it unless prevented by illness or other valid cause. With the destruction of the temple many of the ancient customs of the festival were abandoned, but the booths remained obligatory. The feast is observed to this day and the orthodox Jews preserve as many of the ancient customs as possible under the conditions of modern life. Originally the feast lasted only seven days, but an eighth day was added as a concluding festival. It is known as the Rejoicing of the Law.

SEPTEMBER TWENTY-FIFTH

DISCOVERY OF PACIFIC BY BALBOA

Vasco Nunez de Balboa, the Spanish discoverer, was born in 1475 of a noble, but impoverished, family. Doubtless in an effort to repair the family fortunes, he joined the great mercantile expedition undertaken by Rodrigo de Bastidas in 1501, and established himself in Santo Domingo. However his plantation was not financially successful and to escape his creditors he had himself smuggled aboard a ship, joining the expedition to Darien in 1510. In 1513 he discovered the Pacific Ocean, sighting it on September 25 from "a peak in Darien" and taking possession of it in the name of Spain. The governorship of the territories conquered by Balboa was obtained in 1514 by Pedrarias Davila, whose daughter Balboa married. As the result of a disagreement with Davila, Balboa was accused of plotting to rebel, and beheaded.

SEPTEMBER TWENTY-SIXTH

FEAST OF ST. ISAAC JOGUES

Isaac Jogues, René Coupil and John Lalande, French Jesuit missionaries, were sent to America in 1636 and were killed by the Indians at the Indian village of Ossernenon on the banks of the Mohawk River in eastern central New York. Jogues and his companions were canonized in 1930 and Jogues is venerated as a saint of the church on September 26 with special ceremonies every year at Auriesville, a village on the site of Ossernenon, five miles west of Amsterdam.

It was in 1884 that General John S. Clark, the New York State archeologist, announced that he had found evidence to support the belief that Ossernenon, on a bluff overlooking the Mohawk, occupied the site on which the village of Auriesville had been built many years later. As it was known that Jogues and his companions had been martyred there ten acres of land were bought and a small chapel called Our Lady of Martyrs was erected, and the place began to be visited by pious pilgrims. Its fame has grown with the years. The original ten acres has been increased to five hundred, a coliseum seating 10,000 has been built with four rustic altars to accommodate the worshippers. A life-sized crucifix has been erected on the hill which the three missionaries are supposed to have gone for their evening prayers and stations of the cross have been set up in the grounds. The shrine is visited by a quarter of a million people every year. The three hundredth anniversary of the arrival of the missionaries in America was celebrated there on August 16, 1936, attracting many thousand visitors.

Jogues, who was born in 1607, was sent by the Jesuits to the Huron mission in North America in 1636. He labored among the Hurons until 1639 when he was sent to the Tobacco Nation. In 1641 he went to Sault Ste. Marie and preached to the Algonquins. Then he started for Three Rivers to obtain supplies for his mission but he and Goupil were captured by the Iroquois and taken to the Mohawk villages and tortured. Goupil was killed but Jogues was kept as a slave. He was finally rescued by the Dutch at Rensselaerswyck and sent to New Amsterdam. From there he was sent back to France where he was welcomed with many honors. He soon returned to Canada and two years later went to the Mohawk villages with authority from the Canadian Government to found the Mission of the Martyrs. The Mohawks signed a treaty of peace and he returned to Quebec, but soon went back to work among the Indians. They were no longer friendly and one night in 1646, when he was entering a lodge at Ossernenon to which he had been invited for a feast he was killed by a blow from a tomahawk.

Jogues was one of the early explorers of this continent. He discovered Lake George in New York on May 30, 1636, the eve of the Feast of Corpus Christi, and named it the Lac du Saint Sacrament, a name which it held until 1756, when its present name was given to it by General William Johnson in honor of King George II.

SEPTEMBER TWENTY-SEVENTH

WOMEN IN NATIONAL POLITICS

The Executive Committee of the Democratic National Committee, anticipating the ratification of the Constitutional amendment permitting women to vote, decided on September 27, 1919, to admit women to membership. Its example was soon followed by the Republican National Committee and men and women in equal numbers sit on the national committees of the two great parties. Prior to 1919, women had taken part in state political affairs where they had the vote, and a woman had been elected to the national House of Representatives. In the Eightieth Congress seven women were members.

SEPTEMBER TWENTY-EIGHTH

FRANCES E. WILLARD'S BIRTHDAY

The Woman's Christian Temperance Union observes September 28, the anniversary of the birth of Miss Frances E. Willard, its most distinguished leader, as a Children's Harvest Home and Young Crusader Day. It observes the anniversary of her death (see February 17) as a Memorial Fund Day. Her memory is preserved, outside of the organization in which she was active, by a statue in the National Capitol in Washington, contributed by the State of Illinois. The jury which decides upon those whose statues are to be placed in the Hall of Fame of New York University admitted Miss Willard, and a bust by Lorado Taft was dedicated there in 1923. In 1929 a tablet in her honor was unveiled in the Capitol of Indiana, and her home in Evanston, Ill., is preserved in her memory. Soon after the death of Miss Willard on April 14, 1898, the legislature of Kansas passed a law directing that in every public school in the state at least one fourth of the school day on every September 28 should be devoted to exercises in her memory. Frances E. Willard Day is also observed in the public schools of Delaware, Oregon, and Pennsylvania.

CABRILLO DAY IN CALIFORNIA

In California September 28 is observed by proclamation of the governor in honor of Juan Rodriguez Cabrillo, a Portuguese in the employ of Spain, who discovered California on that day in 1542. On Cabrillo Day in 1935 the Native Sons of the Golden West set up a plaque in memory of the discoverer on the old lighthouse at Point Loma, near San Diego. On December 19, 1940, a bayshore site at San Diego was dedicated, and on Cabrillo Day in 1942, the four hundredth anniversary, a monument was unveiled there. This anniversary was observed throughout the state, particularly by Portuguese residents, but the program at San Diego was the most important. The fourteen-foot statue, carved by Alvaro De Bree, a Portuguese sculptor, in Lisbon in 1939, was presented by Portugal to California. The statue was erected at the foot of Lowell Street, Point Loma, on property owned by the city of San Diego and leased to the United States Navy during World War II, but which was allocated as the eventual site of a small park. Dr. Euclides Goulart da Costa, Portuguese consul at San Francisco, made the dedication address at the unveiling. The same day a new Consolidated PB2Y patrol bomber was dedicated "Cabrillo" in a brief ceremony just before the plane was turned over to the Navy. In San Francisco the Cabrillo Civic Club met on the Saturday preceding the anniversary and celebrated the occasion by two talks on modern history-making events. James G. Smyth, State Administrator of the United States Treasury's war saving staff, delivered an address on "This Economic Battle," and Superior Court Judge Everett C. McKeage spoke on "The Course of the War." Rena Marcell, a well-known Portuguese entertainer, sang and played the accordion.

Cabrillo was a Portuguese navigator who entered the service of Spain, and was sent in 1542 by Viceroy Antonio de Mendoza to explore the coast of the country northwest of Mexico. He explored the shores of what is now Lower California and by the end of September of that year sailed into San Diego harbor. Continuing northward along the coast, he discovered various bays and islands. When within a few miles of San Francisco Bay bad weather forced him to turn back to San Miguel Island where he planned to spend the winter. Here he died on January 3, 1543.

SEPTEMBER TWENTY-NINTH

MICHAELMAS DAY OR
THE FEAST OF ST. MICHAEL AND ALL ANGELS

This day is observed by the Roman and Anglican churches in honor of the archangel Michael and the other angels. Michael is mentioned four times in the Bible, three times in the Old Testament and once in the Epistle of St. Jude in the New Testament. Jude, in rebuking those who spoke evil of others, wrote that "Michael the archangel, when contending with the devil he disputed about the body of Moses, durst not bring against him a railing accusation, but said, 'The Lord rebuke thee.' " This refers to an ancient Jewish tradition that Michael concealed the tomb of Moses and that the devil by disclosing it tried to lead the Jewish people into what is described as "the sin of hero worship." The Fathers of the Church held a theory that Michael appears many times in the Biblical narrative where his name is not mentioned. It was he who stood at the gate of the Garden of Eden "to keep the way to the tree of life." It was through him that God revealed the Ten Commandments to his people. He stood in the way of Balaam and he it was who routed the army of Sennacherib.

St. Michael was the first archangel, prince of the angels and captain of the hosts of heaven. He is believed to be the inspirer of Joan of Arc. He is represented in art as a warrior and hero in battles. Michael was the patron saint of the sick among the early Christians. Hot springs in eastern Asia were dedicated to him. In Egypt the Christians put the Nile under his protection and they celebrated the period of the annual rising of the river in his honor. In Normandy he is regarded as the patron of mariners and the famous church and monastery of Mont Saint Michel was erected in his honor. He was regarded as the angel of mountains and many churches and chapels dedicated to him were erected in Europe on the tops of hills or mountains of which Mont Saint Michel is the most famous. It was built on a rock three hundred feet high a mile from the shore and is regarded as the finest example of French medieval architecture that has survived. The monastery was founded in 708 by the bishop of St. Aubert who, according to the legend, was visited three times by the archangel and commanded to build a monastery and a church on the rocky island. In 1017 Abbot Hildebert II began the erection of the present structures, but they were not completed until 1520. During

SEPTEMBER 30

the French Revolution the monks were ejected from the place and it was made a prison for political offenders. It remained a prison until 1863 when it was leased to the Bishop of Avranches. In 1872 the French Government took it over as a national monument and began the work of restoration.

There is an Italian Society of St. Michael the Archangel, which observes the day with a special celebration beginning on the 26th. A typical observance was that by the society in Boston in 1912. Its members met in their hall in the morning and marched to the Church of the Sacred Heart where a solemn high mass was celebrated and a Franciscan priest from New York preached a sermon on St. Michael. In the afternoon the society held a reception in honor of the presidents, guests and representatives of the forty-five Italian societies in the city. This was followed by a parade and a banquet. There was a band concert in North Square and the celebration ended with a display of fireworks on the Common.

SEPTEMBER THIRTIETH

FEAST OF ST. JEROME

The feast of St. Jerome, one of the greatest scholars of the early Christian church, is celebrated on September 30, the date of his death at Bethlehem in 420. He is honored by all branches of the Christian church, while his feast day is observed regularly in the Catholic churches. Probably its most picturesque observance occurs at Taos, N.M., where the Indians hold what is called a San Geronimo Festival.

Saint Jerome was born at Stridon, a town on the border of Dalmatia, in about the year 340, of wealthy Christian parents. His early secular education was obtained at Rome where he became a fine Greek and Latin scholar, while living the careless life of the youth of the city. He fell ill while traveling in Syria and heard a voice saying: "Thou are not a Christian but a Ciceronian." He took this as a rebuke for his interest in the classics. He spent some time in a monastery at Bethlehem and while in the East studied Hebrew with a converted Jew. He visited Antioch and Constantinople and spent the years from 382 to 385 in Rome where he became acquainted with several noble Christian women. When he returned to Palestine in 386 two of them went with him and one of them built a monastery for men over which Jerome presided. She also built a monastery for women which she superintended. He translated the Bible into Latin and wrote many theological works as well as a large number of letters which have been preserved.

He is frequently represented in Christian art accompanied by a lion because of a legend about him. It seems that he was sitting at the gate of the monastery in Bethlehem when a lion came up to him and held out his paw. Jerome looked at it and found that it was pierced by a

502

large thorn. He removed the thorn, put healing lotions on the wound, bound it up, and had the animal lie down in his cell till it was healed. Thereafter the lion is said to have followed him about like a dog. Jerome told the lion to watch an ass used in carrying firewood so that it might not stray from the pasture. One day while the lion slept the ass disappeared, and the lion returned to the monastery with a drooping head and a look of shame. Jerome thought the lion had killed the ass and made him carry the firewood thereafter. After a time the lion decided to hunt for the missing animal. When a caravan led by an ass passed by, the lion recognized the ass which had been stolen, and he drove the whole caravan, camels, drivers and all, into the gate of the monastery where the men of the caravan admitted that they had stolen the ass. Jerome rejoiced at the proof of the faithfulness of the lion, pardoned the thieves and set them free.

Pinta—Santa Maria—Nina

OCTOBER

The fields are harvested and bare,
And Winter whistles through the square.

October dresses in flame and gold
Like a woman afraid of growing old.

—ANNE MARY LAWLER

October was the eighth month in the ancient Roman calendar, as its name indicates. When the calendar was revised it retained its name in spite of several efforts to change it. A month had been named for Julius Caesar and another for Augustus. Germanicus Caesar, a distinguished general and a kinsman of Augustus's had won fame by his campaigns against the Germans and the Senate voted to honor him by changing the name of October to Germanicus. Some years later the name was changed to Antoninus in honor of the emperor Antoninus Pius, but this was not popular. Then the name was changed to Faustinus, in honor of Faustina, the wife of Antoninus. The name was changed a fourth time to Hercules, to honor the emperor Commodus. He had called himself the Roman Hercules and had insisted that he be worshipped as a god, and as Julius Caesar and Augustus had months named for them he thought he should be honored in the same way. But none of these attempts to give the month a different name was permanently successful. The Saxons had three names for it—Win-monath, or the time for making wine; Teo-monath, or tenth month, and Winterfylleth because winter was supposed to begin with the full moon of October. The Romans who held a festival in honor of Mars in March, the beginning of the season for military campaigns, held another festival in October, dedicated to him, as it marked the close of military activities.

OCTOBER FIRST

MISSOURI DAY

The first Monday in October is known in Missouri as Missouri Day—it fell on October 1 in 1945. It does not mark any anniversary in the history of the state, but the reason for setting apart such a day is stated in the act of the legislature of March 2, 1915, which reads:

The first Monday of October of each and every year shall be known and designated as Missouri Day and shall be and is hereby set apart as a day commemorative of Missouri history to be observed by the teachers and pupils of schools with appropriate exercises. That the people of the State of Missouri and the educational, commercial, political, religious and fraternal organizations of Missouri be requested to devote some part of the day to the methodical consideration of the products of the mine, field and forest of the state and to the consideration of achievements of the sons and daughters of Missouri in commerce, literature, statesmanship, science and art and in other departments of activity in which the state has rendered service to mankind.

In obedience to this law the Superintendent of Schools of the State prepared a manual in which he said:

The observance of Missouri Day in the schools should not be limited to a day, but for some time previous should be connected with the regular work of the school in the various subjects, such as literature, reading, history, civics, geography and nature study. The work may well culminate on the day itself in a program of some kind in each room, in the school assembly, in a parent-teachers association meeting or in a community gathering. The preparation of such program with its attendant activities will afford an excellent means of motivation of the regular school work for securing valuable information, developing worthwhile habits and attitudes and instilling high ideals. It will also serve to establish a closer bond between the school and the community. The school will contribute of its method and material, of its youthful energy and enthusiasm. The oldest settler will give of his knowledge and experience, of his collection of mementos and keepsakes. There will be a unity of purpose, interest and endeavor; a resultant of love and respect for the state and its institutions, of appreciation for its struggles and achievements and of devotion of energies to its continued development and progress.

The manual contains suggestions for a program for the celebration in the schools and a list of the Missourians who have gained fame in various activities. The day is regularly observed in the schools and by patriotic organizations and women's clubs. Appropriate sermons are preached in the churches on the Sunday preceding the first Monday. Although the day is not a legal holiday it is observed more generally than some of the holidays.

OCTOBER 2

MOUNTAIN STATE FOREST FESTIVAL

On the completion of that part of the Seneca Trail in the Monongahela National Forest in West Virginia in 1930, the citizens of Elkins planned a celebration. The national forest has been enlarged since 1930 until it extends over 800,000 acres in three states. The Seneca Trail which passes through it was one of the famous Indian trails, used by them in going from New York to the Gulf of Mexico.

The first Mountain Forest Festival in 1930 continued for three days, with a pageant and games. A year or two later a three-day horse show was arranged, and wood-chopping contests were introduced to interest and attract the foresters. The arrangements are in charge of the Elkins Business Men's Association. The first director general was George H. Dornblazer. In order to arouse interest in the festival throughout the state, at Mr. Dornblazer's suggestion the senior state senators, the members of the national House of Representatives and the two United States Senators were each asked to name a young woman to serve as a princess in the court of the forest queen who was to be crowned during the festival.

The festival in 1936 began on October 1. President Roosevelt attended, crowned Miss Mary Jane Bell as Queen Silvia VII and made an address. Following the coronation there was a pageant based on the ancient Egyptian myth of creation showing how Ra, the sungod, brought forth the world out of nothingness, how he became arrogant and how Osiris and Isis besought him to let them bring order out of the chaos which had resulted from his misrule. The story was told on floats drawn through the streets of the city. There were sports and contests of several kinds on the second day and on the third day the visitors were escorted over the roads and trails in the National Forest or were entertained by athletic contests by members of the Civilian Conservation Corps, and a horse show. The festival attracts about 100,000 visitors to Elkins every year.

OCTOBER SECOND

THE VEILED PROPHET FESTIVAL AT ST. LOUIS

In 1878 a group of about twenty business men of St. Louis met to consider what could be done to stir the pride of the people in their city, and to attract visitors to it. They decided on an annual festival or pageant and ball, presided over by the Veiled Prophet of Khorassan, that powerful and mysterious ruler whose story is told in the first part of Thomas Moore's *Lalla Rookh* which begins:

> In that delightful Province of the Sun
> The first of Persian lands he shines upon,
> Where all the loveliest children of his beam,
> Flowrets and fruits, blush over every stream,
> And, fairest of all streams, the Murga roves

506

Among Merou's bright palaces and groves;—
There on that throne, to which the blind belief
Of millions raised him, sat the Prophet-Chief,
The Great Mokanna. O'er his features hung
The Veil, the Silver Veil, which he had flung
In mercy there, to hide from mortal sight
His dazzling brow, till man could bear its light,
For, far less luminous, his votaries said,
Were even the gleams, miraculously shed
O'er Moussa's cheek, when down the Mount he trod
All glowing from the presence of his God!

It was arranged that the Veiled Prophet should arrive in the city by boat on the Mississippi River, accompanied by his "krewe," on the first Tuesday after the first Monday in October. Accordingly he arrived on October 8, 1878, wearing a veil of crystal strands, which concealed his face but made it possible for him to recognize those around him. He led a parade through the streets in which there were many floats representing the Festival of Ceres, telling the story of agriculture. Roman candles and Greek fire lighted his way, and at the end of the parade he was welcomed by a committee of gentlemen who escorted him to a ball. His identity was not known to the public and it has been customary from the beginning to keep secret the name of the man who impersonates the Veiled Prophet as well as the names of those who masquerade as his krewe.

He presided alone at the ball until 1894 when he selected a queen from among the beautiful young women of the city. The first was Miss Hester Bates Laughlin, on whose head was placed a copy of the crown of Queen Victoria. Before that he had chosen from among the debutantes of the previous season a partner for the royal quadrille. The records are incomplete and it was not until 1885 that note was made of his partner. In that year she was Miss Virginia Joy. In 1887 President and Mrs. Cleveland stopped in St. Louis in the course of a tour of the West and were present at the ball. Mrs. Cleveland sat on the throne beside the Veiled Prophet and it was her presence that suggested the selection of a Queen of the ball which began a few years later. The ball was held in the Merchants Exchange building until 1909 when it was moved to the Coliseum and the ceremonies were made more elaborate by a formal reception by the maids and matrons of honor. The invitations to the ball are anxiously awaited by the society ladies of the city, for each invitation is accompanied by a piece of silver, either a spoon or a fork or a similar utensil.

In 1909, the hundredth anniversary of the founding of the city, the celebration continued for a week and four thousand invitations were issued for the ball in the Coliseum. It became customary after 1904 to present to the Queen of the ball a jewel-set crown of great value which became her property.

In 1928 the celebration was more elaborate than usual in observance of its fiftieth anniversary. The subject of the street parade was "Through the Centuries." In previous years it had been "Progress of Civilization," "Arabian Nights," "Greek Mythology," "Epochs in the History of the Eighteenth Century," as well as many other interesting and romantic themes. In 1919 it was "Victory of Peace."

The parade and the ball were originally on the same day. In time it was arranged that the ball should be held on the evening of the day following the parade. The parade in 1934 was on October 2, as the month began on Monday, October 1, and the ball was on the evening of October 3. The parade represented "The Great Adventurers," with Adam, Columbus, Daniel Boone, Magellan, Captain Kidd and many others posing on floats with their companions. There were so many of them that they extended over a mile of streets. For the ball the bare walls of the Coliseum had been covered with drapery of various colored fabrics and lighted by colored globes. Ten thousand guests were invited. The Queen was escorted to the throne of the Veiled Prophet, her ermine-edged train held by two pages. She knelt before the throne to receive a jeweled crown of platinum. After she took her place beside the Veiled Prophet he gave a. signal and a company of costumed knights began an elaborate drill for her amusement. The knights were masked and after the drill the maids and ladies of the Court of Honor were invited to dance with the Great Adventurers who had appeared in the parade. These were also masked. This ball opens the social season in the city and it surpasses in splendor all those which follow it. The ball and the parade are arranged by an organization of business men the members of which are known only to one another and who bear the whole expense.

OCTOBER THIRD

FOUNDER'S DAY AT LEHIGH UNIVERSITY

On a convenient day in the autumn of every year Lehigh University at Bethlehem, Pa., honors Asa Packer, its founder, by appropriate exercises. Large numbers of alumni assemble on that day and it is the custom to confer honorary degrees on distinguished citizens. Founder's day fell on October 3 in 1934.

Asa Packer was born at Groton, New London County, Conn., on December 29, 1805, and died in Philadelphia on May 17, 1879. He was a poor boy and after spending a few years in the local district school he began to work in a tannery at North Stonington. When his employer died he worked as a farm laborer for a while and not being satisfied with this he set out on foot for Pennsylvania, arriving at Brooklyn, Susquehanna County, in 1822. He learned the carpenter's trade there and worked at it for several years. In 1823 he built a cabin on some land in Springville, Susquehanna County, which he had bought, and where he lived for ten years. When the Lehigh Valley Canal was completed he bought and operated a canal boat carrying coal from the Lehigh Valley to Philadelphia. He bought coal lands with his savings and laid the foundations of the fortune which he later accumulated. In 1831 he operated a store and boatyard and later obtained contracts for locks on the upper Lehigh River. In 1838 he was building boats at Potsville to be used on the canal to carry coal to New York, and mined and transported coal for the Lehigh Coal & Navigation Company. He also bought mines at Hazelton and operated them on his own account. He was elected to the state legislature in 1843 and while a member obtained the passage of a bill creating Carbon County, with Mauch Chunk as its county seat. For five years after the new county was set up he was an Associate Judge of the County Court. He was elected to the national House of Representatives as a Democrat in 1852 and served two terms, and became one of the most influential members of his party in Pennsylvania. He received the votes of the Pennsylvania delegation to the National Democratic Convention in 1868 as its candidate for the presidential nomination, and in 1869 he was the Democratic nominee for governor of his state.

He interested himself in railroads in 1851 when he obtained a controlling interest in the Delaware, Lehigh, Schuylkill & Susquehanna Railroad Company, which was incorporated to build a coal carrying system. The name was changed in 1853 to the Lehigh Valley Railroad Company. He financed the building of the road and persisted in spite of many prophecies of failure. The profits, however, from the mining and transportation business which the road developed, made him the richest man in Pennsylvania. He had long seen the need for better educational facilities for the young men in the northeastern part of the state and in 1865 he set apart one hundred and fifteen acres in Bethlehem and $500,000 in cash for such an institution. The institution was chartered as Lehigh University in 1866. In his will Mr. Packer left $1,500,000 as an endowment fund and $500,000 for a library. The university offers a course in the liberal arts and courses in engineering and cognate subjects. In the fall of 1947 a total of 963 students were enrolled and the faculty numbered 284.

ENDING OF THE SIEGE OF LEYDEN

The resistance of the Netherlands to the tyranny of the Spanish produced many heroic deeds. Probably the most heroic was the opening of the dykes and sluice gates to let the sea flood the land when the Spanish armies were besieging Leyden. The siege ended on October 3, 1574, when the Spaniards fled in disorder as a Dutch fleet under command of Admiral Boisot, neared the city, sailing over the flooded land. There are many descendants of the Dutch of that time in the United States. Some of them organized the Holland Society of New York in 1885. The Dutchess County branch of the society holds a dinner every year in Poughkeepsie on October 3 in celebration.

OCTOBER 4

The siege of Leyden, one of the most beautiful cities of the Netherlands, began on October 31, 1573, and continued until March 21, 1574, when the besieging force was withdrawn to defend the frontier. Prince William advised the people to prepare for a resumption of the siege by storing food and munitions of war, but his advice was not taken, and when the besiegers returned on May 26 with eight thousand men the city was unprepared for the renewal of the siege which lasted until October 3. On July 30 the commander of the Spaniards offered to pardon the citizens if they would open their gates and accept the authority of King Philip. But the offer was spurned. On August 3 the dikes were broken down in sixteen places and the gates at Schiedam and Rotterdam were opened and the sea began to flow over the land. The Spanish commander became alarmed but his advisers told him that he had nothing to fear, yet the waters continued to rise. On September 1 Admiral Boisot with a few shallow-draft vessels and eight hundred sailors, wearing crescents in their caps with the inscription, "Rather Turkish than Popish," began to move toward the beleaguered city. Their progress was slow but when the wind blew in the right direction and piled up the waters from the sea they moved rapidly, defeating the Spanish at point after point. In the meantime the people in the city were starving. On October 3, an anniversary sacred to all Hollanders, Admiral Boisot entered Leyden. And on the next day a northeast wind, blowing furiously, rolled the ocean back to its bed and the dikes were repaired and the sluice gates were closed and in a few days the land was dry again.

As a reward to the city for its refusal to surrender, the University of Leyden was founded. Its charter was issued in the name of King Philip and contains much irony in the writing of which the Hollanders must have found great joy.

OCTOBER FOURTH

BIRTHDAY OF RUTHERFORD B. HAYES

Rutherford Birchard Hayes, nineteenth President of the United States was born in Delaware, Ohio, on October 4, 1822. He was the son of Rutherford Hayes, a farmer, and Sophia Birchard. The father died before the son was born and he was brought up by his uncle Sardis Birchard. He prepared for college at an academy in Norwalk, Ohio, and at the private school of Isaac Webb in Middletown, Conn. He entered Kenyon College at Gambier, Ohio, in 1838 and was graduated as valedictorian in the class of 1842. He read law in the office of Sparrow & Matthews in Columbus, Ohio, and spent a year and a half in the Harvard Law School.

In 1845 he was admitted to the bar and began to practice law in Lower Sandusky, Sandusky County, the home of his uncle. The name of the town was later changed to Fremont in honor of John C. Fremont. He remained in Lower Sandusky for five years and in 1850 opened a law office in Cincinnati, where he built up a profitable practice. He interested himself in politics and was a delegate to the Republican State Convention in 1855. He was elected city solicitor of Cincinnati in 1858. In 1861 he accepted the post of major in the Twenty-third Ohio Regiment, commanded by Colonel William S. Rosecrans, was in active service in the field until 1864, and was breveted a major general of volunteers in 1865. He was elected to Congress in 1864 from the Second Ohio Distirct (the Cincinnati district) by a large majority, resigned his commission in the army and took his seat in the House of Representatives in December 1865, and was reelected in 1866. When the Republicans of Ohio nominated him for governor in 1867 and elected him he resigned his seat in Congress. He was reelected governor in 1869. As governor he instituted many reforms. His uncle, Sardis Birchard, had died in the meantime, leaving to him the estate of Spiegel Grove at Fremont. At the expiration of his service as governor he retired to Fremont.

The Democrats had carried the state in 1873 and in 1875 the Republicans persuaded him to accept the nomination for governor and he was elected by the largest majority he had ever received, and at once became a national figure. There was a formidable greenback movement in Ohio and Hayes as governor combatted its theories of fiat money. His Ohio friends began to put him forward as a candidate for president. They succeeded in arranging for the Republican Convention to meet in Cincinnati where he had many supporters. When the convention met, Blaine was the most popular candidate with about twice as many delegates pledged to him as were pledged to any other aspirant. Other rivals were Roscoe Conkling, Oliver P. Morton and Benjamin H. Bristow. Hayes was nominated on the seventh roll call with one more than the necessary number of votes. The nomination was made unanimous and Blaine, even before the result was known, sent him a telegram of congratulation. The Democrats nominated Samuel J. Tilden of New York who had made a splendid record as governor of the state. As the campaign proceeded it became evident that whatever the result, the decision would be close. The early returns indicated the election of Tilden, but the vote in Louisiana, Florida and South Carolina was disputed. The Republicans claimed 185 electoral votes for Hayes, or one more than they admitted had been cast for Tilden. The Democrats claimed the election of Tilden. It took the appointment of a special commission to decide the dispute. The commission gave 185 votes to Hayes and he was declared elected.

He entered office determined to serve only one term as he had announced in his letter of acceptance that he did not think a president could discharge his duties most effectively if he entertained the thought of succeeding himself. A bill providing for the resumption of specie payments, suspended because of the financial necessities of the Civil

War, had been passed in the last months of the Administration of President Grant. Bills for the repeal of the resumption act and for the free coinage of silver were passed by the House of Representatives in the beginning of his term, but the vigorous demand for the preservation of the financial honor of the government made in his first message prevented the Senate from acting on the proposal to repeal the resumption act. He did much to remove disaffection in the South by withdrawing Federal troops which had been stationed there during the reconstruction period.

His wife was an ardent advocate of total abstinence from intoxicating liquors and abandoned the custom of serving wine at state dinners. The White House chef, however, served at the first dinner a sorbet reinforced with liberal quantities of liquor. According to the gossip of the time Mrs. Hayes was delighted with the flavor and instructed the chef to serve the sorbet at formal dinners thereafter. It came to be called by the foreign diplomatists "the life saving station." On his retirement from office Mr. Hayes returned to Fremont, enlarged the modest farm house into a mansion and assembled an extensive library in which he spent much of his time. He interested himself in many humane movements and was president of the American Prison Association from 1883 until his death on January 17, 1893. The heirs of Mr. Hayes have deeded the Fremont estate of twenty-five acres to the State of Ohio and have erected a memorial museum and library on the grounds with an endowment of $500,000.

FEAST OF ST. FRANCIS OF ASSISI

St. Francis of Assisi, one of the most devout and humble heroes of the Christian church, was canonized by Pope Gregory IX two years after his death on October 3, 1236, and October 4 was set apart as his feast day. His life has inspired poets and painters for many centuries. Churches have been named in his honor and a Franciscan friar gave his name to the Bay of San Francisco on the Pacific coast.

He was born at Assisi in Umbria in 1181 or 1182. There is no record of the exact date. He was the son of Pietro Bernardone, a rich merchant, and was christened Giovanni. His father later changed his name to Francisco, meaning the Frenchman, because of his fondness for France. He received the rudiments of an education and at the age of fourteen his father took him into business with him. He was gay and romantic, leading the youths of his own age in their revels and singing with delight the songs of the troubadours. He delighted in song to the day of his death, singing even in his last illness. When he was about twenty he joined the people of his town in a battle with the men of the neighboring city of Perugia and was taken prisoner and held for a year during which he was seriously ill. When he was released and after he recovered his health he decided to follow a military career and set out with an expedition against Naples but had to turn back because of illness.

The night before he set out, he had a dream in which he saw a vast hall hung with armor all marked with the cross and a voice said, "These are for you and your soldiers." He began to think of religious things and became so absent minded that his companions asked if he were thinking of getting married. He replied, "Yes, I am about to take a wife of surpassing loveliness," referring to Lady Poverty. He had always been generous, giving freely to the poor and needy. He was praying one day in an ancient chapel outside the town when he heard a voice saying, "Go, Francis, and repair my house." He went to his father's warehouse, took a large quantity of fine cloth and sold it, taking the money to the priest in charge of the chapel. The priest refused to receive the money and Francis, to escape his father's wrath, hid himself in a cave for a month. Finally his father found him and took him home, beat and bound him and locked him in a dark closet, from which his mother released him. His father then took him before the city authorities and demanded that he surrender his right to his inheritance. He insisted that as he had entered the service of God he was no longer responsible to the civil authorities. Thereupon he was taken before the bishop where he stripped off his clothing, gave the garments to his father and said, "Hitherto I have called you my father on earth; henceforth I desire to say only, 'Our Father who art in Heaven.'" It was then that he espoused the Lady Poverty, and clad in a garment provided by the bishop he wandered forth into the hills singing hymns of praise as he went.

He worked for a time in the kitchen of a monastery and then returned to Assisi where he begged for stones to restore two or three chapels, carrying the stones and laying them in the walls with his own hands. One of these was the Chapel of St. Mary of the Angels, known as the Portiuncula, where he died. While hearing mass in this chapel in February 1208, he was impressed by the reading of the gospel lesson in which the followers of Jesus were enjoined to go forth without gold or silver or shoes, and decided to obey this injunction. He immediately threw away what poor garments he wore, dressed himself in a coarse woolen tunic tied with a rope about the waist and went forth preaching penance, brotherly love and peace.

His devoutness had by this time impressed the people of Assisi and they listened respectfully to him. It was not long before a canon of the cathedral and a magnate of the town joined him and in a short time he had eleven followers who called themselves the Penitents of Assisi. Francis wrote some simple rules for their guidance and then he and the others went to Rome where they received the approval of the Pope. Out of this small beginning the Order of St. Francis expanded rapidly.

Francis planned to preach to the Moors in an effort to convert them. He went to Spain and made an unsuccessful attempt to get to Morocco. He finally went to Palestine where he obtained for the Franciscans the guardianship of the holy places. He was especially interested in the observance of Christmas and is credited with the introduction of the Crib—that is, Mary, the infant Jesus, the wise men and the cattle in the stable—in the churches for the Christmas season. He regarded all living things as his fellow creatures. One story of him is that when he learned that a wolf was ravaging the flocks about Gubbio he went into the fields where he found his "brother the wolf" and led him into the town and told the people that the animal was hungry and urged them to feed him. Thereafter the wolf was harmless. He preached to his "Little brethren the birds," which listened so devoutly that he chided himself for not having thought of preaching to them before. The half-frozen bees are said to have crawled to him to be fed and a hunted rabbit took refuge near him. He preached not dogma, but kindliness and gentleness and forbearance, leaving theological doctrine to the priests, and is credited with reviving practical Christianity at a time when it was needed.

OCTOBER FIFTH

BIRTHDAY OF CHESTER A. ARTHUR

Chester Alan Arthur, twenty-first President of the United States, was born in Fairfield, Franklin County, Vermont, on October 5, 1830. He was the son of the Reverend William Arthur, a Baptist clergyman from Ireland who settled in Vermont. The son, Chester, the eldest of four children, prepared for college in the schools of his native state and entered Union College at Schenectady in the class of 1849. After graduation he taught school for two years and was for a time principal of the academy at Pownal, Vt. He had been studying law and in 1851 he went to New York City to complete his preparation.

In 1852 he was associated with William M. Evarts in freeing eight slaves who had been taken to New York by Jonathan Lemmons of Virginia, who expected to sail for Texas with them. A writ of habeas corpus was obtained in behalf of the slaves and the New York court ordered their release. The legislature of Virginia directed the attorney general of the state to intervene for the recovery of the slaves. The case was taken to the Supreme Court of the United States which sustained the action of the New York court. In 1856, Arthur appeared as counsel for a colored girl who had been ejected from a street car under the rule of the operating company that Negroes were not to be allowed in the same car with white passengers. He obtained a verdict of $500 for the girl and forced the abrogation of the rule.

He was a delegate to the convention at Saratoga which organized the Republican party in the state. He had enlisted in the state militia and before the Civil War was judge advocate of the Second Brigade. Governor Edwin D. Morgan made him engineer-in-chief on his staff and later quartermaster general. While serving in this capacity he equipped and supplied and forwarded to the front the large number of soldiers which went from New York to serve in the Union armies.

He resumed the practice of law in 1865 and interested himself in politics in the city. President Grant appointed him Collector of the Port of New York in November 1871, and reappointed him in 1875. When Mr. Hayes became President in 1877 he issued an order forbidding the civil servants of the government to take an active part in political management. Mr. Arthur was at that time chairman of the Republican Central Committee of New York City, and Alonzo B. Cornell, Naval Officer of the port, was chairman of the Republican Central Committee of the state. These gentlemen ignored the President's order and were ultimately removed and their successors were confirmed by the Senate. Arthur's administration of the office had been efficient and he had introduced many reforms in the conduct of its business, but in accordance with the custom of the times he had expected the employees to work for the success of the party to which they owed their appointment.

On his retirement from the Custom House he again resumed the practice of his profession and continued his interest in political affairs. He was influential in bringing about the nomination and election of Cornell as governor. He was nominated for Vice President by the Republican National Convention in 1880 to appease Senator Conkling and his associates who were disgruntled because of the nomination of Garfield for President instead of Grant whom they had supported. After the inauguration on March 4, 1881, he presided over the Senate without taking any part in the dispute over the confirmation of the appointments made by the President. But when Senators Conkling and Platt resigned as a protest against the appointment to the collectorship of the port in New York, Arthur went to Albany to use his influence in behalf of the re-election of the senators, but he was unable to bring it about.

When Garfield died on September 19, 1881, Arthur took the oath of office as President in his own house in New York and three days later took the oath again before the Chief Justice of the United States in Washington. He entered the White House with the reputation of a practical politician and the politicians of his party expected him to cooperate with them. But he had a higher ideal of the presidential function and disappointed the party workers. He vetoed a Chinese exclusion bill the provisions of which violated a treaty with China and he also vetoed a river and harbor bill which carried extravagant and wasteful appropriations.

What is regarded as the gravest political mistake of his administration was his insistence on the nomination of Judge Folger, his Secretary of the Treasury, for Governor of New York in 1882. The Democrats nominated Grover Cleveland, the reform mayor of Buffalo, and denounced federal interference in state elections. Cleveland was elected and because of his victory was nominated for President two years later.

OCTOBER 5

Arthur wished to succeed himself in the presidency, but he had alienated the party workers and had not won the support of the reformers so he received little support in the convention of 1884 which nominated Blaine. He retired from office on March 4, 1885, and died on November 18 in the following year.

BIRTHDAY OF EDWARD L. TRUDEAU

It has been customary for a long time to observe the anniversary of the birth of Dr. Edward Livingston Trudeau, one of the pioneers in the outdoor treatment of tuberculosis, at the sanitarium in the village of Trudeau in the Adirondack Mountains in northern New York. Dr. Trudeau was born in New York City on October 5, 1848, of parents of French descent. He was educated in Paris and returned to the United States at the age of eighteen. He obtained an appointment to the United States Naval Academy, but did not enter the academy because he found it necessary to nurse his brother who had fallen ill with tuberculosis. After his brother's death he began the study of medicine in the College of Physicians and Surgeons in New York, was graduated in 1871, and began to practice his profession.

But it was not long before he became ill with the disease which killed his brother. He was ordered South but the southern climate did not agree with him and in 1873 he went to Paul Smith's in the Adirondacks. He was so weak that after arriving at Plattsburg by train he had to rest several days before his could complete the journey into the mountains forty-two miles by stage coach. His physician had told him that he would not live six months. The mountain air improved his health and he decided to remain during the winter, and lived outdoors as much as possible. He gained strength rapidly and concluded that similar treatment would benefit other sufferers. He built a little shack for their accommodation, and in the course of time through gifts from philanthropically inclined persons he built a village, a sanitarium and a laboratory adjoining the village of Saranac Lake, which have become famous because of the cures which have been effected there. The village was named in his honor a few years ago.

Dr. Trudeau was one of the organizers of the National Association for the Study and Prevention of Tuberculosis in conjunction with Dr. Lawrence Flick of Philadelphia, Pa. He was president of the Association of American Physicians in 1905. The Saranac Laboratory for the study of tuberculosis, founded by him in 1894, was the first of its kind in America. The Christmas seal of the National Tuberculosis Association for 1934 contained a picture of the first cottage in commemoration of the fiftieth anniversary of its erection. In the same year on the anniversary of his birth the celebration was unusually elaborate, with representatives present from the national association as well as from various county associations in New York and the state association.

As Dr. Trudeau had proved that tuberculosis is not necessarily fatal, interest in its treatment grew rapidly. In 1905 the Reverend Newell Dwight Hillis, pastor of Plymouth Church in Brooklyn, N.Y., suggested that all the churches in the country set apart one Sunday for consideration of the importance of the better treatment of the sufferers. In 1909, the suggestion was made a second time and the churches of Brooklyn observed Tuberculosis Sunday. In 1910, the National Association for the Study of Tuberculosis interested itself in the movement and obtained approval of it from President Taft and from Charles Evans Hughes, who was then Governor of New York. As a result the day was widely observed on April 24 in that year. Dr. Trudeau died in 1915 and is buried in the village which he founded for the treatment of tuberculosis.

OCTOBER SIXTH

GERMAN DAY

The first permanent German settlement in America was made at Germantown, Pa., on the arrival of thirteen families on October 6, 1683. Two hundred years later, in 1883, the anniversary of the arrival of these colonists was celebrated as German Pioneer Day, by large numbers of citizens of German descent. This is believed to be the first formal notice taken of the importance of the German migration to this country.

The projector of the plan said that the annual celebration of German Day would remind the nation not only of the first settlement in this country, but of one of the great original sources out of which the nation itself, its growth, prosperity and power originated. In order to unite the citizens of German descent in perpetuating the memory of this first settlement and for other purposes the National German American Alliance was formed in 1901 and was incorporated by Act of Congress on February 25, 1907. Among the incorporators were citizens of Pennsylvania, Maryland, New Jersey, New York, Texas, Indiana, Idaho, Ohio, Minnesota and the District of Columbia. The Alliance voted to work with the Ancient Order of Hibernians in furthering the interests common to both organizations. At the celebration of German Day in New York in 1908 Mathew Cummings, president of the Hibernian organization, was one of the principal speakers. He said among other things:

We deny in the most positive language that this is an Anglo Saxon nation. We deny that England is the mother country, and we deny that the great progress and achievements of this country have been brought about solely through the efforts and influence of the Puritans or the descendants of the Puritans. All Europe is our mother, not England. . . . Neither the Germans nor the Irish ever believed that it was necessary to denationalize a people in order to fit them for American citizenship. On the contrary we have always believed that the people who possessed racial pride, and who kept alive the national characteristics and traditions of their race made the best American citizens. I am proud to say that on January 22, 1907, the Ancient Order of Hibernians, representing the Irish race in America, and the German American Alliance, representing the German race, signed a written agreement that henceforth they would work together as a unit on all questions of national interest to both races.

German Day was celebrated in various centers of German population for many years under the direction of the German American Alliance. When the first World War began in 1914 the members of the Alliance naturally sympathized with the Fatherland. They were charged with German propaganda. It was even said that they were supplied with money by Germany, and they were accused of meddling in politics in the interest of Germany. They denied the charges, but a committee of the United States Senate was appointed to inquire into the activities of the organization. Its leaders concluded that under the circumstances its usefulness had ended and the Alliance was formally dissolved on April 12, 1918.

The migration of Germans to Pennsylvania came about through the influence of William Penn. He had learned of the persecution of the separatists on the continent who were tortured and put to death. Elizabeth, the granddaughter of King James I, was the abbess of Herford in Westphalia. She had corresponded with Penn and George Fox and was the protector of various groups of separatists. Penn went to Westphalia in 1677 with some associates to ask her protection for the Quakers. Elizabeth was a woman of determined character. An offer to make her the wife of the King of Poland was made to her on condition that she become a Catholic but she declined it and finally entered the abbey of Herford to devote herself to pious contemplation. Penn tried to convert her to the belief of the Quakers but failed. She was in sympathy with it, however. Penn then went to Frankfort and had interviews with the leading Protestants there. In 1682, as a result of his representations these men formed the Frankfort Company to arrange for the migration of Germans to America. Frankford Village, now a part of Philadelphia, was named for this company.

The first impulse to migration, however, came from Crefeld, a town on the Rhine near the border of the Netherlands. Penn had visited the Quakers and Mennonites there during his visit to the continent in 1677. In 1682 Penn deeded to three citizens of Crefeld five thousand acres each in Pennsylvania. In the autumn of that year Francis Daniel Pastorious heard of the Frankfort Company and went to London as its agent and in the spring of 1683 he bought a tract of twenty-five thousand acres. He was the only member of the Frankfort Company who came to America. He was born in Somerhausen, Germany, on September 25, 1651, and died on September 27, 1719. He was educated at the University of Strasburg and the law school of Jena. He knew the ancient languages as well as French, Dutch, English and Italian. He practiced law in Frankfort and then traveled for two years in Holland,

England, France and Switzerland, returning to Frankfort in time to hear of Penn's enterprise in America. He put himself at the head of the colonization movement and sailed for America on June 10, 1683, reaching Philadelphia on August 20. Thirteen families followed him from Crefeld, sailing from London in the ship "Concord" on July 24, 1683, arrived in Philadelphia on October 6 and took up the land in Germantown which had been bought by Pastorius. This was the first permanent German settlement in North America. There had been previous attempted settlements in Maryland and on the lower Delaware River but they came to naught.

The German-American Alliance and other German societies planned the erection of a monument to Pastorius in Germantown, now a part of Philadelphia, in the early part of this century. Congress in March 1911, appropriated $25,000 for such a monument on condition that a similar sum be raised by private subscription. The money was raised and a monument was erected. As there was no portrait of Pastorius the sculptor designed a structure surmounted by a female figure representing "Civilization" with sculptures on the base showing the German colonists. The first World War broke out just as the monument was to be dedicated. It was charged by sensitive patriots that it was a piece of German propaganda and that the female figure surmounting it was "Germania." The feeling was so acute that the monument was boxed in to prevent vandals from destroying it, and it remained concealed for several years. It was finally exposed to public view and now stands as a tribute to the able and distinguished German who served the Pennsylvania colony well during his life in this country.

OCTOBER SEVENTH

BIRTHDAY OF JAMES WHITCOMB RILEY

James Whitcomb Riley is one of the few poets the anniversary of whose birth was observed annually while he was still alive. Riley was born in Greenfield, Ind., on October 7, 1853, and died in 1916. Arrangements were made in 1912 to celebrate the anniversary of his birth in nearly all the public schools of Indiana. He wrote the following greeting to the children which was read in the schools:

To the School Children Generally:

It may be well for you to remember that the day you are about to celebrate is the birthday of many good men, but if I may be counted the least of these I will be utterly content and happy. I can only thank you and your teachers with a full heart and the fervent hope that the day will prove an equal glory to us all. To the very little children I would say, be simply your own selves, and though even parents, as I sometimes think, do not seem to understand us perfectly, we will be patient with them and love them no less loyally and tenderly.

519

OCTOBER 7

The anniversary fell on Monday in that year. On the following Wednesday Riley drove from his house in Lockerbie Street, Indianapolis, to his birthplace in Greenfield to be the guest of the children. Eight hundred of them marched out to meet his automobile as it entered the town. When the car reached his old home children bearing flowers threw the blossoms into it and almost covered the poet with them. A loving cup was presented to him. This was the beginning of an annual observance which has continued to this day in Indiana. In 1913 Riley wrote the following rhymed acknowledgment of the honor conferred on him:

> O child so mild
> In pure worth, and so wild
> With delight, take the love
> Of an "elderly child."

In 1915, in addition to the celebrations in the public schools, a dinner in Riley's honor was given in Indianapolis. Former Vice President Charles W. Fairbanks presided and introduced the speakers and announced the toasts. Among the decorations in the banquet hall was prominently displayed the following extract from one of his poems:

> 'Cause I'm happier in these posies,
> And hollyhawks and sich,
> Than the humming bird that noses
> In the roses of the rich.

President Woodrow Wilson was not present, but wrote as follows:

I wish that I might be present to render my tribute of affectionate appreciation to him for the many pleasures he has given me along with the rest of the great body of readers of English. I think he has every reason to feel on his birthday that he has won the hearts of his countrymen.

In the morning Riley had visited the public schools of the city. In the afternoon a number of his poems were interpreted in song and dance in one of the theatres before a large audience and throughout the state his poems were recited in the schools, and addresses were made in his honor. Following his death a James Whitcomb Riley Memorial Association was formed. It has preserved his home in Lockerbie street as he left it and keeps it open daily for visitors. It is customary to have exercises on the lawn on the anniversary and to place a wreath on the tomb in the Crown Hill Cemetery. As a permanent memorial to the poet the association has built, through popular subscription amounting to $3,000,000 dollars, a hospital for children in Indianapolis named for him.

Riley's father was a well-to-do lawyer but the profession did not appeal to the boy. He was at first a sign painter. Then he joined a company of strolling players for whom he wrote songs and remodeled plays. He joined the staff of the Indianapolis *Journal* in 1873, to which

520

he contributed his first verse in 1875. He tried to sell his verse in other places but was unsuccessful and concluded that it was because he was not known. To prove that he could write poetry he wrote a poem in the style of Edgar Allan Poe, copied it in imitation of Poe's handwriting on the fly leaf of an old book contemporary with Poe and then announced the discovery of a hitherto unknown poem by that genius. It was accepted as such for some time and even after Riley admitted the hoax certain English critics still insisted that it was written by Poe. The outcome of the incident was Riley's discharge from the newspaper on which he was working. He continued to write and at last found a publisher. For many years he traveled about the country reading his verse, sometimes alone and sometimes with other readers. It was in 1883 that his first book appeared. He was elected to the American Academy of Arts and Letters and received the gold medal of the National Institute of Arts and Letters. His fame was established on a sure foundation long before he reached the age of forty. He shared with former President Benjamin Harrison the honors of Indiana day at the Columbian Exposition in Chicago in 1893, being welcomed with tumultuous applause when Mr. Harrison introduced him to the Indianians who had assembled on the fair grounds.

FOUNDER'S DAY AT THE BERRY SCHOOLS

Martha McChesney Berry was born October 7, 1866 near Rome, Georgia. The date of her birth is celebrated as Founder's Day by the Berry Schools for mountain boys and girls which she founded at Mount Berry, Ga., in 1902. She had attended private schools and enjoyed the advantages of European travel, but her purpose in founding the Berry Schools was to afford educational opportunity to underprivileged and illiterate children in the South. The attendance at the schools increased so rapidly that Miss Berry was compelled to raise about one hundred and fifty thousand dollars a year by personal effort to supplement the income from the endowment. In 1925 the Roosevelt Medal was awarded to Miss Berry for her services to the nation, and in 1928 she received an award of five thousand dollars from the *Pictorial Review* for her twenty-six years of labor on behalf of Southern youth, these being but two notable examples of the many public tributes in recognition of her achievements. She died February 27, 1942.

OCTOBER EIGHTH

BIRTHDAY OF JOHN CLARKE

The anniversary of the birth of John Clarke, one of the founders of Rhode Island, is observed annually by the First Baptist Church of Newport, which he also founded. Clarke is one of the pioneers of religious liberty in America and is credited with obtaining from Charles II the 1663 charter of Rhode Island in which liberty of conscience is guaranteed. He was born in Westhorpe, Suffolk, England, on October 8, 1609. He came to America in 1637 as one of the friends of Anne Hutchinson and landed in Boston in November of that year. The Massachusetts General Court had just taken rigorous action· against the Antinomians. Clarke allied himself with those who were condemned and had to flee for safety to Exeter, N.H. Early in 1638 he with a company of about three hundred sailed for Narragansett Bay and founded a colony on Aquidneck Island. In the spring of the following year several families, including Clarke, founded Newport and also organized a Baptist church. He soon became one of the most influential men in the colony. He wrote the code of laws attached in 1647 to the Roger Williams charter and went to England in 1651 to look after the interests of the new settlement and remained there twelve years until he finally obtained a new charter from the king in 1663. In the course of his petition he wrote of the colonists:

That it is much on their hearts (if they may be permitted) to hold forth a lively experiment that a most flourishing civil state may stand and be best maintained, and that among our English subjects, with full liberty of religious concernments.

These words from the petition are inscribed on the west front of the State Capitol in Providence.

The section of the charter granting religious liberty reads in part:

Now, know ye, that we . . . have therefore, thought fit and do publish, grant, ordain and declare that our royal will and pleasure is that no person within the said colony, at any time hereafter shall be in any wise molested, punished, disquieted, or called in question for any difference in opinion in matters of religion . . . but that all and every person and persons may, from time to time and at all times hereafter, freely and fully have and enjoy his and their own judgments and consciences in matters of religious concernments.

When the provisions of the charter became known in England doubt was expressed about the power of the king to make such a liberal grant of freedom, but this doubt did not affect the validity of the grant and its provisions remained in the constitution of the state until 1842 when a new constitution was adopted. Clarke was a member of the General Assembly of Rhode Island and was deputy governor three times. He died on April 28, 1676.

OCTOBER NINTH

CHICAGO FIRE DAY

The anniversary of the great fire which destroyed the larger part of the city of Chicago on October 8 and 9, 1871, has been observed almost from the year following the fire. In the course of time it became a sort of civic holiday. On the twenty-fifth anniversary in 1896, during the McKinley-Bryan presidential campaign, the celebration of the day was combined with a political demonstration in support of sound money and against the free coinage of silver as advocated by Bryan. About seventy thousand citizens marched in the parade through the business section of the city. All vehicles were excluded from the streets and large crowds assembled on the sidewalks to watch the paraders.

In 1911, at the suggestion of the Chicago Association of Commerce, arrangements were made to celebrate the anniversary as Fire Prevention Day. When through the influence of the insurance companies the President of the United States was persuaded to call upon all cities of the country to observe Fire Prevention Week during the first week in October the anniversary of the fire which fell within those seven days was included in the greater celebration.

There are at least three accounts of the origin of the fire. The most popular is that while Mrs. O'Leary was milking a cow on Sunday afternoon, October 8, the animal kicked over a lamp and set fire to the straw on the floor of the stable. Michael Ahearn, a reporter who was assigned to the fire, said in 1911, that he interviewed Mrs. O'Leary about the story of the cow kicking over the lamp and she said that it was not true. Mr. Ahearn said further:

> There was a social gathering in the neighborhood that night in honor of the arrival of a young man from Ireland. One of those present told me in after years that two women of the party went to the O'Leary shed to get some milk for the punch. One woman held a lighted lamp while the other milked the cow. They thought they heard some one coming and in their haste to escape the lamp was dropped setting fire to the place. That, I believe, is the true cause of the fire.

The third story is that some young men were having a beer party in a shed adjoining the O'Leary stable and that one of them dropped a lighted pipe in the straw setting fire to it. At any rate there is agreement that the fire started in or near Mrs. O'Leary's stable.

Conditions were favorable for the spread of fire. There had been a severe drought for two months. Most of the buildings of the city were wooden, and a strong wind was blowing. The fire spread from the small building where it started to the lumber yards but the fire department was powerless to stop it. General Philip Sheridan in command of the Western Department of the army sent high explosives into the city and blew up scores of buildings in the path of the flames and checked its spread somewhat, and he lent army tents to shelter the people whose homes had been destroyed. The fire was extinguished by a heavy rain on Monday night. It is estimated that nearly twenty thousand buildings were burned and that a hundred thousand persons, out of a total population of three hundred and twenty-four thousand, were rendered homeless. Panic prevailed and men and women had to fight their way over the bridges across the river. Exorbitant prices were charged for the hire of vehicles to carry people out of the danger zone and those who could not hire a vehicle put their treasures in trunks and tried to drag them to safety along the sidewalks. Thieves began to loot all the deserted houses. Until relief could be provided from other cities the prices of what food had not been burned rose to extravagant figures. Frank Harris, in the story of his experiences as a cowboy in the Southwest, tells of his arrival in the city a short time before the fire broke out, with a train load of cattle. They were unloaded at the stockyards. When these were threatened he was warned to remove the cattle to a place of safety, so he drove them out into the country and put them in a farmer's field. The farmer sold some of them on his own responsibility but Harris said that he made a handsome profit from the sale of those that were left.

When the task of rebuilding the city began, the grade of the streets was raised several feet and within a score of years a larger and much more beautiful city welcomed the world to the Columbian Exposition in celebration of the four hundredth anniversary of the discovery of America by Columbus, at one of the finest international exhibitions ever held.

FRATERNAL DAY IN ALABAMA

The legislature of Alabama in 1913 made October 12 a legal holiday in honor of the discovery of America by Columbus, following the example of many other states in providing for the observance of Columbus Day. In 1915, however, the act making Columbus Day a holiday was repealed and in its place an act was passed setting apart the second Tuesday in October (it fell on October 9, 1945) as Fraternal Day. This is a day in which, according to the head of the Department of Archives and History of the State, "all religions, creeds and beliefs could unite in good will." There is seldom any formal celebration, but the people, relieved from their accustomed work, spend the day in recreation of various kinds and the flag is displayed on public buildings.

LEIF ERIKSON DAY

Leif Erikson Day has been observed annually in the public schools in Colorado, since 1943, by educational programs held on October 9, or on the preceding school day when this date falls on a school holiday. It commemorates the discovery of North America about 1000 A.D. by Leif Erikson, or Ericson, and the school programs usually deal with this portion of America's early history. Leif Erikson was the son of Eric the Red, a Norseman, who discovered Greenland in 985 A.D., sailing thither from Iceland. It is said that he called the new territory Greenland in order to induce colonists to settle there. In any case, he founded a colony on the southwest coast, and ruins, coffins, and runic inscriptions mark the spots they inhabited. The adventures of his son Leif, who discovered land to the west of Iceland which he named Vinland, are described in the Icelandic sagas. The site of Leif Erikson's discovery and settlement are placed by different authorities on Labrador, Newfoundland and on the mainland farther south, but there seems no doubt that, whatever the exact location, it was on the North American continent.

OCTOBER TENTH

OKLAHOMA HISTORICAL DAY

Oklahoma Historical Day was inaugurated by the 1941 state legislature which passed a resolution directing the governor to proclaim October 10 of each year as a day for the observance of the founding of the first non-Indian settlement within the boundaries of what is now the State of Oklahoma. The schools celebrate the day by special programs, and it is further recognized by county and municipal officers who also issue proclamations calling attention to the significance of the anniversary.

The settlement of Salina was preceded by the granting of a monopoly for fur trading with the Osage Indians to the Chouteau family in 1794 by the Spanish crown. The monopoly was revoked in 1800 and given to Manuel Liza, and in order to preserve his trade Pierre Chouteau induced the Osages to move outside his previous trading area. This was in 1802, and in that year a trading post was established on the location of the present town of Salina, Oklahoma. The Chouteaus had travelled and traded in the vicinity for some years previously, but it is conceded by authorities on the early history of the region that the establishment of the post in 1802 was the first white settlement. Meanwhile, France had acquired the territory known as Louisiana in 1800, and in 1803 the United States made the Louisiana Purchase which included Oklahoma as part of the enormous tract taken over from the French.

OCTOBER ELEVENTH

PULASKI DAY

The memory of Count Casimir Pulaski is kept green by the Military Order of Pulaski which observes the anniversary of his death on October 11 by a dinner at Washington at which his services to the colonies during the Revolution are recounted. The Military Order of Pulaski was formed on August 15, 1918, and incorporated in the District of Columbia. The preamble to its constitution reads:

As our country was founded by persons of various nationalities and as the present war [World War I] shows how important it is, for the safety and welfare of America, that we be united as one nation, and as in the present war many are aiding to free the world from oppression and injustice; and bearing in mind the services performed by the illustrious Pole for the preservation of our independence; in order to keep afresh in the memory of our descendants and to preserve the history of our country, we, the undersigned, . . . do now institute, form and organize an order to be called the Military Order of Pulaski, named for the illustrious Count and General Casimir Pulaski, who lost his life in the defense of our liberties in the Battle of Savannah, Georgia, October 9, 1779.

Membership is restricted to members of the Aryan race who are descendants of officials or military officers of the colonial and revolutionary period whose ancestors settled in America prior to 1740. The Captain-Commander-General of the order in 1935 was Eugene C. Bonniwell, Judge of the Municipal Court of Philadelphia, and the Secretary-General was Charles Ludwell Wingate, of Washington, D.C.

While the observance of the anniversary of Pulaski's death was originated by this military order it is participated in by a large number of organizations of citizens of Polish descent, including the Polish National Alliance and the Polish Army Veterans Association. Ignace Werwinski, a business man of South Bend, Ind., began to advocate the observance of the one hundred and fiftieth anniversary of the death of Pulaski in 1929 and petitioned President Hoover to designate October 11 as Pulaski Day to be observed throughout the country. The President accordingly issued a proclamation to that effect and appointed a commission to arrange for the observance. Committees were appointed in the states with a Polish population and there was an adequate observance of the anniversary.

Pulaski was born in Lithuania, Poland, on March 4, 1748, the son of Count Joseph Pulaski. He was active in revolutionary movements in Poland and when his army was defeated his estates were confiscated and he was compelled to flee the country. He went to Turkey and joined its army, and later he went to France where he met Franklin who persuaded him to go to America to assist the colonies in their fight against England. He arrived in Philadelphia in 1777 and served in the army as a volunteer. Because of his gallantry at the Battle of Brandywine he was appointed chief of dragoons with the rank of brigadier general. In 1778 he organized an independent corps of cavalry and light infantry which was ordered to the South, and reached Charleston, S.C., on May 9, 1779. In the autumn of the same year he commanded the French and American cavalry at the siege of Savannah, Ga., and was fatally wounded during the battle of October 9 and died two days later on board the "Wasp" in the harbor. The people of Savannah have erected a monument to his memory the cornerstone of which was laid by Lafayette in 1825.

In 1939 President Franklin D. Roosevelt issued a proclamation, in accordance with an Act of Congress setting aside October 11 as the day for commemoration of Pulaski's death. Following this proclamation more than a score of states have done likewise. In Maryland, Nebraska, and Pennsylvania Pulaski Day is observed by proclamation of the governor. In New York City the day is usually observed by a parade. The Pulaski Skyway, a four-lane elevated highway between New York and Philadelphia, is named in his honor.

Y.M.C.A. FOUNDER'S DAY

Sir George Williams, founder of the Young Men's Christian Association, was born on October 11, 1821. Prior to 1932 a few local associations had observed the anniversary, but in that year and in every year since it has been observed by the associations throughout the world. On that day the problems of youth are discussed by competent speakers and suggestions are made about the way the association may meet the changing needs of the times.

George Williams was born in Somersetshire, England, and was converted to Christianity in 1837 at the age of sixteen. In 1841 he became a junior assistant in the dry goods firm of George Hitchcock & Company in London. In 1843 he induced some of the employees of the firm to hold regular prayer meetings and in June 1844, he and eleven others formed a society which they called the Young Men's Christian Association. It grew in numbers and branches were formed in various cities. From 1863 to 1885 Williams was treasurer and in 1885 he became president of the association. He also became the head of the firm with which he was first employed and its name was changed to Hitchcock, Williams & Company. He was knighted in 1894 and died in 1905.

In December 1851, branches of the association were organized in Boston and in Montreal, the first on the American continent. Within three years forty more were formed and the first international convention was held at Buffalo, N.Y., on June 7, 1854. A confederation of the various associations was formed with a central committee and annual conventions were held until the outbreak of the Civil War. The enlistment of young men in the armies weakened many branches and those that survived were occupied chiefly with work among the soldiers. At the close of the war the association grew rapidly. New buildings were erected and the activities of the associations were expanded to include gymnasiums, reading rooms and libraries, in addition to religious work including devotional meetings and Bible training classes. In 1858 student associations were formed at the University of Michigan and the University of Virginia. In 1877 a national intercollegiate association was formed with a general secretary. In 1872 an association was organized in Cleveland, Ohio, especially for railroad employees.

The movement spread to other countries including Japan, China, India, Ceylon, Egypt, Turkey, as well as France, Germany and other European countries, and to the Latin Americas. The membership in some seventy countries is now well over two million.

OCTOBER 11

BIRTHDAY OF HARLAN FISKE STONE

Harlan Fiske Stone, the twelfth Chief Justice of the United States, was born at Chesterfield, N.H., on October 11, 1872. His mother, Ann Sophia Butler Stone, had taught school in Chesterfield before her marriage and his father, Frederick Lauson Stone, was a farmer in the township. Two years after his birth the family moved to Amherst, Mass., so that his eldest brother could attend the agricultural school there. Harlan went to the public school in Amherst and lived the typical life of a farmer's son, milking cows, plowing, reaping, and pitching hay. After two years of high school he entered the agricultural school and distinguished himself as the instigator of "every ducking party, nightshirt parade and chapel rush which featured college life in those days." One escapade proved his undoing and he was expelled. In spite of this, and the fact that he had attended high school for only two years, he was accepted by Amherst College in the class of 1894. He proved himself a fireball in college, tutoring, selling insurance and typewriters, managing the *Amherst Student*, winning his Phi Beta Kappa key in his junior year, and delivering the class oration. In addition to these activities, he found time to play right guard on the famous team of 1892 which defeated Williams 60-0, and to serve as class president for three years. Not unnaturally, he was chosen "the man who would become most famous" and, when his classmates voted on the greatest benefit the College had received from the town of Amherst, they agree it was "Harlan Fiske Stone."

After he was graduated from college he taught at Newburyport High School in order to earn money for law school. He then went to the Columbia University School of Law, supporting himself by teaching history in Adelphi Academy in Brooklyn, and in 1898 received his law degree and was immediately admitted to the bar. He first went with the law firm of Sullivan and Cromwell and later transferred to the firm of Wilmer and Canfield. He supplemented his law practice by teaching at Columbia, as a lecturer from 1899 to 1902, and as a professor from 1902 to 1905. In 1905 he resigned to give all his time to his firm, which had become Satterlie, Canfield and Stone. He cultivated the connections that a partnership with a son-in-law of J. P. Morgan brought within reach and during these years he was "busy making money." Yet in 1907, when Nicholas Murray Butler invited him to become dean of the Law School, Mr. Stone accepted on the condition that Dr. Butler would make no appointments without consulting the law faculty. Dr. Butler went over Mr. Stone's head immediately and the latter resigned, but in 1910 a group of professors and lawyers again asked Dr. Butler to draft Mr. Stone and he again accepted. This time Dr. Butler kept his word on professorial appointments. Dean Stone, while still carrying on his duties as a member of the downtown law firm, taught several classes, wrote on legal subjects, instituted reforms in the teaching and examining of law students, and managed to see any student who had a problem and sought his advice. It was said that his "kindliness of manner . . . and sense of fairness . . . made Stone loved and revered perhaps more than any other . . . professor of that day."

In 1923 Mr. Stone resigned from the deanship of the Columbia Law School to enter the law firm of Sullivan and Cromwell, which had a large corporation and estate practice. There he was considered "a hard-working, solid sort of person, willing on occasion to champion the rights of mankind, but safe nevertheless." He was appointed by President Calvin Coolidge as the Attorney General in April 1924; one of his first acts was to rid the Bureau of Criminal Investigation of holdovers from Mr. Daugherty's "Red scare reign." Its head, William J. Burns, was ousted and J. Edgar Hoover selected in his place. The Attorney General then opened his guns against the Aluminum Corporation of America, which was controlled by the family of Andrew Mellon, at that time Secretary of the Treasury. Mr. Stone had barely started antitrust proceedings when, in March 1925, he was made an Associate Justice of the Supreme Court.

As a Justice people began to say of him that he was "always right the second time"; while his first reaction was toward the conservatism of his Wall Street days, his next was likely to be one of broad humanitarianism. He was somewhat influenced by Oliver Wendell Holmes and by Justice Brandeis and came to be a pleader for a broader view of the Constitution to suit new needs. Often he stood with the liberals of the Court against the conservatives; Brandeis, Holmes and Stone dissent became a famous phrase. On June 12, 1941, he was nominated Chief Justice by President Franklin D. Roosevelt. His views, as expressed in his Supreme Court opinions, were that law itself was a "human institution for human needs" and that it was "not an end, but a means to an end—the adequate control and protection of those interests, social and economic, which are the special concern of government and hence of law—and that end is to be attained through reasonable accommodation of law to changing economic and social needs."

Mr. Stone married Agnes Harvey of Chesterfield, N.H., in 1899 and they had two sons; Lauson, a lawyer and partner in the New York firm of Ignatius and Stone; and Marshall, a professor of mathematics at Harvard. The Chief Justice died in office on April 22, 1946.

OCTOBER TWELFTH

COLUMBUS DAY

So far as can be learned the first celebration of the discovery of America by Christopher Columbus occurred in New York City on October 12, 1792, three centuries after the event. It was arranged by the Society of St. Tammany, or Columbian Order, founded by William Mooney on May 12, 1789. There had been other societies in different parts of the country named for "Saint Tammany," an Indian sage, in ridicule of the societies named for St. George, St. Andrew and St. David. Mooney retained the "saint" in the title of his society and it remains there to this day. The society gave a dinner, accompanied by elaborate ceremonies, on the three hundredth anniversary of the discovery of America. A monument was erected in the headquarters of the society as part of the decorations. This temporary structure is said to be the first monument to Columbus raised in the United States. The second, outside of those in Washington, was erected by the subscriptions of Italian citizens in Fairmount Park, Philadelphia, in 1876, at the time of the celebration of the centennial of the Declaration of Independence.

There had been few if any celebrations of the anniversary between that of the Tammany society in 1792 and 1892. In celebration of the four hundredth anniversary of the discovery of America a monument to Columbus was erected at the southwestern entrance to Central Park in New York and the place was named Columbus Circle in memory of the discoverer. In 1892 elaborate preparations were made for the observance of the quadricentennial and a great international exposition was planned, supported by a Federal appropriation. There was acute rivalry among several cities for the favor of Congress, but Chicago was finally selected as the site for the exposition and a great world's fair was held there attracting millions of visitors from this and other countries. As it was impossible to complete the buildings in 1892 the fair was not held until the following year. But that the actual anniversary might not be ignored Congress on June 29, 1892, adopted a joint resolution directing the President to call upon the people to observe "the four hundredth anniversary of the discovery of America on the 21st of October, 1892, by public demonstrations and by suitable exercises in their schools and other places of assembly." As the change in the calendar had not been made when Columbus sailed the date of the discovery, October 12, is according to the old calendar. Some precisionist in Congress thought that the celebration should be on a day that corresponds by present reckoning to the day of the discovery. This would have put it on October 23, but as that fell on Sunday and as it was desirable that there should be exercises in the schools, the joint resolution fixed Friday, October 21, as the day to be observed.

There were celebrations in all parts of the country in obedience to the proclamation by President Harrison. The next year the celebration on October 12 at the Columbian Exposition in Chicago was the most elaborate arranged up to that time. The day was not yet a legal holiday in any of the states, and did not become such for several years. Governor Alvah Adams, of Colorado, issued a proclamation in 1905 calling on the people of the state to observe October 12 and the next year Mayor Dunne of Chicago issued a similar proclamation to the people of that city. But the

Knights of Columbus had been actively urging the passage of laws in the various states making the day a legal holiday. In 1908 the New York legislature passed a bill making the day a holiday, but it was vetoed by Governor Charles Evans Hughes because of defects in its phraseology and because he was not convinced that there was any popular demand for another holiday. The veto aroused such a vigorous protest that he said if the defects in the measure were corrected and if there should develop popular sentiment in its favor he would sign the bill if it should be passed by the next legislature. Timothy Sullivan, a senator representing the Italian district in New York City, who had been largely influential in the passage of the original bill, exerted himself to bring about its passage in a form to satisfy the governor. The bill was signed on March 23, 1909, and the first observance of the new holiday was on October 12, in that year.

Two Italian cruisers were sent to New York harbor for the occasion and their crew took part in a parade which ended at the Columbus monument in Columbus Circle. Sixty Italian societies were in the procession. Other organizations joined in the demonstration and the Knights of Columbus held a meeting in Carnegie Hall addressed by Governor Hughes. The day was observed as a holiday in Connecticut, New Jersey, Pennsylvania, Maryland and Montana for the first time in 1909. It was made a holiday in Massachusetts and Rhode Island in 1910, and President Taft reviewed the parade on its first observance in Boston. It attracted the largest crowds seen in the city since the parade of the Grand Army Encampment in 1904. October 12 is now a legal holiday in more than two thirds of the states.

The discoverer of America is known here save among the Italians as Christopher Columbus, an Anglicized form of Cristofero Colombo, the name by which he was known to his parents in Genoa where he was born sometime between August 26 and October 31, 1451. When he entered the service of Spain his name became Cristobal Colon. It is in this form that his name was given to a city on the Isthmus of Panama. His father was a weaver and according to the best records the son was working at his father's trade in Italy in 1472. After making several voyages he decided to devote himself to maritime exploration. He vainly sought support from the king of Portugal and from the rulers of Spain and twice set out for France in search of help from the French king. He finally obtained from Ferdinand and Isabella of Spain the support which he needed. He was authorized to search for and take possession of certain islands which he said lay beyond the Sargasso sea. He sailed from Palos on August 3, 1492, with three ships, a crew of ninety men and thirty companions. Early on the morning of October 12 land was sighted and he disembarked on an island which he named San Salvador. This is supposed to be what is now known as Watling island. On his second voyage with a fleet of seventeen vessels carrying fifteen hundred persons he reached the island of Dominica on November 3, 1493, where he tried

OCTOBER 12

to found a colony and set up a government. He made two other voyages, on the last touching the coast of Central America. He arrived in Spain from his last voyage in November 1504. His efforts to obtain the rewards promised to him failed and he died at Valladolid on May 20, 1506. His body was laid in the Carthusian monastery in Seville. In 1542 it was removed to the cathedral in Santo Domingo. When the island was ceded to the French in 1795-96 what was supposed to be his remains were removed to the cathedral in Havana and when Spain lost Cuba in 1898 these bones were taken back to Seville and placed in the cathedral there. The authorities of Santo Domingo, however, insist that the bones which were removed to Havana were not those of Columbus and that his ashes are still where they were deposited in 1542.

UNIVERSITY OF NORTH CAROLINA DAY

University Day is a traditional observance on October 12 each year at the University of North Carolina, Chapel Hill, N.C. The celebration commemorates the laying of the cornerstone of Old East, the first building, on October 12, 1793. Provided for in the state constitution of 1776, the university was chartered in 1789 and formally opened, as the first state university in the United States, in 1795. The ceremonies vary little from year to year, although there are sometimes added features, as in 1943 when the program was concluded with a twenty-minute pageant depicting the laying of the cornerstone. In that year there was also an exhibition of university portraits which had recently been restored. The University Day celebration is open to the public and there is usually a large attendance. The 1946 ceremonies began in the customary manner with a procession of faculty members in caps and gowns who assembled at the Old Well and, led by the University band, proceeded to Memorial Hall where the exercises were held. President Frank P. Graham made the convocation address to the largest student body in the history of the university, numbering close to seven thousand. The Reverend I. Harding Hughes, class of 1911 and chaplain of St. Mary's School, conducted devotional exercises, and Chancellor House led the traditional responsive reading in memory of alumni who had died since the previous anniversary. Following the reading a minute of silence was observed in their honor and the university Glee Club sang two numbers. In other years distinguished visitors frequently contributed addresses. General A. A. Vandergrift, commandant of the United States Marines and a veteran of Guadalcanal, was the principal speaker during the 1944 exercises. Dr. Harold W. Dodds, president of Princeton University, which was linked to the University of North Carolina by close faculty ties in the early years of the latter institution, delivered an address at the 1943 exercises, and Governor Broughton also participated.

An account of the proceedings on October 12, 1793, when the cornerstone of the building now known as Old East was laid, records

OCTOBER 12

that a long procession marched toward the site previously selected by a Board of Commissioners. The charter provided that the site should not be within five miles of the permanent seat of government or any courthouse, a prohibition occasioned by the drunkenness and rowdyism during court week. Among the many localities considered, Chapel Hill appeared the most suitable and was eventually chosen, in part for the liberality of the donations of land offered, totalling nearly twelve hundred acres; and in part for its accessibility at the crossing of the "great roads" from Petersburg to Pittsboro, and from Newbern toward Greensboro and Salisbury. A chapel of the Church of England stood at the northeast corner of the crossroads, which was situated on a plateau, and from this the place derived its name. The plateau was covered with primeval forest except for small clearings and a narrow branch road along which marched the body of distinguished and public-spirited sponsors, attended by a large crowd. The orator of the day, Dr. Samuel E. McCorkle, was one of the most noted educators of his time and a member of the first board of trustees of the new university.

During its early years the institution struggled with both penury and the ignorance and lawlessness rife in the region. Judge Archibald Murphy, one of the first students and later a professor at the university, reported in 1827 that before the University of North Carolina came into existence there were not more than three schools in the entire state at which the rudiments of a classical education could be acquired. Libraries were practically nonexistent except as the private property of a few professional men. The first class to be graduated contained only seven students; the second, nine; the third, three. In 1808 there were thirteen, but in 1811 only one. However, by 1858 a class of ninety-six was graduated and, after the setback of the Civil War, the university resumed a slow but steady growth culminating in a record enrollment for 1946.

FARMERS' DAY

The Florida Legislature of 1915 created Farmers' Day in the belief that a day set aside for farmers would stimulate interest in agriculture in the state. October 12 was designated for the purpose and made a legal holiday. In a furtherance of this aim, the vast swamps in the southern part of the state, known as the Everglades, are being drained and provided with roads to make available large potential agricultural wealth. This drainage district embraces over four hundred million acres, of which one quarter is owned by the state and is valued at one hundred and five million dollars. The interior, central area of the state is suitable for raising citrus fruits and has been successfully developed, Florida leading in the production of grapefruit. Tobacco, rice, maize, oats and peas are grown, and in southern coastal Florida out-of-season fruits and vegetables, such as strawberries and tomatoes, are ready for the northern markets during the winter months. The raising of high grade cattle is a growing industry on the Gulf Coast.

Since Columbus Day is observed in Florida, the two holidays coincide and there has been little, if any, celebration of Farmers' Day aside from the usual observances of a legal holiday.

OCTOBER THIRTEENTH

LAYING THE CORNERSTONE OF THE WHITE HOUSE

The cornerstone of the President's house in Washington, sometimes called the Executive Mansion but popularly known as the White House, was laid on October 13, 1792. In March of that year a prize of $500 and a building lot was offered for a design for the building. Many plans were submitted, but that of James Hoban, an architect of Charleston, S.C., won the prize. The building is said to be modeled on the mansion of the Duke of Leinster in Dublin. It is one hundred and seventy feet long and eighty-six feet deep. The East Room is forty by eighty feet. Hoban was engaged at a salary of one hundred guineas a year to superintend its construction. It was far enough advanced by the autumn of 1792 for the laying of the cornerstone, but it was not completed until 1800 and John Adams was the first President to occupy it.

Until the Administration of Theodore Roosevelt it was the office of the President as well as his residence. President Roosevelt had an office built adjoining it and connected with it by a corridor. This structure has since been enlarged to accommodate the growing clerical force of the President. During the Administration of President Coolidge a new roof was put on and other extensive repairs made. It was seriously damaged by fire when the British burned Washington in the War of 1812 and the stone walls were painted white to cover the stains of smoke. Naming a public building from its color is not unprecedented; the Alhambra in Spain, built of red bricks, was named "The Red" castle by the Moors, "hambra" meaning "red" in Arabic.

OCTOBER FOURTEENTH

BIRTHDAY OF DWIGHT DAVID EISENHOWER

Dwight David Eisenhower, who became Supreme Commander of the Allied Expeditionary Force in World War II, was born October 14, 1890, in Denison, Tex., son of David J. and Ida Elizabeth Stover Eisenhower. The third of six sons, he grew up in Abilene, Kan.; during the war the town celebrated Eisenhower Day and the General sent a cablegram in recognition of the honor. "If the home folks try to high hat me and call me by my title instead of Dwight," it read, "I will feel I am a stranger.

The worst part of high military rank is the loneliness that prevents comradeship. I wish I could be home and gather at the cafe with the gang."

Prime Minister Winston Churchill of Great Britain also recognized
and expressed the terrible responsibility to which General Eisenhower
referred modestly in this cablegram. The trend of the war had been
reversed in 1942 at Stalingrad and El Alamein, and by early 1944 the
United States was almost fully armed. Mr. Churchill and President
Roosevelt proclaimed the invasion of western Europe as necessary and
imminent. The invasion was the greatest gamble and the most complex
operation in the history of warfare; the design was the product of hundreds of brains, but its successful performance was the responsibility of
one man, the supreme commander. About two months before D-Day
the General and his top commanders were gathered around a sand-table
model of the target beaches. After they had spoken in turn, piecing
together the total picture of the proposed operation, Prime Minister
Churchill said: "I have confidence in you, my commanders. The fate of
the world is in your hands." General "Ike," as he was popularly called,
proved worthy of the Prime Minister's confidence, and the following year
witnessed the unconditional surrender of Germany.

The Eisenhower family are what is termed "old Americans." Their
ancestors migrated from Germany in the seventeenth century, because of
religious persecution, and settled in Switzerland for about a hundred
years, thereafter sailing for the New World. Contrary to what many
people suppose, there has been no military tradition in the family. His
father was an employee of the United Telephone Company, now Southwestern Bell, until his retirement. "Ike" worked summers to help finance
his own and his brothers' education, and thought of entering Annapolis.
He was turned down because of his age, twenty-one, and went to West
Point instead, receiving his B.S. in 1915. He was commissioned 2nd
lieutenant of Infantry in June of that year. In September he joined the
19th Infantry at Fort Sam Houston, Tex., was promoted to 1st lieutenant
on July 1, 1916, and to captain in May 1917. He then served with the
57th Infantry of Leon Springs, Tex., and was attached as instructor to
the R.O.T.C., Fort Oglethorpe, Ga., and the Army Service Schools in
Fort Leavenworth, Kan. In 1919 he organized the 65th Battalion Engineers at Camp Meade, Md., and for a few months commanded Camp
Colt, Gettysburg, Pa. While there he was promoted to the temporary
rank of major and was awarded the Distinguished Service Medal for his
"marked administrative ability in the organization, training and preparation for overseas service of technical troops of the Tank Corps." Before
the Armistice, which ended World War I, he had reached the temporary
rank of lieutenant colonel. He commanded the Tank Corps troops at
Camp Dix, N.J., until December 1918 and at Fort Benning, Ga., until
March 1919. He was then ordered to Fort Meade, Md., where he served
as executive officer and later commanded various tank battalions until
January 1922. During this period he reverted to his permanent rank of

captain, but was promoted to major July 2, 1920, and was graduated
from the Infantry Tank School. His next assignment was the Panama
Canal Zone where he served as executive officer at Camp Gaillard until
September 1924. Upon his return to the United States he became recrea-
tion officer, Headquarters 37th Corps Area, Baltimore, Md., until December 1924. Before attending the Command and General Staff School at
Fort Leavenworth, Kan., in 1925, he was recruiting officer at Fort Logan,
Col. In 1926 he joined the 24th Infantry at Fort Benning, Ga., and the
next year was transferred to Washington, D.C., for service with the
American Battle Monuments Commission. After his graduation from the
Army War College, Washington, D.C. on June 30, 1928, he returned to
duty with the Commission. From November 1929 to February 1933 he
was assistant executive in the office of the Assistant Secretary of War,
Washington, D.C., during which time he was graduated from the Army
Industrial College. He then served in the office of the Chief of Staff
until September 1935 when he sailed for Manila as assistant military
adviser to the Philippine Islands. On July 1, 1936, he was promoted to
lieutenant colonel. While helping to devise the islands' defense it was
necessary for him to fly from place to place and, tiring of being a passenger, he took instruction in flying and obtained his pilot's license at the
age of forty-eight.

The then lieutenant colonel joined the 15th Infantry at Fort Ord,
Calif., in February 1940 and accompanied this regiment to Fort Lewis,
Wash. On November 30, 1940, he was assigned as chief of staff of the
3rd Division at Fort Lewis and three months later became chief of staff
of the 9th Army Corps there. He was assigned as chief of staff of the
3rd Army, San Antonio, Tex., on June 24, 1941, having been promoted
to the temporary rank of colonel on March 11 and becoming temporary
brigadier general on September 29 of that year. During the Louisiana
maneuvers in the fall of 1941 General Eisenhower, as chief of staff of
the Blue Army, "kept good-humored command of the most complicated
situation the United States Army, model 1941, had ever met." He defeated the "enemy" army under Lieutenant General Ben Lear and was
made a major general by President Roosevelt. In recognition of his
reputation as one of the finest staff officers in the Army he was also
given the job of chief of staff of the new Operations Section of the
General Staff. In line with the eventual opening of a second European
front the War Department, on June 25, 1942, designated Major General
Eisenhower as commander of the new war theatre. An Allied force headquarters was created in London with a staff of British, as well as American, officers working under General Eisenhower. He was promoted to
the rank of lieutenant general and appointed commander in chief of the
American Expeditionary Force in North Africa. After a period of preparation attended by great secrecy, American and British forces landed on
November 7, 1942, at various points on the Mediterranean and Atlantic
coasts of French North Africa. On February 11, 1943, the insignia of a

four-star general was conferred upon him and in December 1944 he became one of the seven men in the history of the United States designated as General of the Army. Following the successful conclusion of the African campaign, Italy was invaded by Allied forces under the General and eventually, in June 1944, came the great Allied invasion of Normandy which led to V-E Day.

Eisenhower retired from the Army in 1948 and was inducted as president of Columbia University in New York City in June of that year. Attempts were made to draft him as the Democratic candidate for the presidency of the United States, but he declined the honor.

OCTOBER FIFTEENTH

FEAST OF ST. THERESA

The Roman Church observes October 15 as the feast of St. Teresa, the founder of the order of Barefoot Carmelite nuns. She was born at Avila, Old Castile, Spain, in 1515, the daughter of Don Alonzo Sanchez de Cepeda. She was educated by the Augustinian nuns at Avila and was led to devote herself to the religious life while reading the letters of St. Jerome to an uncle. At the age of twenty she entered the Carmelite Convent of the Incarnation in her native place. She was displeased by what she regarded as the lax discipline of the convent and the abandonment of the ancient severities of the order. In 1562 she founded the order of Barefoot Carmelites and took up her residence in their convent, and did much to restore the simplicity of life in the order. She wrote her life which is regarded as one of the most remarkable spiritual autobiographies in the history of the church comparable with the *Confessions* of St. Augustine. She died in 1582 and was canonized in 1622. October 15 was fixed as her feast day.

ETHER DAY

This day is observed periodically in the Massachusetts General Hospital in Boston as the anniversary of the first public use of ether to deaden pain in a surgical operation. The ether was administered by Dr. William Thomas Green Morton (1819-1868), a dentist. In 1844 he had begun the study of medicine with Dr. Charles T. Jackson of that city, continued his studies in the Harvard Medical School, but was not graduated. While studying with Dr. Jackson he learned that sulphuric ether was useful as a local anesthetic, and later used it in his dental operations, after experimenting with it on animals. He told Dr. John C. Warren, a Boston surgeon, of his experiments and at Dr. Warren's request he administered the ether to a patient in the Massachusetts General Hospital on October 15, 1846. The operation was for the removal of a tumor from the jaw. The insensibility to pain produced by the ether was, at the suggestion of Dr. Oliver Wendell Holmes, called anesthesia. The report of the operation was described by Dr. Henry J. Bigelow in an article in the *Boston Medical and Surgical Journal* for November 18, 1846. Within a month after its use Dr. Morton obtained a patent in this country and soon after he obtained another patent in England. A proposal to buy the patent for $100,000 was made in Congress so that the use of ether might be made free to the medical profession but Dr. Morton refused to sell.

The first use of ether as an anesthetic, however, antedated that in the Massachusetts General Hospital by more than four years. The credit belongs to Dr. Crawford W. Long (1815-1878), who had opened an office in Jefferson, Ga., a small village several miles from any railroad. He learned that the druggists' clerks were in the habit of inhaling ether for their own amusement. He experimented with it upon himself and discovered that it not only made him unconscious but insensible to pain. On March 30, 1842, he administered it to James M. Venable, a patient suffering from a tumor of the neck. He removed the tumor successfully and the patient, when he recovered from the effects of the anesthetic, was surprised that the operation was over. He had felt no pain. Thereafter Dr. Long used ether frequently in his operations, but he lived so far from the centers of population that what he was doing did not become known until 1849. Then there was a dispute for a time over the priority of Dr. Morton's use of ether. But Dr. Long was soon forgotten. In 1877, however, Dr. J. Marion Sims of New York examined all the available evidence and concluded that the credit for the first use of an anesthetic in surgery belonged to Dr. Long.

OCTOBER SIXTEENTH

APPLE TUESDAY

During the Louisiana Purchase Exhibition in St. Louis in 1904 several fruit growers discussed ways and means for improving the market for their crop. Some one proposed that a day be set apart on which the attention of the visitors to the fair should be attracted to the virtues of the apple and through them the whole country should be taught to appreciate the fruit more fully. The third Tuesday in October was accordingly agreed upon and it was named Apple Tuesday. It was then announced that on that day an apple would be given to every visitor to the fruit exhibit. The apples were contributed by the exhibitors and they had to provide more than twenty-five thousand before the demand was met.

The New York Fruit Growers Association, at its meeting at Geneva in February 1905, voted to observe the day selected at St. Louis as Apple

Tuesday—it fell on October 16 in 1934—and to urge the fruit growers in other states to follow its example. The suggestion was adopted and expanded. In some states the school boards were induced to arrange for special instruction in the public schools on that day in the best methods of planting, pruning and cultivating fruit trees. Hotel and restaurant proprietors were asked to serve apples more generously than on other days and every citizen was urged to eat at least one apple.

The day was first celebrated in New England in 1907 by a pilgrimage of fruit growers to a farm in Wilmington, Mass., on which the Baldwin apple is supposed to have been discovered. The farm is marked by a granite shaft surmounted by an apple with the inscription:

This pillar, erected in 1895, by the Rumford Historical Society, marks the estate where in 1793 Samuel Thompson, esq., discovered the first Pecker Apple, later named the Baldwin.

The apple was first called "Pecker" because the attention of the discoverer was attracted to the tree by the frequent presence of large numbers of woodpeckers upon it. The claim of Mr. Thompson to the honor of discovering the apple is disputed by adherents of William Butters on whose land the Pecker tree stood and by supporters of Colonel Baldwin who first put the apple on the market and gave it its name. While the Baldwin is one of the most famous apples of American origin, new varieties have been developed until at the National Apple Show at Spokane, Wash., in 1908, two hundred and fifty different varieties were regarded as sufficiently distinctive to make them eligible to compete for prizes. Governor Ralston of Indiana, in his proclamation calling upon the people of the state to observe Apple Tuesday in 1913 said that "each person in the state should eat at least one apple on that day in accordance with the tradition that 'an apple each day keeps the doctor away.' "

Many of the apple trees in Ohio and Kentucky grew from seeds planted by "Johnny Appleseed," as John Chapman who moved to Ohio from Massachusetts in the early days was called. He took an iron kettle filled with apple seeds and wherever he stopped he would plant a few of the seeds with the remark, "Maybe sometime some one will come along here and be hungry and then they will have apples to eat and they are God's food." He wandered from Ohio into Kentucky taking his apple seeds with him. The settlers who followed him called him blessed.

OCTOBER SEVENTEENTH

OPENING OF THE DELAWARE AND CHESAPEAKE CANAL

The canal connecting the Delaware river and Chesapeake Bay was formally opened on October 17, 1829. It is fourteen miles long and was built at a cost of $2,250,000 provided by the Federal Government, the states of Delaware, Maryland and Pennsylvania and private citizens. Because of the difference in level between the river and the bay, four locks were built. It was originally owned and operated by a private corporation. Its depth was about ten feet which was regarded as deep enough for the boats likely to use it. In the present century agitation began for dredging it to sea level so that the locks could be removed, and deepening and widening it to accommodate larger boats. By 1918 it had been arranged for the Federal Government to buy it for $2,514,000, about the amount of the outstanding bonds and to deepen it in accordance with plans of the War Department so that it might serve a military purpose. The work of deepening it to twelve feet and widening it to one hundred and fifty feet was completed in 1927 and the waterway was formally reopened on May 14 of that year.

OCTOBER EIGHTEENTH

CARNEGIE INSTITUTE FOUNDER'S DAY

The Carnegie Institute of Pittsburgh, Pa., observes Founder's Day every year in commemoration of the dedication to public use of the Carnegie Library in that city by Andrew Carnegie on November 5, 1895, and the announcement on that day by Mr. Carnegie of the creation of an endowment of the Institute. The date is fixed by the Board of Trustees. It is the occasion of the opening of the international art exhibition in the gallery of the Institute and occurs in October. In 1934 it was observed on October 18, with exercises in the great Music Hall of the Institute, when an address was made by Samuel Harden Church, the president of the board, and the names of the winners of the prizes awarded to the paintings on exhibition were announced. In 1945 the date selected was October 11 and the chief speaker was Dr. Solomon B. Freehof, Rabbi, Rodef Shalom Temple, Pittsburgh, who delivered an address on "The Older Virtues." In 1946 the date was October 10 and the Hon. Kenneth C. Royall, Under Secretary of War, spoke on "Production and Peace." In 1947 October 9 was chosen, but instead of the usual platform celebration a reception was held in the foyer of Carnegie Music Hall, after which the guests toured the art galleries of the city for a preview of "Painting in the United States, 1947." The foregoing are illustrative of the varied manner in which the occasion is celebrated. Among the Founder's Day orators in the past have been five Presidents of the United States, namely Grover Cleveland, William McKinley, William Howard Taft, Woodrow Wilson and Calvin Coolidge. John Morley crossed the ocean especially to deliver a Founder's Day address, and Paul Doumer, who later became President of France, has been one of the orators. The Institute is supported by an endowment of $22,000,000.

The one hundredth anniversary of Carnegie's birth on November 25, 1835, was widely celebrated in 1935. There were exercises in Dunfermline Park, Scotland, the gift of Mr. Carnegie to the town in which he was born. An address was made by John H. Finley as the representative of six Carnegie trusts in the United States. A special session of the governing board of the Pan American Union was held in Washington in the Hall of the Americas, the gift of Mr. Carnegie to the Union. It was addressed by Cordell Hull, who was then Secretary of State. In Pittsburgh, there was a special observance of Founder's Day at the Carnegie Institute, addressed by D. S. Freeman. At The Hague Peace Palace, built by Mr. Carnegie, there was an exhibit in his honor of material relating to his efforts to bring about international peace as well as reports on the activities of the various organizations in this country which he endowed. And in New York there was a concert in Carnegie Music Hall, which he built, in which the Philharmonic-Symphony Orchestra and the Oratorio Society of the city participated. There were special exhibits in the New York Public Library and in the libraries throughout the country which he had helped.

Mr. Carnegie was the son of a hand loom weaver of Dunfermline, Scotland. As weaving was gradually transferred from home to factories the elder Carnegie found his occupation disappearing and followed some relatives to America, settling in Allegheny, Pa., in 1848. The boy obtained work in a cotton factory at $1.20 a week and later was hired as a telegraph messenger boy at $2.50. He learned telegraphy and was promoted to an operator's key at $4. In 1853 he became private secretary and telegraph operator to Thomas A. Scott, of the Pennsylvania Railroad Company. In the course of time he succeeded Scott as superintendent of the Pittsburgh division of the railroad. During the Civil War he went to Washington to assist Scott who had been put in charge of military transportation. At the close of the war he resigned from the railroad company and devoted himself to the iron business in which he was already interested. Eight years later he decided to concentrate his attention on the manufacture of steel. He had learned of the new Bessemer process while in Europe selling railroad securities. He introduced this process into the United States in 1873 and within sixteen years steel production in this country exceeded that in England for the first time. He organized the Carnegie Steel Corporation and attracted to it a large number of able men. His company, until a short time before it was sold to the newly organized United States Steel Corporation for $250,000,000, was a partnership in which he owned the majority interest.

After he sold his steel interests in 1901 he devoted himself to giving away his fortune in a way to benefit mankind. It is estimated that his gifts amounted to $350,000,000. Of this sum he gave $60,000,-000 to public libraries, $20,000,000 to small colleges, $29,000,000 to the Foundation for the Advancement of Teaching, $10,000,000 each to the Endowment for International Peace, the Scottish Universities

Fund, and the United Kingdom Trust Fund. His largest single gift was to the Carnegie Corporation, amounting to $125,000,000. He was three times elected lord rector of St. Andrews University and once rector of Aberdeen University and received honorary degrees from many American universities. He died on August 11, 1919, and is buried in Sleepy Hollow Cemetery on the Hudson River a few miles from New York City.

ALASKA DAY

October 18, the anniversary of the transfer of Alaska from Russia to the United States, is a holiday in the territory, known as Alaska Day (see Seward Day, March 30). The treaty arranging for the transfer was signed in Washington on March 30, 1867. American commissioners were sent to Sitka, the capital, with proper authorization to accept the formal surrender of the territory, and it was on October 18, 1867, that the Russian flag was lowered from the flagstaff in front of the Russian Governor's residence and the flag of the United States raised in its place. The ceremony was accompanied by a salute to the flag fired by Russian cannon. With the transfer Great Britain remained the only European power with possessions on the mainland of North America. The Federal Government erected barracks at a number of points and for ten years an army officer represented the authorities in Washington. Then the troops were withdrawn and a naval officer stationed at Sitka represented the Government. After a time this arrangement lapsed and Alaska was left without either civil or military government until 1884 when a civil government, was set up, and in 1912 a territorial government was organized in the usual form with a delegate in Congress. The capital is Juneau.

FEAST OF ST. LUKE

St. Luke, whose festival is celebrated on October 18, is one of the most learned of the early followers of Jesus. He wrote a record of the remarkable events connected with His life and death. It is generally admitted that he was a Gentile and that he was a physician. He wrote the Gospel known by his name and the Acts of the Apostles. The preface to the Gospel is interesting for it announces that since many had written of the things which were believed by the Christians "it seemed good to me also, having had perfect understanding of all things from the very first, to write to thee in order, most excellent Theophilus, that thou mightest know the certainty of those things, wherein thou hast been instructed." It is not known who Theophilus was, but it is supposed that he lived in Antioch.

Luke, having been converted by Paul, went with him on two or three of his missionary journeys and accompanied him to Rome. Although Paul was imprisoned at Rome there is no record of any imprisonment of Luke. After the death of Paul he wrote his Gospel and after-

wards the Acts, and it is supposed that he planned a third telling of
Paul's work in Rome. But if he did write such an account it has not
survived. He died in about the year 68. There is a tradition that he was
an artist and drew portraits of Mary and Jesus. A portrait of Mary,
ascribed to him, is in Rome. He is the patron saint of painters.

OCTOBER NINETEENTH

BIRTHDAY OF JOHN ADAMS

John Adams, the second President of the United States and the first
distinguished man in what became one of the most notable families in
America, was born in Braintree, Mass., on October 19, 1735 (old style).
His son became President of the United States, his grandson was minister
to England during the Civil War and his great, great grandson was
secretary of the Navy in the Cabinet of President Hoover. Other descendants rose to distinction in private life. John Adams was descended
from Henry Adams, an English yeoman, who came to this country about
1636 and settled in Braintree. The descendants of Henry were farmers
until the birth of John in the fourth generation.

John Adams was graduated from Harvard College in 1755 and
taught school at Worcester with some thought of becoming a minister,
but when he began to doubt the truth of some of the Calvinistic doctrines
popular at the time he entered on the study of the law and was admitted
to the bar in 1758. His clients occupied little of his time at first, and
he wrote a series of essays on canon and feudal law for the Boston
Gazette. When the news of the passage of the Stamp Act reached
Massachusetts he drafted resolutions of protest adopted by Braintree
which set the example to other towns in the state. He was elected to
the General Court of Massachusetts in 1769 and his law practice began
to increase. He had already been employed in several important cases
including the defense of John Hancock on the charge of smuggling.
In 1774 he was elected as one of the delegates to the First Continental
Congress and assisted in drafting the Declaration of Rights. He was a
member of the committee which drafted the Declaration of Independence
and it was on his motion that George Washington was appointed
General of the American army. On November 28, 1777, he was
elected commissioner to France and sailed in February of the next year
with his son John Quincy Adams who was then ten years old. He
exerted himself unsuccessfully to obtain a loan from France or Holland,
and returned to the United States in 1779. He was again sent to Europe
with instructions to negotiate a commercial treaty with England. He
was engaged in various other diplomatic missions including the negotiation of a treaty of peace with England. In February 1785, he was
appointed minister to England and after an unsuccessful effort to reach

an agreement with the British over various disputed points involved in the peace treaty he asked to be recalled in 1788.

On his return he was elected to the House of Representatives established by the new Constitution, but did not take his seat as he was elected Vice President with Washington as President. He wrote to his wife when the result of the election was known:

> My country has in its wisdom contrived for me the most insignificant office that ever the invention of man contrived or his imagination conceived.

But as there was frequently a tie in the Senate he was able by his vote to decide many important questions, including the power of the President to remove men from office, commercial reprisal on Great Britain and the policy of neutrality. He was elected Vice President a second time and in 1796 when it was known that Washington was unwilling to serve for a third term Adams was elected President in spite of the efforts of Alexander Hamilton to defeat him, and Thomas Jefferson was chosen Vice President. He pledged himself to follow the policies of Washington. His administration was stormy, what with troubles with France and dissension in his cabinet, and he was unpopular when he retired at the end of his first term.

He took no further part in public affairs beyond writing letters and articles. The enmity between him and Jefferson which arose because of political differences was removed in the course of time and the two men engaged in a correspondence for years, exchanging reminiscences and expressing their views on current affairs. He died on July 4, 1826, only a few hours after the death of Jefferson in Virginia. He was buried in the crypt of the First Congregational Church in Quincy, near the house in which he had spent his later years. Beside the pulpit in the church there is an appropriate inscription on a marble tablet surmounted by his bust. On the other side of the pulpit is a similar tablet to the memory of his son, John Quincy Adams, whose body lies beside that of his father.

YORKTOWN DAY

The anniversary of the surrender of Lord Cornwallis at Yorktown, Va., on October 19, 1781, is one of the most notable in the history of the country. The surrender brought the Revolutionary War to a virtual end, which was formally recognized by Great Britain when the treaty of peace was signed a year and a half later. The surrender itself was celebrated when the news of it was spread abroad. As there was no telegraph in those days this took time. It was three o'clock in the morning of October 22 that an express rider reached Philadelphia, then the national capital, with the news. He was conducted to the residence of Thomas McKean, the president of Congress by a German night watchman. The watchman then went about his rounds proclaiming in a loud voice: "Basht dree o'clock and Gornwallis isht taken."

A public celebration was postponed until the arrival of the official report. This came two days later, borne by Colonel Tench Tilghman, an aide to General Washington. Congratulations were exchanged among the members of Congress, the officers of the state and the French minister, at noon the state flag was displayed on the State House and a salute of artillery fired in the State House yard and by the vessels in the harbor. In the afternoon Congress, the State Council, the French minister and others marched to the Dutch Lutheran Church to attend a thanksgiving service conducted by the Reverend Mr. Duffield, one of the chaplains of Congress. In the evening all the houses in the city were illuminated and there was a display of fireworks on the following evening. Congress voted special honors to Washington, Rochambeau, commander of the French land allies, and De Grasse, commander of the French naval force.

On November 3 twenty-four stands of British colors reached the city and were escorted by a company of volunteer cavalry to the State House where they were presented to Congress. Later in November, General Washington and Mrs. Washington arrived in Philadelphia from Virginia and were received with great enthusiasm. The French minister gave a concert in their honor at which an original oratorio composed in honor of Washington was sung. The rejoicings in the national capital were typical of those in the other cities and towns.

The celebration of the surrender itself marked the beginning of a long series of celebrations in succeeding years. A resident of Bedford, Mass., a village between Lexington and Concord, found among his papers in 1910 the following document: "Bedford, October 11, 1830. We the undersigned, severally promise to pay the sums set against our names towards defraying the expenses of a volunteer parade on the 19th of October to celebrate the battle of Lord Corn Wallis, and pay the same on or before the day of the parade." The amount raised was $64.75, a considerable sum for a village of only a few hundred inhabitants to raise in those days. James Russell Lowell, in *The Biglow Papers* refers to the customary celebrations in this way:

> Recollect wut fun we hed, you'n I an' Ezry Hollis
> Up there to Waltham Plain last fall, a-havin' the Cornwallis?

Mr. Lowell has explained that a "Cornwallis" was "a sort of muster and masquerade, supposed to have had its origin soon after the Revolution, and to commemorate the surrender of Lord Cornwallis. It took the place of the old Guy Fawkes procession." The Cornwallis was an annual event in many Massachusetts towns prior to the Civil War, after which it was abandoned. There was usually a sham fight between the Continentals and the British helped by Indian allies. Prominent figures in it were men representing Washington, Cornwallis and an Indian chief. Massachusetts chapters of the Daughters of the Revolution revived the celebration of the day in the present century by holding receptions in honor of distinguished citizens.

As the hundredth anniversary of the surrender approached, plans were made for a national celebration on the battlefield itself. Ten days after the surrender in 1781 Congress had adopted a resolution appropriating $100,000 for a monument at Yorktown. As the money was not available the resolution was forgotten. On June 7, 1880, however, Congress revived the appropriation and plans for the monument were made, as well as plans for a four-day celebration the next year. The cornerstone of the monument was laid on October 18, 1881. On the next day Robert C. Winthrop delivered a commemorative oration in the presence of thousands of people. Representatives of the families of Lafayette, Rochambeau and Von Steuben were present as guests of the nation. On October 20 there was a military review, and on the 21st a review of the ships of the navy which had been assembled there for the occasion. The day has been observed at Yorktown with more or less elaborate ceremonies since that year. In 1906, the one hundred and twenty-fifth anniversary, a special celebration was arranged by the Society of the Signers of the Declaration of Independence and the Yorktown Historical Society of the United States.

The one hundred and fiftieth anniversary was the occasion of another celebration lasting four days. Lord Cornwallis, a descendant of the British general who surrendered, who was in the United States as the guest of the Masonic Order of Pennsylvania, accepted an invitation to be present, and descendants of Lafayette, Rochambeau and Von Steuben were there as they had been at the celebration of the one hundredth anniversary. Lord Cornwallis unveiled a bust of his ancestor which had been set up at Yorktown and, in the course of an address, said:

> I feel that it would be as agreeable to him as it is delightful to me that a member of the family can be here today. War is behind, peace is in the future, let us hope, forevermore.

Governors of five of the original thirteen states were present and made brief addresses. President Hoover delivered a historical oration. On the first day of the celebration there was a pageant representing events in the history of each of the thirteen colonies and the signing of the Declaration of Independence.

The Federal Government has bought about 2000 acres in and around Yorktown and put the land under the supervision of the National Park service. The tract is known as the Colonial National Monument.

PEGGY STEWART DAY

The anniversary of what is called the Peggy Stewart Tea Party in Annapolis, which occurred on October 19, 1774, is observed by the people of Maryland. They celebrate the destruction of the brig "Peggy Stewart" and its cargo of tea by the outraged citizens of Annapolis who resented the attempt to land it. The tea party is the subject of a series of mural paintings in the Court House in Baltimore.

On May 14, 1774, Williams & Company, merchants of Annapolis, had ordered a cargo of 2320 pounds of tea from London. This was before the agreements to import no tea had gone into effect. On July 23 the tea left London in the "Peggy Stewart," owned by Anthony Stewart of Annapolis, and named for his daughter. The brig arrived in the harbor of Annapolis on October 14. In the meantime the opposition to the importation of tea had become bitter. As soon as the arrival of the vessel was known handbills were circulated summoning the citizens of the city and the county to a meeting to decide what should be done about the tea. The members of the Committee of Correspondence learned that the ship and cargo had been entered at the custom house and that the duty on the tea had been paid by Stewart.

The committee called a meeting of the people and ordered the captain of the brig, its owner, the owners of the tea and the deputy collector of the port to attend. When the meeting opened a member of the Williams firm said that the committee might decide what was to be done with the tea. It might be stored in Annapolis, reshipped to London or the West Indies or anywhere else. The captain of the brig explained that the tea had been put on board without his knowledge. And Stewart explained that his action in entering the ship at the custom house was due to humanity, as he could not land his crew or the fifty-three indentured servants on board until after that formality. They had been on board during a long sea voyage and as the vessel was leaking he was anxious to get them on shore. The tea was still on board. When the meeting was asked whether the tea should be landed the reply was a unanimous "No." A committee was appointed to supervise the unloading of the rest of the cargo and Stewart and the members of the firm of importers were compelled to sign the following apology:

We, James Williams, Joseph Williams and Anthony Stewart do severally acknowledge that we have committed a most daring insult and act of the most pernicious tendency to the liberties of America; we, the said Williams, in importing the tea, and said Stewart, in paying the duty thereon; and thereby deservedly incurred the displeasure of the people now convened, and all others interested in the preservation of the constitutional rights and liberties of North America; do ask pardon for the same; and we solemnly declare for the future, that we never will infringe any resolution framed by the people for the salvation of their rights, nor will we do any act that may be injurious to the liberties of the people; and to show our desire of living in amity with the friends to America, we do request this meeting or as many as choose to attend, to be present at any place where the people shall appoint, and we will there commit to the flames or otherwise destroy as the people may choose, the detestable article which has been the cause of this our misconduct.

The indignation against Stewart was so violent that some zealots demanded that he be tarred and feathered. Others, less bitter, demanded that he burn the ship. The meeting, however, voted against destroying the vessel. The feeling against him was so intense that on the advice of Charles Carroll of Carrollton he agreed to burn the ship himself. So when the meeting adjourned he sailed the ship across the harbor to Windmill Point, now a part of the space between Bancroft Hall of the Military Academy and the harbor line, and with his own hand set fire to the ship and its cargo of tea. Stewart was hanged or burned in effigy in various places in Maryland and ultimately fled to England for safety. Thomas C. Williams, of the Williams firm, who had supervised the shipping of the tea from London, arrived in New York the day the people in that city heard of the entry of the tea at Annapolis. He had to flee for his life and hide himself in the woods. A price was set on his head and he had to escape by night from Philadelphia, where he had taken refuge. After a time the indignation against him subsided and on January 12, 1775, he published in the *Maryland Gazette* an apology for his part in the transaction and humbly asked for permission to live in Annapolis. The Maryland Tea Party differed radically from that at Boston, for it was arranged openly and the destruction of the tea was voted at a public meeting attended by the leading citizens of the town (see Boston Tea Party, December 16).

OCTOBER TWENTIETH

BIRTHDAY OF DANIEL E. SICKLES

Daniel E. Sickles, soldier and politician, was born at New York on October 20, 1825. He was a printer in his youth but studied law at the New York University and was admitted to the bar in 1846. He was elected to the State Legislature the next year as a Tammany Democrat. He was secretary of legation at London from 1853 to 1855 and on his return was elected to the State Senate, served one term, and then was twice elected to the national House of Representatives. While living in Washington he shot and killed Francis Barton Key, the son of the author of "The Star Spangled Banner," for debauching his wife, and was acquitted of the charge of manslaughter. At the outbreak of the Civil War he raised a brigade in New York and became colonel of one of its regiments. During the war he served as a brigadier general and major general of volunteers and at the Battle of Gettysburg he lost a leg, but continued in the service. After the war he served for a time in the regular army and was retired in 1869 as a major general. In the same year he was appointed Minister to Spain, remaining in Madrid four years. He was again elected to the national House of Representatives in 1892 and served one term. When he was about to announce his candidacy for reelection his attention was called to the provision in the Constitution that "no person holding any office under the United States shall be a member of either house during his continuance in office." He decided that he was ineligible as he was drawing retired pay as a major general, and withdrew his candidacy. He died in 1914.

OCTOBER TWENTY-FIRST

WILL CARLETON DAY

The Legislature of Michigan, in 1923, passed a law setting aside October 21 as Will Carleton Day to be observed in the public schools of the state by reading Carleton's poems and studying the life of the poet. The day is the anniversary of the birth of Carleton. He was born on a farm two miles east of Hudson, Mich., in 1845. He grew up on the farm, attended country schools and was graduated from Hillsdale College in 1869. He then became editor of the *Standard*, a weekly newspaper, published in Hillsdale. Later he became editor of the Detroit *Weekly Tribune*.

While reporting a divorce trial in 1871 he was impressed by the domestic tragedy involved and wrote the poem "Betsy and I Are Out" and printed it in his newspaper. It was widely copied. Encouraged by its popularity he wrote other poems based on the everyday life of the people, and sent some of them to *Harper's Weekly*. "Out of the Old House, Nancy," "Over the Hill to the Poor House," and "Gone with a Handsome Man," were published in that periodical in quick succession. In 1873 Harper & Brothers published his first volume, *Farm Ballads*, and within eighteen months sold forty thousand copies of it. This was followed by *Farm Legends*, in 1875, *Young Folks' Centennial Rhymes*, in 1876, and *Farm Festivals*, in 1881. His last volume, *Songs of Two Centuries* appeared in 1902.

In 1878 he left Michigan and took up his residence in Boston, Mass. Four years later he married and moved to Brooklyn, N.Y., where he lived for the remainder of his life. He earned a large income by giving readings from his poems on the lecture platform throughout the country. It is said that "Over the Hill to the Poor House" shamed many men who had allowed their parents to be treated as paupers, into withdrawing them from the poor house and taking care of them in their own homes. Will Carleton, who was christened William McKendree Carleton, died at his home in Brooklyn on December 18, 1912. It was eleven years later that his native state honored his memory by setting apart a day to be named for him.

THE ENGLISH THANKSGIVING DAY

The English express their thankfulness for the harvests by religious services in the churches in October instead of in November as is the American custom. In 1922 a group of Americans interested in increasing the friendliness between the two counties arranged to hold a thanksgiving service in St. Paul's Chapel in New York after the English manner. St. Paul's Chapel was erected in 1766 when the British ruled

America; when Trinity church was burned during the Revolution, the chapel was saved. It was to St. Paul's that Washington went to worship after his first inauguration. Several other Protestant Episcopal churches have followed the example set by St. Paul's in celebrating a harvest day.

The services in St. Paul's in 1934 were held on Sunday afternoon, October 21. The chapel was decorated with autumn leaves, fruits, ferns and vegetables symbolic of the harvest of the crops. Sir Gerald Campbell, British Consul General in New York, was present as the representative of the British Government. Captain Wayne B. Watson, of the Seventh Regiment of the New York National Guard, represented Governor Lehman. And there were delegations present from the British Great War Veteran's Association, Sons of St. George, Daughters of St. George, American Legion, Sons of the American Revolution, Daughters of the American Revolution, Daughters of 1812, Colonial Daughters of the Seventeenth Century and other patriotic organizations. The festival service was sponsored by the International Magna Charta Day Association. The official delegates marched through the church yard in a procession led by a Salvation Army Band playing "Onward, Christian Soldiers." An appropriate sermon was preached by the Very Reverend Milo H. Gates, dean of the Cathedral of St. John the Divine, and an address was delivered by Dr. John H. Finley, associate editor of the *New York Times.* Dr. Finley quoted the following passage from the Magna Charta which he characterized as "the finest fruit of sixty centuries of human struggle and evolution":

> No free man shall be seized or imprisoned or dispossessed or outlawed or in any way destroyed; nor will we condemn him, nor will we commit him to prison, except by legal judgment of his peers or by the law of the land.

During the progress of the services Sir Gerald Campbell, following the custom of the British squire at similar exercises in England, read the two Scripture lessons at the prescribed place in the ritual.

The British festival in late October doubtless has its origin in the ancient Druid harvest festival on November 1. The English and the Scotch, however, had a special festival at the end of the grain harvest in August which was accompanied by many curious customs. In northern England the reapers, when the grain was harvested, would make an image with a head of wheat ears, dress it in a white gown tied with colored ribbons and hoist it on a pole. They would carry this to the barn where the farmer would serve a generous supper to them. This figure was called a "kern," or harvest queen. In Scotland it was called "the maiden." The youngest girl in the harvest field was allowed to cut the last bunch of standing grain and this bunch was fashioned into the maiden with the head of ears of grain. A ribbon was tied about just below the ears to make a neck, and a skirt of paper finished the costume. And this was preserved over the fireplace in the farm house. These customs are said to be dying out if they have not already disappeared altogether.

OCTOBER TWENTY-SECOND

REVOCATION OF THE EDICT OF NANTES

The Edict of Nantes, granting tolerance to Protestants in France, was formally revoked on October 22, 1685, resulting in the migration of large numbers of Huguenots to other countries. It is estimated that twenty-five thousand fled to America to enjoy religious freedom. Their descendants have formed Huguenot societies in various parts of the country which are joined in a federation. There are no accurate figures on the total migration, but it is estimated that at least three hundred thousand French Protestants left the country. Some estimates run as high as five hundred thousand. The Huguenots had been industrious workmen. As a result of their flight from persecution, the number of silk looms in operation at Lyons had fallen from eighteen thousand to four thousand by the end of the seventeenth century and of three thousand ribbon mills at Tours only sixty remained and the woolen trade of Poitou was ruined. (See April 13, Huguenot Day.)

ANNIVERSARY OF THE DEATH OF JEAN GROLIER

The Grolier Society was founded in 1884 in New York City, a society of bibliophiles named after the famous French bibliophile, Jean Grolier de Servières. He was born in Lyons in 1479 and died October 22, 1565, and the anniversary of his death is observed annually by the Grolier Society with a banquet, or special meeting of its members, or in some similar manner. The Society is interested in beautifully bound and printed books. It has a club house in New York City, with a library and lecture hall. It also publishes books and has issued Catalogs of Early and Original Editions from Langland to Wither, and books on printing and book-binding.

Jean Grolier was attached to the court of Francis I. He owned about three thousand books, a remarkable private collection for his era. Some three hundred and sixty of these have come to light. They are handsomely bound in brown calf, both sides ornamented with floral arabesques. His library was dispersed in 1675.

OCTOBER TWENTY-THIRD

BIRTHDAY OF FRANCIS HOPKINSON SMITH

Francis Hopkinson Smith, one of the most versatile Americans of his generation, was born at Baltimore, Md., on October 23, 1838. He was first a clerk in an iron foundry in his native city. Then he studied engineering and became a contractor. One of the structures which he built is the Race Rock Lighthouse, off New London, Conn., which he regarded as his greatest achievement. Besides being an engineer he was a painter in water colors and charcoal and a novelist and essayist. He received many awards and medals for his paintings. He wrote *Colonel Carter of Cartersville*, a novel describing Southern manners. The hero is regarded as typical of the old Southern gentleman. *Caleb West, Master Driver*, was one of his most popular books. He wrote several other novels and books of travel, and a work on American illustrators. And he lectured throughout the country to the satisfaction and delight of large audiences.

OCTOBER TWENTY-FOURTH

PENNSYLVANIA DAY

The Legislature of Pennsylvania on June 22, 1931, set apart October 24 to be observed as Pennsylvania Day in honor of the birth of William Penn, the founder of the state. Penn was born on October 14, 1644, (old style) but the celebration of the anniversary has been changed to October 24, under the new calendar. Governor Gifford Pinchot issued a proclamation on October 20, 1931, calling upon the citizens of the state to observe the anniversary. He said: "The character and principles of William Penn and his devotion to what he conceived to be right should ever be kept before our people. The story of Pennsylvania should be the central theme in the coming observance. Our devotion should ever grow to the colony William Penn founded, the ideals which he ennobled and the Commonwealth which has grown out of Penn's holy experiment."

The Legislature had directed the observance of the day in anticipation of the celebration in 1932 of the two hundred and fiftieth anniversary of the founding of the Commonwealth in 1682. It has been observed ever since. The celebration in 1932 was most elaborate. The Post Office Department issued a commemorative stamp, there was a pageant in Philadelphia, bronze tablets were set up at five different places associated with the career of Penn in America, and brief commemorative addresses by radio broadcast were made by the Queen of Holland, the Kings of England and Sweden, President Hoover, Governor Moore of New Jersey, Governor Buck of Delaware, the Mayor of Philadelphia, the Mayors of London and Deal, England, and the Mayors of Chester, Pennsylvania, and New Castle, Delaware. Prior to 1931, Pennsylvania had celebrated March 4, the anniversary of the day in 1681, when the charter to Pennsylvania was issued t Penn by Charles II. This celebration had been authorized by an act passed in 1927.

The memory of Penn had not been ignored in the state before the two acts mentioned were passed by the Legislature. The Society of Friends had kept it green. The Friends' Historical Society of Phila-

OCTOBER 24

delphia in 1917 affixed to the north entrance of the City Hall a bronze tablet engraved with the prayer which Penn wrote for the city on board the "Endeavor" on June 12, 1684. The original letter containing it was found in Chile in 1915, by Albert Cook Myers, who had been devoting his life to the collection of all available information about Penn. The prayer follows:

And thou, Philadelphia, the virgin settlement of this province, named before thou wert born, what love, what care, what service, what travail have there been to bring thee forth and preserve thee from such as would abuse and defile thee. O that thou may be kept from the evil that would overwhelm thee, and that, faithful to the God of thy mercies in the life of righteousness, thou mayest be preserved to the end. My soul prays to God for thee that thou mayest stand in thy day of trial, that thy children may be blest of the Lord and thy people saved by His power.

In 1916 and in previous years October 14 had been informally celebrated as the anniversary of Penn's birth, and in 1918 Governor Brumbaugh issued a proclamation calling on the people to observe November 7 as William Penn Day in celebration of the first landing of Penn on the soil of the state in 1682. The Pennsylvania Department of Public Instruction has issued a pamphlet containing suggestions for the celebration in the schools and colleges of the state.

William Penn was born at Tower Hill, London, in 1644. He was the son of Sir William Penn, who became a vice admiral in the English navy at the age of thirty-one, and the possessor of a considerable fortune. He sent his son to Christ Church College, Oxford, where the youth became interested in the teachings of the Friends and refused to wear the ecclesiastical gown required by the regulations of the university. He not only refused to wear the gown and to attend the services of the Established Church, but he and some companions of like views tore the gowns from the backs of some fellow students. For this offense he was expelled from the university. When he arrived at his home his father, according to tradition, gave him a sound beating. Then he provided him with plenty of money and sent him to London in the hope that he might be attracted by the gaiety of the city and abandon his curious beliefs, but the plan was not successful, for the youth shunned society. His father then sent him to France in company with several riotous youths in the hope that on the continent he might "reform." In Paris he was received at the court of Louis XIV and entered upon a life of pleasure, roistering with his companions.

He returned to England in 1664 and studied law at Lincoln's Inn for a year or more. His father sent him to Ireland to manage his estate there and to superintend a fort at Cork. He was in line for a commission as captain in the army when he was arrested in Cavalier costume at a Friend's meeting. His father then called him back home where the elegance and extravagance of the aristocracy in London offended him and in 1668, at the age of twenty-four, he finally asso-

553

ciated himself definitely with the Society of Friends. He preached in the streets against feasting, pride and luxury and was imprisoned in the Tower for nine months by the Bishop of London. Before this, he had fought a "duel" in the street with a man whose salutation he had failed to notice. The man challenged him at once and Penn, drawing his sword —he still wore the Cavalier costume—fought until he had disarmed his adversary. Then he explained that he had not heard the salutation as he was absorbed in his own thoughts. When he was released from the Tower he resumed his preaching and was again arrested and haled into court. He acted as his own counsel and berated the court for its action. The judge charged the jury to bring in a verdict of "Guilty of speaking unlawfully in Gracious street." The jury returned a verdict of "Guilty of speaking in Gracious street." The Judge threatened the jury with starvation unless they brought in the verdict which he had ordered. After two days without food the jury found a verdict of "Not guilty." Thereupon the judge sentenced them and Penn to Newgate Prison for contempt of court. After a time their friends obtained their release.

Penn's father concluded at about this time that his son would not change his views and made a will leaving to him an estate yielding about $1500 a year, equivalent nowadays to about $30,000. He also left to him a claim of £12,000 against the King, being money lent by him, which he had been unable to collect. After his father's death young Penn went to Holland and Germany with Fox and Barclay to win converts to the belief of the Friends. In 1676 he and several associates founded a Friends' colony in West Jersey. He became interested in the possibilities of religious freedom in the New World, and asked the King for a grant of territory in liquidation of the debt to his father, which had grown to £16,000 with the unpaid interest. It is said that he appeared before the King with his hat on while pleading his case. Charles II, with amused tolerance, is said to have remarked "When another man is in my presence one of the two must be uncovered," and then he took off his own hat. He granted to Penn the territory now included in the states of Pennsylvania and Delaware. The great seal was affixed to the grant on March 4, 1681. Penn spent the next eighteen months in recruiting settlers for his colony and in the meantime sent out his cousin to become its first governor.

He sailed for America in the following year, arriving at the Delaware River in October and landing first at New Castle, Delaware. Late in that month or early in November he moved up the river to the present site of Philadelphia where a city had been laid out according to his plans, with the streets crossing one another at right angles, one of the first city plans in the history of the world so arranged. Although he had received a grant of land from the King he recognized the title of the Indians to it. It is generally believed that he made a treaty of peace and amity with the Indians under an elm at Shakamaxon on the Delaware, now a part of the City of Philadelphia. No copy of this treaty has ever been found and some antiquarians doubt that it was ever made. But Voltaire, who was twenty-four years old when Penn died, has been quoted as saying that

> This was the only treaty made between these people (meaning the heathen) and the Christians which was not ratified by oath and that was never broken.

Penn spent four years altogether in his colony. On his second visit he built a large country house at Pennsburg on the Pennsylvania shore of the Delaware River opposite Burlington, N.J., the foundations of which were unearthed in 1933. He was charged with treason and conspiracy and deprived of his colony for a time, but it was restored to him. When he returned to England from his last visit to his colony he found that he had been ruined by the manipulations of his steward, whose heirs made fraudulent claims against him and he allowed himself to be thrown into prison to escape their extortions. He was stricken with paralysis which affected his mind and after lingering a few years he died on May 30, 1718, and was buried near London.

THE UNITED NATIONS CHARTER

The United Nations conference on international organization assembled at San Francisco, Calif., on April 25, 1945, to draft and adopt a charter. On October 24, 1945, the Union of Soviet Socialist Republics deposited its instrument of ratification, the twenty-ninth state to do so, and the United Nations Charter thereby came into force, superseding the League of Nations which it resembles in structure and aims. Secretary of State James F. Brynes then signed the protocol formally attesting the Charter, and it was adopted by the United States Senate with only two dissenting votes. As promulgated by Chapter XIX, the Charter came into being upon the deposit of ratifications by China, the Soviet Union, the United Kingdom of Great Britain and Northern Ireland, the United States, and by a majority of other signatory states. Before the end of 1945 fifty-one states had deposited their ratifications, and during 1946 several more countries applied for membership.

The foundations of the Charter were laid during a succession of meetings by the leading powers, more importantly at the Conference of Foreign Secretaries in Moscow in 1943, and at Dumbarton Oaks in Washington, D.C. It was expanded at Yalta and, after considerable revision, signed in San Francisco on June 26, 1945. As an international organization proposing to maintain world peace and security and to promote respect for fundamental human freedoms, the United Nations is similar to the League of Nations, but with the difference that the Charter formulates a more realistic recognition of the need for the potential use of force to make its rulings effective.

Of the several organs provided for in the Charter, the General Assembly occupies a controlling position and constitutes the framework and meeting ground of the United Nations. The first session of the

General Assembly met in London on January 10, 1946. The next session convened in New York on October 23, following the acrimonious Paris Peace Conference, to consider the admission of several nations which had applied for membership, and to decide the all-important issue of the veto right of the Big Powers on the Security Council as well as to vote on numerous less vital matters.

THURSDAY OF FAIR WEEK IN SOUTH CAROLINA

Thursday of State Fair Week is a legal holiday in South Carolina and is celebrated in Columbia, Richland County, where the State Fair is held annually during the third full week in October. In 1946 the holiday fell on October 24. This date marked the thirty-fifth year the Carolina-Clemson football game had been played on Thursday of Fair Week, the occasion attracting a large crowd from all parts of the state as usual. The Fair itself has been an annual event since the middle of the last century and has steadily grown in the variety and importance of its exhibits and the size of the attendance. In addition to the classic entries of livestock, agricultural products, flowers, needlework and samples of cooking and preserving, the 1946 State Fair included a model airplane exhibit; an art exhibit with separate classifications for professionals, amateurs and children; educational exhibits by the Future Farmers of America, featuring livestock; the boys' and girls' 4-H Club exhibits; and a canning contest open to all women enrolled in Home Demonstration Extension Work. There were also many amusement concessions characteristic of an agricultural fair, and the city of Columbia enjoyed a gala air during the entire week with the hotels, restaurants, shops and streets packed by cheerful crowds. Thursday was the big day when the football classic, followed by banquets and similar celebrations, took place, and the banks and many places of business were closed.

PANIC OF 1929

On October 24, 1929, the prices of stocks, which speculation had forced to unprecedented highs, suddenly broke and plummeted downward with such rapidity that ticker tape recordings were totally unable to keep pace with the disaster. The New York Stock Exchange and the brokerage offices presented scenes of bedlam which were reflected in serious financial loss throughout the country. Many individuals were ruined and on that day and during the weeks immediately following there were numerous spectacular suicides. However, despite the enormous drop in stock prices no money panic ensued. The New York banks, in conjunction with the Federal Reserve Bank, met all legitimate demands for credits and the liquidation was carried out on as orderly a basis as the severity of the crisis would permit. Prior to the crash the Federal Reserve authorities had attempted to control the speculative mania without success. The trend of stock prices had been upward since 1924.

In 1927 the Federal Reserve inaugurated an easy money policy, partly
to aid business which was experiencing a slight recession, and partly
to assist foreign nations which had been losing gold to the United States.
Unfortunately, the low money rates resulting from this policy encouraged
speculation on the stock market and prices began to rise alarmingly.
Early in 1928 the Federal Reserve Board recognized the necessity of
action, and discount rates at the Reserve banks were gradually raised
from the current 3.5 per cent until, by the end of the year, they had
reached 5 per cent at all but the four western Reserve Banks. Reserve
bank holdings of government securities were also sharply reduced and
open market rates hardened decidedly, the call loan rate being 8.6 per
cent by December. In spite of the rate increases speculation in stocks
continued unabated and accordingly, in February 1929, the Board changed
its policy to one of direct pressure on member banks not to increase
their loans to brokers. This proved effective insofar as member banks
were concerned, but failed to check speculation because of a huge increase
in non-banking loans to brokers placed through the agency of the New
York banks. Although there was a recession in stock prices in March
and declines in certain stocks at various times throughout the spring and
summer, the final crash did not occur until the end of October. The
bankers formed a pool to support the market with temporary success,
but the bull trend was definitely broken and prices moved inexorably
downward until they reached appalling lows in the summer of 1932.

OCTOBER TWENTY-FIFTH

FEAST OF ST. CRISPIN

The feast of St. Crispin, the patron of shoemakers, saddlers and
tanners, is observed on October 25. Crispin was a Roman of distinguished family who became a Christian. He and Crispinian, sometimes
called his brother, went to Gaul as missionaries and settled at Soissons
where they preached to the people by day and made shoes at night to
support themselves. They sold the shoes to the poor for a low price
and, according to their legend, angels provided them with leather.
During the Diocletian persecutions they were arrested and commanded
to change their faith, but refused. It is said that they were stretched on
a rack and tortured, that millstones were tied about their necks and they
were thrown into the Aisne, but that they swam to the opposite shore
of the river. Then an attempt was made to burn them to death but
they suffered no harm. Thereupon they were beheaded on October 25,
285 or 286. A large church was built over their grave at Soissons in
which a golden shrine for the head of one of them was set up.

OCTOBER TWENTY-SIXTH

LAYING THE CORNERSTONE OF DARTMOUTH HALL

The Earl of Dartmouth, whose ancestor was its patron and for whom Dartmouth College at Hanover, N.H., was named, laid the cornerstone of a new Dartmouth Hall on October 26, 1904, to replace the original hall which had been burned. The college was founded as a charity school for Indians at Lebanon, Conn., by the Reverend Eleazer Wheelock who was its first president. Dr. Wheelock went to England and Scotland in 1766 and raised £10,000 for its support. The money was put in the hands of a board of trustees of which the Earl of Dartmouth was chairman. Plans were then made for the enlargement of the school and through the influence of Governor Wentworth large tracts of land were obtained and in 1769 King George III granted a charter to Dartmouth College, incorporating twelve persons by the name of the Trustees of Dartmouth College and giving them full power to govern the institution and to fill vacancies. In 1816 the Legislature of New Hampshire passed an act amending the charter providing for the appointment of eleven new trustees by the governor and for a board of overseers to control the conduct of the trustees. The old trustees refused to accept the amended charter and brought suit to recover possession of the college property which the new board had seized. The State Supreme Court sustained the validity of the amended charter. The case was taken to the Supreme Court of the United States where Daniel Webster appeared for the old trustees. He argued that the college was a private and not a public corporation and that the charter of such a corporation was a contract. The court agreed with him, holding that the amendment of the charter by the state without the consent of the corporation was a violation of the constitutional provision that no state should pass any law impairing the obligation of contracts. This decision, in what is known in legal history as the Dartmouth College Case, was one of the most far reaching made up to that time for it established the power of the Federal courts to invalidate an act of a state legislature and it guaranteed the inviolability of private contracts.

OCTOBER TWENTY-SEVENTH

NAVY DAY
BIRTHDAY OF THEODORE ROOSEVELT

Since 1922 the anniversary of the birth of Theodore Roosevelt, twenty-sixth President of the United States, and also the anniversary of the report of a special committee of the Continental Congress in 1775 in favor of buying merchant ships as the foundation of an American navy have been observed with special ceremonies. The two anniversaries fall on the same day, October 27. It was in 1922 that the American Navy League suggested to President Harding that the day be observed. The Navy League was founded in 1903 by a group of patriotic citizens interested in impressing upon the public the need of an adequate navy and the uses which it would serve.

Theodore Roosevelt was then President and he was in hearty sympathy with the purposes of the League. As Assistant Secretary of the Navy in the Cabinet of President McKinley he had exerted himself to increase the efficiency of the fighting ships. It was thought fitting that as his birthday occurred on the same day on which the first proposal for an American navy was made the two should be observed together. Therefore all the navy yards were opened and the public was invited to visit them on October 27, 1922. There were parades and dinners in many cities. Admiral Hillary P. Jones, commander in chief of the Atlantic fleet, acting under orders, laid a wreath on the Roosevelt tomb at Oyster Bay, N. Y. Secretary Denby of the Navy Department laid a wreath on the tomb of the Unknown Soldier in Arlington Cemetery and there were ceremonies before the statue of John Paul Jones in Potomac Park in Washington. Special memorial services were held in the churches in New York City, and there were pilgrimages to the birthplace of Roosevelt at 28 East Twentieth Street in that city, the house which has been purchased by a memorial association to be maintained as a Roosevelt museum. In the evening there was a meeting in Carnegie Hall addressed by prominent citizens who celebrated the fame of Roosevelt. The day was also observed in London where the military attaché of the American Legation placed a wreath on the grave of the Unknown Soldier in Westminster Abbey. There were similar exercises at the tomb of the Unknown Soldier in Paris, with an address by the naval attaché of the American Legation, and a response by the chief of staff of the French navy.

When the time approached for the second observance of the day in 1923, President Coolidge addressed the Secretary of the Navy in the following words:

It has been pleasing to learn of the plans to continue this year the observance of October 27, birthday of the late President Roosevelt, as Navy Day. The date is appropriate in view of the part President Roosevelt played in making our modern navy, of his historical writings dealing with it, and of the demonstrations which as President he gave regarding the effective utilization of naval power as an instrument of peace.

Theodore Roosevelt was born in New York City in 1858, the son of a successful merchant of the same name. The family came to America from the Netherlands. He was a sickly child but by a course of strenuous exercises he developed a body which could endure the severest hardships. When he entered Harvard College in 1876 he was a skillful boxer. He taught a Sunday school class for some time while he was in college but when he organized boxing matches among his pupils there was some objection and he withdrew from the Sunday school. While in college he became interested in that part of the War of 1812 which was fought upon the sea and began to study it, and in 1882, two years after his graduation, he published *The Naval War of 1812*, which is recognized as a standard history so fair that he was asked by the English editors of the *Encyclopaedia Britannica* to write for them the article on that phase of the war for their great work. He was elected to the Assembly of the New York State Legislature in 1881 and was reelected twice. In 1884 he was made a delegate-at-large to the Republican National Convention where he favored the nomination of George F. Edmunds and opposed that of James G. Blaine. The convention, however, nominated Blaine, a result which led Roosevelt to write to a friend that his political career was ended and that he would thereafter devote himself to literature.

At about this time his mother and his first wife died and he bought a ranch in North Dakota to which he went to escape from his old surroundings. He remained there for two years and in 1886 the Republicans of New York City nominated him for mayor, but he was defeated. President Harrison appointed him to the National Civil Service Commission in 1889 and President Cleveland, whom he had known as Governor of New York while serving in the legislature, continued him in the office. He resigned in 1895 to become president of the Board of Police Commissioners in New York where he did his best to free the force from the control of politicians. He resigned from this office in 1897 to become Assistant Secretary of the Navy under John D. Long in President McKinley's Cabinet. He did much to improve the marksmanship of the naval gunners by arranging for regular target practice.

When the war with Spain began he resigned from the Navy Department and, in cooperation with Leonard Wood, raised a cavalry regiment which became known as the Rough Riders. He was its lieutenant colonel with Leonard Wood as colonel. Although he had been a member of a New York militia regiment he did not think he was fitted to serve as commander. After four months' service in Cuba during which he was promoted to the rank of colonel, the regiment returned to the United States and was mustered out. He had become a popular hero and the Republican organization in New York nominated him for governor after he had refused to accept the nomination from a group of independents who wished him to oppose the regular organization of his party. He was elected and served one term or two years to the satisfaction of the people but to the dissatisfaction of his party leaders. He desired a renomination but before the time for the state convention arrived he was nominated for Vice President by the Republican National Convention in 1900 which had renominated President McKinley. The ticket was elected and Roosevelt took the oath as Vice President on March 4, 1901. President McKinley died from an assassin's bullet on September 14, and the Vice President became President by succession.

He was elected President in 1904 and announced that he would not be a candidate to succeed himself four years later.

His administration is notable for recognizing the republic of Panama which had revolted from Colombia, thus clearing the way for building the Panama Canal; for sending a naval fleet around the world at a time when there was fear of a war with Japan, an act which calmed the Japanese jingos; for his enforcement of the anti-trust laws; for his successful mediation in the Russo-Japanese war, an act for which the Nobel peace prize was awarded to him; and for his utilization of the Hague Arbitration Tribunal in the settlement of a long standing dispute with Mexico, thus demonstrating for the first time that the tribunal was a useful instrument. In 1909, when he retired from the White House, he went to Africa with an expedition to hunt big game for the American Museum of Natural History in New York and for the National Museum in Washington. A wing has been added to the museum in New York to house the specimens which he brought back with him. As the presidential campaign of 1912 approached he began to interest himself actively in politics in an effort to find a candidate in his party more satisfactory to the progressive elements than Mr. Taft seemed to be. Failing to find anyone else he entered the lists, and when the Republican National Convention met he and his friends insisted that a majority of the delegates favored him. Contesting delegations, however, had been sent from several states. They favored Mr. Taft. Enough of them were seated to give the nomination to Taft. It has been asserted and denied that Roosevelt actually had a majority of the legally elected delegates. When the contestants were seated a large body of the delegates left the convention hall and not long afterward a bolting convention was held which nominated Roosevelt. While making a speech at Milwaukee, Wis., he was shot by a fanatic but not seriously wounded. In November he carried enough states to give him eighty-eight electoral votes while Taft received only eight. The two Republican candidates divided the Republican vote so that Woodrow Wilson, the Democratic candidate, was elected carrying states which but for the party division would have gone Republican.

When the United States entered the first World War in 1917 Roosevelt wanted to raise an army division and go to Europe as its commander, but President Wilson would not consent. During all his life he had written much—an edition of his works, exclusive of his state papers has been published in twenty-five volumes—and in his later years he wrote for the magazines and newspapers. His death was hastened— he died on January 6, 1919—by an illness which he contracted during an exploring expedition up the River of Doubt in South America, undertaken as a last adventure. He is buried in the cemetery at Oyster Bay, N.Y., the village near his home, Sagamore Hill. The grave is decorated every year by pilgrims who visit the place for the purpose and airplanes circle above the cemetery and drop flowers on the tomb. The pew which he occupied in Christ Episcopal Church in the village has been marked by a tablet setting forth the fact that it had been his for thirty years.

OCTOBER TWENTY-EIGHTH

FEAST OF ST. SIMON

The feast of St. Simon, one of the Apostles, is celebrated by the Roman church on October 28, while the Greek church celebrates it on May 10. Little is known of him beyond the fact that he is named as one of the Apostles in the New Testament record. The Greek church identifies him as the bridegroom at the feast at Cana where Jesus turned water into wine. The Abyssinian church identifies him as bishop of Jerusalem and according to its tradition he was crucified after he had preached in Samaria. According to various accounts he preached in almost every part of the then known world, including Britain, Northern Africa, Persia and Spain. One account says that he died in Spain. Where his bones lie is as uncertain as where he preached. Tradition places them at Babylon, Rome and Toulouse. At Rome what are regarded as his relics are under the Altar of the Crucifixion in St. Peter's Church. The best accepted tradition is that he met his death by being sawed in two. He is the patron of tanners.

REPUBLIC OF CZECHOSLOVAKIA DAY

In 1935 the General Assembly of Maryland passed a joint resolution directing the governor to proclaim October 28 of each year as a day for the observance and commemoration of the founding of the Republic of Czechoslovakia. The United States was the first country, through public announcement of the Secretary of State on June 13, 1918, to express sympathy with the purpose of Thomas G. Masaryk and his fellow countrymen to establish a republic. It was founded on October 28, 1918, and Masaryk was elected in November of that year as its first President; he was subsequently reelected three times, the last time in May 1934, at the age of eighty-four. Czechoslovakia was one of the states of Europe created at the end of the first World War; it was formed from all or parts of Bohemia, Moravia, Silesia, Slovakia and Ruthenia, its frontiers delimited by the Treaty of Versailles in 1920. During the war the Czechs, who were conscripts of Austria Hungary, had deserted in large numbers to the Russians with whom they were closely affiliated racially. The rapid decline of the Central Powers in 1918 was seized upon as the opportune time for the declaration of Czech independence which had long been desired, and on October 28 the local government of Prague was taken over and the Republic proclaimed.

The resolution of the Maryland Assembly further directed that the anniversary should be commemorated with suitable patriotic and public exercises in honor of "this great sister Republic in Europe"; and the governor was authorized to call upon state officials to display the flag of the United States on all government buildings, and to invite the people to observe the day in schools and churches.

Czechoslovakia Day is celebrated in Baltimore, and various smaller communities in Maryland where persons of Czech descent have settled, by banquets accompanied by patriotic speeches, and by special religious services. The date is also observed by Czechs throughout the United States; for example, in Masaryktown, Fla., where it is known as Czecho-slovakian Independence Day.

DEDICATION OF THE STATUE OF LIBERTY

Bartholdi's statue of "Liberty Enlightening the World," on Bedloe Island in New York harbor, was dedicated with elaborate ceremonies on October 28, 1886. The statue was presented to the people of the United States by the French people as a memorial of the friendly feelings between the two countries. In 1874 a French-American Union was organized in France which solicited subscriptions for such a memorial and raised a million francs. Frederick August Bartholdi, a French sculptor, submitted a model which was accepted, the United States Government set apart Bedloe Island as the site for it, and $300,000 was raised to build a suitable pedestal. The statue was formally delivered to the American minister in Paris on July 4, 1880. It arrived in the United States in 1884 and was set up on its pedestal in 1886 and dedicated on October 28th. It is the largest statue ever built as it is one hundred and fifty feet and one inch high. With its pedestal it is one inch less than three hundred and six feet above low water mark. It stirs the imagination of foreigners arriving in the United States and Americans, returning from Europe, welcome the sight of it as a symbol of home.

On October 28, 1936, the fiftieth anniversary of the original dedication, the statute was rededicated with elaborate ceremonies. President Franklin D. Roosevelt made the principal address, and President Albert Lebrun of France spoke by wireless from France.

OCTOBER TWENTY-NINTH

A HISTORIC ELECTION

The election for the choice of a member of the New York Assembly held in St. Peter's Protestant Episcopal Church at East Chester, now a part of the city of Mount Vernon, is of historical importance because out of it grew the failure of the Governor of the colony to restrict the freedom of the press. (See August 5, Acquittal of John Peter Zenger.) Lewis Morris had been removed as Chief Justice of the Supreme Court by Governor Cosby because he would not submit to dictation. Judge Morris became a candidate for the Assembly and a creature of the Governor was entered against him. At the election on October 29, 1733, it was charged that Quakers were not allowed to vote, that the Sheriff tried to intimidate voters and that the Governor had sent a lot of nonresident sailors from the waterfront of New York and had tried to have their votes counted. John Peter Zenger published an account of what happened in the New York *Weekly Journal*, founded by the opponents of the Governor. This led to his arrest on a charge of libel of which he was acquitted.

The two hundredth anniversary of the election was celebrated at the church in 1933 attended by owners and editors of newspapers from all parts of the country. Colonel Robert R. McCormick of the Chicago *Tribune* delivered an address on the career of Zenger and on the importance of defending the freedom of the press. This was at a time when the newspaper publishers were demanding that the constitutional guarantees of a free press should be inserted in the newspaper code to be drafted under the provisions of the Industrial Recovery Act of 1933.

OCTOBER THIRTIETH

JOHN MITCHELL DAY

Soon after the settlement of the strike of coal miners in 1900 and 1902, under the leadership of John Mitchell, then president of the United Mine Workers of America, the anthracite miners in Pennsylvania set apart October 30 to be observed as a holiday every year in honor of their leader. The mine workers, with the exception of the engineers, firemen and pump men, lay down their tools on that day and celebrate with parades and mass meetings. The strike of 1902 continued so long that there was a serious coal famine and President Roosevelt made plans for having the army take over the mines, but negotiations conducted through Mr. Mitchell brought about a settlement of the strike and an increase in wages for the miners. Mr. Mitchell was then only thirty-two years old and had been president of the United Mine Workers for four years.

He was born in Braidwood, Ill., on February 4, 1870. His father combined coal mining with farming. His mother died when he was two and a half years old and his father was killed when he was six. He had little formal schooling and began working in a mine when he was twelve. He joined the Knights of Labor in 1885 but in the course of a strike three years later he became convinced that the miners should have a union of their own. When the United Mine Workers of America was organized he became a member of the local branch in Spring Valley,

Ill., where he was working. In 1894 he joined a strike, but when it was settled he was not rehired. He was soon invited to become secretary-treasurer of a branch of the union and three years later he was elected to the state executive board of the union in Illinois. The next year he was elected vice president of the union at its national convention and succeeded to the presidency before the year was out when the president resigned to accept a government job.

In preparation for the strike in the anthracite fields of Pennsylvania in 1902 he exerted himself successfully to draw into the union the immigrant miners from eastern and southern Europe and to win their loyal support. He remained at the head of the United Mine Workers until 1908. He had won the confidence of both the miners and their employers and after his retirement from the presidency of the union he was made head of the trade agreement department of the National Civic Federation. He resigned from this post in 1911 because his union felt that he could not consistently hold it and remain a member of the union and demanded that he withdraw from one or the other. He was appointed in 1915 chairman of the State Industrial Commission in New York and held that office until his death on September 9, 1919. He has been generally regarded as one of the ablest labor leaders which the union movement has produced.

OCTOBER THIRTY-FIRST

HALLOWE'EN

The mystic rites and ceremonies with which Hallowe'en was originally observed had their origin among the Druids centuries before the dawn of the Christian era in their celebration on the eve of the festival of Samhain. In the course of time there was added to them some of the rites peculiar to the Roman festival of Pomona who presided over the harvests. The early Christian church adopted the eve and the day following and gave new names to them, as it did with many other non-Christian observances. Many of the ancient rites were brought to this country from Europe but they no longer have any mystic significance save among the credulous, and are observed only in a sportive spirit by young people who wish to spend a frolicsome evening. The name is of Christian origin and refers to the eve of All Hallows or All Saints' Day, which falls on November 1.

November 1 among the Druids was the beginning of the year and a festival of the sun god. They lighted fires in his honor. They believed that on October 31, the end of the old year, the lord of death gathered together all the souls of the dead who had been condemned to enter the body of animals and decided what form they should take for the next year. They believed that the souls of the good entered the body of another human being at death. And they also believed that the punishment of the wicked could be lightened by gifts and prayers to the god. The cat was sacred and it was long believed that cats had once been human beings and had been changed into that form as punishment for evil deeds. Although the Druids were outlawed by the Romans during their rule in Great Britain their rites survive even to the present time, but without their mystic meaning. Ireland has many traditions of Druidic origin. November 1 was Samhain, or summer's end. On its eve the spirits came out of the cave of Cruachan in Connaught, called the gate of hell. When it was unlocked copper colored birds came out with the spirits. They killed farm animals and stole babies leaving changelings in their place. These changelings could be gotten rid of by maltreatment or by boiling egg shells in their presence. The boiling of the egg shells would induce the imp to confess that in all his centuries of life he had never seen the like and thus prove that he was a demon. Brides were also stolen and there are many interesting stories about them.

The fairies, too, were more powerful during the Vigil of Samhain than at other times. One of the traditions about St. Patrick is that he was put to sleep by fairy music on the day before Samhain. Another tradition is that the fairies, angered because they were not receiving the ancient honor, sent a minstrel to Tara, who put it under a charm and burned it with his breath. Ireland, too, has a story about the origin of the jack-o'-lanterns carried on Hallowe'en. It seems that a stingy man named Jack was barred from heaven because of his penuriousness and forbidden to enter hell because of his practical jokes on the devil so he was condemned to walk the earth with his lantern until Judgment Day.

Hallowe'en is a time when it was once supposed that witches and ghosts were most likely to wander abroad. The belief in witchcraft is very old. Evidences of it are found in the Bible. The ancient Egyptians and the Romans believed in witches and so did the American Indians. The opinion of the Christian Church about witches varied during the first thousand years or thereabouts. At one time it regarded belief in witches as a delusion and at another time it accepted the existence of witches and condemned intercourse with them as a form of traffic with the devil. By the end of the fifteenth century, however, it had adopted a policy of punishing witches with extreme severity. The accused were tortured into a confession and then were burned. During the following two centuries thousands of women were slain after they had been charged with practicing witchcraft. A single judge in Nancy is said to have put to death eight hundred of them within six years. At Toulouse four hundred were executed at a single time and in Treves seven thousand were punished by death. In England in 1603, under King James, parliament enacted a law against intercourse with witches which provided that:

If any person shall use any invocation or conjuration of any evil or wicked spirit; or shall consult, covenant with, entertain, employ, feed or reward any evil or cursed spirit to or for any intent or purpose; or take up any dead man, woman or child out of the grave, or the skin, bone or any part of the dead person, to be employed or used in any manner of witchcraft, sorcery, charm or enchantment; or shall use, practice or exercise any sort of witchcraft, sorcery, charm or enchantment; whereby any person shall be destroyed, killed, wasted, consumed, pined or lamed in any part of the body; that every such person, being convicted, shall suffer death.

Samuel Johnson, in his notes on "Macbeth," quotes this statute as evidence that the introduction of witches into the tragedy would be accepted by the people of the time as doing no violence to the probabilities even when the witches vanish into thin air. Disbelief in witches came to be regarded as proof of atheism, an opinion which John Wesley held as late as 1768.

There were many persecutions for witchcraft in America in the seventeenth century in the colonies of Massachusetts, Connecticut and Virginia. Through the influence of Cotton Mather there were many executions of so-called witches in Salem, Mass., toward the end of that century. The panic was so great about this time that, according to a tradition, a woman who had made an apple dumpling was charged with witchcraft. Her accusers insisted that she could not have got the apple inside the dumpling without the exercise of unholy magic. She proved her innocence by making a dumpling in court and was acquitted. The last trial for witchcraft in England was in 1712, but the accused was not executed.

Various methods of divining the future were used on Hallowe'en and the results were accepted in all seriousness. One of the dishes served at supper in Ireland on that eve was known as callcannon or colcannon. It consisted of mashed potatoes, parsnips and chopped onions. A ring, a thimble, a china pig, a doll and a coin were stirred into it and when it was served the one who found the ring was to be married within a year, the finder of the doll would have children, the one who got the thimble would never marry and whoever was fortunate enough to get the coin would have wealth. This was varied sometimes by baking a ring and a nut in a cake. The one who got the slice of cake containing the ring would marry and the finder of the nut would marry a widow or a widower. If the kernel of the nut was shriveled the finder would never marry. Marital prospects were also sought by burning nuts in the coals in the fireplace. A girl would put three in the coals, and name one for herself and the other two for her lovers. If one of the nuts burnt quietly beside that named for the girl it meant that that lover was true to her, but if the nuts separated there would be no happy relations between the girl and either of the lovers. A test used by lovers was the sowing of hempseed. They would take a handful of the seed and go out into a field and sow it, repeating during the process this rhyme:

> Hempseed, I saw thee,
> Hempseed, I saw thee,
> And her that is to be my true love,
> Come after me and draw thee.

If he had the courage to look back over his shoulder he would see the apparition of his truelove following him and reaping hemp. A girl would throw a ball of blue yarn out the window after dark and hold fast to one end of the yarn. Then she would wind it over her hand from left to right, or widdershins, and repeat the creed backward. If this charm worked the end of the yarn still out the window would be held by someone so that she could wind no more. Then she would ask "Who holds?" and the name of her sweetheart would be wafted through the window by the wind.

Another custom was for a young man to put nine grains of oats in his mouth and take a walk and continue walking until he heard the name of a girl mentioned. He would then know that his wife would have that name. Just before midnight a girl would go out alone, unseen by anyone, to a brook running south and dip in it the sleeve of a shirt, take it home and hang it by the fire to dry. Then she would go to bed and try to stay awake until midnight in the hope that she might see her future husband come and turn the sleeve to dry on the other side. It was believed also that if a girl put a glass of water with a sliver in it beside her bed and would say before she fell asleep:

> Husband mine that is to be,
> Come this night and rescue me,

she would dream of falling off a bridge into the water and the spirit of the man she was to marry would rescue her. If she wanted her future husband to give her a drink she had to eat a cake made of flour, soot and salt before she went to bed.

The Scotch observed some of the Irish customs and had others of their own. In the Highlands in the eighteenth century each family would carry lighted torches into the fields on October 31 and march about the fields sunwise or from right to left in the belief that good crops would thus be ensured for the coming year. At dark the torches were taken home and thrown into a heap for a bonfire. Each member of the family would put a stone in the fire and mark a circle around it. When the fire was burned out the ashes were raked over the stones. If any stone was found misplaced in the morning or if there was a footprint near it the person to whom the stone belonged believed that he would die within a year. In another part of Scotland it was believed that the witches were out on Hallowe'en stealing milk and harming the cattle. Boys got peat torches and carried them about the fields, widdershins, that is from left to right, in order to frighten the witches away.

The belief in witches survives in the most surprising regions. German farmers in eastern Pennsylvania paint magic signs on their barns to warn the witches away although in recent years some of them have insisted that the signs were merely ornamental. But there have been murders in that region by men who insisted that they had been bewitched and that they could be freed from the enchantment only by the death of the person responsible.

There were various beliefs about fairies in Scotland. One of them is that they meet at crossroads. If a man would take a three-legged stool on Hallowe'en to a place where three roads cross and sit on it at midnight he would hear the names of those who were to die during the year. If, however, he took various garments with him and threw one to the fairies as they spoke each name the fairies would be so pleased that they would revoke the death sentence. The witches held a party on Hallowe'en and the women, who seemed like other people during the rest of the year, but had sold their souls to the devil, would put a stick in their beds annointed with the fat of murdered babies. This would change itself into their likeness and they would fly up the chimney on a broomstick attended by black cats. They met the devil at a place arranged by him to which he rode on a goat. They drank out of horses' skulls and danced in a circle from west to east, or widdershins, a direction contrary to that followed at the ancient Baal festivals from which many of the Hallowe'en customs are derived. The devil played a bagpipe for the dancing and the revelers were lighted by a torch between the horns of the goat. When the torch was burned out the witches gathered the ashes which were supposed to be especially potent in incantations.

Scottish children made jack-o'-lanterns carved from large turnips with a candle inside similar to the pumpkin lanterns of American children. Scottish children, too, believed that if they piled cabbage stalks about the doors of the house the fairies would bring them a new brother or sister. The young people would go in pairs into the fields blindfolded and each would pull a cabbage. The size and shape would indicate the appearance of the future husband or wife. The stalks were placed over the door and numbered. And if, for example, a youth was the third person entering the door, his name would be the name of the husband of the girl whose stalk was number three. The Irish custom of putting a ring, a thimble and other objects in a cake was also common in Scotland. They also put nuts in the fire and named them as the Irish did, and sowed hempseed after the Irish custom. It was believed that if a girl went into her room at midnight on the fatal eve, sat down before her mirror, cut an apple into nine slices, and held each slice on the point of her knife before eating it she might see in the mirror looking over her shoulder the face of her future lover and he would ask for the last slice. Burns in "Hallowe'en" has described a party in which most of the ancient customs are followed by the young people, but with a touch of skepticism not characteristic of the earlier days.

In England many of the Scotch and Irish customs prevailed, in addition to some of their own. One was for a youth or maiden to pare an apple with the paring all in one piece, to swing it around the head three times and then drop it over the left shoulder when it was expected to fall on the floor in the shape of the initial of the sweetheart's name. They ducked for apples as the Irish and Scotch did, and they would tie a lighted candle on one end of a stick and an apple on the other and suspend it from the middle and set it spinning. The game was to bite the apple as it swung past and to avoid getting burnt by the candle. This candle game is supposed to be a relic of the fires lighted on the hills on the eve of Samhain in the ancient days.

The use of fruit and nuts for divination on Hallowe'en is borrowed from the Roman festival of Pomona, the goddess who cared for the fruits. A grove was dedicated to her near Ostia and a harvest festival was held there on about the first of November, during which it is supposed offerings of the winter stores were made to her, and the horses, rested from their summer toil, were pitted against one another in races.

When families from the Old World came to America they brought their Hallowe'en customs with them. Many of the customs have survived, with variations, but belief in the virtue of the rites has become tenuous and the Hallowe'en parties common in all parts of the country are gatherings of young people for a frolic, even as they were in part in Scotland at the time when Burns wrote his poem describing one of them. The jack-o'-lantern is made from a pumpkin. The houses are decorated with yellow paper ornamented with pictures of the lanterns, with witches riding on broom sticks, and with black cats in different postures. Sometimes papier-mâché skeletons are used to create a ghostly atmosphere and frighten timid girls. And in recent years the guests have often appeared at parties in masquerade costumes which have no relation to the traditions of the occasion.

Belief in witchcraft was once common in America. The witches were charged with making waxen images of their victims and causing their illness by sticking pins in the image or making them waste away by melting the images before the fire. This is an old superstition entertained by the savages of Africa, by the American Indians, as well as by other peoples of widely varying civilizations and localities. It was believed that iron was a protection against the power of the witches and that it was especially potent if in the shape of a horseshoe. And those who believe in the power of the sign of the cross believed that if it were made in the presence of a witch she would become impotent.

The imps which frolic on Hallowe'en nowadays are chiefly mischievous small boys. They carry off gates, ring doorbells, adjust devices for making mysterious rappings on windows, or balance a bag of flour or a pail of water over a door to fall on whoever passes through.

There are numerous cat superstitions connected with the time. If a cat sits quietly beside a person, that means peace and prosperity. If the cat rubs herself against one, that means good luck and greater good luck if the cat jumps into one's lap. If the cat yawns that means an opportunity awaits which must not be neglected. And if a cat runs from one that means that the person has a secret which will be disclosed within a week.

A Pennsylvania belief is that if one goes out of the front door backward, picks up grass or dust and wraps it in paper and puts it under the pillow one will dream with certainty of what the future holds. In Maryland the girls put an egg on the stove to fry and open wide the doors and windows. Then the man they are to marry will come in and turn the egg. At supper the girls stand behind the chairs confident that their future husband will come and sit in front of them. In the South a custom originating from the taking of omens from the struggles of victims in the fires of Druidic sacrifices was once common. Alcohol was put in a bowl and lighted and "fortunes" in the shape of figs, orange peel, raisins, almonds and dates, wrapped in tinfoil were thrown into the flame. The girl who snatched out of the burning the best thing would meet her future husband within a year. There is a belief that pills made of a hazelnut, a walnut and nutmeg grated together and mixed with butter and sugar will produce dreams. If the dream is of gold the husband will be rich, if of noise he will be a tradesman and if of thunder and lightning he will be a traveler. Another dream superstition is described in the rhyme:

> Turn your boots toward the street,
> Leave your garters on your feet,
> Put your stockings on your head,
> You'll dream of the one you're going to wed.

And another superstition is that if one eats a crust of dry bread before going to bed on Hallowe'en any wish that one may have will be fulfilled.

Hallowe'en in the present century has been made the occasion for historical pageants having little or nothing to do with the magic lore of the season. The custom of a carnival parade with the marchers in fantastic costumes has become general in many parts of the country. The season has come to be regarded as a time for merrymaking rather than for serious consultation of magic oracles. This is a modern development, but the custom of children going about the neighborhood wearing masks and fancy costumes and asking at the houses for apples and cookies and candies on Hallowe'en is a survival from the seventeenth century. The Irish peasants then went about asking for money with which to buy luxuries for a feast and demanding in the name of Columb Kill, or St. Columba, that fatted calves and black sheep be prepared for the feasting. St. Columba had by that time taken the place in the Irish traditions of Samhain, the old lord of the dead. St. Columba was a priest who in the sixth century had been ordered to convert the Picts and founded a monastery on Iona island off the coast of Scotland. (See June 9, Festival of St. Columba.)

PROTESTANT REFORMATION DAY

The Lutheran Church observes October 31, or the Sunday nearest to that date, as the beginning of the Protestant Reformation. It was on All Saints' Eve in 1517 that Martin Luther nailed his famous thesis to the door of the castle church in Wittemberg, Germany. Luther was born at Eisleben on November 10, 1483. His father was a poor miner. When the boy was thirteen years old he was sent to school at Madgeburg and then for four years at Eisenach. He supported himself in part by begging. In his eighteenth year he entered the university at Erfurt and received his bachelor's degree at the age of nineteen, his master's degree three years later, and began the study of law. At about this time an epidemic of the plague sweeping over Germany led to the temporary closing of the university. On his way back to Erfurt on July 2, 1505, Luther was overtaken by a violent thunderstorm and was so thoroughly frightened that he vowed to St. Anna that if he were saved he would become a monk. Two weeks later he entered the Augustinian friary at Erfurt.

In due time he took the vows of poverty, chastity and obedience, and in 1507 was ordained a priest. In 1508 he was called to teach philosophy in the new university at Wittemberg but soon left to lecture on theology at Erfurt. He made a business journey to Rome in the winter of 1510-11 and was scandalized by the luxury and vice which he found there. He resumed his work at Wittemberg in 1511 as professor of biblical exegesis, a post which he held for the remainder of his life. He was troubled about his own salvation and by the teaching of the church that salvation could be won by works and by the purchase of indulgences. He finally concluded that salvation was dependent on faith and not on works and began to teach this.

An indulgence proclaimed by Pope Leo X in 1515 was exploited by the archbishop of Mainz. John Tetzel, the chief agent of the archbishop, traveled about Germany preaching the importance of buying indulgences not only for the living but for the dead, reaching the neighborhood of Wittemberg in 1517. Luther was convinced that this preaching was demoralizing and injurious to his people. Therefore, on All Saints' Eve he nailed on the door of the castle church a thesis of ninety-five points, challenging the theory of indulgences. It was written in Latin but was soon translated into German and printed and circulated throughout the country. It was received with great enthusiasm by the people. In February 1518, the Pope ordered the general of the Augustinians to compel Luther to recant. At the general chapter of the order, held at Heidelburg in May, Luther, instead of recanting, defended his views in a public debate. He was then summoned to appear before the Cardinal Legate Cajetan at Augsburg to answer for heresy. He appeared in October, but maintained his position and appealed from the Pope to a General Council of the Church. For this offense the Cardinal Legate was ordered to seize him and send him to Rome, but the elector of Saxony protected him from the agents of the Church.

In 1519 Luther, in a debate at Leipzig, approved some of the doctrines of John Huss, who had been burned as a heretic a century before. Thereupon the Pope issued a bull of excommunication against him. When the bull arrived at Wittemberg, Luther accompanied by the faculty and students of the university, took it and a copy of the canon law to a meadow and burned them in a bonfire. For this offense he was summoned before the German Emperor, German princes, and ecclesiastics, who had assembled in the Diet at Worms (April 1521), and once more commanded to recant. He again refused, was declared an outlaw, and his followers were threatened with extermination. But this decree was never fully carried out as nine tenths of the German people supported Luther, according to a report to Rome by the Papal Nuncio. But Luther had to remain in hiding in Wartburg castle for several months.

When it was safe for him to reappear in public he returned to Wittemberg and assumed the leadership of the religious reform which he had started. In 1530 his followers, beginning to be known as Lutherans, met at Augsburg and drew up a confession which contains the doctrines of the Lutherans to this day.

Luther condemned the monastic system and the celibacy of the clergy. On June 13, 1525, he married Catharine von Bora, a former nun. By her he had six children, and he maintained in his home several orphaned nephews and nieces, and was in the habit of entertaining the poor students in the university. His conversation was so entertaining that these students wrote down everything that they heard him say and it was later published as his *Table Talk*. He died on February 18, 1546. Luther asserted the superiority of private judgment over authority in religious matters. This is the basic tenet of Protestantism.

One of Luther's great achievements was the translation of the Bible into German. The four hundredth anniversary of the completion of the work was celebrated in 1934.

ADMISSION DAY IN NEVADA

The Territory of Nevada, created by Congress in 1861, was admitted to the Union as a state on October 31, 1864, by proclamation of President Lincoln, issued in accordance with the provisions of an act passed on March 31 of that year. The anniversary is a legal holiday in the state and is observed by the display of flags on all public buildings. Although the population of the region was small the political conditions growing out of the Civil War made it desirable that there should be two more Northern senators in Congress and another state to ratify the amendment to the Federal Constitution abolishing slavery. So this state was created, with a constitution prohibiting slavery within its borders.

The territory from which Nevada was formed came into the possession of the United States from Mexico by the treaty of Guadaloupe-Hidalgo on February 2, 1848. It was included in Utah Territory when

573

that territory was organized, but when the territorial government was set up it was separated from Utah. The first white man to enter the region is said to have been Francisco Garces, a Franciscan friar, who passed through it on his way to California from Mexico. In 1767 the Spanish Government of Mexico had expelled the Jesuits and the priests were driven out and took refuge in the north. In 1771 the region known as California was divided, with the southern portion falling to the Jesuits and the northern portion to the Franciscans. The priests were followed by trappers and in 1825 exploration from the East began with the expedition of Jedediah Smith. He was followed by Peter Ogden some years later and in 1850 the Mormon church began to send colonists into the southern part of Nevada. With the discovery of gold in California the gold seekers crossed the region and the Mormon settlers supplied their need for provisions. The inhabitants of the Carson valley sought annexation to California in 1853 and again in·1856 but without success.

Pilgrims Thanksgiving

NOVEMBER

The Wind from the North
Is strong and proud,
And he pounds on my door
In a fashion loud—
One for life,
And two for death,
And November looses
A bitter breath.

—ANNE MARY LAWLER

November was the ninth month in the old Roman calendar, its name, like the names of September, October and December, being derived from the Latin numbers. When the calendar was revised by Pope Gregory, making the year begin with January instead of March, November became the eleventh month without any change of its historic name. The Roman Senate, however, sought to change it in the first century. The fifth month had been named for Julius Caesar and the name of the sixth month had been changed in honor of Augustus, the first Roman emperor. Tiberius, the second emperor, was born in November so it was proposed that his name should be given to the month in order that he might be as distinguished as his predecessor. Tiberius declined the honor, remarking, "What will you do if you have thirteen Caesars?" referring to the condition which would exist when each of the twelve months had been named for an emperor. The Saxons called it Windmonath, as the winds then blew furiously and the fishermen drew their boats on the beach to wait for the calmer weather of the spring. They also called it "Blot-monath," or Bloodmonth, as it was the time of slaughtering the animals for winter food.

NOVEMBER FIRST

FEAST OF ALL SAINTS

This feast was first observed on May 13, the anniversary of the dedication of the Pantheon in Rome to the Virgin Mary and all the martyrs by Pope Boniface IV, in 609 or 610. Pope Gregory III more than a hundred years later consecrated a chapel in St. Peter's to all the saints and fixed November 1 as the date for the feast in their honor. Pope Urban IV once explained that the feast was instituted to provide for the veneration of saints who might have been overlooked during the year. There were so many martyrs that there were not days enough to make it possible to set apart a separate one for each. The feast in the Roman church is of the highest rank and its observance displaces all others. The feast was one of those retained by the Protestants after the Reformation and it is observed by the Anglican church. November 1 is a legal holiday in Louisiana.

One of the martyrs remembered on this day is St. Caesarius of Africa. He was a Christian deacon who had crossed the Mediterranean to Italy and landed at Terracina in the year 300. At that time it was the custom for a youth to offer himself as a sacrifice to Apollo, the patron of the city. He was feasted and honored for weeks in advance and on the day of the special honors to the god, the youth, after the ceremonies, rushed from the temple and threw himself into the sea from a precipice. Caesarius saw the ceremonies and was present when the youth leaped from the cliff. He condemned the sacrifice of life as a useless folly and his words were overheard by two priests of Apollo. They seized and bound him and haled him before the governor. He was condemned to death and bound in a sack and cast into the sea from the same cliff from which the youth had leaped.

NOVEMBER SECOND

BIRTHDAY OF JAMES K. POLK

James Knox Polk, the eleventh President of the United States, was born in Mecklenburg County, North Carolina, on November 2, 1795, the son of Samuel Polk, a farmer and surveyor. His ancestors, bearing the name of Pollock, had come to America from the north of Ireland early in the eighteenth century and settled in the South. They shortened their name to Polk after they had been in this country a few years. Their descendant who became President was graduated from the University of North Carolina in 1818 and then went to Nashville, Tenn., where he studied law with Felix Grundy, a distinguished criminal lawyer who later became United States Senator from Tennessee. He was admitted to the bar in 1820. Three years later he was elected to the state House of Representatives, and in 1825 was elected to the national House of Representatives, as a Democrat. He was Speaker of the House in the Twenty-fourth and Twenty-fifth Congresses and was one of the chief supporters of the administration of President Andrew Jackson, and he supported the policies of Martin Van Buren who succeeded Jackson in the presidency. After serving fourteen years in Congress he was elected Governor of Tennessee in 1839, but was defeated by the Whig candidate when he ran for reelection in 1841 and again in 1843.

Van Buren had been defeated by the Whig candidate, William Henry Harrison, in the presidential election of 1840 and his friends immediately began to plan for his nomination in 1844. When the convention met in Baltimore he had a majority of the delegates. His opponents obtained the adoption of the rule of the convention of 1832 under which the vote of two thirds of the delegates was required to nominate. On the first roll call Van Buren had one hundred and forty-six votes, or a majority of twenty-six, but thirty-two less than two thirds. The roll was called seven times but without a nomination. Among the eight candidates for whom votes were cast the name of Polk had not appeared. On the eighth roll call the New Hampshire delegates voted for Polk and he received a total of forty-four votes. On the ninth there was a stampede to him and he received every vote. Thus he is known in American history as the first "dark horse" to win a presidential nomination.

Polk was elected over Henry Clay, the Whig candidate, receiving one hundred and seventy electoral votes to one hundred and five won by Clay. The election was so close, however, that a change of 7918 votes in four states would have given the victory to Clay. During Polk's term the dispute with England over the northwestern boundary was settled, and the war with Mexico was fought which resulted in the acquisition of California and New Mexico. He signed a tariff act based on the theory of a tariff for revenue only, and supported the establishment of the sub-treasury system, but he was opposed to the expenditure of public money for internal improvements and vetoed a bill appropriating a large sum for improving rivers and harbors. He died in Nashville, on June 15, 1849, a little more than three months after his term expired.

The Polk Memorial Association, founded through the efforts of Mrs. George W. Fall of Nashville, the niece and adopted daughter of Mrs. Polk, acquired the boyhood home of Polk in Columbia, Maury County, and has preserved it as a shrine. It was formally opened on November 23, 1929. In it are deposited the historical and personal relics of Polk. His birthday is observed by the Memorial Association with exercises at his tomb on Capitol Hill in Nashville, and with a pilgrimage to the shrine in Columbia.

BIRTHDAY OF WARREN G. HARDING

The Harding Memorial Association observes the anniversary of the birth of Warren G. Harding, twenty-ninth President of the United States, by exercises at his tomb at Marion, Ohio, on November 2 every year. In 1934 President Franklin D. Roosevelt sent a wreath to be laid on the tomb at the time of the observance. The address was delivered by the Reverend Walter A. King, who had been pastor of Trinity Baptist Church in Marion, the church which Mr. Harding attended and of which he was a trustee.

Mr. Harding was born on a farm at Caledonia, now Blooming Grove, Morrow County, Ohio, in 1865. He was the eldest of eight children born to George T. Harding, a farmer and later a physician. He spent three years as a student at Ohio Central College at Iberia, Ohio, leaving it in 1882. In that year his father moved to Marion, the county seat of Marion County, and the son studied law for a time but gave it up. He had learned the printer's trade by working on the Caledonia *Advertiser* and in 1884 he obtained employment on the *Democratic Mirror* in Marion. Although he was not of voting age he was an enthusiastic supporter of Blaine, then the Republican candidate for President. The *Democratic Mirror* supported Cleveland. Harding threw up his job and immediately after election he joined with John Warwick in buying the Marion *Star*, for $300. It was a four-page weekly paper with a circulation of not more than five hundred and it was in such financial straits that it was about to be sold by the sheriff. Harding soon bought out his partner and concentrated his energies in an effort to make the property financially successful. He married Florence Kling De Wolfe, a widow, on July 8, 1891, and his wife assisted him in the work on the *Star*. When he bought the paper Marion had a population of less than 5000, but as the population of the city grew he was able to make his paper grow along with it. He turned the weekly *Star* into a daily and built it up into a valuable property appraised at about half a million dollars at the time of his death.

He was elected to the Ohio State Senate in 1898 and served two terms, declining reelection for a third term. He was nominated for Lieutenant Governor, however, in 1902 on the ticket with Myron T. Herrick and was elected. He was nominated for governor in 1910 but was defeated by Judson Harmon, the Democratic candidate. He had earned a reputation as an orator and was chosen by President Taft to make the nominating speech at the Republican National Convention of 1912. In 1914 he was elected to the United States Senate by a plurality of 102,000 and began to attract national attention. He was the temporary chairman of the Republican National Convention of 1916 and made what is known as the keynote speech. His friends began to make plans for entering him in the race for the nomination for president in 1920. He entered the convention that year with little support among the delegates. When it became evident that it was impossible to nominate the candidates with the greatest strength he was brought forth as a compromise and was nominated on the tenth roll call with nearly seven hundred votes to one hundred and fifty-six recorded for the next highest. He was elected by an overwhelming majority both in the popular and in the electoral vote.

He formed a Cabinet in which were some of the best and some of the worst men in the party. The distinguishing achievements of his administration were the establishment of a federal budget system with a Director of the Budget and the holding of an international conference on the reduction of armaments which resulted in the negotiation of treaties fixing the maximum naval armament of the principal powers, subject to revision in 1935. He had promised the people of Alaska that he would visit that territory and on June 20, 1923, he left Washington, against the advice of his physician, to fulfill his promise. He landed at Seattle on his return and left for San Francisco on July 27. The next day it was reported that he was suffering from ptomaine poisoning. On his arrival at San Francisco he went immediately to a hotel for rest. Bronchopneumonia developed and he died on August 2 from what was described in the physician's certificate as an embolism. The body was taken to Washington for a state funeral on August 8, and was buried at Marion on August 10.

A memorial association was almost immediately organized to provide a suitable monument over his grave. By contributions from school children and others a fund of more than $800,000 was raised. This, through interest and other accretions, reached about $1,000,000 before the monument was dedicated. It is an open structure one hundred and two feet in diameter surrounded by columns of Georgia marble. The bodies of the President and his wife, who survived him only a short time, are buried in a vault beneath the floor. It was dedicated on June 16, 1931, by an address by President Herbert Hoover. Calvin Coolidge, who had become President upon the death of Harding, presided. President Hoover, in the course of his address, said that Harding as President had been betrayed by his friends, thus referring to the various scandals that had marred his term in office, scandals that did not become fully known until after his death.

ALL SOULS' DAY

The observance of this day is peculiar to the Roman church. The Office of the Dead is recited by the clergy and requiem masses are said. According to the *Catholic Encyclopedia* "the theological basis for the feast is the doctrine that the souls which on departing from the body are not perfectly cleansed from venial sins, or have not fully atoned for

579

past transgressions are debarred from the Beatific Vision, and that the faithful on earth can help them by prayers, alms, deeds and especially by the sacrifice of the mass." The festival was introduced by St. Odilo, abbot of Cluny, who is said to have been the first to prescribe that the commemoration of all the faithful departed should be made in his monasteries on the next day after the Feast of All Saints. He lived in the tenth and eleventh centuries. His festival occurred on January 1, but in later times was fixed for November 2.

NOVEMBER THIRD

BIRTHDAY OF EDWARD DOUGLAS WHITE

Edward Douglas White, ninth Chief Justice of the United States, was born in La Fourche parish, Louisiana, on November 3, 1845. He was named for his father. His grandfather, James White, emigrated from Ireland to Pennsylvania in the late eighteenth century and then removed to Tennessee and later to Louisiana, where he became the first judge of the western district of the territory after it was ceded to the United States. James White's son, the father of the Chief Justice, served as Governor of Louisiana and as a member of the national House of Representatives. Edward attended Mt. St. Mary's College at Emmitsburg, Md., and at the age of fifteen entered Georgetown College. When the Civil War began in 1861 he returned home and enlisted as a private in a Confederate infantry regiment. While serving on the staff of General W. N. R. Beale he was taken prisoner by the Union army in July 1863, and was not released until the end of the war. He then began to study law in the office of Edward Bermudez at New Orleans and was admitted to the bar in 1868. He was a member of the Louisiana State Senate from 1874 to 1878 and in the latter year was appointed to the State Supreme Court. The state constitution was amended in 1878 making the minimum age of judges thirty-five years. As he had not yet reached that age he was forced to retire and resume his law practice. He led the successful fight against the Louisiana lottery with such skill that he came to be recognized as one of the ablest lawyers in the state and a political force to be reckoned with. He was elected to the United States Senate as a Democrat in 1890, and before his term expired he was appointed by President Cleveland an Associate Justice of the Supreme Court.

He wrote many notable opinions. He dissented from the majority in the Northern Securities case, insisting that the acquisition of stock by a parent company in its subordinate companies was not illegal. He also dissented in the income tax case. Upon the death of Chief Justice Fuller in 1910 President Taft, a Republican and a Unitarian, recognized the great judicial abilities of Justice White, a Democrat and a Catholic, and appointed him to the vacancy. The appointment was confirmed by the Senate unanimously without the usual preliminary of referring it to a committee, so profoundly was he respected.

As Chief Justice he immediately began reforms in the procedure of the court for the purpose of expediting business and in conjunction with two associate justices he revised the code of equity rules which had been framed fifty years earlier and had not been changed in all that time. In a Standard Oil case he declared in his opinion that judges should be governed by "the rule of reason" in interpreting obscure or conflicting laws, a pronouncement which aroused a great deal of discussion at the time. In the suit for the dissolution of the United States Steel Corporation, he agreed with the majority that the public interest would not be served by an attempt to restore the corporation to its original constituent members. On his death on May 19, 1921, he was described as a great Chief Justice ranking with the ablest who had preceded him.

NOVEMBER FOURTH

FEAST OF ST. CHARLES BORROMEO

Charles Borromeo, one the most distinguished and devout ecclesiastics of the Church in the sixteenth century, was born at Arona on the southern shore of Lake Maggiore in the castle of his father, Count Gilbert Borromeo, on October 2, 1538. His memory is honored by many Roman Catholic churches in the United States, which are named for him. The theological seminary in the archdiocese of Philadelphia, one of the largest in the country, bears his name.

He belonged to a distinguished family. Not only was his father one of the richest noblemen of Lombardy, but his mother belonged to the family of the Medici. He was religiously inclined and at the age of twelve years his father allowed him to receive the tonsure and not long afterward made him titular abbot of the monastery of Sts. Fratinian and Felinus at Arona. He studied under a tutor in Milan and entered the University of Pavia at the age of fourteen. His father died in the summer of 1558 and although he was not the eldest son he was asked to take charge of the family estates.

Pope Paul IV died in the summer of 1559 and the conclave called to choose a successor elected Charles Borromeo's uncle, Cardinal de Medici, after a session of nearly three months. He took the name of Pius IV. The following January the youth was summoned to Rome by his uncle, the new Pope, who gave him charge of the administration of all the Papal States, and on January 31, when he was a few months more than twenty-one years old, the Pope made him a cardinal-deacon. About a week later the archbishop of Milan resigned and Charles was appointed ad-

NOVEMBER 4

ministrator of the vacant see and legate of Bologna, Romagna and the
March of Ancona and protector of the Kingdom of Portugal, of Lower
Germany and of the Catholic cantons of Switzerland. He was active
in bringing about the reassembling of the Council of Trent in 1562
which had been suspended for ten years and in enforcing obedience to
its decrees.

When his elder brother died in 1562 he became the head of the
family but he looked upon the death as a warning to him to devote
himself entirely to religious matters. His family, however, urged him
to abandon his ecclesiastical activities and to marry. The Pope himself
suggested it. But he resisted their importunities and in 1563 was secretly
ordained a priest. He was active in correcting abuses in the monasteries
and convents and in arousing the priests to an appreciation of the importance of the spiritual life. He was so active in these matters that he
aroused the antipathy of some of the priests and a plot was made against
his life resulting in the firing of a pistol at him at short range while he
was at prayer. Fortunately he was not wounded. The plotters were
discovered and handed over to the civil authorities. Two of them were
hanged and two were beheaded.

He was interested in the religious life of the people as well as in
that of the priests for he organized the Confraternity of Christian Doctrine for the instruction of the children. This has been described as the
beginning of what has come to be known as the Sunday school. Credit
for beginning the instruction of the children in religious matters is given
to him in an inscription on a statue outside the Essex Unitarian Church
in Kensington, London.

When the plague broke out in Milan, in the summer of 1576, he
was convinced that it was sent as a punishment for the sins of the people,
but he devoted himself to the care of the stricken after making his will
and preparing himself for death. He also persuaded the secular clergy
to assist him in looking after the suffering. At this time he decided to
do penance for the people and walked barefoot in a procession with a
rope about his neck. He won a wide reputation for piety, for good
works and for devotion to the Church. He became critically ill in
October 1584, but he continued the performance of his duties till his
strength was exhausted and he died on November 4. The people of
Milan immediately began to adore him as a saint and kept the anniversary
of his death as though he had been canonized. On November 1, 1610,
twenty-six years after his death, he was canonized by Pope Paul V who
fixed November 4 as his feast day.

WILL ROGERS DAY IN OKLAHOMA

In 1947 the Oklahoma legislature passed a statute making November 4 a legal holiday in the state, to be known as Will Rogers Day in
honor of the famous native son. The first observance of the day, which

took place in the same year, was centered at Claremore, Oklahoma, birthplace of Rogers and the location of a memorial. The Claremore Chamber of Commerce, the Oklahoma Will Rogers Memorial Commission, and the Variety Club International sponsored the celebrations, the chief feature being an hour and a half parade with sixteen bands. The distinguished guests included Governor Roy J. Turner, former governors Robert S. Kerr, and Leon C. Phillips, Edgar Guest, poet and close friend of Will Rogers, Bob Hope, the radio comedian, and Will Rogers, Jr. Approximately twenty-five thousand persons were present, many from distant parts of the country.

Will Rogers was born in 1879 in what was then known as Indian Territory, later to become the state of Oklahoma. He was educated at Kemper Military School at Boonville, Ohio, a curious preparation for his subsequent renown as one of America's best-loved humorists in both the fields of acting and writing. He made his first stage appearance at Keith's Union Square Theater in New York City in 1905, the beginning of a notable career in "show business" which ended only with his death. He appeared with the Ziegfield Follies in 1907, and the innovation of the homespun, gum-chewing, lariat-throwing humorist, in contrast with the display of feminine pulchritude, was so piquant as to achieve instantaneous, overwhelming success, making him famous. In addition to appearing in numerous Broadway hits, Rogers also starred in motion pictures and became well-known as an after-dinner speaker and journalist. In 1924 and 1928 he covered the meetings of the national political conventions for the New York Times; he also published several books in which shrewd observations on life and politics were clothed in his inimitable dry wit. He died August 15, 1935, together with Wiley Post, in an airplane crash at Point Barrow, Alaska.

NOVEMBER FIFTH

GUY FAWKES DAY

The celebration of November 5, the anniversary of the discovery of the Guy Fawkes gunpowder plot of 1605 to blow up the House of Parliament in London was brought to this country by early colonists. The code of laws for New York in 1665 ordered that every minister should preach a sermon on November 5 in commemoration of the deliverance from the plot. The New York *Gazette* of November 7, 1737, contained the following account of the celebration in that year:

Saturday last, being the fifth of November, it was observed here in memory of the horrid and treasonable popish gunpowder plot to blow up and destroy King, lords and commons and the gentlemen of his majesty's council. The Assembly and Corporation and others the principal gentlemen and merchants of this city, waited upon his honor, the Lieutenant Governor at Fort George, where the royal healths were drunk as usual under the discharge of cannon, and at night the city was illuminated.

It was customary throughout the colonies to light bonfires at night and to carry an effigy of Guy Fawkes in a procession through the streets of the towns. The custom survives into the present century among the boys of Portsmouth, N.H., and Marblehead, Mass., who frolic around bonfires on that day without any clear understanding of the original significance of the celebration.

The plot originated among the Catholics who were resentful because James I, on ascending the throne of England, did not grant them religious freedom. The conspirators succeeded in hiding thirty-six barrels of gunpowder in a cellar below the chamber of the House of Lords. The barrels were covered with coal and wood, but their presence was discovered in the course of time and on the early morning of November 5 a party of soldiers went into the cellar where they found Fawkes who had been selected as the man to explode the powder. The other conspirators fled, but some of them were found. Four were slain while resisting arrest and seven others were taken alive. They and Fawkes were tried and put to death in January 1606, at the west end of St. Paul's Churchyard. Parliament appointed November 5 as "a holiday for ever in thankfulness to God for our deliverance and detestation of the Papists." A special service for the day formed part of the ritual of the Church of England which was used until 1859 when it was ordered removed from the Book of Common Prayer as out of harmony with the spirit of the times.

NOVEMBER SIXTH

ELECTION DAY

By Act of Congress, passed in 1845, the Tuesday after the first Monday in November is fixed as the date for the choice of presidential electors. This date has come to be the recognized date for local elections in virtually all of the states. Before 1845 the law provided that presidential electors should be chosen within thirty-four days preceding the meeting of the electors. The date for this meeting was fixed for December 3. In the election of 1840, the voting began in Ohio and Pennsylvania on October 30 and it ended in North Carolina on November 12. While the first Tuesday after the first Monday in November remains election day, in 1887 Congress changed the date for the meeting of the presidential electors from December 3 to the second Monday in January. Election day is a legal holiday in all the states and territories, except Alaska, Connecticut, the District of Columbia, Hawaii, Illinois, Massachusetts, New York, Ohio, the Philippines and Vermont. In Illinois it is a legal holiday in Chicago, Springfield, East St. Louis, Galesburg, Dan-

ville, Cairo and Rockford. In Ohio it is a half holiday. In Maine it is
a legal holiday only for the courts. The courts in Maine also close on the
state election day which occurs biennially on the second Monday in September. In most of the states elections are held every two years. When
there was an annual election in Connecticut that state was famous for its
election cake, a rich confection served to visitors to the state capitol on
election day. The day fell on November 6 in 1945.

APPOINTMENT OF THE FIRST CATHOLIC BISHOP

John Carroll of the famous Carroll family of Maryland and a
descendant, on his mother's side, of the Calverts, the founders of the
colony, was appointed a bishop in 1789, the first Catholic bishop in the
United States. The authorities differ on the date of the appointment,
some placing it on November 6 and others on November 14. As there
was no authority in the United States to consecrate him he went to England and was consecrated at Lulworth Castle on August 15, 1790. He
was later made archbishop with his headquarters at Baltimore.

He was born at Upper Marlboro, Md., on January 8, 1735. As there
were no Catholic schools in the United States, when he was thirteen years
old he was sent with his cousin, Charles Carroll of Carrollton, to
St. Omer's in France, a well known Jesuit college. He later studied at
Liège in Belgium, taught there for a while and then spent a year or so
as tutor for English noblemen. In 1773 or thereabouts he returned to
America and lived quietly with his aged mother. In 1776 at the suggestion of Franklin, he was named by Congress as one of the commissioners
to visit Canada and try to induce the Canadians to join in the revolt
against Great Britain. Eight years later he was named prefect-apostolic
for the United States, and made bishop in 1789. In 1808 Baltimore was
made an archdiocese and Bishop Carroll was made archbishop. He interested himself in education and founded Georgetown College in 1791
for the benefit of Catholic youth as the University of Pennsylvania was
the only college to which Catholic students were admitted. He built the
cathedral in Baltimore, and died on December 3, 1815.

NOVEMBER SEVENTH

AMERICAN TROOPS LAND IN AFRICA

Control of the northern African coast during World War II was
strategically necessary if the Mediterranean was to be controlled, and in
turn the Mediterranean must be safe for the Allies before an invasion of
southern Europe was possible. On November 7, 1942, American and
British troops under General Dwight D. Eisenhower commenced landing

operations under cover of darkness along the coast in Morocco and Algeria to meet the increasing menace of the Axis in this territory.

The conflict in Africa had started in July 1940 when the British attacked the French fleet at Mers-el-Kebir to prevent warships of their former allies falling into the hands of the Axis. The battle had swept across the rim of northern Africa six times but the Germans could not hold their gains because they did not control the Mediterranean. Marshal Rudolfo Graziani had begun an attack against Egypt on August 6 simultaneously with an invasion of British Somaliland. He reached Sidi Barrani, but the British started a lightning counter-offensive and drove the Italians back as far as Benghasi. However, the British, forced to send troops to Greece at this time, retreated even more rapidly. Athens fell on April 27, 1941, and the British staged a costly evacuation from Peloponnesus. Three weeks later the Germans invaded Crete with an airborne force and within ten days this important island in the eastern Mediterranean was held by the Axis. During November 1941 the British had launched another offensive in Africa and this attack relieved Tobruk.

On December 8, 1941, the day after the Japanese bombed Pearl Harbor, the United States had declared war against Japan and on December 11 against Germany and Italy. The Germans had become active in North Africa again in 1941. On June 21 their forces, led by Marshal Erwin Rommel, captured Tobruk in a surprise thrust which carried to within sixty miles of Alexandria, Egypt. Despite the calls for men and munitions in the Pacific and the Far East—Great Britain had declared war against Japan simultaneously with the United States—air and tank forces were rushed to Africa and eventually the tide was turned. The British Eighth Army under General Sir Bernard L. Montgomery scored a great victory at El Alamein October 23, 1942, and started its march westward across northern Africa to meet General Eisenhower's forces which had made good their beachheads after the landings on November 7. Later the Germans and Italians were trapped at Cape Bon, May 12, 1943. The Battle of Africa was ended and the stage set for the invasion of Italy, the "soft underbelly of the Axis."

NOVEMBER EIGHTH

MOUNT HOLYOKE COLLEGE FOUNDER'S DAY

Beginning in 1891 Mount Holyoke College, at South Hadley, Mass., has celebrated the anniversary of the opening of Mount Holyoke Seminary by Mary Lyon on November 8, 1837. Mary Lyon, one of the pioneers in the higher education of women, was born in Buckland, Franklin County, Mass., on February 28, 1797. Her father, Aaron Lyon, died when she was less than seven years old, leaving eight children to the care of his widow. Mary, as she grew older, studied in the academies at Ashfield and Amherst. She learned easily and it is told of her that she mastered English grammar in four days and Latin grammar in three. She taught school in the intervals of her study at the two academies and when she was twenty-four she shocked her friends by entering the seminary conducted by the Reverend Joseph Emerson at Byfield. Everyone thought she was too old to go to school. She remained at Byfield for two terms and then became associate principal of the academy at Ashfield. When Miss Zilpah P. Grant, who had been a fellow student with her at Byfield, opened a seminary at Ipswich she made Miss Lyon her assistant.

Miss Lyon, during these teaching years, became convinced that there should be a seminary for young women which was not dependent for its existence upon the life of the person who opened it, that it should be on a permanent foundation as the colleges are. She succeeded in interesting some men in her project and on September 6, 1834, when she was thirty-seven years old, a group of men met her at Ipswich to consider ways and means for founding such a seminary. The ladies seminaries of the time were conducted for the daughters of the well to do. Miss Lyon wanted a seminary so conducted that "the rich will be glad to avail themselves of its benefits, and so economical that people in very moderate circumstances may be equally and as fully accommodated." For two years she was the inspiration of the men who began to raise money for the proposed seminary, and on October 7, 1836, she wrote:

> I have lived to see the time when a body of gentlemen have ventured to lay the corner stone of an edifice which will cost about $15,000, and will be an institution for the education of females.

The seminary was opened in November of the next year with Miss Lyon as its principal. It offered a course of study covering three years, modeled largely on the courses offered at Amherst College. It was immediately popular and at the beginning of the second year four hundred girls who sought admission had to be turned away for lack of room. The teachers were women, but members of the faculties of Williams and Amherst Colleges supplemented their instruction by giving lectures to the students. The original course of study included mathematics, English, science, philosophy and Latin. Music and modern languages were added later. There was no course in domestic science for Miss Lyon did not think that subject had a proper place in a literary institution, but to reduce the cost of operating the seminary, she had the students do the housework, doubtless assuming that they had learned how in their own homes.

The seminary which she founded obtained a college charter in 1888. It had in the meantime received gifts which had made possible the enlargement of the physical plant, and the employment of more and better trained teachers. Miss Lyon died on March 5, 1849, and is buried on the campus of the institution which she founded. She occupies a high place in the history of the education of women in America.

NOVEMBER NINTH

SADIE HAWKINS DAY

Sadie Hawkins Day originated as the invention of Alfred Gerald Caplin, the cartoonist, for his comic strip entitled "Li'l Abner." He introduced the day in 1938, as an occasion upon which the maidens and spinsters of the mythical town of Dogpatch might lawfully pursue the unattached males of the community in a free-for-all race, the males being obliged to "marry up" with the females who caught them. Mr. Caplin did not realize he was filling a gap in the American cultural pattern, but such was apparently the case, since the day has subsequently been observed in many localities throughout the United States, particularly on a large number of college campuses where the Dogpatch ceremony, humorously reenacted, is an annual occurence on November 9. Most Old World countries have a similar day and the lack in America was presumably felt, leading to the enthusiastic adoption of Sadie Hawkins Day by the marriageable young people. In France St. Catherine's Day supplies the desired opportunity to unmarried females for acquiring a mate, although what must have begun as a serious custom, intended to solve a social problem, has degenerated there and everywhere into a mere game or hilarious ceremony without actual matrimony resulting. In the United States the Sadie Hawkins Day observance is also incorporated in various promotional and publicity programs. But wherever the day is celebrated, on the campuses or elsewhere, the captured male is simply the temporary property of his captor, the enforced partner at a dance or some mock ceremony, and is spared the permanent bond of marriage.

However, no such lenience is shown the victims of the Dogpatch race. In Mr. Caplin's comic strip Sadie Hawkins Day is a desperate crisis for the bachelors, and Dogpatch the scene of the type of melodrama that has made the strip and its author-illustrator famous. "Li'l Abner" started on August 13, 1934, in eight newspapers. In 1946 it was syndicated to upwards of five hundred papers with a combined circulation of twenty-seven million which, together with advertising fees, grossed an income of two hundred thousand dollars for its creator, who is popularly known as Al Capp.

NOVEMBER TENTH

UNITED STATES MARINE CORPS DAY

The United States Marine Corps has for many years observed November 10 as the anniversary of its organization. It was on this day in 1775 that the Continental Congress, sitting in Philadelphia, authorized its formation in the following resolution:

Resolved, That two battalions of marines be raised, consisting of one colonel, two lieutenant colonels, two majors, and other officers as usual in other regiments; and that they consist of an equal number of privates with other battalions; that particular care be taken that no persons be appointed to office or inlisted into said battalions but such as are good seamen, or so acquainted with maritime affairs as to be able to serve to advantage by sea when required; that they be inlisted and commissioned to serve for and during the present war between Great Britain and the colonies unless dismissed by order of Congress; that they be distinguished by the names of the first and second battalions of American Marines, and that they be considered as part of the number of the continental army before Boston.

General Washington, in command before Boston, was asked to draw from his army the men to fill the two battalions, but he objected as the resolution required the marines to be good seamen or acquainted with marine affairs and it would be disorganizing to his army to go through it and remove such men from the various companies and put them in a different organization. Accordingly arrangements were made to enlist the force as a new organization. On November 28, Samuel Nicholas of Philadelphia was commissioned by John Hancock, the president of the Continental Congress, as the first captain of marines and he began to enlist the force by opening headquarters in the Tun Tavern in Water Street at the corner of Wilcox's alley in Philadelphia.

There had been three companies of marines in America before the organization of the corps which Captain Nicholas began, but they were a British force. Robert Mullen, the proprietor of the Tun Tavern, received a commission as captain after Captain Nicholas had enlisted him. This tavern is recognized by the marines as the birthplace of the corps. It was torn down in 1900, but in 1925, during the celebration of its hundred and fiftieth anniversary, the corps placed a bronze tablet on the site of the building, and in 1926, the Sojourners Clubs, whose members are commissioned officers of the United States Army, Navy and Marine Corps belonging to the Masonic order, placed another tablet on the site in commemoration not only of the organization of the corps but also in memory of the meetings of the first American lodge of Masons which were held in the tavern.

The first expedition of the marines at sea was in 1776, when a detachment of them under Captain Nicholas left Philadelphia for the Bahamas to capture British ammunition and stores held there. And the first concert by the Marine band, which became famous years later under the leadership of John Philip Sousa, was given at the City Tavern at Philadelphia in 1800 just before the capital was moved from that city to Washington. The corps was abolished, along with the army and navy at the close of the Revolutionary War for reasons of economy. But in 1794 it was ordered that marines were to be part of the complement of every naval vessel built under the direction of Congress. On July 11, 1798, Congress ordered the creation of the corps as at present organized, named it the United States Marine Corps, and directed that it be available for service under the direction of the Secretary of the Navy when needed

When Washington was made the capitol that city appropriately became the headquarters of the army, the navy, and the marine corps.

The corps has a brilliant record. Its members fought with Washington at Trenton and Princeton and they were on the "Bon Homme Richard" with John Paul Jones. They had an active part in the Civil War, both on land and sea, and their record during the Boxer uprising in China is one of the most brilliant pages in their history. In the first World War they astounded the Germans who named them "Devil Dogs," by the fierceness with which they fought. They are proud of their record and boast of it in their hymn which they sing on every appropriate occasion:

From the halls of Montezuma
To the shores of Tripoli,
We fight our country's battles
On the land as on the sea.
First to fight for right and freedom
And to keep our honor clean,
We are proud to claim the title
Of United States Marine.

Our Flag's unfurled to every breeze
From dawn to setting sun,
We've fought in every clime or place
Where we could take a gun
In the snow of far-off northern lands
And in sunny tropic scenes
You'll find us always on the job—
The United States Marines.

Here's health to you and to our corps
Which we are proud to serve.
In many a strife we've fought for life
And never lost our nerve.
If the Army or the Navy
Ever looks on Heaven's scenes,
They'll find the streets are guarded
By United States Marines.

The hundred and fiftieth anniversary of the establishment of the corps was celebrated on November 10, 1925, in Philadelphia, where it was first recruited. There was a parade with the army and navy participating and the heads of the War and Navy Departments present. There was a dinner at which speeches were made glorifying the corps and a ball attended by the beauty and the fashion of the city.

NOVEMBER ELEVENTH

ARMISTICE DAY

Hostilities in the first World War, which began late in July 1914, were suspended at eleven o'clock on the morning of Monday, November

11, 1918, after the signing of an armistice by the contending powers. A peace delegation called upon Marshal Foch, the allied commander at Spa, and asked for mercy. The marshal told the Germans that he had the terms of a protocol which if signed would bring peace. Dr. Frederick Ebert, the German Chancellor, had on Sunday night authorized the delegation to sign. The authorization reached the delegation at two o'clock on Monday morning and at five o'clock they signed. Then an order was sent out to the various armies to cease firing and hostilities ended at eleven o'clock.

The announcement that the war was ended was flashed to all parts of the world, followed almost instantly by enthusiastic demonstrations in the cities of the United States, to say nothing of the communities in the other countries which had been engaged in the conflict. Women wept and men became almost hysterical; there were impromptu parades in the streets; church bells were rung; people in offices threw ticker tape out of the windows and tore telephone books into scraps and threw them on the marchers. The spontaneous rejoicing was more enthusiastic and more general than ever before known over any previous event in the history of the country. It was even greater than that of the previous week when a premature report had come from France that the armistice had been signed. That report lacked verification, but there was a feeling that the war was at an end.

Soon there came to be universal agreement that the anniversary should be observed. On November 11, 1919, President Wilson issued the following proclamation:

To my fellow-countrymen: A year ago our enemies laid down their arms in accordance with an armistice which rendered them impotent to renew hostilities, and gave to the world an assured opportunity to reconstruct its shattered order and to work out in peace a new and juster set of international relations. The soldiers and people of the European Allies had fought and endured for more than four years to uphold the barrier of civilization against the aggressions of armed force. We ourselves had been in the conflict something more than a year and a half. With splendid forgetfulness of mere personal concerns we remodeled our industries, concentrated our financial resources, increased our agricultural output and assembled a great army, so that at the last our power was a decisive factor in the victory.

We were able to bring the vast resources, material and moral, of a great and free people to the assistance of our associates in Europe who had suffered and sacrificed without limit in the cause for which they fought. Out of this victory there arose new possibilities of political freedom and economic concert. The war showed us the strength of great nations acting together for high purposes, and the victory of arms foretells the enduring conquests which can be made in peace when nations act justly and in furtherance of the common interests of men.

To us in America the reflections of Armistice Day will be filled with solemn pride in the heroism of those who died in the country's service and with gratitude for the victory, both because of the thing from which it has freed us and because of the opportunity it has given America to show her sympathy with peace and justice in the councils of the nations.

The day was celebrated with parades of veterans, by public meetings and religious services. All business was suspended for two minutes beginning at the hour when firing ceased at the front.

It had been necessary to bury many of the dead without identification. On Armistice Day in 1920 the body of such an unknown soldier was buried under the Arc de Triomphe in Paris and in Westminster Abbey in London. A Cenotaph was erected in a public square in London in honor of the unknown dead and in Paris a perpetual flame was lighted over the tomb beneath the famous arch. In 1921 the body of an unknown American soldier was brought from France and on Armistice Day buried in Arlington Cemetery with elaborate ceremonies, including a parade from the National Capitol across the Potomac River to the cemetery. President Harding made an appropriate address. A splendid tomb has been erected beside which soldiers stand guard and at which memorial exercises are held every year. Congress in 1926 adopted a resolution directing the President to issue an annual proclamation calling upon the people to observe the day. In 1938 President Franklin D. Roosevelt signed a law which made November 11 a legal holiday in the District of Columbia. It is now a legal holiday in all the states, and in Alaska, Hawaii, Puerto Rico, and the Virgin Islands as well, although not generally observed since World War II.

MARTINMAS

St. Martin of Tours, whose festival is observed on this day, is one of the best beloved saints of the church. He was born at Sabaria, now Szombathely, Hungary, about 316. His father was a military tribune, who, while Martin was still a boy, was transferred to Pavia, Italy. The boy accompanied his father and when he had reached the legal age was enrolled in the Roman army in accordance with the regulations for military service. He had become a Christian and was so benevolently disposed that he gave away whatever he had to those in greater need than he. This disposition is responsible for one of the traditions about him. His regiment had been sent to Amiens in Gaul not long after he entered it. At the gates of the city he is said to have seen a half-naked beggar shivering in the cold. He took off his cloak, cut it into two parts, put one part over the beggar and donned the other. He bore patiently the jeers of his fellow soldiers who laughed at his scanty cloak. According to the legend about him he had a vision that night in which he saw Jesus clad in the part of his cloak which he had given to the beggar and Jesus in the vision was saying to the angels, "Martin, the catechumen, hath clothed Me in his garment." The part of the cloak which he kept was preserved in the oratory of the Frankish Kings and the place in which it was deposited was called a chapel, from the word "chape" meaning a cloak.

After a time Martin was freed from military service and enrolled himself among the pupils of St. Hilary at Poitiers. He visited his family in Italy and then returned to Gaul where he obtained permission from Hilary to live the solitary life at some distance from Poitiers. He continued thus for about ten years, occasionally going about the country to preach to the people many of whom he converted to Christianity. When the second bishop of Tours died the clergy wished to make Martin bishop, but he would not consent. So he was told that the wife of one of the rich men of the city was fatally ill and wished him to prepare her for death. He went to the city and was welcomed so enthusiastically by the people that he yielded to their entreaties and consented to accept the bishopric. One of the legends about him deals with a pilgrimage on foot to Rome. Satan met him and jeered at him for traveling in a way not suitable to his high office. According to the legend Martin touched Satan who was instantly changed into a mule. Martin mounted him and continued his journey. Whenever the mule lagged Martin would spur him on at full speed until at last Satan exclaimed in Latin:

> Signa te signa: Temere me tangis et angis;
> Roma tibi subito motibus ibit amor.

Each line is a palindrome, reading the same way backward or forward. The English is: "Cross thyself: thou plaguest and vexest me without necessity; for owing to my exertions thou wilt soon reach Rome, the object of thy wishes." Martin died in Candes in his diocese on November 11, in either 397 or 400; the exact year is in doubt. There are many Roman Catholic and Anglican churches named for him in this country.

WASHINGTON ADMISSION DAY

In the State of Washington the 1939 legislature created a holiday for the schools, known as Armistice and Admission Day, which is observed annually on November 11. When this date falls on a nonschool day the Friday preceding it is set aside for programs celebrating the history of the state; when it falls on a school day it is a holiday for all common schools and institutions of higher learning.

As is true of most of the present states, the territory now included within the boundaries of the State of Washington was originally claimed by several nations. Probably the first white man to sight the Washington shore was the Spaniard, Juan Perez, who discovered Nootka Sound and Mt. Olympus in 1774. The English and Americans followed, and in 1778 Captain James Cook visited Nootka and opened the Northwest fur trade. Later George Vancouver mapped Puget Sound which, together with Hood's Canal and Mt. Rainier, he named in 1792. The same year Robert Gray sailed up the Columbia River, named it in honor of his ship, and gave America her first claim to the Oregon country. This claim was strengthened when Lewis and Clark crossed the continent, reaching the

Pacific in 1805; and again in 1811 when John Jacob Astor of the American Fur Company founded Astoria which was taken over by the British in 1812, but restored in 1818. Spain and Russia surrendered their claims to the region, in 1819 and 1824 respectively, after England and the United States had agreed, in 1818, to hold the territory jointly for ten years. In 1827 this agreement was extended indefinitely, but the American settlers eventually organized a provisional government in "Oregon," stirring up public opinion to the point where the slogan for the Democratic Party in 1843 was "fifty-four forty or fight," referring to the proposed northern boundary of the territory. This determined stand led to the acceptance by England in 1846 of the forty-ninth parallel as her southern boundary. Until 1853 Washington was a part of Oregon Territory. However, the region was so vast and travel so slow and difficult that the settlers north of the Columbia desired their own capital conveniently located. They petitioned Congress to organize the Territory of Columbia with the result that the Territory of Washington was created in 1853. The area was greater than that of the present state since it included a part of what later became the State of Idaho. From 1867 on there was a campaign for statehood, a constitution being drafted in 1878, but it was not until November 11, 1889, that Washington was admitted to the Union. Thereafter the state prospered, growing rapidly with the completion of the Great Northern Railroad in 1892, and the Klondike gold rush in 1897, which helped make Seattle the gateway to Alaska and the Orient.

NOVEMBER TWELFTH

BIRTHDAY OF JOSEPH HOPKINSON

Although Joseph Hopkinson distinguished himself in several other ways he is remembered chiefly as the author of "Hail Columbia," a patriotic song that preceded "The Star Spangled Banner" by almost a score of years. He was born in Philadelphia, Pa., on November 12, 1770, and was graduated from the University of Pennsylvania at the age of sixteen. He studied law, was admitted to the bar and began to practice at Easton, Pa., but soon opened an office in Philadelphia where he was well known. His father was Francis Hopkinson, one of the signers of the Declaration of Independence and a man of standing in the city. The younger Hopkinson was one of the three lawyers engaged by Associate Justice Samuel Chase of the United States Supreme Court to defend him in the impeachment proceedings before the Senate which resulted in an acquittal. He was elected to the National House of Representatives in 1814 and served three terms. In 1828 President Adams appointed him Judge of the Federal Court for the Eastern District of Pennsylvania, a position which he held until his death in 1842. He was vice president of the American Philosophical Society, president of the Academy of the

Fine Arts and one of the founders of the Pennsylvania Horticultural Society and a trustee of the University of Pennsylvania.

"Hail Columbia" was written in 1798. According to his own account Gilbert Fox, a young singing actor of his acquaintance, needed a popular song for a benefit performance and asked Hopkinson to write one for him. England and France were at war at the time and Americans were taking sides with much bitter feeling, so Hopkinson set out to write a song which would arouse, as he said, "an American spirit which should be independent of and above the interests and passions and policy of both belligerents, and look and feel exclusively for our own honor and rights." Fox sang the song at his benefit performance to the wildest applause. He had to repeat it several times while the audience joined in the chorus. Men began to sing it on the streets the next day and it became popular throughout the country.

NOVEMBER THIRTEENTH

EDWIN BOOTH'S BIRTHDAY

The anniversary of the birth of Edwin Booth, one of the most distinguished American actors, is observed by the Players Club of 16 Gramercy Park, New York. On each recurring November 13, the president of the club, accompanied by a group of its members, leaves the club house and enters Gramercy Park where he places a wreath on the statue of Booth erected there, and makes a brief address. The club was founded by Booth and he was its first president. In 1888 he bought for it the house in Gramercy Park for $75,000 and fitted it up as a club house, reserving for his own use a suite of rooms on one of the upper floors. He had previously lived at 29 Chestnut street, Boston, Mass. He died in his rooms in the club house on June 7, 1893. After his death the Board of Directors of the Players Club arranged a memorial service in the Concert Hall of the Madison Square Garden on the anniversary of his birth. Joseph Jefferson, who had succeeded Booth as president of the club, presided and made a touching address on the personality and career of his life long friend. Other addresses were made by Henry Irving, Tommaso Salvini and Parke Godwin. George E. Woodberry read an elegy which he had written for the occasion and the symphony orchestra played the funeral music which Booth had selected for his performance of "Hamlet."

Booth was the son of Junius Brutus Booth, an English actor who had come to America and bought a large farm at Bel Air, Md., twenty-three miles from Baltimore, where the son was born in 1833. He was named Edwin for Edwin Forrest and Thomas for Thomas Flynn but in later years he dropped the second name. While he was still a young boy

Edwin traveled about the country with his father. When he was not yet sixteen years old he made his first appearance on the stage at the Boston Museum as Tressel in "Richard III." He played occasional juvenile parts with his father during the next three years and in 1851, at the National Theater in New York his father forced him to appear in his place as "Richard III." The next year he went with his father to California where he acted in various plays. In 1854 he went to Australia with Laura Keene, but the venture was unsuccessful and he returned to San Francisco. He played in the West until 1857 when he returned to the East and scored a brilliant success as Sir Giles Overreach in Boston on April 27 in that year. This success repeated in other cities lifted him to the top of his profession. In 1860 he married Mary Devlin, described as a charming young actress, who died in less than three years leaving a little daughter, Edwina. He made successful tours of England and this country, but when his brother shot Lincoln in 1865 he retired from the stage for nearly a year only to be welcomed heartily by the public when he returned to it. He built a theater of his own but lost it by bankruptcy in the panic of 1873. He repaid his debts and continued a successful career on the stage. In the 'eighties he toured England, Germany and Austria. His last appearance on the stage was on April 4, 1891, in "Hamlet" in the Brooklyn Academy of Music.

NOVEMBER FOURTEENTH

A PROTESTANT EPISCOPAL ANNIVERSARY

The Protestant Episcopal Church celebrated in 1934 the one hundred and fiftieth anniversary of the consecration of Samuel Seabury as the first American bishop of the church. Seabury was born at Groton, Conn., in 1729 and was graduated from Yale College in 1748. Later he studied medicine and theology at Edinburgh. He was ordained a priest of the Church of England in 1753, returned to America and served as pastor of churches in New Brunswick, N.J., and Jamaica and Westchester, N.Y., until 1775. He was obliged to resign his pastorate because of his loyalist sentiments and was imprisoned for his opinions. On March 25, 1783, the Episcopal clergymen of Connecticut elected him as bishop. The church in America was under the jurisdiction of the bishop of London, and when Seabury went to London to be consecrated, the bishop, for political and other reasons, refused to act. After waiting for more than a year for the bishop to reconsider his decision Seabury went to Scotland and on November 14, 1784, was consecrated by the bishops of Aberdeen and Moray, and Ross, and the coadjutor bishop of Aberdeen. When he returned to America in the summer of 1785, his authority was recognized by the church in New England, and the church throughout the country was relieved for it was no longer necessary for the candidates for admission to the priesthood to go to London for their ordination. With an American bishop the work of organizing the church as a body independent of the Church of England began. This was completed at the General Convention of 1789 which met in Philadelphia and ratified the constitution, established the prayer book and adopted the necessary canons. Bishop Seabury died at New London, Conn., in 1796.

BIRTHDAY OF JACOB ABBOTT

Jacob Abbott, a Congregational clergyman and the most popular writer of children's books of his generation, was born at Hallowell, Me., on November 14, 1803. He was graduated from Bowdoin College in 1820, and the next year taught in the Portland Academy where Longfellow was one of his pupils. He was on the faculty of Amherst college for four years until 1828 when he opened a school for young women in Boston. After preaching for a few years he opened a school in New York City which he directed until 1851, after which he devoted the remainder of his life to travel and writing. He had, however, begun to write many years earlier. His first book, *The Young Christian*, was published in England in 1832, and translated into French and Dutch. In 1834 he began the publication of the "Rollo Books" of which he wrote twenty-eight volumes. They took Rollo through a long series of activities described in a simple and entertaining manner while moral precepts were interspersed throughout the narrative. Boys and girls read them for the story and probably absorbed unconsciously some of the moral lessons. Abbott died on October 31, 1879.

NOVEMBER FIFTEENTH

THE FIRST CONSTITUTION

Soon after the Continental Congress adopted the Declaration of Independence in 1776 a committee reported to the Congress a draft of the Articles of Confederation. It was not until November 15, 1777, that the articles were finally adopted and submitted to the states for ratification. The record in the *Journal of the Congress* notes:

A copy of the confederation being made out and sundry small amendments made in the diction, without altering the sense, the same was agreed to as follows: Articles of Confederation and Perpetual Union, between the States

Then follow the names of the thirteen states preceding the text of the document. It contains many of the provisions which were later put in the constitution drafted by the convention of 1787, the preamble of which recites that it is made "in order to form a more perfect union."

597

This means that the conditions of the "perpetual union," set up by the Articles of Confederation were not wholly satisfactory and needed revision. The Continental Congress provided for what came later to be called "an indissoluble union of sovereign states," but it took the Civil War to demonstrate that the Constitution of 1787 was intended to provide for such a union.

NOVEMBER SIXTEENTH

FEAST OF ST. EDMUND

St. Edmund, archbishop of Canterbury, is honored by both the Roman and Anglican churches. Several American churches have been named for him. He was born at Abingdon, near Oxford, in England in about 1175. His father was a merchant of Oxford and a very devout man. Edmund began his education in the grammar school at Oxford and later went to Paris with his brother to study the liberal arts, and was graduated there. For six years he lectured on the liberal arts at Paris and at Oxford. He is said to be the first who lectured on Aristotle at Oxford, where he soon became a theological lecturer noted for his eloquence. He gave his fees and the revenues from several benefices to charity. In 1222 he became the treasurer of Salisbury Cathedral and in 1227 he was appointed to preach the Crusade in England. He was favorably regarded in Rome, so favorably in fact, that Pope Gregory IX insisted on his election as Archbishop of Canterbury over the objections of the monks attached to the cathedral. As archbishop he opposed the use of foreign councillors by the King, until the King and a papal legate who was sent to England at the royal solicitation, deprived the archbishop of his authority. He unsuccessfully resisted what he regarded as the encroachments of the papal authority in England and finally withdrew to Pontigny. Because of his poor health he later went to Soissy where he died on November 16, 1240. His admirers at once demanded his canonization, but it was not until 1247 that Pope Innocent IV raised him to sainthood and fixed the day of his death as the date for his feast.

NOVEMBER SEVENTEENTH

CONGRESS FINDS A PERMANENT HOME

The Congress of the United States had no definitely fixed abode until 1800. It first met at Philadelphia, the largest city in the country, but for various reasons and at various times it was compelled to abandon that city and sat at York and Lancaster, Pa., at Princeton, N.J. and at

Baltimore and Annapolis, Md. It was sitting at New York when Washington was inaugurated in 1789, but not long afterward returned to Philadelphia. That city expected to be the permanent seat of the government and it built a President's house, but eventually it was arranged to move the national capitol south to the banks of the Potomac. Congress adjourned its last session in Philadelphia on May 20, 1800. The seat of government was moved to Washington early in June and Congress held its first session there on November 17. Only the north wing of the Capitol had been completed and the Treasury Building was the only public structure ready for the occupancy of the executive departments. Since then the Capitol has been enlarged and monumental structures have been erected for the use of the various departments of the government.

NOVEMBER EIGHTEENTH

BIRTHDAY OF ASA GRAY

Asa Gray, whose textbooks on botany were standard for many years, was born at Paris Furnace, N.Y., on November 18, 1810, the son of a tanner. He studied medicine in a physician's office and obtained the degree of doctor of medicine in 1831. He became acquainted with John Torrey, a distinguished botanist in New York city, who obtained for him in 1836 the position of curator of the New York Lyceum of Natural History. In the same year he published his *Elements of Botany*, the first of a remarkable series. Two years later he was appointed professor of natural history in the University of Michigan, but he never occupied the post. After spending some time in Europe studying botany he was appointed Fisher professor of natural history at Harvard University which he soon made the center of botanical instruction in the United States. He was the founder of the famous Harvard herbarium. For ten years he was president of the American Academy of Arts and Sciences. He was one of the early supporters of Darwin's theory of natural selection and defended it against those who insisted that it was contrary to the teachings of the Bible.

NOVEMBER NINETEENTH

BIRTHDAY OF JAMES A. GARFIELD

James Abram Garfield, the twentieth President of the United States, was born in Cuyahoga County, Ohio, on November 19, 1831. His father was Abram Garfield, descended from an ancestor who came to Massachusetts in 1630 with John Winthrop, the first governor of the colony. Abram Garfield moved from New England to Ohio in 1827 and obtained a contract for construction work on the Ohio Canal. He soon bought a farm and built a cabin upon it, and it was in this cabin that his son James was born. He died in 1833, leaving to his widow the responsibility of rearing his family of four children of whom James was the youngest. When James was old enough he began to work on the farm and remained there until he was seventeen. He then was hired to drive horses on the towpath of the Ohio Canal in the construction of which his father had been engaged. The next year he entered Geauga Seminary at Chester, Ohio, and in 1851 he transferred his studies to the Western Reserve Eclectic Institute at Hiram, now known as Hiram College, and prepared for Williams College from which he was graduated in 1856. He was employed as a teacher in the institute at Hiram immediately after his graduation and was soon elected as its president. The institute was under the patronage of the Disciples Church of which he was a member and a lay teacher. In 1858 he began the study of law and was admitted to the bar in 1861.

He had been active in the Republican campaign of 1856 and in 1859 was elected to the State Senate. When the Civil War began he assisted in raising the Forty-second Ohio Volunteer Infantry Regiment and although he had no military experience he was made its lieutenant colonel and then colonel. By study of the military manual he mastered his duties and turned his recruits into soldiers. He had demonstrated his efficiency so well that a few days after his regiment joined the army of Major General Buell in Kentucky he was put in command of a brigade. By January 1862, he had risen to the rank of brigadier of volunteers. In the following winter he sat in the court in Washington which inquired into the charges against Fitz-John Porter, and in the spring of 1863 he was sent to join the army of General Rosecrans, and was made chief of staff. He showed great courage in the Battle of Chickamauga in September 1863, and for his bravery was promoted to the rank of major general of volunteers.

He was nominated to represent the Nineteenth Ohio District in the national House of Representatives and elected while in the field. At the solicitation of President Lincoln he resigned from the army and took his seat in Congress in December 1863. His service in the House was distinguished and he early became one of its leaders. He was re-elected every two years until 1879 when he was elected to the Senate. He never took his seat in the Senate, however, as he was nominated for President by the Republican National Convention in 1880. The leading aspirants in the convention were Blaine, Grant and John Sherman. Garfield was the leader of the Sherman delegation and made the nominating speech which became famous as a splendid piece of political oratory. When it was evident after the roll has been called thirty-four times that it was impossible to nominate Blaine, Grant or Sherman, sixteen of the twenty Wisconsin delegates voted for Garfield on the thirty-fifth roll call and on the next there was a stampede to him and he was named unanimously. Garfield has been criticised for accepting the nomination under the circumstances. He was elected in November with a small plurality of the popular vote but with a majority of fifty-nine electors.

The wing of the party which had sought the nomination of Grant, a wing led by Senator Roscoe Conkling of New York, became hostile to him because he did not consult it regarding the appointments to be made. The appointment of a collector for the port of New York was especially distasteful to Conkling and when Garfield refused to yield to his demands Senator Conkling and his colleague, Thomas C. Platt, resigned and appealed to the Legislature of the State for reelection to vindicate them. There was a bitter contest in the legislature which resulted in their defeat. This struggle over the distribution of patronage is said to have incited Charles J. Guiteau, a disappointed office seeker, to shoot Garfield on July 2, 1881, while the President was waiting in a Washington railroad station for a train to take him to a reunion at Williams College. After being nursed for eleven weeks in the White House without favorable results he was removed to Elberton, N.J., where he died on September 19.

His body was taken to Washington where it lay in state in the rotunda of the Capitol on September 22. There were impressive funeral ceremonies on the next day. The body was then taken to Cleveland, where after lying in state for a day beneath a pavilion in Monument Park, it was escorted on September 26 by a military and civic procession to Lake View Cemetery and placed in a vault to await the erection of a suitable memorial on the lot set apart for it. The day was observed throughout the country as a day of mourning, and a number of European royal courts ordered the observance of a period of mourning for the death of the President. This was said to have been the first time that such respect had been shown to the memory of the head of a republic. A year or two later the Garfield Republican Club of the Nineteenth Ohio Congressional district began to hold an annual dinner in his memory on the anniversary of his birth and continued it for more than twenty-five years.

DEDICATION OF THE NATIONAL CEMETERY AT GETTYSBURG

The battle of Gettysburg, Pa., on July 1, 2 and 3, 1863, marked the defeat of the efforts of the Confederates to invade the North. Approximately 160,000 men were engaged in the battle, about half on each side. The total of killed, wounded and prisoners taken was about 45,000, of which 5750 were killed. The Union and Confederate dead were buried on the field, but the Confederate dead were later removed to a cemetery in Richmond. There are 3654 graves of Union Soldiers at Gettysburg. Soon after the battle it was decided to make the burying ground a National Cemetery, and it was dedicated as such on November

19, 1863. The speakers at the dedicatory ceremonies were President Lincoln and Edward Everett of Massachusetts, a distinguished orator. Mr. Everett delivered a long oration but Mr. Lincoln made only the following brief speech of about three hundred words, which has come to be regarded as a classic:

> Four score and seven years ago our fathers brought forth on this continent a new nation, conceived in liberty and dedicated to the proposition that all men are created equal. Now we are engaged in a great civil war, testing whether that nation, or any nation so conceived and so dedicated, can long endure. We are met on a battlefield of that war. We have come to dedicate a portion of that field as a final resting place for those who gave their lives that the nation might live. It is altogether fitting and proper that we should do this. But, in a larger sense, we cannot dedicate—we cannot consecrate—we cannot hallow—this ground. The brave men, living and dead, who struggled here have consecrated it far above our poor power to add or detract. The world will little note, nor long remember what we say here, but it can never forget what they did here. It is for us, the living, rather to be dedicated here to the unfinished work which they who fought here have thus far so nobly advanced. It is rather for us to be here dedicated to the great task remaining before us—that from these honored dead we take increased devotion to that cause for which they gave the last full measure of devotion—that we here highly resolve that these dead shall not have died in vain—that this nation, under God, shall have a new birth of freedom and that government of the people, by the people, for the people, shall not perish from the earth.

The National Cemetery covers seventeen acres. A tract of thirty-eight square miles, however, which includes the battlefield, has been bought and is preserved as a park. It is adorned with monuments to the commanders of the Union armies and to the various regiments engaged in the battle. In 1934 there were 851 such memorials along with more than 400 cannon of the kind used in the battle. It is visited by thousands of persons every year and students of military tactics make frequent excursions to the battlefield to study the strategy of the two armies.

The fiftieth anniversary of the dedication of the cemetery was celebrated throughout the country in 1913. The most elaborate exercises were those held in Illinois, the state from which Lincoln was elected to the presidency. At Springfield the exercises were in charge of the Illinois Historical Society, and were held in the State Capitol. Governor Dunne presided and delivered an address. Other addresses were made by the State Superintendent of Public Instruction and the president of the Historical Society. Among those present were many veterans of the Civil War who had heard Lincoln speak at the dedication ceremony. They signed their names in a register in the library of the Historical Society. The Superintendent of Public Instruction had asked the teachers in all the public schools to have the pupils learn the address and recite it at exercises in the schools during the day, and it is estimated that a million children took part in these exercises. At the University of Illinois in Urbana the "President's Hymn" written by Dr. William A. Muhlenberg in 1863 and dedicated to Lincoln, was sung, the prayer dedicating the cemetery and the peroration of Edward Everett's address were read and the university band played Chopin's Funeral March. In Chicago the anniversary was observed by the Chicago Historical Society, the Chicago Association of Commerce and other organizations. (See July 1, Battle of Gettysburg.)

NOVEMBER TWENTIETH

FIRST NATIONAL G.A.R. ENCAMPMENT

The Grand Army of the Republic, composed of men who had served in the United States army, navy and marine corps during the Civil War, held its first national encampment at Indianapolis, Ind., on November 20, 1866. The organization had been formed at Decatur, Ill., in the preceding April through the efforts of Dr. B. F. Stephenson and W. J. Rutledge of the Fourteenth Illinois Infantry Regiment. Its purpose was to strengthen the fraternal feeling among those who had served under the flag, to perpetuate the memory of those who had died and to assist their widows and orphans. In 1869 its convention adopted the rule that the organization should not be used for partisan purposes, partisan discussion or political manipulation. Its members, however, fell into the habit of supporting for public office veterans of the war and the politicians of the time catered to the "soldier vote." Its membership grew until in 1890 it was more than four hundred thousand. The observance of Memorial Day on May 30 originated with the Grand Army of the Republic.

NOVEMBER TWENTY-FIRST

INVENTION OF THE PHONOGRAPH

Although the principle on which instruments for recording and reproducing human speech was known as early as 1855 it was not until Thomas A. Edison announced on November 21, 1877, that he had invented a phonograph that there was a practical application of it. Edison's first crude device consisted of a funnel with a diaphragm at its base, to which a pointed needle was attached. This was connected with a threaded cylinder around which tinfoil was wrapped and the funnel was adjusted so that by turning a crank it would move in such a way as to allow the needle to run in the threads of the cylinder. When one spoke into the funnel and turned the crank the needle made indentations in the tinfoil corresponding to the sounds of the voice. Then the funnel could be moved back to the place from which it started and by turning the crank again the words uttered would be reproduced. They were husky and rather indistinct, but they demonstrated that the problem of mechanical reproduction of human speech had been solved. Since then the device has been perfected so that the natural quality of the voice is preserved, and music and all other sounds can be recorded and reproduced at pleasure. The business of making records and instruments for reproducing them expanded to large proportions. The voices of distinguished men and women in public speech and song have been preserved in records so that future generations may hear them.

NOVEMBER TWENTY-SECOND

FEAST OF ST. CECELIA

St. Cecelia, whose feast is celebrated on November 22, is one of the best known and most venerated of the Christian saints. She is the patroness of church music. She is credited with inventing the organ and is frequently represented in art as sitting at an organ surrounded by angels.

St. Cecelia, the daughter of a noble Roman family, became a Christian in her early childhood. When she was of marriageable age she was bethrothed to Valerian, a youth who was not yet a Christian. According to her legend she converted him on their wedding night by telling him that she was betrothed to an angel who jealously guarded her body. Valerian asked to see the angel and she sent him to the Appian Way where he met Pope Urban, who baptized him. Valerian returned to his bride, and according to the legend, an angel appeared and crowned the two with roses. She was later ordered to offer sacrifices to idols and when she refused she was condemned to death by suffocation in an overheated bath. But she did not die, and the efforts of an executioner to behead her also failed. She survived three days and was buried ultimately in a church in Rome. Her name appears in the records of the church in the fourth century and about the middle of the fifth century the story of her martyrdom began to be written. When the Academy of Music was founded in Rome in 1584 she was made its patroness. There are musical associations in the United States as well as in Europe named for her. Imaginary portraits of her have been painted by Raphael, Domenichino, Carlo Dolci and many others.

NOVEMBER TWENTY-THIRD

BIRTHDAY OF FRANKLIN PIERCE

Franklin Pierce (pronounced Purse), fourteenth President of the United States, was born at Hillsborough, N.H., on November 23, 1804. He was the son of Benjamin Pierce, a farmer who had held several public offices including that of governor of the state. His father sent him to Bowdoin College from which he was graduated in 1824, one year ahead of Nathaniel Hawthorne and Henry Wadsworth Longfellow. He studied law in Portsmouth, N.H., and Northampton, Mass., and was admitted to the bar in his native county in 1827. Two years later he was elected to the New Hampshire legislature and his father was chosen governor for the second time at the same election. He served four terms and was Speaker of the House in 1831 and 1832. He was elected to the national House of Representatives in 1833, and four years later to the United States Senate.

He was a Jacksonian Democrat but was opposed to internal improvements. He was also a nationalist and believed in the perpetuation of the Union. His salary as a senator, on which he was dependent, was not large enough to meet his expenses and he resigned from the Senate in 1842 and joined his family in Concord. He practiced law there for the next ten years and won a reputation as a successful pleader before juries. During this period he managed most of the Democratic campaigns in the state. President Polk appointed him Federal District Attorney for New Hampshire and in 1946 asked him to become Attorney General in his Cabinet. Pierce declined the honor and also refused to accept appointment as United States Senator.

He enlisted as a private in the Mexican War but when he was called up in 1847 he was appointed colonel and then promoted to the rank of brigadier general. He led an army from Vera Cruz to reinforce General Scott in his attack upon the Mexican capital. Illness prevented him from active participation in the capture of the city. At the end of the war he resigned from the army and resumed the practice of law and his participation in political affairs. He supported the fugitive slave law, an attitude which attracted attention in the South.

Levi Woodbury was regarded by the New Hampshire Democrats as an available candidate for President, but he died in 1851 and the party leaders in the state began to talk of Pierce as his successor to be proposed to the National Convention. So far as appeared on the surface the Democrats in other parts of the country did not take his aspirations seriously. They were divided in their support of Buchanan, Douglas, Marcy and Cass. James W. Bradbury, a United States Senator from Maine, aware of the unwillingness of the supporters of these men to yield, planned to bring Pierce forth as a compromise candidate. The convention, which met in Baltimore on June 1, 1852, adopted the two-thirds rule. The roll was called thirty-five times with little change in the vote for the contending candidates none of whom received the necessary two thirds. On the thirty-fifth roll call Pierce had fifteen votes. He received fifteen more on the next vote. On the forty-ninth roll call, however, there was a stampede to him and all but six votes were cast for him. In the election he received two hundred and fifty-four electoral votes to forty-two for General Winfield Scott, the Whig candidate.

As President he sought to conciliate the Northern and Southern wings of his party by dividing the offices between them. He used the surplus in the treasury to reduce the national debt and he urged a reduction in the tariff to prevent the accumulation of another surplus. He planned the annexation of Cuba and negotiations were begun for the acquisition of Hawaii and for a naval base in Santo Domingo, and Russia was asked whether she would sell Alaska. He directed Pierre Soule, the minister to Spain, to consult with James Buchanan and John Y. Mason, American ministers to Great Britain and France respectively, about the annexation of Cuba. They met at Ostend in October 1854, supposedly in secret, and signed a report known as the Ostend Manifesto, to the effect that as France and Great Britain were occupied with the Crimean War the time might be opportune for acquiring Cuba. The nature of the report leaked out and strong opposition to the annexation of Cuba developed in the North. Consequently the project fell through. Nothing was accomplished regarding Alaska, Hawaii or Santo Domingo. Pierce had difficulties also in Kansas and Nebraska which alienated some of his supporters. He hoped to be nominated to succeed himself, but his party named James Buchanan, who had been out of the country during the controversies over the extension of slavery.

On his retirement Pierce made a tour of Europe. When the Civil War broke out he supported the administration mildly at first but was soon criticizing the policies of President Lincoln, and became unpopular even in his own state. He died on October 8, 1869. The estimation in which he was held by his critics is revealed by a contemporary punning comment on his name:

He may be a big purse in New Hampshire, but he is a pretty slim purse when spread over the whole country.

REPUDIATION OF THE STAMP ACT

On November 23, 1765, the court of Frederick County, Maryland, ordered that its business should be carried on without the use of the stamped paper required by the Stamp Act. This anniversary has been celebrated for many years in Frederick, the capital of the county. A tablet has been set up in the Court House commemorating the action of the men who refused to recognize the validity of the law. Each year the Daughters of the American Revolution meet in the Court House on or about November 23, when the original decision is formally read by the clerk of the Circuit Court. The by-laws of the Sergeant Lawrence Everhart Chapter of the Sons of the Revolution of Frederick provide that the chapter shall meet annually on the anniversary and celebrate the courageous act of the court of the county.

Revenues had long been raised in England through the sale of stamps to be affixed to various documents and papers and commodities.

Early in the eighteenth century Sir William Keith, who had been Governor of Pennsylvania, proposed to the King that these stamp duties be extended to the colonies.

Disregarding various warnings concerning the attitude of the colonists, Parliament passed the Stamp Act which was approved by the King on March 22, 1765, to become effective on November 1. The act levied a stamp tax of from three pence to ten shillings on legal papers. College diplomas were taxed two pounds, charters issued by the governors, six pounds; licenses to sell wine, four pounds; deeds, from two to five shillings; playing cards, one shilling a pack; and pairs of dice, ten shillings. Printed papers of a single sheet had to pay a tax of a penny for every copy and the tax was larger for printed papers of more than one sheet and every advertisement in a newspaper had to pay a tax of one shilling.

Protests against the act were made in many cities and plans were adopted to cease trading with England until the act was repealed. The act was printed in New York with a death's head at the top instead of the royal arms. Patrick Henry, a young member of the Virginia General Assembly, denounced the act most bitterly and obtained the adoption of a resolution declaring that:

> The General Assembly of the colony have the sole right and power to lay taxes and impositions upon the inhabitants of this colony and that every attempt to vest such powers in any person or persons whatsoever other than the General Assembly aforesaid has a manifest tendency to destroy British as well as American freedom.

Although this resolution was expunged from the record on the day after its adoption, the news of it spread throughout the country and the sentiments that it contained were echoed generally. The aroused people in many places destroyed the stamps which came from England and many courts following the example of the court of Frederick County ruled against their use on legal papers.

The British became alarmed at the vigor of the protest and a bill for the repeal of the act was introduced in Parliament. Benjamin Franklin, who was in London as the American agent, was summoned before the House of Commons, sitting as a committee, on January 28, 1766, to explain the attitude of the colonies. He was asked if the act could be executed with the help of a military force and replied that it could not be, for the military force would find no one in arms and could not compel people to take the stamps who refused to use them. "They will not find rebellion," he explained, "they may make one."

The act was finally repealed in March 1766, but the spirit of revolt which had been aroused was not calmed and it reached its culmination on July 4, 1776, with the adoption of the Declaration of Independence.

FEAST OF ST. CLEMENT

The feast of St. Clement, who is Clement I in the list of the Popes, is celebrated by the Roman and the English churches. By some authorities he is said to have been the third Pope. Others, with better evidence, say that he was the fourth. It has been assumed that he is the person referred to by Paul in his letter to the Philippians in which he wrote:

> And I entreat thee also, true yokefellow, help those women which labored with me in the gospel, with Clement also, and with my other fellow laborers, whose names are in the book of life.

But this is doubted, as St. Clement is supposed to have been a Roman and not a resident of Philippi. There is extant a letter which he wrote to the church at Corinth which is supposed to contain evidence that he was a Jew. And there is a theory that he was the son of a freedman in the household of the Emperor Domitian. But this is all conjecture, for almost nothing is known of his life and death.

There is an apochryphal account of his martyrdom giving traditions about him, but this is not older than the third century. It tells of his banishment by Trajan to the Crimea, of his quenching the thirst of two thousand Christians by a miracle, of the conversion of the people, and the building of seventy-five churches. In the ninth century St. Cyril, on his way to the Crimea, discovered some bones together with an anchor. These were believed to be the bones of St. Clement and were taken to Rome and deposited in the high altar of the basilica of St. Clement. The presence of the anchor with the bones recalled another tradition about the martyrdom of the saint. According to this tradition Clement was condemned to death for providing water for the thirsty workers in a quarry to which he had been sentenced by Trajan. An anchor was tied to him and he was thrown into the sea. When the Christians prayed the waters of the sea retreated revealing a shrine in which his body was resting, still tied to the anchor. For many years, according to the tradition, the waters receded on the anniversary of his death and remained so for three days. Because of this tradition he is represented in Christian art with an anchor.

NOVEMBER TWENTY-FOURTH

BIRTHDAY OF ZACHARY TAYLOR

Zachary Taylor, twelfth President of the United States, was born in Orange County, Virginia, on November 24, 1784. There have been conflicting statements about the year and the month of his birth. Old books say that he was born in 1790 and some say it was on September 24, others on November 24. The issue was settled beyond dispute when a committee planning for the celebration of the one hundred and fiftieth anniversary of his birth found in the manuscript division of the Library of Congress an autobiographical sketch in Taylor's own handwriting in which he said: "I was born in Orange County, State of Virginia, November 24, 1784."

He was the son of Colonel Richard Taylor, an officer in the Revolutionary War, and one of the first settlers in Louisville, Ky., then a part of Virginia, to which he moved when Zachary was a small child. Young Taylor lived in Louisville until his twenty-fourth year, working on a plantation, and receiving only an elementary education. When an elder brother, who had received a commission as a lieutenant in the army, died in 1808, Zachary was appointed to the vacant commission. Two years later he was made a captain. In 1812, with fifty men, most of whom were ill, he defended Fort Harrison on the Wabash against a large force of Indians led by Tecumseh. He was made a major in recognition of his gallantry on this occasion. During the War of 1812 he was employed in fighting the Indian allies of Great Britain. In 1822 he built Fort Jessup and from 1832 to 1836 his headquarters were at Fort Crawford, Wis. After an important victory over the Seminoles in Florida he was made a brigadier general, and put in command of the United States forces in Florida. On his appointment to the command of the Southwestern Department in 1840 he bought a plantation near Baton Rouge, La. In 1846 when the United States declared war on Mexico and fifty thousand volunteers were called for, General Taylor was ordered to invade Mexico. On September 9 with six thousand six hundred men he attacked Monterey, defended by about ten thousand regular troops of the Mexican army and won a victory. This and other brilliant military achievements created great enthusiasm throughout the country and the Whig politicians, who had begun a year before to talk of him as a candidate for President, became still more enthusiastic in urging him upon their party. General Taylor had at first been reluctant to allow his party to consider him for its candidate. On July 18, 1846, he wrote from Matamoras, Mexico, to General T. Young of Newcastle, Del.:

Your remarks in relation to my being a candidate for the presidency are very flattering, but I think you will know without the necessity of saying so to you, that I am not and never shall be an aspirant for that honor. My opinion has always been against the elevation of a military chief to that position.

Yet he was nominated by the Whigs in 1848 and was elected. He received one hundred and sixty-three electoral votes to one hundred and twenty-seven for Lewis Cass, the Democratic candidate.

When he took office on March 4, 1849, the Whigs were in the minority in Congress with the balance of power between them and the Democrats held by the Free Soil party. The short period during which he served—he died on July 9, 1850—was filled with discussions about the Mexican boundary, the admission of California as a state and the extension of slavery.

At the time of his death, among the eulogies delivered outside of Congress was one by Abraham Lincoln, whose term as a member of the

House of Representatives had expired with the inauguration of President Taylor. Among other things Lincoln said:

I cannot help thinking that the American people in electing General Taylor to the presidency, thereby showed their high appreciation of his sterling, but unobtrusive qualities, did their country a service and themselves an imperishable honor. It is much for the young to know that treading the hard path of duty as he treaded will be noticed and will lead to high places.

When the one hundred and fiftieth anniversary of President Taylor's birth approached, the Southern Society of New York and the people of Virginia began to plan for its observance. A committee was appointed of which President Franklin D. Roosevelt was honorary chairman, Governor George C. Perry of Virginia, chairman ex officio, and Hugh Gordon Miller of New York the general chairman. It arranged a dinner at the Waldorf Astoria Hotel in New York on November 24, 1934, presided over by Eugene W. Stetson, president of the Southern Society. The principal speaker was Josiah W. Bailey, United States Senator from North Carolina, who was introduced by John W. Davis, at one time Democratic candidate for President. Archibald W. Watson, a great-nephew of President Taylor, presented in behalf of the society its gold medal to Hugh Gordon Miller, in recognition of what he had done to honor Taylor.

NOVEMBER TWENTY-FIFTH

FEAST OF ST. CATHERINE

Of the six saints known by the name of Catherine, St. Catherine of Alexandria and St. Catherine of Siena are probably the best known (see Feast of St. Catherine of Siena, April 30). Catherine of Alexandria whose feast is celebrated on November 25, is usually known without any explanatory phrase. She was born in the latter part of the fourth century, the daughter of noble parents at Alexandria, and early espoused Christianity. When she was only eighteen years old she appeared before the Emperor Maximus II who was persecuting the Christians, and sought to convince him that it was iniquitous to compel persons to worship false gods. According to legend the emperor called on his learned men to argue with her. They failed to prove her reasoning unsound and several of them declared themselves Christians, and were at once put to death. The emperor, furious at the outcome, ordered that she be scourged and imprisoned. The empress, interested in the courageous young woman, went to the prison with the head of the army. Catherine converted both of them and they were put to death. The emperor then ordered her to be slain by torture on the wheel, but a stroke of lightning severed the cords by which she was bound, and killed the executioner and several of the bystanders. As she survived the lightning she was beheaded, and the tradition says, her body was carried to Mt. Sinai by angels where a church and monastery were later built in her honor. In the Middle Ages her feast was celebrated with more elaborate ceremonies than the feasts of the apostles and for six centuries she was one of the most venerated saints of the church. She is usually represented in Christian art with the wheel to which she had been bound. The piece of fireworks called the Catherine wheel is named in allusion to her. She is the patroness of wheelwrights and mechanics. As she remained a virgin she is the patroness of schools for girls, and, as she confuted the arguments of the idolaters summoned by Maximus, she is regarded with veneration by theologians and philosophers. She is said to have appeared to Joan of Arc and to have become her divine adviser.

EVACUATION DAY IN NEW YORK

The celebration of the anniversary of the evacuation of New York by the British on November 25, 1783, is not so elaborate as it once was when the event was fresher in the minds of the people. Arrangements for the evacuation were made by General Washington and Governor Clinton in a conference with Sir Guy Carleton, the British commander. On the morning of November 25 the American troops, under General Knox, encamped at Harlem, marched down to the present junction of Third avenue and the Bowery. They remained there until one o'clock in the afternoon, as the British insisted that they were not to leave until noon. By that hour the British had embarked at Whitehall, Sir Guy Carleton sailing for England, and before three o'clock General Knox took possession of the city, welcomed by the cheers of the people. A salute was fired at the Battery. Governor Clinton gave a dinner to General Washington and the other officers of the army at Fraunce's Tavern. In the evening the city was brilliantly illuminated, with bonfires blazing at the corners of the streets. Many citizens sent up rockets from their houses.

The event was commemorated annually for many years with elaborate ceremonies. Bouck White, in *The Book of Daniel Drew*, makes his hero describe a celebration in the 1830's. Drew was then proprietor of the New Bulls Head Tavern on the Boston Post Road, at what is now Third Avenue and Twenty-third Street. Mr. White makes him say:

On such a holiday as Evacuation Day when the people celebrated the evacuation of the city by the British troops in the War of the Revolution my house would be filled with young drovers and farm hands come in to see the sights. Sometimes I would put three in a bed and also stow some away in the barn to sleep in the haymow. These celebrations were something worth seeing. There would be a parade in the morning by mounted and foot soldiers, artillery, the fire companies, the Tammany Society, target companies and such like. At these times the City Hall Park, which had a great iron fence around it, would be surrounded by booths where they sold roast pig, cider, eggnog and spruce beer. The day would close with a display of fireworks.

611

NOVEMBER 26

The Old Guard, a historic military organization, observes the day by parading to the Battery, raising a flag and firing a salute. This demonstration is usually followed by a dinner, at which patriotic addresses are made, often held at Fraunce's Tavern where Governor Clinton entertained the officers of the army on the afternoon of the day when the city was evacuated. The Empire State Society of the Sons of the American Revolution also has an occasional celebration in the form of a dinner on the evening of Evacuation Day. In 1933 the one hundred and fiftieth anniversary was observed by the Sons of the American Revolution, and the Connecticut and New York chapters of the Society of the Cincinnati.

NOVEMBER TWENTY-SIXTH

JOHN HARVARD DAY

It has been the custom of the authorities of the Harvard Memorial Society of Harvard University in Cambridge, Mass., to decorate the statue of John Harvard, the first benefactor of the college, on the anniversary of his birth ever since the statue was put in place in 1884. Arrangements for designing and erecting this statue were made in 1883. They were described by Joseph H. Choate in an address at the alumni dinner at the commencement exercises in that year as follows:

It is now 245 years since John Harvard died in Charlestown, bequeathing his fair name, his library and the half of his estate to the infant college in the wilderness, then just struggling into existence and matriculating its first freshman class of nine. He surely moulded better than he knew. He died all unconscious of the immortality of glory that awaited him, for it was not until after his death that the General Court voted, in recognition of his generous gifts, to change the name of the little college at Newtowne to Harvard College. And now, after eight generations of graduates have been baptized in his name, a pious worshipper at his shrine, turning his face toward Mecca, has presented to the alumni a bronze statue of our prophetic founder, which is to be erected at the head of the delta, and to stand for coming ages as the guardian of the genius of the college. Let me read the letter which precedes the gift; and I will say that the writer and the giver, a gentlemen here present, from whom and of whom I hope we shall hear more by and by, is Mr. Samuel J. Bridge of Boston. The letter is as follows:

To the President and Fellows of Harvard College:

Gentlemen:—I have had the pleasure of offering you an ideal statue in bronze, representing your founder, the Reverend John Harvard, to be designed by Daniel C. French of Concord, and to be placed in the west end of the enclosure in which Memorial Hall stands. If you do me the honor to accept this offer, I promise to contract at once for the work, including an appropriate pedestal, and I am assured that the statue can be in place by June 1, 1884.

I am sure, gentlemen, that I can assure the generous donor in your name of the hearty thanks of all the alumni of the college, those who are here today and those who are scattered throughout the country and the world.

The statue was unveiled with appropriate exercises on October 15, 1884. This is not the first memorial to Harvard erected by the alumni, for in 1828 they raised a granite shaft over his grave in the burying ground in Charlestown, Mass.

612

The celebration of the anniversary of his birth varies in elaborateness from year to year. On the three hundredth anniversary, in 1907, the exercises were especially notable. The exact date of the birth is not known, but there is a record of the baptism on November 29, 1607. It is assumed that he was born at least three days earlier, as it was the custom to postpone baptism for three days after a child was born. November 26 is, therefore, regarded as the probable date. The celebration of its tercentenary began with a memorial service in Appleton Chapel in the morning. Addresses were made by Professor Francis G. Peabody, D.D., on "John Harvard's Religion," and by the Reverend Lyman Abbott, D.D., on "The Church and the College." In the evening there was a dinner, given by the Harvard Memorial Society in Memorial Hall. It was attended by more than five hundred alumni representing the Harvard clubs in all parts of the country. Charles W. Eliot, president of the college, presided. Addresses were made by many distinguished persons, including the Right Reverend William Lawrence, Protestant Episcopal Bishop of Massachusetts, and Sir Courtney Peregrine Ilbert, clerk of the British House of Commons. A poetic tribute to the founder was read by Professor LeBaron R. Briggs, dean of the college. Here is the first stanza:

> Yes, thou art known; we feel we see thee near us.
> Though Art be blind, though History be dumb.
> Down through the centuries thou com'st to cheer us
> Even as of old the saints of God have come.

Three days later, on November 29, the students celebrated by a torch light procession so that if perchance Harvard were born on that date its three hundredth anniversary might not pass without appropriate recognition.

John Harvard, whose father was a builder, was born in Southwark, London, and was graduated from Emmanuel College, Cambridge, in 1635. He was ordained as a dissenting minister and in 1637 started for New England. He became a freeman of Massachusetts on November 2 of that year. He preached in Charlestown and died on September 3, 1638, only about a year after his arrival in this country. His will disposed of an estate of £1500, a considerable sum in those days. Half of this along with his library he left to endow a school for the education of the youth of the colony. On this foundation has been built the great institution now known as Harvard University.

NOVEMBER TWENTY-SEVENTH

THANKSGIVING DAY

Thanksgiving Day, as a national religious festival celebrated on the same day throughout the country, dates from 1863. The credit for bringing this about is usually given to Mrs. Sarah J. Hale. In 1827, while editor of the *Ladies' Magazine* in Boston, she began to urge the observance of a uniform day throughout the country for the expression of thanks for the blessings of the year. She continued her agitation in a desultory manner until the *Ladies' Magazine* was consolidated with *Godey's Lady's Book* of Philadelphia. As editor of *Godey's* she wrote editorial after editorial in support of the plan. She also wrote personal letters to the governors of all the states and to the President and succeeded in persuading many governors to fix the last Thursday in November as a day of thanksgiving. Her editorials supplemented her letters and served to create public sentiment in favor of the proposed arrangement. *Godey's Lady's Book,* under her editorship, had a circulation of 150,000, the largest of any periodical of any kind in the country.

Her last editorial on the subject, printed in the September issue for 1863, is worth preserving outside of the files of the magazine as an example of the kind of propaganda which she used. The title she gave to it was "Our National Thanksgiving." She began it with a text from the Bible, printed in small type, and wrote what might be called a sermon based on the text:

Then he said unto them, Go your way and eat the fat and drink the sweet and send persons unto them for whom nothing is prepared; for this day is holy unto the Lord; neither be ye sorry, for the joy of the Lord is your strength.—Nehemiah, VIII: 10.

Thus commanded the inspired Leader of the Jews when they kept the "Feast of Weeks"; in a time of national darkness and sore troubles shall we not recognize that the goodness of God never faileth, and that to our Father in heaven we should always bring the Thanksgiving offering at the ingathering of the harvest?

Wise lawgivers and great patriots have acknowledged the salutary effect of appointed times for national reunions which combine religious sentiment with domestic and social enjoyment; thus feelings of benevolence are awakened and gratitude to the giver of all the blessings is seen to be the great duty of life. Owing to the different economy of different churches among Protestant denominations, except the Christian Sabbath, all our religious commemorations are partial and local.

Can we not then, following the appointment of Jehovah in the "Feast of Weeks," or Harvest Festival, establish our yearly Thanksgiving as a permanent American National Festival which shall be celebrated on the last Thursday in November in every State of the Union? Indeed, it has been nearly accomplished. For the last twelve or fourteen years the States have made approaches to this unity. In 1859 thirty States held their Thanksgiving Festival on the same day— the last Thursday in November. It was also celebrated that year on board several of the American fleets—ships in the Indian ocean, the Mediterranean and on the Brazil station; by the Americans in Berlin at our Prussian Embassy; in Paris and in Switzerland; and American missionaries have signified their readiness to unite in the Festival if it should be established on a particular day that can be known as the American Thanksgiving. Then in every quarter of the globe our nationality would be recognized in connection with our gratitude to the Divine Giver of all our blessings. The pious and loving thought that every American was joining in heart with the beloved family at home and with the church to which he belonged, would thrill his soul with the purest feelings of patriotism and the deepest emotions of thankfulness for his religious enjoyments.

Would it not be a great advantage, socially, nationally, religiously, to have the day of our American Thanksgiving positively settled? Putting aside the sectional feelings and local incidents that might be urged by any single State or isolated territory that desired to choose its own time would it not be more noble, more truly American, to become national in unity when we offer to God our tribute of joy and gratitude for the blessings of the year?

Taking this view of the case, would it not be better that the proclamation which appoints Thursday, the 26th of November as the Day of Thanksgiving for the people of the United States of America, should in the first instance emanate from the President of the Republic—to be applied by the Governors of each and every State in acquiescence with the chief executive's advices?

Mrs. Hale had written to President Lincoln as well as to his predecessors, urging the plan upon him and she undoubtedly sent to him a copy of this editorial. At any rate on October 3, 1863, he issued the first national Thanksgiving Proclamation setting apart the last Thursday in November as the day to be observed. The Proclamation reads:

The year that is drawing toward its close has been filled with the blessings of fruitful fields and healthful skies. To these bounties, which are so constantly enjoyed that we are prone to forget the source from which they come, others have been added, which are of so extraordinary a nature that they cannot fail to penetrate and soften the heart which is habitually insensible to the ever watchful providence of almighty God. In the midst of a civil war of unequaled magnitude and severity, which has sometimes seemed to foreign states to invite and provoke their aggressions, peace has been preserved with all nations, order has been maintained, the laws have been respected and obeyed, and harmony has prevailed everywhere except in the theatre of military conflict; while that theater has been greatly contracted by the advancing armies and navies of the Union.

Needful diversions of wealth and strength from the fields of peaceful industry to the national defense have not arrested the plow, the shuttle, or the ship; the ax has enlarged the borders of our settlements, and the mines, as well of iron and coal as of the precious metals, have yielded even more abundantly than heretofore. Population has steadily increased notwithstanding the waste that has been made in the camp, the siege and the battle-field, and the country, rejoicing in the consciousness of augmented strength and vigor, is permitted to expect continuance of years with large increase of freedom.

No human counsel hath devised, nor hath any mortal hand worked out these great things. They are the gracious gifts of the most high God, who, while dealing with us in anger for our sins, hath nevertheless remembered mercy.

It has seemed to me fit and proper that they should be solemnly, reverently and gratefuly acknowledged as with one heart and one voice by the whole American people. I do, therefor, invite my fellow citizens in every part of the United States, and also those who are at sea and those who are sojourning in foreign lands, to set apart and observe the last Thursday of November next as a day of thanksgiving and praise to our beneficent Father who dwelleth in the heavens. And I recommend to them that, while offering up ascriptions justly due to him for such singular deliverances and blessings, they do also, with humble penitence for our national perverseness and disobedience, commend to his tender care all those who have become widows, orphans, mourners or sufferers in the lamentable civil strife in which we are unavoidably engaged, and fervently implore the interposition of the almighty hand to heal the wounds of the nation and to restore it, as soon as may be consistent with the Divine purposes, to the full enjoyment of peace, harmony, tranquility and union.

In the North there was a general response to this proclamation. Services were held in the churches of all denominations on the appointed day and sermons were preached appropriate to the occasion.

Pursuant to a Congressional Joint Resolution, approved by President Roosevelt December 26, 1941, Thanksgiving Day is now the fourth Thursday of November and is observed in every State of the Union and in the District of Columbia. It was originally regarded with almost the same reverence as was shown for Sunday. Religious services were held in the churches and after the services the families gathered around the table at a bounteous dinner at which the principal dish was roast turkey, with pumpkin pie for dessert. It occasionally happened that the church was decorated for the occasion with the products of the farm in order that the members of the congregation might see for themselves that evidence of fruitfulness for which they were to express their thanks. Shocks of corn, sheaves of wheat, pumpkins and apples and the like were massed about the platform and wreathed about the pulpit itself. The religious services are still held in the churches, but it has become a day for sport as well.

An old world custom attached itself to Thanksgiving Day in many eastern cities when the children in the different neighborhoods dressed themselves in clothes of their elders, covered their faces with masks and paraded the streets blowing tin horns. Some of the children solicited money from the people they met or went from house to house with baskets asking for contributions of fruit or vegetables to help them celebrate the day. Their elders usually laid in a stock of oranges, bananas and apples to be ready for the children, and gave them freely to those who came. This custom is said to be a survival of the old Scotch wassail custom of New Year's day transferred to Thanksgiving. On New Year's the poor in Scotland went about the streets with a bowl asking for contributions to help fill it so they might drink "waes hael," or good health, to one another.

While the first national celebration of the day was held in 1863 the first international celebration was held in Washington in 1909. It was conceived by the Rev. Dr. William T. Russell, rector of St. Patrick's Catholic Church in that city, and held in obedience to a request from Cardinal Gibbons. Dr. Russell planned what he called a Pan American celebration to be attended by the representatives of all the Latin-American countries in the national capital. As these countries are Catholic it was natural that a Catholic church should be selected for the celebration. President Taft and members of his Cabinet attended the services along with the diplomatic representatives of the Latin-American Republics. The account of the celebration published by St. Patrick's church says:

> Thanksgiving Day, 1909, will be remembered in the future as the first Pan American Feast Day. As the Secretary of State remarked to the Cardinal, about 90 per cent of all the people on the Western Hemisphere were represented before the altar of St. Patrick's Church. It was the first time in the history of the Western World that all the Republics were assembled for a religious function. It was the first time in the history of the world that twenty-one Republics assisted

together at the Holy Mass. Dr. Russell was cordially congratulated upon the "inspiration," as the Ambassador of Brazil expressed it, of bringing together upon our national feast day the nations of North, Central and South America. For over a year Dr. Russell had in mind such a celebration. . . . In June last he suggested the idea to Mr. John Barrett the Director of the Pan American Bureau. Mr. Barrett was enthusiastic over the proposed celebration, encouraged it and promised his efforts to bring it to a success. . . . When asked what prompted him in planning a Pan American Thanksgiving celebration, Dr. Russell said: "My purpose was to bring into closer relations the Republics of the Western World. As Christianity had first taught the brotherhood of man, it was appropriate that the celebration should take the form of a solemn Mass. For it is at the holy sacrifice that all nations, all languages, all conditions meet on an equal footing of brotherhood. For sixteen centuries the followers of Jesus Christ, go where he might, would be sure to meet the brethren, be their race, nation, color or language what it might, before the altar of the Holy Sacrifice. The Mass, more than any other single influence, has been efficacious in teaching and developing the truth that all men are brethren in Jesus Christ. For this union of nations it was meet that we should thank God and I felt no day could be more fitting than our national Thanksgiving Day."

The Pan American celebration, begun by Dr. Russell, has continued from year to year.

The practice of setting apart a day for thanks did not originate in New England, although Governor Bradford of the Plymouth colony issued the first Thanksgiving proclamation. It is probably as old as the worshiping spirit. Although some students maintain that Thanksgiving Day in America was suggested by the Hebrew Feast of the Tabernacles, its origin goes back to the time when men first began to understand their dependence on a Higher Power. Those who never heard of the Feast of the Tabernacles gave thanks, and those who worship strange gods express their gratitude for mercies to the Powers which they venerate. Few other Christian nations, however, have a yearly festival of thankfulness such as is observed in the United States. The victory of Constantine was celebrated at Constantinople for years on September 24, and July 21 was observed at Alexandria's as a day of thanks for the cessation of earthquakes, but these anniversaries have long since been forgotten in the cities where they were observed. Many special days of thanksgiving have been kept in England. After the Black Prince defeated the French at Poictiers in 1356 the Archbishop of Canterbury ordered that thanksgiving should be celebrated for eight days in all England. Special thanksgiving services were held in St. Paul's Cathedral after the defeat of the Spanish Armada in 1588 and for various other military triumphs as well as for the recovery from illness of members of the royal family. But for more than two hundred years England had a national thanksgiving day established out of gratitude for the failure of the plot to blow up the King and the House of Lords on November 5, 1605.

The first New England day of thanks for the harvest was in the autumn of 1621 under orders from Governor Bradford. The colonists went out into the forests and shot a number of turkeys and took them to the settlement to be cooked for the dinner. A number of Indians heard of the celebration and they entered the settlment carrying with them several deer. The Indians and the settlers feasted together. It was twenty-three years later when the Governor of the Dutch colony of New York issued a thanksgiving proclamation. During the Revolutionary War a day of national thanksgiving was annually recommended by Congress, but after the peace in 1784 there was no national call for thankfulness until Washington in 1789 ordered a day of thanksgiving for the adoption of the Constitution. This was the first thanksgiving proclamation issued by any President. Madison set a day to give thanks for peace in 1815 and Lincoln, in 1862 and 1863 recommended special days of thanks for victories.

It has frequently been the custom for clergymen to preach political sermons on Thanksgiving Day. In the early years of the nineteenth century their sermons were extremely partisan. In Massachusetts most of the Congregational pastors were opposed to Jefferson and denounced him and his theories. Governor Elbridge Gerry was an ardent supporter of Jefferson. As it was customary to read the Governor's Thanksgiving proclamation at the beginning of the services Mr. Gerry one year wrote a proclamation so long that it took more than two hours to read it. By the time it was finished most of the congregation, anxious to get home in time for the dinner awaiting them, left the churches, and the Clergymen denounced Jefferson to empty pews. General Benjamin F. Butler, another Massachusetts Governor, who was unpopular in the state, played a different kind of trick upon the people. His public utterances were always criticized severely, and when he issued a Thanksgiving proclamation it was denounced as a typical Butler document. When his critics had said their say about one of his Thanksgiving proclamations he explained that he had copied it verbatim from one issued by Governor Christopher Gore, one of the most pious and highly respected men who had held the office.

NOVEMBER TWENTY-EIGHTH

FEAST OF ST. STEPHEN THE YOUNGER

St. Stephen the Younger was a monk of Constantinople. He was the son of a wealthy family of the city who began his novitiate at the monastery of St. Auxentius at the age of fifteen, and pursued his studies so diligently and grew in the esteem of his associates so rapidly that at the age of thirty he was made abbot of the monastery. In the eighth century, in which he lived, a bitter controversy arose over the use of pictures and statues in the churches. Pope Gregory the Great (590-604) had written about paintings and statues:

It is one thing to worship a picture and another to learn from the language of the picture what that is which ought to be worshiped. What those who can read learn by means of writing, that do the uneducated learn by looking at a picture. . . . That, therefore, ought not to have been destroyed which had been placed in the churches, not for worship, but solely for instructing the minds of the ignorant.

But about a hundred and fifty years later Leo III, the Eastern emperor, began to demand the removal of the paintings and statues of holy men and women from the churches. The warfare against such things was continued by Constantine, his successor, and in February 754, Constantine assembled a council of three hundred and eighty-eight bishops, mostly of the East. The council condemned the use of images and the emperor demanded that all his subjects throughout the empire should swear on the cross that they detested them.

A large number of monks had already fled to Italy where there was no prohibition against setting up paintings and statues in the churches. St. Stephen refused to take the oath and protested against it. He was taken from the monastery by soldiers, tried and condemned to be beheaded. The sentence was changed so as to provide that he should be scourged to death in the prison. As he lived in spite of the scourging certain partisans of the emperor went to the prison and dragged him into the streets with his feet tied with cords and killed him with stones and clubs. This was in 764, and November 28 has been fixed as his feast day.

The controversy over the use of works of art in the churches continued for a hundred and fifty years. It was resumed during the Protestant reformation when in England and on the Continent the iconoclasts tore down the statues of the saints in the churches and destroyed the beautiful stained glass windows in which the saints were pictured. But this feeling of hostility died out in the course of time and now even the most protestant of the Protestant churches are adorned with stained glass windows representing both Jesus and the apostles and even Mary, the mother of Jesus, although their members may not be aware that St. Stephen the Younger died in defense of such adornments.

NOVEMBER TWENTY-NINTH

BIRTHDAY OF MORRISON R. WAITE

Morrison Remick Waite, seventh Chief Justice of the United States, was born at Lyme, Conn., on November 29, 1816. He was the son of Henry M. Waite, who for twenty years was a Judge of the Superior Court of Connecticut and for fifteen years Chief Justice of the Supreme Court of the state. He was educated at Yale College, and was graduated in 1837 in the same class with William M. Evarts and Samuel J. Tilden. He began the study of law in his father's office and continued it in the office of Samuel L. Young at Maumee City, Ohio. Mr. Young took him into partnership on his admission to the bar in 1839. The office of the firm was moved to Toledo in 1850, where its practice and its reputation increased. Mr. Waite was soon recognized as one of the leading lawyers in the state, second only to Allen G. Thurman. When Thurman was raised to the bench Waite was the acknowledged leader of the Ohio bar and held that reputation until he was appointed to the bench of the United States Supreme Court.

He was a Whig and when that party was dissolved he became a Republican. He served one term in the Ohio Senate to which he was elected in 1848. He was one of the American counsel before the Alabama Claims Commission, sitting at Geneva in 1871, as an associate of William M. Evarts and Caleb Cushing. Mr. Evarts won popular acclaim for his able presentation of the case and Mr. Waite won fame among lawyers for his preparation of the case which Mr. Evarts defended in his address. He was elected by both political parties to the Ohio Constitutional Convention of 1874 and was its president.

When Chief Justice Chase died President Grant, in 1874, appointed Mr. Waite to the vacancy on the bench of the Supreme Court. His reputation, save among lawyers, had not extended beyond the borders of Ohio and the appointment was bitterly criticised. Its confirmation was opposed in the Senate by Charles Sumner, but Allen G. Thurman, then serving his first term as a United States Senator, spoke in defense of the ability of Mr. Waite and did it so effectively that the appointment was confirmed unanimously. On the bench he was called upon to consider many of the questions arising under the amendments to the Constitution adopted following the Civil War and he maintained the balance between state and federal rights with absolute impartiality. He died in Washington on March 23, 1888.

DEATH OF MARCUS WHITMAN

Ever since 1897, fifty years after Marcus Whitman was killed by the Indians at Wailatpu, Wash., on November 29, 1847, the anniversary has been observed in the region which he served as a missionary. The fiftieth anniversary was observed by the Presbyterian church in many parts of the country. A statue of Whitman was erected on the Witherspoon building, the Presbyterian headquarters in Philadelphia, and a monument was set up over the grave near the site of the mission which he founded not far from Whitman College at Walla Walla. Whitman College was founded in 1859 by Cushing Eells, a colleague of Whitman's, and named in his honor.

Whitman has been credited with saving Oregon for the United States at a time when the Hudson's Bay Company was exerting itself to have the British jurisdiction extended over the region. This claim is based on his winter ride from Oregon territory to Washington, D.C., when the Senate was considering the Ashburton Treaty. The treaty, which was ratified before he reached Washington, left the northern boundary uncertain. Whitman, however, impressed Daniel Webster, then Secretary of State, with the value of the territory, and as a result when the boundary was fixed, the Oregon territory became the property of the United States.

Marcus Whitman was born at Rushville, N.Y., on September 4, 1802. After a preliminary education he entered the Berkshire Medical Institute at Pittsfield, Mass., to prepare himself for a career in medicine. After graduation he practiced for four years in Canada. In November 1834, he attended a meeting at Wheeler, N.Y., addressed by the Reverend Samuel Parker, a missionary commissioned by the American Board of Foreign Missions to go to Oregon. Mr. Parker told the story of the four Indian chiefs who had visited St. Louis to get the white man's Bible (see Birthday of Cushing Eells, February 16). They returned to the Northwest without it as they could not read English and as they had no written language into which it could be translated. This incident had led the missionary bodies in the East to decide to take Christianity to the Indians who had been asking about it. After listening to Mr. Parker's address Dr. Whitman volunteered to serve as a missionary. He accompanied Mr. Parker to Oregon the next year with instructions to examine the field and report to the American Board. They were welcomed by the Indians, were satisfied with the prospects, and Mr. Parker remained while Dr. Whitman returned with his report. The report was so favorable that the Board commissioned the Reverend H. H. Spalding to return with Whitman. While in the East, Whitman married and he and his bride with Mr. and Mrs. Spalding started overland by wagon and in due course reached the neighborhood of Walla Walla through a pass in the Rocky Mountains which the agents of the Hudson's Bay Company had said were impassable.

He and his associates labored peacefully for seven years. In September 1842 Dr. Whitman, at a dinner at Fort Walla Walla attended by Englishmen, heard the diners boasting of the prospects for British control through immigration of Englishmen, and concluded that Washington should be warned. Within twenty-four hours he had started for Washington on horseback with a single white companion, an Indian guide, and three pack mules. After terrible hardships he reached St. Louis then traveled by stage to Washington.

When he learned there that it was thought that Oregon was worthless and that the Rocky Mountains were impassable he described the fertile valleys and the rich forests and said that he had crossed the mountains in a wagon and that he had it still. His report changed the official attitude in the national capital.

When he returned to Oregon he found that some of the Indians had become hostile. On November 29, 1847, they attacked the mission which he had built and killed him with a tomahawk, shot his wife, and killed thirteen others. Their bodies were buried in an unmarked grave, which was found many years later and the body of Whitman identified by the mark of the tomahawk on the skull.

An association formed by patriotic citizens of Oregon, Washington and Idaho, states carved in whole or in part from the old Oregon territory, have erected a monument near the site of the mission and removed the bones to a mausoleum beside it. At this spot memorial services are held every year. In 1931, the chapter of the Daughters of the Revolution at Walla Walla, Wash., assisted by the Kiwanis club, beautified the grounds around the monument. The memory of Dr. Whitman is kept green, not only in the region where he became a Christian martyr, but by the General Assembly of the Presbyterian Church and by the Council of Congregational Churches.

NOVEMBER THIRTIETH

BIRTHDAY OF MARK TWAIN

Samuel Langhorne Clemens, better known as Mark Twain, some of whose books have come to be regarded as classics of American literature, was born at Florida, Mo., on November 30, 1835. His father was descended from Virginian ancestors and his mother belonged to an English family in which there was an earldom. His parents moved to Hannibal, Mo., on the Mississippi River in 1839. When his father died in 1847 he had to help support his mother, and learned the printer's trade in the village newspaper shop. When he was eighteen he traveled about the country working as a journeyman printer in St. Louis, New York, Philadelphia and Keokuk, Iowa. In 1857 he was apprenticed to a river pilot on the Mississippi and spent four years on the river, the last two and a half as a licensed pilot.

When the Civil War began he joined a company of volunteers undecided on which side to fight, but he soon left it and went to Nevada where his brother was secretary to the territorial governor. He prospected for gold without success and in 1862 became a reporter on a newspaper in Virginia City and wrote sketches which he signed "Mark Twain" from a term used on the Mississippi to indicate the depth of the channel at two fathoms. He went to California as a reporter in 1864 and while there wrote the story of "The Jumping Frog." This gave him a wide reputation for it was reprinted in all parts of the country. He was sent by his newspaper to the Sandwich Islands to write whatever interested him. His articles broadened his reputation and on his return he lectured in the West. He planned a writing tour around the world for a California paper and went to New York where he delivered a lecture in Cooper Union to a delighted audience and then joined a party of travelers who were visiting the Mediterranean and the Holy Land on the "Quaker City." This trip resulted in *Innocents Abroad*, published in 1869, which added to his reputation.

He did not write *The Adventures of Tom Sawyer* until 1876 and *The Adventures of·Huckleberry Finn* did not appear until 1884. These two books are regarded by many critics as his best and most distinctive works. Not satisfied with his dealings with publishers he established a publishing business of his own at Hartford, Conn., where he had taken up his residence after his marriage in 1870. It prospered for a time and then failed. In order to pay its debts he made a lecture tour around the world in 1895 and 1896 and succeeded in meeting the claims of his creditors. Harper & Brothers took over the publication of his long list of books and in 1905 arranged an elaborate celebration of the seventieth anniversary of his birth at which distinguished men and women of letters were present to pay tribute to his genius.

The one hundredth anniversary of his birth was celebrated in 1935 under the direction of a committee of notable persons. It began with the lighting of a memorial airplane beacon at Hannibal, by President Roosevelt on January 13, and continued with the opening of a memorial museum in the same city on April 25 when the model of a monument to him was unveiled. The monument shows the man seated with his arm around Tom Sawyer and with many of the other characters which he created grouped about the base of the statue. The celebration came to a climax on November 30 with public meetings and dinners in various parts of the country. The Hannibal museum contains the academic gown which he wore when Oxford University conferred on him the degree of Doctor of Letters, an honor which he prized highly as a tribute to a man without a university education. He died in 1910.

FEAST OF ST. ANDREW

St. Andrew, the brother of Peter and one of the Twelve Disciples, was martyred on a cross shaped like the letter X on November 30, A.D. 60, during the reign of Nero. The day is observed as a feast day by all branches of the Christian church. Andrew was a follower of John the Baptist and through his influence became a follower of Jesus. He introduced Jesus to his brother Peter and they both abandoned their work as fishermen and joined themselves to Him. There are few details about him in the New Testament. It is recorded, however, that on the occasion of the feeding of the five thousand, it was Andrew who remarked "There is a lad here which hath five barley loaves and two small fishes; but what are they among so many?" He was present at the Last Supper, witnessed the Ascension, and was among those present on the Day of Pentecost.

It is supposed that he went forth to preach Christianity among the nations, but there is no authentic record of his journeyings. According to tradition he preached in Cappadocia, Galatia, Bithynia, Thrace, Macedonia and Achaia. It is generally agreed that he was crucified by order of Aegeas, the Roman Governor, at Patrae in Achaia. His bones were taken from Patrae to Constantinople and deposited in the Church of the Apostles there about A.D. 357, according to an accepted tradition. In the thirteenth century they were taken to Italy and placed in the cathedral of Amalfi. There is a Scotch legend, however, that in the fourth century the bones were taken to Scotland by St. Regulus. The ship in which Regulus was traveling was wrecked on the Scotch coast near the present town of St. Andrews, the seat of the university by that name. St. Andrew was adopted in the course of time as the patron saint of Scotland. He is also the patron saint of Russia.

He is the patron of societies of Scotchmen and men of Scotch descent in all parts of the world, who have organized St. Andrew's Societies for the relief of the needy. The oldest St. Andrew's Society in the United States was organized in Charleston, South Carolina in 1738; the next two were in Philadelphia in 1749, and in New York in 1756. The founders of the Philadelphia society met in a tavern, and perfected arrangements for taking care of the needy Scotch families in the city. The society has celebrated St. Andrew's day with a dinner every year since its organization, save in the year 1776 when most of its members were under arms. Among its earlier members were many men distinguished in the history of the country, including three or four signers of the Declaration of Independence. Its dinners as well as those of the St. Andrew's Societies in other cities are conducted in accordance with a prescribed ritual. The diners in Philadelphia are led into the banquet room by a company of pipers. Following the pipers a man bears the sword of General Hugh Mercer, a former member who was killed at the Battle of Princeton. Then comes a huge ram's head properly escorted. In the top of the head is a snuff box ornamented with a large cairngorm. And last a loving cup, presented to the society on the one hundred and fiftieth anniversary of its founding, is borne in. These trophies are deposited on the head table before the presiding officer. The diners frequently wear the tartans of their clans, and the room is decorated with the American and British flags and the flags of the Blatch Watch, the Cameron Highlanders, and the state and city flags.

On the occasion of the annual dinners of the St. Andrew's Societies congratulatory telegrams are exchanged among them. The society in Edinburgh usually cables to the American societies and the Scotchmen meeting in Canada in honor of St. Andrew and the land of their nativity exchange felicitations with their fellow Scots meeting for the same purpose in the United States.

Accounts of the early dinners of the Philadelphia society indicate that dining customs in the eighteenth century differed from those in the twentieth. It is recorded of the dinner in 1788 at which forty-five gentlemen sat down that the beverages consumed included "thirty-eight bottles of Madeira, twenty-seven bottles of Claret, eight bottles of Port wine, twenty-six bottles of porter, two bottles of cider and two bowls of punch." Before the Revolution a toast was always drunk to the King. Nowadays the President of the United States and the King of Great Britain are toasted.

Besides the Patriotic societies of Scotchmen there is a Protestant Episcopal Brotherhood of St. Andrew. It was founded in St. James's Parish in Chicago by James H. Houghteling and others interested in the spread of Christianity among men. There is a junior department for work among boys. It holds an annual convention, and publishes a monthly paper. Chapters of the brotherhood have been organized in England and her colonies.

Christmas Home-coming

DECEMBER

Shout now! The months with loud acclaim,
Take up the cry and send it forth;
May, breathing sweet her Spring perfumes,
November, thundering from the North.
With hands upraised, as with one voice,
They join their notes in grand accord;
Hail to December! say they all.
It gave to Earth our Christ, the Lord!

—J. K. Hoyt

December was the tenth month in the ancient Roman calendar when there were only ten months in the year. In the fifth century B.C. two months were added, February following December and January preceding March. The order of these two extra months was changed sometime later. Commodus, following the example of the Senate which sought to flatter the emperors by naming months for them, ordered that December should be known as Amazonius in honor of his mistress who had been represented as an Amazon in a painting. But the people preferred the old name, which has survived to this day. The Saxons called it Mid-winter-monath, as, according to their reckoning, it was half way between the autumn and the spring. The Christian Saxons called it Heligh-monath, or Holy month, in allusion to the birth of Jesus on the twenty-fifth. They also called it Se uro geola, meaning anti-yule in probable reference to Druidistic customs. The French called Napoleon III the man of December, as his election to the presidency, his coup d'état and his proclamation of himself as emperor all occurred in this month.

DECEMBER FIRST

MOTHER SETON DAY

This day has been observed more or less formally by the Sisters of Charity of St. Vincent de Paul throughout the United States as the anniversary of the founding of their order in this country by Elizabeth Ann Bayley Seton. Mrs. Seton was born in New York city in 1774, the daughter of Dr. Richard Bayley and his wife Charlotte Barclay. Her mother's mother was Helen Roosevelt, of the family from which Theodore Roosevelt and Franklin Delano Roosevelt sprang. In 1794 she was married to William Seton, a New York merchant, and accompanied him to Italy in 1803. He died in Pisa not long after arriving in Italy, leaving his widow with five small children. She returned to New York and in 1805 became a Roman Catholic and was baptized in St. Peter's Church in Barclay Street. She soon moved to Baltimore and opened a school for girls. She, however, was consumed by a desire to devote her life to religion and in 1809 she consecrated herself by vows to charitable and religious work. On December 1 of that year she founded the American branch of the Sisters of Charity of St. Vincent de Paul in Emmitsburg, Md. This society had its origin in France in 1631 through the efforts of St. Vincent de Paul assisted by Madame Louise le Gras. The Archbishop of Paris raised the society to the order of "The Daughters of Divine Love." In 1668 its rule was confirmed by Pope Clement IX.

Mrs. Seton expected to have a colony of French sisters of the order sent to this country, but the political troubles in France at the time made this impossible and her sisterhood remained independent until 1850 when it became affiliated with the French body. The one hundredth anniversary of the founding of the order in this country was celebrated in 1909 in the parochial schools and academies throughout the United States and in the charitable institutions with which the sisterhood is connected. The day was declared a holiday in the parochial schools. In New York a solemn pontifical mass was celebrated in St. Patrick's Cathedral. The mass was sung by Archbishop Farley of the New York archdiocese. He was assisted by two hundred clergy including the Bishops of Brooklyn, Albany and Newark. The sermon was preached by Monsignor James M. McGean, pastor of St. Peter's Church in the parish in whose chapel Mother Seton was received into the Catholic Church. The Pope sent his blessing through a letter from Cardinal Merry del Val. Fifteen hundred young girls from the parochial schools and orphan asylums occupied seats in the chancel and sang the processional, "Blessed is the faith," and the recessional, "Holy God, we praise thy name." Mother Seton died in 1821 at the age of forty-seven.

DECEMBER SECOND

BEGINNING OF ADVENT

The season of Advent begins in the Roman and Anglican churches on the Sunday nearest to the Feast of St. Andrew, which occurs on November 30. It fell in 1945 on December 2. It may fall as early as November 27 and as late as December 3. It is observed by special services in a period including four Sundays. It is regarded as a season in which the faithful must prepare themselves for the advent of the Savior on December 25. An elaborate ritual is prescribed by the Roman Church for the services during the season. The solemnization of matrimony is forbidden between Advent Sunday and Christmas. It is resumed on December 26.

Church historians have been unable to decide with any certainty when the celebration of Advent was introduced. The preparation for the Feast of the Nativity, or Christmas, did not begin before the observance of that feast was instituted and there is no evidence of the celebration of Christmas before the end of the fourth century. Some sections of the Church observed December 25 then and others observed January 6, and it was not until some time later that December 25 was fixed as the proper date. A synod, which met in 581, ordered that the preparation for the Nativity should begin on November 11. In 650 Advent was celebrated in Spain over five Sundays. The ecclesiastical year begins with Advent, and the date of various other religious observances depends on its date.

PROMULGATION OF THE MONROE DOCTRINE

President Monroe, in his annual message to Congress on December 2, 1823, announced the opposition of the United States to the extension of the control of European powers over territory on the American continents in what has come to be known as the Monroe Doctrine. In referring to boundary disputes between the United States on the one hand and Russia and Great Britain on the other, the President said that "the American continents . . . are henceforth not to be considered as subjects for future colonization by any European powers." And then in referring to the proposed action of the Holy Alliance to assist Spain in recovering control over the South American countries which had rebelled against Spanish rule he said:

With the governments who have declared their independence and maintained it . . . we could not view any interposition for the purpose of oppressing them or of controlling in any other manner their destiny by any European power in any other light than a manifestation of an unfriendly disposition to the United States.

This declaration was approved by Columbia, Brazil and Argentina at the time. It was in pursuit of this policy that the French were asked to withdraw from Mexico, where during the Civil War they had set up a monarchy with Maximillian on the throne. And it was cited as justification for the demand by President Cleveland that the boundary dispute between Great Britain and Venezuela should be settled by arbitration for the protection of the Venezuelan rights against destruction by the use of force.

DECEMBER THIRD

BIRTHDAY OF GILBERT STUART

Gilbert Stuart, best known for his portraits of Washington, of which he painted about forty, was born near Newport, R.I., on December 3, 1755. He began to paint portraits when he was thirteen years old after having taught himself the art. When he was fifteen a friend took him to Scotland but within a year he returned to America where his talent was recognized and he had many commissions for portraits. He went to London at the age of twenty and after three years made the acquaintance of Benjamin West with whom he lived and worked for four years. He became a successful painter of portraits but lived so lavishly that he had to flee to Dublin in 1787 to escape his creditors. He remained there five years after which he returned to America. In 1794 he settled in Philadelphia and the next year he painted his first portrait of Washington. In 1796 he painted a full length Washington portrait for the Marquis of Lansdowne. There was so great a demand for portraits of Washington that he painted many replicas from his originals. He also painted portraits of John Adams, Jefferson, Madison and Monroe as well as portraits of George III and George IV and of many other distinguished persons. He died in 1828.

DECEMBER FOURTH

WASHINGTON TAKES LEAVE OF HIS OFFICERS

Nine days after the British evacuated New York in 1783 the Revolutionary army entered the city. On December 4 Washington invited the officers to meet him in the great public room of Fraunce's Tavern at the corner of Broad and Pearl streets so that he might bid them farewell. When they had assembled Washington entered the room and taking a glass of wine in his hand, said: "With a heart full of gratitude, I now take leave of you. I most devoutly wish that your latter days may be as prosperous and happy as your former ones have been glorious and honorable." Then he tasted the wine and continued: "I cannot come to each of you to take my leave, but shall be obliged to you if each will come and take me by my hand." General Knox, who succeeded him in command of the army, was the first to approach. The other officers followed and Washington kissed each on the forehead and they and he were moved to tears by the parting. When he left to board the ferry on the first part of his journey to Annapolis where Congress was sitting, he walked between two lines of infantry drawn up between the tavern and the ferry. He resigned his commission and returned it to Congress on December 23.

DECEMBER FIFTH

BIRTHDAY OF MARTIN VAN BUREN

Martin Van Buren, eighth President of the United States and tenth Governor of New York, was born at Kinderhook, N.Y., on December 5, 1782. His father, Abraham Van Buren, was a farmer who had served in the Revolutionary armies. He was descended from Dutch immigrants from the village of Buren in Holland. It is from that village that the family derived its name. He received his early education in the local schools and at the age of fourteen became an office boy in the employment of a local lawyer. He later studied law there, was admitted to the bar in 1803, and in 1807 moved to Hudson, N.Y., where he opened an office and immediately interested himself in politics.

After serving as county surrogate, state senator, and Attorney General, he was elected to the United States Senate in 1821 and re-elected in 1827. In the Senate he voted to restrict the admission of slaves into Florida, tried to change the manner of electing the President and to bring about the enactment of a general bankruptcy law. He was elected Governor of New York in 1828 and resigned from the Senate. President Jackson, whose policies he had supported, made him Secretary of State in 1829, and in that office he succeeded in settling disagreements with England over the West Indies. In June 1831, President Jackson sent him to England as the American minister, but the Senate, when it met in the following winter, failed to confirm him, with the deciding vote of Vice President Calhoun against him. He was nominated for Vice President in 1832 on the ticket with Andrew Jackson and elected.

In his *Autobiography* he says that Jackson, who was opposed to the reelection of a President, had proposed that he (Jackson) should resign after being reelected so that the Vice President might become President. But Van Buren declined to be a party to any such arrangement. He was himself elected President in 1836, defeating the Whig candidate, General William Henry Harrison. During his term the evils predicted by those opposed to Jackson's dealings with the United States Bank broke upon the country and there was a financial panic which brought ruin to thousands and threw hundreds of thousands out of employment. Buren called a special session of Congress in September 1837, to do what it could to relieve the distress. He urged a bankruptcy law for corporations, and the establishment of an independent treasury system. He was renominated by the Democrats in 1840, but the country held him responsible for the business depression, as it held President Hoover responsible for the depression which began in 1929, and he was succeeded by General Harrison whom he had defeated four years earlier. He received only sixty electoral votes out of a total of two hundred and ninety-four and carried only seven states. He retired to Lindenwald, an estate which he had bought near Kinderhook, his birthplace, and became known as the "sage of Kinderhook," when he was not called "the old fox," in allusion to his political astuteness. He was nominated for President over his protests as the candidate of the Free Soil Party in 1848, and although he did not carry a state he received votes enough to prevent the election of Lewis Cass, the Democratic nominee. Thereafter he lived quietly at his estate at Kinderhook except for two years spent in European travel. He died on July 24, 1862.

DECEMBER SIXTH

FEAST OF ST. NICHOLAS

The feast of St. Nicholas is celebrated in the Greek and Latin churches on December 6. Very little is known about him, save that he was bishop of Myra in Lycia in the fourth century. Whether he died in 345 or 352 is uncertain. He is one of the most popular saints and the identification of him by the Germans as Santa Claus, the patron of children and the giver of gifts at Christmas has made him popular in all countries and among all sects.

There are many legends about him. One is that even in his infancy he was religiously inclined and refused to suckle his mother on Wednesdays and Fridays, the fast days. It is supposed that he was born at Parara, in Lycia, and that in his youth he made a pilgrimage to Egypt and Palestine. After his return, tradition says that he was made bishop of Myra, was imprisoned during the persecution by Diocletian, was released by Constantine, and was present at the Council of Nicaea. In 1087 what were supposed to be his remains were taken by Italian merchants from Myra to Bari in Italy. These relics are still preserved in the church of San Nicola in Bari.

Another legend is that he inherited great wealth and devoted it to charity. One instance of his benevolence is preserved in the legend concerning a nobleman of the city who had become so poor that he contemplated abandoning his three daughters to a life of sin. Nicholas, when he heard of this, went to the nobleman's home secretly three nights in succession and threw a bag of gold into a window on each visit, and thus saved the daughters from infamy. This incident is supposed to be responsible for his connection with the giving of gifts. Nicholas is sometimes represented bearing three purses symbolical of his generosity. It used to be the custom in various parts of Europe for the parents to put gifts of sweetmeats and toys in the shoes or stockings of their children on St. Nicholas' eve. In convents the young lady boarders would leave their stockings at the door of the abbess's room with a note recommending themselves to the generosity of St. Nicholas. The next morning the abbess would summon them and show them their stockings filled with sweetmeats by the saint.

Still another legend is that when he learned that an inn keeper in a time of famine was in the habit of stealing children, killing them, cutting up their bodies and serving them to his patrons, the saint made the sign of the cross over the dismembered bodies, restoring the children to life. The representations of him in Christian art with a tub containing three children relates to this tradition. He is the patron saint of sailors and of children, of scholars, parish clerks, travelers and pawnbrokers. And his protection was besought against robbers so that the robbers were sometimes called clerks of St. Nicholas. Many churches in the United States and in England as well as on the continent of Europe are named for him.

It has long been the custom of the St. Nicholas Society of New York City to observe St. Nicholas Day. The society was founded by Washington Irving in 1835 and he was its first secretary. A dinner was given to him in New York on May 30, 1832, on his return from Spain where he had been the United States Minister, and in the course of his address acknowledging the compliments paid to him he remarked that there was a St. Andrew's Society for Scotchmen, a Saint George's Society for Englishmen and a St. Patrick's Society for Irishmen, but that there was no society for the original New Yorkers and their descendants. He proposed the organization of such a society. As a result of his efforts the St. Nicholas Society was organized on February 28, 1835, with a constitution providing that any person of full age and good moral character residing in the city who had lived there in 1785 or was descended from any person living in the city at or prior to that date was eligible for membership. St. Nicholas was adopted as the patron saint of the society because he was particularly dear to the Dutch founders of the city, as the ship that brought them to America had a statue of the saint on its deck, and the first church built in the city was dedicated to him.

The society holds a dinner every year on St. Nicholas Day at which some old customs are observed. When the diners are at their places a trumpeter blows a blast in observance of Peter Stuyvesant's order that the "burghers guard should be daily paraded within the fort at the sound of the trumpet." Long-stemmed clay pipes, known as church wardens, are smoked, and the president when making his annual address dons a cocked hat. The brass weathercock which adorned Federal Hall came into the possession of Washington Irving when the building was demolished and he gave it to the society. At the annual dinner the weathercock is formally escorted into the room and placed at the head table before the president while the members stand and wave their napkins. The weathercock is then turned so that it points to the northeast to indicate that the early Dutch settlers feared encroachment from the British in Connecticut. The motto of the society is "Oranje Boven," meaning "Orange Above," which was a battle cry of William of Orange. It is always displayed at the dinner. The Minister of the Netherlands at Washington attended the dinner in 1893 and on behalf of the Queen Regent awarded the cross of the Order of Orange Nassau to Frederick J. dePeyster, a former president, and in 1925 Queen Wilhelmina presented to the society a bronze medal in commemoration of the twenty-fifth anniversary of her coronation.

DECEMBER SEVENTH

PEARL   HARBOR

About November 22, 1941, Japanese fleet units left the Inland Sea and headed north. This was the start of the sneak attack on Pearl Harbor, official records concerning which were released after the end of World War II. According to these records, the units gathered and made ready for sea at Tankan Bay, near desolate Etorfu Island in the southern Kuriles. On November 27, six aircraft carriers, two fast battleships, two heavy cruisers, a light cruiser, destroyers and submarines steamed into the Pacific. They followed little-used sea lanes and had orders to sink on sight any vessel they encountered, even Japanese. In the early morning of December 7, before daylight, the task force was about two hundred miles north of Pearl Harbor; from the decks of its carriers three hundred planes took off. An enlisted man in one of the United States services was practicing with radar in Honolulu at the time. He detected the planes approaching one hundred and thirty-two miles away, reported them, but was ignored. Just before eight o'clock they were over Pearl Harbor, beginning their deadly business of unloading bombs and torpdoes on the ships and docks of the American navy, and the army airfields. Five battleships were sunk or put out of commission, three cruisers damaged, three destroyers sunk, and over three thousand men killed or missing. The army lost ninety-seven of its nearly three hundred planes. By far the greatest military disaster in the history of the United States, the event was made more shocking by the fact that two Tokyo envoys were visiting the State Department in Washingon, D.C., in their so-called peace negotiations, almost simultaneously with the attack. On the following day the United States declared war against Japan, and against Germany and Italy on December 11.

633

It was not until after the end of World War II, on August 29, 1945, that President Truman released the findings of the army and navy boards of inquiry which had attempted to fix the blame for the disaster. The navy "found no serious offenses committed nor serious blame incurred" by any of its personnel. The army report extended its censure to include Secretary of State Cordell Hull and Chief of Staff General George C. Marshall. President Truman and Secretary of War Stimson defended General Marshall. Court martials were not recommended, but the reports told a regrettable tale of unpreparedness, and lack of cooperation between the service branches. However the subsequent performance of all branches of the service during the war were such that it was generally felt their record had been redeemed and Pearl Harbor avenged.

DELAWARE DAY

The anniversary of the adoption of the Federal Constitution by Delaware on December 7, 1787, was observed for several years by the Sons of Delaware and the Daughters of the American Revolution. In 1933, however, the Kiwanis and Rotarian Societies and the Society of the Patrons of Husbandry, popularly known as the Grange, began to urge a formal and official celebration of the anniversary by the state. At a special session of the legislature late in the year a resolution was adopted authorizing the governor to issue a proclamation calling upon the citizens to display the state and national flags on December 7 of each year and to invite the schools, churches and civic organizations to observe the day with appropriate ceremonies. Accordingly on December 7, 1933, there was the first state-wide celebration of the event.

Soon after the approval of the draft of the Constitution by the convention sitting in Philadelphia a copy of it was sent to the General Assembly of Delaware. When the people of the state learned of this, four different petitions were submitted to the General Assembly asking for immediate ratification. Within a month arrangements were made for the election of delegates to a ratifying convention. Ten delegates from each of the three counties of the state were elected to attend a convention at Dover, which met on December 7 and ratified the Constitution unanimously. Delaware was thus the first state to approve the document. Pennsylvania ratified it five days later, but only by a two-thirds vote.

LIBRARY DAY IN WEST VIRGINIA

The first Friday in December (it fell on December 7 in 1945) has long been observed in the schools of West Virginia as Library Day. The purpose of the celebration is to arouse public interest in the school libraries and to raise money for the purchase of books. When the celebration began there were only 8000 books in the libraries. Within ten years this number had been increased to 176,000.

In place of the usual school exercises the day is given up to the reading of essays by the pupils and the delivery of addresses by citizens. At the opening the roll is called and each pupil is expected to respond by a brief quotation about books or reading. The session closes with a request for contributions of books or money with which to buy them.

DECEMBER EIGHTH

FEAST OF THE IMMACULATE CONCEPTION

This feast, observed on December 8, is recognized in the calendars of the Anglican and Roman churches as well as in the calendar of the Eastern church. It celebrates the preservation of the Virgin Mary from the stain of original sin from the moment of her conception by her mother. It originated in the monasteries of Palestine as early as the seventh century and was first known merely as the Feast of the Conception of Mary. The dogma of the immaculate conception of Mary was of much later growth and was not formally adopted by the Latin church until it was promulgated by Pope Pius IX in 1854. The doctrine is that although Mary was born of Anne, her mother, as all other children are born, she was preserved from all stains of original sin as soon as her soul entered her body. After the decree of 1854 the day was known in the Latin church as the Feast of the Immaculate Conception. The Greek church still celebrates it as the Conception of St. Anne without reference to the new Latin dogma.

The monks of Palestine observed the anniversary for years before it was celebrated in the cathedrals. By the tenth century it had become a fixed feast, approved by church and state. In the Western church it was observed on December 8 and its popularity grew while interest in it waned in the Eastern church. The first record of it in the West appears in the calendar of Winchester Cathedral, dating from about 1030, and it is, therefore, agreed that the Winchester monks introduced it into England before the Norman Conquest in 1066. The Normans, however, caused its public observance to be abandoned. There is a tradition at variance with the record at the Winchester Cathedral that the observance of the feast was introduced into England in 1070 by the abbot of Ramsey who had been saved from shipwreck by an angel after he had promised to celebrate the feast at his monastery. The Normans, at any rate, adopted the feast in spite of their orders against its observance in England. The Norman students at the University of Paris chose it as their patronal feast and during the Middle Ages it was known as the Feast of the Norman Nation.

Along with the observance of the feast a controversy grew up over the meaning of the terms used and Pope Alexander VII in 1661 issued a decree defining them. A new office for use in the celebration was pre-

635

scribed in 1863, nine years after the doctrine had been formally promulgated by the Roman church. In 1904 the golden jubilee of the promulgation of the dogma was celebrated with great splendor. Mary, in her immaculate conception, was elected principal patron of the United States at the first council of Baltimore in 1846, since which time her feast has been observed in this country as a double feast of the first class with a vigil.

The Syrian and Chaldean churches celebrate the feast on December 9. The schismatic Abyssinians and Copts keep it on August 7 while the Catholic Copts observe December 10. It is observed by Catholics in other places on different dates in thankfulness for deliverance from calamities.

DECEMBER NINTH

BIRTHDAY OF JOEL CHANDLER HARRIS

The anniversary of the birth of Joel Chandler Harris is observed in the public schools of Georgia by a program devoted to his life and works, as Indiana and Michigan observe the anniversary of the birth of James Whitcomb Riley and Will Carleton, respectively. Harris was born near Eatonton, Putnam County, Georgia, on December 9, 1848. His mother, Mary Harris, had eloped with an Irish laborer who deserted her before their child was born.

Joel lived with his mother in Eatonton for the first fourteen years of his life and attended one of the two academies in the village. His mother read *The Vicar of Wakefield* to him and through that he became interested in literature and formed a desire to write. When he was fourteen he became an apprentice in the printing office of Joseph Addison Turner who was publishing *The Countryman,* a weekly paper, on his plantation about nine miles from the village. Turner lent books to him and gave him instruction in the art of writing. This stage of his career ended abruptly in 1864 when the left wing of Sherman's army swept through Putnam county, leaving desolation in its wake. He then found employment as a printer in Macon and late in 1866 went to New Orleans as secretary to William Evelyn, publisher of the *Crescent,* but after six months he returned to Eatonton. He worked for a time on the Monroe *Advertiser,* and in 1870 went to the Savannah *Morning News* as a humorous writer. He married in Savannah, and when a yellow fever epidemic broke out in the city in 1876 he took his family to Atlanta where he obtained employment on the *Constitution,* with which he remained until 1900.

While employed on this newspaper he wrote some of his Uncle Remus and Brer Rabbit stories in which he used the dialect of the middle Georgian Negroes with which he had become familiar in his boyhood. These attracted the attention of D. Appleton & Company who asked him to assemble them for publication in book form. His *Uncle Remus: His Songs and His Sayings* was published in 1880. Three years later *Nights with Uncle Remus* appeared. During his life six more books dealing with Uncle Remus were published and two appeared after his death. Harris always insisted that the tales were those which he had heard from the Negroes and that he was merely a compiler. But, however that may be, the stories are an important contribution to the folklore of this country. He wrote many other books besides these dealing with the Negroes. As an editor of the Atlanta *Constitution* he wrote political editorials, feature articles and book reviews. He was the editor of *Uncle Remus's Magazine* for about a year before his death on July 3, 1908. His home, Wren's Nest, in Atlanta is preserved as a memorial.

DECEMBER TENTH

BIRTHDAY OF THOMAS H. GALLAUDET

Thomas H. Gallaudet, the pioneer teacher of the deaf in the United States, was born on December 10, 1787, at Philadelphia, Pa., of Huguenot ancestors who had fled to America from France at the time of the revocation of the Edict of Nantes. When he was thirteen years old the family moved to Hartford, Conn. He entered Yale College and was graduated in 1805. He spent the next seven years in studying law, teaching, in a business office, and traveling for his health. He then decided to study for the ministry and was graduated from the Andover Theological Seminary in 1814. At about the time of his graduation he became acquainted with Alice Cogswell, a deaf child, and urged her father to hire a special teacher for her. Her father, joining with others, sent Gallaudet to Europe to study the methods in use there for teaching the deaf, and he spent several months at the Royal Institute for Deaf Mutes at Paris. In 1816 he returned to America with Laurent Clerc, a teacher from the French institution, and with his aid raised the money to open the first free school for the deaf in the United States, in Hartford in 1817. He was made principal of the school and held the post for thirteen years. His oldest son became a minister to the deaf and his youngest son assisted in founding a school for the deaf in Washington, which developed into Gallaudet College. The deaf people of the country, grateful for what he did for them, have erected a monument to his memory on the grounds of the college.

WYOMING DAY

In 1935 the legislature of Wyoming designated December 10 of each year as Wyoming Day, and provided for its observance in the

637

DECEMBER 10

schools and throughout the state "by appropriate exercises commemorating the history of the territory and state and the lives of its pioneers, and fostering in all ways the loyalty and good citizenship of its people." The proclamation is made annually by the Governor of Wyoming in recognition of the action of the Wyoming Territorial Governor on December 10, 1869, in approving the first law found anywhere in legislative history which extends the right of suffrage to women.

The event commemorated grew out of the organized women's rights campaign which, from 1848 onward, had attracted nationwide attention. It was apparent that sooner or later prejudice would give way and the desired legislation be passed. However, that the new Territory of Wyoming should be the first to accord the franchise to women was totally unexpected, and the account of how it came about is a picturesque chapter in pioneer history. In the middle of the nineteenth century a sparse population was scattered along the trails leading from Council Bluffs to Oregon and California. But when the Union Pacific Railway was completed halfway across Wyoming, in 1867, a city of tents sprang up almost overnight at the last stop, called Cheyenne. Thousands poured into the region and the Congress of the United States was petitioned for the protection of an organized government. Thus, in 1869, the Territory of Wyoming was created and the election of delegates to its first legislature planned for September of that year. Shortly before the election, the twenty most influential men running for office were invited to dinner at "the shack of Mrs. Esther Morris, who had followed her husband and three sons into the trackless West." Mrs. Morris had heard Susan B. Anthony speak and become imbued with enthusiasm for the cause of women's suffrage. She, therefore, presented the case to her guests and succeeded in persuading each candidate to pledge that, if elected, he would introduce and support a women's suffrage bill. William H. Bright, one of the men present, was elected president of the council, as the upper house of the legislature was called. When the legislature met he kept his promise to Mrs. Morris and, in addition to pleading the cause on its merits, suggested that as Democrats they would increase the prestige of the party as advocates of progress by passing such a bill; whereas should this action eventually be taken by the Republicans the shoe would be on the other foot. The bill was finally passed by both houses after much lively and acrimonious debate. When it went before the Republican Governor, John W. Campbell, he, perforce, was compelled to sign it or admit the implication that his party was unprogressive. It it said that the women of Wyoming were astounded by the legislation which was an important milestone in the progress of events leading to universal franchise for women. Incidentally, Mrs. Esther Morris was appointed justice of the peace at South Pass City and, although the rowdy element tried to intimidate her, administered the cases brought before her so justly that none were appealed to a higher court.

638

DECEMBER ELEVENTH

INDIANA DAY

By act of the Legislature of Indiana, December 11, the date of the admission of the state to the Union, is designated as Indiana Day. The governor is directed to issue a proclamation providing that "suitable exercises having reference to the historical event to be commemorated thereby may be held in the public schools of the state and by citizens generally throughout the state in appropriate and patriotic observance of the anniversary of the admission of the State of Indiana to the Union." It was in 1816 that the state was admitted, in accordance with an enabling act of Congress, approved on April 16 of that year.

French trappers and fur traders who appeared within the present limits of the state in 1679, are supposed to be the first white men to enter the region. LaSalle, however, crossed the northwestern part in 1670. The Miami and Wabash Indians welcomed the French settlers who came later. The French built Fort Ouatanon, on the Wabash, in 1720 and Fort Vincennes in 1727. The first permanent settlement, however, was made in 1734 in the neighborhood of Fort Vincennes. The French settlers, who had some Negro and Indian slaves, lived in friendly relations with the Indians for many years. The territory came into the possession of the English in 1763, but in 1778-79 George Rogers Clark drove the British out. Troubles with the Indians soon began and continued until 1795 when General Wayne established peace. In May 1800, Indiana Territory was organized. It included all that part of the Northwest Territory lying west and north of the Ohio river. Some time later Michigan and Illinois were set off from this territory reducing Indiana to its present area. Its capital, first at Vincennes, was removed to Croyden in 1813 and to Indianapolis in 1825. The Indians, because the whites were occupying their lands, were making trouble in 1811 and General William Henry Harrison, later President of the United States, defeated Tecumseh and his followers in a decisive battle on the Tippecanoe River in Tippecanoe County. Early in the nineteenth century many Southern families moved into the territory and sought to legalize slavery. In 1816, however, the constitutional convention definitely forbade slavery and Negroes and mulattos were forbidden by law to migrate to the state. This law remained in force until after the Civil War.

HANUKKAH, OR THE FESTIVAL OF LIGHTS

Hanukkah or Channukah, the Jewish festival known also as the Feast of Dedication, the Feast of the Maccabees, and the Festival of Lights, begins on the twenty-fifth day of the month Kislew, which fell on December 11 in 1945. It continues for eight days as does the Feast of the Tabernacles. The elders of the congregation of Israel, under

639

the leadership of Judas Maccabeus, instituted it in the year 165 B.C., in honor of the dedication of the altar and the purification of the temple after it had been desecrated by Antiochus Epiphanes, three years earlier on the same day, when he set up a pagan altar in the temple and offered sacrifices to Zeus Olympius. The Jews had recovered the temple, had kindled anew the fires on the altar and lit the lamps and the candles. The dedication of the altar was celebrated with sacrifices and songs similar to those on the Feast of the Tabernacles. It is described in the Talmud as the Feast of Illumination, the illumination consisting of eight lamps lighted on the first night and one less on each succeeding night, or beginning with one lamp and increasing by one until eight were lighted on the last night.

According to a rabbinical tradition the custom of observing the festival for eight days with lamps arose from the miracle which is said to have occurred at the rededication of the temple. A small cruse of consecrated oil that had not been polluted by the pagans was found in the temple. It lasted eight days until new oil could be prepared and consecrated. Silver and bronze and copper lamps and candlesticks of elaborate design were made for use during the festival, each with places for eight wicks or eight candles. The Hanukkah lamps in the houses were not intended to be used for reading but were to be placed so that the passers by in the street could see them. There was to be one light for each person in the house, placed near the door, and if the house had more than one outside door lamps were to be placed at each. When the lamps are lighted the person who lights them and those looking on recite:

Blessed be the Lord our God, King of the Universe, who has sanctified us by Thy commandments and enjoined us to kindle the Hanukkah lamp.

There are beautiful specimens of the lamps in the Cluny Museum in Paris, the Victoria and Albert Museum in London and in the possession of private collectors. Some of them are modern and others were found in the excavations at Jerusalem.

DECEMBER TWELFTH

BIRTHDAY OF JOHN JAY

John Jay, the first Chief Justice of the United States, was born in New York City on December 12, 1745. He was the sixth son in the family of eight children born to Peter and Mary Van Cortlandt Jay. His paternal grandfather was Augustus Jay, a Huguenot exile who had settled in New York about 1686. His father was a rich merchant. He was graduated from King's College, now Columbia University, in 1764, studied law in the office of Benjamin Kissam, was admitted to the bar in 1768, and practiced his profession for several years. His first public employment was as secretary to a royal commission in 1773 appointed to fix the boundary between New York and New Jersey.

The outbreak of the Revolution put an end to his law practice for he was drafted into public service as a member of the New York Committee of Correspondence. He was sent as a delegate from New York to the First and Second Continental Congresses where he represented the interests of the business men who opposed independence lest it should result in disorder. But when the Declaration of Independence was adopted he embraced whole heartedly the cause of the colonies. From 1776 until 1778 he was busy with public affairs in New York, helping to draft its constitution, and as chief justice of the state interpreting the document. He took his seat in the Continental Congress again in December 1778, and early in the month was elected as its president, a post which he held until September of the next year when he was sent as plenipotentiary to Spain with instructions to persuade that country to recognize the independence of the United States. He failed in this because of commitments made by Spain to France, but he did obtain a loan of $170,000.

In the spring of 1782 he was summoned to Paris by Franklin where he assisted Franklin and John Adams in negotiating the treaty of peace with Great Britain. He declined appointments as Minister to Paris and as Minister to London which had been offered to him and returned home intending to resume his law practice. But he learned when he arrived on July 24, 1784, that Congress had made him secretary for foreign affairs. He served in this capacity until the ratification of the Constitution and the organization of the new government, and until Thomas Jefferson, who had been made Secretary of State, arrived to take up his duties in March 1790. Washington, after his election as the first President, offered to Jay any office which he might desire. Jay said he would like to be Chief Justice of the United States, and was the first to serve in that capacity. He had served five years when he resigned in 1795. His interpretation of the Constitution in the case of Chisholm vs. Georgia led to the adoption of the Eleventh Amendment.

Jay had been Federalist candidate for Governor of New York in 1792 against George Clinton, but he had been defeated. When he returned from England in 1795, after negotiating the treaty of 1794, he found that the Federalists had elected him governor and he resigned from the Supreme Court. He served two terms as governor, but declined to become a candidate for a third term in 1800, and also declined to accept reappointment to the Supreme Court. On the completion of his service as governor he retired at the age of fifty-five to his farm of 800 acres at Bedford, Westchester County, New York, where he lived the life of a political sage until his death on May 17, 1829.

DECEMBER 12

FEAST OF THE VIRGIN OF GUADALUPE

The feast of the Virgin of Guadalupe which falls on December 12 is celebrated in the Southwest where Spanish influence prevails. There are elaborate celebrations of it at Santa Fe and at many Indian pueblos in New Mexico. The legend of the Virgin is one of the most interesting in the religious history of North America. According to this legend a recent convert to Christianity, named Juan Diego, was hurrying down Tepayac Hill, three miles northeast of Mexico City, to hear mass in the city on Saturday, December 9, 1531, when the Virgin appeared to him and told him to tell the bishop to have a temple built where she stood. She was at the same place on Saturday evening and on Sunday evening, waiting for an answer. Diego had delivered the message, but the bishop had been skeptical. After carefully questioning Diego the bishop told him to ask the vision for a sign to prove that she was the Virgin. Diego spent all day Monday caring for an uncle who was grievously ill and at daybreak on Tuesday, December 12, fearing that his uncle was dying, he was hastening to the city for a priest. To avoid the vision of the Virgin, still on the hill, he went around it, but the Virgin saw him and went down to meet him and said, "What road is this thou takest, son?" A conversation followed during which the man explained his mission. The vision, calling herself Holy Mary of Guadalupe, cured his uncle and again told him to go to the bishop with the message about the temple. For a sign she told him to go up among the rocks and gather roses, although it was not the season wher roses were in bloom, but he went and found them and gathered them in his long cloak of coarse cloth. The Virgin arranged the roses and told him to keep them out of sight and untouched till he reached the bishop. When he arrived at the episcopal residence he unfolded his cloak and the roses fell out, and to his astonishment the bishop and his attendants were kneeling before him. He looked and there on the cloak was a life-sized picture of the Virgin as he had seen her.

The picture was guarded and a shrine was built where the Virgin had stood. It was simple when first erected. In 1622 a more elaborate structure was reared and a much finer one was built in 1709. During the eighteenth century other structures were reared, including a parish church, a convent and a church for the Capuchin nuns. The shrine itself has been decorated in the Byzantine style.

The picture, still preserved, is on coarsely woven stuff like sacking. Two strips of the cloth, about seventy inches long and eighteen inches wide, are held together by coarse stitching, the seam running through the center of the figure. The figure is surrounded by the sun, moon and stars, and rests on a crescent supported by an angel. It wears a mantle of blue green and a rose-colored figured tunic under the mantle. A careful inquiry has been made by the ecclesiastical authorities into the authenticity of the tradition and they have agreed to accept it. Pope

Benedict XIV made Our Lady of Guadalupe the patron of Mexico and the day on which she gave her sign to Diego a holiday of obligation.

DECEMBER THIRTEENTH

FEAST OF SANTA LUCIA

Santa Lucia, or St. Lucy, is one of the lesser saints of the Roman Catholic Church. Her feast day is December 13 and is observed by the Church with a mass designated in the Catholic missal, which terms her a virgin-martyr. She was one of the early Christian martyrs, was executed as a Christian at Syracuse in Sicily in 304. She is a patroness against diseases of the eyes. According to Swedish tradition Santa Lucia is also the patroness of the harvest and of light, and her day as well as the end of harvest. All threshing must be done by that day as well as all spinning and weaving for the year. The feast is often observed by Americans of Swedish descent and "Lucia buns" are served for breakfast. Among those of Italian descent it is traditional to serve boiled wheat on Santa Lucia's day.

DECEMBER FOURTEENTH

DEATH OF WASHINGTON

Washington, after his retirement from the presidency, took up his residence on his estate at Mount Vernon, Va. On December 12, 1799, he rode about the estate for several hours in the cold and snow and as a result of the exposure he came down with an acute attack of laryngitis. His doctors bled him several times as that was the customary treatment, but it failed to relieve him and he died on December 14. When the commander of the British fleet heard of the death he ordered the flags on every ship to be lowered to half-mast. Napoleon Bonaparte, then First Consul of France, announced the death to the army and ordered black crape to be suspended from all the flags in the French service for ten days, and a funeral oration was delivered before him and the civil authorities. John Marshall, then a member of the House of Representatives, made formal announcement of the death to Congress on December 29, and the next day Congress voted to erect a marble monument in Washington and recommended that the people wear crape on their left arms for thirty days. Later Congress arranged for memorial exercises on February 22, 1800. Plans were made for the burial of Washington in a crypt under the rotunda of the Capitol, but the family preferred that the burial should be at Mount Vernon. The proposed monument was not built until many years later.

DECEMBER FIFTEENTH

ADOPTION OF THE BILL OF RIGHTS

On December 15, 1791 the first ten amendments to the Constitution, popularly known as the Bill of Rights, were ratified by three fourths of the states and became a part of the Constitution. The one hundred and fiftieth anniversary of this significant occasion, December 15, 1941, was designated Bill of Rights Day by presidential proclamation and the people were called upon to observe it by displaying the flag and meeting together for such prayers and ceremonies as seemed appropriate. Since this date followed on the heels of the Pearl Harbor disaster when the nation was arming against the then powerful and victorious Axis, the democratic ideology expressed in the Bill of Rights was seized upon as a sort of battle cry and reiterated throughout the war in speech and in print, perhaps most notably in President Franklin D. Roosevelt's famous speech, "The Four Freedoms."

The Bill of Rights grew out of criticism of the Constitution as drafted by the Convention of 1787, many contending that it did not afford sufficient protection to the rights of individuals and the states. Richard Henry Lee of Virginia inquired: "Where is the contract between the nation and the government? The Constitution makes no mention but of those who govern, and never speaks of the rights of the people who are governed." Accordingly, after considerable argument and disagreement, twelve amendments were voted at the first session of the First Congress in New York on September 25, 1789, and submitted to the states for ratification. Two, relating to apportionment of Representatives, and to the pay of Congressmen, were rejected. The other ten, duly ratified, were a guarantee, as was the Magna Charta before them, of the rights of free men against tyranny; freedom of religion and speech, the right of the people to assemble peaceably, the right to petition the Government, the right of private property, the right of trial by jury, and various other guarantees which, together, established the United States as a true democracy, a government of, by and for the people.

DECEMBER SIXTEENTH

THE BOSTON TEA PARTY

One of the most famous incidents in the course of the protest of the American colonies against taxation without representation is known as the Boston Tea Party. Its anniversary is observed in Massachusetts by the Daughters of the Revolution and the Daughters of the American Revolution. There is a Tea Party Chapter of the Daughters of the American Revolution in Boston. Frequently when its celebrations of the anniversary take the form of luncheons or dinners, little brown tea pots are placed at the plates of guests. There is a mural painting in the State House in Boston showing the men throwing the tea overboard.

The colonies had protested against import taxes on goods entering America and merchants had agreed not to import anything from Great Britain as long as the taxes were continued. The British exporters protested to Parliament because of the loss of trade and some of the taxes were repealed, but the tax on tea remained. On the petition of the English East India Company an arrangement was made for suspending the export tax which would enable the colonists to buy their tea as cheaply as if the import tax had been removed. But this did not satisfy the colonists. As a matter of principle, they refused to allow any tea to be landed in their ports and the ships went back to England with their cargoes. There was great indignation in Boston and mass meetings were held to protest against the continuance of the tax. In November 1773, two ships laden with tea were moored at a wharf in Boston, and an attempt was made to land the cargo, supported by the royal governor and his friends, but it failed. The Boston *Weekly News-Letter* of December 2, 1773, contained the following call for a meeting of protest:

FRIENDS! BRETHREN! COUNTRYMEN! That worst of plagues, the detested T-E-A, shipped for this port by the East India Company, is now arrived in this Harbor; the Hour of Destruction or manly Opposition to the Macchinations of Tyranny stares you in the face; every Friend to his Country, to Himself, or to Posterity, is now called upon to meet in Fanueil Hall, at Nine o'clock T-H-I-S D-A-Y (At which Time the Bells will ring), to make a united and successful Resistance to the last, worst and most destructive Measure of Administration.

There was a later meeting in the Old South Meeting House and early in the evening of December 16, a company of sixty men, disguised as Indians, boarded the ship, tore open the hatches, and threw the tea overboard. The people of Boston offered to pay for what had been destroyed, but that did not appease the Government in London. In March of the next year Parliament passed by an almost unanimous vote a bill closing the port of Boston to all commerce by water and removing the seat of government to Salem. The passage of the bill was made easy by tales about the barbarism of the people of Boston circulated in England. It was said, for instance, that the Bostonians had a regularly appointed committee whose duty it was to tar and feather officers of the crown and their friends.

DECEMBER SEVENTEENTH

AVIATION DAY

The anniversary of the first successful flight in a heavier than air machine by the Wright brothers at Kitty Hawk, N.C., on December 17, 1903, has been observed in many ways in the intervening years. One of the celebrations of the day in 1934 was arranged under orders of

Claude A. Swanson, Secretary of the Navy, who directed that all the available airplanes of the Navy Department should take to the air at 10:30 o'clock in the morning and remain in flight for half an hour.

Sir Hiram Maxim of England, Otto Lilienthal of Germany, and S. P. Langley of the United States, had made many systematic experiments in an effort to build a flying machine supported by planes. And Octave Chanute, an American engineer, had made an aeroplane without a motor which would soar and carry a man for a short distance. Mr. Langley built an aeroplane with a steam motor, but his experiments with it were not successful, although it is now known that his theory of artificial flight was sound.

Orville and Wilbur Wright of Dayton, Ohio, began experiments early in the century with a gliding apparatus similar to that used by Chanute. They finally devised a machine with a sixteen horse-power four-cylinder gasoline engine. The wings could be warped and the machine was equipped with a rudder in front for elevating it. At a test at the Kill Devil sand hills, near Kitty Hawk, on December 17, 1903, four success-ful flights were made. In one of them the machine with a passenger rose by its own power, remained in the air fifty-nine seconds and traveled a distance of eight hundred and fifty-two feet. It was thus demonstrated for the first time that it was possible for man to fly. The Wright brothers continued their experiments and on October 5, 1905, with a new machine they made a flight of twenty-four and a half miles, remaining in the air thirty-eight minutes and three seconds, returning to the starting point. The machine had a maximum speed of thirty-eight miles an hour.

The development of the aeroplane proceeded slowly until the beginning of the first World War in 1914 when unlimited money became available for perfecting the machine for use in military operations. Planes were equipped for carrying explosive bombs and dropping them on the enemy. They were fitted with rapid fire guns for use in attacking other planes and there were many battles in the air fulfilling Tennyson's prophecy of "the nations' airy navies dropping down a ghastly dew." In the interval between the two world wars commercial aviation made tremendous strides, the size and speed of the planes constantly increasing and the record for nonstop and distance flights repeatedly topped. World War II witnessed a repetition of the aerial fighting of the earlier war, but with planes whose maneuverability, carrying capacity, and speed so far outstripped the models of World War I as to make the latter de-risively termed "crates." Commercial airlines now girdle the globe and the airplane has become a permanent and important means of trans-portation both for passengers and freight.

WHITTIER'S BIRTHDAY

It is customary in many public schools to observe the anniversary of the birth of John Greenleaf Whittier on December 17 with special exercises intended to interest the pupils in the man and in what he wrote. The program suggested by the Superintendent of Schools in one of the states included, in addition to songs by the pupils and a composition on Whittier's boyhood, recitations of "The Barefoot Boy," "Maud Muller," "Mabel Martin," "The Frost Spirit," "Centennial Hymn," and selections from "Snowbound." Other programs include "The Eternal Goodness," one of Whittier's best known shorter poems. It runs in this way:

> And if my heart and flesh are weak
>   To bear an untried pain,
> The bruised reed He will not break,
>   But strengthen and sustain.
>
> No offering of my own I have,
>   Nor works my faith to prove;
> I can but give the gifts He gave,
>   And plead His love for love.
>
> And so beside the silent sea
>   I wait the muffled oar;
> No harm from Him can come to me
>   On ocean or on shore.
>
> I know not where His islands lift
>   Their fronded palms in air:
> I only know I cannot drift
>   Beyond His love and care.

This poem expresses the religious sentiment which dominated his whole life. His early American ancestors became members of the Society of Friends and he was known as the Quaker poet. He was born in Haverhill, Mass., on December 17, 1807, and in his youth worked on his father's farm. He began to write while still a lad and his first poem was published when he was eighteen in the *Free Press*, an anti-slavery paper edited by William Lloyd Garrison. In 1827 and 1828 he studied in the Haverhill Academy, and in 1829 became editor of the *American Manufacturer*, published in Boston. He was employed as an editor of papers in Haverhill and in Hartford, Conn., until 1831.

His first volume, *Legends of New England*, consisting of poems and prose sketches, was published while he was in Hartford. He was a delegate to an anti-slavery convention in Philadelphia, in December 1833, and was a member of the Massachusetts Legislature in 1835 and 1836. In 1838 he went to Philadelphia to edit the *Pennsylvania Freeman*, an anti-slavery paper. His attacks upon slavery were so vigorous that a mob sacked and burnt his printing office in May of that year. But he remained in charge of the paper until 1840. On his return to Massachusetts he wrote many poems intended to arouse public sentiment against slavery, as well as many descriptive and narrative poems. When the *Atlantic Monthly* was established he became a frequent contributor. The esteem with which he had come to be regarded is indicated by his choice as a presidential elector for Massachusetts in 1860 and 1864. He was recognized as one of the men whose influence was effective in bringing about the abolition of slavery. His later years were spent with relatives at Danvers, Mass. He died, however, at Hampton Falls, N.H., on September 7, 1892, while on a visit there.

DECEMBER EIGHTEENTH

BIRTHDAY OF LYMAN ABBOTT

Lyman Abbott, one of the best known religious leaders of his time, was born at Roxbury, Mass., on December 18, 1835, the son of Jacob Abbott, the author of the "Rollo books." When he was three years old the family moved to Farmington, Me., and in 1843 to New York City where he entered New York University. He was graduated in 1853, and joined two brothers who were practicing law. After remaining in the law office two years he decided to prepare himself for the ministry and studied with his father and his uncle, J. S. C. Abbott. He was ordained as a Congregational clergyman in 1860 and became pastor of a church in Terre Haute, Ind., where he remained until 1865, when he became corresponding secretary for the American Union Commission, a group of clergymen and laymen interested in reconstruction after the Civil War. At the same time he served as pastor of a Congregational Church in New York.

He added to his income by writing book reviews for *Harper's Magazine* and in 1870 the American Tract Society made him editor of its new periodical the *Illustrated Christian Weekly*. He held this post until 1876 when he became associated with Henry Ward Beecher in the editorship of the *Christian Union*, the name of which he changed to the *Outlook*, after the withdrawal of Beecher from the editorship. Under his direction the *Outlook* became the leading religious weekly in the country. On the death of Beecher in 1887 Lyman Abbott succeeded him as pastor of Plymouth Church in Brooklyn which continued to prosper under his leadership. He resigned the pastorate in 1899 and spent the remainder of his life directing his paper and lecturing throughout the country. He wrote many books which influenced religious thought, and in his later years he was one of the leaders of the liberal wing of the Protestant church. He died on October 22, 1922.

DECEMBER NINETEENTH

WASHINGTON ENCAMPS AT VALLEY FORGE

After the battles of Brandywine and Germantown and the occupation of Philadelphia by the British in the autumn of 1777, Washington took his army of about eleven thousand men on December 19 to Valley Forge, in the rolling country twenty-four miles northwest of Philadelphia, and set up a fortified camp for the winter. One of the reasons for selecting this place was a desire to be in a position to prevent the British from making a move against Congress, which was then sitting at York, Pa. Another reason was the defensibility of the site. One side was protected by the Schuylkill and another by a steep precipice surmounted by a lofty hill from which all the surrounding country could be seen. Through failure of the commissary department and the quartermaster general the men suffered severely from cold and hunger during the winter. Yet under the training of Baron von Steuben they were turned into a well drilled and disciplined army. Washington broke camp on June 18, 1778, and reoccupied Philadelphia.

A large part of the site of the camp at Valley Forge has been bought by the State of Pennsylvania and turned into a public park. The old earthworks have been preserved and reproductions of some of the huts occupied by the soldiers have been erected. The Federal Government has put up a memorial arch on one of the hills and there are other monuments on the grounds. Just outside of the park a memorial chapel, in the gothic style, adorned by stained glass windows of great beauty, has been built. There is a Cloister of the States with thirteen bays adjoining the chapel as well as a museum, and a chime of bells has been set up by the women's patriotic societies. The chapel is a popular place for weddings—there is at least one there every day of the year. Among the buildings in the park is the house which Washington occupied as his headquarters, furnished in the style of the period.

The site of the Valley Forge encampment was thickly wooded when Washington took his army there. The soldiers immediately began to cut the trees to make cabins for their shelters. The huts were made weatherproof by mud and clay plastered on the logs to fill the crevices. When Washington evacuated the camp the farmers who owned the land tore down the huts and used the logs for firewood or for fences. During the political campaign of 1840, when General William Henry Harrison was the Whig candidate, Matthias Pennypacker of Phoenixville, an ardent Whig and an ancestor of a future Governor of Pennsylvania, decided to build a cabin from the logs that had been taken from the Valley Forge huts. He found only one that was sound, but he built a cabin using this log in it, mounted it on a wagon and drove it about the country to arouse the voters in what was then called a log cabin and hard cider campaign. At the close of the campaign he preserved the log. It was safely guarded by his son and grandson. Joseph P. Stockwell obtained it from the grandson and in 1935 presented it to the Pennsylvania chapter of the Sons of the American Revolution. In January 1936, it was deposited with the Pennsylvania Historical Society where it is preserved along with many other relics of the Revolutionary War.

DECEMBER TWENTIETH

LOUISIANA PURCHASE

When the United States took possession of what was loosely known as the Louisiana territory on December 20, 1803, it completed one of the greatest real estate deals in history. The region turned over to this country by France was more than a million square miles in extent, and cost about twenty dollars a square mile. Out of it have been carved many states now inhabited by millions of Americans. The population at the time of the purchase was about ninety thousand.

The transfer came about through the activities of Thomas Jefferson, who was President at the time. Louisiana had been transferred to France by Spain in 1800 and Jefferson was fearful of the consequences. Accordingly James Monroe was sent to Paris to cooperate with Robert R. Livington, the minister to France, in negotiations. As war between England and France had been resumed, the French, fearful lest the English should seize the territory, were ready to sell. After negotiating for some time an agreement of sale was reached on April 30, 1803, and the United States took possession in the following December. Jefferson, however, was doubtful of his constitutional authority to make the purchase and proposed the adoption of a constitutional amendment ratifying his acts, but as the country was pleased with what he had done and no one seriously questioned its wisdom, Jefferson finally decided that the less said about the constitutional question the better. The one hundredth anniversary of the purchase was celebrated by a great international exhibition at St. Louis in 1904.

DECEMBER TWENTY-FIRST

FEAST OF ST. THOMAS

This festival, falling on December 21, was instituted in the twelfth century. An ancient writer says that an early place in the Christian year was assigned to it because it was to Thomas that Jesus showed the wounds of the crucifixion after his resurrection and thus resolved the doubts of his disciple. Thomas was one of the Twelve Apostles. He was a Jew and is supposed to have been a native of Galilee. There is little authentic information about him save in the New Testament, and that is slight, but he is the subject of many traditions for which there is little foundation. There is extant a book called *The Acts of St. Thomas* which relates that on the dispersion of the Apostles he was told to go to India. On his refusal Jesus appeared and sold him as a slave to an Indian prince to serve as a carpenter. The prince turned a vast sum of money over to him and instructed him to build a palace more gorgeous than that of the Roman emperor, after which the prince started on a journey. Thomas, instead of building the palace, distributed the money among the poor and ill. When the prince returned and learned what had been done he was angry and sent Thomas to prison and ordered the jailor to put him to death. But the prince's brother died just then and while he sat beside the catafalque on which the dead body lay, the corpse sat upright and said:

The man whom thou tortured is a servant of God. I have been in Paradise and the angels showed me a wondrous palace, built of gold, silver and precious stones and they said: "This is the palace which the architect Thomas built for thy brother Gondoforus."

The prince thereupon hastened to the prison and released Thomas and told him what he had heard. Thomas then said to him:

Knowest thou not that they who wouldst possess heavenly things care little for the gauds of this world? There are in heaven such palaces without number for those who purchase the possession of them through faith and charity. Thy riches, O king, may prepare thee for such a palace but they cannot follow thee.

On account of this legend Thomas has been made the patron saint of masons and architects. A representation of the legend appears in one of the windows of the Cathedral of Bourges presented by the company of builders of the city. Another legend is that Thomas saw a large beam floating in the sea near the coast. The prince, with the aid of many men and elephants tried to pull it ashore but failed. Thomas, wishing to use it in building a church, attached a light cord to it and drew it easily to the beach.

In support of the tradition that Thomas preached in India it is cited that there is in Malabar a large group of persons who call themselves Christians of St. Thomas, who for centuries had been under the jurisdiction of the patriarch of Babylon. They still use a form of Syriac as the language of their liturgy. St. Thomas's Day falls on the winter solstice. The English have an old rhyme referring to it in this way:

St. Thomas gray, St. Thomas gray,
The longest night and shortest day.

DECEMBER TWENTY-SECOND

FOREFATHERS' DAY

New England Societies throughout the nation celebrate December 22 as the anniversary of the landing of the Pilgrim Fathers at Plymouth, Mass., in 1620. The actual landing, however, did not take place until January 4, 1621. The passengers on the "Mayflower" sighted Cape

Cod on November 9, 1620, and on November 11 the ship anchored in what is now the harbor of Provincetown. Several expeditions were sent out to explore the land but reported on their return that the region was not suitable for settlement. On December 16 a party of seventeen was sent out for a more extended examination of the surrounding country. They reached Plymouth harbor on December 21, found it good and the adjoining region satisfactory. They then returned to the "Mayflower" with their report and the ship sailed southward reaching Plymouth on January 4 and landed its passengers.

The first celebration of the anniversary was arranged by the Old Colony Club of Plymouth on December 22, 1769. It selected the date from the record in the diary of George Morton which had been printed. The misplacing of a comma led to the belief that the exploring party had arrived at Plymouth on December 22 instead of on December 21. The precedent thus set has been generally followed, although some New England Societies hold their celebration on December 21, others on December 20 and still others on December 23. The Plymouth celebrations have been notable. Among the orators who have addressed the Old Colony Club on the occasion have been Daniel Webster, Edward Everett, Rufus Choate and Charles Sumner. William Cullen Bryant wrote a poem to be read at one of the celebrations.

Plymouth Rock, on which tradition says the Pilgrims landed, is a large boulder, the only rock of any size in the neighborhood. They did not land on a "stern and rock bound coast," as Felicia Hemans has it in her poem. The people of Plymouth have always prized the rock. In 1774, when they were resenting the maltreatment of the colony by the British, they decided to move it to a more honorable position and on October 5 of that year five thousand of the colonists gathered at Plymouth to assist or be present while it was moved to the center of the Town Square. While the workmen were lifting it from its place it split in two, and one of the spectators remarked that this was prophetic of the separation of the American colonies from the mother country. Half of the rock was dragged by twenty yoke of oxen to the square in front of Pilgrim Hall. It remained there until 1880 when it was carried back to its original site and a dressed stone canopy supported by pillars was erected over it. In the early days of the present century the hack drivers in Plymouth who carried visitors to the historic spots about the town would sell to their customers chips of stone, described as pieces broken from the rock when it was moved back to its original site. The credulous, failing to reflect that tons of broken stone had probably been sold in this way since 1880, bought the souvenirs as authentic.

The Pilgrims, as is well known, were Separatists, setting up a church independent of the Church of England. They suffered persecution in England and with John Robinson as their pastor they migrated to Amsterdam and later to Leyden in Holland. Robinson found that the prospects for the permanence of his church in Holland were not good, and in 1617 he and Bradford and Brewster organized a movement to emigrate to America. A majority of the members of the church sailed from Delftshaven for England in the "Speedwell" to join others at Plymouth, England. The "Mayflower" sailed from Plymouth on September 6. The "Speedwell" was forced to abandon the voyage. They had intended to settle in Virginia, but storms drove them north to the Massachusetts coast. They planned to found a church without a bishop and a state without a king. Yet in the compact to which they signed their names on board the "Mayflower" before they landed they described themselves as "loyal subjects of our dread sovereigne Lord, King James, by the grace of God, of great Britaine, France and Ireland, defender of the faith, etc." This compact declared that:

We, whose names are underwritten, . . . doe, by these presents solemnly and mutually in the presence of God and of one another, covenant and combine ourselves together into a civill body politick, for our better ordering and preservation and furtherance of the ends aforesaid; and by virtue hereof to enacte, constitute and frame such just and equall laws, ordinances, acts, constitutions, and offices, from time to time, as shall be thought most meete and convenient for the generall good of the Colonie, unto which we promise all due submission and obedience.

This was signed at Cape Cod on November 20 (November 10, Old Style) 1620.

A Society of Mayflower Descendants was organized near the close of the last century by men and women whose ancestors arrived at Plymouth on the famous ship. The descendants of John Alden and Priscilla Mullins, who were among the passengers, have organized a special society of their own, doubtless because of the interest in these two pilgrims aroused by Longfellow's poem, "The Courtship of Miles Standish." New Englanders have migrated to all parts of the country and they have formed New England Societies which annually observe Forefathers' Day. The oldest of these societies is in Charleston, S.C. A New England Society was formed in New York City in 1805, and there are similar societies in Philadelphia, Cincinnati, Chicago, St. Louis and other cities. There are also state societies the members of which are of New England descent.

The Pilgrim migration of 1620 was followed a few years later by a migration of Puritans from England to the region around Boston, forming the Massachusetts Bay Colony. It was said of the Puritans that they came to America to worship God in their own way and to compel others to do the same. For a time no one was allowed to hold office in the Massachusetts Bay Colony who was not a church member. But the Plymouth colony never had any such rule. The Puritans banished Roger Williams to Rhode Island because they regarded his religious views as unsettling to the state. They believed in witches and punished them by death. Yet on the whole the Puritan influence was good and it is always glorified at the dinners of the New England Societies.

ST. FRANCES XAVIER'S DAY

December 22 is the feast day of St. Frances Xavier, the first American citizen ever canonized, who thus may properly be termed an American saint although she was born in Italy, the daughter of Italian farmers. Francesca Cabrini was the last of thirteen children, her birthplace Saint Angelo, near the town of Lodi in northern Italy. She took her vow of chastity at fourteen, repeating it before she was twenty. Two orders rejected her because of her frail health and she therefore became directress of an orphanage. She was in her late thirties when the Bishop of Lodi sent for her and told her she was to become a missionary, but, as he knew of no missionary order for women, she would have to found one. In 1889 she arrived in New York with a band of five sisters, established herself in the slums and immediately opened the first of the many charitable institutions which were to make her famous. Eventually she became a naturalized American citizen, and when she died in Chicago on December 22, 1917, at the age of sixty-seven, had established no less than sixty-seven charitable institutions, one for each year of her life. She was the founder of the Missionary Sisters of the Sacred Heart under whose auspices hospitals, orphanages, and schools were opened in London, Paris, Buenos Aires, and Rio de Janeiro, as well as in many American cities.

Blessed Mother Frances Xavier Cabrini, as she was known before her canonization, was the personal friend of Pope Leo XIII who said of her that she possessed "real sanctity" and "a great mind." She had keen business sense and amazing self-confidence, in addition to an intellectual clarity that made her appear direct, headstrong and daring, although these qualities were tempered by genuine modesty and a charm felt by all who met her. Sainthood is recognized in the Roman Catholic Church only after long examination proves that the candidate is characterized by exceptional virtue and has performed well-authenticated miracles. Joan of Arc's canonization was debated five hundred years and, according to church decree sainthood proceedings may never be instituted until fifty years after a candidate's death. However, upon the death of Mother Cabrini reports of miracles attributed to her began pouring in from all parts of the world. As a result, the Vatican waived the requirement, "in view of the need for strong spiritual currents in the world today." In 1937 the Blessed Mother was declared venerable, and the following year beatified and accredited by the church with two miracles selected from thousands reported. On July 7, 1946, she was canonized in an elaborate ceremony at St. Peter's in Rome.

Perhaps the most famous miracle accredited to St. Frances Xavier occurred shortly after her death. Peter Smith of New York, later an ex-sergeant who served on Okinawa, became blind directly after his birth at Columbus Hospital, Chicago, in 1921, due to the carelessness of a nurse who accidentally bathed his eyes in a 50 per cent solution of nitrate of silver instead of the usual 1 per cent solution. He also contracted pneumonia from inhaling the acid fumes and was given up by the doctors. The hospital superior then pinned a relic of Mother Cabrini to his gown, while she and the sisters spent the night in prayer. Dr. Michael F. Horan and two of his colleagues testified at an ecclesiastical hearing that improvement was noted the next morning. Seventy-two hours later Peter Smith was a normal child, his sight restored.

The impressive rites of canonization, performed in St. Peter's basilica in Rome, were attended by more than forty thousand persons. The basilica, hung with red damask and brilliantly lighted by countless candles, was an appropriate setting for the majestic pageantry and symbolism of the ceremonies. Pope Pius XII stood at the altar, surrounded by the cardinals and other prelates who bared their heads, and read the pronouncement that proclaimed Mother Cabrini a saint. Cardinal Salotti, prefect of the Sacred Congregation of Rites which conducted the examination for cause of canonization, expressed thanks, and the Pope then intoned the ancient Latin hymn in praise to God, the Te Deum. Thereafter the Pontiff spoke in Latin of the life of St. Frances Xavier, whom he called "a humble child who distinguished herself not by tribute or richness of power, but by virtue." He saw in her life an admonition to the world, declaring that "men need as never before the splendor and fruit of saintliness. Nations and peoples will learn from her—who ardently loved her fatherland and spread the treasures of her charity and her labors even to other lands— that they are called to constitute a single family that must not be divided in ambiguous and stormy rivalry, nor dissolve itself in eternal hostilities."

DECEMBER TWENTY-THIRD

BIRTHDAY OF JOSEPH SMITH, JR.

Joseph Smith, Jr., the founder of what is popularity known as the Mormon Church, was born in Sharon, Vt., on December 23, 1805. The anniversary is regularly observed by his followers by holding memorial services at which addresses on his life and work are made. His father was a farmer said to be expert in locating sites for wells by the use of a forked wand. His mother was deeply religious and believed that she would become the mother of a prophet. The family moved to Palmyra, N.Y., in 1816 and after living there a short time settled on a tract of land near Manchester, a few miles south of Palmyra. The boy's education was limited to reading, writing and elementary arithmetic.

In the spring of 1820, when he was fourteen years old, there was considerable religious excitement in the neighborhood. The different denominations engaged in bitter rivalry and the boy was mentally disturbed by the religious excitement. After reading in the Bible that if any man lack wisdom let him ask of God and it shall be given unto him he decided to ask God which denomination had the truth and which he should join. He went into a retired place in the woods and prayed, and according to his account he beheld a pillar of light over his head from which appeared two personages floating in the air. One of them called him by name and pointed to the other saying, "This is my Beloved Son. Hear Him." Then he asked which denomination held the truth and was told that none of them did.

Three years later, on September 21, 1823, he had a second vision when an angel named Moroni appeared to him revealing the hiding place of some golden tablets containing the history of the ancient people of America. The next day, according to his account, the angel appeared to him again and guided him to the hill Cumorah near Manchester where he found the plates but was not allowed to take them away with him. On the anniversary of this date for the next three years he visited the hill and saw the plates but was told each time that it was too soon to reveal them to the public. In the spring of 1827 he married the daughter of a Pennsylvania farmer. On September 22 of that year he visited the hill again and was allowed to take the plates away with him. The message on them was written in strange characters. Nearly three years were spent in the translation. Smith was assisted in this work by his wife, by a school teacher and by a farmer. The translation was published under the title of *The Book of Mormon,* in Palmyra in 1830. Smith's father went about the country selling it at the price of $1.25.

While the translation was in progress, according to the Mormon account, John the Baptist appeared on May 15, 1829, to Joseph Smith, Jr., and Oliver Cowdery, the school teacher assisting him, and made them priests after the order of Aaron. They, thereupon, began to make converts and to found a church which was organized on April 6, 1830, under the laws of New York as the Church of Jesus Christ of Latter-Day Saints.

The church grew in membership and sent missionaries into other states. Its headquarters were in Ohio for a time and then in Missouri, from which it was driven by Governor Boggs. They took refuge in Illinois on the banks of the Mississippi a few miles above Warsaw and built the town of Nauvoo, which prospered and was fostered by the state government until July 12, 1843, when Joseph Smith had a revelation in favor of the practice of polygamy. A schism developed in the church and the practice of polygamy was denounced by a newspaper started by one of the schismatics. The paper was suppressed and the printing plant where it was published was destroyed by a mob. The owner of the paper obtained an order at Carthage, Ill., for the removal of Smith to that town—he was Mayor of Nauvoo—on the charge of riot. Smith was released but was later lodged in jail at Carthage on the charge of treason. The jail was attacked by a mob and he was killed on June 27, 1844. (See July 24.)

DECEMBER TWENTY-FOURTH

CHRISTMAS EVE

The old English custom of welcoming Christmas on the preceding eve by singing carols was early introduced in America, especially in those parts of the country in which the rigid simplicities of Puritanism were not insisted upon. The celebration of Christmas was forbidden in Massachusetts for a time but when the observance of the festival became general the occupants of the houses on Beacon Hill in Boston placed candles in the front windows on Christmas eve, and the waits going about the city singing carols would pause before these houses and sing their merry songs.

Waits were originally night watchmen, but the name in course of time came to be applied to companies of musicians. There were such companies in England as early as the late fourteenth century. The name was sometimes applied to the town band. In modern times the name is applied in England to musicians who play or sing in the evening for two or three weeks before Christmas.

The Boston custom of placing lights in the windows on Christmas eve spread to other cities. With the growing use of electricity, wreaths with electric lights in them took the place of candles. Carol singing is common in many American communities. The church choirs go about the town singing before the houses of the pastor and the leading members of the churches and there is a special Christmas eve service in many of the churches, when the Christmas entertainment for the Sunday school is not held at that time.

Christmas Eve is known in the Roman and Anglican churches as the Vigil of Our Blessed Lord Jesus.

DECEMBER TWENTY-FIFTH

CHRISTMAS, OR THE FEAST OF THE NATIVITY

This is the most important feast in the whole Christian year, the anniversary of the birth of Jesus. The story of the birth is told in the Gospel of St. Luke in this way:

DECEMBER 25

And it came to pass in those days that there went out a decree from Caesar Augustus, that all the world should be taxed. (And this taxing was first made when Cyrenius was Governor of Syria.) And all went to be taxed, every one to his own city. And Joseph also went up from Galilee out of the city of Nazareth, into Judea, unto the city of David, which is called Bethlehem (because he was of the house and lineage of David), to be taxed with Mary his espoused wife, being great with child. And so it was that, while they were there, the days were accomplished that she should be delivered. And she brought forth her first born son and wrapped him in swaddling clothes, and laid him in a manger, because there was no room for him in the inn.

And there were in the same country shepherds abiding in the field, keeping watch over their flock by night. And lo, an angel of the Lord came upon them, and the glory of the Lord shone round about them; and they were sore afraid. And the angel said unto them, "Fear not; for, behold, I bring you good tidings of great joy, which shall be to all the people. For unto you is born this day in the city of David a Savior, which is Christ the Lord. And this shall be a sign unto you: Ye shall find him wrapped in swaddling clothes, lying in a manger."
And suddenly there was with the angel a multitude of the heavenly host, praising God, and saying, "Glory to God in the highest, and on earth peace, good will toward men."

And it came to pass, as the angels were gone away from them into heaven, the shepherds said one to another, "Let us now go even unto Bethlehem, and see this thing which is come to pass, which the Lord hath made known unto us," And they came with haste, and found Mary and Joseph, and the babe lying in a manger. And when they had seen it they made known abroad the saying which was told them concerning this child. And all they that heard it wondered at those things which were told them by the shepherds. But Mary kept all these things and pondered them in her heart.

Although December 25 is observed as the anniversary of the birth of Jesus the exact date of the birth is not known. January 6 was observed by the Christians in Palestine as the date of both the birth and the baptism of Jesus as early as the fourth century. But there was doubt in the mind of the Bishop of Jerusalem over the correctness of the date. He wrote to the Bishop of Rome asking him to consult the archives in that city to discover if possible the real date of the birth. The Bishop of Rome made an investigation and replied that Jesus was born on December 25. But modern scholars are of the opinion that this date was fixed arbitrarily. Egyptian theologians had fixed the date as May 20. Others had put it on April 19 or 20 and still others on January 6. In fact there is no month in which reputable scholars have not fixed the date of the birth.

The day was not one of the early feasts of the Christian church. In fact the observance of birthdays was condemned as a heathen custom repugnant to Christians. The earliest record of any celebration comes from Clement of Alexandria who lived in the latter part of the second century and the early part of the third. The name for the day in English dates from the eleventh century when it was called Cristes Maesse. In Dutch it is known as Kerst-misse, and in Latin as Dies Natalis. Noel, the French name for this day is derived from the Latin word "natalis," meaning birthday. The Italians call the day Il Natale and the Germans

Weihnachtsfest. The English, besides calling the day Christmas, frequently speak of it as Yuletide. The scholars, however, have been unable to find any satisfactory explanation of this name.

An attempt has been made to connect the celebration of Christmas with the Roman Saturnalia and with the worship of Dionysus at Delphi, but the ecclesiastical authorities frown upon it. Yet it is admitted that many pagan customs centering around the first of January were adopted by the Christians in the celebration of the nativity. The giving of presents on January 1 by the Romans has survived as the giving of Christmas remembrances, or as it is sometimes called the exchange of presents.

The first hymn to the nativity was written in the fourth century. The earliest German Christmas lieder date from the eleventh century. The French songs and the English carols were first sung in the thirteenth century. An Arab geographer quoted in the tenth century a tradition that trees and flowers blossomed on Christmas and in the thirteenth century a French epic tells of candles appearing on the flowering trees. In England the rod of Joseph of Arimethea, a thorn' bush at the Glastonbury cathedral, was said to blossom on Christmas. When the calendar was changed, dropping ten days, two thousand people gathered about the thorn bush at Glastonbury in 1752 to see if it would blossom. When the flowers failed to appear they refused to accept the new calendar. The custom of decorating the houses with greens is derived from this belief in the blossoming of trees and plants at Christmas. Yet one archibishop forbade the use of greens on the assumption that the custom was of heathen origin. The use of mistletoe is without doubt traced to the Druids, who regarded it with reverence long before the Christian era. In celebration of the winter solstice the Druid priests gathered mistletoe and piled it on the altar of their god and burned it in sacrifice to him. The priests clad in white ceremonial robes for the occasion, went into the oak groves where the mistletoe grew on the trees and cut it with a golden sickle. Not only was the plant placed on the altar but sprigs of it were distributed among the people and hung up in their houses. The plant was regarded as a symbol of future hope and peace. Whenever enemies met under the mistletoe they would drop their arms, forget their enmities and embrace. It is believed that the custom of kissing under the mistletoe grew out of this ancient practice. In some parts of England the mistletoe was used with holly in decorating the churches at Christmas. In other parts it was banned because of its connection with Druidical ceremonies. Its use as part of the Christmas decorations in private houses is common in the United States. A sprig is fastened to a chandelier in the living room and the youths regard it as their privilege to kiss any pretty girl who wittingly or unwittingly stands under it. There was a time in England when it was hung only in the kitchens and the youth who kissed a girl standing under it plucked one of the white berries for every kiss.

659

The Christmas tree, as it is now known, is of German origin, although antiquarians profess to trace it to ancient Egypt. The first authentic mention of a Christmas tree in Germany was in 1605 when one was set up in Strassburg. There is a tradition, however, that Martin Luther, in the previous century, took an evergreen tree home to his children and decorated it for Christmas and thus introduced the custom. The lighting of it with candles undoubtedly grew out of the belief that candles appeared miraculously on various trees at the Christmas season. It was not until 1840 that the custom of setting up a Christmas tree was introduced into England. It was taken there by Princess Helena of Mecklenberg and the Prince Consort. It was introduced into the United States at an earlier date by the German immigrants. It was not used in Massachusetts, however, until 1860 when John C. Bushmann, a German, set up a tree in Westfield, and invited the people to see it.

There was a time during the Puritan ascendancy in England when the observance of Christmas was forbidden. A law was passed in 1644 making December 25 a market day and ordering that the shops be kept open. The making of plum puddings and mince pies was forbidden as a heathen custom. This law was repealed after the Restoration, but the Dissenters ridiculed the celebration of Christmas by calling it "Fooltide" in burlesque of Yuletide. The General Court of Massachusetts passed a law in 1659 making the observance of Christmas a penal offense. This law was later repealed as the English law had been, but it was many years before there were any general Christmas celebrations in New England.

One of the early German celebrations in America was arranged in 1741 by Count Nicholas Ludwig von Zinzendorf, who had recently arrived in the country to join the Moravians at what is now Bethlehem, Pa. On Christmas day the Count holding a lighted candle and singing a German hymn, led the settlers into a stable attached to the first house built by them. The Moravians to this day observe Christmas with services modeled on those instituted by Count Zinzendorf. Lighted candles are distributed to those present and the congregation sings "Christ Whose Glory Fills the Skies." It was the Christmas revels of the Hessians in the British army at Trenton in 1776 which made the victory of Washington easier than it would otherwise have been. Washington crossed the Delaware on Christmas night, found the British army sleeping off the effects of the celebration and took it by surprise.

The Lord of Misrule, a mock potentate ruling over Christmas sports in England appears in the United States during the carnival festivities in the Southern cities. In England, however, in the sixteenth and seventeenth centuries the King and the nobles had such an official attached to their courts during the Christmas season who arranged various diversions for the amusement of the people. In London he would parade the streets with a large mounted retinue clad in gorgeous costumes of velvet adorned with gold chains, and accompanied by musicians.

The use of fireworks on Christmas is common in Italy, France and Spain. The French settlers in Louisiana introduced this custom in America and it spread to many other Southern states so that while fireworks are associated with the Fourth of July in the North they are regarded in the South as an indispensable accompaniment of Christmas. The day was observed in the South much earlier than in the North.

The French had a Christmas celebration in New England several years before the Pilgrims arrived at Plymouth, but it was an isolated event. Under the lead of De Monts they made a settlement on St. Croix Island off the coast of Maine in 1604. On December 25, while everyone was well and the food supply seemed abundant, they held religious services in the chapel which they built and spent the rest of the day in sports of various kinds after the manner of their home country. But before spring came most of the colonists were dead and those who survived went to Nova Scotia near the present site of Annapolis. A note on a New England Christmas in 1774 appears in the diary of Lieutenant Barker, an English officer stationed at Boston, who wrote:

Bad day, continued snow till evening when it turned out rain and sleet. A soldier of the Tenth was shot for desertion, the only thing done in remembrance of Christmas Day.

The wassail bowl was filled for Christmas in England and the English brought it to America where it frequently serves its ancient purpose. Here is an ancient recipe for the beverage with which it was filled:

Cook a little grated nutmeg, two cloves, a pennyweight of powdered ginger, a tiny blade of mace, five or six allspice berries and an inch or two of stick cinnamon in a gill of water until it boils once or twice. Mix this with the contents of four bottles of wine and heat the whole over a moderate fire, dissolving in it about a pound of sugar. Beat the yolks of twelve eggs until light and frothy, then fold them throughout the whites which should also have been beaten to as stiff a froth as possible. Put the beaten eggs into a big punch bowl or old wassail bowl. Remove the wine from the fire, pour it over the eggs, beating the whole constantly till light and frothy. While still foaming add twelve hot baked apples.

The belief in Santa Claus as the giver of Christmas presents comes to us through the Germans. It derives from the legend of St. Nicholas—Santa Claus is a German corruption of the name—who lived in the fourth century. St. Nicholas learned that three young women had no suitors as their father was too poor to provide them with a dowry. So one night he filled three bags with gold and threw them into the windows of the rooms occupied by the young women and they soon were happily married. Unexpected gifts were thereafter said to come from St. Nicholas. His feast day occurs on December 6, and in Germany in the course of time he came to be described as the giver of Christmas presents. The children put their shoes and stockings beside the fireplace on Christmas eve in the hope that he would fill them with goodies. The myth that Santa Claus descends the chimney to find the stockings comes from the Norsemen. The legend is that at the winter solstice the goddess Hertha appeared in the fireplaces in their great halls and brought with her happiness and good fortune.

Dr. Clement Clarke Moore, a professor in the General Theological Seminary in New York, put the myth in the form in which it is accepted in the United States. It was in his poem "The Visit of St. Nicholas." He invented the sleigh and the reindeer and his description of St. Nicholas was suggested by the appearance of a German man-of-all work in his employ. The sleigh bells were suggested by the bells on his own horse as he was driving home on a winter evening. This was in 1822. He wrote the poem for his children and read it to them on Christmas Eve in that year. It begins, as everyone knows:

> 'Twas the night before Christmas, when all through the house
> Not a creature was stirring, not even a mouse;
> The stockings were hung by the chimney with care,
> In hopes that St. Nicholas soon would be there:
> The children were nestled all snug in their beds,
> While visions of sugar plums danced in their heads:
> And mamma in her 'kerchief and I in my cap,
> Had just settled our brains for a long winter's nap;
> When out on the lawn there arose such a clatter,
> I sprang from my bed to see what was the matter.
> Away to the window I flew like a flash,
> Tore open the shutters and threw up the sash.
> The moon on the breast of the new-fallen snow,
> Gave the luster of mid-day to objects below,
> When, what to my wondering eyes should appear,
> But a miniature sleigh and eight tiny reindeer,
> With a little old driver, so lively and quick,
> I knew in a moment it must be St. Nick.

In the autumn of the next year Miss Harriet Butler, daughter of the Reverend David Butler, rector of St. Paul's Church in Troy, N.Y., was visiting Dr. Moore and saw the poem. She got Dr. Moore's consent to make a copy of it which she took back to Troy. She sent it anonymously to the editor of the Troy *Sentinel* in the holiday season and he printed it with a complimentary introduction. A copy of the newspaper was sent to Dr. Moore who was annoyed that the verses which he had written to amuse his children should be printed. They were reprinted by newspapers in other parts of the country and republished during the Christmas season every year. In 1829 the editor of the Troy *Sentinel*, in response to many inquiries, announced that the poem was written by a gentleman who belonged "by birth and residence to the City of New York, and that he is a gentleman of more merit as a scholar and writer than many of more noisy pretensions." In 1830 the poem was printed in Troy for use as a "Carrier's Address" such as the men who delivered the newspapers gave to their customers in the holiday season. It was adorned with a wood engraving of St. Nicholas in his sleigh driving over the housetops. It was included in 1837 in *The New York Book of Poetry,* but anonymously. It was not until 1838 that Dr. Moore publicly admitted that he wrote the poem. The announcement was made in the Troy *budget.* He included it in his collected poems in 1844 and in 1848 it was published separately by Henry M. Onderdonck of New York in a little book illustrated with many crude wood engravings. Since then innumerable editions of it have been published.

Little children accept the Santa Claus myth without question, but as they grow older they begin to have doubts. One of them .in 1897 wrote to the New York *Sun* asking whether there is a Santa Claus. Its answer, written by Francis P. Church and printed as an editorial article, has become almost as famous as Dr. Moore's poem. Here it is:

We take pleasure in answering thus prominently the communication below, expressing at the same time our great gratification that its faithful author is numbered among the friends of the *Sun*:

Dear Editor—

I am eight years old. Some of my little friends say there is no Santa Claus. Papa says "If you see it in *The Sun* it's so." Please tell me the truth, is there a Santa Claus?

VIRGINIA O'HANLON

Virginia, your little friends are wrong. They have been affected by the skepticism of a skeptical age. They do not believe except they see. They think that nothing can be which is not comprehensible by their little minds. All minds, Virginia, whether they be men's or children's, are little. In this great universe of ours man is a mere insect, an ant, in his intellect as compared with the boundless world about him, as measured by the intelligence capable of grasping the whole of truth and knowledge.

Yes, Virginia, there is a Santa Claus. He exists as certainly as love and generosity and devotion exist, and you know that they abound and give to your life its highest beauty and joy. Alas! how dreary would be the world if there were no Santa Claus! It would be as dreary as if there were no Virginias. There would be no childlike faith then, no poetry, no romance to make tolerable this existence. We should have no enjoyment, except in sense and sight. The eternal light with which childhood fills the world would be extinguished.

Not believe in Santa Claus! You might as well not believe in fairies. You might get your papa to hire men to watch in all the chimneys on Christmas eve to catch Santa Claus, but even if you did not see Santa Claus coming down, what would that prove? Nobody sees Santa Claus, but that is no sign that there is no Santa Claus. The most real things in the world are those that neither children nor men can see. Did you ever see fairies dancing on the lawn? Of course not, but that's no proof that they are not there. Nobody can conceive or imagine all the wonders there are unseen and unseeable in the world.

You tear apart the baby's rattle and see what makes the noise inside, but there is a veil covering the unseen world which not the strongest man, nor even the united strength of all the strongest men that ever lived could tear apart. Only faith, poetry, love, romance, can push aside that curtain and view and picture the supernal beauty and glory beyond. Is it all real? Ah, Virginia, in all this world there is nothing else real and abiding.

No Santa Claus! Thank God! he lives and lives forever. A thousand years from now, Virginia, nay, ten times ten thousand years from now, he will continue to make glad the heart of childhood.

DECEMBER 25

The custom of sending Christmas cards to one's friends originated in England in 1846. It was suggested by Sir Henry Cole to Joseph Cundall, a London artist who had a drawing made by J. C. Horsley, R.A., and lithographed in black and white and colored by hand. About a thousand copies of it were sold. It was not until eighteen years later that the custom of sending the cards became popular. Even then it was not general. In the course of time the King and the Queen and the Prince of Wales adopted the custom and employed distinguished artists to paint an appropriate picture for each of them, which was reproduced in colors.

Christmas cards were introduced in the United States in the late 1870's by Marcus Ward & Company of London who had a monopoly of the market for a time. The English cards were so popular that L. Prang & Company of Boston began to compete for the trade with considerable success. In the spring of 1880 the Boston firm offered prizes amounting to $2000 for the best designs for such cards with Samuel Coleman, Richard M. Hunt and E. C. Moore as the judges. Nearly six hundred designs were submitted. The competition was so successful that Prangs arranged another prize competition for cards to be issued in 1881 with John LaFarge, Louis C. Tiffany and Samuel Coleman as the judges.

About this time the shops in the large cities, finding the demand for greeting cards so great, began to fill their show windows with them a month or more before Christmas. In the intervening years their popularity has increased and millions of them are sent through the mail at every Christmas season. They are made in an almost endless variety of styles and prices with designs suitable for persons of all ages and tastes.

Early in the present century the custom of setting up a Christmas tree in a public place and decorating it with colored lights was adopted in many American cities. In 1909 the people of Pasadena, Calif., instead of setting up a tree in the city, selected a tall evergreen on Mount Wilson, decorated it with lights and tinsel and loaded it with gifts which were distributed on Christmas day. In 1912 a tree was set up in Madison Square in New York and on the Common in Boston for the first time. And in 1914 a tree was placed in Independence Square in Philadelphia. In each of these cities choirs gathered around the trees on Christmas eve and sang carols.

Christmas is distinctly a Christian festival, but in modern times the day has been observed by the Jews as well as by the Christians. They give gifts and send Christmas greetings to their friends. The reason for this was explained by Rabbi Eichler in a sermon in Temple Ohabei Shalom at Boston in the Christmas season of 1910, in which he said:

664

Is there a reason why he (the Jew) cannot conscientiously join the world in celebrating Christmas? To this the loyal Jew must answer with an emphatic 'No.' Christmas has a double aspect, a social and a theological side. The Jew can and does heartily join in the social Christmas. . . . Gladly does he contribute to the spirit of good will and peace, characteristic of the season. . . . At the very time in which the Christian world celebrates Chritsmas, the Jews celebrate Hanukka—the feast of lights—commemorating the victory of the heroic Maccabeans over the idolatrous and tyrannical Graeco-Syrian empire. Through that victory Judaism was preserved and the subsequent development of Christianity made possible. It was from the light of Israel's sanctuary that Christianity lit its torch. The Hanukka lights, therefore, justly typify civilization and universal religion.

For centuries Christmas has been celebrated in Bethlehem where Jesus was born. Constantine the Great built a church on the site of the birthplace in the early part of the fourth century. It was destroyed, and another church built in the fifth or sixth century and additions have been made to it since that time. A dispute over the right to possess the key to the Holy Grotto beneath the church, supposed to be the site of the manger, was one of the causes of the Crimean War. The Russians insisted that the Greek church should have the key, but the dispute was decided in favor of the French and the Latin church. The church, known as the Church of the Nativity, is now shared by various communions. The choir belongs to the Greeks alone while the Grotto of the Nativity is open to the Roman, the Greek and the Armenian churches which hold services there in turn. The Christmas services in 1934 were conducted by the acting Greek Patriarch. As midnight of Christmas Eve approached a procession of priests led by the acting Patriarch moved slowly to the transept, swinging censers as they marched. At the stroke of midnight a curtain was drawn back revealing a figure of the Christ child lying on rich cloths. The congregation began to sing "Hallelujahs" and the Patriarch lifted the Babe and carried it down to the manger in the grotto and reverently laid it there. One by one the worshippers moved up to the manger and kissed it. As the worshippers left the church the bells rang in joyful notes. While the services in the church were in progress the Jerusalem Young Men's Christian Association was conducting a service in the shepherd's field outside Bethlehem where the shepherds watched their flocks on the Holy Night. Hymns and carols were sung and bread and meat, prepared as the shepherds prepared their food in the field, were eaten.

Reproductions of the manger known as the crib are set up in the Catholic churches every Christmas season, with the Holy Child, Mary and Joseph, the Wise Men, and the cattle. There is a tradition that on Christmas Eve the cattle in their stalls kneel in adoration. The crib remains in the churches until Twelfth Night. Small cribs are frequently part of the Christmas decorations in Catholic families.

DECEMBER TWENTY-SIXTH

BATTLE OF TRENTON

It was the custom of the citizens of Trenton, N.J., for many years in the early part of the nineteenth century to observe the anniversary of the defeat of the British at that place on December 26, 1776. In 1876, the one hundredth anniversary of the battle brought these celebrations to a climax. Then no particular note of the event was taken until the one hundred and twenty-fifth anniversary in 1901.

The celebration in that year began with a reproduction of the battle by the members of the state militia organizations. It was planned that the forces holding the town, impersonating the Hessian troops, should wear the Hessian uniform, but as the militiamen objected, both attacking and defending forces wore the the same uniform. Colonel Q. O'M. Gilmore, impersonating the Hessian commander, defended the town in command of the First Battalion of the Second New Jersey Regiment, the battery of Camp Garfield and the Sons of Veterans. General William H. Cooper impersonated General Washington and commanded the Second and Third Battalions of the Second Regiment and the Third Battalion of the Third Regiment and one platoon of Battery B. He was supported by Colonel John J. Shinn in command of the First and Second Battalions of the Third Regiment and the Philadelphia City Troop. This troop fought in the battle itself, one hundred and twenty-five years earlier. The sham battle began at eight o'clock in the morning, the hour of the original battle, the attacking army sweeping down the streets driving the imitation Hessians before it. After the battle there was a parade including the militia and various civic organizations. It was reviewed at the Capitol by Governor Foster M. Voorhees and his staff. In the afternoon addresses on the battle were delivered in the Taylor Opera House by Governor Voorhees, Mayor Frank O. Briggs of Trenton, and Professor Woodrow Wilson of Princeton University. The Right Reverend John Scarborough, bishop of New Jersey, and the Right Reverend James A. McFaul, bishop of Trenton, offered the opening and the closing prayers. The one hundred and fiftieth anniversary of the battle was celebrated under the direction of the New Jersey Historical Society by a parade and a public dinner on December 29, 1926, as December 26 fell on Sunday. The President of the United States and the governors of the original thirteen states were invited guests.

The Battle of Trenton marked a turning point in the Revolutionary War. General Howe was so sure that the backbone of the rebellion had been broken after the success of his troops in New Jersey in the early winter that he gave General Cornwallis leave to return to England. General Washington knew that about fifteen hundred of the enemy, chiefly Hessians, were stationed at Trenton where they felt so secure that they had not placed any cannon for their protection. On the night of Christmas Washington gathered about two thousand men on the shore of the Delaware river at McConkey's ferry (now Taylorsville) and prepared to cross for an attack early on the morning of December 26. He had been sending men up and down stream for several days assembling all the large flat-bottomed boats used by the river men and in these he took his men across to the New Jersey shore. He reasoned that the Hessians, who celebrated Christmas with much drinking, would be in no condition to resist him. He reached the pickets on the outskirts of the town before his approach was discovered, he forced the pickets back and after sharp fighting for thirty-five minutes, utterly routed the enemy. Colonel Rahl, the Hessian commander, was fatally wounded and a thousand prisoners were taken, besides a large number of small arms and six brass cannon. Because of this unexpected defeat General Howe cancelled the leave of General Cornwallis and kept him in America for further operations against the revolutionists.

FEAST OF ST. STEPHEN

The martyrdom of Stephen, the first Christian to suffer death because of his faith, is celebrated on December 26, the day after Christmas. Stephen was not only the first Christian martyr, but he is one of the first deacons. When the Greek Christians complained about the distribution of food to the needy, the twelve apostles called the people together and told them to select "seven men of honest repute, full of the Holy Ghost and wisdom, whom ye may appoint over this business." Stephen and six others were chosen and presented to the apostles who prayed and laid their hands upon them setting them apart for the work. The number of believers increased and, according to the account in the Acts of the Apostles, "Stephen, full of faith and power, did great wonders and miracles among the people." He debated with various Jews in the synagogues and confounded them by his reasoning. Through jealousy they persuaded witnesses to say that they had heard him speak blasphemously against Moses and against God and he was arraigned before the council. He made a long defense, reciting the history of the children of Israel and concluded it with a vigorous denunciation of his accusers, saying:

Ye stiffnecked and uncircumcised in heart and ears, ye do always resist the Holy Ghost. As your fathers did, so do ye. Which of the prophets have not your fathers persecuted? And they have slain them which showed before of the coming of the Just One; of whom ye have been now the betrayers and murderers.

This aroused in the council a vindictive spirit and Stephen was condemned to be stoned. "And the witnesses laid down their clothes at a young man's feet, whose name was Saul. . . . And Saul was consenting unto his death." The record continues: "And devout men carried Stephen to his burial and made great lamentation over him."

667

It was not known where he was buried, but in 415 Lucian, a priest, had a vision in which he was told that the burial place was in Caphar Gamala, some distance north of Jerusalem. What were supposed to be his bones were disinterred and carried to a church on Mount Zion and in 460 they were removed to a church built on the spot where, according to tradition, Stephen had been stoned, outside the Damascus Gate of Jerusalem. There is now a church on the site built by the Dominican Fathers.

Virtually nothing is known of Stephen before his ordination as deacon. His name is Greek which suggests that he was a Jew born in a place where Greek was spoken. In the fifth century a tradition arose that "Stephen" was only a Greek form of the Aramaic name "Kelil." This name was found inscribed on a slab on what Lucian regarded as the tomb disclosed to him in a vision. But whatever his name or nativity he is revered by all Christendom as the first believer to give up his life for his faith.

DECEMBER TWENTY-SEVENTH

FEAST OF ST. JOHN THE EVANGELIST

This day is observed by the Roman and Anglican churches in honor of John, known as "the beloved disciple." It is also observed by the Masonic fraternity. John was the son of Zebedee and Salome and the brother of James the Greater. He and his brother were called "sons of thunder" by Jesus. They worked as fishermen with their father in the Lake of Genesareth. It is believed that they were followers of John the Baptist before they became followers of Jesus. John and Peter were sent into Jerusalem to arrange for the Last Supper and John sat next to Jesus at the supper. He alone of the disciples remained at the foot of the cross on Calvary and took Mary in charge. He and Peter were the first to hasten to the grave after the Resurrection. After the Ascension he was active in directing the affairs of the Christians. Although there is no definite information on the subject it is supposed that he remained in Palestine for twelve years until the persecutions of Herod Agrippa I forced the disciples to flee to various provinces of the Roman Empire. According to the Christian writers of the second and third centuries John lived in Asia Minor in the last years of the first century and had his headquarters at Ephesus. One of them says that he wrote his Gospel at Ephesus. He was banished to the isle of Patmos during the reign of Domitian (81-96) as he was charged with trying to subvert the religion of the Roman Empire. While there he wrote the book of The Revelation. After his release from Patmos it is supposed that he returned to Ephesus where he died at a great age in the year 99 or 100, the only one of the twelve disciples who died a natural death. All Christian sects honor him and name their churches for him.

DECEMBER TWENTY-EIGHTH

BIRTHDAY OF WOODROW WILSON

South Carolina in 1928 made the anniversary of the birth of Woodrow Wilson, the twenty-eighth President of the United States, a holiday. The anniversary, however, had been observed in different cities before that year.

On December 28, 1924, less than a year after his death, the Woodrow Wilson Foundation, with headquarters in New York, held a meeting and made its first award of a prize of $25,000 to Viscount Cecil of London for his efforts toward peace. The establishment of this foundation was inspired by the award to Mr. Wilson of the Nobel peace prize in 1920. Mrs. Charles E. Simonson and Mr. Charles L. Tiffany, both of New York, thought that there should be a foundation similar to that endowed by Nobel and that it should be named for Woodrow Wilson in recognition of his services in behalf of peace. The foundation was established at a meeting at Mr. Tiffany's house on December 23, 1920, and the organization was perfected on March 15, 1921 at a meeting at the Hotel Biltmore. It was planned to raise an endowment of $1,000,000; and at a meeting on December 27, 1922, it was announced that $800,00 had already been raised. The fund was turned over to a body of trustees and, on December 28, a committee went to Washington to inform Mr. Wilson, on his birthday what had been done in his honor. An award is made from time to time from the income of the Foundation to the individual or group that has rendered meritorious service to democracy, public welfare, liberal thought or peace through public justice. Among those to whom the award has been made are Viscount Cecil, Elihu Root, and Charles Augustus Lindbergh, for his lone flight to Paris.

Wilson was born at Staunton, Va., on December 28, 1856, the son of the Reverend Joseph R. Wilson, a Presbyterian clergyman, and Janet Woodrow. His paternal grandfather was James Wilson who came to America from Ireland in 1807, and published a chain of newspapers. His maternal grandfather, for whom he was named, was Thomas Woodrow, a graduate of Glasgow University. Wilson studied for a year at Davidson College in North Carolina and then entered Princeton University from which he was graduated in 1879. He then entered the law school of the University of Virginia from which he was graduated in 1881. He practiced law in Atlanta for about a year after which he entered Johns Hopkins University for post-graduate study of jurisprudence. While there he wrote a thesis on "Congressional government" in preparation for receiving the degree of doctor of philosophy. This was published and was immediately welcomed as a contribution to the history of government in the United States.

He went to Bryn Mawr college in 1885 as associate professor of history and political economy, where he remained for four years. In 1888 he went to Wesleyan University at Middletown, Conn., as professor of history and political economy. In 1890 he was called to Princeton, his alma mater, as professor of jurisprudence and political economy. In 1895 he was made professor of jurisprudence and in 1897, professor of jurisprudence and politics a post which he filled during the remainder of his service at Princeton. In 1902 he was elected president of the university. As president he sought to reform the social habits of the students by regulating their clubs, which aroused opposition. He introduced the preceptorial system designed to bring the students and their instructors into intimate relationship. When the graduate college was founded he found himself in radical disagreement with the dean in charge of it.

He had won distinction outside of Princeton by addresses on public affairs and when the nomination for Governor of New Jersey was offered to him in 1910 by the Democrats he accepted it as conditions in the university were no longer agreeable to him. He had written a *History of the United States* in 1902, published by Harper & Brothers. Not long afterward Colonel George Harvey, the head of the publishing company, began to urge him upon the consideration of the country as a candidate for President of the United States. When he was elected governor in a state that had been Republican for many years Colonel Harvey became more insistent on his availability for the presidency. As governor, Wilson brought about the passage of much "reform" legislation.

His name was presented to the Democratic National Convention at Baltimore in June 1912. Champ Clark of Missouri was the leading candidate and received a majority of the votes on a number of roll calls. As Clark was supported by Tammany, William Jennings Bryan denounced the Tammany delegates and turned the tide in favor of Wilson who was named on the forty-sixth roll with the necessary two-thirds vote of the delegates. There was a split in the Republican party in 1912, the so-called "progressive" wing objecting to the renomination of President Taft. When Taft was nominated a bolting convention was held which nominated Theodore Roosevelt. Wilson was elected with four hundred and thirty-five electoral votes, while Taft received eight and Roosevelt eighty-eight.

When the World War began in 1914 Wilson issued a proclamation calling upon the people to be neutral in thought as well as in deed. When the "Lusitania" was sunk on May 7, 1915, with the loss of one hundred American lives he still remained neutral and in a speech to newly naturalized citizens in Philadelphia he said that a nation might be "too proud to fight." He, however, protested to Germany and one of his notes was couched in such vigorous language that William Jennings Bryan, his Secretary of State, resigned.

He was nominated by acclamation to succeed himself when the Democratic National Convention met in 1916. The Republicans nominated Charles Evans Hughes, a justice of the United States Supreme Court. The Democrats asked support for their candidate on the plea that "he kept us out of war." Hughes carried the Eastern states and on election night it was thought that he had won. Colonel House, then one of Wilson's intimates, was with him as the returns came in and he has been quoted as saying that Wilson thought he had been defeated and that he had decided to resign; but first planned to ask Vice President Marshall and his Secretary of State to resign and then appoint Hughes as Secretary of State. Wilson would then resign and Hughes would become President under the law providing for succession to the office. But when the California vote was reported, Wilson was elected. A change of two thousand votes in California, however, would have given the election to Hughes.

The conduct of Germany gradually became so intolerable that on April 2, 1917, Wilson appeared before Congress and in an address asked for the declaration that a state of war existed. The necessary resolution was passed within four days and preparations for war were begun. A draft bill was passed, about four million men were put in training in the course of months, and about two million sent to France. Following the armistice on November 11, 1918, Mr. Wilson arranged to go to Europe to attend the Peace Conference, and sailed on December 4. He was received in London, and Paris and Rome with great enthusiasm. When the Peace Conference assembled at Versailles in January he proposed that the peace treaty should contain the Covenant of a League of Nations with provisions for avoiding war in the future. This was finally accepted; and the League was formed, but he was unable to persuade the Senate to ratify the treaty containing the Covenant. He made a tour of the country in an effort to arouse sentiment in support of his program. The negotiations in France had exhausted his strength and on September 26, 1919, he found himself unable to continue and returned to Washington, where in a few days he had a stroke which incapacitated him for weeks and from which he never fully recovered. On his retirement he bought a house in Washington where he lived until his death on February 3, 1924. His last public appearance was on Armistice Day, 1923, when he made a short speech from the porch of his house. Mr. Wilson's admirers in different cities are accustomed to meet each year to celebrate the anniversary of his birth.

CHILDERMAS

December 28 is observed in the Anglican, Greek and Roman Churches in commemoration of the massacre of the young children by

Herod. The story of it is told in the Gospel of St. Matthew. The Wise Men of the East had arrived in Jerusalem and made inquiries concerning the birth of the King of the Jews, which had been made known to them by the appearance of his star. After telling of this the narrative of St. Matthew continues:

> Herod, when he had privily called the wise men, inquired of them diligently what time the star appeared. And he sent them to Bethlehem, and said "Go and search diligently for the young child; and when ye have found him, bring me word again, that I may come and worship him also." When they had heard the King, they departed; and, lo the star which they saw in the East, went before them, till it came and stood over where the young child was. When they saw the star, they rejoiced with exceeding great joy. . . . And being warned of God in a dream that they should not return to Herod, they departed into their own country by another way. . . . Then Herod, when he saw that he was mocked of the wise men, was exceeding wroth, and sent forth and slew all the children that were in Bethlehem, and in all the coasts thereof, from two years old and under, according to the time which he had diligently inquired of the wise men.

The number slain has been variously estimated. The Greek liturgy puts it at fourteen thousand boys. The Syrians estimate the number at sixty-four thousand, and medieval authors at one hundred and forty-four thousand. Modern writers have reduced the number to correspond with the probabilities. As Bethlehem was a small town one of them has conjectured that not more than ten or twelve were killed. Another reduces the number to six.

The day is known by different names, including the Feast of the Innocents, the Feast of the Holy Innocents, and the Childermas Day. The Roman and Anglican Churches observe it on December 28, the Greek Church on December 29, and the Chaldeans and Syrians on December 27. These dates are fixed arbitrarily as nothing is definitely known about when the children were slain, but it must have been within two years of the birth of Jesus as the children more than two years old escaped. The Roman Church began to celebrate the feast not later than the end of the fifth century. It was once the custom in England, France and Germany to elect a boy bishop on December 6, the Feast of St. Nicholas, who officiated at that feast and also at the Feast of the Holy Innocents. He sat in the bishop's chair while the choir boys occupied the stalls of the canons.

There is a popular superstition in England that Childermas is an unlucky day. Those who entertain this superstition do not marry on that day. The coronation of Edward IV, set for December 28, was put off till the next day. Not only is the day itself considered unlucky, but the day of the week on which it falls is regarded as unpropitious for beginning any new undertaking. It was once the custom to whip all children on the morning of Childermas that they might remember the murder of the innocents by Herod.

DECEMBER TWENTY-NINTH

BIRTHDAY OF ANDREW JOHNSON

Andrew Johnson, the seventeenth President of the United States and the only one whom Congress tried to remove by impeachment proceedings, was born at Raleigh, N.C., on December 29, 1808. His father, Jacob Johnson, a sexton and bank porter in Raleigh, died when the boy was only four years old. When he was ten he was apprenticed to a tailor. As he was not able to go to school he spent much of his leisure trying to educate himself. Just before his term of apprenticeship expired he went to Laurens Court House, S.C., and obtained work as a journeyman tailor. In 1826, when he was eighteen he moved to Greenville, in east Tennessee, which he made his home for the rest of his life. He worked at his trade there for about a year when he married Eliza McCardle, who taught him arithmetic and helped him to improve his writing. When he was twenty he organized a party of working men in opposition to the planters and was elected alderman in Greenville and twice reelected. When he was twenty-two he was elected mayor and served three years. He joined a debating society composed of the students of Greenville College in an effort to improve himself in public speaking. When his term as mayor expired he was elected to the state legislature, was defeated for reelection, but was later elected for two terms to the state senate. In 1843 he was elected to the national House of Representatives and served five terms, after which he was elected governor for two terms. When his last term as governor was expiring he was elected to the United States Senate by the state legislature which the Democrats then controlled.

When the Civil War began he did not follow the example of many other Southern Senators by withdrawing, but continued in his place. He was made military governor of the state by President Lincoln. In 1864 he was nominated for Vice President on the ticket with Lincoln and was elected as a Union Democrat. When Lincoln was assassinated, six weeks after his second inauguration, Johnson announced that he would retain the Lincoln Cabinet and continue the Lincoln policies. He strove to make it easy for the Southern states to resume their places in the Union, assuming with Lincoln, that they had never really been outside of the Union, and that their ordinances of secession were invalid. But there was unfortunately a spirit of vindictiveness entertained by some of the Northern political leaders. When he vetoed what he regarded as the unwise acts of Congress they were passed over his veto and when Congress passed the Tenure of Office Act forbidding the removal of officers appointed with the approval of the Senate unless the Senate consented to the removal he vetoed that. It was passed over his veto. He removed Edward M. Stanton, his Secretary of War, but Stanton insisted that the removal was illegal. Thereupon

673

the House of Representatives adopted a resolution charging him with high crimes and misdemeanors in office. This was on February 24, 1868. The articles of impeachment, consisting of eleven specifications were prepared and on March 5, the Senate, with Chief Justice Chase presiding, was organized as a court for the trial, which began on March 13, and has been described as "a solemn theatrical fiasco." The vote on two of the specifications was taken on May 26 with the result that one less than the necessary two thirds supported the charges. The other charges were dropped and the attempt to convict the President fortunately failed. A historian of the trial has said, "The single vote by which Andrew Johnson escaped conviction marks the narrow margin by which the presidential element in our system escaped destruction." Although Johnson made no attempt to obtain a renomination he received sixty-five votes on the first roll call in the Democratic National Convention which met a few weeks after his acquittal.

On his retirement from the presidency in 1869 he sought election to the Senate but was unsuccessful, and in 1872 he made an attempt to be sent to Washington as representative-at-large from Tennessee, but failed. But the Tennessee Legislature elected him to the Senate in 1874, and he took his seat in the special session called by President Grant on March 5, 1875. About two weeks later he made a speech attacking the policies of the administration. He died on July 31, 1875, praised for his integrity and his loyalty to the Constitution.

DECEMBER THIRTIETH

GADSDEN PURCHASE

James Gadsden of South Carolina, born May 15, 1788, was engaged in the promotion of railroad building for many years. As president of the South Carolina Railroad Company he planned joining the small lines in the South and connecting them with the Pacific coast by a road near the southern boundary of the United States. In 1853 he became convinced that the best route lay along the southern bank of the Gila River which, however, was in Mexican territory. Through the influence of Jefferson Davis he was appointed minister to Mexico with instructions to buy enough territory from Mexico to permit the construction of the proposed railroad. He reported to Washington that he could get more land from Mexico than was originally thought possible and he was authorized to buy as much as he could get for $50,000,000. Mexico was not willing to sell that much land, but Santa Anna was in financial straits and finally agreed to sell for $10,000,000, a tract of 45,535 square miles, bounded on the east by the Rio Grande, on the north by the Gila River and on the west by the Colorado. A treaty agreeing to the sale was signed in the Mexican capital on December 30, 1853. The land lies in New Mexico and Arizona. Its southern boundary was fixed as the boundary between the two countries, and ended boundary disputes. Gadsden, however, was more interested in a route for his proposed transcontinental railroad than in settling boundaries. The treaty was ratified by the Senate and proclaimed on June 30, 1854. It was so unpopular in Mexico that Santa Anna was banished.

The plans for a railroad across the continent were checked by the Civil War and the first railroad to the Pacific coast was built much farther north than the Gila River; but a railroad now runs along the southern bank of that stream as Gadsden had planned.

DECEMBER THIRTY-FIRST

NEW YEAR'S EVE

The approaching advent of the New Year has been celebrated in the United States from early times on the evening of December 31. The old world custom of ringing bells, blowing horns and shooting firearms as the hour of midnight approaches became general. In the course of time hotels and restaurants in the cities arranged New Year's eve celebrations. Because they were popular, reservations had to be made in advance and high prices were charged for seats at the tables. On New Year's eve in 1919, the last before the prohibition amendment to the Constitution went into effect, these celebrations degenerated into drunken orgies in all the principal cities. During the period of national prohibition the popularity of the celebrations in the hotels and restaurants declined. But with the repeal of the prohibition amendment they began to take on their old-time flavor with more or less riotous merrymaking.

It was the custom for years for the revellers to march down Broadway in New York to Trinity Church at the head of Wall street, blowing their horns and ringing their bells and tickling unsuspecting persons with a feather on a long stick. As midnight approached they would suddenly become silent waiting for the chimes in the church tower to welcome the New Year with sacred hymns. When the chimes ceased playing the noise began again. In Philadelphia the revellers would march down Chestnut street to Independence Hall and wait for the bell to ring in the New Year.

In addition to the secular celebrations many religious denominations hold special services on New Year's eve from nine or ten until twelve o'clock. The Methodist Episcopal Church, which was the earliest to adopt this custom calls them "watch-night" services. In 1934 St. George's Methodist Episcopal Church in Philadelphia held its one hundred and sixty-fifth watch-night services. The church was founded in 1769 and in 1770 held what has been called the first such service in America. The Presbyterians, Baptists, and Lutherans, among many others, hold such services now.

FEAST OF ST. SYLVESTER

The anniversary of the death of St. Sylvester, who was Pope from 314 until he died in 335, is observed on December 31. Little is known about his early life or about his administration as Pope. There are many legends about him which have no historical foundation. He is said to have baptized Constantine the Great who had been afflicted with leprosy but was instantly cured by the baptism. It is known however, that during his pontificate Constantine built several great churches in Rome, including the Lateran, the Church of the Holy Cross, and St. Peter's in the Vatican. He was the son of a Roman named Rufinus and his mother was Justina. During his reign the first list of Christian martyrs was compiled, and he encouraged the establishment of a school of singing for the improvement of the church services. He built a church over the Catacomb of Priscilla and was buried in it. Excavation in Rome in the early part of this century disclosed the ruins of this church. The day of his death was set apart as a feast day by Pope Gregory IX in 1227. It is observed by the Anglican as well as by the Roman Church. St. Sylvester's Day is celebrated in Germany and in Belgium with various kinds of horseplay in anticipation of the advent of the New Year.

APPENDICES

CALENDAR

The word calendar is derived from the Latin *calendarium* meaning an interest or account book, and is akin to the Latin verb *calare*, to call. The first day of the Roman month was known as the Calends, the day on which the priests called the people together to announce to them sacred days and festivals to be observed during the month. The calendar of the western world is the Gregorian calendar introduced by Pope Gregory XIII in 1582.

The ancient Roman year began on March 25th and consisted of ten months, the last six of which were numbered, Quintilis, Sextilis, September, October, November, and December. Two months were added by Numa, January at the beginning and February at the end of the year. This order was reversed in 452 B.C.

Even after the addition of the two new months, the calendar did not correspond with the solar year, and by the time of Julius Caesar there was a discrepancy of about three months between the actual spring equinox and the calendar equinox. Julius Caesar therefore decreed that the calendar year should correspond with the solar year and fixed its length at three hundred and sixty-five days, with an extra day every fourth year. The first Julian year was 46 B.C.

But Julius Caesar's astronomers were in error in their computations. The spring equinox, which had fallen on March 21 when the Julian calendar was adopted, by 1582 was on March 11. Pope Gregory XIII therefore ordered that ten days be dropped so that the day which was October 5, 1582, by the Julian calendar should be October 15, and the new year should begin January 1, instead of March 25. He also ordered that each year divisible by four should be a leap year, except the years numbering the centuries which should have the extra day only when divisible by four hundred. Thus 1900 was not a leap year.

The Gregorian calendar was introduced in Spain, Portugal, and parts of Italy on the same day that it was adopted in Rome, in the Catholic states of Germany the following year, and in France at about the same time. The Protestant German states did not adopt it until 1700. In Great Britain and in her American colonies, where there was objection to everything originating in Rome, the old calendar, with the new year beginning on March 25th, was used. Because of the confusion arising from the use of a different calendar from that used on the Continent, the British Parliament passed an act in 1750 adopting the Gregorian calendar, with the new year beginning on January 1st. The Julian calendar had become eleven days slow by that time. It was therefore ordered that September 3, 1752, should be September 14, not only in Great Britain but in her American colonies as well. In the course of time the dates of events prior to 1752 were changed to correspond to the new calendar. Washington was born on February 12, Old Style, and he observed the anniversary on that date, but at about the beginning of the nineteenth century the day began to be observed on February 22.

How the new calendar was regarded at the time of the change by some of the French is indicated by the comments of Montaigne. In the eleventh chapter of the Third Book of his Essays he wrote:

Two or three years are now past since the year hath been shortened ten days in France. Oh how many changes are like to ensue this reformation! It was a right removing of heaven and earth together, yet nothing removeth from its own place. My neighbors find the season of their seed and harvest time, the opportunity of their affairs, their lucky and unlucky days, to answer just those seasons to which they had from all ages assigned them. Neither was the error heretofore preceived, nor is the reformation now discerned in our use, so much uncertainty is there in all things, so gross, so obscure and so dull is our understanding. Some are of opinion this reformation might have been repressed after a less incommodious manner; substracting according to the example of Augustus, for some years, the bisextile or leap day, which in some sort is but a day of hindrance and trouble, until they might more exactly have satisfied the debt, which by this late reformation is not done. For we are yet some days in arrearages. And if by such a means we might provide for time to come, appointing that after the revolution of such or such a number of years that extraordinary day might forever be eclipsed, so that our misreckoning should not henceforth exceed four and twenty hours. We have no other computation of time but years. The world hath used them so many ages, and yet it is a measure we have not until this day perfectly established. And such, as we daily doubt, what form other nations have diversely given the same and which was the true use of it. And what if some say, that the heavens in growing old compress themselves towards us and cast into an uncertainty of hours and days? And as Plutarch saith of the months, that even in his days astrology could not yet limit the motion of the moon.

DAYS OF THE WEEK

Sunday, the first day, gets its name from the Anglo-Saxon "Sunnandaeg" from "sunnan" meaning sun and "daeg" meaning day. It is thus regarded as a name surviving from ancient sun worship. As the Resurrection occurred on the first day of the week the early Christians began to assemble for worship on that day instead of on the Jewish Sabbath, which is Saturday. It is known as Sonntag among the Germans. The French call it Dimanche and the Italians Domenica. Both words are derived from the Latin, Dominus, meaning "the Lord." It is frequently called "the Lord's day" in the United States. By the beginning of the fourth century Sunday had been made a holy day by the church when secular labor was forbidden. Strict observance of the day was ordered by the English Puritans and the New England Puritans early passed laws regulating its observance. Many states now have Sunday laws forbidding certain activities. Their validity is defended as a proper exercise of the police power.

The name of Monday also comes from the Anglo-Saxon in which it was Monandaeg, or Moonday. The moon was worshipped as the wife of the sun, and her name was given to the second day of the week. Many superstitions are connected with the moon. It was known as Luna among the Romans and it was believed that if the light of the moon shone on anyone while he was asleep he would lose his reason. Thus we have the word lunatic. The phases of the moon were once believed to have an effect on crops and other things. For example the bacon from pigs killed in the old of the moon would shrivel in the pan when it was fried and seed planted in the time of the new moon would grow better than when planted when the moon was waning. And it was believed that the efficacy of certain medicines depended upon the state of the moon when they were taken.

Tuesday is named for the old god Tyr. In Anglo-Saxon the name was Tiwesdaeg. Tyr in the Norse mythology was the god of war. A wolf spirit named Fenrir was troubling the world and Tyr volunteered to bind it. A chain had been made of what was called the hardest things in the world, including the footsteps of a cat, the beards of women, the roots of stones, and the breath of fishes. According to the legend it was so strong that it could not be broken. Fenrir would not consent to be bound unless the gods would promise to take the chain off again and would send a god to put his hand in his mouth. Tyr put his hand in the wolf's mouth and then bound him. The wolf was so angry at being bound that he bit off Tyr's hand. The French name for Tuesday is Mardi, derived, like the English name, from the god of war, who was known as Mars.

Wednesday is named from the Norse god Odin, or Wodin, and in Anglo-Saxon was called Wodnesdaeg. Odin was the father of Tyr

681

and was known as the god of storms. According to the old sagas, Odin and his brothers slew Ymir, or Chaos, and from his body created the world. His flesh became the dry land, his bones the mountains and his blood the sea. His skull became the vault of the heavens. Odin's seat is in Valhalla, where he welcomes brave warriors after his death and treats them to the pleasures in which they took greatest delight on earth.

Thursday in Anglo-Saxon was Thunresdaeg, named for Thor, the Norse god of Thunder. His chariot, drawn by he-goats caused the thunder when it was drawn through the heavens. He was also the strongest of the gods. He had a magic hammer with which he killed the giants. A giant Thrym, however, got possession of it and refused to give it up unless the goddess Freya would marry him. Thor dressed himself in Freya's garments and visited Thrym. The hammer was returned to him and with it he killed his host.

Friday is named for Freya, the goddess whom Thrym wished to marry. In Anglo-Saxon the day was called Frigedaeg. Freya was the wife of Odin. As a day had been named for her husband and for her son Thor the ancients decided to name a day for her lest she be jealous and work evil upon them. The Norsemen regarded Friday as the luckiest day of the week, but among Christians it has been regarded as unlucky as it was the day on which Jesus was crucified. The day is the Mohammedan Sabbath as it is the Mohammedan belief that Adam was created on Friday. There is a Moslem legend that it was on Friday that Adam and Eve ate of the forbidden fruit and that they died on Friday. The belief that Friday is an unlucky day is older than Christianity, for the ancient Romans and Buddhists regarded it as a day of bad omen.

Saturday is the only day in the English week named for one of the old Roman gods. The Anglo-Saxon called it Saterdaeg, for Saturn. He was the Roman god who presided over the sowing of the seed. His festival was celebrated on December 17, following the winter sowing. It was known as the Saturnalia, and because of the wildness of the revels during the festival the name has come to mean a time of wild revelry and tumult. Saturn has been identified with the Greek god Cronos. According to a Roman legend he was an ancient king of Latium and was welcomed to Rome by the Italian god Janus, for whom January is named.

There are various theories about the origin of the week of seven days as a measure of time. One is that it is based on the moon's phases covering twenty-eight days. On the theory that the week came from Babylonia it is assumed that the number seven for its days is derived from the sun and the moon and the five planets, Saturn, Jupiter, Mars, Venus and Mercury. As seven has been regarded as a sacred number, that may have had some connection with the establishment of the week. But the measure of time by seven days has been in use so long that its origin is lost in the mists of antiquity.

RHYMES OF THE DAYS AND SEASONS

Monday for wealth;
Tuesday for health;
Wednesday is the best day of all.
Thursday for crosses;
Friday for losses;
Saturday, no luck at all.

Monday's child is fair of face,
Tuesday's child is full of grace,
Wednesday's child is full of woe,
Thursday's child has far to go,
Friday's child is loving and giving,
Saturday's child works hard for a living.
And a child that's born on the Sabbath day
Is fair and wise and good and gay.

Sneeze on Monday, you sneeze for danger;
Sneeze on Tuesday, you'll kiss a stranger;
Sneeze on Wednesday, you sneeze for a letter;
Sneeze on Thursday, for something better;
Sneeze on Friday, you sneeze for sorrow;
Sneeze on Saturday, your sweetheart to-morrow;
Sneeze on Sunday, your safety seek—
The devil will have you the whole of the week.

Cut your nails on Monday, cut them for news;
Cut them on Tuesday, a pair of new shoes;
Cut them on Wednesday, cut them for health;
Cut them on Thursday, cut them for wealth;
Cut them on Friday, cut them for woe;
Cut them on Saturday, a journey you'll go;
Cut them on Sunday, you'll cut them for evil,
For all the next week you'll be ruled by the devil.

They that wash on Monday
Have all the week to dry;
They that wash on Tuesday
Are not so much awry;
They that wash on Wednesday
Are not so much to blame;
They that wash on Thursday,
Wash for shame;

RHYMES OF THE DAYS AND SEASONS

They that wash on Friday,
Wash in need;
And they that wash on Saturday
Oh, they are slovens, indeed.

Thirty days hath September,
April, June and November;
All the rest have thirty-one;
February twenty-eight alone—
Except in leap year, at which time
February's days are twenty-nine.

The authors of the preceding rhymes are unknown, but it was Sarah Coleridge who wrote the following verses about the months:

January brings the snow,
Makes our feet and fingers glow.
February brings the rain,
Thaws the frozen earth again.
March brings breezes, loud and shrill
To stir the dancing daffodil.
April brings the primrose sweet,
Scatters daisies at our feet.
May brings flocks of pretty lambs
Skipping by their fleecy dams.
June brings tulips, lilies, roses,
Fills the children's hands with posies.
Hot July brings cooling showers,
Apricots and gillyflowers.
August brings sheaves of corn,
Then the harvest home is borne.
Warm September brings the fruit;
Sportsmen then begin to shoot.
Fresh October brings the pheasant;
Then to gather nuts is pleasant.
Dull November brings the blast;
Then the leaves are whirling fast.
Chill December brings the sleet,
Blazing fire and Christmas treat.

684

SIGNS OF THE ZODIAC

The zodiac is the name given by the ancients to an imaginary band extending around the celestial sphere with its center in the ecliptic, or the apparent path of the sun. This band is sixteen degrees wide and includes the orbit of the five planets which were known to the astronomers when they named it. The planets were Mercury, Venus, Mars, Jupiter and Saturn. The name comes from a Greek word for "animal" and means "relating to animals." It was so called as the constellations were regarded as animals. The stars in the zodiac were grouped into twelve constellations and the zodiac was divided into twelve sections of thirty degrees and each was named for a different constellation. When the division was made each constellation was in its proper place, but because of the precession of the equinoxes they are now out of place. The constellation Aries, or the Ram, which was originally in the first section of the zodiac, is now in the second section, or the place occupied at first by Taurus, or the Bull. In about 25,800 years the precession will have completed the circuit of the heavens and Aries will occupy its proper place. The twelve signs of the zodiac, as the constellations are known, correspond roughly to the twelve months of the year. Capricornus, or the Goat, is the sign for January. It is named for the goat which, according to the legend, nursed the young gods of the sun. Aquarius, or the Water-bearer, is the sign for February. It is named in allusion to the heavy rains which flooded the Nile. Pisces, or the Fishes, is the sign for March, and is supposed to refer to the resumption of labor in the fields. The sign for April is Aries, or the Ram. It refers to the first month of the ancient Babylonian year when sacrifices of rams were made. Taurus, or the Bull, is the May sign, in allusion to the sun which the ancients regarded as a bull. Gemini, or Twins, is the sign for June, named for Castor and Pollux, the twin sons of Zeus and Leda. Cancer, or the Crab, is assigned to July, as the retreat of the sun is associated with the backward motion of the crab. The sign for August, is Leo, or the Lion, as this was the hottest month and the lion was the ancient symbol for heat. September's sign is Virgo, or the Virgin, in allusion to the Babylonian myth of Ishtar. The sign for October is Libra, or the Scales, referring to the balancing of day and night at this season. November is known for Scorpio, or the Scorpion, in allusion to the darkness which follows the decline of the sun after the autumn equinox. And the sign for December is Sagittarius, or the Archer, named for the Babylonian god of war.

HOLIDAYS IN THE UNITED STATES

January 1—New Year's Day, observed in all the states and territories.

January 8—Battle of New Orleans, or Jackson Day, in Louisiana.

January 19—Robert E. Lee's Birthday, observed in Alabama, Arkansas, Florida, Georgia, Kentucky, Louisiana, Mississippi, North Carolina, South Carolina, Tennessee, Texas, and Virginia.

January 20—Inauguration Day in the District of Columbia, beginning in 1937.

January 30—Birthday of Franklin D. Roosevelt, a legal holiday in Kentucky.

February 12—Abraham Lincoln's Birthday, observed in Arizona, California, Colorado, Delaware, Illinois, Indiana, Iowa, Kansas, Kentucky, Michigan, Minnesota, Missouri, Montana, Nebraska, Nevada, New Jersey, New York, North Dakota, Ohio, Oregon, Pennsylvania, South Dakota, Tennessee, Utah, Vermont, Washington, West Virginia, Wisconsin, Wyoming, and observed by proclamation of the Governor in Arkansas and Massachusetts. It is also a holiday in Alaska, Hawaii, Puerto Rico, and the Virgin Islands.

February 12—Georgia Day in Georgia in celebration of the landing of Oglethorpe.

February 14—Admission Day in Arizona.

February 22—George Washington's Birthday, observed in all the states and territories.

March 2—Independence Day in Texas.

March 7—Arbor Day in California.

March 15—Birthday of Andrew Jackson, a legal holiday in Tennessee.

March 17—Evacuation Day, a legal holiday in Suffolk County, Massachusetts.

March 25—Maryland Day in Maryland.

March 30—Seward Day in Alaska.

April 12—Halifax Independence Day in North Carolina.

April 13—Birthday of Thomas Jefferson, a legal holiday in Virginia and observed by proclamation of the Governor of Nebraska. It is also a public, but not a bank holiday in Missouri and Oklahoma.

April 19—Patriot's Day in Maine and Massachusetts.

April 21—San Jacinto Day in Texas.

April 22—Opening of Oklahoma Territory, a legal holiday in Oklahoma.

April 26—Confederate Memorial Day in Alabama, Florida, Georgia and Mississippi.

April 26—World War Memorial Day in Georgia.

May 10—Confederate Memorial Day in North Carolina and South Carolina.

May 20—Anniversary of the signing of the Mecklenburg Declaration of Independence in North Carolina.

May 30—Memorial or Decoration Day, observed in all the States except Alabama, Arkansas, Florida, Georgia, Louisiana, Mississippi, North Carolina and South Carolina.

May 30—Confederate Memorial Day in Virginia.

June 3—Confederate Memorial Day in Kentucky, Louisiana, and Tennessee.

June 3—Birthday of Jefferson Davis, a legal holiday in Alabama, Arkansas, Florida, Georgia, Louisiana, Mississippi, South Carolina, Texas and Virginia.

June 14—Flag Day in Pennsylvania.

June 15—Pioneer Day in Idaho.

June 17—Bunker Hill Day, a legal holiday in Suffolk County, Massachusetts.

June 20—West Virginia Day in West Virginia.

July 4—Independence Day, observed in all the States and Territories.

July 13—Birthday of General Nathan Bedford Forrest in Tennessee.

HOLIDAYS IN THE UNITED STATES

July 24—Pioneer Day in Utah.
August 1—Colorado Day in Colorado.
August 14—Victory Day in Michigan.
August 16—Battle of Bennington Day in Vermont.
August 30—Birthday of Huey P. Long, a legal holiday in Louisiana.
September 9—Admission Day in California.
September 12—Defenders' Day in Maryland.
October 1—Missouri Day, observed in the public schools of Missouri.
October 12—Farmer's Day in Florida.
October 12—Columbus Day, observed in Alabama, Arizona, California, Colorado, Connecticut, Delaware, Florida, Georgia, Illinois, Indiana, Iowa, Kansas, Kentucky, Louisiana, Maryland, Massachusetts, Minnesota, Montana, Nebraska, Nevada, New Hampshire, New Jersey, New Mexico, New York, North Dakota, Ohio, Oklahoma, Oregon, Pennsylvania, Rhode Island, Texas, Utah, Vermont, Virginia, Washington, West Virginia, Wisconsin, and Wyoming.
October 18—Alaska Day in Alaska.
October 24—Pennsylvania Day in Pennsylvania.
October 31—Admission Day in Nevada.
November 1—Feast of All Saints in Louisiana.
November 4—Will Rogers Day in Oklahoma.
November 11—Armistice Day, a legal holiday in all the states and in the District of Columbia. Also in Alaska, Hawaii, Puerto Rico and the Virgin Islands.
December 7—Delaware Day in Delaware.
December 25—Christmas, observed in every State and Territory.
December 28—Woodrow Wilson's Birthday in South Carolina.

The holidays which do not fall on a fixed date every year include the following:
Shrove Tuesday. In Alabama, Florida and Louisiana.
Good Friday in Arkansas, Connecticut, Delaware, Florida, Illinois, Indiana, Louisiana, Maryland, Minnesota, New Jersey, North Dakota, Pennsylvania, South Carolina, and Texas; also in five counties in Arizona.
Arbor Day on a date fixed by the Governor on a proclamation, save in California when it falls on Luther Burbank's birthday, March 7, and in a few other states where there is a fixed date. For details see April 22.
State Election Day in Louisiana, the third Tuesday in April.
Fast Day in New Hampshire, the last Thursday in April.
Labor Day, the first Monday in September, observed in all the States and Territories.
Fraternal Day in Alabama, the second Thursday in October.
Thursday of State Fair Week in South Carolina, in the third full week in October.
General Election Day, which is on the first Tuesday after the first Monday in November, is a full holiday in every state and territory except Alaska, the District of Columbia, Illinois, Massachusetts, Ohio and Vermont. In Ohio it is a half holiday. In Illinois it is a holiday only in the cities of Chicago, Springfield, East St. Louis, Galesburg, Danville, Cairo and Rockford. In Maine it is a legal holiday only for the courts which also close on the State Election Day, the second Monday in September in alternate years.
Thanksgiving Day, the fourth Thursday in November, observed in all the states and territories.

687

INDEX

Abbott, Jacob, birthday of, 597
Abbott, Lyman, birthday of, 648
Adams, John, birthday of, 543
Adams, John Quincy, birthday of, 387
Admission Day in Arizona, 122
Admission Day in California, 472
Admission Day in Nevada, 573
Admission Day in Washington, 593
Advent, beginning of, 628
Agassiz, Louis, birthday of, 305
Agnes, Saint, eve of, 48; feast of, 51
Alabama claims, 212
Alabama, Fraternal Day in, 524
Alamo Day, 161
Alaska Day, 542
Alaska, Seward Day in, 195
Albany, becomes capital of New York, 164
Alden Kindred of America, celebration of John Alden Day, 436
All Fools' Day, 199
All Saints, feast of, 576
All Souls' Day, 579
"America," winner of international yacht race, 449
American Academy of Arts and Letters, chartering of, 225
American Colonies, confederation of, 287
American Indian Day, 277
American troops arrive in France in 1917, 359
American troops land in Sicily in 1943, 386
American troops land in Africa in 1942, 585
Americanism Day in Pennsylvania, 257
Andrew, Saint, 623
Anne, Saint, 415
Annunciation, feast of, 188
Anthony of Padua, Saint, 340
Anthony, Susan B., fined for voting, 351
Anthony the Great, Saint, 40
Apple Blossom festival, Shenandoah Valley, 259
Apple Blossom festival, Wenatchee, Wash., 262
Apple Tuesday, 538
Appleseed, Johnny, 539
Appomattox Day, 213

April Fools' Day, 199
April, origin of name, 198
Arbor Day, 232
Arizona Admission Day, 122
Armistice Day, 590
Army Day, 208
Arthur, Chester A., birthday of, 514
Ascension Day, 273
Asheville, North Carolina, Rhododendron festival, 343
Ash Wednesday, 119
Assumption of the Virgin Mary, feast of, 440
Astor, John Jacob, birthday of, 397
Atlantic cable, the first successful, 416
Atlantic Charter, 440
Atomic bomb, first use of, 428
Atonement, Day of, 491
Audubon, John James, birthday of, 242
Augustine of Canterbury, Saint, 302
Augustine, Saint, 454
August, origin of the name, 423
Aviation Day, 645

Balboa discovers Pacific, 498
Balloon ascension, the first in America, 26
Barnabas, Saint, 337
Barry, Commodore John, anniversary of death, 478
Bartholomew, Saint, 450
Bastille Day, 390
Beard, Daniel Carter, birthday of, 354
Bede, Saint, 304
Bell, Alexander Graham, birthday of, 157
Bennington, Vermont, battle of, 441
Berry, Martha McChesney, birthday of, 521
Bill of Rights, adoption of, 644
Bird Day, 221
Blaine, James G., birthday of, 73
Blessing the Berries in Boyle County, Kentucky, 350
Blizzard of 1888, 166
Boone, Daniel, 328
Booth, Ballington, birthday of, 417
Booth, Edwin, birthday of, 595
Booth, William, founder of the Salvation Army, 214
Boston Evacuation Day, 177

689

INDEX

Boston Massacre, 160
Boston Tea Party, 644
Boy Scout Day, 86
Braddock, General Edward, 384
Brandywine, battle of, 475
Bretton Woods Agreements, 421
Bridget, Saint, 76
British Empire Day, 299
Brown, John, birthday of, 271
Brownsville, Texas, Charro Fiesta, 101
Bryan, William Jennings, birthday of, 181
Buchanan, James, birthday of, 235
Buena Vista, battle of, 143
Bunker Hill Day, 349
Burbank, Luther, birthday of, 161
Burns, Robert, birthday of, 55
Burr, Aaron, birthday of, 81

Cabrillo, Juan Rodriguez, discovers California, 500
Cabrini, Blessed Mother Frances Xavier, Saint, 654
Calendar, 679
California Admission Day, 472
Cameron, Simon, birthday of, 162
Candlemas, 77
Cape Henry Day in Virginia, 243
Capitol building in Washington, D.C, laying cornerstone of, 489
Carleton, Will, birthday of, 549
Carnation Day, 64
Carnegie Institute Founder's Day, 540
Carroll, John, first Catholic bishop in the United States, 585
Casseday, Jennie, birthday of, 334
Catherine of Alexandria, Saint, 610
Catherine of Siena, Saint, 249
Cecelia, Saint, 604
Centennial Exposition, Philadelphia, 274
Chapman, John (Johnny Appleseed), 539
Charles II, birthday of, 306
Charles Borromeo, Saint, 581
Charleston, South Carolina, earthquake, 460
Charro Fiesta in Brownsville, Texas, 101
Chase, Salmon P., birthday of, 30
Chatauqua Day, 431
Cherokee Strip Day in Oklahoma, 483
Cherry Festival at Traverse City, Michigan, 400
Cheyenne, Wyoming, Frontier Day in, 411
Chicago Fire Day, 522
Childermas, 671

Child Health Day, 255
Children's Day, 335
Chincoteague Island, Virginia, pony penning, 414
Chinese New Year, 103
Christmas, 657
Christmas Eve, 657
Christopher, Saint, 414
Chrysostom, Saint, 60
Cinco de Mayo, 266
Circumcision, feast of, 13
Citizenship Day, 286
Clare, Saint, 437
Clarke, John, birthday of, 521
Clark, Francis E., birthday of, 477
Clement, Saint, 608
Cleveland, Grover, birthday of, 178
Cody, William F., birthday of, 147
Colorado Day, 424
Columba, Saint, 332
Columbia University, opening of, 382
Columbus, Christopher, sails from Spain, 426
Columbus Day, 529
Confederate Memorial Day, 240
Connecticut charter, 275
"Constitution" and the "Guerriere," 446
Constitution Day, 484
Constitution of the Continental Congress ratified, 597
Constitution of the United States ratified, 353
Continental Congress, the first, 467
Conwell, Dr. Russell H., founder of Temple University, birthday of, 123
Coolidge, Calvin, birthday of, 377
Cooper, James Fenimore, birthday of, 471
Copley, John Singleton, birthday of, 367
Cotton carnival, Memphis, Tennessee, 282
Cotton gin, patented by Eli Whitney, 169
Cowbellian de Rakian, Mobile carnival society, 13
Crater Day, 419
Crispin, Saint, 557
Crockett, David, birthday of, 443
Crosby, Fanny, birthday of, 184
Cuba, U.S. withdraws from, 61
Custer, Colonel George A., 358
Czechoslovakia, anniversary of founding of Republic of, 562

Daffodil Festival in Washington, 190
Dana, Charles A., birthday of, 432

690

Dartmouth Hall, laying the cornerstone of, 558
David, Saint, 153
Davis, Jefferson, inauguration of, 135; birthday of, 323
D-Day, 327
December, origin of the name, 626
Declaration of Independence, American, 367
Declaration of Independence, Colony of Rhode Island, 261
Declaration of Independence, Mecklenburg, 287
Defenders' Day in Maryland, 476
Delaware and Chesapeake Canal, opening of, 539
Delaware Day, 634
Democratic National Committee admits women to membership, 499
De Molay Day, 180
Derby Day, 263
Dewey Day, 254
Dickens, Charles, birthday of, 82
Dolly Madison Day, 290
Dominic, Saint, 426
Dow, Neal, birthday of, 182

East Chester, N.Y., election of 1733, 563
Easter, 200
Eddy, Mary Baker, birthday of, 394
Edison, Thomas Alva, birthday of, 91; invents phonograph, 603
Edmund, Saint, 598
Eells, Cushing, birthday of, 130
Eisenhower, Dwight David, birthday of, 534
Election Day, 584
Eliot, John, birthday of, 428
Ellsworth, Oliver, birthday of, 248
Emancipation proclamation, 11
Emerson, Ralph Waldo, birthday of, 301
English Thanksgiving Day, 549
Epiphany, eve, 15; feast of, 15; Greek Church, 47
Erikson, Leif, anniversary of his discovery of America, 524
Esther, Fast of, 164
Ether Day, 537
Exaltation of the Cross, feast of, 481
Expatriation treaty with Great Britain, 223
Evacuation Day, in Boston, 177; in New York City, 611

Farmers' Day in Florida, 533
Farragut, Admiral David G., birthday of, 380
Fast Day in New Hampshire, 241
Fast of Esther, 164
Father's Day, 347
February, origin of the name, 75
Field, Eugene, birthday of, 464
Fillmore, Millard, birthday of, 22
Flag Day, 341
Flag, of Washington's Army, 13; adoption of present design, 207
Florida ceded to the United States, 397
Florida, Farmers' Day in, 533
Forefathers' Day, 651
Forrest, Edwin, birthday of, 163
Forrest, Nathan B., birthday of, 389
Four Freedoms, 21
Fourteenth Amendment to the Constitution, 416
Francis of Assisi, Saint, 512
Franklin, Benjamin, birthday of, 36
Fraternal Day in Alabama, 524
Frontier Day in Cheyenne, Wyoming, 411
Fuller, Melville W., birthday of, 90
Fulton, Robert W., and the "Clermont," 435

Gadsden purchase, 674
Gallaudet, Thomas H., birthday of, 637
Gallup, New Mexico, Inter-tribal Indian ceremonial, 456
Galveston, Texas, tornado, 472
Garfield, James A., birthday of, 599
Gasparilla Carnival, 89
German Day, 517
George, Saint, 237
Georgia Day, 99
Gettysburg, battle of, 365
Gettysburg National Cemetery, dedication of, 601
Girl Scout Day, 167
Girard College Founder's Day, 291
Gold Clause, repeal of, 326
Good Friday, 192
Gordon, Anna Adams, birthday of, 405
Grand Army of the Republic, first national encampment, 603
Grant, Ulysses S., birthday of, 245
Gray, Asa, birthday of, 599
Greek Independence Day, 210
Grolier, Jean, anniversary of the death of, 551
Ground Hog Day, 78
Guadalupe, feast of the Virgin of, 642
Guy Fawkes Day, 583

691

INDEX

Hague Peace Palace, gift of, 229
Hale, Nathan, hanging of, 494
Halifax Resolutions Day, 217
Hallowe'en, 565
Hamilton, Alexander, birthday of, 28
Hanukkah, 639
Harding, Warren G., birthday of, 578
Harris, Joel Chandler, birthday of, 636
Harrison, Benjamin, birthday of, 447
Harrison, William Henry, birthday of, 87
Harvard, John, birthday of, 612
Hawaii, annexation of, 382
Hawaii, Kamehameha Day in, 336
Hayes, Rutherford B., birthday of, 510
Henry, Patrick, speech for the revolution, 184
Hippolytus, Saint, 437
Historical Day, in Oklahoma, 525
Holidays, list of legal, 686
Holmes, Oliver Wendell, birthday of, 455
Holmes, Oliver Wendell II, birthday of, 162
Holy Name, feast of the, 33
Hoover, Herbert Clark, birthday of, 433
Hopkins, Mark, birthday of, 79
Hopkinson, Joseph, birthday of, 594
Hospital Day, 276
Hughes, Charles Evans, birthday of, 215
Huguenot Day, 220
Hundredth Night at West Point, 158
Hussey's reaper, first exhibition of, 366
Hutchinson, Anne, banishment of, 458

I Am an American Day, 286
Idaho, Mormon Pioneer Day in, 410
Idaho Pioneer Day, 345
Ignatius de Loyola, Saint, 420
Ildefonsus, Saint, 54
Illinois, creation of Territory of, 79
Immaculate Conception, feast of, 635
Inauguration Day, 49
Income tax amendment to the Constitution, 146
Independence Day, 367
Indian ceremonial, Gallup, New Mexico, 456
Indian treaty, the first, 183
Indiana Day, 639
Initiative and referendum, decision on validity of, 135
Inter-Tribal Indian ceremonial, Gallup, New Mexico, 456
Irving, Washington, birthday of, 206
Isaac Jogues, Saint, 498

Jack Jouett Day in Virginia, 326
Jackson, Andrew, censured by the Senate, 189
Jackson Day in Louisiana, 24
Jackson, "Stonewall," birthday of, 50
Jacksonville, Texas, tomato festival, 325
James, Saint, 257
James the Greater, Saint, 413
Jamestown, Virginia, settlement of, 281
Jane Frances de Chantal, Saint, 448
Januarius, Saint, 490
January, origin of the name, 1
Jay, John, birthday of, 640
Jefferson, Joseph, birthday of, 136
Jefferson, Thomas, birthday of, 218
Jerome, Saint, 502
Jerusalem, destruction of, 404
Jewish New Year, 474
Joan of Arc, Saint, 313
John the Baptist, Saint, 456
John the Evangelist, Saint, 668
John Maro, Saint, 157
Johnny, Appleseed, 539
Johnson, Andrew, birthday of, 673
Jones, John Paul, birthday of, 398
Jousting tournament at Natural Chimneys, Virginia, 443
July, origin of the name, 364
June, origin of the name, 317

Kamehameha Day in Hawaii, 336
Kansas Day, 62
Keller, Helen, birthday of, 359
Kentucky Statehood Day, 318
Kidd, Captain William, hanging of, 298

Labor Day, 465
Labor Sunday, 464
Lady Day, 188
Lafayette, Marquis de, birthday of, 468
"Lame duck" Amendment to the Constitution, 82
La Salle's last journey, 30
Lawrence, Saint, 434
League of Nations' Day, 27
Leap Year, 679
Lee, Ann, birthday of, 150
Lee, Robert E., birthday of, 43
Lehigh University Founder's Day, 508
Leyden, siege of, 509
Library Day in West Virginia, 634
Lights, festival of, 639
Lincoln, Abraham, birthday of, 92
Lindbergh lands in Paris, 294
Lithuania, anniversary of founding of Republic of, 132
Longfellow, Henry Wadsworth, birthday of, 147

692

Long, Huey P., birthday of, 458
Los Angeles, California, birthday celebration, 466
Louisiana, Jackson Day in, 24
Louisiana purchase, 650
Louis, Saint, 451
Lowell, James Russell, birthday of, 141
Loyal Temperance Union Day, 405
Lucy, Saint, 643
Luke, Saint, 542
Lusitania, sinking of, 268
Lyon, Mary, founder of Mount Holyoke College, 586

MacArthur, Douglas, birthday of, 58
McDonogh Day in New Orleans, 261
McGuffey, William H., birthday of, 494
McKinley, William, birthday of, 64
Madison, James, birthday of, 170
Magna Charta Day, 346
Maine, admitted to the Union, 169
"Maine" (battleship), anniversary of destruction of, 126
Manheim, Pennsylvania, Rose Day, 336
March, origin of name, 152
Mardi Gras, 104
Marine Corps Day, 588
Maritime Day, 295
Mark, Saint, 240
Marshall, John, birthday of, 495
Martha, Saint, 417
Martinmas, 592
Maryland Day, 185
Maryland Defenders' Day, 476
Maryland Tea Party, 546
Mary Magdalen, Saint, 406
Marquette, Jacques, birthday of, 321
Matthew, Saint, 493
Matthias, Saint, 143
May Day, 251
May, origin of the name, 250
Mecklenburg Declaration of Independence, 287
Medical School, established by the College of Philadelphia, 259
Meeker, Ezra, "Days of", in Washington, 418
Memorial Day, 308
Memphis, Tennessee, cotton carnival, 282
Michaelmas Day, 501
Michael, Saint, 268; 501
Michigan Day, 57
Military Academy, United States, founding of, 172
Miami royal poinciana festival, 331

Mint, establishment of, 203
Missouri Day, 505
Mitchell, John, 564
Mobile, New Year in, 13
Monroe Doctrine, promulgation of, 628
Monroe, James, birthday of, 246
Mormon Church, founding of, 209
Mormon Pioneer Day in Idaho, 410
Mother's Day, 279
Mother Seton Day, 627
Mountain state forest festival in West Virginia, 506
Mount Holyoke College Founder's Day, 586
Mule Day in Columbia, Tennessee, 204
Mummers' parade, Philadelphia, 5

Nantes, revocation of the Edict of, 551
National Aviation Day, 445
National Bank Act, 146
National Cemetery at Gettysburg, dedication of, 601
National Maritime Day, 295
Navy Day, 558
Navy, United States, rebuilding of in 1794-95, 189
Nebraska State Day, 155
Nevada, Admission Day in, 573
New Church Day, 351
New Hampshire Fast Day, 241
New Orleans, McDonogh Day in, 261
New Year's Day, 2
New Year's Eve, 675
New York City, evacuation of, 611
New York City Fire Department, beginning of, 258
Nicholas, Saint, 631
Nimitz, Chester William, birthday of, 144
Nineteenth Amendment to the Constitution, 452
North Carolina, University of, anniversary of laying cornerstone of first building, 532
November, origin of the name, 575
Norwegian Independence Day, 284

October, origin of the name, 504
Ohio's first legislature, 51
Oklahoma, Cherokee Strip Day in, 483
Oklahoma Historical Day, 525
Oklahoma Territory, anniversary of opening of, 234
Oklahoma, Will Rogers Day in, 582
Orange Day, 389

INDEX

Osteopathy, beginning of, 355
"Our Lady of Mt. Carmel," feast of, 395

Packer, Asa, founder of Lehigh University, 508
Paine, Thomas, birthday of, 68
Palm Sunday, 187
Panama Canal, 23
Pan American Day, 222
Panic of 1873, 492
Panic of 1929, 556
Pasadena Rose Bowl football game, 10
Pasadena Tournament of Roses, 8
Pasch Monday, 202
Passover, feast of, 226
Patrick, Saint, 173
Patriots' Day in Mass. and Me., 227
Paul, Saint, 56; 362
"Peacemaker", explosion of, 149
Pearl Harbor attacked by the Japanese, 633
Peary, Robert E., birthday of, 267
Pendleton, Oregon, round-up, 480
Pennsylvania, Americanism Day in, 257
Pennsylvania Day, 552
Penn treaty with the Indians, 355
Pension Fund for College Teachers, endowment of by Andrew Carnegie, 224
Pentecost, feast of, 286
Perry, Oliver Hazard, birthday of, 449
Peter, Saint, 361; 282
Petersburg Memorial Day, 334
Petroleum Day, 453
Philadelphia Centennial Exposition, 274
Philadelphia mummers' parade, 5
Philippine Islands, independence of, 377
Philip, Saint, feast of, 257
Phonograph, invention of, 603
Pierce, Franklin, birthday of, 604
Pioneer Day in Idaho, 345
Pioneer Day in Utah, 408
Poe, Edgar Allan, birthday of, 45
Poinciana festival in Miami, 331
Polk, James K., birthday of, 576
Ponce de Leon seeks fountain of youth, 212
Pony penning on Chincoteague Island, Virginia, 414
Portland, Oregon, rose festival, 338
Priestly, Joseph, birthday of, 168
Princeton, battle of, 14
Prohibition and repeal, 36
Protestant Reformation Day, 572

Pulaski, Count Casimir, anniversary of death, 525
Purim, feast of, 164

Randolph, John, birthday of, 322
Republican party, founding of, 380
Revolutionary soldiers riot at Philadelphia, 353
Rhode Island Declaration of Independence, 261
Rhododendron festival, Asheville, North Carolina, 343
Rhymes of the days and seasons, 683
Riley, James Whitcomb, birthday of, 519
Roch, Saint, 442
Rockefeller Foundation chartered, 282
Rockefeller, John D., birthday of, 383
Rogers, Will, birthday of, 582
Roosevelt, Franklin D., birthday of, 71
Roosevelt, Theodore, birthday of, 558
Rose Bowl football game, 10
Rose Day at Manheim, Pennsylvania, 336
Rose festival, Portland, Oregon, 338
Rosh Hashana, 474
Royalist Fast Day in Virginia, 69
Rumford, Count, birthday of, 188
Rural Life Sunday, 258
Rutledge, John, 407

Sadie Hawkins Day, 588
St. Agnes, eve of, 48
St. Agnes, feast of, 51
St. Andrew, feast of, 623
St. Anne, festival of, 415
St. Anthony the Great, feast of, 40
St. Anthony of Padua, feast of, 340
St. Augustine, festival of, 454
St. Augustine of Canterbury, feast of, 302
St. Barnabas, feast of, 337
St. Bartholomew, festival of, 450
St. Bede's Day, 304
St. Bridget, festival of, 76
St. Catherine of Alexandria, feast of, 610
St. Catherine of Siena, feast of, 249
St. Cecelia, feast of, 604
St. Charles Borromeo, feast of, 581
St. Christopher, feast of, 414
St. Chrysostom, feast of, 60
St. Clare, feast of, 437
St. Clement, feast of, 608
St. Columba, feast of, 332
St. Crispin, feast of, 557

694

St. David's Day, 153
St. Dominic, feast of, 426
St. Edmund, feast of, 598
St. Frances Xavier, feast of, 654
St. Francis of Assisi, feast of, 512
St. George's Day, 237
St. Hippolytus, feast of, 437
St. Ignatius de Loyola, feast of, 420
St. Ildefonsus, feast of, 54
St. Isaac Jogues, feast of, 498
St. James the Greater, feast of, 413
St. James the Less, feast of, 257
St. Jane Frances de Chantal, feast of, 448
St. Januarius, feast of, 490
St. Jerome, feast of, 502
St. Joan of Arc, festival of, 313
St. John the Baptist, decollation of, 456
St. John before the Latin Gate, feast of, 267
St. John the Evangelist, feast of, 668
St. John's Day, 356
St. John Maro, festival of, 157
St. Lawrence, feast of, 434
St. Lucy, feast of, 643
St. Luke, feast of, 542
St. Louis, feast of, 451
St. Louis, Missouri, Veiled Prophet festival, 506
St. Mark's Day, 240
St. Martha, feast of, 417
St. Mary Magdalen, feast of, 406
St. Matthew, feast of, 493
St. Matthias, feast of, 143
St. Michael and All Angels, feast of, 501
St. Michael, feast of the apparition of, 268
St. Nicholas, feast of, 631
St. Patrick's Day, 173
St. Paul's Day, 362
St. Paul, feast of the conversion of, 56
St. Peter and his companions, festival of, 282
St. Peter's Day, 361
St. Philip, feast of, 257
St. Roch, festival of, 442
St. Simon, feast of, 562
St. Stephen, feast of, 667
St. Stephen the Younger, feast of, 618
St. Swithin's Day, 392
St. Sylvester, feast of, 676
St. Theresa, feast of, 537
St. Thomas, feast of, 650
St. Timothy, feast of, 54
St. Titus, feast of, 14
St. Valentine's Day, 120
St. Veronica, festival of, 32

St. Vincent de Paul, feast of, 403
Salvation Army Founder's Day, 214
San Francisco Fire, 225
Santa Fe Fiesta, 462
San Jacinto Day in Texas, 229
Santa Lucia, feast of, 643
Schwenkfelder Thanksgiving Day, 496
Seabury, Samuel, first bishop of the Protestant Episcopal Church in the United States, 596
Senora Conquistadora, Fiesta de la, 303
September, origin of the name, 461
Seton, Elizabeth Ann Bayley, 627
Seventeenth Amendment to the Constitution, 315
Seward Day in Alaska, 195
Shakespeare, William, birthday of, 236
Shenandoah Valley Apple Blossom Festival, 259
Shrove Tuesday, 104
Sickles, Daniel E., birthday of, 548
Simon, Saint, 562
Sisters of Charity of St. Vincent de Paul, observance of Mother Seton Day, 627
Sixteenth Amendment to the Constitution, 146
Smith, Francis Hopkinson, birthday of, 551
Smith, John, president of the Council of Jamestown, Virginia, 474
Smith, Joseph, Jr., birthday of, 655
Soldiers' Hospital Day, 451
South Carolina, Thursday of State Fair Week in, 556
Spanish Peace Treaty, 88
Sponge Divers at Tarpon Springs, Florida, blessing of, 20
Stamp Act, signing of, 184; repudiation of, 606
Statehood Day in Kentucky, 318
State Day in Nebraska, 155
Statehood Day in Tennessee, 319
Statue of Liberty, dedication of, 563
Stephen, Saint, 667
Stephen the Younger, Saint, 618
Steuben, Baron von, birthday of, 486
Stewart, Peggy, (brig), anniversary of the destruction of, 546
Stone, Harlan Fiske, birthday of, 528
Street letter boxes inaugurated, in Boston, 425
Stuart, Gilbert, birthday of, 629
Swedenborg, Emanuel, birthday of, 67
Swedish Midsummer Festival, 357
Swiss Independence Day, 425
Swithin, Saint, 392
Sylvester, Saint, 676

INDEX

Tabernacles, feast of, 497
Taft, William H., birthday of, 481
Talulah, Louisiana, lynching of five
Italians, 403
Taney, Roger B., birthday of, 175
Tarpon Springs, Florida, blessing of
sponge divers at, 20
Taylor, Zachary, birthday of, 608
Temple University Founder's Day, 123
Tennessee, Mule Day in Columbia, 204
Tennessee Statehood Day, 319
Texas, Alamo Day in, 161
Texas Independence Day, 156
Texas, San Jacinto Day in, 229
Thanksgiving Day, 613
Theresa, Saint, 537
Thomas, Saint, 650
Timothy, Saint, 54
Titus, Saint, 14
Tomato festival, Jacksonville, Texas,
325
Tomato tom-tom, Yoakum, Texas, 332
Tournament of Roses, Pasadena, 8
Transcontinental Railroad, the first, 272
Transfiguration, feast of, 430
Traverse City, Michigan, cherry festi-
val, 400
Trenton, New Jersey, battle of, 666
Trudeau, Edward L., birthday of, 516
Truman, Harry S., birthday of, 270
Tuskegee Institute Founder's Day, 208
Twain, Mark, birthday of, 622
Twelfth Night Revels, 18; in New Or-
leans, 19
Twentieth Amendment to the Consti-
tution, 82
Tyler, John, birthday of, 191

United Nations charter, 555
United States Marine Corps Day, 588
United States, recognition by France,
33; withdraws from Cuba, 61
Utah Pioneer Day, 408

Valentine, Saint, 120
Valley Forge, Washington encamps at,
648
Van Buren, Martin, birthday of, 630
V-E Day, 268
Veiled Prophet festival in St. Louis,
506
Vermont Day, 159
Vermont's Declaration of Independ-
ence, 34
Veronica, Saint, 32
Versailles treaty, 360

Vincent de Paul, Saint, 403
Vinson, Frederick Moore, birthday of,
52
Virginia, Cape Henry Day in, 243
Virginia, Jack Jouett Day in, 326
Virginia, jousting tournament at Nat-
ural Chimneys in, 443
Virginia, Royalist Fast Day in, 69
Virgin of Guadalupe, feast of, 642
Virgin Islands, transfer of, 196
Virgin Mary, nativity of, 472
V-J Day, 438
Volunteers of America, Founder's Day,
417

Waite, Morrison, birthday of, 619
Walton, Izaak, birthday of, 432
War Department of the United States,
creation of, 431
Washington Admission Day, 593
Washington, Booker Taliaferro, found-
er of Tuskegee Institute, 208
Washington Daffodil Festival, 190
Washington, "Days of Ezra Meeker"
in, 418
Washington, D.C., burned by the Brit-
ish, 239; first session of Congress in,
598
Washington, George, birthday of, 137;
death of, 642; takes leave of his of-
ficers, 629
Washington monument, Baltimore, Md.,
137
Washington monument, Washington,
D.C., 136
Webster, Daniel, birthday of, 42
Week days, origin of names, 681
Wenatchee, Washington, Apple Blos-
som Festival, 262
West Point Hundredth Night, 158
West Point Military Academy, found-
ing of, 172
West Virginia Day, 352
West Virginia, Library Day, 634
West Virginia, mountain state forest
festival in, 506
Whistler, James Abbott McNeil, 384
White, Edward Douglas, birthday of,
580
White House, Washington, D.C., lay-
ing the cornerstone of, 534
Whitman, Marcus, death of, 620
Whitman, Walt, birthday of, 314
Whitney, Eli, patents cotton gin, 169
Whitsunday, 293
Whittier, John Greenleaf, birthday of,
646

Widows of Presidents pensioned, 196
Wilkes, Captain John, commands first United States government exploring expedition, 445
Willard, Emma, birthday of, 142
Willard, Frances E., anniversary of death of, 133; birthday of, 499
Williams, Roger, arrival in America, 80
Williams, Sir George, birthday of, 527
Wilson, Woodrow, birthday of, 669
Wittenmyer, Annie, birthday of, 451
Woman suffrage convention, the first, 402
World Court, organization of, 348
World War I, 360

Wright, Orville and Wilbur, anniversary of their first successful air plane flight, 645
Wyoming Day, 637

Yale, Elihu, birthday of, 207
Y.M.C.A. Founder's Day, 527
Yoakum, Texas, tomato tom-tom, 332
Yom Kippur, 491
Yorktown Day, 544

Zenger, John Peter, acquittal of, 427
Zodiac, signs of, 685